Beyond Austerity

Beyond Austerity

Reforming the Greek Economy

edited by Costas Meghir, Christopher A. Pissarides, Dimitri Vayanos,
and Nikolaos Vettas

The MIT Press
Cambridge, Massachusetts
London, England

This book was set in ITC Stone Sans Std and ITC Stone Serif Std by Toppan Best-set Premedia Limited. Printed and bound in the United States of America.

Library of Congress Cataloging-in-Publication Data is available.

ISBN: 978-0-262-03583-5

10 9 8 7 6 5 4 3 2 1

Contents

Preface

Greece has received more than its fair share of media attention from 2010 onward. Although it represents only 0.15 percent of the world's population and 0.3 percent of the world's GDP, it made the cover page of the *Economist* magazine nine times between 2010 and 2015, and was the subject of numerous articles and opinion pieces in other top international media. Greeks would have happily given away that media attention in exchange for better economic performance. Between 2008 and 2014 their incomes shrank by more than a quarter, their houses lost more than a third of their value, and the unemployment rate more than tripled to reach 27 percent. Even bank deposits ceased being viewed as safe: a bank run took place in the summer of 2015, leading to the imposition of capital controls. As of early 2017 the economy appears to have stabilized but shows only a few signs of recovery, and Greece's place inside the eurozone (EZ) can still not be taken for granted.

Greece attracted media attention not only because of its own economic plight but also because of its central role in the broader crisis experienced by the EZ. The EZ crisis made clear that the ambitious project of introducing a common currency in Europe had important structural deficiencies that needed to be addressed. The deficiencies impacted a number of EZ economies, but Greece was the most vulnerable and hardest hit. Greece was also the only country whose future in the EZ has been put seriously in doubt, and this uncertainty has tested the strength and the limits of the monetary union.

Most of the articles written on Greece in the media have focused on the effects of austerity on Greek economy and society, on the negotiations between Greece and its creditors, on whether Greece can or should repay its debt, and on whether Greece may be better off outside the EZ. Analysis of the pathologies that made Greece vulnerable to the crisis and of the actions that Greece should undertake to address them has been more limited. For example, it is often claimed that Greece's public sector is large and inefficient, but what are the inefficiencies and how can they be fixed? What actions should be undertaken to reform Greece's pension system, which is one of the most expensive in the European Union but provides inadequate protection against old-age poverty? What changes are needed to the regulations governing Greece's product and labor markets, and what are the costs stemming from the way that these markets are currently regulated?

Answers to questions such as the above are essential for a proper understanding of the Greek crisis. Greece's pathologies have made it particularly vulnerable and are the main reason why the crisis has lasted for eight years and shows no signs of ending. They are also the reason why Greece's economic performance has been weak over a horizon much longer than the crisis. (The decade of high growth prior to the crisis was preceded by a decade and a half of relative stagnation.) Unless the pathologies are addressed, Greece's weak economic performance will continue. And so will the flow of media articles commenting on issues other than the main causes of the weak performance. For example, commentators will keep arguing about austerity and the decline in Greek living standards—which are consequences of the weak performance—about debt relief—which is desirable but far from being a full solution to Greece's problems—and about the benefits to Greece of exiting the EZ—which is unlikely to solve problems that existed for many years before entry, and will bring its own problems and challenges.

In this book we seek to provide an in-depth analysis of the Greek economy before and during the crisis, and of policy options going forward. Each chapter of the book focuses on a specific policy area, and an introductory chapter provides an overview and draws out common themes. There are fourteen chapters in addition to the introductory one. Two pertain to the macroeconomy: the costs and benefits of Greece's participation in the EZ, and Greece's international competitiveness and export performance. Four concern markets and their regulation: product markets, privatizations, the labor market, and the financial system. Two concern public finances: taxation and pensions. And the remaining six mostly concern the public sector: education, healthcare, the justice system, corruption, and different aspects of the public administration. The chapters share the same broad structure: first an analysis of the Greek economy before the crisis, then a description of the main developments during the crisis, and finally ideas and policy options going forward.

A distinguishing feature of the book is its focus on Greek institutions and how they shape outcomes at both the micro- and the macroeconomic levels. We argue that Greek institutions require a deep overhaul, and in some cases should be redesigned from scratch. Policy actions undertaken during the crisis generated some improvements, but these were often partial fixes rather than long-term solutions. The chapters of the book propose ideas and policy options for more comprehensive and radical change.

The institutional changes that the book chapters propose have common themes, which we summarize here and develop in greater depth in the introductory chapter. One theme is that markets should become more open and regulatory barriers to entry should be reduced. Another is that social protection for the weak should be improved, and this can be done while also strengthening incentives for wealth creation in markets. And another is that the public administration should become more transparent and nonpolitical, with less centralized control by the state. Accomplishing these changes would improve economic performance and facilitate Greece's transition to the "new growth model" that it must adopt. Under that model, investment and exports should constitute larger fractions of the gross domestic product (GDP), while consumption and debt should be playing a smaller role. How fast Greece will eventually exit the crisis will depend on how fast it makes that transition.

Given our book's emphasis on the Greek economy and how to reform Greek institutions, a natural audience for the book is readers interested in Greece and the crisis that it has been experiencing. Yet, the material covered in the book is relevant well beyond Greece—and even beyond the EZ.

Crucial to the EZ's long-term survival is that productivity growth does not diverge across EZ member countries. This is because in the absence of the currency-devaluation tool, such divergence would lead to high unemployment in the underperforming countries. Fiscal stabilization would only be a short-term fix and in any case it is not available as a tool, given the limited political will to perform fiscal transfers across countries. Policies should hence be devised to raise productivity in underperforming countries and to make their markets more flexible so that they can better adjust to change. Such policies are described in this book.

While the policies that we describe are important for countries within the EZ, where the environment is less forgiving of factors that lower productivity growth, such policies should be part of the agenda in any well-functioning economy. This is all the more so in the current circumstances: growth in advanced economies has slowed down since the 2007–2008 global financial crisis, financial leverage is high in both the private and the public sector, and populism is riding high as a result. Sensible economic reforms to raise productivity, and to improve public finances as well as the functioning of the state more broadly, could help deal with many of these problems.

The chapters of the book are written so as to be accessible to readers without formal training in economics. At the same time the analysis tends to build on rigorous arguments from modern economics, and to draw on lessons offered by academic research and by the policy experience of other countries. In particular, the chapters make extensive use of data and comparisons between Greece and other European countries. In this light, the book can be used as a supplementary text in undergraduate or graduate courses covering European economics and politics, or the Greek economy and crisis.

The set of authors mainly consists of academics who are experts in the fields covered in their respective chapters. It also includes some from outside academe with extensive experience on policy making or evaluation.

The writing of the chapters was not a linear process and lasted over a long time period, with some of the chapters moving in parallel with the actual developments in Greece. Combining insights from academic research with a reading of the fast-changing policy landscape in Greece was a demanding task. Exchanges of views and comments among the authors took place at various times and in different ways during the process, including at a preliminary workshop in Athens in May 2013. Naturally not all authors may agree with the content of chapters other than their own, although the themes emerging from the chapters have much in common.

We are grateful to LSE's Hellenic Observatory for making funds available to employ research assistants to collect and organize data pertaining to some of the chapters. Research assistants who worked on specific chapters are thanked at the respective chapters, and so are numerous academics, policy makers, and practitioners, who have provided comments on the chapters. We owe a special thanks to Kostas Peppas and Michalis Vasileiadis for valuable research assistance across several chapters of the book, and to three anonymous reviewers for very helpful comments on the book. We are also grateful to Dana Andrus, Laura Keeler, Jane Macdonald, and Emily Taber at the MIT Press for being patient with our delays and for their valuable feedback on aspects of the publication process.

We hope that this book will contribute toward a better understanding of the Greek economy, its weaknesses as well as its potential, the ways in which it differs from other European economies, and the features that it has in common. We also hope that, as deep, complicated, and prolonged the current crisis has been in Greece, there will be a way to prosperity and growth in Europe and definitely including Greece.

Costas Meghir, Christopher A. Pissarides, Dimitri Vayanos, and Nikolaos Vettas
Athens, London, and New York
January 16, 2017

I Introduction

1 The Greek Economy before and during the Crisis—and Policy Options Going Forward

Costas Meghir, Christopher A. Pissarides, Dimitri Vayanos, and Nikolaos Vettas

1.1 Introduction and Roadmap

In this chapter we review the performance of the Greek economy before and during the crisis. This provides useful background and motivates the more in-depth analysis in subsequent chapters. We also present policy options for Greece going forward, drawing to a significant extent on the conclusions of subsequent chapters.

Section 1.2 reviews Greece's economic performance in the decades before the crisis. On the macroeconomic side, we review the evolution of GDP per capita and productivity (section 1.2.1), debt, consumption, and investment (section 1.2.2), and wages and prices (section 1.2.3). On the microeconomic side (section 1.2.4), we review the quality of the institutions pertaining to the business environment (product market regulation, justice system, access to finance, and labor market regulation), and to social protection and public good provision (pensions, welfare system, health care, and education). We also identify interconnections between institutional quality and macroeconomic outcomes.

As of 1970, Greece's GDP per capita was above that of Ireland, Portugal, and Spain.[1] Greek government debt was about 15 percent of GDP, a low ratio, comparable to Portugal's and Spain's. During the 1980s, Greece experienced relative stagnation and was overtaken by both Ireland and Spain in terms of GDP per capita. Government debt also rose sharply, reaching about 70 percent of GDP in 1990. Better economic management during the 1990s turned the large budget deficits of the 1980s into primary surpluses. It also led to fast growth, starting from the mid-1990s, and to an increase in corporate investment from its low levels over the previous twenty years.

Greece's fast growth continued after euro entry and until 2007, when the global financial crisis erupted. By 2007, Greece's GDP per capita had become almost equal to that of Spain. The fast growth following euro entry, however, was resting on weak foundations. First, it was driven almost entirely by investment from domestic firms and households, rather than by increases in total factor productivity (TFP). Second, it was financed to a large extent by borrowing from foreigners. By 2007, Greece was borrowing 15.8 percent of its GDP from foreigners on an annual basis, with the capital inflows financing a trade deficit (imports minus exports) of 12.4 percent of GDP. Greece became highly reliant on foreign borrowing because of a combination of (1) low private sector savings from the mid-1990s onward and (2) high government deficits after euro entry and especially in the years leading to the crisis. While some of the funds that were borrowed from abroad were used to finance cost-reducing investments in the corporate sector, their main effect was to increase aggregate demand. This can be seen by the rapid increases in prices and wages: for example, wage competitiveness relative to Germany declined by 30 percent between 2000 and 2007.

On the microeconomic front, the fast GDP growth after euro entry was not accompanied by sufficient efforts to create an attractive business environment. Various legal and regulatory obstacles generated high costs for firms to operate and to enter new markets. One of the important consequences of the high entry costs was the low level of foreign direct investment (FDI). For example, over the period 2001 to 2007, Greece received the lowest FDI among all EU28 countries, despite the fast growth in its GDP and its lower wage costs relative to many of the other countries. High entry costs were probably a main driver of the low TFP growth.

Low institutional quality pertained not only to the business environment and the creation of wealth by the private sector but also to the redistribution of wealth and other basic functions of the public sector. Metrics such as the poverty rate, the fraction of social benefits received by the poorer segments of the population, and the out-of-pocket expenditures in education and health care placed Greece well below the median OECD country—and at levels comparable to Italy, Portugal, and Spain. Provision of public goods, such as education and health care, was also overly expensive relative to the quality of the output.

The global financial crisis put an end to Greece's ability to borrow large amounts of money from abroad. With borrowing from foreign investors being no longer possible, the process that led to Greece's fast GDP growth prior to the crisis had to run in reverse. The adjustment to a zero trade deficit was made harder by Greece's large government deficit and debt, as well as by the poor quality of its institutions. Italy, Portugal, and Spain had some of the same problems, but Greece stood out because it had all of them combined (although the level of private sector debt was lower than in Portugal and Spain).

To cope with the lack of market access, Greece agreed in May 2010 to follow an adjustment program designed and monitored by the "Troika" of the European Commission

(EC), the European Central Bank (ECB), and the International Monetary Fund (IMF). That first program was followed by a second and a third. Portugal, Ireland, and Cyprus followed similar programs, while Spain followed a more limited program focused on its banking sector. The programs in Cyprus, Greece, Ireland, and Portugal entailed access to loans on favorable terms in exchange for fiscal tightening and structural reforms. Unlike typical IMF programs, they did not involve a currency devaluation, since all four countries were members of the eurozone (EZ), or a restructuring or default on the debt. Debt restructuring and some forgiveness ("haircut") for Greece only took place in 2012.

We review the economic policy that was followed in Greece during the crisis in section 1.3. We start with the macroeconomic developments (section 1.3.1), then describe the structural reforms that were implemented at the microeconomic level (section 1.3.2), and end with an overall assessment (section 1.3.3).

Greece's adjustment programs eliminated the primary budget deficit and almost eliminated the trade deficit by 2014. Progress was also made with structural reforms. On the negative side, Greece's GDP per capita declined by 26.3 percent between 2007 and 2014. This decline was much larger than in Ireland (10.6 percent), Italy (12 percent), Portugal (7.9 percent), and Spain (10 percent). The larger decline was due to some extent to Greece's worse economic fundamentals, and indeed designing an adjustment program for Greece was a big challenge given the state of its economy. At the same time the policy actions that were followed had important shortcomings, stemming from a combination of design flaws and EZ-level political constraints, on one hand, and lack of domestic "ownership," on the other. These factors were reinforcing each other: lack of ownership had adverse effects on the mix of policy actions that were implemented, and conversely was exacerbated by shortcomings in the programs' execution that were partly due to design flaws and political constraints.

A key shortcoming concerned the way "internal devaluation" worked in Greece. To engineer the declines in prices and wages that were a necessary part of the adjustment to a zero trade deficit, the Troika emphasized changes in labor market regulation. Such changes facilitated the adjustment of wages, and it was hoped that this would spill over into prices and boost Greek exports. But while the drop in wages was much larger than in Ireland, Portugal, and Spain, the rise in exports was smaller than in those countries. The trade deficit was eliminated mostly through a reduction of imports, brought about by the drop in incomes. Key reasons for the weak export response were the uncertainty about Greece exiting the EZ, which depressed investment; the lack of access to finance because of the distressed state of the banks; the limited degree of product-market reform, especially early on in the programs; and tax rises on key business inputs.

An additional shortcoming was that fiscal tightening was too rapid and effectively took priority over the structural reforms. Emphasizing structural reforms early on in the program and leaving some of the fiscal tightening to a later stage would have required more funding by the Troika but would have given a better chance to the reforms to succeed. The fiscal tightening was also inefficient in its mix, being more reliant on tax rises than on expenditure cuts, and reducing public investment more than other expenditure categories.

The above shortcomings concern the policies designed to eliminate the deficits. The policies designed to deal with the government debt were also suboptimal. While Greece lost market access in 2010 and its debt was widely viewed as unsustainable, the restructuring and reduction of the debt took place only in 2012. Delay meant that Greece found itself saddled with more debt. This is because debt payments to private investors between 2010 and 2012 were made in full through additional loans by the other EZ countries and the IMF. Delay also exacerbated in various ways the liquidity and solvency problems of Greek banks, and the uncertainty about EZ exit. Last but not least, delay contributed to the perception that financial assistance given to Greece was designed to benefit foreign countries and their banks. This helped make debt rather than the reforms the main political issue. It also gave credibility to political parties and commentators who belonged to the political fringes and were openly hostile to reforms, but were arguing for debt relief.

Section 1.4 presents policy options going forward. We start (section 1.4.1) by sketching where Greece should aim to be 20 years from now (with "now" being 2016). We next examine how the transition to that desirable long-run state could be accomplished (section 1.4.2).

In a nutshell, a desirable long-run state for Greece is one where all types of markets are more open, the public administration is more efficient, transparent, and nonpolitical, and significant emphasis is given to education and human capital. Reaching that state would require Greece to catch up with (or do better than) the EU average on key measures of institutional quality and economic performance such as the ease of doing business, the quality of product market regulation, the efficiency of courts, the performance of the education and health care systems, the investment and outcomes in innovation and R&D, and the quality of social protection. Currently Greece stands close to the bottom at most of these rankings. Many of the chapters in this volume describe in greater detail aspects of Greece's desirable long-run state, and key points are summarized in section 1.4.1.

The policies that we propose for the transition take into account the current adverse macroeconomic environment. They also seek to remedy shortcomings of the adjustment process, identified in section 1.3. A fundamental policy goal for the transition is to attract new investment. This is necessary to boost exports and productivity, and to make up for the massive cumulative disinvestment that has taken place during the crisis. Attracting investment requires removing the uncertainty about the future direction of the economy, including its position inside the EZ. This requires that a broad political consensus is formed in Greece in favor of key reforms.

A drastic redesign of fiscal policy is an additional requirement for attracting investment (and for improving economic performance more generally). Corporate taxes, including the implicit tax rate on labor, are high in Greece relative to both EU averages and Greece's neighbors, and should be reduced significantly. A commitment is also needed not to increase these tax rates for many years to come, and to make up for any budget shortfalls mostly through expenditure cuts. Expenditure cuts could target mainly wages in privileged segments of the public sector and various types of spending in pensions. They should be sufficient to make up for the lower tax rates and to finance a welfare system that possibly takes the form of a minimum guaranteed income. Future increases in tax revenue should come only from lower tax evasion and the broadening of the tax base (rather than from higher tax rates). Efforts to track tax evaders should be intensified, and lower tax rates would reduce incentives to evade.

Greece's strategy to attract investment and raise productivity should also include privatizations of state assets, such as real estate, utilities, and transportation infrastructure. In the third adjustment program, the privatization agency has been given useful additional flexibility on how to manage its assets. Perhaps the agency's remit could be expanded further to taking on some nonperforming loans (NPLs) from the banks. This would accelerate the resolution of the NPLs, attract new investment in those firms that are viable, and strengthen the banks. In addition to these measures, structural reforms should continue, especially in opening up product markets and in improving the education system, the justice system, and the public administration more broadly.

While some have argued that Greece should leave the EZ, we firmly believe that it should stay in. This is not only because the short-run costs of leaving are huge, but also because EZ membership provides a disciplining device for continuing with the necessary reforms.[2] While in Greece there is broad political consensus in favor of staying in the EZ, Greece's EZ partners should also do their part to remove the uncertainty by not encouraging Greece to exit the EZ, as they are better off with a reformed Greece inside the EZ than with an unreformed Greece outside it. In particular, Greece should be provided with a clearer path for debt relief. Debt relief could consist in extending maturities and locking interest rates at their low current levels, and should be made conditional on measurable reform efforts.

1.2 The Greek Economy before the Crisis

1.2.1 Income and Productivity

Figure 1.1 plots the gross domestic product (GDP) per capita for Greece and other EZ countries from 1970 onward. As comparison countries, we select Ireland, Italy, Portugal, and Spain (the largest EZ countries hit by the sovereign debt crisis), and also Germany. GDP per capita is adjusted for inflation, so its growth is in real terms, and is expressed in 2014 dollars. It is also adjusted for purchasing power parity (PPP), to account for the fact that the same good may be trading at different prices across countries.

In 1970, Greek GDP per capita was above that of Ireland, Portugal, and Spain. During the 1980s, Greece experienced relative stagnation, and was overtaken by both Ireland and Spain. Greece grew faster during the period 1996 to 2000 and especially from 2001, when it entered the EZ, to 2007. By 2007, Greek GDP per capita had become almost equal to that of Spain's.

GDP per capita is the income that corresponds to each citizen of a country, and can be viewed as a rough measure of productivity: how much income the average citizen

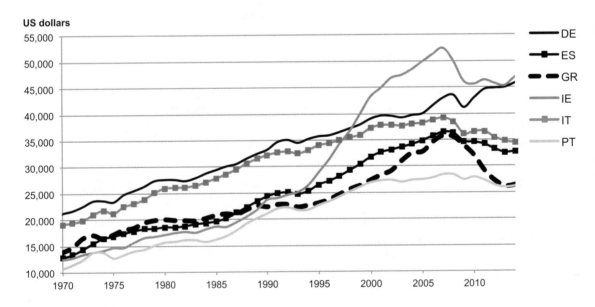

Figure 1.1

GDP per capita for Greece and other EZ countries, 1970 to 2014.

The data come from the Conference Board Total Economy Database. GDP is expressed in 2014 US dollars and is adjusted for PPP using 2011 weights. In this and subsequent figures we use the country codes employed by the European Central Bank (ECB): DE = Germany, ES = Spain, GR = Greece, IE = Ireland, IT = Italy, PT = Portugal.

generates. We next turn to more precise measures of productivity. One such measure is labor productivity per person employed, obtained by dividing GDP by the number of persons employed.

Figure 1.2 plots labor productivity in Greece and the comparison countries from 1970 onward. As with GDP per capita, Greece was ahead of Ireland, Portugal, and Spain in 1970. It was overtaken by Ireland and Spain in the late 1970s, and the gap with these countries increased significantly in the 1980s and early 1990s. Labor productivity in Greece increased rapidly during 1996 to 2007, and Greece caught up with Spain in 2006. Note that the growth rate of labor productivity in Greece during 1996 to 2007 was much faster than in Italy, Portugal, and Spain: labor productivity was flat in Spain during that period, while it declined slightly in Italy. Labor productivity in Greece in 2007 was 91 percent of that in Germany.[3]

A second measure of productivity is total factor productivity (TFP). Unlike labor productivity, it takes into account changes in the amount of capital that is used. TFP increases when a country can produce more output from given inputs of labor and capital, such as by a technological innovation that renders labor and capital more productive. If instead the output produced from given labor and capital inputs does not

US dollars

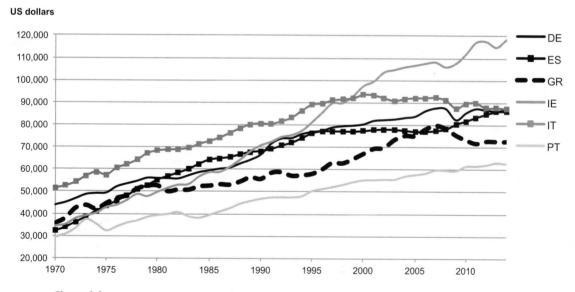

Figure 1.2
Labor productivity per person employed in Greece and other EZ countries, 1970 to 2014. The data come from the Conference Board Total Economy Database. Labor productivity per person employed is expressed in 2014 US dollars and is adjusted for PPP using 2011 weights.

change and growth occurs because the capital input is increased, such as when more factories are built, then labor productivity increases but TFP does not change. Improvements in TFP are necessary for sustainable long-run growth of a country's GDP per capita. Indeed, capital accumulation without growth in TFP can generate growth only in the short run because decreasing returns to capital eventually kick in (i.e., additions to capital become less and less productive). As we show below, the fast growth of Greek GDP per capita during 1996 to 2007 fits that scenario closely, as TFP growth was almost zero during that period. Figure 1.3 plots TFP in Greece and the comparison countries from 1996 onward.

TFP in Greece grew at an annual rate of 0.4 percent over the period 1996 to 2000, prior to euro entry, and 0 percent from 2001 to 2007. The average over the pre-crisis period 1996 to 2007 was 0.2 percent. This is slightly lower than the EZ average of 0.4 percent (not plotted). Greece performed better than Italy (–0.4 percent), Portugal (–0.4 percent), and Spain (–0.8 percent), where TFP growth was negative. At the same time it lagged behind Germany (1 percent) and Ireland (1.2 percent).

Since TFP growth in Greece during 1996 to 2007 was slow, the fast growth in GDP and labor productivity must have been driven primarily by capital accumulation.

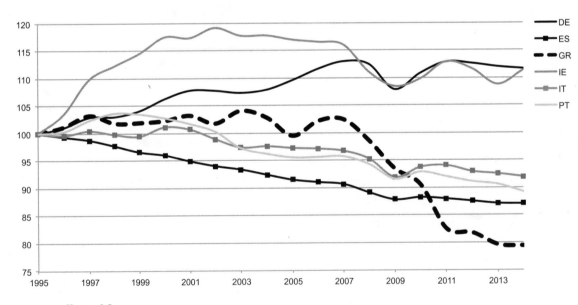

Figure 1.3
Total factor productivity (TFP) in Greece and other EZ countries, 1996 to 2014.
The data come from the Conference Board Total Economy Database. TFP is set to 100 for all countries in 1995, and the figure shows growth in subsequent years.

Table 1.1 decomposes real GDP growth into five sources: increases in labor quantity (number of hours worked), increases in labor quality (fraction of skilled workers in the labor pool), increases in ICT capital (pertaining to Information and Communications Technology, e.g., computers), increases in non-ICT capital, and TFP growth. The decomposition is performed over three periods: 1996 to 2000, 2001 to 2007, and 2008 to 2014.

Table 1.1 shows that the main contributor to Greece's fast growth in GDP during the period 1996 to 2007 was non-ICT capital. Accumulation of non-ICT capital, such as investment in buildings and machinery, accounted for about half of GDP growth. Section 1.2.2 confirms that corporate investment increased significantly during 1996 to 2007 (albeit starting from a low base). Public investment increased as well due to an expanded program of public works (new motorways and bridges, a new airport for Athens, 2004 Athens Olympics).

The slow TFP growth in Greece is an important concern. The same applies to other southern European countries such as Italy, Portugal, and Spain. Policy attention in all these countries should be on how to raise TFP.

Understanding the drivers of TFP growth has been the subject of a large body of academic research. A strand of that research emphasizes human capital accumulation, research and development (R&D), and innovation (e.g., Romer 1990; Barro 1991). A more recent strand of research emphasizes the quality of a country's institutions as measured, for example, by the efficiency of government, the control of corruption, and the protection of property rights (e.g., Hall and Jones 1999; Acemoglu, Johnson,

Table 1.1
Growth decomposition in Greece, 1996 to 2014

	1996–2000	2001–2007	2008–2014
Labor quantity	0.4%	0.8%	−2.1%
Labor quality	0.7%	0.7%	0.3%
ICT capital	0.7%	0.7%	0.7%
Non-ICT capital	1.4%	1.8%	0.4%
TFP growth	0.4%	0%	−3.6%
GDP growth (sum of the above)	3.6%	4.0%	−4.3%

Source: The data come from The Conference Board Total Economy Database (TED).
Note: The table reports the average contribution of each productive input to annual GDP growth during the periods 1996–2000, 2001–2007, and 2008–2014. The contribution of each input is taken directly from the TED (which decomposes growth into the inputs reported in table 1.2 for each year starting from 1995).

and Robinson 2001; Acemoglu and Robinson 2012). Understanding institutional quality and its drivers requires going to the microeconomic level—and the same applies to human capital and R&D. We provide an overview for Greece in section 1.2.4, and indeed most of the subsequent chapters of this book are devoted to an in-depth analysis of Greece's economic institutions.

We end this section by presenting data on foreign direct investment (FDI). A number of studies find that FDI is positively correlated with TFP growth (e.g., Javorcik 2004; Alfaro, Kalemli-Ozcan, and Sayek 2009; Baltabaev 2014). Such a correlation may arise because foreign firms can bring in new and more efficient production techniques. Moreover their presence can make competition more intense, which can further raise productivity. We view data on FDI as interesting beyond the direct correlation with TFP. This is because FDI in Greece (inward FDI) is particularly low, and the microeconomic-level inefficiencies that may be behind this could be affecting TFP in other ways as well.

According to Eurostat figures, FDI in Greece was 1 percent of GDP on average during the period 2001 to 2007. This was the lowest value among the 28 countries of the European Union. The median among the EU28 was 4.5 percent. During the period 2008 to 2012, FDI in Greece dropped to 0.7 percent of GDP. This was the third-lowest value among the EU28, and the median was 2.7 percent.

The low relative level of FDI in Greece during the period 2008 to 2012 may be attributed partly to the severe economic crisis. Yet the relative level of FDI was even lower during 2001 to 2007, the period of high GDP growth.[4] This suggests that the main driver of low FDI in Greece is poor institutional quality—in particular, legal and administrative obstacles that make it unattractive for foreign firms to invest and produce in Greece. Such obstacles can generate an oligopolistic market structure that benefits domestic incumbents and makes them hostile to reform. All these factors impact productivity negatively. We look at them in more depth in section 1.2.4 and especially in subsequent chapters of the book, chapters 4 (on product markets), 6 (labor market), 7 (financial system), 12 (justice system), 14 and 15 (public administration).

1.2.2 Debt, Consumption, and Investment

Figure 1.4 plots government debt for Greece and the comparison countries from 1970 onward, as percentage of GDP. Figures 1.5 and 1.6 plot the government's primary deficit and the interest payments on debt, respectively. The primary deficit is defined as the deficit net of the interest payments on debt. (Hence adding figures 1.5 and 1.6 yields the deficit.) The primary deficit identifies a government's contribution to debt without "penalizing" it for debt inherited from previous governments. To show the primary

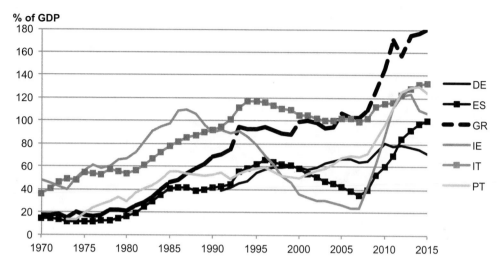

% of GDP

Legend: DE, ES, GR, IE, IT, PT

Figure 1.4

Government debt in Greece and other EZ countries, 1970 to 2014, as percentage of GDP. The data come from AMECO (series "General government consolidated gross debt: Excessive deficit procedure").

deficit and interest payments more clearly, in figures 1.5 and 1.6 we drop all comparison countries except for Italy, which is the most comparable to Greece in terms of the size of its public debt. We also add the average of the EU countries. We start figures 1.5 and 1.6 in 1985 because most of the series are not available before then.

During the 1970s, government debt in Greece was about 15 percent of GDP. That percentage was comparable to Portugal's and Spain's, and significantly below Ireland's and Italy's. Because of large primary deficits during the 1980s, debt rose sharply. Better economic management during the 1990s turned these primary deficits into primary surpluses. Yet during the early 1990s debt continued to rise, and by 1993 it had reached 94.4 percent of GDP, a percentage only lower than Italy's. This was partly because of the high interest rates: interest payments on debt during the early 1990s were between 10 and 12 percent of GDP. The combined effect of (1) the primary surpluses, and (2) a sharp reduction in interest rates in anticipation of euro entry that lowered drastically interest payments on debt, caused debt to stabilize and even decrease—to 88.5 percent of GDP in 1999.

Budget discipline decreased after euro entry, and there was a return to primary deficits starting in 2003. Primary deficits ballooned, to 5.0 and 10.3 percent of GDP, respectively, in 2008 and 2009. By contrast, Italy maintained primary surpluses after euro

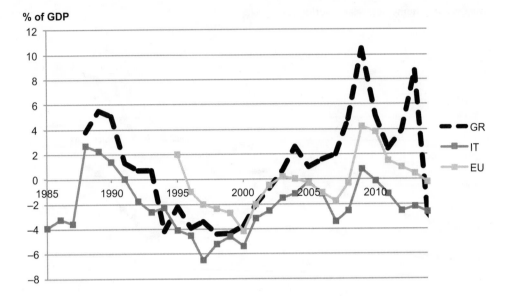

Figure 1.5
Government primary deficit in Greece, Italy, and the EU average, 1985 to 2014, as percentage of GDP. The data come from the European Commission (series "Net lending or net borrowing excluding interest; General government").

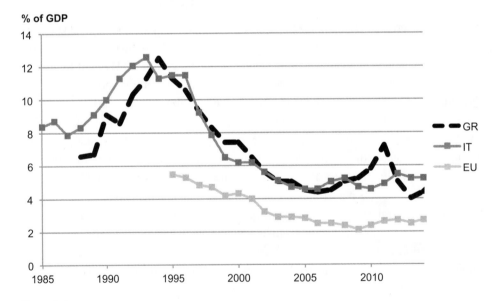

Figure 1.6
Interest payments on government debt in Greece, Italy, and the EU average, 1985 to 2014, as percentage of GDP. The data come from the European Commission (difference between the series "Net lending or net borrowing excluding interest; General government" and "Net lending or net borrowing; General government").

entry, with the exception of a small primary deficit in 2009. Because of the lax budget discipline in Greece, debt to GDP rose to 126.8 percent in 2009 despite the fast growth in GDP during 2000 to 2007.

Figures 1.7 and 1.8 provide a more detailed account of the evolution of government finances by plotting revenue and expenditure separately. Figure 1.7 plots current revenue, which includes income taxes, consumption taxes, and social contributions, but excludes items such as privatization proceeds (where revenue is derived in the current year by foregoing revenue in future years). Figure 1.8 plots current expenditure net of interest payments on debt. This includes compensation of public employees, and social transfers such as pensions, health care, and unemployment insurance but excludes items such as investment by the government (whose cost is paid in the current year but return accrues in future years). Excluding noncurrent items such as asset sales and investment allows better comparability of revenue and expenditure across different years and countries.

The current revenue of the Greek government, as a percentage of GDP, has been lower than in Italy and the EU average. This is mainly because of tax evasion. The gap between Greece and the EU average narrowed during the 1990s. The gap in expenditure

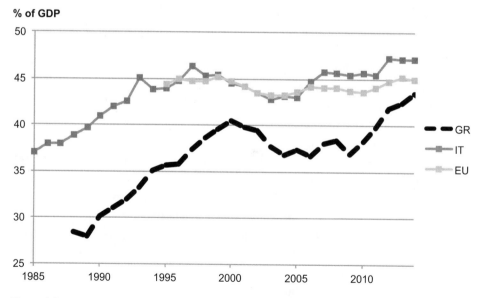

Figure 1.7

Government's current revenue in Greece, Italy, and the EU average, 1985 to 2014, as percentage of GDP. The data come from the European Commission (series "Total current revenue; general government").

% of GDP

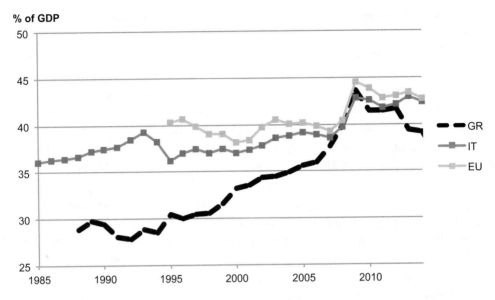

Figure 1.8
Government's current expenditure net of interest payments on debt in Greece, Italy, and the EU average, 1980 to 2014, as percentage of GDP. The data come from the European Commission (difference between the series "Total current expenditure; General government" and "Interest; General government").

narrowed as well, but primary surpluses were realized because the increase in expenditure was smaller than that in revenue. After euro entry, expenditure continued to rise, and did so particularly rapidly after 2006, when it reached the EU average. At the same time, revenue declined further below the EU average, and the combined effect caused the rapid increase in the deficit.

A large government debt means that a country's residents have a large future tax liability. This does not necessarily mean, however, that their net worth is low. Indeed, if all the debt is held domestically, then the taxes that the government must collect from its residents to repay the debt will go back to the same individuals in the form of debt repayments.[5] A large debt means that a country's residents have low net worth only if (some of) the debt is held by foreigners. We next review Greece's indebtedness to foreigners.

We define a country's net indebtedness to foreigners (NIF) as the difference between (1) claims held by foreigners on the country's government and private sector and (2) claims held by the country's government and private sector on foreigners. When NIF is positive, foreigners hold more claims on the country than the country holds on them, and hence the country is indebted to foreigners. This indebtedness is in a broad sense because NIF includes not only debt claims but also equity and derivatives claims. Debt claims held by foreigners include, for example, holdings of the country's government debt and of debt issued by the country's firms. Equity claims held by foreigners include, for example, foreign direct investment (FDI) in the country as well as shares of the country's firms bought in the stock market. Figure 1.9 plots NIF for Greece and the comparison countries from 1970 onward, as percentage of GDP.

Figure 1.9 shows that NIF for Greece has been positive during the entire period 1970 to 2014, meaning that Greece owed to foreigners more than what it was owed. NIF was a relatively small fraction of GDP until the late 1990s. From then on, it increased sharply to a much larger fraction of GDP—99.9 percent of GDP in 2007. The sharp increase of NIF for Greece is comparable to Portugal's and Spain's, while Ireland experienced a more abrupt increase.

Figure 1.10 plots the different components of NIF, to determine which ones accounted for the sharp increase. Both liabilities (claims of foreigners on Greece) and assets (claims of Greece on foreigners) increased since the late 1990s, and the increase concerned both debt and equity. The increased capital flows were a consequence of the financial liberalization that took place in Greece in the late 1980s and the 1990s, and of

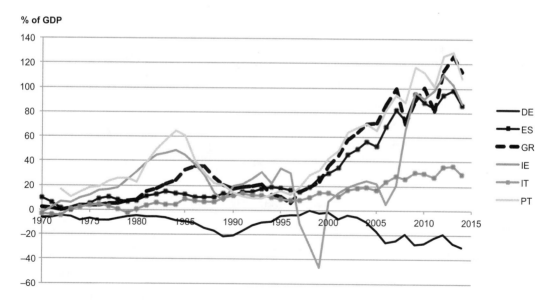

Figure 1.9
Net indebtedness to foreigners for Greece and other EZ countries, 1970 to 2014, as percentage of GDP. The data come from Lane and Milesi-Ferretti (2007).

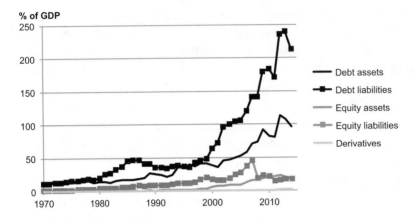

Figure 1.10
Components of net indebtedness to foreigners in Greece, 1970 to 2014, as percentage of GDP.
The data come from Lane and Milesi-Ferretti (2007).

Greece's growing financial integration with the euro area. At the same time debt claims were far larger than equity claims, meaning that foreigners' investment in Greece was primarily through bonds and other types of debt rather than through FDI or stock purchases (and likewise for the investment of Greek residents in foreign countries). Hence the sharp increase in NIF was primarily the outcome of debt liabilities increasing faster than debt assets. Indeed the NIF series for Greece almost coincides with the net external debt series, which is the difference between debt liabilities and debt assets.[6]

We next examine how the behavior of Greece's NIF was replicated in that of exports and imports, investment, and savings. This provides a fuller account of the evolution of the Greek economy before the crisis, as well as more insight into the mechanisms at play.

The basic macroeconomic identities linking NIF, exports, imports, investment, and savings are

Increase in NIF = – Net exports – Net current transfers – Capital gains   (1)

and

Savings – Investment = Net exports + Net current transfers.   (2)

According to equation (1), a country's NIF increases if the sum of net exports and net current transfers is negative.[7] Net exports are defined as exports minus imports. Net current transfers are the foreign aid, workers' remittances, interest and dividend payments, and so on, that the country receives from other countries, net of what it pays to them.[8] Intuitively, if the country must pay for imports an amount larger than what it earns from exports plus the net transfers it receives from other countries, then the country has to transfer resources to foreigners. This depletes the country's assets and eventually the country must borrow from foreigners.

According to equation (2), the sum of a country's net exports and net current transfers is negative if the country's savings are not sufficient to finance investment.[9] This identity becomes intuitive when combined with equation (1): if the country's savings are not sufficient to finance investment, then the country must borrow the difference from foreigners. In such cases NIF increases because of equation (1).

Figures 1.11 and 1.12 plot net exports and net current transfers, respectively, for Greece, Portugal, Spain, and the EU average from 1970 onward, as percentage of GDP.

Net current transfers for Greece averaged 5.1 percent of GDP per year during the period 1970 to 1995. After that period they dropped significantly, averaging 1 percent during 1996 to 2007. The drop had several causes: (1) EU subsidies became smaller as funds were re-directed to newly entering countries that were poorer than Greece, (2) workers' remittances became smaller as Greece was historically a net sender of migrants (who were sending their earned money back to Greece) but became a net receiver, and (3) Greece's external debt kept increasing and so were the required interest payments. Portugal experienced a similar drop in net current transfers.

Since net exports for Greece were negative during the entire period 1970 to 2014, the country was importing more than it was exporting. Greece's trade deficit, defined

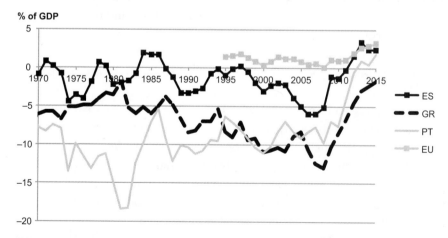

Figure 1.11
Net exports for Greece, Portugal, Spain, and the EU average, 1970 to 2014, as percentage of GDP. The data come from AMECO (series "Net exports of goods and services").

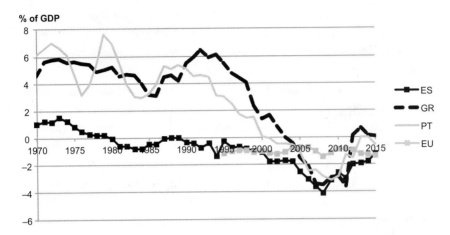

Figure 1.12
Net current transfers for Greece, Portugal, Spain, and the EU average, 1970 to 2014, as percentage of GDP. The data come from AMECO (sum of the series "Net current transfers" and "Net primary income").

as imports minus exports, averaged 5.6 percent of GDP per year during the period 1970 to 1995, and was roughly offset by net current transfers (5.1 percent). As a consequence of the transfers Greece's net indebtedness to foreigners (NIF) was kept at manageable levels. But while net current transfers dropped significantly after the mid-1990s, the trade deficit did not drop in a compensating manner. Instead, it *rose*, to 9.8 percent during 1995 to 2007. The combined drop in net current transfers and rise in the trade deficit drove, from equation (1), the sharp increase in NIF. The sharp increase in NIF in Spain was driven by same combined drop in net current transfers and rise in the trade deficit. In the case of Portugal the drop in net current transfers was instead the main driver.

According to figures 1.11 and 1.12, the sharp increase in Greece's NIF from the mid-1990s was associated with a sharp drop in net exports and in net current transfers. According to equation (2), the combined drop in these two variables was associated with an equally sharp drop in the difference between savings and investment. We next examine the latter two variables to identify the drivers of that drop. Figure 1.13 plots investment in Greece, Portugal, Spain, and the EU average from 1970 onward, as a percentage of GDP.[10]

Investment in Greece was high in the 1970s, averaging 30.6 percent of GDP per year over the period 1970 to 1979. It remained relatively stable in the region of 20 to 25 percent of GDP from the 1980s until the crisis. In the late 1990s, investment increased to the top of that region and remained at that level until 2007.

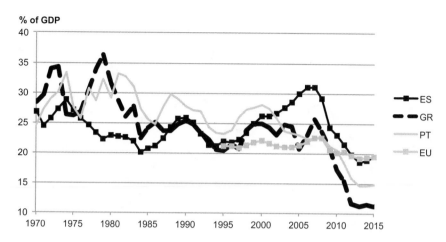

Figure 1.13

Investment in Greece, Portugal, Spain, and the EU average, 1970 to 2014, as percentage of GDP. The data come from AMECO (series "Gross fixed capital formation—Total economy").

The relatively mild variation in investment from 1980 until the crisis masks much sharper variation in the different components of investment. Figure 1.14 plots corporate investment in Greece and the comparison countries, and figure 1.15 does the same for residential investment.

During the period 1970 to 1995, corporate investment in Greece was well below Portugal's and Spain's: it averaged 8.1 percent of GDP per year, while the corresponding averages were 13.5 percent for Portugal and 13.1 percent for Spain. The low level of investment reflected Greece's relatively low growth rate of GDP during that period. As a consequence of better economic management during the 1990s, and a stock market boom in anticipation of euro entry, corporate investment rose significantly. It averaged 10.4 percent of GDP per year during the period 1996 to 2007, and the gap with the other countries narrowed. The increase in investment was reflected in the sharp pickup of growth during that period. It is also consistent with the evidence in table 1.1 that capital accumulation was the main contributor to Greece's fast growth in GDP from the mid-1990s until the crisis.

In contrast to corporate investment, residential investment was higher in Greece than in all comparison countries until the mid-1990s. From the mid-1990s onward and until the crisis, Greek residential investment stabilized at a lower level, and picked up somewhat toward the end of that period. From 2001 to 2007, Greece was overtaken by Spain, consistent with the debt-fueled real-estate boom in that county.

The predominance of residential relative to corporate investment in Greece is consistent with the evidence shown in chapter 7 (on the financial system) that when

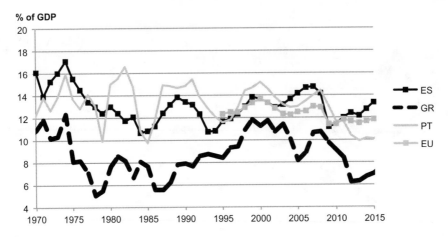

Figure 1.14
Corporate investment in Greece, Portugal, Spain, and the EU average, 1970 to 2014, as percentage of GDP. The data come from AMECO (difference between the series "Gross fixed capital formation—Private sector" and "Gross fixed capital formation—Dwellings").

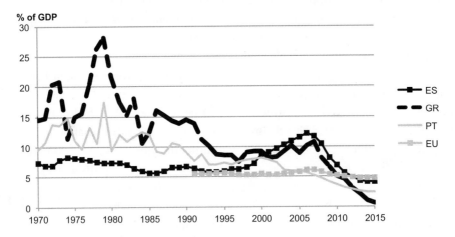

Figure 1.15
Residential investment in Greece, Portugal, Spain, and the EU average, 1970 to 2014, as percentage of GDP. The data come from AMECO (series "Gross fixed capital formation —Dwellings").

compared to their EZ counterparts, Greek households hold a larger fraction of their wealth in real estate than in financial assets. Real estate seems to be the preferred savings vehicle for Greek households, to a larger extent than in the comparison countries. Explanations that chapter 7 puts forward for this behavior include lack of trust in capital markets due to insufficient investor protection, no incentives (and until 2014 tax disincentives) to save in private pensions, and a history of high inflation. Because firms have limited access to household savings, their cost of capital is high, and this depresses corporate investment.

Figure 1.16 plots savings in Greece, Portugal, Spain, and the EU average from 1970 onward, as percentage of GDP. The figure shows a large drop in savings since the mid-1990s. In fact savings in Greece have been dropping since the 1970s.

The savings in figure 1.16 are the sum of government savings and private sector savings. Government savings are the difference between current revenue (figure 1.7) and current expenditure (obtained by adding figures 1.6 and 1.8). Figures 1.6 to 1.8 indicate that government savings in Greece declined sharply from about 0 percent in the late 1990s to about −12 percent in 2009. This sharp drop is reflected in the sharp drop in (total) savings shown in figure 1.16. Since a decline in savings is associated with an increase in net indebtedness to foreigners (NIF), one could attribute Greece's high NIF to the government's lax budget discipline after euro entry. Yet why was NIF low in

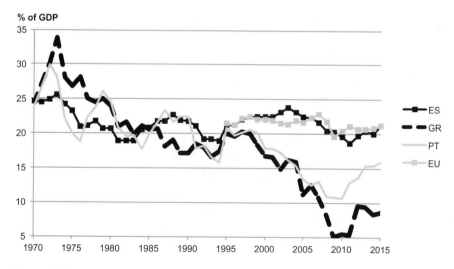

Figure 1.16
Savings in Greece, Portugal, Spain, and the EU average, 1970 to 2014, as percentage of GDP. The data come from AMECO (series "Gross national saving").

the 1980s, when budget discipline was equally lax? The answer lies in the behavior of private savings, plotted in figure 1.17.

Private sector savings in Greece dropped sharply from the mid-1990s: from 26.1 percent of GDP in 1995, they decreased to an average of 16.4 percent in 2000 to 2007. That average was the lowest among all comparison countries (not all of which are reported in figure 1.17), and significantly below the EU average of 20.8 percent. Moreover the 9.7 = 26.1 − 16.4 percent drop from 1995 to 2000–2007 was the most severe among all comparison countries.

The sharp increase in Greece's NIF from the mid-1990s was due to a combination of high government deficits after euro entry and a drop in private sector savings in the run-up to euro entry.[11] Private sector savings became insufficient to finance the government's deficits. From 1999 onward (and until 2008), they became insufficient to even finance private sector investment, as can be seen by comparing the series in figure 1.17 to the sum of the series in figures 1.14 and 1.15.

The low level of private sector savings in Greece since the late-1990s could have been the result of many factors. The financial liberalization that took place in Greece in the late 1980s and the 1990s, and the sharp decline in interest rates in anticipation of euro entry led to a boom in consumer credit, documented in chapter 7, and hence to a decline in savings. The large stock of housing accumulated in the 1970s and

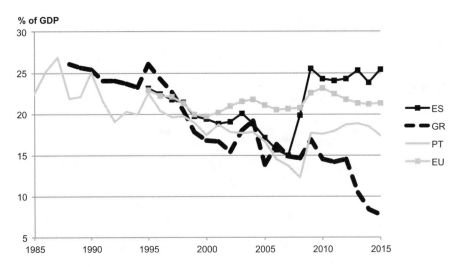

Figure 1.17
Private sector savings in Greece, Portugal, Spain, and the EU average, 1980 to 2014, as percentage of GDP. The data come from AMECO and the European Commission (difference between AMECO series "Gross national saving" and EC series "Gross saving; General government").

1980s might have made households more secure about their wealth and less inclined to save further. The pension system that was made increasingly generous in the 1980s might have further reduced households' need to save. Because of the lower savings, the increased investment needs by Greek firms in the run-up to and after euro entry had to be covered partly outside of Greece.

In theory, an increase in a country's NIF can be beneficial and sustainable if it is used to finance improvements in the country's productive capacity and ability to export. Figure 1.14 shows that corporate investment increased in Greece from the mid-1990s, and so productive capacity did increase. At the same time, as figures 1.15 to 1.17 show, most of the increase in NIF was associated with increases in consumption. Indeed, lower private savings, lower government savings, and higher residential investment, all reflect higher consumption. Hence the high NIF was most likely unsustainable.

1.2.3 Wages and Prices

We next examine the behavior of wages and their relationship to labor productivity. We look both at real wages (i.e., wages adjusted for price inflation) and nominal wages.

The ratio of the average wage in a country to the country's labor productivity per person employed is referred to as real unit labor cost (RULC). This ratio can be computed using either the real or the nominal wage, provided that productivity is measured in the same terms. RULC is also the ratio of the aggregate compensation of all employees to GDP, as can be seen by multiplying numerator and denominator by the number of persons employed. Hence RULC measures the fraction of GDP going to labor. Figure 1.18 plots RULC in Greece and the comparison countries from 1990 onward.

RULC in Greece has been fairly stable, around 50 percent, which means that wages were roughly keeping up with labor productivity. Thus the rapid increase in real labor productivity during the period 1996 to 2007 (figure 1.2) was reflected in an equally rapid increase in real wages.[12]

We next compute the ratio of the average nominal wage to real labor productivity. This is referred to as nominal unit labor cost (NULC), and differs from RULC because it incorporates information about price inflation. NULC allows us to compare the cost of producing the same unit of real GDP across countries, without adjusting by each country's price level. This makes it useful as a measure of competitiveness, especially from the point of view of a firm that wants to produce a good to sell to the global market and must decide on which country to produce it in. NULC has pitfalls when used as a measure of competitiveness (e.g., Knibb 2015), but it is useful for a first-pass

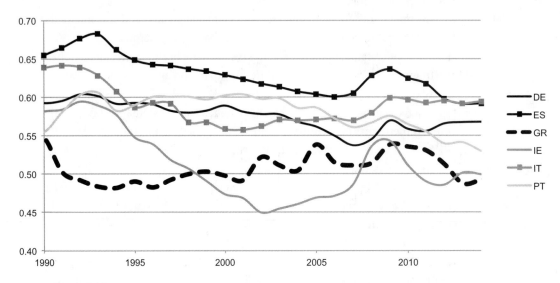

Figure 1.18
Real unit labor cost in Greece and other EZ countries, 1990 to 2014. The data come from AMECO.

approach. Figure 1.19 plots the NULC in Greece and the comparison countries from 2000 onward.

NULC stayed roughly constant in Germany prior to the crisis. It increased in all the other countries, however, reflecting their higher price inflation relative to Germany. Hence all those countries lost competitiveness relative to Germany. In measuring Greece's competitiveness relative to Germany by the ratio of their respective NULCs, we find that the loss of competitiveness for Greece between 2000 and 2007 was 29.6 percent. That was second-highest after Ireland (36 percent).

1.2.4 Markets and Institutions

1.2.4.1 Business Environment Figure 1.20 plots an index of the quality of the business environment for Greece and the comparison countries. The index is constructed based on the World Bank *Doing Business* reports. These reports rank countries each year according to factors such as the number of procedures required to start a business, the legal protection of creditors and shareholders, the level and complexity of corporate taxes, and the efficiency of courts in enforcing contracts. The reports go back to 2004, and country rankings were first calculated in the 2006 report. The number of countries covered in the reports increased over time, from 155 in the 2004 report to 189 in the 2016 report. Because the report for a given year is computed using information collected in the previous year, we associate each report to the year preceding the one

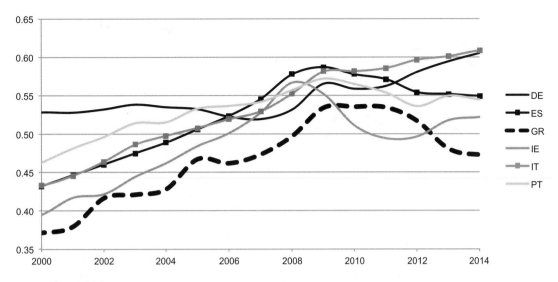

Figure 1.19
Nominal unit labor cost in Greece and other EZ countries, 2000 to 2014. The data come from AMECO.

mentioned in the report. Hence figure 1.20 starts in 2005, using the index computed from the 2006 report.[13]

Figure 1.20 shows that before the crisis Greece's business environment was significantly worse than in all comparison countries. For example, in the last pre-crisis year 2007, Greece ranked 100th. This placed it in the bottom half of the countries in the report, and at a significant distance from the remaining comparison countries—next came Italy ranked 53rd, Spain ranked 38th, and Portugal ranked 37th. Greece's ranking improved significantly in 2011 to 2014.[14] As we explain in section 1.3, the improvement was due to reforms that were required as part of the adjustment programs. Yet, despite the improvement, Greece remained close to the bottom of the EU28 countries: as of 2015, it was 26th out of 28. Greece's relative position did not change because other EU countries with comparatively low rankings before the crisis also reformed (e.g., Italy in the figure). Thus, while the reforms required as part of the adjustment programs helped Greece improve its global ranking, they were not sufficiently ambitious (in design or implementation) to help it overtake other EU countries.

The quality of a country's business environment is determined by a number of factors including product market regulation, the justice system, access to finance, and labor market regulation. These factors are accounted for in the World Bank *Doing Business* rankings, and are further considered in subsequent chapters of this book, where they are analyzed in depth in regard to Greece.

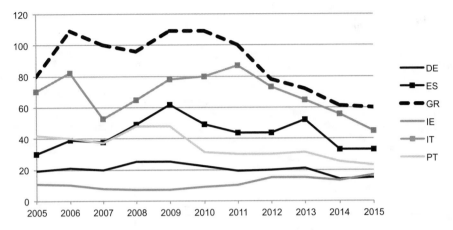

Figure 1.20
Quality of the business environment in Greece and other EZ countries. Country rankings in the World Bank *Doing Business* reports. We associate each report to the year prior to the one mentioned in the report.

Product Market Regulation   Product market regulation (PMR) is the set of state-provided rules that govern how the markets for goods and services operate. These rules can affect, for example, the ease with which new firms or individuals can enter into a market, or the extent to which competition can take place within a market. Efficient rules should generally facilitate entry and competition. Indeed entry lowers production costs because more efficient firms can enter. Entry also renders competition more intense. This results in incentives to further reduce costs and to also reduce "markups" of prices over costs (i.e., lower prices even if costs were unchanged). Lower costs and prices increase economywide productivity and make consumers better off. PMR in Greece was inefficient prior to the crisis, and improvements during the crisis have been limited (as of 2016). There are typically a large and overly complicated number of regulations, and entry in many markets is discouraged or explicitly disallowed. Moreover in the markets where regulation is truly necessary, such as due to fixed costs that can sustain only few firms that form an oligopoly and charge high prices, implementation is often weak and inefficient. Finally, state-owned or controlled firms play a significant role in some markets. Because these firms are prone to political interference, they are typically inefficient, with high production costs. Because they are also politically powerful, they can distort competition in their favor. The poor state of PMR in Greece is reflected, for example, in the OECD PMR index. That index aggregates many dimensions of PMR, such as entry costs and state ownership, and higher values mean heavier PMR. As of

2008, the index value for Greece was 2.21. That was the second-highest value among the 34 OECD countries for which the index was computed; the highest value was 2.65 for Turkey, and the OECD average was 1.57.[15]

The state of PMR in Greece is reviewed in depth and with the use of examples in chapter 4 (on product markets). Chapters 14 and 15 (on public administration) provide further evidence on the complexity of regulations in Greece and on the role played by state-owned firms. Chapter 5 (on privatizations) further elaborates on the size and inefficiency of state-owned firms and on the trade-offs involved in moving firms from state to private ownership.

Justice System   A key factor contributing to the quality of the business environment is whether contracts can be enforced efficiently. Indeed firms are reluctant to invest and enter new markets if they are worried that disputes that may arise with their trading counterparties will not be resolved fairly and quickly. Contract enforcement by the Greek justice system was, and still is, inefficient because of the long delays that are involved. For example, according to the 2008 World Bank *Doing Business* report, the average time to resolve a dispute in Greece was 819 days. The EZ average was 507 days, and Greek courts were the third slowest in the EZ after Slovenia's (1,350 days) and Italy's (1,210 days). The state of the justice system in Greece is reviewed in depth in chapter 12 (on the justice system). That chapter describes the inefficiencies in the system, analyses their underlying causes, and gives a comprehensive blueprint for reform going forward.

Access to Finance   Another factor contributing to the quality of the business environment is whether firms with good investment projects can raise the necessary funds to implement them and can do so at competitive rates. Evidence surveyed in chapter 7 (on the financial system) suggests that Greek firms face high costs of raising equity capital from households: their debt-to-equity ratios (leverage) are higher than those of their counterparts in other European countries, and they rely less on small minority shareholders and more on large controlling ones. Moreover, compared to their EZ counterparts, Greek households hold a larger fraction of their wealth in real assets rather than financial ones, and most of their financial assets portfolio consists of bank deposits, with limited investment in stocks, bonds, and mutual funds. (The household evidence is consistent with the preponderance of residential relative to corporate investment shown in section 1.2.2.) These features were present before the crisis, and they still remain important. One likely cause for the high cost of equity capital is the weak protection of small shareholders. Chapters 7 (on the financial system) and especially 12 (on the justice system) review evidence on investor protection. According to the 2008 World Bank *Doing Business* report, creditor protection (strength of legal rights index) was the weakest in Greece and Italy among all EZ countries, and shareholder protection (strength of investor protection index) was the weakest in Greece. Both indicators measure the quality of laws (*de jure*) rather than the actual implementation; inadequate implementation due to large court delays further weakens protection. Chapters 7 and 12 also review bankruptcy laws in Greece, especially in the context of the NPL problem that has developed since the beginning of the crisis, and show that bankruptcy in Greece is a highly inefficient process.

Labor Market Regulation   Labor market regulation (LMR) is the set of state-provided rules that govern the relationship between workers and firms. These rules can affect the ease with which firms can dismiss workers, employ part-time workers, or request workers to put in overtime. Efficient rules should give firms flexibility to adapt quickly to changes in their environment, for example, by dismissing workers if product demand decreases, or by asking them to work overtime if demand increases temporarily. Labor market flexibility is what enables firms to invest, and as the empirical evidence surveyed in chapter 6 (on the labor market) shows, this can have positive effects on employment and wages. As chapter 6 also points out, labor market flexibility should be accompanied by a robust state-provided system of social insurance, a point to which we return later in this section. LMR in Greece prior to the crisis was restrictive and inefficient. This can be seen, for example, by the OECD Employment Protection Legislation (EPL) index. That index aggregates many dimensions of LMR, such as the costs for a firm to dismiss workers, either individually or collectively, and the costs to employ part-time workers. Higher values of the index mean heavier LMR. As of 2008, the index value for Greece was 2.97. That was the fifth-highest value among the 30 OECD countries for which the index was computed; the highest value was 3.46 for Turkey, followed by 3.39 for Luxembourg, 3.23 for Mexico, and 3.11 for Spain. The OECD average was 2.23. Other dimensions of labor market regulation were also restrictive. For example, overtime was prohibitively expensive. And the implicit tax rate on labor, defined as the difference between what a firm pays for a worker minus what the worker actually receives as disposable income, expressed as a percentage of what the firm pays, was one of the highest in the OECD for some worker categories, hence discouraging job creation. Heavy regulation is conducive to regulation evasion and the formation of an informal labor market, in which workers receive only limited protection. Chapter 6 reviews in depth the regulatory distortions in the Greek labor market, and their implications for market outcomes. It also presents a conceptual framework to evaluate the costs and benefits of LMR.

Summary Despite its fast GDP growth during the period 1995 to 2007, Greece failed to provide an attractive legal and regulatory environment for firms to operate in. The low levels of FDI, as described in this section, and the low corporate investment are likely consequences of this. The various costs that firms face to enter markets and operate in them raise production costs and are the key driver of the low productivity discussed above. Entry costs further contribute to the formation of oligopolistic market structures with few domestic incumbents. This is at the expense of domestic consumers as well as of the economy at large because high prices in one industry sector raise the costs of firms' activities in other sectors.

An additional negative consequence of the high regulatory burden (both PMR and LMR) is that firms have strong incentives to remain small, as to remain below the regulators' (and tax collectors') radar. Chapter 3 (on international trade) shows that small firms indeed account for a much larger fraction of employment and GDP in Greece relative to other European countries of similar size. Small firms are typically less efficient than large firms and find it more difficult to export. Hence the effect of heavy regulation on firm size is an additional channel through which regulation impairs productivity, and can account for the relatively low exporting capacity of the Greek economy.

1.2.4.2 Social Protection Figure 1.21 plots the poverty rate for Greece and the comparison countries. The poverty rate is computed using the OECD definition, as the percentage of people whose income falls below 50 percent of the median household income. Income is computed after taxes and transfers, and hence takes into account welfare payments to the poor.

The poverty rate in the four southern European countries, Greece, Italy, Portugal, and Spain, is significantly higher than in Germany and Ireland. Within this group of southern countries, Greece's poverty rate was second highest after Spain's during 2004 to 2009 and became the highest from 2010 onward. Other measures of income inequality, such as the Gini coefficient, paint a similar picture, with inequality being the highest in the southern countries, and Greece being close to the top of that group.

The evidence on higher income inequality in the southern countries, does not take into account informal sources of income; for example, transfers between family members may be more frequent and substantial in the European south than in the north.

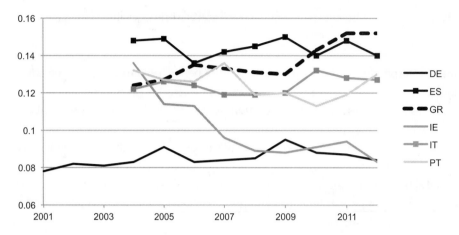

Figure 1.21
Poverty rate in Greece and other EZ countries. The data come from the OECD. The poverty rate is defined as the percentage of people whose income falls below 50 percent of the median household income. Income is computed after taxes and transfers.

Nevertheless, as figure 1.21 suggests, the formal system of social protection in the southern European countries is not as robust as in the northern countries. The chapters that follow analyze in depth different aspects of social protection, and public sector efficiency more broadly, in the case of Greece.

Pensions   Pensions provide social protection to the old, and especially those who could not save enough during their working lives. In the *pay-as-you-go* (PAYG) system, the pensions of the old are paid by the taxes and social contributions of the young. Its polar opposite is the *funded* system, whereby the pensions of the old are funded from their savings, and there are no transfers across generations. Typical pension systems have elements of both: pensions are funded by taxes and social contributions as well as by savings that carry tax incentives. Greece's pension system is almost exclusively PAYG, with voluntary pensions based on private savings playing a smaller role than in other EZ countries.[16] More important, the system is costly, inefficient, and socially unfair. These problems have remained despite some improvements to the system. As chapter 11 (on pensions) documents, in 2007 pensions absorbed more than 12 percent of GDP in Greece, which was the second-highest percentage in the EU after Italy. Nevertheless, old-age poverty was high, indicating that the high expenditure on pensions was directed inefficiently.[17] That inefficiency was partly due to the fragmentation of the pension system: rules that map lifetime contributions to pensions, and even retirement ages, differed across professional groups, with politically powerful groups such as employees in state-owned enterprises or the public sector, enjoying special privileges at the expense of others. A related source of inefficiency was that while contributions were large, they bore only a weak link to pensions paid out. Contributions were thus viewed as a (large) tax on labor, driving up the cost of employment and incentivizing contribution evasion. Further sources of inefficiency were that pension funds were required to invest their limited resources in Greek government bonds, hence forgoing diversification; their managers were often political appointees with no asset-management experience; and regulatory oversight was weak. Chapter 11 (on pensions) analyses in depth the drawbacks of Greece's pension system, evaluates the improvements made during the crisis, and proposes a detailed blueprint for completing the system's reform.

Welfare System and Unemployment Insurance The welfare system provides social protection to those with low income. Such protection can take, for example, the form of a minimum guaranteed income. The welfare system is related to the system of unemployment insurance, which can provide time-limited unemployment benefits. Figure 1.22 plots the expenditure on unemployment benefits and on active labor market programs for Greece and the comparison countries. Active labor market programs are meant to help the unemployed find a job by providing them with training and other assistance. They account for a small part of the total in figure 1.22.

Greece's expenditure on the unemployed was the lowest among all comparison countries during 1995 to 2010, and the second lowest in 2011. This is not because unemployment in Greece was low. During 1995 to 2011 it ranged from first to fourth highest among the comparison countries. Thus Greece's unemployment insurance system seems to offer limited protection to the unemployed.

A similar conclusion holds for the protection that Greece's welfare system offers to those with low income. OECD computes the fraction of public social benefits that goes to different population groups, sorted by income. In 2014 (first year in which results were reported) only 7 percent of social benefits in Greece went to the lowest quintile (fifth) of the population. That was the second-lowest percentage among 35 OECD countries; the lowest was Turkey (4.5 percent) and the OECD average was 20.1 percent. Conversely, 31.1 percent of social benefits went to the highest quintile. That was the fifth-highest percentage in the OECD; the highest was Mexico (55.9 percent), Portugal (40.1 percent), Turkey (39.1 percent), and Italy (31.1 percent), and the OECD average was 20.3 percent. Thus Greece's welfare system provides limited protection to the poor and some key social benefits, such as pensions, benefit disproportionally the well-off.

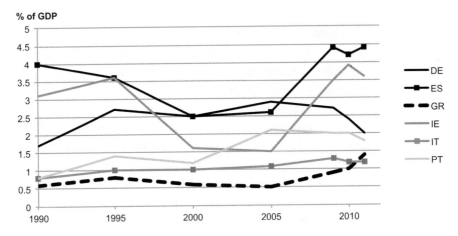

Figure 1.22
Expenditure on unemployment benefits and active labor market programs in Greece and other EZ countries, as percentage of GDP. The data come from the OECD.

Similar conclusions hold for the other southern European countries, consistent with the evidence on poverty rates in figure 1.21. Building on these observations, Chapter 10 (on taxation) sketches how a comprehensive welfare system could be set up in Greece, and evaluates quantitatively a number of alternatives. Chapter 6 (on the labor market) similarly emphasizes the absence of a robust unemployment insurance system in Greece, and sketches how a modern such system could be set up.

Health Care Health care systems include an element of social protection: if, for example, income-based social contributions are used to finance uniform access to health care services across the population, then there is a redistribution from the rich to the poor (because the social contributions are income based) and from the healthy to those in poor health. An additional aspect of health care systems is cost efficiency, that is, whether money is spent in those medical procedures or those pharmaceuticals that yield the highest health benefit per unit of money spent. Greece's health care system scored poorly on both counts before the crisis. It still does so despite some improvements. As chapter 9 (on health care) documents, although Greece spent a similar proportion of its GDP on health care as the other comparison countries, it was overly reliant on expensive inputs. For example, it had the highest number of practicing doctors per capita in the OECD while its number of nurses per head was one of the lowest; it was performing the highest number of CT and MRI scans per capita together with Italy; and it had one of the highest expenditures in pharmaceuticals. At the root of these problems, present both before and during the crisis, was a lack of accountability of health care suppliers, such as hospitals, for cost overruns. Overspending in some aspects of health care provision meant low quality in key other aspects, such as long waiting times in public hospitals. To bypass long waiting times, patients incurred high out-of-pocket expenses, including informal payments to physicians. Out-of-pocket expenses in Greece in 2008 were 38 percent of total health care expenditure, compared to 26 percent in Portugal, 21 percent in Italy and Spain, 9 percent in the United Kingdom, and 8 percent in France. Thus Greece's health care system provided limited social protection. Chapter 9 (on health care) analyses the drawbacks of Greece's health care system, evaluates the improvements made during the crisis, and proposes key further improvements.

Education Education is one of the main drivers of long-term economic growth. A well-educated population tends to be more productive and adapt better to technological change. Moreover a country's ability to do basic research and innovation, and to be among the leaders in high value-added industry sectors, depends on its education system and especially on the quality of its universities. Because education tends to be one of the main components of public expenditure, cost efficiency is an important consideration, as in the case of health care. And as with health care, education has a social-protection component: tax-financed public education provides the poor with education that they could not afford otherwise. Broad access to a well-functioning educational system is a prerequisite for social mobility, whereby young people can develop their talents and pursue productive careers independently of their parents' status and wealth, with wide benefits for the economy and society.

The performance of Greece's educational system before the crisis was mediocre, and initial attempts to reform parts of the system during the crisis have mostly been reversed. Greece ranked 24th and 23rd, respectively, out of 31 OECD countries in 2007 in terms of the percentages of the population who had completed secondary and tertiary education. The 2009 PISA tests for 15-year-olds placed Greece 24th for reading, and 27th for mathematics and science, within the same group of 31 counties. And Greece had no university in the top 200 according to the 2007 Shanghai Jiao Tong ranking, while countries with similar population to Greece, such as Belgium and Israel, had three or more universities in the top 150. One may be tempted to attribute Greece's underperformance to the relatively low proportion of its GDP that is spent on education: as of 2005, Greece was spending 4.2 percent of its GDP on education, while the OECD average was 5.8 percent. Yet the OECD-reported spending for Greece corresponds almost exclusively to public education and does not include two large out-of-pocket expenditures incurred by Greek households: tuition costs for private tutoring centers (*frontistiria*) to prepare high-school students for university entrance exams, and tuition and living costs for university students studying abroad.[18] Taking these expenditures into account, Greece's overall expenditure on education is likely to lie above the OECD average. At the root of the inefficiencies is lack of a systematic and effective evaluation system for schools and universities, combined with their minimal autonomy from the state. According to a 2009 PISA survey, Greece and Turkey scored the lowest in the OECD on measures of schools' autonomy to allocate resources and to set up their curriculum and their assessment methods. Likewise universities are closely controlled by the Ministry of Education in terms of their resources, personnel decisions, admissions criteria and targets, and programs of study. Faculty members and academic units are given weak incentives for high performance on research and teaching. Chapter 8 (on education) analyses the drawbacks of Greece's education system, as well as the failed attempts to reform it, and sketches key directions for improvement.

Summary   Greece's performance in the areas of social protection has been well below the median OECD country. This can be seen from measures such as the poverty rate and the fraction of social benefits received by the poorer segments of the population. It can also be seen from the relative importance of out-of-pocket expenditures on health care and education. Moreover the provision of health care, education, pensions, and welfare was, and still is to a lesser extent, overly expensive relative to the quality of the output. The inefficiencies are partly driven by a lack of performance measurement and evaluation: there is neither a way to direct funds to the more efficient units nor any incentives for efficient management within these units. An additional source of inefficiencies in social protection is that politically powerful groups are enjoying special privileges at the expense of others; that was especially important for pensions and health care before the crisis.

The inefficiencies in the provision of public services have led to the emergence of privately provided services, although in many instances the overall benefit has been limited. For example, the main out-of-pocket expenditure of Greek households on education is directed toward private tutoring centers that prepare high school students for university entrance exams. These centers have effectively replaced high school coursework, thus creating only low additional value.

1.2.4.3 Politicians and the Economy   Many of the institutional features described in this section are related to another key feature of the Greek economy: the control that politicians exert over economic activity. By political control, we refer to the influence exerted by the government on industry regulators, other public agencies such as those in charge of statistics and tax collection, and broader segments of the public sector such as state-owned firms, schools and universities, hospitals, and local authorities. One indicator of political control is whether industry regulators and heads of other public agencies or state-owned firms change routinely when the political party in power changes, and do not have fixed terms or are not allowed to complete them.

Political control is different from the issue of state versus private ownership. For example, an industry can be mostly privately owned, but politicians can have significant influence over the firms in that industry because they control the regulator. Conversely, universities or hospitals can be public but can have an arm's-length relationship with politicians, e.g., such that their funding is decided by a public agency based on preset performance metrics.

Unfortunately, internationally comparable indexes of political control that capture the above-mentioned characteristics do not seem to exist. It is nevertheless possible to form an impression of the degree of political control in Greece from indexes that measure related characteristics and from anecdotal evidence.

Political influence over Greece's statistical agency prior to the crisis is well known, as it led to the underreporting of the government deficit. A requirement of Greece's first adjustment program was that the statistical agency should have full independence. There were significant improvements in that respect, although allegations of efforts at political meddling continued and have culminated with the attempted prosecution of the agency's first director since the agency became independent.

Tax collection prior to the crisis was the responsibility of the Ministry of Finance, and hence was under full political control. Following sustained demands by its official creditors, Greece established an independent agency in charge of tax collection in 2013. Directors ("General Secretaries") of that agency were supposed to have a five-year term. The first director, however, was forced to resign in 2014, and the second director was forced to resign after the 2015 election that led to a new party taking over. Thus independence seems to be only nominal. Note that control over tax collection gives the political party in power huge sway over the economy: it can reward firms that support it by lobbying the tax-collection agency to not audit these firms or not levy penalties against them, and it can punish other firms.

The importance of state-owned firms can be measured by the OECD index "Scope of state-owned entreprises." This index measures the share of industry sectors in which the state controls at least one firm, and it is a sub-index of the PMR index. As of 2008, the index value for Greece was 3.60. This was the tenth-highest value among 31 OECD countries. State-ownership in Greece was higher than in countries such as Denmark, Germany, the Netherlands, and the United Kingdom, but lower than in France, Italy, Spain, and Sweden. Thus, while Greece had high state-ownership by OECD standards, it was not an outlier. Measures of state-ownership, however, can understate the degree of political control in Greece.

The banking sector, analyzed in chapter 7 (on the financial system), provides a good case study. Prior to the recapitalization in 2013, the state held negligible or no stakes in any of the four largest banks. Yet the top management at the largest bank, the National Bank of Greece (NBG), was replaced when the political party in power changed. The government could engineer this change partly through its influence on state pension funds, which were holding minority stakes in NBG. Additional evidence for political control is that Greek banks were the most "home biased" in the EZ in terms of their government bond portfolio: as of 2010, 98 percent of that portfolio was invested in Greek government bonds rather than being more broadly diversified across the EZ. This lack of diversification cost Greek banks dearly following the bankruptcy of the Greek state. Chapter 7 argues that political pressures to banks were an important driver of the lack of diversification.[19]

Political control is also apparent in the health care and education sectors. For example, directors of public hospitals change routinely when the political parties in power change, and new appointments are often members or sympathizers of the new party. And as chapter 9 (on health care) notes, the Ministry of Health gets involved directly in negotiating prices for pharmaceuticals or hospital treatments, while it should have only general oversight and leave operational control to an independent public agency. Likewise schools and universities are micromanaged by the Ministry of Education to a much greater extent than in other countries. For example, public universities in countries such as Germany, the Netherlands, Switzerland, and the United Kingdom have significant discretion over how to manage their budget, including how many faculty and staff to employ, what salaries to pay senior faculty, and how many students to admit. In Greece, no such discretion exists: staffing numbers must be negotiated with the Ministry of Education, and all salaries and admissions targets are centrally set. Moreover, public funding to the universities in the other countries depends on preset measures of performance, but a relationship between funding and performance is virtually nonexistent in Greece.

Political control of the forms described above is damaging to the economy. Political appointees to public agencies, state-controlled firms, hospitals, and the like, are generally chosen based on party loyalty rather than their skills for the job. This leads to mismanagement and inefficiencies in the public sector, which is a key characteristic of the Greek economy, and is further documented in several chapters of this book, especially chapters 8 (on education), 9 (health care), 14 and 15 (public administration). Incentives in the private sector become distorted as well. Firms endeavor to be in good terms with politicians rather than to develop innovative products or production methods. Such incentives can give rise to corruption, as firms may pay bribes and political contributions to get favors from politicians. Corruption is another key characteristic of the Greek economy (e.g., Greece ranked 26th out of 28 EU countries according to the World Bank "control of corruption" indicator in 2013), and is further analyzed in chapter 13 (on corruption). Corruption imposes important costs to firms, and is a likely driver of Greece's low FDI.

1.3   The Greek Economy during the Crisis

1.3.1   Macroeconomic Performance

The main macroeconomic developments in Greece since the beginning of the crisis can be seen from the figures and tables in sections 1.2.1 to 1.2.3. GDP per capita declined by 26.3 percent between 2007 and 2014. The drop in GDP and the concomitant increase in unemployment, from 8.5 percent in 2007 to 26.6 percent in 2014, caused a sharp decline in living standards. Labor productivity per person employed declined by 8.9 percent, despite the sharp decline in the number of persons employed. The growth decomposition in table 1.1 indicates that the decline in labor productivity was driven by a decline in TFP, whereby less output was produced from given inputs of labor and capital, rather than a decline in the capital input. The decline in TFP was obviously not due to Greek firms forgetting how to use their existing technologies; TFP instead declined because labor and capital inputs were underutilized.

During the crisis Greece tightened sharply its public finances. In 2009 its primary deficit was 10.3 percent of GDP, and it turned into a primary surplus of 0.4 percent in 2014.[20] Likewise government savings, which differ from primary surplus because they exclude noncurrent items such as investment or privatization receipts, rose from –9.9 percent of GDP in 2009 to –0.9 percent in 2014. The fiscal tightening was achieved by cuts in public expenditure and increases in tax revenue, with the latter playing a somewhat larger role. Indeed the government's current expenditure decreased from 47.3 percent of GDP in 2009 to 44.4 percent in 2014, a change of 2.9 percent (= 47.3 – 44.4), and the government's current revenue increased from 37.4 percent of GDP in 2009 to 43.5 percent in 2014, a change of 6.1 percent (= 43.5 – 37.4).

The fiscal tightening in Greece was much sharper than in other EZ countries hit by the sovereign crisis. Government savings in Greece increased by 9.0 percent of GDP from 2009 to 2014 but increased by only 5.3 percent in Ireland, 1.2 percent in Italy, 3.7 percent in Portugal, and 1.1 percent in Spain. Thus Greece experienced much more severe austerity than the other countries. Greece's sharper fiscal tightening from 2009 to 2014 reflected fiscal conditions at both ends of that time interval: government savings in 2009 were the lowest in Greece relative to the other countries, and government savings in 2014 were the highest.[21]

Public debt increased significantly during the crisis, from 103.1 percent of GDP in 2007 to 177.1 percent in 2014. This change resulted from a number of factors: deficits during that period; the drop in GDP, which reduced the denominator of the debt-to-GDP ratio; and the debt restructuring that Greece agreed with its creditors in 2012 (PSI), which partly offset the previous effects. An approximate calculation of the contribution of each factor is as follows: Public debt in 2007 stood at 240 billion euros. The cumulated primary deficits during 2008 to 2014 were 76.4 billion, and the cumulated interest payments on debt were 75.8 billion.[22] Still, the PSI brought debt down by 107.1 billion, but Greece had to take a new loan of 25 billion to recapitalize its banks, which had incurred large losses on their holdings of Greek government bonds as a result of the PSI.[23] The cumulative effect of these factors was to bring debt to 310.1 billion (= 240 + 76.4 + 75.8 – 107.1 + 25), which is close to the AMECO-reported figure of 317.1 billion for 2014. Had GDP stayed at its 2007 value, the debt of 317.1 billion would have been 136.2 percent of GDP, but because of the drop in GDP it stood at 177.1 percent of 2014 GDP.

All these calculations are in nominal rather than present-value terms. That is, debt is computed by adding the principal (face value) payments that are due in all future years, rather than by adding all principal and coupon payments after discounting them at appropriate market interest rates. Computing debt in nominal rather than in present-value terms overstates Greece's debt because during the crisis much of the debt was extended to long maturities at below-market interest rates.[24] For example, interest payments on Greek debt in 2015 were 4.2 percent of GDP, lower than in Italy (4.3 percent) and Portugal (4.9 percent). By contrast, Greek debt stood at a significantly higher fraction of GDP (180.2 percent) than Italian (133.1 percent) and Portuguese (124.4 percent) debt. This means that the average interest rate on Greek debt was smaller than in Italy and Portugal, despite Greek debt having a longer average maturity and higher country risk.[25,26]

The crisis saw the elimination of not only Greece's primary budget deficit but also its trade deficit. In 2007 Greece's trade deficit was 12.4 percent of GDP, and it shrank to 2.4 percent in 2014. Net current transfers increased as well, from –3.4 percent of GDP in 2007 to 0.2 percent in 2014. The trade deficit had to shrink because the pre-crisis level was unsustainable. Indeed in 2007 Greece's net exports plus net current transfers were –15.8 percent (= –12.4 – 3.4) of GDP, which means from equation (1) that Greece was borrowing from foreigners an extra 15.8 percent of its GDP on an annual basis. Net exports plus net current transfers increased to -2.2 percent (= –2.4 + 0.2) in 2014.

The elimination of the trade deficit could, in principle, be accomplished through a combination of rising exports and declining imports. Declining imports played a significantly larger role than rising exports when comparing Greece to Ireland, Portugal, and Spain. We provide evidence for this in section 1.3.3, in the context of our discussion of internal devaluation. A more in-depth analysis is performed in chapter 3 (on international trade).

We next examine how the sharp increase in net exports and net transfers was reflected on savings and investment. The difference between savings and investment, which from equation (2) is the same as the sum of net exports and net transfers, rose by 13.6 percent (= 15.8 – 2.2) of GDP from 2007 to 2014. Savings dropped slightly, by 2.4 percent of GDP. Hence the rise in net exports and net transfers reflected an even larger drop in investment, by 16 percent (= 13.6 + 2.4) of GDP. The drop in investment in Greece was larger than in Ireland (10.7 percent), Portugal (8.2 percent), and Spain (11.9 percent). The discrepancy becomes even larger when investment is expressed in absolute terms rather than as a percentage of GDP, given Greece's larger drop in GDP. The drop in savings in Greece was larger than in the other three countries, although the effects were comparable: savings dropped by 1.6 percent of GDP in Spain, and rose by 1.3 percent in Ireland and 2.4 percent in Portugal. A key difference between Greece and the other three countries was that government savings rose in Greece but dropped in the other countries, while the opposite happened with private savings.

Wages declined significantly during the crisis. The decline in the average real wage between 2009 and 2014 was 19 percent. It was driven partly by the decline in real labor productivity and partly by the decline in real unit labor cost. The corresponding decline in the average nominal wage was 16.3 percent.[27] The large decline in wages helped Greece recover some of the competitiveness that was lost during the pre-crisis years. While Greece's loss of competitiveness relative to Germany (as measured by the ratio of their respective nominal unit labor costs shown in figure 1.19) was 29.6 percent between 2000 and 2007; it became only 11.1 percent between 2000 and 2014.

1.3.2 Structural Reforms

During the crisis, Greece legislated a number of structural reforms. Most of the reforms were required as part of the adjustment programs agreed with the EC/ECB/IMF Troika, although some important reforms were domestically driven. Some of the reforms had a significant impact. Others had no impact either because there was insufficient follow-up on their implementation or because they were diluted by subsequent pieces of legislation (Ioannides and Pissarides 2016). Below we list the main reforms by area, following roughly the same order as in section 1.2.4. Figure A.3, available at https:// mitpress.mit.edu/books/beyond-austerity, summarizes the timing of the main reforms, and figures A.1 and A.2 do the same for the political events and fiscal measures, respectively. The book ends with a comprehensive timeline of the reforms and other events during the crisis.

Product Market Regulation   A series of reforms were intended to make product market regulation (PMR) less onerous for firms and to reduce barriers to entry and competition. Law 3853/2010 reduced the complexity of starting a business, creating a "one-stop shop." Law 3919/2011 abolished restrictions to entry and competition in a number of professional services. Law 3982/2011 simplified procedures for obtaining permits in technical and manufacturing activities. Law 4014/2011 simplified the granting of environmental permits. Law 4072/2012 simplified legal aspects of business incorporation. Law 4177/2013 allowed stores to open on Sundays. Law 4254/2014 eliminated restrictions to entry and competition following up on some of the recommendations of an OECD study commissioned by the Greek government in 2012. Taken together, these reforms contributed significantly to the improvement in Greece's ranking in the World Bank *Doing Business* reports from 2010 to 2014, shown in figure 1.20.

In addition to the efforts to improve PMR, Greece embarked on a privatization program. Following up on an agreed action in the first adjustment program, it set up in 2011 a privatization agency, the Hellenic Republic Asset Development Fund (HRADF), with a stated target to sell 50 billion euros' worth of assets from 2011 to 2015. The assets included stakes in state-owned firms, public infrastructure such as airports and seaports, and public land. Privatizations fell much below the 50 billion target: as of December 2015, assets worth less than 10 billion have been privatized.[28] On the positive side, progress was made in eliminating regulatory and legal barriers slowing down privatizations, and in organizing the assets to be sold (cleaning up ownership titles, etc.).

Justice System   Reforms focused on speeding up court proceedings and reducing delays. Laws 3900/2010 and 4055/2012 introduced the concept of the "model trial," whereby a decision from one trial could be transposed automatically to cases deemed similar. The latter law also sought to reduce incentives by judges to adjourn cases (e.g., required that the same judge must preside over a case that he or she had adjourned) and by defendants, plaintiffs, and lawyers to cause delays; transferred a sizable portion of cases to lower level courts; strengthened out-of-court mediation; and allowed courts to expand on their use of interns by hiring recent law-school graduates. Some of these provisions brought significant benefits: for example, the introduction of the model trial helped resolve thousands of cases regarding pensions and social security benefits. Yet court delays have increased significantly during the crisis: from 819 days in 2007 (as reported in the 2008 World Bank *Doing Business* report) to 1,580 days in 2015. Significant cuts in judges' pay and in other resources available to courts, an increase in crisis-related cases such as NPLs in the financial sector, and strikes by lawyers and notaries have been important contributing forces.

Access to Finance   The main focus of policy actions was to restore the financial health of the banks so that they could start lending again to the real economy. Losses on Greek government bonds following the PSI had decreased dramatically the capital of all Greek banks and had rendered most of the large ones insolvent. Things were made worse by the projected losses on private sector loans due to the recession. Recapitalizing the banking system was a difficult task given that the problem was systemic; in other words, all banks needed assistance.

The first, and main, recapitalization involved mostly public funds and was completed in the summer of 2013. The recapitalized banking system centered at four large banks, and most of the remaining banks were absorbed by these banks. This resulted in a dramatic increase in industry concentration, which became the largest in the European Union. The increase in concentration was harmful for competition, but it meant that banks could increase their capital levels more easily in the future through oligopoly profits and hence would be more robust to future uncertainties.

The first recapitalization was followed by a second that took place in the spring of 2014 and was accomplished purely by private funds. The state of the banks remained precarious, however, because their large portfolio of NPLs was highly sensitive to economic downturns. And indeed, following the policies of the first SYRIZA-ANEL government and the imposition of capital controls in June 2015, a third recapitalization was required and took place in the fall of 2015. Banks remain still (as of 2016) highly sensitive to the state of the economy.

In addition to recapitalizing the banks, efforts were made to improve bankruptcy laws, to deal with the large and growing problem of NPLs of firms and households. Law 3869/2010 provided a process through which households could obtain relief on their private debts (but not debts to the state, which were effectively given senior status). Partly because of long delays in the courts, the law created strong incentives for strategic default, which subsequent laws 4161/2013 and 4336/2015 sought to address. Law 4013/2011 gave more leeway to firms in financial distress to negotiate reorganization plans with their creditors. Law 4336/2015 established the profession of corporate bankruptcy administrators, made claims by secured creditors of a firm more senior to those by the state and employees, and set tighter deadlines for the verifications of creditor claims.

Labor Market Regulation   The labor market received significant policy attention during the crisis. A series of reforms and other policy actions were intended to make labor market regulation less restrictive, and to reduce wage costs so to recover some of the competitiveness that was lost in the pre-crisis years. Law 3863/2010 made individual dismissals easier for firms by reducing the notice periods and the severance payments given to those dismissed. As a result of this law, the employment protection legislation (EPL) index for Greece became close to the OECD average. Law 3863/2010 also made collective dismissals easier by raising the threshold beyond which such dismissals would need approval by the Ministry of Labor. Laws 3899/2010 and 4024/2011 allowed for agreements that firms would negotiate with representatives of their own employees to supersede agreements made at the level of the industry sector. The preconditions for employee representation at the level of each firm were also simplified. The effect of these laws was to render sector-level agreements essentially irrelevant. Law 4046/2012 reduced the national minimum wage by 22 percent for those over 25 years of age and by 32 percent for those below that age. It also included provisions on the termination on existing contracts and the negotiation of new ones so that the reduction of the minimum wage could percolate over the entire wage scale. These laws and other policy interventions contributed to the large decline in wages during the crisis.

Pensions   Pensions are another area that received significant policy attention during the crisis. The main goals were to make the system sustainable and to reduce the inequities within it. Law 3863/2010 raised retirement ages and reduced pension entitlements. It also abolished a large number of pension providers by consolidating them into a single provider (IKA/ETAM). The consolidation, however, was mostly cosmetic because preexisting differences in retirement ages and pension entitlements were preserved within the consolidated fund for a long transition period. Moreover, while under the new rules pension entitlements were to be reduced if career lengths remained at their low current level (about 25 years of contributions), entitlements would become more generous than under the old system if career lengths increased to European norms (40 years of contributions) as a result of longer working lives or smaller contribution evasion. The law also entailed extensive "grandfathering," in the sense that those above 50 years of age could keep the entitlements they had under the old system. The law triggered a wave of early retirements, as employees were concerned that subsequent laws might worsen the terms at which they retire. Early retirements in the public sector were also encouraged by the government so that targets on personnel cuts would be met. Thus, while the law addressed (partially) the long-term sustainability of the pension system, it increased the cost relative to the old system in the short and medium term (until at least 2020). The shortfall was covered by cuts to the pensions of existing pensioners. Between 2010 and 2013, there were ten consecutive cuts. The cumulative cut for private sector pensions ranged from 14 percent for those earning a 700 euros pension to 44 percent for those earning 3,500 euros, while the cumulative cut for public sector pensions was slightly larger. Most of these cuts were presented as temporary, and promises were made each time that no further cuts would take place. This undermined trust in the pension system and risks, fueling a vicious cycle of disintermediation: the young seek to minimize their contributions to the system because they expect their future pensions to be cut, triggering the need for further cuts to current pensions and further loss of trust. The sustainability of the pension system still remains a problem and is high up in the policy agenda.

Health Care   A key reform in health care was a consolidation of all public health insurers into a single fund, the National Health Fund (EOPYY). This was analogous to the consolidation of pension providers into a single provider, and indeed both reforms were part of the same law (3863/2010). While this reform was significant, a mechanism through which EOPYY can negotiate contracts with health care suppliers, such as hospitals and pharmaceutical companies, has not yet been fully set up. Under such a mechanism, EOPYY could obtain more advantageous prices, hence saving on public funds, by exploiting its monopsony position and the competition among the suppliers. Most of the savings on health care were instead achieved in a cruder and more untargeted manner. For example, expenditure on pharmaceuticals was reduced mainly through restrictions on the introduction of new pharmaceuticals, through across-the-board price cuts, and by shifting part of the expenditure from the public sector to the patient.

Education   The most important reform on education concerned the universities. Unlike most other reforms described in this section, this reform was not required as part of the adjustment programs but was domestically driven. Law 4009/2011 gave universities more autonomy to manage their resources. It also instituted a more robust system for evaluating the performance of each university by an independent authority (which was preexisting but whose role was upgraded) and for upholding quality standards within each university for faculty promotions, and the like. It established modern governing structures within universities by mandating the creation of a university council that would formulate the university's policy over the long run, monitor the rector, and have a significant say over the choice of future rectors and area deans by vetting candidates up for election by the faculty body. The law also eliminated student voting for rectors: that practice had led to collusion between candidate rectors, on one hand, and student representatives of political party youths, on the other, with the latter extracting concessions from the former in exchange for their votes and those of their student followers. The law also made it possible for universities to accept private donations such as for endowed chairs. Key provisions of this law were watered down by subsequent governments, and the SYRIZA-ANEL government elected in January 2015 has signaled its intention to abolish the law completely.

Public Administration   Some of the reforms in public administration were intended to put in place infrastructure necessary for the success of the adjustment programs. The strengthening of the statistical agency's independence in 2010, the establishment of an independent agency in charge of tax collection in 2013 (Law 4093/2012), and the establishment of a general secretariat for the coordination of reforms (Law 4109/2013), can all be interpreted in that spirit. These initiatives have had some success, but there is much scope for improvement. Other reforms concerned the internal organization of the public sector. Law 3845/2010 established a single payment authority for all public employees. This made it possible to better control public expenditure and to reduce the fragmentation in compensation policies across different segments of the public sector. Law 3852/2010 (aka the Kallikratis law) restructured local government, mainly by making regional governors elected officials rather than appointees by the central government, and by transferring more resources to regions. Law 3861/2010 (aka the Diavgeia or Transparency law) required that all laws and acts by the central and local governments be posted promptly on the Internet. This provided some transparency and accountability. The Opengov initiative, established in 2010, also aimed at improving transparency, mainly by making appointments at the higher levels of the public administration a more open procedure. This initiative led to the appointment of some well-qualified outsiders without political connections, but it was watered down in 2012 and effectively abolished in 2015. Law 4172/2013 allowed the dismissal of public employees and the closure of entire public agencies if the positions held by the employees or the role performed by the agencies was deemed to be no longer necessary. The law also facilitated mobility within the public sector. These provisions strengthened those in Law 4093/2012, which also provided a stricter disciplinary framework for public servants. A third set of reforms was intended to make regulations concerning the private sector simpler and more efficient. This was the case for Law 3853/2010 (aka the one-stop shop), mentioned in the context of PMR, and Law 4048/2012. The latter law required the public administration to provide impact assessments for new regulation. Its implementation has been ineffective as the assessments include little evidence and have become a mere bureaucratic exercise.

1.3.3 An Assessment of the Economic Policy during the Crisis

To assess the economic policy followed during the crisis, it is useful to describe what had to be accomplished and to define an evaluation criterion. Recall from section 1.2.1 that starting in the late 1990s, Greece's net indebtedness to foreigners (NIF) rose rapidly. During the period 2001 to 2007, Greece's net exports plus net current transfers averaged –10.9 percent of GDP per year, which means, from equation (1), that Greece was borrowing from foreigners an extra 10.9 percent of its GDP on an annual basis. The funds were entering the economy in several forms, such as increased government spending e.g. higher wages in the public sector and higher pensions, and more plentiful bank loans for households and firms. Some of the bank loans were used to finance cost-reducing investments in firms, hence increasing aggregate supply. Yet the funds that were borrowed from abroad were mainly used to finance higher consumption, including residential investment, hence boosting aggregate demand (section 1.2.2). The dominant role of aggregate demand relative to aggregate supply can be seen by the large increases in wages and prices (section 1.2.3). The trade deficit widened both because higher prices meant that Greek products became more expensive in the global market, and because higher wages meant that Greek citizens had more to spend, including on imported goods.

The situation mentioned above was unsustainable. Greece could not keep borrowing from foreigners an extra 10 percent of its GDP every year forever: such borrowing had to stop and Greece had to eventually pay back the accumulated debt. In principle, the unsustainable situation could have continued past 2007, but the global financial crisis acted as a trigger making markets understand the problem.

An end to the inflow of new borrowed funds would mean an end to the demand stimuli, and hence a decline in GDP. Wages and prices would also have to decrease so that the trade deficit would be eliminated. Lower wages and prices would cause the trade deficit to shrink through two mechanisms, converse of the ones that operated in 2001 to 2007: lower prices would mean that Greek products would become cheaper in the global market, and lower wages would mean that Greek citizens would have less to spend, including on imported goods. The first mechanism would boost exports of the cheaper Greek products and reduce imports of the more expensive foreign ones. The second mechanism would reduce imports.

In addition to the trade deficit, the government deficit would also have to be eliminated because it was financed mostly by borrowing from foreigners. Structural reforms that would make the business environment more attractive (section 1.2.4) would be key to facilitating the adjustment. Indeed, since such reforms would enable Greece to boost its exports, wages would not have to drop by as much to eliminate the trade deficit, and the same would be true for GDP.

The adjustment programs started in 2010, when Greece first lost market access. Most of the adjustment had been completed by 2014: both the trade deficit and the government deficit had become close to zero by that year.

The criterion that we use to assess the economic policy during the crisis is whether the adjustment was made as painlessly as possible. We also examine whether as a result of the policy Greece was put in a position to resume a more sustainable growth path at the end of the adjustment.[29]

Given that Greek GDP per capita declined by 26.3 percent between 2007 and 2014, the adjustment can be characterized as everything but painless. It is useful, however, to compare Greece to other southern European countries hit by the crisis, in terms of their pre-crisis macroeconomic fundamentals and their subsequent decline in GDP. Table 1.2 compares Greece to Italy, Portugal, and Spain, based on the last pre-crisis year 2007.

Relative to the other three countries, Greece had the largest trade deficit and was the most reliant on foreign borrowing. Italy's trade deficit and NIF were small. Portugal's and Spain's NIF were only slightly smaller than Greece's, but their trade deficit was about half as large.

Greece's situation was worse than that of the other countries on the fiscal front as well. Its government debt was comparable to Italy's but significantly larger than Portugal's and Spain's. Moreover gross government savings, defined as the difference between current revenue and current expenditure, were negative in Greece in 2007, while they were positive in Italy and Spain, and only slightly negative in Portugal. Thus Greece's government had significantly less room for maneuver to cushion the effects of adjustment on the economy. The lax fiscal policies of Greek governments prior to the crisis were in fact doubly irresponsible: not only they eliminated any room

Table 1.2

Macroeconomic conditions before the crisis and subsequent decline in GDP per capita for Greece, Italy, Portugal, and Spain

	ES	GR	IT	PT
% Change in real GDP per capita 2007–2014	−10.0	−26.3	−12.0	−7.9
Net exports 2007 (% of GDP)	−6.0	−12.4	−0.4	−7.6
Net indebtedness to foreigners 2007 (% of GDP)	82.3	99.9	28.5	94.5
Gross government savings 2007 (% of GDP)	6.8	−4.1	2.1	−0.6
Government debt 2007 (% of GDP)	35.5	103.1	99.7	68.4
Loans of domestic banks to domestic firms and households 2007 (% of GDP)	162.8	92.4	90.3	138.2

Sources: Sources for the data in the first five rows are given in section 1.2.1. The data on bank loans come from the ECB and the Bank of Greece.

for maneuver during the crisis, but they also made the necessary adjustment larger as lower government savings before the crisis resulted in lower national savings and hence a sharper increase in NIF.

Greece's combination of a high trade deficit and government deficit, on one hand, and a high NIF and government debt, on the other, was particularly problematic. Indeed policies designed to eliminate the deficits would unavoidably reduce GDP but, with lower GDP debts would become less sustainable.

Greece's situation was better than Portugal's and Spain's with respect to private sector leverage. Private sector leverage in Greece, defined as the ratio of loans by Greek banks to Greek firms and households over GDP, was about two-thirds that of Portugal and Spain, and similar to Italy's. Thus Greek firms and households could experience a larger decline in income without getting bankrupt, compared to their Portuguese and Spanish counterparts. Likewise Greek banks had a smaller exposure to private sector loans than Portuguese and Spanish banks. At the same time Greek banks were holding large positions in Greek government bonds, which were particularly risky given Greece's fiscal situation.

Table 1.2 indicates that on balance, Greece entered the crisis with worse macroeconomic fundamentals than the other southern European countries. Its microeconomic fundamentals were also worse (section 1.2.4). This underscores how challenging it was to design an adjustment program for Greece.

The comparison between Greece and Italy is particularly informative: Italy had no trade deficit and low NIF, positive government savings, and government debt and private sector leverage that were comparable to Greece's. It was not in an adjustment program and its economic policy was not dictated by the Troika. Yet it experienced a 12 percent decline in GDP per capita. This suggests that no matter how well Greece's adjustment programs were designed and implemented, it would have been difficult to avoid a decline in GDP larger than 12 percent. Of course, this does not imply that the decline should have been as large as 26.3 percent, or that the adjustment programs were optimally designed and implemented. We believe that there were important shortcomings, which we next review.[30]

We focus on four aspects of the programs' design and implementation. The first three concern the mix of policy actions, and the fourth the domestic "ownership" of the programs. While it is tempting to associate the former with the Troika and the latter with the Greek government and society, the picture is more complicated. Indeed lack of ownership had adverse effects on the mix of policy actions that were implemented. And conversely, lack of ownership was exacerbated by shortcomings in the programs' execution that were partly driven by flaws in design and implementation.

Internal Devaluation   The declines in wages and prices that were a necessary part of Greece's adjustment could not take place through the currency devaluation because Greece was part of the EZ. To engineer these declines, the Troika opted instead for "internal devaluation," a policy that emphasizes a reduction in domestic wages. The changes in labor market regulation summarized in section 1.3.2 were designed partly with that goal in mind, and they contributed to the 19 percent decline in real wages between 2009 and 2014.

Internal devaluation reduces the trade deficit through the two mechanisms described earlier in this section. Because wage costs for domestic firms decline, prices decline, and so domestic products become cheaper in the global market. This boosts exports and reduces imports. Moreover lower wages reduce domestic demand, including demand for imports.

Internal devaluation in Greece worked primarily through the second mechanism. In particular, lower wages failed to have a significant impact on prices and exports. Their main effect was instead to depress imports through lower domestic demand. One way to see this is to compare Greece to Ireland, Portugal, and Spain. We perform this comparison in table 1.3 for the period 2009 to 2014.

While nominal wages dropped by 16.3 percent in Greece between 2009 and 2014, they remained constant or rose slightly in the other countries. The large drop in Greek wages was not reflected in prices: the consumer price index (CPI) cumulatively rose by 7.4 percent between 2009 and 2014, an increase that was smaller than in Portugal and Spain but larger than in Ireland.[31] Moreover, while Greek exports rose, the increase

Table 1.3

Changes in wages, prices, exports, and imports, in Greece, Italy, Portugal, and Spain, between 2009 and 2014

	ES	GR	IE	PT
% Change in nominal wages	1.0	−16.3	2.9	0.0
% Change in prices (CPI)	8.9	7.4	4.1	12.0
% Change in exports	29.2	17.8	33.5	33.3
% Change in imports	6.5	−17.5	24.7	5.1

Sources: The data on wages and prices come from the OECD ("Average annual wages current prices" and "consumer price index"). The data on exports and imports come from AMECO, and these variables are expressed in real terms (2010 prices).

was significantly smaller than in the other countries. And Greek imports dropped, while imports in the other countries rose. The large drop in Greek wages thus does not appear to have had a significant impact on exports, whose rise was driven mainly by an improvement in global economic conditions. By contrast, there was a large negative effect on imports.

Because internal devaluation essentially failed to stimulate exports, the wage reduction that was necessary to eliminate the trade deficit was overly large. Moreover it was associated with an overly large drop in aggregate demand and in GDP, and an overly large rise in unemployment.[32] Chapter 3 (on international trade) estimates that the weak response of exports and consequent large drop in wages during the adjustment process accounted for at least one-third of the decline in Greek GDP between 2007 and 2012. This points to what we view as a key shortcoming in the design of the Greek adjustment programs: an emphasis on wage reduction without due consideration as to whether it would trigger significant price reductions. This problem was acknowledged by the IMF, which admitted that the Troika should or would have done things differently if they knew the outcomes when the program was drawn up (see Ioannides and Pissarides 2016 and Wyplosz and Sgherri 2016 for discussion and references).

The large wage reduction was not reflected on prices and exports because of several reasons. One reason, which accounts not only for the relatively weak response of exports during the crisis but also and more broadly for the low exporting capacity of the Greek economy, is the small size of Greek firms compared to their counterparts in other European countries. Small firms typically find it harder to export than large firms because exporting involves fixed costs which are independent of firm size.

A second reason, which accounts more specifically for the response of exports during the crisis, has to do with the macroeconomic environment. Uncertainty about a possible EZ exit acted as a powerful deterrent to all types of investment, including entry by new firms. Investment and entry would have raised export capacity and put downward pressure on prices. Uncertainty also hampered the integration of Greek firms into international trading networks, and this further lowered exports (and imports). The uncertain macroeconomic environment also had an effect through lack of access to finance. Corporate loans became hard to get and interest rates increased dramatically, partly because of the liquidity and solvency problems of Greek banks. This further reduced investment and entry.

An additional reason why the large drop in wages was not reflected in prices was the low degree of competition. As pointed out in section 1.2.4, product markets in Greece are not open competitive markets but ones that are closed, regulated, and controlled by oligopolies or by severe regulatory barriers to entry. In such markets, wage reductions are more likely to be taken in as increased profits than to be passed on to price reductions. Policies undertaken during the crisis aimed at reducing barriers to entry, but the effect was limited both because uncertainty and lack of access to finance discouraged investment and entry (as mentioned above) and because the policies themselves and their implementation were limited in scope in many cases.

A final reason accounting for the limited response of prices was that firms' fiscal burdens increased significantly as a result of the overall fiscal tightening. For example, firms' energy costs (which constitute a large fraction of costs in some industry sectors) rose sharply because of a 60 percent increase in energy taxes between 2009 and 2014.[33] Some tax regulations intended to improve compliance also increased costs in possibly counterproductive ways.[34]

Internal devaluation might have been more successful if the sequencing of the reforms had been different. In particular, labor market reform was pursued more vigorously than product market reform at the early stages of the programs. While this is understandable because product market reform is more complicated to design and implement (due to the large diversity of regulations across different product markets), greater emphasis on product markets early on might have resulted in more entry, larger price declines, and a stronger response of exports. Likewise product market reform should have been accompanied by greater efforts to improve firms' access to finance. And keeping firms' fiscal burdens manageable should have been more of a priority on the fiscal front.

Fiscal Tightening   While fiscal tightening and structural reforms were both essential to the success of the adjustment programs, the programs ended up relying excessively on fiscal tightening, and especially on "horizontal" measures such as across-the-board tax rises and cuts to pensions and public sector wages. To a large extent, this was a consequence of the lack of domestic ownership: as we argue later in this section, ownership is essential for the successful implementation of structural reforms. But the Troika was to blame as well. Indeed the programs were designed to achieve (among other targets) a rapid reduction of the government deficit. Given that structural reforms take time to implement and to have discernible impacts, the deficit reduction had to be accomplished mainly by horizontal measures. Moreover the Troika was intransigent about fiscal targets being met, but did not show the same insistence that the reforms are implemented successfully. Inadequate implementation of the reforms meant that more horizontal measures were made necessary.[35]

Prioritizing the structural reforms early on in the program (and insisting on their implementation), while leaving some of the fiscal tightening to a later stage, would have given a better chance for the reforms to succeed and would probably have resulted in a smaller drop in GDP. Fiscal leeway would have made it possible, in particular, to provide some protection or compensation to those standing to lose from the reforms. (The importance of fiscal leeway for the success of reforms is illustrated nicely by the German Hartz reform program of 2002 to 2005, the most famous recent case of successful reforms in Europe.[36]) Of course, a program allowing for a slower reduction in the deficit would have required more funding by the Troika.

Fiscal tightening relied on tax rises more than on expenditure cuts: current revenue increased by 6.1 percent of GDP during the period 2009 to 2014 (37.4 percent of GDP in 2009 and 43.5 percent in 2014), while current expenditure decreased by 2.9 percent of GDP (47.3 percent of GDP in 2009 and 44.4 percent in 2014). The counterparts of these numbers during the period 2009 to 2011 were 3.9 and −2.4 percent, respectively, which suggests that tax rises were the only source of fiscal tightening during the first two years of the program. The greater focus on tax rises especially early in the program was suboptimal given the empirical evidence that adjustment programs in which most of the savings come from expenditure cuts yield smaller declines in GDP (e.g., Alesina and Ardagna 2010). A further aspect in which the fiscal tightening was suboptimal was that public investment (roads, ports, public buildings, etc.) was one of the hardest-hit expenditure categories despite being one of the most crucial for a speedy recovery. During the period 2009 to 2011, public investment was cut by 2.1 percent of GDP. That was about half of its 2009 level.[37]

Debt Restructuring, the Banks, and Uncertainty about EZ Exit The shortcomings reviewed so far concern the policies designed to eliminate the trade deficit and the government deficit. The policies designed to deal with the debt were also suboptimal.

The main shortcoming was that debt relief to Greece was delayed: while Greece lost market access in 2010 and its debt was widely viewed as unsustainable, relief came only in 2012.

Debt relief was delayed mainly for reasons outside Greece. EZ governments and the ECB were concerned that a Greek default would cause problems to EZ banks and the EU economy more generally. A number of EZ banks, especially in Germany and France, were holding large positions in Greek government bonds, and a Greek default would have reduced their capital significantly. There was also a concern that following a Greek default, investors would put in doubt the solvency of other crisis-hit EZ countries, and this could imply further losses for the banks as well as runs on deposits. These concerns were particularly acute in 2010 because European economies and financial systems were weak after the global financial crisis of 2007 to 2009. The US government had similar concerns because its economy and financial system were also fragile. Delaying or avoiding a Greek default, by providing loans to Greece, could give time to the banks to reduce their exposures to the debt of Greece and other crisis-hit countries, and to EZ governments to set up EZ-wide mechanisms that would ensure the stability of the banking system. But while delayed debt relief to Greece seemed to be the best solution from a global viewpoint, it had significant negative consequences for Greece.

One negative consequence was that Greece found itself saddled with more debt than had it been allowed to default in 2010. This is because it had to rely on loans by the other EZ countries and the IMF to make debt payments to private investors between 2010 and 2012. Hence a significant fraction of the debt to private investors was substituted by debt to EZ countries and the IMF. The additional debt (relative to a default-in-2010 scenario) did not burden Greece's budget until 2014, since Greece was running primary deficits and hence was not making net payments to its debt. (It was paying debt by taking on new loans.) Yet the expectation of higher future debt payments might have reduced growth prospects and investment.

An additional negative consequence of the delay was uncertainty. Greek banks were holding large positions in Greek government bonds, and hence were highly exposed to a default by the Greek government. Had a default taken place promptly in 2010 and the banks been recapitalized shortly thereafter, uncertainty about their solvency would have been eliminated. Instead, uncertainty persisted, triggering a steady decline in deposits.

Delay contributed to uncertainty through an additional channel, by maintaining the possibility of a large and disorderly default. A disorderly default, which could have resulted from a breakdown in negotiations between the Greek government and the

Troika over new loans, could have disrupted significantly the Greek economy, given the large size of Greece's debt. Fears of such a disruption discouraged investment and added to the decline in bank deposits. The perceived likelihood of EZ exit also increased because a collapse of the banks would have eventually required Greece to issue a new currency. The threat of EZ exit was used indirectly by foreign politicians as a device for Greece to reach agreement with the Troika.

Uncertainty about the banks, the economy, and EZ exit was more pronounced in Greece than in Ireland, Italy, Portugal, and Spain. Figure 1.23 illustrates this by plotting bank deposits by domestic households from January 2009 onward. Deposits are normalized to one on January 2009. Deposits dropped by 45 percent in Greece between January 2009 and July 2015, while they dropped only slightly in Ireland and rose in Italy, Portugal, and Spain.[38] Thus depositors' fears about losing their savings due to a haircut or a conversion to a devalued currency were more pronounced in Greece.[39]

Ownership A key problem with the adjustment programs was the lack of domestic ownership. None of the big political parties in Greece sought to systematically or credibly explain to voters why the adjustment was necessary and why structural reforms would be beneficial. Parties in government presented the reforms as something imposed by the Troika as a condition for making the loans. Parties in opposition argued that the adjustment could be avoided altogether, that the reforms were mostly harmful, and blamed foreigners for both.[40] Most of the media projected a similar message. As a result the unavoidable fiscal tightening and decline in GDP and wages were viewed by many

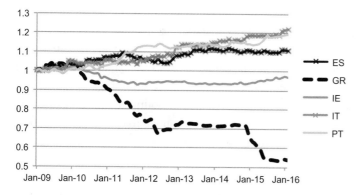

Figure 1.23
Bank deposits in Greece and other EZ countries, 2009 to 2016. The data come from the ECB. Deposits are normalized to one for all countries on January 2009.

voters as imposed by foreigners and as entirely avoidable. By 2012 a majority of voters were in favor of parties openly hostile to the adjustment programs.

Lack of domestic ownership is a serious impediment to reforms, no matter how much pressure there is by outsiders. Outsiders can request that a reform be legislated through Parliament but cannot perform most of the follow-up that is necessary for the reform's successful implementation. Follow-up is necessary especially because there always exist vested interests that stand to lose from the reform and will try by all means in their disposal to undermine it.

Our account of the reforms in section 1.3.2 is consistent with a lack of ownership. Many reforms were characterized by a lack of ambition, being attempts to provide fixes to an existing system rather than to transition to a different and better system.[41] Tellingly, some of the most ambitious reforms were ones not required by the Troika, such as the university reform and the reform on public sector transparency (Diavgeia law).

The lack of ownership was evident not only in the design of reforms but also in their implementation. In some cases this was manifested by a lack of follow-up after a reform was legislated. In other cases government ministers actively sought to dilute the reforms with subsequent actions or pieces of legislation, expecting that the Troika would not notice or protest.[42] And even in cases where government ministers sought to implement a reform, resistance at lower levels of the administration, or pure lack of administrative capacity, made implementation difficult or unsuccessful.[43]

Lack of ownership was exacerbated by the perception that the program was not meeting its overall targets. Many specific targets that were announced were missed by a wide margin. For example, it was initially planned that Greece would gain access to the markets in 2012. Yet the program was prolonged significantly, and as of 2016 it was still unclear when the crisis would end and Greece would gain market access. Another example was the 50 billion stated target for privatization revenue to be raised between 2011 and 2015; actual revenue was below 10 billion. A final example was the repeated tax rises as well as cuts to pensions and public sector wages. Each of these was billed by the government as the "last and final" one. Some of the announced targets were overly ambitious, perhaps to make the program politically acceptable to creditors or to Greek voters. The design flaws covered earlier in this section were also one of the reasons why targets were not being met.

Opposition to the adjustment programs was also fueled by the perception that financial assistance to Greece was designed to benefit foreign countries and their banks—a perception that was partly justified because of the delayed debt relief. Hence an additional cost of the delay was to make debt rather than the reforms the main political issue, and so to detract attention and support from reforming the economy. Instead, political parties and commentators who belonged to the political fringes and were openly hostile to reforms gained credibility because they were arguing for debt relief.

1.4 Policy Options Going Forward

1.4.1 The Long Run

To organize our discussion of Greece's policy options going forward, we start from the long run: where Greece should aim to be 20 years from now (with "now" being 2016). In section 1.4.2 we examine how the transition to the desirable long-run state could be accomplished.

In a nutshell, a desirable long-run state for Greece is one where all types of markets are more open, the public administration is more efficient, transparent, and nonpolitical, and significant emphasis is given to education and human capital. As section 1.2.4 shows, Greece lags behind most EU and OECD countries on these dimensions. For example, it scores close to the bottom (within these groups of countries) in rankings measuring the ease of doing business, the quality of product market regulation, the efficiency of courts, the performance of the education and health care systems, the investment and outcomes in innovation and R&D, the quality of social protection, and so on.[44] The degree of control that the political party in government has over the public sector and economic activity more generally is also particularly large in Greece.

Improvements on all these dimensions are critical for Greece's long-run growth. Indeed a large body of academic research summarized in section 1.2.1 has shown that countries' long-run growth depends to a significant extent on their human capital and ability to innovate as well as on the quality of their institutions. So while Greece is likely to recover some of the large drop in GDP that it suffered during the crisis, it is also likely to experience long-run stagnation if it does not improve on the dimensions noted above. Long-run stagnation would bring about a significant decline in Greece's relative standing among EU countries in terms of GDP per capita. A decline has taken place during the past 30 years: Greece dropped from 13th among the EU28 in 1985 to 19th in 2015 in terms of its GDP per capita, and was surpassed not only by Ireland and Spain (as mentioned earlier in this chapter) but also by former communist countries such as the Czech Republic, Estonia, and Slovakia. That relative decline could become a foretaste of things to come.

Many of the chapters in this volume describe in greater detail aspects of the desirable long-run state for Greece. The theme of opening up markets and reducing regulatory barriers to entry is emphasized particularly in chapters 4 (on product markets) and 6 (on the labor market). Chapter 4 argues that Greece should formulate a national competition and competiveness policy. Among other things, that policy should include the establishment of a new public agency tasked with evaluating the effects of new and existing regulations—with a view to abolishing regulations that do not promote entry and competition. Agencies with such a remit and the required political independence exist in many advanced countries. Chapter 6 proposes the abolition of most labor market regulations, except for those pertaining to health, safety, and discrimination. Chapter 6 also emphasizes that the deregulation of the labor market should be combined with the establishment of a robust system of social insurance that protects workers from the consequences of unemployment and low pay.

Social protection is taken up not only in chapter 6 but also in chapters 10 (on taxation) and 11 (on pensions). A theme common to all three chapters is that Greece can improve social protection while also providing more powerful incentives for wealth creation in markets. Improvements for social protection are necessary both to address the current poor state of social protection in Greece (section 1.2.4) and to ensure that the wealth created by opening up markets in the future will be spread more evenly throughout the economy.

Chapter 10 proposes the establishment of a simple and integrated tax and welfare system to replace Greece's fragmented tax system and essentially nonexistent welfare system. All three designs that are considered involve a minimum guaranteed income. Their main differences concern the relative weight of consumption versus income taxes, and the possible introduction of a negative tax rate ("earned income tax credit") that subsidizes work by low-paid individuals. Chapter 11 proposes the establishment of a multipillar pension system similar to those adopted by many advanced countries. Under that system, the state would provide a minimum pension to protect against old-age poverty, as well as a pension that would depend on contributions but be significantly smaller relative to current levels. The state pension would be complemented by individual retirement accounts with tax incentives, and possibly by occupational pensions that, unlike in the current system, would not carry state subsidies. Because pension contributions would be significantly smaller under the proposed system, the implicit tax on labor would be small. That would stimulate job creation and discourage contribution evasion. Additional benefits of the proposed system are that it would boost household savings and promote the development of capital markets. The cost of capital for firms would thus decrease, and corporate investment would increase. Realizing these benefits would also require improvements in financial regulation and enforcement. The latter issues are taken up in chapter 7 (on the financial system).

The theme of making the public administration more efficient, transparent, and nonpolitical is emphasized particularly in chapters 8 (on education), 9 (health care), 12 (justice system), and 14 (public administration). Chapter 14 proposes reforms to the public administration that include making the evaluation and disciplinary processes for civil servants more rigorous and less formalistic, benchmarking the performance of public agencies against key performance indicators that can be monitored publicly, and devolving more powers and accountability to lower levels of the administration. Chapter 12 proposes an across-the-board reform of the Greek justice system that is based on some of the same principles. The proposals include changes to the rules governing the evaluation and promotion of judges so to better reward performance and reduce political influence, devolution of powers to courts to manage their resources, more investment in information technology, more emphasis on judges' training in business-related disciplines, the establishment of specialized tribunals to handle cases where special expertise is needed such as in tax evasion and bankruptcy cases, and improvements to the system producing new legislation.

Improvements in incentives and accountability, together with less centralized control by the relevant government ministries, are central to the reforms proposed in chapters 8 (on education) and 9 (on health care) Chapter 8 proposes reforms that include evaluating schools and universities more rigorously, based on students' performance in the former case, and research output and quality of teaching programs in the latter; giving schools and universities more autonomy, such as in selecting teachers and managing budgets and curricula for schools, and full operational responsibility for universities; and making more resources available to attract and reward individuals with high academic achievements, as this will help improve the overall quality level and reduce Greece's brain drain. Chapter 9 proposes reforms that include the rigorous implementation of contracting mechanisms, whereby the single health care fund (EOPYY) negotiates supply contracts with hospitals and pharmaceutical companies, and leverages the competition among them to reduce cost; the devolution of more budgetary and operational independence to public hospitals; and a more arm's-length relationship between EOPYY and the Ministry of Health.

1.4.2 The Transition

A transition to the long-run state described in section 1.4.1 would require a sustained effort lasting for many years. Greece has not only to catch up with (or do better than) the EU average on various dimensions of institutional quality but must also do so in an adverse macroeconomic environment. Indeed its economy has been shrinking every year from 2008 to 2015, with the exception of a small positive (real) growth rate in

2014. Negative growth is also expected for 2016. The cumulative and deep recession has had a number of adverse knock-on effects: massive unemployment and the depreciation of workers' skills, a brain drain, a huge number of NPLs and hence weak banks, massive cumulative disinvestment and the depreciation of the capital stock, and low domestic savings.[45]

Policies for the short and the medium run should aim to boost exports and corporate investment. Both variables should make up a larger fraction of GDP under the new growth model that Greece should seek to put in place, compared to their values before and during the crisis. The necessity of boosting exports follows directly from our discussion of internal devaluation in section 1.3.3: given that Greece cannot be running large trade deficits going forward, export growth is necessary for wages and GDP to increase. Growth in corporate investment is necessary for export growth and more generally for productivity growth, especially if it comes in the form of FDI or investment in new technologies. Investment growth also has to make up for the accumulated disinvestment during the crisis.

Export growth will be associated with a shift in the composition of economic activity, away from sectors that produce "nontradables" (i.e., products geared for domestic consumption) and toward sectors producing "tradables" (i.e., products that can be sold internationally). Such a shift has already begun, although it has been slow, reflecting the slow pickup of exports.[46] Job creation in the tradables sectors holds the key to reducing the massive unemployment.

In the rest of this section we propose policy actions aimed at stimulating investment and exports, and at moving the economy toward the desirable long-run state. Some of these actions seek to redress shortcomings of the adjustment programs reviewed in section 1.3.3. Some actions are specific to Greece, while others also concern its EZ partners.

Inherent in many of the actions that we propose is the need to remove uncertainty about the future direction of the Greek economy. This requires that a broad political consensus be formed in Greece in favor of key reforms. Once uncertainty has been removed, and even if the actual progress with some of the reforms is slow, investment is likely to be high, leading to fast growth. Investment will be attracted by the combination of reduced uncertainty and the low valuations at which Greek assets are currently trading (as of 2016) precisely because of the high uncertainty.[47]

An additional channel through which lower uncertainty will stimulate investment is through the return of deposits to the banks. Greek banks have experienced a severe deposit flight, unlike other crisis-hit countries in the EZ (figure 1.23). Lower uncertainty will induce depositors to bring back their savings to the banks. Banks will then be able to start lending again to the real economy, and domestic savings will play a more productive role—to finance investment rather than be stashed under mattresses.

Redesign Fiscal Policy   Fiscal policy should be redesigned drastically to encourage investment and job creation. The tax rises that have been imposed on households and firms as part of the adjustment programs have resulted in rates that are overly large and that discourage economic activity and tax compliance. As of 2015, the top rate for corporate income stood at 29 percent, well above the EU28 average of 22.8 percent and the rates in neighboring countries such as Bulgaria (10 percent), Croatia (20 percent), Cyprus (12.5 percent), and Romania (16 percent). The top rate for personal income and the standard VAT rate were also above their EU28 averages: 48 percent versus 39.3 percent, and 23 percent versus 21.6 percent, respectively.[48] Contributions to (state) pensions are also large, and together with the high personal tax rates, they result in high implicit tax rates for labor. Table 1.4 compares implicit tax rates for labor for all OECD-reported worker categories in Greece with other OECD countries. Tax rates in Greece are higher than the OECD average for all worker categories, and the highest or second-highest for some of the main categories, such as married individuals with two children in a one-earner family earning the average wage.

Going forward, it is important to reduce significantly both the corporate tax rate and pension contributions in order to encourage investment and job creation.

Table 1.4

Implicit tax rates on labor for various worker categories in Greece and the OECD

	Greece	OECD average	Greece's ranking (1 = highest tax rate, 34 = lowest tax rate)
Single, no children, 67% of average wage	35.7	32.2	16
Single, no children, 100% of average wage	40.4	36.0	14
Single, no children, 167% of average wage	48.0	40.4	9
Single, 2 children, 67% of average wage	37.5	17.9	1
Married, 2 children, 100–0% of average wage	43.4	26.9	1
Married, 2 children, 100–33% of average wage	40.9	28.5	2
Married, 2 children, 100–67% of average wage	41.4	31.3	6
Married, no children, 100–33% of average wage	39.5	32.9	11

Sources: The data come from the OECD publication *Taxing Wages 2013–2014*. Implicit tax rates on labor are expressed as a percentage. The last column reports Greece's ranking among the 34 OECD member countries as of the time of the publication.

Crucially, there should be a commitment, supported by a broad political consensus, not to increase these tax rates for many years to come. Indeed a major deterrent for firms contemplating to invest in Greece is the uncertainty that tax rates may increase in the future. A commitment to keep tax rates low, and to make up for budget shortfalls mostly through expenditure cuts, would remove this uncertainty and result in large inflows of investment, including FDI. Such a commitment could be specified in the Constitution. A historical precedent exists: in an effort to attract FDI, the 1952 Constitution stipulated that taxation of investments financed by inflows of foreign capital would be determined by a single law (and hence could not be changed in the future), and that law was passed in 1953 (Law 2867/1953). Stable tax rates and high FDI were powerful drivers of Greece's high growth rates in the 1950s and 1960s.

A commitment to lower tax rates would mean that any increases in tax revenue in the future should come only from lower tax evasion. Efforts to track tax evaders, especially large ones, have been insufficient and should be intensified. Lower tax rates would also reduce incentives to evade.

The cuts to corporate taxes and pension contributions could be paid for by a combination of measures. Consumption taxation (VAT) could be increased somewhat. Most of the savings, however, should come from cutting expenditure. Public investment is low and should not be cut further; it should instead be raised because it is important for economic recovery and for export growth.[49] Expenditure cuts should instead target wages in privileged segments of the public sector (where lobbying has resulted in wages well above those in other segments and in the private sector) and various types of spending on pensions. State subsidies to the pensions of some occupations (obtained through lobbying) should be eliminated. Incentives could also be given to motivate the large consortium of pensioners currently in early retirement to re-join the workforce. And while some cuts to state pensions would be unavoidable as a consequence of smaller pension contributions, the proposal of recognition bonds in chapter 11 (on pensions) could reduce their extent: recognition bonds are in effect voluntary pension contributions that are fully "owned" by the contributors rather than being part of a general "pot" and hence are not perceived as a tax. Chapter 11 shows in a calibrated example that the transition to a system with lower state-pension contributions could realize gains of the order of 8 percent of GDP even during the transition period.

Last but not least, it is important to establish a robust welfare system to protect the unemployed and those with low incomes. This could take the form of a minimum guaranteed income, perhaps coupled with a negative tax rate ("earned income tax credit") that subsidizes work by the low-paid.

Improve the Allocation of Productive Assets—Privatizations and NPLs A requirement of Greece's third adjustment program was to revamp the privatization agency established in the first adjustment program by giving it more flexibility on how to manage its assets. Targets on revenue to be raised over specific horizons became less strict, and the agency was given more freedom to lease its assets over long periods instead of selling them. The governance structure of the agency was also revamped. The goal is to privatize key state assets such as infrastructure and utilities. A series of successful privatizations would increase economywide productivity by transferring assets to more efficient management. It would also bring in much-needed revenue to the state and new investment.

The remittance of the privatization agency could be expanded by allowing the agency to take on some NPLs off the balance sheets of Greek banks. The banks could be given as compensation bonds issued by the agency, which would be backed by the revenue produced by the agency's assets. Effectively, the agency could partly assume of the role of a "bad bank." The advantages of a bad bank, over the current solution of letting each bank deal with its NPLs, include better incentives to resolve the NPLs and put productive assets back to efficient use, economies of scale, and better availability of loans for new firms. At the same time, transferring NPLs to a bad bank at market values, as of 2016, may necessitate a further recapitalization of the banks. The privatization agency could contribute to such a recapitalization by buying the loans at above market prices (which in some cases may be fire-sale prices). In exchange, it could be given shares in the banks. Efficient resolution of NPLs (by the banks and the privatization agency) would also require significant changes to bankruptcy laws and their practical implementation, especially to facilitate the liquidation of bankrupt firms' assets. All these issues are taken up in chapter 7 (on the financial system).

Some of the shares of the privatization agency could be transferred to EZ core institutions, such as the European Stability Mechanism (ESM), in exchange for a reduction in Greece's debt. This would give the EZ more of a stake in Greece's growth.

Proceed with Key Structural Reforms A gradual but systematic effort should be devoted to pursuing the structural reforms presented in section 1.4.1. Priority in the short run should be given to opening up product markets, and improving the education system, the justice system, and the public administration more broadly. Proposals along these lines, which cover also the short run, are in chapters 4 (on product markets), 8 (education system), 12 (justice system), and 14 (public administration).

Stay in the EZ   Staying in the EZ is important for Greece, both for the short and the long run. In the short run, an EZ exit would create huge adjustment problems relating to Greece's banks, foreign trade, output, and employment. The dramatic events in the summer of 2015, when Greece came close to exiting the EZ, provide a glimpse into these problems. In the long run, staying in the EZ would provide the critical discipline and encouragement for continuing with the reforms. Indeed, EZ institutions will continue to pressure Greece and other EZ countries to reform and make their economies more efficient because this is viewed as necessary for the monetary union as a whole.[50] Moreover staying in the EZ but not reforming will be painful for Greece: Greece would be constantly losing competitiveness relative to the other countries, and would have difficulty exporting and creating jobs. These issues are discussed in greater depth in chapter 2 (on the macroeconomy) where it is also argued that any beneficial effects of EZ exit on Greece's trade surplus are likely to be small.

Uncertainty about Greece's position in the EZ is damaging for investment and growth. A broad political consensus exists in Greece in favor of staying in the EZ (although this may change if Greece is unable to reform its economy in the next few years and the economy keeps shrinking or stagnating). Greece's EZ partners should also do their part to remove the uncertainty by not encouraging Greece to exit the EZ, as they are better off with a reformed Greece inside the EZ than with an unreformed Greece outside the Union. Removing the uncertainty requires the EZ, in particular, to provide Greece a clearer path for debt relief. Debt and Greece's EZ position have become connected because a default on the debt by Greece has been viewed as a trigger for an EZ exit.

Agree on a Path for Debt Relief   Greece did not benefit from debt relief in 2010, when it lost market access. Relief on the debt held by private investors came in 2012 in the form of the PSI. There was also some relief on the debt held by EZ taxpayers because that debt came with long maturities and below-market interest rates. Moreover there has been a grace period on interest payments for most of the latter debt (ESM loans) until 2022. As a consequence of these actions, interest payments on Greece's debt are relatively small in the short run, and the debt's high value in nominal terms overstates its value in present-value terms (section 1.3.1). Yet the interest payments on the debt can become large in the more distant future, since much of the debt comes with floating interest rates that can increase if global rates increase. This creates uncertainty, and thus suppresses investment. Also, on the grounds of fairness Greece has a strong case for debt relief: the relief that it has obtained is smaller than what it would have gotten had it defaulted in 2010, and the main reason why it was not allowed to default at that time was to safeguard the stability of the EZ (and the global) financial system, benefiting thus other EZ countries.[51]

Debt relief should take the form of extending maturities and locking in interest rates at their low current levels. This would keep interest payments manageable and would reduce uncertainty. Such changes could be agreed on the part of the debt that is held by EZ taxpayers, since it constitutes the majority of the debt and can be restructured more flexibly than the part held by private investors.

At the same time, debt relief should be used as a tool to incentivize reforms, which are necessary for Greece's long-run prosperity within the EZ. Relief should occur gradually and be made conditional on measurable reform efforts.[52] Incentives based on debt relief are likely to be more effective than threats of EZ exit because they provide a positive path for the economy going forward: the end goal is an economy that is both reformed and has a sustainable level of debt. Debt relief could also serve as a powerful signal: by providing relief the creditors could be signaling to the markets and other third parties their commitment to support the Greek economy, as long as progress is being made with structural reforms.

Notes

We would like to thank, without implicating, Harris Dellas, Aristos Doxiadis, Manolis Galenianos, John Geanakoplos, Gikas Hardouvelis, Philip Lane, Stelios Papadopoulos, Elias Papaioannou, Evangelia Papapetrou, Kostantinos Peppas, Ricardo Reis, Georges Siotis, Michalis Vassiliadis, and Nikos Zonzilos, for assistance, suggestions, and comments during the preparation of this chapter.

1. Throughout this chapter, GDP per capita is measured in real terms and is adjusted for purchasing power parity.

2. The argument that an EZ exit will allow Greece to repudiate or reduce its debt unilaterally is flawed. Even after an EZ exit, Greece will need to collaborate closely with other EZ countries on issues such as trade and security, but unilateral moves will isolate it internationally. Greece will be in a better position to negotiate debt relief inside the EZ.

3. The corresponding percentage for GDP per capita was smaller (83 percent) because a smaller fraction of the population is employed in Greece compared to Germany. This is due to the limited participation by some population groups, such as the men outside the ages of 25 to 55 and the women of all ages, in the labor force. Chapter 6 (labor market) provides more detailed evidence on workforce participation.

4. The low FDI during the high-growth years indicates that the increase in corporate investment during 1996 to 2007, shown in section 1.2.2, was driven almost exclusively by domestic firms. The latter fact is consistent with the small TFP growth during that period.

5. This is not to say that there are no costs to large government debt even when it is all domestically held. A significant cost is that the government must impose high taxes to service the debt, and these distort economic activity by reducing the incentives of firms and individuals to produce.

6. The increase in net external debt was the main driver of the sharp increase in NIF not only in Greece but also in Portugal and Spain (not shown in figure 1.9). In the latter two countries, however, equity flows were relatively more important than in Greece. The smaller size of equity flows in Greece is consistent with the low FDI, shown in section 1.2.1. It is also consistent with the broader evidence shown in chapter 7 (financial system) on the limited extent of risk-sharing in the Greek economy.

7. Equation (1) also includes a term equal to the capital gains that the country makes on claims it holds on foreigners, minus the capital gains that foreigners make on claims they hold on the country. We ignore this term except for our discussion of default in section 1.4.

8. A distinction is generally made between net current transfers and net primary incomes, with the latter including items that are "earned" rather than "transferred," such as workers' remittances. Equations (1) and (2) hold for the sum of the two variables, and for simplicity, we aggregate them into a single variable (which we term "net current transfers").

9. A country's savings are defined as the country's income minus consumption minus government spending. Income is GDP plus net current transfers.

10. Figure 1.13 plots AMECO series "Gross fixed capital formation—Total economy," which measures investment net of inventories. Equation (2) holds when investment includes inventories. This is done by AMECO series "Gross capital formation—Total economy." We plot the former series because we can decompose it into corporate and residential investment (figures 1.14 and 1.15). Because of measurement errors, (2) does not hold exactly prior to 1995 in AMECO data. Yet we plot the series also before 1995 because they reveal useful information.

11. This point is also emphasized in Meghir, Vayanos, and Vettas (2010), who review more generally the state of the Greek economy before the crisis and make reform proposals. Galenianos (2015) also emphasizes the combined role of government and private sector savings in driving the increase in Greece's NIF. The latter paper argues more generally that the key driver of the euro crisis was external debt rather than government debt.

12. Figure 1.18 shows also that RULC is smaller in Greece than in most comparison countries. This is partly due to the fact that Greece has a larger share of the self-employed, whose income is not included in the aggregate compensation of all employees but is included in the GDP.

13. Unfortunately, the data from the World Bank *Doing Business* reports do not allow us to trace changes to the business environment in Greece during the period 1970 to 2005, and hence to map to the measures of macroeconomic performance presented in sections 1.2.1 and 1.2.2. A discussion of microeconomic policies in Greece during the period 1974 to 2000 can be found in Bryant, Garganas, and Tavlas (2002), who also provide a broader account of the evolution of the Greek economy during the same period. As these authors point out, weaknesses at the

microeconomic level were not addressed, or were made worse, until the early 1990s. From 1995 onward, there were significant improvements in product market and labor market regulations. Moreover some large privatizations took place starting in the early 1990s, and a significant program of financial liberalization took place from 1987 onward. Chapter 7 (financial system) provides an account of this financial liberalization program, and chapter 5 (privatizations) provides an account of privatization activity from 1991 until 2015. The lack of sound microeconomic policies during the 1980s is likely to have been the main driver of Greece's macroeconomic stagnation during that period. Conversely the pickup in GDP growth and corporate investment from 1995 onward owe in part to the improvements in the business environment during the 1990s.

14. The addition of countries covered in the reports between 2010 and 2014 only strengthens Greece's improvement. Six countries were added during that period.

15. Internationally comparable indexes of competition intensity (which is partly a consequence of PMR) are harder to find. Some evidence in the case of Greece comes from Katsoulacos and Vettas (2004), who report that out of 208 industry sectors, only 82 have a sufficient degree of competition, as measured by a Herfindahl index below 2000.

16. Chapter 7 (financial system) documents that voluntary pensions in Greece are small, and points out to tax disincentives as a possible cause.

17. According to the OECD, the poverty rate in those above the age of 75 was higher in Greece than in all comparison countries in figure 1.21, except for Spain.

18. Greece is one of the few OECD countries where a system of private tutoring centers has been set up to prepare high school students for university entrance exams. Greece also has one of the largest percentages, among OECD countries, of university students studying abroad: second highest after Ireland as of 2005.

19. Cypriot banks invested in Greece also acquired a high number of Greek government bonds, which contributed to their bankruptcy in 2013. The Cypriot banks bought the bonds partly as a quid pro quo for obtaining licenses to open more branches in Greece.

20. These numbers are slightly different than in figure 1.5 because they come from the Spring 2015 report of the European Commission, whereas figures 1.5 to 1.8 are drawn based on the Spring 2014 report. We use the Spring 2014 report for these figures because the data in that report go farther back in time. We should also note that the large primary deficit in 2013 shown in figure 1.5 was due to a one-off expenditure for the recapitalization of the banks, and does not reflect any fiscal loosening. Fiscal tightening during the crisis can be seen more clearly in figures 1.7 and 1.8, which report current revenue and expenditure, respectively. These series do not include one-off items.

21. The comparison remains the same if 2009 is replaced by the last pre-crisis year 2007. In our comparison we use government savings instead of primary surplus because the former include only current revenue and expenditure, and this allows for a cleaner comparison.

22. We compute these numbers by multiplying primary deficit as percentage of GDP (figure 1.5) and interest payments as percentage of GDP (figure 1.6) by GDP, and adding the results over the years 2008 to 2014.

23. Bank recapitalization used up an additional 15.1 billion, which was counted in the primary deficit (so as part of the 71.5 billion). For more details on the bank recapitalization process, including the third recapitalization that took place in 2015, see chapter 7 (financial system).

24. Computing debt in nominal terms yields the same result as in present-value terms if market interest rates are equal to the debt's coupon rate, namely its interest rate. Then extending the debt's maturity has no effect on its present value. When instead the debt's coupon rate is smaller than market interest rates, its present value is smaller than its nominal value, and it declines when maturity is extended. To take a simple example, suppose that market interest rates are 5 percent, and consider a bond with 5-year maturity and face value 100. The bond's nominal value is 100. If the bond has coupon rate 5 percent, then its present value is also 100, and it does not change when the bond's maturity is extended to 30 years without a change in the coupon rate. If, however, the coupon rate is 3 percent, then the bond's present value is 91.3 when maturity is 5 years and 69.3 when it is 30 years.

25. Interest payments on Greek debt in 2015 were 7.5 billion. The data on debt and interest payments come from AMECO. In the case of Greece, the calculation of interest payments depends on whether accrued interest on the loans by the European Stability Mechanism (ESM) that has to be paid after a grace period ending in 2022 is taken into account. Depending on the calculation method, this yields a range of 6 billion to 9 billion for 2015.

26. Zettelmeyer, Trebesch, and Gulati (2013) show that present-value calculations yield a larger relief for the PSI compared to nominal calculations. During the PSI, old bonds with nominal value 199.2 billion were exchanged for new long-term bonds with nominal value 62.4 billion plus short-term EFSF bonds with nominal value 29.7 billion. Adding the 25 billion euro loan that Greece took to recapitalize its banks, debt relief for Greece was $1 - (62.4 + 29.7 + 25)/199.2 = 41.2$ percent in nominal terms. However, debt relief in present-value terms was 53.1 percent using a 5 percent discount rate and 54.6 percent using an 8 percent discount rate (table 4 in Zettelmeyer, Trebesch, and Gulati 2013). Kazarian (2014) and Schumacher and Weder di Mauro (2015) compute debt to GDP for Greece in present-value terms and find that it is smaller by more than 50 percent of GDP than when computed in nominal terms. Kazarian (2014) argues that the corresponding discount for Ireland, Italy, Portugal, and Spain is significantly smaller.

27. The wage data are from the OECD (series "Average annual wages 2014 constant prices" for real wages, and "Average annual wages current prices" for nominal wages").

28. The HRADF got abolished by the SYRIZA-ANEL government in 2015. It got a reincarnation with a broader mandate, however, under the third adjustment program agreed in the summer of 2015.

29. We focus on the policy followed in Greece and isolate it from broader issues at the EZ level, such as whether countries with a trade surplus such as Germany should have stimulated their

aggregate demand to enable deficit countries such as Greece, Portugal, and Spain to gain some competitiveness relative to them.

30. Estimating the contributions of different factors to the decline in GDP requires a macroeconomic model. Gourinchas, Philippon, and Vayanos (2017) develop a model to perform that exercise.

31. Greece entered into negative inflation territory (declining prices) in 2013, and inflation continues to be negative as of 2016.

32. There was a two-way connection between lower wages, on the one hand, and lower aggregate demand and higher unemployment, on the other. Wages decreased in response to the drop in aggregate demand and the rise in unemployment. This is the outcome of a market concession when workers' "outside option" in labor negotiations with firms worsens as unemployment rises and it becomes difficult to find another job. Conversely, declining wages meant that Greek citizens had less to spend, and this fed back to lower aggregate demand and higher unemployment.

33. For example, in steel mills, energy costs account for 50 percent of total costs while wage costs account for only 15 percent. Iron and steel exports declined by more than 50 percent in Greece between 2011 and 2014, while no such decline was observed in Portugal (Pelagidis and Mitsopoulos 2016).

34. One example of a counterproductive regulation is Law 4174/2013, which held firms' managers and shareholders personally liable for tax debts that the firms were unable to pay (e.g., due to a firm's bankruptcy). Liability was assumed "by default" regardless of whether the firms were unable to pay the debts because of reasons beyond their control or because of intentional fraud. This effectively abolished limited liability.

35. For example, a reform designed to make the pension system sustainable was legislated in 2010 but was phased in very gradually. The reform triggered a wave of early retirements, as employees became concerned that subsequent laws might worsen their retirement terms. Early retirements in the public sector were also encouraged by the government so that targets on personnel cuts could be met. As a result of the gradual phase-in and the early retirements, expenditure on pensions in the short and medium term increased significantly. The shortfall was financed by repeated horizontal cuts in the pensions of the current pensioners. See chapter 11 (pensions) for more detail.

36. The Hartz program was initiated by Chancellor Gerhard Schroeder in response to a slowing down of the economy and high unemployment. Germany was labeled the "sick man of Europe" before the reforms. The reforms increased the flexibility of labor and product markets and switched from passive unemployment support to active policies that provided incentives for job creation and self-employment. The reforms were successful in bringing unemployment down during the recession at any given level of job vacancies, which is a clear case of reducing structural impediments to the operation of the market (Pissarides 2013). Yet it took four years for the reforms to have an impact on the economy, during which time Chancellor Schroeder lost the election and the CDU came to power and oversaw a complete transformation of the German economy. To facilitate the implementation of reform, Germany ran budget deficits that exceeded

the Maastricht thresholds, in the belief that the high deficits were temporary as once the reforms had their impact the government would be able to balance the budget at full employment and bring the debt down again—as indeed happened.

37. Public investment is not part of current expenditure. Our data on public investment come from AMECO (series "Gross fixed capital formation; General government").

38. Out of the 45 percent drop, 17 percent (i.e., 37 percent of the total) occurred between December 2014 and July 2015, as a result of the negotiations between the SYRIZA-ANEL government and the Troika. That was after debt had been restructured (April 2012) and banks had been recapitalized (July 2013). Hence the drop that can be attributed more directly to the delay in restructuring the debt and recapitalizing the banks is the remaining 28 percent.

39. While uncertainty about the banks was the main driver of the drop in household deposits, deposits also dropped because of the overall decline in household savings: with disposable incomes dropping sharply, households reduced their savings to finance consumption. Figure 1.17 shows the sharp decline in private savings during the crisis.

40. Prime Minister Alexis Tsipras went further, and criticized openly the reforms while in government. After his government had finally agreed to a new adjustment program in July 2015, he said that he did not agree with the reforms, he would not have agreed to them if he had a free choice, but given the options presented to him, this was the least injurious one.

41. One example was the pension reform, which sought to make the current pay-as-you-go system more viable, but without contemplating a switch to a modern multipillar system, such as those adopted by many countries around the world.

42. Section 1.3.2 includes many examples of poor implementation. Two indicative ones are that the independent authority set up in 2013 to collect taxes remained subject to strong political pressures, and the single health insurance provider set up in 2010 was not given sufficient tools to negotiate contracts with hospitals and pharmaceutical companies.

43. An example of administrative resistance was the refusal by tax collectors to enforce a legislated tax reform. And an example of lack of administrative capacity was that when the government initiated in 2012 the process of clawing back social benefits from those who were not entitled to them, it could not make significant progress because the Ministry of Health lacked sufficient personnel.

44. The rankings reported in section 1.2.4 mostly concern years before the crisis. The rankings mentioned in this paragraph, however, have not improved during the crisis, and have become worse in some cases.

45. According to the World Bank, nonperforming loans accounted for 34.4 percent of all loans in 2015. That percentage increases by more than 40 percent when restructured loans are included.

46. For example, employment in the tourism sector (tradable) grew by 4.8 percent between 2008 and 2014, and employment in the agriculture sector (also tradable) dropped by only 4 percent. By

contrast, employment in the construction sector (nontradable) dropped by 68.8 percent and in the retail-trade sector (also nontradable) by 20.7 percent. The data are from Eurostat.

47. By early 2016, the Athens stock market index had dropped to a 25-year low.

48. The data are from Eurostat, and EU28 averages are simple (rather than weighted) averages.

49. For example, many museums and archeological sites are open during limited hours or not at all because of lack of staff.

50. ECB President Mario Draghi has forcefully advocated that view. See, for example, https://www.ecb.europa.eu/press/key/date/2015/html/sp150522.en.html.

51. Philippon (2015) estimates that a fair debt relief for Greece based on these grounds should be 30 percent of GDP.

52. For a proposal along these lines, see Meghir, Vayanos, and Vettas (2012). The idea of conditioning debt relief on reforms dates back to the Highly Indebted Poor Countries (HIPC) initiative launched in 1996 by the IMF and World Bank. That initiative was targeted to poor countries, mainly in Africa, and made debt relief conditional on poverty-reducing reforms.

References

Acemoglu, D., S. Johnson, and J. Robinson. 2001. The colonial origins of comparative development. *American Economic Review* 91: 1369–1401.

Acemoglu, D., and J. Robinson. 2012. *Why Nations Fail: The Origins of Power, Prosperity, and Poverty*. London: Profile Books.

Alfaro, L., S. Kalemli-Ozcan, and S. Sayek. 2009. Foreign direct investment, productivity, and financial development: An empirical analysis of complementarities and channels. *World Economy* 32: 111–135.

Baltabaev, B. 2014. Foreign direct investment and total factor productivity growth: New macro evidence. *World Economy* 37: 311–334.

Barro, R. 1991. Economic growth in a cross-section of countries. *Quarterly Journal of Economics* 106: 407–443.

Bryant, R., N. Garganas, and G. Tavlas. 2001. Introduction. In *Greece's Economic Performance and Prospects*, ed. R. Bryant, N. Garganas, and G. Tavlas. Athens: Bank of Greece and Brookings Institution.

Galenianos, M. 2015. The Greek crisis: Origins and implications. Research paper 16. ELIAMEP Crisis Observatory.

Gourinchas, P.-O., T. Philippon, and D. Vayanos. 2017. The analytics of the Greek crisis. *NBER Macroeconomics Annual* 31: 1–81.

Hall, R., and C. Jones. 1999. Why do some countries produce so much more output per worker than others? *Quarterly Journal of Economics* 114: 83–116.

Ioannides, Y., and C. Pissarides. 2016. Is the Greek debt crisis one of supply or demand? *Brookings Papers on Economic Activity*. Washington, DC: Brookings Institution.

Javorcik, S. 2004. Does foreign direct investment increase the productivity of domestic firms? In search of spillovers through backward linkages. *American Economic Review* 94: 605–627.

Katsoulacos, Y., and N. Vettas. 2004. A sectoral analysis of the Greek economy (in Greek: Χαρτογράφηση Κλάδων Ελληνικής Βιομηχανίας). Working paper. Athens University of Economics and Business.

Kazarian, P. 2014. Unique insights into sovereign credit risk using IPSAS framework. Presentation at the IIF Executive Programme on Country and Sovereign Credit Risk Management. http://www.mostimportantreform.info/Credit_Rating_Agency.pdf.

Knibb, M. 2015. A critique of nominal and real macro unit labour costs as an indicator of competitiveness. *World Economic Association Newsletter* 5: 5–7.

Meghir, C., D. Vayanos, and N. Vettas. 2010. The economic crisis in Greece: A time of reform and opportunity. http:// greekeconomistsforreform.com.

Meghir, C., D. Vayanos, and N. Vettas. 2012. Greece needs growth not austerity. Bloomberg op-ed, http://www.bloombergview.com/articles/2012-11-20/greece-needs-growth-not-austerity/.

OECD. 2015. Taxing wages 2013–2014. OECD report. Paris.

Pelagidis, T., and M. Mitsopoulos. 2016. *Who's to Blame for Greece? Austerity in Charge of Saving a Broken Economy*. New York: Palgrave Macmillan.

Philippon, T. 2015. *Fair Debt Relief for Greece: New Calculations*. Washington, DC: VoxEU.

Pissarides, C. 2013. Unemployment in the Great Recession. *Economica* 80: 385–403.

Romer, P. 1990. Endogenous technological change. *Journal of Political Economy* 98: 71–102.

Schumacher, J., and B. Weder di Mauro. 2015. *Diagnosing Greek Debt Sustainability: Why is it so Hard? Brookings Papers on Economic Activity*. Washington, DC: Brookings Institution.

Wyplosz C., and S. Sgherri. 2016. The IMF's role in Greece in the context of the 2010 stand-by arrangement. Background paper BP/16-02/11. Independent Evaluation Office, IMF.

Zettelmeyer, J., C. Trebesch, and M. Gulati. 2013. The Greek debt restructuring: An autopsy. *Economic Policy* 28: 515–563.

II The Macroeconomics of the Crisis

2 Greece and the Euro

George-Marios Angeletos and Harris Dellas

2.1 Introduction

Greece's participation in the eurozone (EZ) has an arduous history. Greece was the only long-standing EU country whose admission had to be postponed due to a lack of satisfaction of the entry criteria. Its entry was accompanied by debate on whether various performance criteria—such as inflation—were satisfied[1] and whether the entry value of the nominal exchange rate (drachmas per euro) was sensible and consistent with long-term external balance.[2] Greece's international competitiveness was subsequently further eroded by an inflation (in prices and wages) that significantly exceeded the eurozone average. Inflation was fueled by economic activity due to credit growth and a significant increase in government spending. EZ membership contributed by reducing the cost of government borrowing. Membership was perceived as providing an implicit sovereign debt guarantee by the eurozone at large, and this made the issuance of Greek government debt cheap. Deficits ballooned despite the strong growth (fiscal policy was strongly procyclical). Worsening competitiveness and fast-growing public debt (from an already high level) sowed the seeds of the current malaise in Greece. A troubled relationship from the outset has now turned into a crisis.

In this chapter we evaluate the economic aspects of this relationship. We start by discussing whether Greece's entry in the EZ made good *economic* sense. We then describe what went wrong and the underlying reasons. Last we evaluate the costs and benefits from Greece's continued membership in the EZ and how these costs and benefits may relate to the decision to honor debt obligations to official creditors.

2.2 The Entry

The optimum currency area (OCA) theory originated in a debate over the merits of fixed versus floating exchange rates. The intent was to arrive at a framework for studying the costs and benefits associated with a currency union. In its earliest manifestation, OCA theory aimed at identifying the characteristics that make it less costly for a potential member of a currency union to forgo independent monetary policy and surrender the use of its exchange rate instrument. The following criteria are used to determine whether a country is suitable (i.e., faces a lower cost) to join a currency union:

1. *Labor mobility* Regions between which there exists high labor mobility are viewed as better candidates for currency-union membership because such mobility provides a substitute for exchange-rate flexibility in promoting external adjustments (Mundell 1961). To better understand the meaning of labor mobility across regions let us consider two states in the United States, such as Texas and California. If California suffers an adverse demand shock (people wanting to eat fewer fruits and vegetables) and if wages are rigid, any resulting increase in unemployment could be halted by Californian growers lowering their products' prices (by an exchange rate change in a region that has its own currency) or by unemployed Californian workers moving to Texas. Because moving from California to Texas is easy, Californian workers do not suffer much when their state does not have access to the exchange rate instrument (currency devaluation). The same considerations apply if Texas suffers a state-specific shock. Hence labor mobility can make an exchange rate adjustment less necessary.

   A related argument concerns the role of real wage flexibility in alleviating the costs of participation in a currency union. If wages are not rigid, then costs adjust downwardshould an adverse shock occur, keeping unemployment from rising, and thus making exchange rate adjustment less necessary.

2. *Similarity in production structure* Countries that produce and trade similar goods or have similar industries are prone to symmetric terms-of-trade shocks, so exchange rate adjustments become less necessary. Such countries are considered to be better candidates for currency unions than countries whose production and trade structures are markedly different (Mundell 1961). The similarities in production structures between two countries can be inferred from the share of their bilateral intra-industry trade in their total bilateral trade. In the EZ, for instance, intra-industry trade is more prevalent within the core countries than across core and periphery countries.

3. *Degree of commodity diversification* Highly diversified economies are considered better candidates for currency unions than less diversified economies. In fact diversification provides good insulation against any type of shocks, lessening the need for frequent changes in the terms of trade via the exchange rate (Kenen 1969). The composition of trade (the distribution of the shares of exports across various categories) also is a measure of the diversity of an economy.

4. *Openness and size of an economy*   According to McKinnon (1963), small and highly open economies should prefer fixed exchange rate arrangements. Indeed, nominal exchange rate changes in such economies do not affect the terms of trade and thus international trade competitiveness, but do affect the nominal prices of imported goods and thus the overall domestic price level. Thus exchange rate adjustments do not accomplish much at the output front but rather diminish price stability. Small and highly open economies are thus more suited than larger or more closed economies for membership in a currency union.

   For McKinnon, the disconnect between the nominal exchange rate and terms-of-trade movements was due to presumed values of the various trade elasticities that somehow made the price of the domestic traded goods move one to one with changes in the nominal exchange rate. A natural and transparent way to get this disconnect, so that the effect of a change in the nominal exchange rate on trade competitiveness is negated by an offsetting move in domestic prices, is through nominal wage indexation. Exchange rate devaluation makes imported goods more expensive, raising directly the domestic price level. Under wage indexation, wages then go up throughout the economy, pushing the nominal price of exportable goods up, and thus negating the effect of the devaluation on the terms of trade. Italy in the 1980s is a good example of this. Devaluations failed to affect Italy's trade competitiveness as wages adjusted quickly to changes in prices due to formal indexation provisions (*la scala mobile*).

5. *Fiscal integration*   The higher the level of fiscal integration between two areas, the greater their ability to smooth out diverse shocks through endogenous fiscal transfers from high to low economic activity regions (Kenen 1969). Consider the California example used earlier. When California suffers a negative income shock, it transfers fewer federal taxes to the United States but receives more funds (e.g., for unemployment insurance benefits). Unlike the other criteria, the degree of fiscal integration is a policy variable, so it can be selected in a way that makes a currency union more or less costly from the point of view of macroeconomic stability.

6. *Trade integration*   The more concentrated is a country's trade with a subset of partner countries, the greater is the saving in transactions costs associated with the use of a single currency (Eichengreen 1994).

Greece did not satisfy any of the OCA criteria at the time of its entry to the EZ.[3] In the 1990s labor mobility between Greece and other EZ countries was limited, and Greek wages were too rigid (due to the large share of public employment as well as various institutional features of the labor market). Moreover there were no fiscal integration mechanisms in the EZ to ease Greece's entry. While the same drawbacks affected other prospective EZ members, Greece was particularly unprepared for the currency union because it failed by a large margin all the criteria. Greece's production structure was different from that of the large EZ members, its degree of commodity diversification was more limited and, remarkably, for a country of such small size and with large access to waterways, Greece was not particularly open. The last feature is documented in table 2.1, which shows exports as a percentage of GDP for various EU countries of similar size to Greece. Table 2.2 shows the patterns of Greece's bilateral trade with EU countries. As the table indicates, Greece's trade integration with the European Union is much smaller than that of other EZ countries. While we do not

Table 2.1
Exports as a percentage of GDP in EU countries with approximately Greece's population size, 2008 to 2012 average

Austria	55.4
Belgium	81.4
Czech Republic	68.2
Greece	23.4
Hungary	85
Portugal	33.2
Sweden	50

Source: World Bank.
Note: Entries are total exports (goods and services).

Table 2.2
Countries' trade with the EU27 and outside the EU27, euros (million), 2001

	Extra-EU27	Intra-EU27	Percent intra/total
Greece	4,608	8,241	0.64
	13,149	23,719	0.64
Spain	33,363	96,895	0.74
	54,091	118,586	0.68
Belgium	46,922	165,616	0.78
	55,921	143,570	0.72
Portugal	5,043	21,875	0.81
	10,264	33,830	0.76

Source: Eurostat, External and intra-EU trade, a statistical yearbook, data 1958 to 2010.
Note: First row for each country represents exports and the second imports.

have information on Greece's share of interindustry and intra-industry trade with its currency partners, Greece's structure of imports/exports suggests a relatively large share of interindustry trade. The importance of this factor for our analysis is that as Baxter and Stockman (1988) have shown, sectoral shocks play a big role in international business cycles. Countries that have similar structures trade mostly intra-industrially, so their business cycles become synchronized when sectoral shocks occur, and there is no need for asymmetric adjustment via the exchange rate. This lowers the cost of a currency union.

The OCA criteria thus suggest that Greece's adoption of the euro could be detrimental to its macroeconomic stability. But does this imply that Greek entry did not make economic sense?

To address this question, we need to take into account a second branch of the currency union literature that emphasizes the role of policy credibility.[4] This literature shows that a move to a new monetary arrangement can be entirely motivated by a desire to commit to more efficient monetary practices. Hence the loss of monetary control may actually be *beneficial*. Consider a country that suffers from inflation bias à la Barro and Gordon (1983). In this country inflation is high because the monetary authorities have behaved opportunistically; they have inflated the economy and devalued the currency to reap a short-term employment gain. This country ends up suffering from high inflation[5] without any compensating employment gains (because in the long run high inflation does not bring employment gains). Experience has indeed shown that countries with high inflation have difficulty stabilizing their economies using policies at the national level, e.g., by making their central bank independent or unilaterally pegging their currency to that of a more credible country.[6] But they have a better chance of eliminating their inflation bias—practically overnight—by joining a union with credible monetary institutions—like the ECB (Giavazzi and Pagano 1988). Many of the countries that have joined the EZ are understood to have acted according to this logic. And for the most part their monetary union participation has proved to be an unambiguously welfare-improving move in that the success of a stabilization policy is limited when a country lacks monetary policy credibility.[7]

To evaluate whether Greece's adoption of the euro was beneficial, we must take into account both the higher stabilization costs and the credibility gains. This requires combining insights from the two branches of the currency union literature: that on OCA and that on policy credibility. It is possible to combine the two branches and derive the net balance of costs and benefits associated with a currency union as a function of the size of the inflation bias. Clerc, Dellas, and Loisel (2011) demonstrate this approach using a standard, New Keynesian, open economy model. Their model suggests that central banks with strong anti-inflation credentials can anchor inflationary expectations and stabilize the economy at a low cost in terms of output. By the same token, central banks that lack anti-inflation credentials would not be able to make effective use of stabilization policies and would keep inflation under control only with high output losses. These points may be better understood if illustrated by an example.

Suppose that firms in an economy become better able to collude and charge higher markups. This causes inflation to rise and output to decline. The central bank can fight the rising inflation by raising interest rates, but this comes at the cost of further depressing the economy.

The central bank can choose between two policy reactions. One is to raise interest rates sharply and immediately to signal its resolve to fight inflation. The other is to follow a more measured path: raise the interest rate gradually in the present period, while communicating to the markets that interest rates will continue rising until inflation has been contained.[8] The second strategy is superior because the economy adjusts more smoothly and output loss is smaller. But the gradual approach can only be implemented if the central bank's pledges are taken in earnest, that is, if the monetary authorities have credibility. In the absence of credibility, a gradual increase in the interest rate could be interpreted as a sign that the central bank that does not have the capability to take strong measures to control inflation, and so is fueling rather than containing the inflationary expectations.

Delegating the management of monetary policy to the ECB did eliminate the inflation bias and inefficient stabilization policy in Greece. But entry to the EZ also has had its costs in that Greece has not benefited at all from the EZ's monetary stabilization policy. This situation would not have arisen if the shocks that afflicted Greece were common across the EZ countries such as an increase in the cost of energy. But it would arise and represent a problem if a shock only afflicted Greece such as a major oil spill that reduces the demand for Greek tourist destinations, and as a country-specific shock would not solicit any ECB response. A critical factor in the comparison of stabilization costs to credibility gains is thus the commonality of the shocks versus the inflation bias and the degree of inefficiency in the handling of monetary stabilization policy. Clerc, Dellas, and Loisel further show that even countries that suffer from a modest inflation bias (e.g., 3 percent) would benefit from being part of a currency union so long as the international correlation of economic disturbances is positive.

In table 2.3 we present the average CPI inflation differential vis-à-vis Germany for some EU countries. If these differentials are taken to reflect the average inflation bias in these countries relative to Germany, then the analysis of Clerc, Dellas, and Loisel indicates that for a country like Greece, with a double-digit inflation bias, EZ membership

Table 2.3
Pre-EZ inflation differences

	France	Italy	Greece	Spain	Netherlands
1960–98	2.44	4.91	8.46	5.78	0.99
1970–95	3.15	6.77	12.49	7.21	0.75
1970–90	4.08	7.68	12.27	8.21	1.01
1980–90	4.13	7.89	16.69	7.04	−0.05

Source IFS.
Note: Numbers give the average CPI inflation difference of the country under consideration vis-à-vis Germany during the specified period.

was bound to be welfare improving, even in the absence of any commonality of shocks between Greece and the EZ countries.

There are indeed other benefits to EZ participation, such as lower transaction costs and greater comparability—transparency—in international prices, that aid in trade competition. In our view, these benefits are likely to be small. But there is another consideration that made the case for Greek participation in the EZ even more compelling. This is that the elimination of the inflation bias was accompanied by a reduction in inflation volatility.[9] Economic theory suggests that the effect of inflation uncertainty on economic activity and policy effectiveness can be much more severe than the effect of its average level. For instance, higher volatility typically implies higher risk premiums and real interest rates, lower savings and investment, less effective monetary policy, and inability to issue long-term nominal debt. The latter effect has not yet been accounted for in the currency area literature, but is likely to be important because long-term nominal debt serves a useful welfare and resource allocation role. The Greek government was able, for the first time, to issue long-term debt only after having been admitted to the EZ. Similar considerations apply to exchange rate uncertainty, whose main impact is on the volume of international trade. There is in fact a large literature that argues that lowering exchange rate volatility could stimulate international trade and cross-border investment.

To recapitulate, while the exchange rate can be a useful tool for macroeconomic stabilization, countries that lack policy credibility may not be in a position to use it effectively. Such countries may end up with high and volatile inflation rates and high real interest rates with detrimental effects on their short- and long-term macroeconomic performances. For such countries, giving up this policy tool may actually represent a positive development in terms of both macroeconomic stability and welfare. Greece fits this case well.

2.3   The Actual Experience

The delegation of the management of monetary affairs to the ECB led to the taming and stability of inflation in Greece relative to past experience. It was still the case that Greek inflation, while low by historical standards (see figure 2.1), remained above the EZ average (see table 2.4). As a result inflation risk premiums decreased and ex ante real interest rates dropped significantly (and the ex post rates even more, given the higher than EZ average inflation) stimulating spending and thus having a strong expansionary effect on short-term economic activity. The increase in spending came through three main channels. Most important was a so-called intertemporal substitution effect that arose from the fact that low current real interest rates discourage savings and induce people (households and firms alike) to spend more on investment, housing and durable consumption goods. Next in importance was a wealth effect that derived from two considerations. First, given that Greece is not an advanced economy (its level of industrial development is not high), it is a natural borrower on the world financial markets as it wants to borrow against its higher expected future income. The net present value of a borrower's wealth always increases when borrowing costs decline. And second, a government that faces lower borrowing costs incurs a smaller cost—in terms of distortionary taxes—of servicing each unit of public debt. To the extent that growth in the size of public debt falls short of the—negative—growth in borrowing costs, lower rates induce people to expect that they will be facing lower tax liabilities during their lifetime. Under plausible assumptions, they feel richer and spend more.

The last channel proved to be the main ex post cost of EZ membership for Greece: excessive government borrowing and spending. Figure 2.2 shows how yields in long-term government bonds in the currently heavily indebted countries rapidly declined following EZ entry. Figure 2.3 shows in greater detail the spread relative to German bonds on ten-year Greek government bonds for 2001 to 2007 and for 2001 to 2013. Table 2.4 shows the budget and current account deficits, the debt to GDP ratio and GDP growth over these periods, and figures 2.1 and 2.4 depict these macroeconomic developments graphically. The budget deficit was excessive, particularly in light of Greece's relatively strong economic growth. Indeed prudent fiscal policy, as captured by the size of the budget surplus, ought to be procyclical rather than strongly countercyclical as it was in Greece where large deficits materialized even during good times.

The argument that a developing country is a natural borrower and that its government should borrow in order to invest in infrastructure is only part of the Greek debt accumulation story. Very little of the Greek government borrowing went into

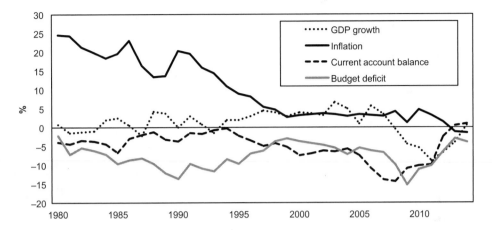

Figure 2.1
Macroeconomic performance in Greece (Bank of Greece)

Table 2.4
Deficit, debt, and inflation

	Deficit/GDP	Debt/GDP	CA/GDP	INF-GR	INF-EU15	GDP growth
2001	−4.5	103.7	−7.23	3.7	2.4	4.2
2002	−4.8	101.7	−6.52	3.9	2.3	3.4
2003	−5.6	97.4	−6.53	3.4	2.1	5.9
2004	−7.5	98.6	−5.78	3.0	2.2	4.4
2005	−5.2	100	−7.64	3.5	2.2	2.3
2006	−5.7	106.1	−11.39	3.3	2.2	5.5
2007	−6.5	107.4	−14.61	3.0	2.1	3.5
2008	−9.8	112.9	−14.92	4.2	3.3	−0.2
2009	−15.6	129.7	−11.17	1.3	0.3	−3.1
2010	−10.7	148.3	−10.13	4.7	1.6	−4.9
2011	−9.5	170.3	−9.89	3.1	2.7	−7.1
2012	−10	156.9	−3.37	1.0	2.5	−6.4

Source: Eurostat.

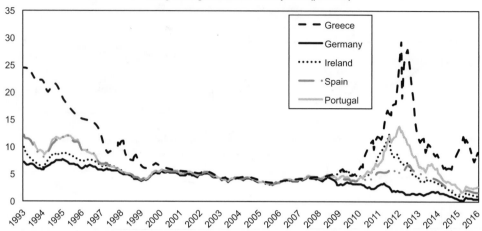

Figure 2.2
Spreads in select European countries (IMF Country report 13/156)

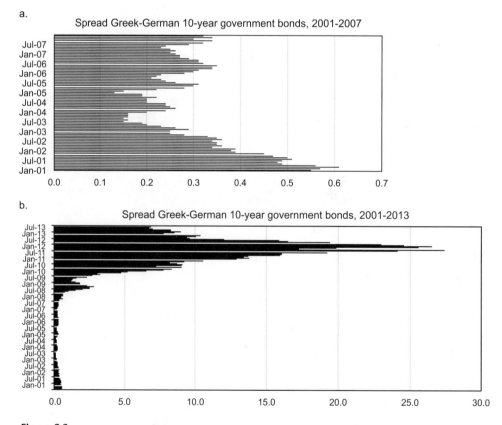

Figure 2.3
Spreads in Greece (Gibson et al. 2014)

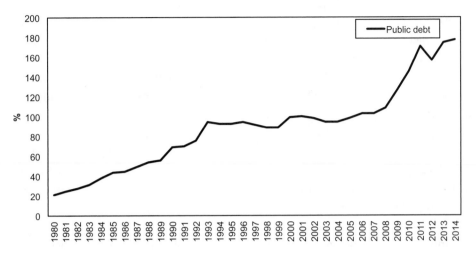

Figure 2.4
Greek public debt (Bank of Greece)

productive investments. Moreover the government continued to borrow heavily, even after it became clear that it was likely to get into repayment trouble. One can use standard political argument considerations (e.g., political myopia) to account for this. But it is also conceivable that it was perfectly rational for the Greek government to continue borrowing heavily even after realizing that the debt path had become unsustainable as international financial markets were pricing Greek debt as if it were safe. The big question is why such fiscal imprudence was tolerated by the markets and made it possible for Greece to issue unsustainably large amounts of public debt. How could the spreads remain so low despite the high level and growth of public debt?[10] Was this an inevitable side effect of participating in a currency union? Fraud (inaccurate statistics reported by Greece) is one explanation, but likely not the main cause. The main cause may be rather that Greece's participation in EZ reduced the perceived Greek sovereign risk. There are two possible explanations for such market sentiment. Lenders seem to have believed that Greece's EZ partners would be obliged to bail Greece out if things went wrong to maintain the cohesion of the currency union and also prevent negative spillovers to other countries (a EZ-wide banking crisis, a run on other heavily indebted EZ governments, etc.). Non-Greek banks held the lion's share of Greek public debt, so a default could call their viability into question. Alternatively, lenders may have believed that the stability and growth pact (SGP) provisions would eventually kick in at some point, forcing Greece to return to a sustainable path of public finances. The point we want to make is that a currency union does not all alone lead to sovereign debt problems. But that it worked this way in the case of Greece as it led to the belief that Greek sovereign default was highly improbable because Greece's EZ partners would either not allow excessive borrowing to occur or would somehow bail Greece out if it run into sovereign debt problems. Greece would have never been able to borrow the amounts it did at such low interest rates had it not been a member of the EZ.

The EZ membership had additional, indirect effects on Greek external imbalances. First, the rate at which drachmas were converted into euros (340 drachmas per euro) was widely perceived at the time as excessively low, meaning the drachma was "over-valued." The explanation for this particular exchange rate choice is that Greece was having trouble satisfying the inflation entry criterion—which was effectively the only criterion applied to Greece at the time—and the Greek government was trying to contain inflation with a policy of high real interest rates and a strong currency.[11] As a result Greece started its euro journey with a "strong" real exchange rate that contributed to international competitiveness problems and further weakened the incessantly weak Greek trade balance. This represented a bad initial condition that is not a general feature of currency unions. While it was not amendable through national monetary policy, the imbalance could have been amended by productivity growth or by low rates of domestic price and wage rate increases. Neither of these materialized. And second, as the Greek government borrowed and spent more, it pushed the price of nontraded relative to traded goods up (government spending tends to fall disproportionately on domestic, and in particular, nontraded goods). Wages in the nontraded sector increased, and this wage increase inevitably spilled over into the traded sector, such as tourism. To the extent that the increase in production costs could not be offset by countervailing forces, such as productivity growth, prices of traded goods increased with a negative impact on international competitiveness. A significant fraction of the deterioration in the Greek foreign accounts can thus be attributed to this indirect "Dutch disease" effect.

According to the literature on self-fulfilling crises (e.g., see Cole and Kehoe 2000), countries fall into one of three categories, the first of which does not lead to crisis, the second leads to crises on the basis of fundamentals, and the third to self-fulfilling crises. In the first category, the fundamentals are so strong as to completely rule out the possibility of default. Countries that are growing robustly or have low debt levels and low deficits fall in this category (e.g., Sweden with a public debt to GDP ratio of 40 percent and a deficit of 0.2 percent). In the second category the fundamentals (debt, deficit, growth) are so weak that a government cannot avoid default even if funds are made available at risk-free rates. Greece is a good example. The government ended

2008 with a debt to GDP ratio of 113 percent; then in 2009 it had a primary deficit of 11 percent and experienced real growth of –3 percent. Even with an interest rate of 4 percent the debt to GDP ratio would have increased by about 20 percentage points to 132 percent![12] At such high levels of debt, anything but exceptionally sustained strong growth and/or large budget surpluses would make public debt explode. In the third category the fundamentals are of intermediate strength, and there are two possible equilibria. If markets expect that with high probability the government will default, they require accordingly high interest rates on the country's newly issued debt, which induces debt to grow fast and can make default self-fulfilling. Or, if markets do not expect default, interest rates remain low, debt growth is limited, and there is no default (again a self-fulfilling scenario). One can easily sketch numerical examples that have this knife edge property. We do not believe that this case applies to Greece (but it may apply to a country like Spain).

2.4   The Road Ahead: Greece's Present and Future with or without the Euro

Greece faces two key macroeconomic decisions: to default or not default on its outstanding debt (and if she defaults, by how much), and to stay inside or exit the EZ. These two decisions may not be mutually independent, and especially because default could potentially force Greece to exit the currency union and even the European Union.

2.4.1   The Default Decision

The decision to default depends on the sovereign's perception of the associated costs and benefits. Those have been extensively studied in the existing literature but only in the context of sovereign default against private creditors. We will argue that the cost of default against official creditors is likely to be significantly higher than that against private creditors.[13]

The benefit from default corresponds roughly to the value of foreign-owned sovereign debt. If Greece defaults on 100 billion euros of foreign-held Greek debt, then Greece's gain is roughly[14] 100 billion that does not need to be transferred to foreigners. The costs of sovereign default listed in the literature include (1) exclusion from private international credit markets (which constrains domestic investment to equal domestic savings, a potentially significant constraint when income is volatile and/or the marginal productivity of domestic capital exceeds the world interest rate as is the case for countries outside the high income ones), (2) seizure of Greek government assets located abroad, and (3) possible adverse effects on international trade either because domestic goods are seized by foreign creditors when they cross the border or because trade relies heavily on foreign trade credit. When a country—like Greece— relies heavily on foreign intermediate goods for domestic production, the trade disruption can have depressing effects on the level of output.

We believe that these costs are only a subset of those that apply when default takes place against official lenders. This is because a credit relationship is part of a broader set of relationships between the borrower and the lender due to participation in the same club,[15] and there can be spillovers across relationships. Consider, for instance, the relationship between Greece and the other members of the EZ. A Greek default on official loans from those countries could trigger retaliation and lower Greece's benefits from membership in the EZ or even the European Union: structural fund payments and other transfers might be cut, ECB credit to the Greek central bank and the Greek banking system might be cut, official lenders might be tempted to adopt policies that are less favorable to Greek interests, support for Greek foreign policy positions might wither, actions may be taken to force Greece to leave the EZ, and so on and on.

As the ongoing crisis constitutes the first instance in which members of the EZ have borrowed large amounts from other members, and since no default against official funds has occurred, we cannot yet know whether official lenders would be in a position to inflict sanctions of the type described above and, if they were, whether they would actually choose to do so. But what matters for the behavior of Greece— and hence for the decision to default or not—is the *perception* of the existence and likely use of such sanctioning powers, rather than the use itself. In our view, the public debate in Europe and statements by policy makers provide ample evidence for a widely shared belief that superior sanctioning powers do exist and official lenders would be willing to use them.

In Germany, for example, which provides most of the official financing, statements of politicians, the debates in parliament, and the public reaction give the impression that the loans have a low probability of default. Indeed such a perception was the sina qua non for large German loan provision at low rates to be politically feasible in the first place, given voters' expressed antipathy to solidarity (transfers) toward Greece. This perception is also founded in the knowledge that a default by Greece on debt held by official creditors amounts to violating EU treaties and breaking national laws, leaving Greece in uncharted and treacherous political territory regarding its future within the European Union.[16] Naturally, time consistency is an issue as it would also be costly for Germany to impose sanctions ex post. Yet, repeat business within the club (lending to Portugal, Ireland, and Spain is but one example) makes reputational considerations important, and not imposing sanctions following a Greek default could undermine Germany's credibility.[17] Note also that to ensure broad political support for enforcement ex post, Germany has required club-wide participation in the official lending operations.

Similar perceptions about the augmented costs of Greek default against official EZ loans are held in Greece: until the January 2015 election voters opted for parties that oppose default and warn about its dire consequences for Greece's membership in the EZ and even the European Union. And even the SYRIZA party elected in power in January 2015 with a promise to renegotiate down the debt, has shelved that promise and agreed that renegotiations would take place in the distant future, Some fringe parties still advocate default, but this position may not reflect the view that official lenders are powerless but rather an underlying desire to actually subject Greece to the wrath of its official creditors and get the country expelled from the EZ and even the European Union. In our view, the evidence thus points to a widely shared belief in both the existence of unusual sanctioning powers on the part of official lenders and their willingness to use them.

2.4.2 The Currency Decision

The arguments in favor and against currency union membership reviewed in section 2.2 in the context of Greece's decision to join the EZ remain relevant for Greece's decision to stay inside or exit the EZ. Greece did not satisfy at the time—and nor can nowadays—the OCA criteria. Yet, it did make economic sense for Greece to join the EZ because this eliminated its inflation bias and reduced inflation volatility. Much has changed since those days: in particular, Greece has accumulated a huge external debt, its banking system is ailing, and its economy has been severely contracting for a number of years with no visible signs of recovery. It has been suggested that exiting the EZ could bring large enough short-term benefits that could compensate for both short (higher inflation) and long-term costs (loss of monetary credibility).

What are the short-term benefits? The standard view is that Greece's current plight has to do with a serious lack of international competitiveness, in that Greek products have become too expensive relative to the products of other countries. This overvaluation of the Greek products is usually inferred from a comparison of the evolution of the general price level in Greece relative to that in other EZ countries. Or, from the examination of the evolution of unit labor costs (see figure 2.5). Overpriced Greek products discourage buyers and contribute to a trade deficit. Because a trade deficit must be financed by borrowing from abroad, that exacerbates Greece's already weak external financial position. More negative impacts on the current level of economic activity and employment arise as imports crowd out domestic production and Greek exports cannot serve as a source of growth for Greece. In contrast, trade surpluses would have not only improved the output and employment outlook but made it possible for Greece to service and eventually repay its euro-denominated external debt.

But how could the trade balance improve? The standard argument is that this could happen if Greek products became cheaper relative to foreign ones. This could be accomplished either by reducing nominal wages and other production costs while remaining in the EZ (internal devaluation). Or, by leaving the EZ and engineering a sizable *real* devaluation[18] of its new currency (external devaluation). Such devaluation could provide a boost to Greek exports and at the same time encourage import-competing production.

Let us first consider the effects of an internal devaluation as it does not involve the complications associated with the introduction of a new currency. Would such devaluation work? That is, would it improve real economic activity and the trade balance? In general, real devaluations induced by large, sudden downward adjustments in nominal wages and prices have been rare. So we need to address this question by looking at the literature that has studied exchange rate induced real devaluations, namely those that occurred during the Bretton Woods period, in the Latin American countries in the post Bretton Woods period, and in individual cases during the EMS (e.g., see Miles 1978; Edwards 1986). The challenge for this type of research is to isolate the contribution of the devaluation as many other changes in the macroeconomic environment take place around the time of the exchange rate change. Moreover devaluations are not exogenous events, so it is conceivable that the observed relation between devaluation and economic activity is the result of some other, third factor such as an increase in world interest rates or a prolonged downturn. This problem of simultaneity is the curse of econometric work.

Theory suggests an ambiguous relationship between real devaluations, economic activity, and the trade balance. There are factors that contribute to a positive association and factors that contribute to a negative association.

Positive Effects

• *Expenditure switching effect* As Greek products become cheaper, consumers would switch their spending away from foreign and toward Greek products. Increasing demand for Greek products would stimulate domestic production and employment and improve the trade balance.

• *Real balance effect* Another positive effect arises from the so called real balance (Pigou) effect. A decrease in the general price level increases the real value of wealth held in the form of nominal assets (e.g., money), inducing higher spending.

Negative Effects

• *Low trade elasticities*   If quantities do not respond sufficiently to changes in international relative prices—that is, trade elasticities are low—then expenditure switching effects will be small. Low trade elasticities derive from the existence of poor substitutes for a country's exports and imports, substantial habit persistence in consumption, and so on.[19] Suppose, for example, that holiday packages on Greek islands are poor substitutes for other countries' similar exports, say holiday packages in Spain. Poor export substitutability means that as the price of holiday packages in Greece declines, the number of tourists who will switch their destinations from Spain to Greece will not be large enough, and Greece's export revenues—the number of packages sold times their new price—will decrease. Lower export revenue implies a deterioration in the trade balance.

• *Cost push effects*   Depending on the structure of a country's international trade, a devaluation could act as a cost push shock: by increasing the prices of imported intermediate goods—such as machinery and oil—it raises the cost of domestic production and thus depresses economic activity and impairs competitiveness. This is particularly critical for a country like Greece that relies heavily on foreign intermediate goods to produce domestic goods. Van Wijnbergen (1985) has developed a model that treats this type of devaluation as a negative (contractionary) supply shock.

The empirical evidence is mixed. More often devaluations are contractionary (Edwards 1986). The effects on the trade balance may be ambiguous as well. When the effects are positive, they often come with a substantial delay, forming the so-called J-curve. That is, following a devaluation, the trade balance initially worsens as the volume of exports and imports does not change in the short run but the value of exports declines (because they are now cheaper) while the value of imports increases (because imports are made more expensive by the devaluation). And only when export and import volumes adjust significantly—which may take a long time—the trade balance shows an improvement. Consequently there is little in past experience to suggest that devaluations are an effective, reliable means of stimulating economic activity and improving the trade balance. Note in figure 2.5 that Greece experienced a significant real devaluation as nominal wages and unit labor costs decreased, but exports remained below their pre-crisis values (see figure 2.6). While the path of exports during the last few years may reflect other factors, such as weak growth in some other European countries or geopolitical developments in Mediterranean countries, there is little to suggest that the internal devaluation has boosted Greece's economic performance.

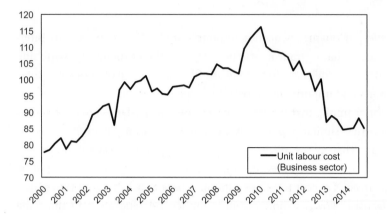

Figure 2.5
Greek unit labor costs, per working day and seasonally adjusted (ECB, Statistical Data Warehouse)

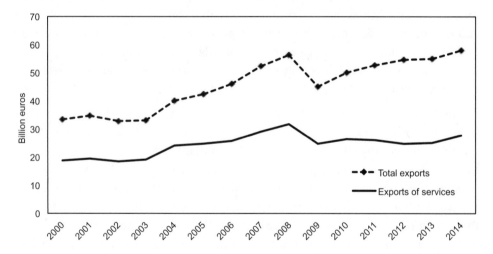

Figure 2.6
Greek exports (Bank of Greece)

Let us next turn to the effects of an *external* devaluation that Greece might undertake after leaving the euro and introducing a new currency. Suppose that the exchange rate chosen represents nominal currency devaluation relative to the parity at the time of entry (e.g., there are 500 new drachmas to a euro). It is important to note that unlike the earlier case of the internal devaluation, where a reduction in domestic prices automatically makes domestic products relatively cheaper (a real devaluation), there can be no guarantee that a nominal devaluation will accomplish the same, that is, translate into a real devaluation. This is because domestic prices may increase following the currency devaluation, negating any effects on competitiveness. Domestic prices increase directly because the cost of imported goods increases due to the cheaper exchange rate and indirectly when wages are indexed to the price level (as it was in Italy in the 1980s), limiting large nominal devaluations to small real devaluations. The empirical evidence in the exchange rate pass-through literature suggests that domestic inflation moves at a slower pace than a change in the nominal exchange rate, with the result that changes in nominal and real exchange rates often go hand in hand. But it is not clear whether these findings are relevant for devaluations, as devaluations represent well-known, often anticipated, large discrete adjustments in the exchange rate. Edwards (1986) argues that if nominal devaluations are supplemented by adequate macroeconomic policies, it is possible to achieve in the short to medium run significant real devaluations. Similar patterns are present in devaluations occurring in the EMS system (i.e., domestic prices did not increase by the amount of the currency devaluation, so domestic products became indeed cheaper following the nominal devaluation). Nevertheless, the fact that these episodes were often accompanied by fiscal and other adjustments makes it difficult to isolate the effect of the devaluation itself.

In addition to the nominal–real devaluation issue, an external devaluation has the potential to affect internal devaluation in one of two ways. The first regards the pricing policies of exporters and importers. Consider the popular pricing scheme of pricing to market in the buyer's currency (Devereux and Engel 2002). An example would be a German exporter of cars to Greece who fixes the price of his cars in Greek drachmas. Consequently devaluation has no effect on the prices charged. With unchanged prices there is no reason for a consumer to switch to buying a domestic car, so devaluation has no effect.[20] The second is, again, a real balance (Pigou) effect but it now works in the opposite direction—that is, it is contractionary—as the domestic price level typically increases following a nominal devaluation, reducing the real value (the purchasing power) of domestic money holdings and thus making domestic households poorer. Lower spending by domestic households can lead to an output contraction.

2.4.3   An Important, Overlooked Consideration

Currently in debate is Greek competitiveness with regard to employment and the trade balance. Proposals to exit the EZ or to stay in and adjust significantly nominal wages and prices aim at allowing Greece to experience a substantial terms of trade deterioration as a means of improving its output and employment outlook. What this debate ignores, however, is that a real devaluation also gives rise to negative welfare effects. And that these effects may be quite pronounced for Greece due to its large external debt. In general, real devaluation involves a trade-off. On the one hand, it may improve competitiveness. But on the other hand, it involves a transfer of income and wealth from Greeks to foreigners. The transfer of income occurs because Greece has to give up more units of domestic goods for each unit of foreign goods it obtains (Greek goods become cheaper). The transfer of wealth occurs because Greece has a negative net international investment position. For instance, consider Greek public debt owned by foreigners. When Greece's real exchange rate depreciates, each foreign-held unit of Greek public debt represents a claim to a larger number of units of Greek goods. Note that these negative income and wealth effects are independent of how the devaluation is being accomplished, that is, whether it happens through a nominal exchange rate or domestic price adjustment. The important thing for the wealth transfer is whether Greece's external debt will remain denominated in euros (naturally, re-denominating the currency of the country's liabilities represents a default).

We now offer a rough estimate of these welfare losses, first those associated with trade (income losses) and then those associated with Greece's international asset position (wealth losses). Let us consider a recent year, say, 2011. Greek imports of goods and services were 62 billion euros (source: Bank of Greece). Without any loss of generality, let us fix the original Greek terms of trade to unity and assume that there is a real devaluation of 25 percent so that one unit of Greek goods now buys only 0.75 units of foreign goods, that is, the new terms of trade—the price of foreign in terms of domestic goods—becomes 0.75. Consequently, while before the devaluation the country needed to generate an amount of 62 billion euros of exports to finance the same amount of imports, the required amount of exports is now equal to 62/0.75 = 83, that is, an extra payment to foreigners of about 20.6 billion. Alternatively, imports may decrease as a result of the devaluation, so the actual transfer needs to be computed using the new imports figure. Suppose that imports also decrease by 25 percent—a rather large decline as trade elasticities may be well below unity—so the new annual level of imports is 46 billion. The implicit transfer to foreigners at the new level of imports is 46/0.75 – 46/1 = 61 – 46 = 15 billion euros. The nominal Greek GDP in 2011 was 208 billion. Say that the devaluation proves expansionary with output growing by 5 percent to 218 billion euros. The devaluation then implies a transfer to foreigners that is equal to 15/218 = 7 percent of GDP on an annual basis (for as long as the Greek terms of trade remain weak). Moreover not only all of the extra output that was produced because of the devaluation (10 billion) is gifted to the foreigners but also some of the remaining output (5 billion) is transferred too. These are substantial numbers. In our scenario, for a devaluation to generate an extra amount of resources to the domestic residents that is equal to the resources it gives to the foreigners (15 billion), it must generate an increase in Greek GDP of the order of 30/208 = 14.4 percent. Such a growth rate does seem outlandish.[21] The calculations can also be cast in terms of employment gains by making assumptions on the value added for a typical Greek worker. But the losses in terms of GDP seem cleaner and quite informative.

Are such losses preventable? That is, could a trade balance be reached without Greece making such a huge indirect transfer of Greek products to foreign consumers through the terms-of-trade deterioration? The answer is affirmative. The volume of trade depends not only on relative prices but also on income. If economic growth in Europe were stronger, there would be higher demand across the board and thus also for Greek products even if these products were not priced so low. That is, more foreign tourists would come to Greece and spend more even at unchanged Greek prices. But while it has been suggested that northern eurozone countries could in this way mitigate the recession in the south, it is not a policy option for Greece.

A more probable approach to balancing trade would be to reduce the relative prices of Greek goods by increasing the supply of these Greek goods (e.g., through a productivity innovation) rather than through administrative or aggregate demand channels. Suppose, for example, that producers of feta cheese find a way to convert the same quantity of milk into a larger quantity of feta. The increase in the supply of feta would lead to lower feta prices. If the elasticity of the demand for feta is not too low, then the price of feta does not drop much when its supply increases and as a result Greek producers of feta benefit because of higher earnings alongside the foreign consumers of feta who benefit because of the lower prices. In this case the Greek trade balance improves. So while the country passes on to foreign consumers some of the benefits of the technological innovation, it still gains both in terms of welfare and the trade balance.

One could similarly compute the international transfer of wealth toward Greece's foreign creditors that arises from devaluation. The most recent value of Greek external debt is approximately 400 billion euros. A 25 percent devaluation implies a once and for all wealth transfer to foreigners worth about 50 percent of the Greek GDP.[22] This is a large transfer and raises the question whether a devaluation is worth undertaking, especially when real devaluations may be ineffective.

These calculations have—to the best of our knowledge—so far been completely ignored in the current debates, which have focused instead on GDP growth and unemployment. Of course, it is quite conceivable that jobs created when devaluations work carry also other tangible (human capital creation) and intangible (social harmony) benefits that need to be included in the overall assessment. Nonetheless, the welfare cost of the devaluation in terms of direct income–wealth transfer to foreigners is huge. If it is also the case that devaluations fail to improve output and employment, then this course of action appears questionable on a welfare basis.

Note that even in the absence of any external debt, a significant, unanticipated reduction in domestic wages and prices within the EZ can have important income redistribution and perhaps also resource allocation effects. As the literature on debt deflation (I. Fisher, Minsky) has pointed out, given the value of nominal obligations, a drop in nominal goods' prices increases the real value of these obligations, redistributing income from debtors to creditors. To the extent that these groups have different marginal propensities to spend, such redistribution from one group (debtors) to another (creditors) could have significant macroeconomic effects. Some recent research is trying to quantify the role of debt deflation in past economic downturns (the Great Depression). It must be said, however, that the current mainstream view is that even when recognizing that firms are on the borrowing side (and they may have to cut down on fresh borrowing and investment to meet their higher debt liabilities), debt deflation may not matter much for macroeconomic performance.

2.4.4   Some Food for Thought

If devaluation does not seem to hold much promise for fixing Greece's bleak macroeconomic outlook even in the short run, are there any other macroeconomic policies that appear more promising? Investment (and in particular foreign investment) could provide much relief in the short term and bring also substantial benefits in the long term. There is little foreign investment in Greece and, in addition, domestic companies are relocating abroad (Bulgaria, Turkey, Cyprus). Naturally, there are many factors that discourage investment in Greece: red tape and excessive regulation, militant unions, corrupt officials, and poor infrastructure (ports, roads) being key among these. However, the largest deterrent of investment is macroeconomic uncertainty. As the recent business cycle literature has pointed out, macroeconomic uncertainty is both a major deterrent to investment and a major source of macroeconomic instability. In the case of Greece much uncertainty also pertains to uncertainty about EZ membership and hence the future value of a company's assets and liabilities, its future tax rates, and so on. Bloom et al. (2012) show that an increase in uncertainty has strong, contractionary effects on economic activity. For instance, they report that an increase in macroeconomic uncertainty led to drops of about 2 percent of GDP in the United States. One could easily imagine much larger effects in Greece given the magnitude of uncertainty present in this country. So measures to reduce macroeconomic uncertainty in Greece, perhaps a constitutional amendment that removes government discretion in the setting of policy, or even delegates aspects of economic management of Greece to foreign official or private entities, could have a large and immediate impact on output and employment. Today Greece's economy lies so far below its maximum technological institutional capabilities that any such measures, together with critical reforms in labor and product markets as well as in public administration, could help unleash the country's growth potential.

Living standards in Greece have declined substantially since the onset of the debt crisis. They were unsustainably high before the crisis, financed by foreign resources, but they cannot be restored to their previous levels whether or not Greece honors its external debt. The reason is that, as is well known, a country's living standards are primarily determined by its labor productivity, and the growth in living standards, by its growth in productivity. Table 2.5 gives some productivity differences across countries (GDP per hour). The numbers paint a bleak picture. As long as the productivity differentials remain stable over time, a Greek worker who works as many hours as an American or German worker can only hope to consume approximately 60 percent of what his German counterpart does. These gaps cannot be narrowed directly by default or exit. But they could worsen if default (or exit from the EZ) leads to shortages of specialized foreign intermediate goods, a weak banking system, less investment, and so on. In this context, EZ membership, to the extent that it makes Greece undertake sensible, productivity-enhancing reforms as a condition for securing official refinancing and remaining in the EZ seems to be the only short- to medium-term action that could lead to a narrowing of Greece's productivity differential vis-à-vis the developed countries. Other chapters in this volume offer more specialized and detailed discussion of how Greece's long-term productivity can be improved.

Table 2.5
GDP per hour, in 1990 USD

	2000	2006	2012
Greece	14.17	16.80	15.83
Germany	27.16	30.12	30.97
Italy	25.43	25.80	25.80
Spain	22.50	23.22	25.70
Portugal	14.53	15.38	16.25

Source: Conference Board Total Economy Database™, January 2013, http://www.conference-board.org/data/economydatabase.

2.5   Conclusions

Greece has had a tumultuous relationship with the euro. Its delayed entry made good economic sense due to monetary policy credibility issues but took place (like Italy's) without satisfactorily meeting all the fiscal requirements. And it involved a drachma/euro conversion rate that was too strong relative to what was thought to represent the equilibrium exchange rate (the rate that is consistent with external balance) at the time. Both of these elements turned out to be costly mistakes. As borrowing costs came down significantly, Greek governments embarked on a debt-financed, unproductive, spending spree that went "unnoticed by the custodians of the growth and stability pact," and thus the already high public debt ballooned. International trade competitiveness, which was already suffering from the overvalued conversion rate, was subsequently eroded by higher government spending. When the true fiscal situation became publicly known at a time when the world financial markets were becoming sensitized to issues of financial risks following the Lehman Brothers' collapse and the Dubai debt moratorium, the die was cast. Interest rates on Greek debt skyrocketed, and Greece defaulted on privately held debt, severely damaging its banking system. European partners and the IMF helped Greece survive with official loans.

In the important debate taking place today on the wisdom of Greece's continued membership in the EZ, given the extreme economic conditions in the country, it is argued that exit and the adoption of a "weaker" currency could provide quick relief by worsening Greece's terms of trade. This could lead to trade surpluses and help both at the employment and the repayment of external debt front. Past experience provides ground for being skeptical about the effectiveness of such a strategy as devaluations do not seem to be a particularly effective output management tool and in addition they cannot help improve long-term economic performance. The same probably applies to internal devaluations that are achieved by price–wage adjustments. So real devaluations—internal or external—cannot be a panacea to Greece's economic malaise even if they could provide temporary relief. In addition we have identified a novel welfare cost—which is quantitatively substantial—that is associated with the conventional strategies of improving international competitiveness (exchange rate or wage adjustment). While not suggesting that such devaluations may not sometimes be useful, we think that increases in competitiveness that arise from productivity growth are a better tool as they can improve the trade balance without any welfare losses.

Finally, we argued that one should not underestimate the potential costs that Greece would suffer in defaulting on its official creditors. Such an unprecedented development

Table 2.6
Composition of Greek government debt in terms of residence of debtholders

	2001	2002	2003	2004	2005	2006	2007	2008	2009
Government debt (% of GDP)	103.7	101.7	97.4	98.9	110.0	107.7	107.5	113.0	129.3
Level of debt (bn euros)	151.9	159.2	168.0	183.2	212.4	224.9	239.5	263.3	299.7
Change in debt (bn euros)	10.9	7.3	8.8	15.2	29.2	12.5	14.6	23.8	36.4
Domestic	4.4	0.0	−8.2	−4.6	−5.0	−0.2	−9.8	−1.1	6.9
Foreign	6.5	7.3	17.0	19.4	34.3	12.7	24.5	24.9	29.5
Debt share held by residents	56.6	54.1	46.3	40.0	32.1	30.2	24.2	21.6	21.3
Domestic banks	26.9	25.1	21.6	18.3	18.5	19.2	17.1	15.2	15.5
Share held by nonresidents	43.4	45.9	53.7	60.0	67.9	69.8	75.8	78.4	78.7

Source: ECB and ELSTAT.

could, in addition to making reform less urgent and likely, jeopardize Greece's position in the European clubs with dire long-term economic and political consequences.

Notes

We are grateful to D. Vayanos and C. Pissarides for valuable suggestions.

1. Even at that time it was suspected that the officially reported rates of inflation were being manipulated. It was also well understood that Greece's fiscal variables were far from satisfying the criteria; see figures 2.1 and 2.2. Italy's admission two years earlier with similarly bad fiscal figures set the precedence for ignoring the fiscal criteria.

2. The drachma's conversion rate was set in advance of Greece's entry. Greece insisted on a strong drachma–euro conversion rate over German objections to contain inflationary pressures that were threatening the satisfaction of effectively the sole entry criterion, namely inflation. Consequently Greece's real exchange rate at entry was too strong, undermining international competitiveness.

3. This remains the case nowadays. Note that there was an expectation at the time that structural reforms, such as the deregulation of labor and product markets, would accompany the formation of the currency area—as countries lost the bargain-basement option of competitive devaluations—and would lessen the impact of asymmetric shocks, making the OCA criteria more likely to be satisfied ex post. Not much of this has happened.

4. By policy credibility, we mean the public's belief that the policy makers will act in a way consistent with promises they made in the past even when such actions are not the best available within the menu of current actions.

5. The literature has identified two major costs associated with a high—but stable—rate of inflation. One cost is associated with the process of changing prices (e.g., printing new menus) and the higher transaction costs people and firms face when they hold too little money as they attempt to evade the inflation tax. The other cost is associated with a larger price dispersion that arises in economies with staggered price setting when inflation is nonzero. See Woodford (2003). We discuss the cost of unstable inflation below.

6. The lack of credibility of the fixed exchange rate systems in the EMS was demonstrated many times before and most prominently in the currency crisis of 1992 that led the United Kingdom to leave the EMS and other countries to effectively move to flexible rates.

7. Another important motivating factor for an EU currency union—which the current paper abstracts from—was the threat that competitive devaluations posed for the process of EU economic integration. When economic conditions weakened, countries were often tempted to gain a competitive advantage over other countries by devaluing their currency and thus making their products relatively cheaper. This created political storms within the European Union as the countries that lost competitiveness threatened to retaliate by disrupting trade relations with the devaluing countries. Such disruptions could have proved fatal for EU survival.

8. The latter strategy represented the policy of forward guidance—or inflation expectations management—as practiced at present by the US and UK central banks, but with the reverse pattern, that is, lowering interest rates and promising to keep them low in the future.

9. It is a well-known empirical fact that higher average rates of inflation are accompanied by more volatile inflation.

10. Gibson, Hall, and Tavlas (2014) provide evidence showing that prior to 2009, the markets failed to incorporate Greece's deteriorating fundamentals into the price of Greek sovereigns.

11. The use of the exchange rate instrument to contain inflation resulted in the appreciation of the drachma during the months preceding the fixing of the drachma–euro parity in June 2000, six months before Greece's entry.

12. This number has been computed as follows: The evolution of nominal debt, $b(t)$, satisfies the equation $b(t) = (1 + R(t-1)) \, b(t-1) + d(t)$, where t denotes year, R is the nominal interest rate, and d is the primary deficit (for simplicity we have assumed that the debt maturity is one year). Dividing through by nominal GDP in period t, $y(t)$ results in $b(t)/y(t) = (1 + R(t-1)) * b(t-1)/y(t-1) * y(t-1)/y(t) + d(t)/y(t) = 1.04 * 1.13 * (1/0.97) + 0.11 = 1.32$.

13. An important factor that bears on default is the composition of debt in terms of the residence of debt holders. It is thought that governments find it easier to default against foreigners than against domestic residents, as the latter have important ways to punish the politicians (votes). While in the early years of the 2000s most Greek debt was held by Greek residents, by 2009 most of it was held by foreigners, mostly financial institutions (see table 2.6). This is in

sharp contrast to other heavily indebted countries such as Japan and Italy and could have played a role in the Greek default.

14. We use the word roughly to indicate abstraction from potential additional effects such as terms-of-trade effects that result from international wealth redistribution in the absence of homotheticity in preferences.

15. This discussion draws heavily on Dellas and Niepelt (2016).

16. The German government spokesman Steffen Seibert argued that the countries of the EZ could not accept a reduction in the value of their loans to Greece because this would contradict EU treaties as well as national legislation in Germany and other countries that prohibit member countries to assume the debts of other countries (Kathimerini, November 27, 2012).

17. Steffen Seibert has argued that debt forgiveness would lead to a huge loss of credibility for Germany and could encourage other countries with debt problems to ask for similar treatment (Kathimerini, November 27, 2012).

18. The exchange rate is the value of domestic currency in terms of the foreign currency. A nominal devaluation of the Greek currency versus the euro means that more drachmas are needed in order to get one euro. A real devaluation means that one euro can buy a larger quantity of Greek goods. That is, Greek products become cheaper relative to EZ products. A nominal devaluation translates into a real devaluation when the prices of the domestic goods do not increase in line with the change in the exchange rate. For instance, if the drachma becomes 10 percent cheaper vis-à-vis the euro (a 10 percent drachma devaluation) and the drachma price of Greek goods increases by 4 percent, then there is a 6 percent (= 10 − 4 percent) real devaluation and the international competitiveness of Greek products increases by this amount.

19. In general, the empirical literature on trade elasticities is quite underdeveloped and there exist no reliable measures (even more so for Greece).

20. This issue is present for currencies already in existence. It may not apply to the case of a new currency, as new prices will have to be set when the new currency is introduced and those prices will have to reflect the parity chosen by the government.

21. This example is quite stylized. One may want to incorporate sustained growth over the period the terms of trade remain weak as well to link imports to the rate of domestic income growth. The exact details may differ but the big picture remains.

22. The most recent estimate of the net international investment position (NIIP) of Greece is 210 billion euros. A 25 percent devaluation implies a transfer of 25 percent of GDP.

References

Barro, R., and D. Gordon. 1983. Rules, discretion and reputation in a model of monetary policy. *Journal of Monetary Economics* 12: 101–21.

Baxter, M., and A. Stockman. 1989. Sectoral and national aggregate disturbances to industrial output in seven European countries. *Journal of Monetary Economics* 21 (2–3): 387–409.

Bloom, N., M. Floetotto, N. Jaimovich, I. Saporta-Eksten, and S. Terry. 2012. Really uncertain business cycles. Mimeo.

Clerc, L., H. Dellas, and O. Loisel. 2011. To be or not to be in monetary union: A synthesis. *Journal of International Economics* 83 (2): 154–67.

Cole, H. L., and T. J. Kehoe. 2000. Self-fulfilling debt crises. *Review of Economic Studies* 67 (1): 91–116.

Dellas, H., and D. Niepelt. 2016. Sovereign debt with heterogeneous creditors. *Journal of International Economics* 99 (1), S16–S26.

Devereux, M., and C. Engel. 2003. Monetary policy in the open economy revisited: Price setting and exchange-rate flexibility. *Review of Economic Studies* 70 (4): 765–83.

Edwards, S. 1986. Are devaluations contractionary? *Review of Economics and Statistics* 68 (3): 501–508.

Giavazzi, F., and M. Pagano. 1988. The advantage of tying one's hands: EMS discipline and central bank credibility. *European Economic Review* 32 (5): 1050–82.

Gibson, H., S. Hall, and G. Tavlas. 2014. Fundamentally wrong: Market pricing of sovereigns and the Greek financial crisis. *Journal of Macroeconomics* 38: 405–19.

Kenen, P. 1969. The theory of optimum currency areas: An eclectic view. In *Monetary Problems of the International Economy*, ed. R. A. Mundell and A. K. Swoboda, 41–60. Chicago: University of Chicago Press.

Malliaropoulos, D. 2010, How much did competitiveness of the Greek economy decline since EZ entry? *Eurobank Research: Economy and Markets* 4 (5).

McKinnon, R. 1963. Optimum currency areas. *American Economic Review* 53: 717–25.

Mundell, R. 1961. A theory of optimum currency areas. *American Economic Review* 53: 657–65.

Wijnberger, S. 1985. Exchange rate management and stabilization policies in developing countries. In *Economic Adjustment and Exchange Rates in Developing Countries*, ed. S. Edwards and L. Ahamed.

Woodford, M. 2003. *Interest and Prices*. Princeton: Princeton University Press.

3 The Challenge of Trade Adjustment in Greece

Costas Arkolakis, Aristos Doxiadis, and Manolis Galenianos[1]

3.1 Introduction: The Other Deficit

In 2009 it became clear that the Greek economy was facing very serious challenges arising from the country's "twin deficits": both the budget of the Greek government and the current account (essentially, the trade balance) of the country were in deficit exceeding 15 percent of GDP. The two deficits required large amounts of financing which were not forthcoming in the aftermath of the global financial crisis of 2007 to 2009, leading to the eruption of the Greek crisis. Since 2009, however, policy makers and the public have focused almost exclusively on the budget deficit and scant attention has been paid to the trade deficit.

Developments in the Greek economy since then suggest that this lopsided focus was misplaced. The budget deficit was rapidly reduced but the trade balance remains a problem: it has declined by less than other countries' and the pattern of improvement creates concerns about its sustainability. Specifically, the reduction of the trade deficit was driven exclusively by lower imports while exports have actually fallen since the crisis erupted which suggests that Greece is not adjusting to the post-crisis economic environment.

This chapter studies the reasons behind Greece's adjustment difficulties. We first show that the underperformance of exports is not due to the economy's inherent inability to produce exportable commodities. In particular, we use Greece's pre-crisis export performance to assess the country's export capability and calculate that exports should have increased by 25 percent between 2007 and 2012. Therefore the fact that exports actually fell in that period is puzzling.

When analyzing the potential reasons for this underperformance, we find that labor markets have adjusted further than in most other countries while product markets seem to be an important impediment to adjustment. Between 2007 and 2012, wages fell by 13 percent relative to the eurozone average, which is a much greater drop than in the other countries of the eurozone periphery and would have sufficed to recover competitiveness had prices followed the same pattern. However, prices actually increased over the same period, which undermined competitiveness and hindered the adjustment. For this reason we conclude that product market rigidities are a primary reason for the lack of adjustment. We also find that exporting has become more difficult since the beginning of the crisis, which accounts for one-third of the decline in Greek GDP. This finding suggests that facilitating the process of exporting should become a top policy priority.

We then discuss three possible explanations for how these frictions might arise: the business environment, the size distribution of firms, and sector-specific factors. We also draw some policy implications from these interpretations.

The rest of the chapter is structured as follows: Section 3.2 gives a brief description of what is measured by the current account balance and a presentation of recent developments. Section 3.3 provides the main quantitative analysis. Section 3.4 discusses possible sources of the frictions observed in the quantitative model.

3.2 The Current Account: Recent Developments and Economic Impact

The current account balance measures the difference between a country's export revenues and import costs (the trade balance), plus two smaller items, net income and net transfers.[2] Essentially, when a country imports more than it exports, it experiences a current account deficit and needs to borrow from abroad or sell assets to foreigners in order to finance the difference (the country experiences net capital inflows); when it exports more than it imports, it lends to foreign countries or buys their assets (net capital outflows). Importantly, the domestic borrower (or lender) might be either the private or the public sector.

Figure 3.1 presents the evolution of the current account balance for Greece, Ireland, Portugal, Spain, and the eurozone as a whole. It is clear that the current account deficit of every peripheral country deteriorated significantly between the late 1990s and the global financial crisis of 2007 to 2009 and improved rapidly since then. At the same time, the current account balance of the eurozone as a whole did not change very much.[3]

The rise and fall of peripheral countries' current account deficits can be attributed to the introduction of the euro and the aftermath of the global financial crisis, respectively.[4] The former eliminated exchange rate risk within the eurozone, thereby encouraging capital flows from the richer European core toward the (relatively) poorer periphery. The latter increased investors' risk aversion, leading to the stop and reversal of capital flows. In other words, the reduction of current account deficits that occurred

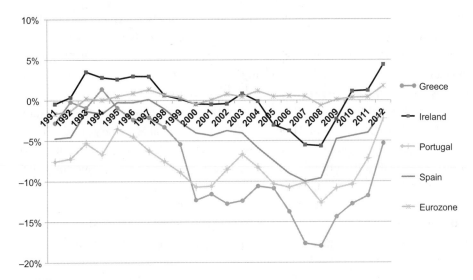

Figure 3.1
Current account balance (% of GDP).
Source: AMECO

in recent years was primarily due to a reduction in the flows of capital toward the European periphery.

In this chapter we focus on the trade balance, which is the most important component of the current account, to study how the various economies, and in particular Greece, adjusted to this reduction in net capital inflows. The most direct consequence of a drop in net capital inflows is that the trade balance must improve since a deficit can no longer be financed from abroad.

The trade adjustment can occur in two distinct ways. First, the country's overall income falls, and depresses consumption, which leads to lower imports, since part of the consumption goods are imported. Second, the country's production shifts from the nontradable to the tradable sector, leading to higher exports and to the displacement of imports from the domestic market. A prerequisite for this shift to occur is the improvement in the competitiveness of the country's tradable sector, which, at least in the short run, necessitates a reduction in wages and prices vis-à-vis foreign competitors. Typically, the adjustment is achieved through a combination of these two ways. However, a more substantial shift toward tradables helps sustain production and employment and therefore leads to less economic and social hardship, for a given level of trade adjustment.

In the ensuing analysis we will compare developments in Greece with those in Ireland, Portugal, and Spain. Comparing Greece to Ireland, Portugal, and Spain is informative because of the shared predicament of all four countries: when the global financial crisis started, they all had very large current account deficits and were forced to quickly reduce them in the subsequent years. Furthermore the adjustment was difficult enough that all four countries experienced economic crises and requested (and received) help from the European Union and the International Monetary Fund.[5] Therefore the comparative aspect of this exercise allows us to disentangle the issues that relate to the overall difficulty of adjustment, which are shared by all four countries, from those that are specific to Greece.

Figure 3.2 shows the change in the trade balance between 2007 and 2012 for the four countries in question as a proportion of the GDP level of 2007. It also shows the decomposition of this change into export expansion and import compression.[6]

All four countries experienced great improvements in their trade balance over these years, in Greece's case by almost 10 percent of pre-crisis GDP. However, the composition of this improvement varies dramatically across countries: in Greece's case it was driven exclusively by a reduction in imports, while exports actually fell over that period (a decline in imports improves the trade balance and therefore enters with a positive sign). Ireland is the mirror image of Greece, with a huge increase in exports and slight increase in imports. Portugal and Spain present a more balanced picture, with

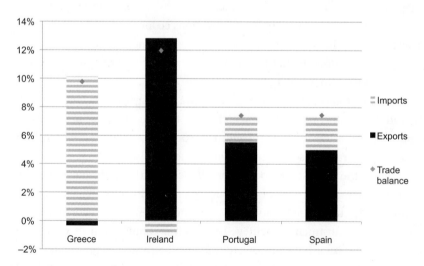

Figure 3.2
Change in trade balance between 2007 and 2012 as a percentage of 2007 GDP
Source: Eurostat

export expansion accounting for about two-thirds of the improvement in the trade balance and import compression for the remainder.

The patterns in figure 3.2 are important because they are indicative of the economic costs that each country sustained during this period: Greece experienced a catastrophic depression while the other countries had severe but relatively milder recessions. For this reason it is crucial to identify the source of the stark differences in how each country closed its trade deficit and, more important, to assess whether policy intervention can improve this pattern.

One difficulty in this comparison is that the countries differed significantly with respect to their trade performance even before the crisis, as depicted in figure 3.3. For instance, Ireland exported and imported twice as much as a share of GDP than Greece did, with Portugal and Spain in the middle.[7] Therefore it is hard to assess whether post-crisis performance is due to each country's deep, inherent characteristics, which are reflected in pre-crisis performance and are hard to change, or are due to factors that are amenable to policy.

To determine whether the difference in adjustment patterns is due to preexisting differences in economic structure or due to more transient features, we resort to economic modeling, which we detail in the next section.

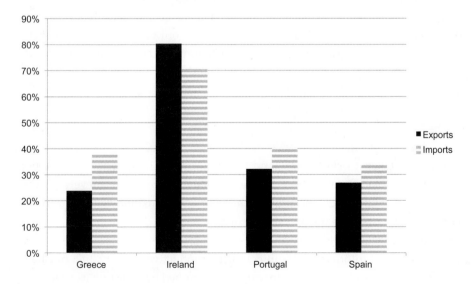

Figure 3.3
Imports and exports as a percentage of GDP, 2007
Source: Eurostat

3.3 Analysis of Trade Adjustment

In this section we quantitatively assess the economic performance of Greece, Ireland, Portugal, and Spain in recent years, and in particular, we examine the effect of the reduction in net capital inflows (and hence the reduction in the trade deficit) on economic activity. The aim is to determine whether the severe recessions faced by these countries, and especially Greece, were the inescapable outcome of the reduction in net capital inflows or if they should be attributed to different causes.

To make this assessment, we need a benchmark of what might be expected to happen when capital flows are reduced with which to compare actual economic performance. To calculate this benchmark we first need to estimate a country's productive capacity independently of capital flows. A country's pre-crisis GDP is informative about its productive capacity because, everything else equal, a productive country has higher GDP. However, the level of GDP also depends on capital flows: when capital flows into a country domestic spending increases, which leads to higher GDP, albeit without immediately affecting productivity.[8] The fact that a high level of GDP can be either attributed to high productivity or high net capital inflows presents us with a significant difficulty since it is exactly the effect of a drop in capital flows that we want to analyze. To resolve this problem, we resort to economic modeling.

We outline in section 3.1 the economic model that we will use to overcome the difficulties described above. In sections 3.2 and 3.3 we use our model to create a benchmark for economic performance that corresponds to long- and short-term adjustment, respectively, and compare the benchmark's predictions with the actual data. Section 3.4 presents the implications of our analysis.

3.3.1 The Model

In this section we outline an economic model of trade, based on the work of Eaton and Kortum (2002) and Dekle, Eaton, and Kortum (2007), and describe how we use data on GDP and trade to determine countries' underlying productivity levels (see the appendix for a more detailed exposition of the model). We first illustrate the logic of the model and then describe the data that we use.

The model's key insight is that the data on the countries' pre-crisis trade performance provide useful information about countries' productive capacity. In a nutshell, a country's inherent level of productivity can be determined by adjusting its GDP with its trade performance. Specifically, a high level of exports is a sign of high productivity while a large trade deficit (i.e., high net capital inflows) means that current GDP is greater than inherent productivity would suggest.

In the model the main determinants of a country's exports and imports are its productivity, the trade costs faced by importers and exporters (e.g., transportation costs, administrative costs of clearing customs and the difficulties of financing international trade) and capital flows.

In more detail, the ability of a country to export a particular good depends on how efficiently the good can be produced, the cost of trading the good (described above), and the cost of inputs, such as the prices of intermediate goods and the wages of workers. The cost of inputs, in turn, depends on the aggregate level of domestic economic activity: high domestic economic activity leads to high demand for intermediate goods and labor, resulting in high prices and wages. A country's imports depend on the ability to finance them, either through export revenue or through net capital inflows.[9]

Everything else equal, a highly productive country has high exports because it can efficiently produce many goods, *and* high imports, because its high level of exports generates the revenue to pay for them.[10] Furthermore a high level of productivity leads to high domestic economic activity (and high GDP), which results in high wages and high prices. In this example, however, the high level of wages and prices is the outcome of high productivity and does not reflect poor competitiveness.

Everything else equal, net capital inflows (which correspond to a trade deficit, as described in section 3.2) increase a country's available resources and lead to high domestic economic activity and, consequently, high GDP, wages, and prices. However, in this case the high level of wages and prices is not a reflection of high productivity and act as a deterrent to exports by inflating the cost of inputs. Therefore, in this case, the high levels of GDP, wages, and prices are the outcome of foreigners' willingness to fund the country, rather than the country's contemporaneous productivity.

The logic outlined above gives the intuition for how we use a country's level of exports and imports, as well as its trade balance, to infer its inherent productivity level: a country's productivity is similar to its GDP, adjusted upward in the case of high exports and downward in the case of low exports.

For our quantitative analysis we use data on GDP, the current account and trade deficits, and bilateral trade flows for 32 countries, which account for 80 percent of global GDP and 98 percent of EU GDP in 2007, as well as a residual "rest of the world" country. The World Bank provides detailed data on the trade of non-oil goods while the United Nations and the Organization of Economic Cooperation and Development provide data on the trade in services. Data on GDP and the current account comes from the Economist Intelligence Unit.

The reason why we use data from more countries than the ones we are immediately interested in (Greece, Ireland, Portugal, Spain) is that we need to account for the complicated bilateral trade patterns that we observe. A country's trade balance might differ across its trading partners; for example, in 2012 Greece had a trade surplus with Turkey and a trade deficit with Germany. Furthermore the cost of trading differs across pairs of countries; for example, it is easier for a Greek firm to export to the United Kingdom than to Australia.

3.3.2   Long-Run Analysis: The Frictionless Model

We begin with the analysis of the economy's long-run adjustment to the reduction of capital flows and resulting reduction in the trade deficit. We first derive estimates of each country's pre-crisis productivity, using the model and 2007 data in the way described in section 3.3.1. We then introduce the level of capital flows from 2012 (corresponding to lower inflows toward the eurozone periphery) and use our estimates to make predictions about GDP, wages, prices, exports, and imports. In other words, we want to isolate the economic effect of lower capital inflows from anything else that might have simultaneously affected the economy.

In the case of Greece, for instance, the fact that the trade deficit is lower in 2012 than in 2007 leads to the prediction that in 2012 the country should export more and import less than in 2007. For this to happen, wages and prices are also predicted to be lower in 2012 than in 2007 so that foreign consumers purchase additional Greek products and Greek consumers purchase fewer foreign products. Finally, Greek GDP is predicted to be lower due to the drop in capital inflows. While the direction of the predicted changes is interesting in itself, the purpose of using our model is to go a step further and make a quantitative statement about how large each of these changes should be.

In this calculation we assume that prices and wages are fully flexible and that workers and productive assets can be seamlessly reallocated across the production of different goods and services, so there is no increase in unemployment.[11] This delivers our "frictionless" benchmark for adjustment. Before describing the outcomes, we should explain why this exercise is a useful benchmark of analysis even though it is based on a very unrealistic depiction of the economy. The frictionless model's predictions correspond to what happens to the economy over the long run, after all adjustment difficulties have been overcome. Any differences between the model's predictions and actual performance can therefore be attributed to the adjustment frictions in the economy, which allows us to identify where such frictions are present and to assess their relative importance. In other words, the point of the exercise is to disentangle the long-run adjustment that the economy needs to perform from the short-run difficulties of this adjustment. We will address the importance of these short-run frictions in section 3.3.3.

We use our frictionless benchmark to calculate the effect of the reduction in the trade deficit on real GDP, the composition of trade, prices and wages. Figure 3.4 plots the predicted and actual reduction in real GDP between 2007 and 2012 for the four countries under analysis.

Three features stand out in this figure. First, the predicted loss of GDP is relatively small for all countries, including Greece: no country is predicted to lose more than 3 percent of real GDP even though the trade adjustment is very significant (7 to 10 percent of GDP) for every country. The implication is that the long-run cost of the reduction in capital flows is small, and it is the short-run adjustment costs that we should mostly worry about. This observation is consistent with international experience that significant changes in the current account do not necessarily have adverse effects on economic activity, to the extent that the change is gradual and there is time to adjust. For instance, Germany went from balanced trade in 2000 to a surplus of 7 percent of GDP in 2007 without experiencing a recession, albeit in a more favorable external environment.

Second, the actual decline in GDP is much larger than the predicted one for every country. This is to be expected, since our model deliberately ignores the frictions of adjustment, as well as other developments of that period such as fiscal austerity. Nevertheless, the magnitude of the difference suggests that adjustment frictions are

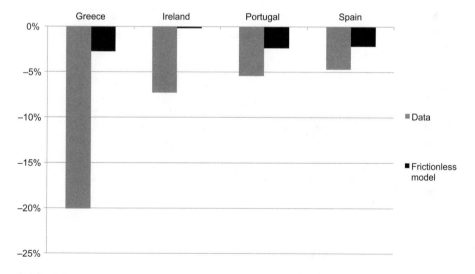

Figure 3.4
Percentage change in real GDP between 2007 and 2012: data compared with frictionless model
Sources: Eurostat, EIU, and authors' calculations

quantitatively important, as the next section will confirm. Third, and most relevant for our study, Greece's performance is considerably worse with respect to the predicted one than the other countries'. This suggests that adjustment frictions might be a bigger problem for Greece than for the other countries. Figure 3.5 identifies the proximate cause of Greece's underperformance: it shows the percentage change in exports and imports between 2007 and 2012 in the data and as predicted by the model.

Given the large improvement in the trade balance experienced by Greece (figure 3.2), the model predicts that, absent frictions, Greek exports would have increased by almost 25 percent between 2007 and 2012. Indeed, according to the model, exports should account for a large part of the adjustment even after taking into consideration Greece's relatively low export base in the preceding years. This change corresponds to an increase in the exports-to-GDP ratio of 5.8 percentage points, a significant but, given time, achievable amount.[12]

But Greek exports instead *fell* during that period! The other side of the coin, of course, is that all of the actual improvement in the Greek trade balance is accounted for by a huge reduction in imports, which was almost three times larger than the one predicted by the model.

By comparison, the exports of the other three countries increased by more than 5 percent. Even though Portugal and Spain still underperformed with respect to the frictionless benchmark, the fact that they experienced an increase in exports

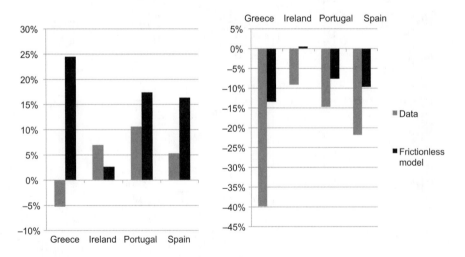

Figure 3.5
Percentage change between 2007 and 2012: data compared with frictionless model for (a) exports and (b) imports.
Sources: Eurostat, EIU, and authors' calculations

suggests that Greece's poor performance is due to domestic reasons rather than global factors.

To explore the reasons why exports underperformed in the Greek case, we examine the changes in labor and product markets. We compare the predicted change in wages and prices in our model and in the data since they are the main channel for recovering competitiveness, and therefore increasing exports.

Figure 3.6 plots the change of wages as predicted in the model and as they happened in reality. We use Eurostat data on the average hourly nominal wage for the whole economy, except for public administration where wages are set under different constraints than the ones under consideration in this study. Nominal wages are deflated for every country using the eurozone GDP deflator.[13] We do not use each country's individual GDP deflator because we want to examine the evolution of a country's wages relative to other eurozone countries.

The model predicts that wages fall in all four countries, which is consistent with the idea that they need to become more competitive. Remarkably, Greece is the only country that comes close to achieving the level of wage reductions predicted by the model. Therefore it does not appear that labor markets are a big source for the difficulty of adjustment. Although this conclusion will be somewhat tempered in section 3.3.3, it certainly does not appear that labor rigidities during the adjustment process were worse in Greece than in other countries.

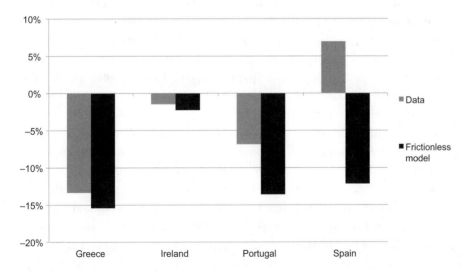

Figure 3.6
Percentage change in wages between 2007 and 2012: data compared with frictionless model
Sources: Eurostat, EIU, and authors' calculations

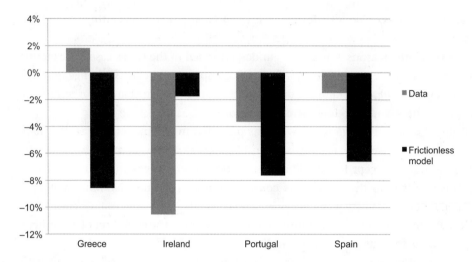

Figure 3.7

Percentage change in prices between 2007 and 2012: data compared with frictionless model

Sources: Eurostat, EIU, and authors' calculations

Finally, figure 3.7 plots the predicted change in the price level and the actual change in prices between 2007 and 2012. We use data from Eurostat's harmonized index of consumer prices and we calculate the difference between the evolution of each country's price level and the eurozone's price level. What is evident from figure 3.7 is that Greece is an outlier in terms of price adjustment: prices increased by almost 2 percent relative to the Eurozone, although they were predicted to fall by more than 8 percent, while the prices of the other three countries decreased over the same period.[14] At the same time, Ireland, Portugal, and Spain experienced much greater increases in their exports than Greece did. Therefore price rigidity is a potential explanation for the underperformance of Greek exports.

To summarize, after comparing the data with the predictions of the frictionless adjustment model, we conclude that (1) Greece's economic performance was not only worse than that of the other peripheral countries but also much worse than expected given the estimates of its inherent productivity level, (2) Greek exports underperformed significantly, (3) wages dropped in Greece almost as much as expected and therefore labor markets are not the prime suspects for the lack of adjustment, and (4) prices *increased* in the face of the worst recession in 70 years and therefore product markets are the prime suspects for the lack of adjustment. An important question, which we address in the next section is the extent to which the lack of exports is responsible for the underperformance in GDP.

3.3.3 Short-Run Analysis: The Frictional Model

We now enrich our analysis by taking into account the short-run difficulties that a country might experience in increasing exports. The purpose of this exercise is to quantify the contribution of sluggish export adjustment in the post-2007 GDP declines of the four countries in question.

As in section 3.3.2, we use our model to make a prediction about economic activity, but our prediction now takes as given each country's actual exports and imports for 2012, in addition to their trade balance. In this way we estimate how much of the drop in output is due to the performance of exports and how much is a residual that should be attributed to other factors. On a technical level we allow trade costs to change between 2007 and 2012 in order to capture the effect that a country's exports do not increase in reality as much as predicted by the frictionless model. For instance, Greece's export underperformance is rationalized as an increase in the trade costs faced by Greek exporters. Given the estimated change in trade costs, we have a new set of predictions regarding GDP, wages, and prices.

We begin by comparing the actual developments in economic output between the data and our new model, in figure 3.8. The main observation is that the model's predictions are closer to the data for all countries. Incorporating the slow adjustment of exports fully explains the output drops in Portugal and Spain and captures about one-third of the recession's magnitude in Greece.

The presence of trade frictions shifts the burden of preserving full employment toward wages and prices. In particular, if the potential for export expansion is limited due to trade frictions, then import compression must take a bigger role in achieving any given improvement in the trade balance. This, in turn, requires that domestic consumption (and hence income) must be further reduced, which can be achieved if wages and prices fall, or, alternatively, if employment falls. In the following figures, we take the first route and assess how much wages and prices need to fall for employment to stay at its 2007 level. The difference between predicted drops in prices and wages and the actual ones is reflected in the substantial unemployment increases in all four countries.

Figure 3.9 shows the predicted change in wages according to the frictional model, which is much greater than in figure 3.6, and the wage reductions observed in the data now fall far short from the predicted amount. Similarly to section 3.3.2, however, the wage drops are closer to the predicted ones in Greece than for the other three countries.

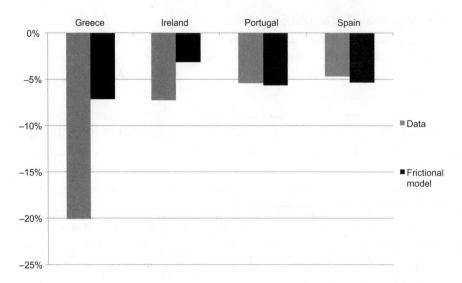

Figure 3.8
Percentage change in real GDP between 2007 and 2012: data compared with frictional model
Sources: Eurostat, EIU, and authors' calculations

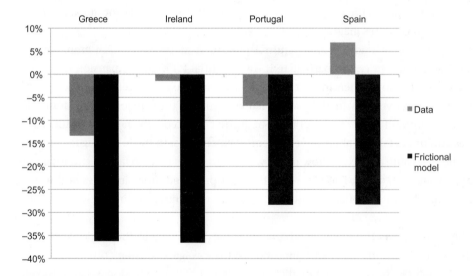

Figure 3.9
Percentage change in wages between 2007 and 2012: data compared with frictional model
Sources: Eurostat, EIU, and authors' calculations

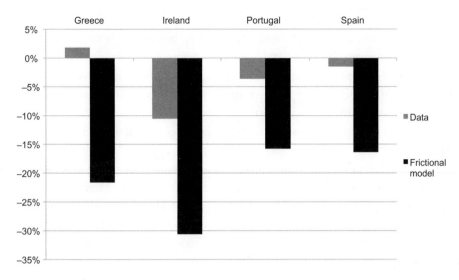

Figure 3.10
Percentage change in prices between 2007 and 2012: data compared with frictional model
Sources: Eurostat, EIU, and authors' calculations

A similar picture emerges when considering the predicted change in prices. Figure 3.10 shows that prices are predicted to fall by a much larger amount and, again, Greece is further than any other country from that prediction.

The conclusion from the second exercise is that taking trade frictions into account can explain at least one-third of the drop in output in Greece. Furthermore the presence of trade frictions magnifies the required adjustment along other margins, such as labor and product markets, for full employment to be preserved. Therefore the gap between the predicted and actual adjustment in prices and wages is now much larger, probably accounting for a large component of the remaining drop in GDP. This point illustrates that lack of adjustment in one front (e.g., exports) leads to greater needs of adjustment in other fronts (e.g., wages).

3.3.4 Policy Implications

Greece's post-crisis economy will have fewer resources at its disposal since capital flows from abroad are likely to be limited. However, our calculations suggest that the output cost of this change is relatively modest, at around 3 percent of pre-crisis GDP, if the necessary adjustment is successful. The most significant, albeit least successful so far, component of this adjustment is that exports should increase by 25 percent in comparison to 2007.

Therefore the growth of exports should be a top policy priority. Our analysis concludes that the lackluster performance of Greek exports is responsible for one-third of the drop in GDP between 2007 and 2012, which is a lower bound since the effect of incomplete price and wage adjustment has not been fully taken into account. Other factors, such as the rapid pace of fiscal contraction, the credit crunch and political uncertainty have undoubtedly also contributed in deepening the crisis. Most of what follows focuses on improving export performance, since our analysis does not address these other issues.

Our exercise suggests that the Greek labor market has adjusted to the requirement of greater competitiveness. The drop in wages between 2007 and 2012 has been almost as steep as needed for long-run adjustment (figure 3.6), and it is also much greater than that observed in Ireland, Portugal, and Spain, which nevertheless exhibited better export performance. It is therefore clear that factors other than labor costs are mostly responsible for export underperformance and that further wage declines are unlikely to make a significant difference.

Prices, however, exhibited very different behavior. Despite the huge decline in domestic demand, prices were higher in 2012 than in 2007 relative to the eurozone, which goes against both the requirements of adjustment for Greece and the experience of the other three countries. This indicates that the adjustment in the product markets of Greece is incomplete and is hindered by severe frictions, such as oligopolistic or regulated market structures. The lack of adjustment in product markets hinders exports both by directly reducing some products' price competitiveness and by increasing the cost of production, since a large share of inputs of an exportable commodity is domestically provided. The exact breakdown of how important each factor is requires a more detailed input–output analysis that is beyond the scope of the present study. One conclusion, however, that can be drawn is that increased competition in domestic markets would help exports.

Finally, a large part of the lag in export performance is attributed by our model to increased trade costs. In practice, this may include various types of barrier or friction, to which we turn in the next section.

3.4   Trade Costs and Barriers to Adjustment

We now focus on three possible explanations of the frictions observed in our model: business environment, as described in international surveys, both before and during the crisis; size distribution of firms; and some sector-specific factors.

3.4.1   Business Environment up to the Crisis

For a country that has been a member of the European Union since 1981, with a good record of GDP growth and with a GDP per capita in 2008 that ranked 38th in the world out of over 200 countries (between New Zealand and Israel), Greece was a (negative) outlier: in some important ways it resembled an emerging third-world economy more than a Western one. It ranked well below most EU and OECD countries in various "competitiveness" and "doing business" indicators, such as those published by the World Economic Forum (WEF) and by the World Bank (WB).

Such indicators are an ex ante evaluation of the environment in which businesses operate. Conceptually they are very different from the measures of productivity used in economic analysis, but they do correlate broadly across countries and over time with GDP per capita and with total factor productivity. Rich developed nations, members of the European Union and of the OECD, cluster toward the top of the rankings, but there are notable exceptions. Greece is one of them.

In 2008 Greece ranked 67th out of 134 countries in the Global Competitiveness Index (GCI) published by WEF (table 3.1). It had the lowest ranking of any OECD member (34 countries), below Turkey (63rd) Hungary (62nd), and Mexico (60th). Its position was only slightly better in 2000; it ranked 34th and 38th out 58 countries in two earlier indexes used by the WEF, surpassing only one or two OECD members.

The GCI is composed of 12 "pillars," and each pillar of several specific indexes. By comparing the country's ranking across indexes, one can get a sense of the nature of the constraints competitive businesses face in each country.

The worst pillars for Greece in 2008 were "Macroeconomic stability," due to very high government deficits and debt and a very low national savings rate, and "Labor market efficiency" due to several indexes, such as inflexibility in wage determination, nonwage labor costs, and rigidity of employment. The best pillars, comparable to other rich countries, were "Market size," "Higher education and training," "Health and primary education," and "Infrastructure." These all relate with the well-being and consumption patterns of individuals and of families; this is where Greece had fared best in recent years.

In the two pillars that relate directly to business organization and strategy—"Business sophistication" and "Innovation"—Greece was the worst ranked OECD member, and in the middle of the overall global list. In the pillar "Institutions," Greece did fairly well on some crime-related indexes, but very badly on issues related to government: burden of regulation, transparency of policy making, and wastefulness of spending.

Overall, the pattern of the indexes suggests a country of high individual consumption, good quality of life, reasonable levels of spending on infrastructure and public

Table 3.1
Ranking of Greece in the 12 pillars of the Global Competitiveness Index

	GCI 2008–2009 Rank (out of 134)	GCI 2013–2014 Rank (out of 148)
Overall rank	**67**	**91**
Basic requirements	**51**	**88**
Institutions	58	103
Infrastructure	45	38
Macroeconomic environment	106	147
Health and primary education	40	35
Efficiency enhancers	**57**	**67**
Higher education and training	38	41
Goods market efficiency	64	108
Labor market efficiency	116	127
Financial market development	67	138
Technological readiness	59	39
Market size	33	47
Innovation and sophistication factors	**68**	**81**
Business sophistication	66	83
Innovation	63	87

services, but with a dysfunctional state and a business sector of low sophistication. All this is compatible with macroeconomic data on savings rates and expenditure patterns. It is also compatible with data on industrial structure, as described in section 3.4.3.

The World Bank reports on the ease of "doing business" monitor a narrower set of indicators, mostly on procedures and regulatory burdens. They confirm that, for a rich country, Greece was a difficult place for businesses to operate. In 2008 it was ranked 100th out of 178 countries (table 3.2). It was by far the worst EU (and OECD) country; second worse was Poland at 78th place.

3.4.2   Business Environment during the Crisis

We now turn to developments after 2009, looking at how these are reflected in more recent WEF and WB reports, and we refer briefly to three major areas of deterioration of the business environment, namely access to finance, political instability, and increases in some operating costs.

From 2010 onward, the Greek government embarked on a program of reform, drafted to a large extent by the troika and designed, among other things, to increase

Table 3.2

Doing business indicators in Greece

	DB 2008 (2007 data) Rank (of 178)	DB 2013 (2012 data) Rank (of 185)	DB 2014 (2013 data) Rank (of 189)
Overall rank	**100**	**78**	**72**
Starting a business	152	146	36
Dealing with licenses	42	NA	NA
Dealing with construction permits	NA	31	66
Getting electricity	NA	59	61
Employing workers	142	NA	NA
Registering property	93	150	161
Getting credit *(legal and procedural aspects only)*	84	83	86
Protecting investors	158	117	80
Paying taxes	86	56	53
Trading across borders	65	62	52
Enforcing contracts	87	87	98
Closing a business	38	NA	NA
Resolving insolvency	NA	50	87

competitiveness and to enable the business sector to become more export oriented. In some important fields, such as the labor market, or in starting new businesses, regulation became much more favorable. However, these changes are not reflected in the GCI, which exhibits strong deterioration in several pillars, as indicated in table 3.1.

The "Institutions" ranking has dropped mainly because of increased perception of corruption, of "favoritism in decisions of government officials," of "burden of government regulation," and even of threat to "property rights." These indicators are based on surveys of businesspeople, rather than on "hard" data, in contrast to the World Bank "doing business" indexes.

"Macro environment" has deteriorated, as the adjustment program has not (yet) decreased fiscal deficits and debt below 2007 levels. "Financial markets" have become very much tighter for businesses. Even the "Labor market" ranking is worse, even though flexibility in setting wages and in hiring and firing has increased substantially; to some extent this may be due to timing, since most of the effects of new legislation kicked in late in 2012 or in 2013.

The WB "doing business" indicators paint a different picture. There is a clear improvement, especially in the 2014 report, based on 2013 data. Establishing new

Table 3.3
Most problematic factors for doing business in Greece

GCI 2008–2009 (weighted % of responses)	GCI 2013–2014 (weighted % of responses)
Inefficient government bureaucracy (26.5)	Access to financing (22.4)
Tax regulations (15.6)	Inefficient government bureaucracy (21.2)
Restrictive labor regulations (12.6)	Tax regulations (14.5)
Corruption (12.0)	Policy Instability (12.0)
Tax rates (6.5)	Tax rates (9.8)

firms has become much easier, so have export procedures. However, the WB rankings are based on a small set of procedures, while other important aspects of regulation are not included. For example, regulations for building new plant or getting environmental permits have not changed, and they are still cumbersome and hampered by corruption. In any case, it will take some time until the technical changes captured in the WB reports work through to business sentiment and begin affecting business practice to a substantial extent.

As table 3.3 shows that the nature of the problems businesses face has changed in important ways. Access to finance has become the top issue, and policy instability is also a major new factor. These issues are discussed below.

Access to Finance[15]   Both bank finance and internal sources of funding have dried up during the crisis. Bank loans to enterprises have contracted in Greece 18 percent between end-2009 and end-2012. According to the ECB, in early 2013, 38 percent of small and medium enterprises in Greece reported "access to finance" as their most pressing problem, and this was by far the highest percentage in the euro area. Forty percent of Greek SMEs reported that access was deteriorating compared to the previous year. Greece was also one of the few countries where interest payments as a proportion of turnover and debt to asset ratios (leverage) were increasing. Indeed most of Greek business deleveraging has not started. The evolution of internal sources of funding is more difficult to monitor, but it is a fair assumption that as sales and profits have plunged liquid assets have dried up as well.

Tax Regulations   Dozens of tax laws and hundreds of decrees have been enacted in four years.[16] Neither businesspeople, nor their accountants, not even tax officials are sure of what is in force, or what will be in force next year. Penalties for noncompliance to this ever-shifting jumble have increased dramatically. In 2013 the penalty for missing any tax filing deadline (not for delaying payment) was set at 1,000 euros for microbusiness, which many cannot afford to pay.[17] The cost of full compliance is also unrealistic for many small and medium-size businesses of low productivity, because of the heavy social security rates; before the crisis, a common solution was to evade payment. The rates have not been adjusted downward in the crisis, so the "tax wedge" on labor was still the highest in Europe in 2012.[18] The combination of falling revenues, stable or rising costs of compliance, increased penalties, and, in some cases, better controls, has led to a huge increase in tax and social security debt. Verified tax debt increased in 2013 by 4 percent of GDP, while over 40 percent of all business owners and self-employed are now in arrears on their own personal social security payments.

Policy Instability   This factor is linked to tax regulations. On the legal front, the risk of personal liability of owners and directors for unpaid debt of their companies to the government has become very high, though no one can predict to what extent tax authorities can enforce the confiscation of private assets. In addition the fear of general political instability and of a possible exit from the eurozone was holding back investment decisions.

High Operating Costs   The GCI and the doing business indicators do not directly address the issue of operating costs. Though average labor cost has dropped after 2010, other costs have remained high, and some have increased. The tax wedge on labor (i.e., social security charges plus payroll tax) is still among the highest in Europe. Indirect tax rates have gone up, affecting not only consumer prices but some intermediate goods as well. Energy-intensive industries claim that they have to pay very high rates for gas and electricity, compared to their competitors abroad.

In summary, Greece came into the crisis with an institutional environment that was not favorable to building competitive businesses. In the crisis, labor costs have decreased, but some of the costs and the uncertainties of doing business have increased. For existing exporters, shortage of finance is perhaps the most important of those, but there are many others. Factor mobility, bureaucracy, corruption, and an overall perception of a deteriorating environment have been important barriers to exporting. In this context, the assumption in section 3.3 about an overall increase in the cost of trade, is realistic.

3.4.3 Size Distribution of Firms

Apart from the institutional environment, some inherent characteristics of Greek firms are also responsible for lags in adjustment. A striking feature of the Greek economy is the size distribution of firms, and particularly the predominance of very small ("micro") firms. In the nonfinancial business economy (NFBE), Greece has the lowest average size of firm in the European Union in terms of number of people employed (3.1 vs. 6.4 in EU27 in 2007), the lowest proportion of employment in "large" firms of over 250 employees (13 vs. 32 percent EU27 average), and the third lowest proportion of value added produced in large firms (27 vs. 42 percent EU27).[19]

Looking beyond the NFBE, in the economy as a whole, self-employment is very high for a European country. Thirty-six percent of all civilian employment is self-employment, including unpaid family members. This is the second highest rate among OECD members, after Mexico, and the highest in the EU27. Romania is close, but then Italy is third with just 26 percent. The average among OECD members is 16 percent and of EU27 17 percent.

Micro firms, namely those that employ up to nine people including the owner, dominate employment in the NFBE, making up 58 percent of the total. This was by far the highest ratio among EU countries. The second highest was in Italy (47 percent), while in EU27 as a whole it was 30 percent. Within the micro-firm size class, the average number of people was 1.9. They accounted for 35 percent of all value added, again the highest proportion in the EU, versus 21 percent in EU27.

This large divergence from EU averages is only partly due to sectoral composition effects. Within manufacturing as a whole, Greek micro firms account for 46 percent of employment and 32 percent of value added versus 14 and 7 percent, respectively, in EU27.[20]

In addition Greek micro firms have a very low productivity per person employed compared to Greek large firms. Value added per person in micro firms is just 29 percent of that in large firms. The corresponding ratio in EU27 is 55 percent. To a lesser degree, comparatively low productivity also applies to small and medium-size Greek firms, so that the whole SME sector in Greece is the least productive of all EU countries when benchmarked against the large corporate sector within the country (39 percent in Greece vs. 66 percent in EU27). Comparative productivities of size classes vary widely across industries and across countries, and to a significant extent the aggregate Greek ratio is due to composition effects.

The data presented here shows that are comparatively very few large firms and very many micro firms in the Greek economy. Smaller firms tend to have much lower productivity almost everywhere. In the case of Greece the productivity differential among

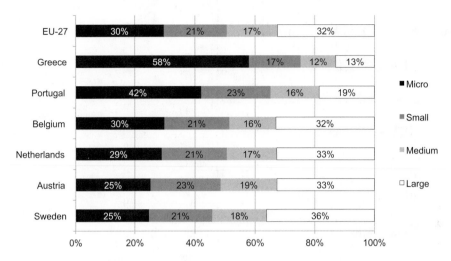

Figure 3.11
Employment by size class, nonfinancial business economy in 2007
Source: European Commission, SME Performance Review Database 2009

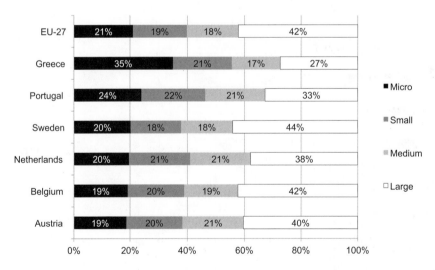

Figure 3.12
Gross value added by size class, nonfinancial business economy in 2007
Source: European Commission, SME Performance Review Database 2009

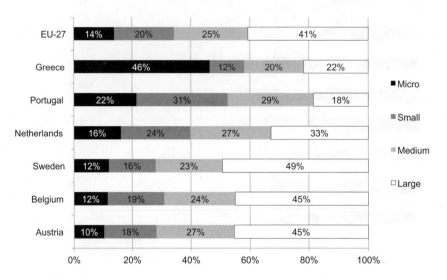

Figure 3.13
Employment by size class, manufacturing in 2007
Source: European Commission, SME Performance Review Database 2009

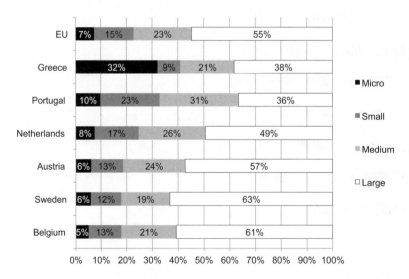

Figure 3.14
Gross value added by size class, manufacturing in 2007
Source: European Commission, SME Performance Review Database 2009

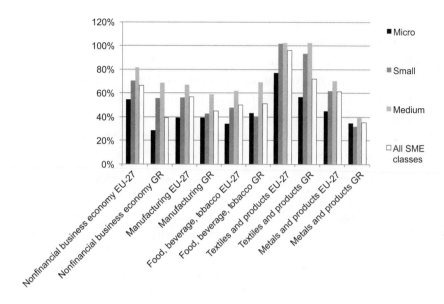

Figure 3.15
Labor Productivity in SMEs as percentage of the productivity of large firms in 2007
Source: European Commission, SME Performance Review Database 2009

size classes is exacerbated by sectoral composition: small firms tend to be in sectors where small size is more of a disadvantage. This means that there is a very limited pool of existing businesses in Greece that can respond quickly to new costs and prices.

Below a certain size, it is hard for firms to move into new markets or to expand production quickly. Expanding to new foreign markets has substantial discovery costs; it requires a management team with sales and marketing capability beyond the existing narrow client base, and this can usually be found only in relatively large firms. Furthermore rapid expansion requires that existing fixed assets of firms can be readily used to increase output. This implies standardized production processes that can scale up by adding labor without much in-house training; this is not usually the case in small artisanal units.

3.4.4 Sectors That Are Not Sensitive to Labor Cost Improvements

Additional reasons for the limited response of exports to the drop in wages have to do with the idiosyncrasies of Greece's two important export industries.

Tourism is the largest tradable industry in Greece, contributing 7 percent of GDP and 9 percent of employment directly, and 17 percent of GDP and 18 percent of employment including indirect and induced demand.[21] The business is very seasonal. Even in low years most accommodation near the coasts is fully booked during peak weeks, and in better years the peak period extends a bit longer. Thus lower costs cannot do much to increase sales in the peak period, and filling up rooms off-peak requires more than low cost. It requires also adding activities that will make the destination attractive in spring or autumn, namely a new type of offering that takes time to devise and coordinate. The capacity constraint does not apply to city breaks, but urban hotels account for a smaller number of beds and Greek cities are not top-of-mind destinations. And again, attracting many more visitors to cities requires more than low-cost offerings.

Deep sea shipping is the next most important export business, contributing between 3 and 6 percent of GDP (direct gross value added), depending on the year. International Greek-owned shipping draws very little of its cost base from Greece. Only about 8 percent of its domestic gross value added is wages and salaries, the rest being profits, depreciation, and amortization.[22] As for other inputs (fuel, parts, supplies) they are mostly sourced elsewhere. Therefore lower domestic labor costs and institutional reforms can do little to increase incomes from this industry. The global shipping cycle has been unfavorable, as shipping rates (e.g., the Baltic Dry Index) peaked in 2007 and 2008, plunged in 2009 and have not fully recovered since.

3.4.5 Policy Implications

The models of section 3.3 attribute any lag in export performance to increased trade costs. In discussing the actual economy, it is useful to break this down into proper trade costs (for existing exporters) and into barriers in factor mobility toward export businesses. Lowering the first type should have an immediate positive effect on exports, while lowering the second will make an impact in the medium term.

Measures for Immediate Impact The largest trade cost that has risen dramatically during the crisis has been bank finance. Providing more and cheaper credit should be of the highest priority. Taxes and levies should also be reviewed for their impact on exports, and those that impact more directly should be lowered or removed; one example is speeding up VAT reimbursement for exporters; another is lowering energy costs for exporters.

Measures for the Medium-Term and Long-Term Impact More persistent frictions derive from the regulatory environment, or they are inherent in particular types of firm. Removing regulatory barriers is likely to have faster results; changing company structures and cultures may take longer.

Despite some reform after 2010, there remain high barriers to starting a business with substantial fixed assets, to complying to all tax and social security regulations, and to introducing new business models. For example, getting planning permits for factories should be streamlined, and zoning regulations for business activity should be much more transparent. The sooner such barriers are removed, the more new businesses can be established in tradable activities. This is crucial in the case of Greece because the number of existing exporters is low, and in some important sectors such as summer tourism, exporters are facing capacity constraints.

Removing barriers to the growth of firms is an important long-term target; this would not only facilitate factor mobility but probably also increase overall productivity. Barriers to growth often derive from the costs of full compliance, since bigger firms are on the radar screen of the authorities more often than small ones. Moreover attracting foreign direct investment can help overcome both the issue of small firm size and the scarcity of capital.

In summary, our analysis suggests a mix of policies that will lower trade costs of existing exporters in the short term, enable many more firms to become exporters in the medium term, and increase productivity in several industries in the longer term.

Appendix

The model that we use in our quantitative work is the multi-country and multi-sector model of Eaton and Kortum (2002) and Dekle, Eaton, and Kortum (2007). To provide the main intuition for our results, in this appendix we describe a parametrized version of the two-county one-sector model of Dornbusch, Fischer, and Samuelson (1977), on which Eaton and Kortum (2002) and Dekle, Eaton, and Kortum (2007) are based.

There are two countries (A and B), each populated by a unit measure of consumers who have love of variety preferences and supply a unit of labor inelastically. There is a unit measure of goods that is produced with a linear technology so that $y_k(i) = z_k(i) * n_k(i)$, where $y_k(i)$ is country k's output of good i, $z_k(i)$ is the productivity of country k in producing good i, and $n_k(i)$ is the number of workers who produce that good. The productivity of country k for producing each good is follows a distribution parametrized by T_k, where a higher value of T_k leads to higher draws, on average. In other words, T_k measures the country's absolute advantage. A good can be consumed domestically or can be exported to the other country and, in the case it is exported, it incurs "iceberg" costs C. The model is static and country A's trade balance ($TB = X_A - M_A$) is exogenously given.

Labor and product markets are perfectly competitive. To find the equilibrium, we need to determine which goods are produced in each country and which goods are exported. Perfect competition means that there is a unique wage in each country and each good has a unique price. Furthermore trade means that the price of a good cannot differ "too much" (i.e., by more than trade costs) across countries. The identity of each good is not particularly relevant and the equilibrium is defined in relation to the aggregate price level and trade.

The exogenous variables of this model are the productivity levels for each country (T_A, T_B), the trade cost (C) and the trade balance TB. The endogenous variables are each country's aggregate production (Y_A, Y_B), which corresponds or GDP, exports and imports (X_A, M_A, X_B, M_B), wages (w_A, w_B) and price levels (p_A, p_B).

We now provide a graphical characterization of the equilibrium and some simple comparative statics, to provide intuition about how we the model interprets the data.

In the first example, the two countries are equally productive ($T_A = T_B$) and trade is balanced ($X_A = M_A = X_B = M_B$). In this case, trivially, output, wages, and prices are also equalized across countries. Still, the set of goods that are produced in each country and the set of goods that are traded (the level of X_A and X_B) have to be determined.

Figure 3A.1 ranks the goods on the horizontal axis according to the relative productivity of country A (i.e., country A's comparative advantage), so that good 0 has the highest $z_A(i)/z_B(i)$ and good 1 has the lowest $z_A(i)/z_B(i)$. The line associating the good index with relative productivity (the double line) is linear to ease exposition.

In equilibrium there are three regions. The first region, consists of the goods in the range (0, i_A), where the relative productivity of country A is above the endogenous threshold z_A. The goods in this region are only produced by country A and are then exported to country B (i.e., country B does not produce them at all and the agents of country B only consume these goods as imports). These are the goods where country A has the comparative advantage, and moreover the advantage is strong enough to outweigh the trade costs.

The second region consists of goods in the range (i_B, 1) where the relative productivity is below the endogenous threshold z_B The goods in this region are only produced in country B and are exported to country A. The third region consists of goods in the range (i_A, i_B) where neither country has a strong comparative advantage. These goods are produced in both countries and are not traded. Notice that this third region would not exist if trade costs were equal to zero ($C = 0$).

In the second example, country A is more productive than country B, or has absolute advantage ($T_A' > T_B'$), and bilateral trade is balanced. In comparison to the first

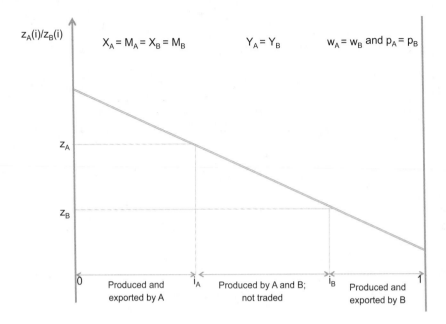

Figure 3A.1
Symmetric productivity, balanced trade

example, the relative productivity of goods shifts in the upper-right direction, as shown in figure 3A.2.

Since the relative productivity of country A is higher, it will export more, which is shown as an expansion in the range of exported goods to $(0, i_A')$.[23] Greater export revenues imply that country A can also finance additional imports which means that country B also exports a greater range of goods, $(i_B', 1)$. Therefore higher productivity for country A means that trade expands for both countries.

Higher productivity in country A, leads to higher output and wages than in the first example, but also to higher prices, since nontraded goods are in greater demand in country A. The higher level of exports means that output, wages and prices are also higher in country B than in the first example, although they are below the level of country A.

In the third example, both countries are equally productive and country A receives a capital inflow (a transfer) from country B, which, as we will see, corresponds to a trade deficit in relation to country B ($X_A'' = M_B'' < M_A'' = X_B''$). Figure 3A.3 compares the new equilibrium with the equilibrium from the first example.

The capital inflow increases the available resources of country A's agents, which increases their consumption both of imports and of locally produced goods. The range

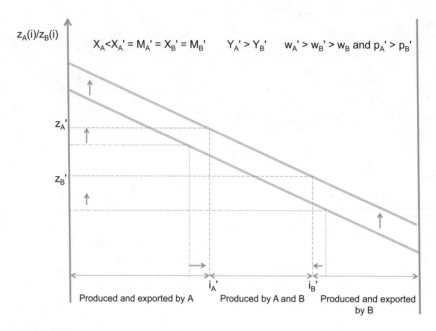

Figure 3A.2
Asymmetric productivity, balanced trade

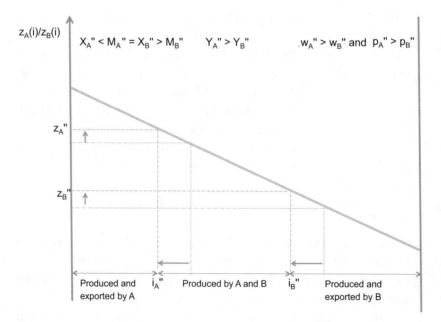

Figure 3A.3
Symmetric productivity, trade deficit for A

of imported goods (B's exports) expands to (i_B'', 1) while the increase in the consumption of nontraded goods leads to an increase in country A's prices and wages. In turn, this makes the export of previously marginal goods unprofitable, shrinking the range of exports to (0, i_A'').

As a result the capital inflow from country B to country A leads to an increase in A's output, wages, prices, and imports and a reduction in its exports. The transfer has exactly the opposite effect on country B. Notice that in this static sense, running a trade deficit (receiving a capital inflow) increases a country's welfare. Of course, this is due to the fact that we ignore the future repayment that country A needs to make to B in exchange for the current inflow, which, however, was probably not too far from Greek thinking before the crisis.

The final example also shows how the economy adjusts, according to the model, to a reduction in net capital flows, such as the one which occurred after 2008 in the four countries of the eurozone periphery. For trade to become balanced, wages and prices need to fall so that previously nontraded goods start being exported (i_A shifts right). Furthermore the decline in prices means that some goods that were previously imported are now produced locally, reducing imports (i_B shifts right). Nominal output is necessarily reduced, but the drop in prices means that real output should fall by a lower amount.

Notes

1. We would like to thank Jonathan Eaton, Theodore Papageorgiou, Andres Rodriguez-Clare, and the volume editors for helpful comments, and Konstantin Kucheryavyy for excellent research assistance.

2. Net income from abroad is the difference between the income that a country's citizens earn abroad and repatriate (as wages or profits) and the income that foreign citizens earn within the country that is sent abroad. Net transfers is the difference between money sent abroad with no expectation of repayment or other benefit (e.g., as foreign aid) and the money that flows in for the same purpose. Typically, net income and net transfers are small and vary relatively little over time.

3. For figure 3.1, the eurozone consists of the 12 countries that adopted the common currency before the crisis: Austria, Belgium, Finland, France, Germany, Greece, Ireland, Italy, Luxembourg, the Netherlands, Portugal, and Spain. For the years before 1999, the eurozone current account balance is calculated by aggregating the data from the individual countries. Between 2007 and 2014, six more countries have joined the common currency, but their current account balance is not included in the figure.

4. See Galenianos (2014) for a detailed account of these developments and their implications.

5. Greece, Ireland, and Portugal received help from the European Union, the European Central Bank, and the IMF to finance their governments' budget deficits and, in Greece's and Ireland's case, to recapitalize their banks. Spain only received funds from the European Union to recapitalize its banks.

6. Global trade collapsed in 2008, and therefore 2007 is a convenient starting point because it is the last "normal" year. Using 2008 as the starting point does not change our results in any significant way. Using 2009 as a base year would show a different picture (i.e., a substantial increase in Greek exports from 2009 to 2012), but the aim of the exercise is to compare the "normal" level of exports (as achieved before the crisis) to what must be achieved to restore income and employment after the crisis; 2009 is therefore not a relevant benchmark.

7. Notice that in 2007 Ireland had a trade surplus (figure 3.3) and a current account deficit (figure 3.1). The primary reason is that net income was strongly negative because a large number of US multinationals are operating in Ireland and repatriate their profits to the United States.

8. Of course, net capital inflows could be invested to create productive capacity and thus lead to higher productivity in the future. However, productivity improvements usually take some time to be realized and the investments are frequently squandered. See Galenianos (2015) for a detailed description of how the introduction of the euro led to optimistic expectations about the prospects of the eurozone periphery, which did not happen.

9. As described in section 3.2, a trade deficit corresponds to borrowing from or selling assets to other countries (experiencing net capital inflows), and a trade surplus corresponds to lending to or buying assets from other countries (experiencing net capital outflows).

10. The balance of trade depends on whether capital flows into or out of the country.

11. We consider the labor market of 2007 as being consistent with full employment for all four countries.

12. For instance, if real GDP grows by 2 percent and real exports by 6 percent annually, this change can be achieved within six years. Greek exports grew by about 6.5 percent annually in real terms between 1999 and 2007.

13. The GDP deflator is calculated in a similar way to the inflation rate, but takes into account the prices for all goods, while the inflation rate focuses on consumption goods.

14. The increase of VAT is partly responsible for the observed price increases in Greece: VAT is responsible for a 3.2 percent price increase in eurozone counties but a 6.6 percent increase in Greek prices, as calculated by Eurostat. Therefore, had VAT increased in Greece at the same rate as in the rest of Europe, Greece would have experienced a 1.8 percent drop in relative prices instead of an increase of 1.8 percent—still much below the 8.6 percent drop predicted by the model.

15. See chapter 7 in this volume (on the financial system) for a detailed analysis.

16. At least ten major tax laws; dozens of tax-related amendments in other laws; and over 800 ministerial decrees.

17. After great outcry, in April 2014 this was lowered to €250.

18. For "one family earner with two children" it was 42 percent, equal to France, and above all other OECD members. See IMF, *Country Report No. 14/151,* p. 12.

19. Data on the size distribution of firms in the NFBE are from the SME Performance Review Database 2009, of the European Commission.

20. An analysis of distribution in selected second-digit NACE sectors confirms that in most industries Greek firms tend to be significantly smaller than their counterparts in other EU countries.

21. World Travel and Tourism Council, *Economic Impact 2013, Greece.*

22. Foundation of Economic and Industrial Research (IOBE), *The contribution of deep sea shipping to the Greek economy,* January 2013 (in Greek).

23. Depending on the elasticity of substitution in consumer preferences, the expansion of exports could also take place in the intensive margin, that is, by exporting higher quantity of each good but the same or smaller range of goods. We have chosen the case where the expansion occurs in the extensive margin as it is easier to visualize.

References

Dekle, Robert, Jonathan Eaton, and Samuel Kortum. 2007. Unbalanced trade. *American Economic Review* 97 (2): 351–55.

Dornbusch, Rudiger, Stanley Fischer, and Paul A. Samuelson. 1977. Comparative advantage, trade and payments in a Ricardian model with a continuum of goods. *American Economic Review* 67 (5): 823–39.

Eaton, Jonathan, and Samuel Kortum. 2002. Technology, geography and trade. *Econometrica* 70: 1741–80.

Galenianos, Manolis. 2015. The Greek crisis: Origins and implications. Research paper 16. Crisis Observatory. Athens.

III Reforming Markets

4 Product Market Regulation and Competitiveness: Toward a National Competition and Competitiveness Policy for Greece[1]

Yannis Katsoulacos, Christos Genakos, and George Houpis

4.1 Introduction

This chapter focuses on the product markets in Greece and how to restore their competitiveness. One of the main determinants of competitiveness is the quality of the set of rules and regulations that govern the operation of markets. These should promote competition, investment, and entrepreneurship. Regulations that are well designed, suitably applied, and effectively enforced can make a country competitive and prosperous.

Greece's low competitiveness is not due to a lack of regulations. Indeed the Greek economy is heavily regulated, and the same applies to Greek product markets, which are among the most heavily regulated in the OECD. Heavy regulation is generally associated with inefficiencies and poor economic outcomes (e.g., see Nicoletti et al. 1999; Blanchard 2004). Many product market regulations present serious obstacles for competition, investment, and entrepreneurship, and thus should be abolished. Deregulations that promote competition usually have a positive impact on productivity through a more efficient use of resources (Nickell 1996; Blanchflower and Machin 1996; Bloom et al. 2012), by making entry easier for more innovative firms (Van Wijnbergen and Venables 1993; Bloom et al. 2016; Blundell et al. 1999; Aghion et al. 2005). Unfortunately, in Greece important regulations such as the Competition Law and network industry regulations that could promote the good operation of markets have not been enforced effectively.

Yet it is precisely because the Greek economy is heavily and inefficiently regulated that large benefits could be reaped from regulatory reform. According to one OECD study (Scarpetta and Tressel 2002), a comprehensive regulatory reform alone could raise the competitiveness of the Greek economy and ultimately the incomes of Greek citizens by more than 15 percent. More recent model-based calibration work carried out by IOBE (2014a) has indicated that deregulation reforms of Greek markets can enhance competition and boost Greece's GDP by 1.7 percent in just one year and 7.8 percent over the long run. Similarly an OECD (2014) competition assessment of Greek laws and regulations in just four sectors[2] of the economy identified 555 problematic regulations and 329 provisions "where changes could be made to foster competition," and it estimated the benefits from enhanced competition—through "rising expenditure, increased turnover and lower prices for the Greek consumer"—at around 5.2 billion euros, or around 2.5 percent of GDP.[3] All in all, there is unanimous agreement that the potential effects for Greece of reforms in product markets on employment, output, productivity, and competitiveness are sizable.

In section 4.2, we provide a brief summary of the competitiveness of the Greek economy and its evolution over time using various internationally comparable indicators that cover many dimensions of competitiveness. In section 4.3, we illustrate, using a number of case studies, the poor regulation of Greek product markets and its possible causes. In section 4.4, we consider in depth a national competition and competitiveness policy plan that aims to improve the regulatory institutions and reduce the regulatory burden. In section 4.5, we look at regulation and reforms in two important markets: energy and telecommunications. We offer some concluding remarks in section 4.6.

4.2 Competitiveness of the Greek Economy and Its Evolution

For at least two decades leading up to the economic crisis in 2009, Greece had been losing competitiveness vis-à-vis other EU and OECD countries. This negative trend was somewhat halted by the reforms implemented under the 2010 Economic Adjustment Programme, and in many sectors there has been clear evidence of slow but steady improvements. We begin with a brief review of the indicators used to gauge the decline and subsequent rise of the competitiveness of the Greek economy, with special emphasis on product market regulations and the business environment.[4] To this end, we utilize data from three international organizations: the World Economic Forum, the World Bank, and the OECD.[5]

The World Economic Forum is an independent international organization that has been publishing the Global Competitiveness Report for over thirty years. The World Economic Forum bases its analysis on the Global Competitiveness Index (GCI), a comprehensive tool that measures the microeconomic and macroeconomic foundations of national competitiveness. The GCI defines competitiveness as the set of institutions, policies, and factors that determines the level of productivity of a country. The level of productivity determines the rates of return obtained by investments in the country, which are fundamental drivers of the country's economic growth. In other words, a more competitive economy is one that is more likely to achieve sustainable growth (see Sala-i-Martín and Artadi 2004). The GCI is a weighted average of many different components, which are grouped into twelve pillars. Figure 4.1 shows the evolution of Greece's overall competitiveness ranking between 2001 and 2014.[6] The increase in the index means that the relative competitiveness of the Greek economy has been steadily declining since 2005. The decline tipped in 2012, and since then Greece's competitiveness has been improving.

The decline in Greece's competitiveness from 2005 onward was driven to a large extent by declines in the efficiency of the goods market and in the quality of the institutions more generally. Figure 4.2 plots the indexes corresponding to goods market efficiency and institutional quality, and shows that they both experienced a strong decline since 2006. If we add to this decline the already low efficiency of the labor market, we can begin to understand the truly disastrous combination that led to the decline of Greece's competitiveness over these years. The figure also shows that although the product and labor markets may be closely interlinked, the inefficiencies of the product markets can exert an independent negative effect on the economy's overall efficiency. Nevertheless, since 2012, all indexes have been improving steadily as a result of new legislation.

Figure 4.3 plots two important sub-indexes of the goods market efficiency index. The first measures the intensity of local competition, and the second the effectiveness

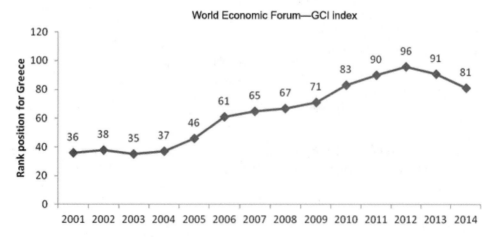

Figure 4.1
Global Competitiveness Index
Source: World Economic Forum, 2001–14

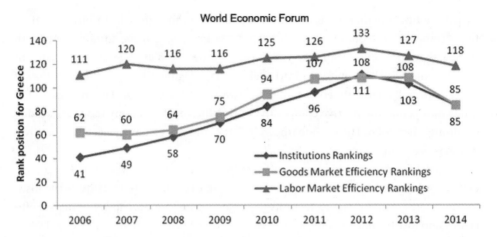

Figure 4.2
Goods and labor markets and institutions
Source: World Economic Forum, 2006–14

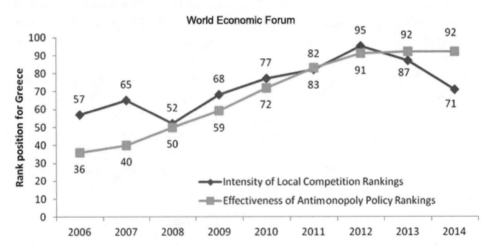

Figure 4.3
Intensity of competition and effectiveness of antimonopoly policy
Source: World Economic Forum, 2006–14

of antimonopoly policy. Greece's relative performance has been low in both areas and has deteriorated rapidly since 2006. The deterioration has been more severe for anti-monopoly policy and that trend has not reversed from 2012 onward: Greece ranked 36th in 2006, 83rd in 2011, and 92nd in 2014. On the other hand the 2009 crisis seems to have ignited strong local market competition, as can be surmised from the fact that Greece improved to the 71st position of the corresponding sub-index in 2014 from the 95th position in 2012.

Figure 4.4 plots three further sub-indexes that measure business sophistica-tion, innovation capability, and FDI and technology transfer. All three sub-indexes have been experiencing a decline since 2006, but things have been improving since 2012.

The second set of indicators comes from the World Bank. The first indicator is from the *Doing Business* report, which presents quantitative indicators on business regula-tions and the protection of property rights that can be compared across 185 countries. These regulations affect eleven areas of the life of a business: starting a business, deal-ing with construction permits, getting electricity, registering property, getting credit, protecting investors, paying taxes, trading across borders, enforcing contracts, resolv-ing insolvency, and employing workers. Based on the 2011 report, Greece was ranked 109th among 183 countries, down from the 80th position in 2006. According to the report, among the most problematic factors for doing business were the inefficient government bureaucracy, access to finance, policy instability, tax regulations, and

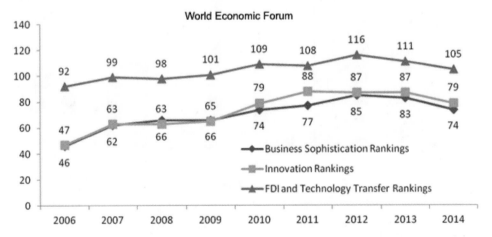

Figure 4.4
Business sophistication, innovation, and FDI
Source: World Economic Forum, 2006–14

corruption. In contrast, the 2015 report ranks Greece in the 72nd position, reversing the trend of the previous years.

In addition to the *Doing Business* indicators, the World Bank had been publishing the *Worldwide Governance Indicators* (WGI) report for the period 1996 to 2013. That report provides aggregate and individual governance indicators for 215 countries. Six dimensions of governance are covered: voice and accountability, political stability and absence of violence, government effectiveness, regulatory quality, rule of law, and control of corruption. Figure 4.5 plots the latter four indicators in percentile rank terms from 0 to 100, with higher values corresponding to better outcomes. The conclusions are consistent with those from the *Doing Business* report: there is evidence of Greece's overall poor regulatory framework and its decline over time (regulatory quality ranking), along with decreasing government effectiveness, and particularly low and declining ranking in corruption and the general rule of law, as compared to other OECD countries.

A final indicator that we consider is the product market regulation (PMR) indicator, published every five years by the OECD. That indicator measures the quality and restrictiveness of product market regulations, various obstacles to entrepreneurship and investment, and the amount of state control in the economy. Figure 4.6 plots

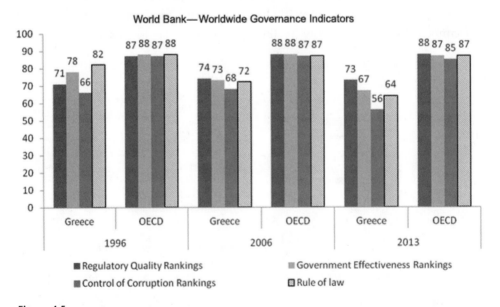

Figure 4.5
Worldwide governance indicators
Source: World Bank, Worldwide Governance Indicators

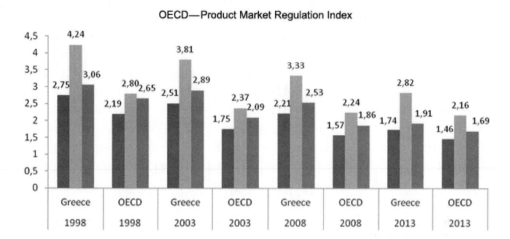

Figure 4.6
Product Market Regulation index
Source: OECD, Product Market Regulation Database

the PMR indicator for Greece for 1998, 2003, 2008, and 2013, and compares with the OECD average. Relative to the OECD average, Greece has heavier product market regulation, more state control, and higher obstacles to entrepreneurship and investment.

All the indicators mentioned above paint a similar picture of Greek product markets before the crisis: high obstacles to entrepreneurship and investment, extensive state control, heavy and inefficient regulations, all contributing to the steady decline of overall competitiveness. The 2012 reforms and changes in the legislation are reversing these negative trends and Greece appears to be gradually closing the gap with the other advanced countries. However, important differences remain that indicate that the deregulation effort to reinvigorate competition in product markets still has a long way to go.

4.3 Taking a Closer Look at the Greek Product Markets

Greek product markets suffer from a lack of effective competition. The main reasons behind this phenomenon are (1) excessive and worthless regulations in a large number of markets resulting in high barriers to entry, protected markets, and "closed" professions and (2) inefficient implementation of regulations such as competition law that can improve market outcomes and social welfare.[7] We briefly examine each of these factors below, before making our policy recommendations.

4.3.1   Excessive and Worthless Regulation

To give a sense of the excessive number of regulations generated by the Greek government between 1995 and 2005, we refer to a recent OECD report (2011), "Functional
Review of the Central Administration in Greece." As recorded in this report, 3,430
laws, 20,580 presidential decrees, 114,905 ministerial decisions, 24,010 regional decisions, and 8,575 decisions of municipal authorities were generated between 1975 and
2005. These add up to 171,500 new regulations or about 5,716 regulations a year (or
477 regulations a month) on average. Even if we do not take into account the regional
decisions and the decisions of municipal authorities, the number of regulations generated in a year was 4,630 on average (or 386 regulations a month[8]). Based on an OECD
(2009a) cross-country comparison study, not only was there a significant increase in
new primary laws between 1997 and 2007, but Greece was the country with the highest
new subordinate regulations across all OECD countries.

To make things worse, the regulations are often poorly conceived because no institutions and mechanisms are in place to determine whether the regulations are necessary,
are proportional to the problem that they were supposed to address, and are adopted
after their effects have been assessed. There is no institutional framework in Greece
to assess regulations, abolish those that are not necessary or create high social costs,
and prevent the creation of new regulations that are expected to yield the same result.
There is neither an authority for the assessment of the effects of regulations (AAER)
nor any other institution or mechanism. Law 4048/12 of 2012 aimed to improve the
regulatory governance and proposed principles and procedures of good regulation.
That law, however, has never been implemented, and it has not provided the appropriate organizational and decision-making structures and processes that are necessary to
address the problems. Moreover it was aimed at new regulation, and not at reducing
the existing (huge) regulatory burden.

Although the institutional framework for assessing the effects of regulations varies
across countries, a central unit or organization with such responsibilities exists in most
advanced countries. In Australia, for example, a major role is played by the independent Productivity Commission. In the United Kingdom, the responsibility lies with a
subgroup of the Cabinet together with the independent Regulatory Policy Committee.
In the Netherlands, the Advisory Board on Regulatory Burden explicitly aims at reducing the regulatory burden as a key government priority to improve the performance of
the economy. In the United States, which has the most extensive experience in assessing the effects of regulation, the Small Business Administration Office of Advocacy has
the powers of an AAER and reports directly to the President. We return with a proposal
for the Greek case based on international experience in section 4.4.

Providing a full list of the regulations affecting the markets for all products in Greece is a task that goes beyond the scope of this chapter. We instead illustrate the degree of over-regulation and inefficiency by using six case studies. The inefficiencies that the case studies reveal are indicative but by no means exhaustive.

4.3.2   Case Studies

Case Study 1: Trucks   The road freight transport sector, which accounts for 98 percent of transportation of goods by land, had until recently one of the strictest regulatory frameworks in the OECD (2001). The government granted licenses to haulage operators (license for vehicle for public use) and set minimum tariffs. No new licenses had been issued since the early 1970s, which meant that the only way to enter the sector was to purchase an existing license at a significant cost in the secondary market, with prices varying between 30,000 and 300,000 euros. The restrictiveness of the legal framework for road freight resulted in high rents for incumbents, inhibited competition, constrained development of outsourcing in trucking services, and resulted in higher prices for almost all consumer goods. A new law in 2010, and subsequent important amendments, deregulated the road freight transport sector; it also led to major strikes by existing license holders that brought the country to a halt. Few new licenses have been issued after the law was passed due to the deep recession and large demand reduction.

Case Study 2: Maximum Markup Regulation for Fruits and Vegetables   Fresh fruits and vegetables are often sold under a maximum markup regulation, imposed both at the wholesale and the retail levels. The typical government justification for imposing maximum markups is consumer protection from the effects of excessive market power. In oligopolistic markets, the main argument in favor of maximum markups is to trim the right tail of the markup distribution, hence limiting the most extreme instances of exploitation of market power. This is expected to put downward pressure on retail prices, without affecting firms with smaller markups (e.g., a competitive fringe), though it entails a risk of creating a focal point for potential collusion.

In June 2011 this regulation was hastily canceled. Interestingly enough, five fruit products (apples, lemons, mandarins, oranges, and pears) were excluded from this regulation. Genakos et al. (2014) collected retail and wholesale data and compared prices of products affected by regulation before and after the policy change, with the unregulated products used as a control group. Genakos et al. found that abolishing markup regulation led to 6 to 9 percent *lower* average retail prices, which amounts to 256 million euros per year aggregate savings for Greek consumers. They provide consistent evidence demonstrating that markup ceilings were a focal point for collusion among wholesalers. Therefore in this case deregulation benefited consumers, whereas the regulation in place had failed to protect consumers.

Case Study 3: "Fresh" Pasteurized Milk   Greek legislation allows that only pasteurized milk with a shelf life of up to five days can carry the word "fresh milk" on its packaging. Greece is the only EU country that regulates the shelf life of milk in this way; EU regulation leaves the shelf life duration at the discretion of the manufacturer, provided that they abide by all relevant regulations regarding the safety of the product. Due to the limited shelf life, importing "fresh" milk from other EU countries is not practicable. This protective environment means that there is limited competitive pressure at all stages of milk production, and as a result Greek consumers are paying one of the highest retail prices for "fresh" pasteurized milk across the European Union (34 percent higher prices on average). Also consumers on (most) islands and remote mountainous villages do not have access to "fresh" milk, and small producers in northern Greece cannot reach the large urban areas. Therefore the five-day restriction creates an inefficient and costly system of collecting and returning expired products from retailers, which amounts to 5 percent of the final retail price of "fresh" pasteurized milk. Although the recent OECD (2014) report recommended abolishing the five-day restriction, the final version of the law that was passed in 2014 only increased it from 5 to 7 days, due to strong opposition from local producers and the industry. Following this change, the effects on the market so far have been negligible, as the threat of milk imports from major EU producing countries is not a credible constraining factor and hence there is no pressure on local producers to modernize and improve their productivity.

Case Study 4: Bread and Bake Off   Until 1992, the price of a loaf of bread was regulated by the state. In 1992, the government lifted all geographic restrictions regarding the establishment of new bakeries and allowed the sale of bread and bread products from other retail channels such as supermarkets. However, licensing requirements to establish a bake-off installation (a small oven to bake ready-made bread rolls) inside a supermarket were made very restrictive. Essentially, installing a small oven was a bureaucratic procedure equivalent to an industrial installation. As a result most supermarkets could not sell bread and despite the "liberalization" the supply of bread was practically restricted to bakeries. In 2004, the EU court censured Greece for its very restrictive regulation of the bake off. Subsequent changes in 2007 and 2010 made the law less restrictive, but supermarkets were still not allowed to mount bake-off services (minimum space and separation requirements, etc.). The current law (passed in 2013) has eased the restrictions, setting the same sanitary requirements for every retail shop that seeks to bake and sell bread. The bakery sector nowadays is one of the most vibrant retail sectors.

Case Study 5: Stevedores and Lawyers   A variety of restrictions also apply to services. The government regulates professions in various ways, such as by setting the number of licenses, geographical restrictions, and compulsory minimum fees. We examine the workings of these regulations for two professional activities at opposite ends of the educational spectrum: stevedores and lawyers.

In Greece stevedores are commonly used for land and port operations (loading and unloading trucks or boats). Their fees were fixed by law (hence no price competition), and the Stevedore Work Regulatory Committee acted as the licensing authority, which meant that the incentives to allow more workers into the profession were severely distorted. Instances of companies paying fees to the Committee, despite not using their services, were not unheard of.

New legislation in 2013 removed legal restrictions concerning the permissible number of stevedores in cities and ports, the permissible number of stevedoring operations contractors in each port, the setting of stevedores' wages, as well as geographical restrictions on practicing the profession. However, because of insufficient monitoring by authorities, the previously existing restrictions are often still in place and the new market rules have not been fully implemented. This is also one of the main reasons for the low level of recorded entries to the stevedore profession after the reforms (IOBE 2014b).

The legal profession had also been subject to a number of restrictions. First, there were geographic restrictions for practicing law within Greece. If, for example, a lawyer was registered with the Bar Association in Athens, he/she could not appear in a court in Thessaloniki or elsewhere in Greece. Second, there were mandatory minimum payments and fixed payment scales for legal services. Third, a lawyer's involvement in real estate transactions was mandatory, and there was also a mandatory payment scale according to the value of the estate. All these restrictions meant that legal services were not competitive and their costs were unnecessarily high. Recent changes in the law (passed in 2013), removed many of these restrictions. However, some restrictions remain, mostly in relation to required fees and payments to the Bar Association (IOBE 2014c).

Case Study 6: Advertising Fee   Greece is the only OECD country that imposes a high tax on advertising: 20 percent for all advertisements in the press and 21.5 percent for

TV and radio. While from an economic perspective this regulation acts as a tax on advertising, the term "advertising fee" is more appropriate because the revenues are used to fund the health and pension benefits of the employees in media (newspapers, magazines, TV, and radio stations) replacing their employer contributions.

With such a high fee the marginal cost of advertising is high. As a consequence advertising expenditure is low, hurting consumers (less information, less competition). Low advertising expenditure means reduced revenue and fewer jobs in advertising agencies. Since, in addition, the cost of tax collection falls on the advertising agencies, the agencies' operating costs are high. This means that small advertising agencies cannot survive, and the advertising market is concentrated. The high cost of advertising goods and services is incorporated into their prices and is ultimately borne by the consumer. Based on the OECD (2014) report, abolishing the advertising fee would increase advertising expenditure by 35 percent, creating more than 800 new jobs in the advertising business alone, while also lowering consumer prices by 1 percent, which amounts to an estimated 1.8 billion euro annual consumer benefit. So far, no changes in the relevant legislation have taken place.

As these case studies demonstrate, it is difficult to isolate a few common problems that could easily be addressed when deregulating Greece's product markets. Perhaps the main lesson is that product market deregulation in Greece will be a long and painstaking process. Changing the primary legislation is just the first step, as the whole deregulation procedure requires careful monitoring and continuous assessment. Just as we need, ex ante, careful considerations for policy reforms, we need also to create a strong culture of, ex post, policy evaluations[9] to learn from successes and failures.

4.3.3 Inefficient Implementation of Regulation

One of the pillars for a competitive environment, and one where the government has a clear role to play, is an effective legislative and institutional framework for dealing with cases where regulation is necessary to achieve efficient market outcomes. Such a framework must encompass competition policy as well as the regulation of network markets with natural monopoly features, in particular, telecommunications and energy. In this section we concentrate mainly on competition policy; we will discuss the regulation of the telecoms and the energy sector in section 4.5.

The legal and institutional framework for protecting competition in Greece has been progressively modernized by a series of amendments[10] to the Competition Law, in accord with EU standards. However, *the extent and effectiveness of enforcement is low*.

The extent and effectiveness of enforcement should be assessed on the basis of its impact in deterring anticompetitive practices by firms and other organizations in the private and the public sector, in identifying a large part of such practices that are not deterred, and in minimizing decision errors in cases where potentially anticompetitive practices are identified and investigated. As emphasized by Buccirossi et al. (2011), various features of a country's legal and institutional framework reflect the effectiveness of enforcement. Greece is behind in all of these features.

• *The Hellenic Competition Commission (HCC) and the sectoral regulatory authorities are prone to political interference, especially with regard to investigations and decisions directly affecting specific markets and firms.* Traditionally, the "political culture" in Greece— and this is true across the spectrum of political parties—favors intervention in the work of the "independent" authorities. In order to move toward real independence, the president and the members of these authorities should be selected from the multi-party committees of the Parliament in which the government (or the ruling party or parties) is involved but doesn't hold the majority.

• *There is no specialized appeals court to petition for a review of decisions by government authorities.* Such a court could be modeled on the standards of the Competition Appeals Tribunal of England, which many other European countries have followed and in which there must be participation of economists, as in England, France, and other countries. It is critical that cases decided by government authorities be open to (re)examination on matters of substance and not simply ruled on the propriety of the legal procedures followed.

• *Potential anticompetitive practices are often evaluated not based on their impact on social welfare[11] (adopting* effects-based legal standards) *but rather on a standard formalistic assessment of the facts (adopting* per se *or* "object based" legal rules).[12] This is injudicious because it focuses on the effects of the examined practices on the "competitors" rather than on "competition and consumer welfare," and reduces welfare because it deters firms from undertaking practices that can improve welfare.[13]

• *Human resources within the regulatory authorities are insufficient, in terms of skills and competence mix.* The HCC is unique in the European Union in that it has not yet (as of April 2015) filled the position of chief economist, who should co-decide on cases examined by the Commission,[14] and also in that in the last ten years none of the few Commission members is specialized in the economics of competition.[15] Similar problems exist in the sectoral regulatory authorities of the telecommunications and (to a lesser extent) energy sectors (EETT and RAE).

• *Infringements are identified with long delays if at all.* Commentators on economic policy issues frequently refer to the HCC's inability to effectively address instances of probable collusion (i.e., cartels).[16] There are even cases where firms wait for a complaint against them to be investigated for more than ten years. The consequences of the Commission's shillyshallying are evidenced by Greece's performance in the relevant index of the World Economic Forum. As noted in section 4.2, Greece position in the WEF's index of the effectiveness of antimonopoly policy has slipped from the 36th place in 2006 to the 83rd place in 2011.[17]

• *There are overlapping competences between the regulatory authorities.* The problem of overlapping competences is endemic in the Greek public administration. The most important instance of overlap concerns the EETT, which regulates the telecommunications industry but does not coordinate with the HCC.

• *The competitive neutrality principle is not upheld.* The HCC has, to a large extent, been treating organizations in the wider public sector more favorably than similar firms in the private sector when it comes to prohibiting anticompetitive practices or notifying the firms to amend any such practices. Such instances have arisen when public organizations act as suppliers or buyers in markets, or in public procurement for providing local government services, information services, and so forth. However, *the Commission has performed significantly better in recent years in terms of advocacy and outreach activities,* and we discuss this important dimension of its activities in the section that follows.

4.4   Toward a National Competition and Competitiveness Policy

4.4.1   Key Requirements
We believe that the deficiencies in product market regulation identified in section 4.3 can be dealt with only if the Greek government implements a national competition and competitiveness policy (NCCP). A NCCP would include competition policy in the more narrow sense, that is, competition law meant to condemn and deter anticompetitive practices. Such practices include the formation of cartels, as well as some vertical mergers and practices by dominant firms. The enactment of competition law, however, is not sufficient to create conditions of effective market competition. Creating such conditions requires a NCCP that is based on three pillars.

First an effective legislative and institutional framework must be in place for those cases where regulation is necessary to achieve efficient outcomes. The NCCP should focus both on competition policy and on regulation of network markets with natural monopoly features (especially telecommunications and energy). As noted in section 4.3.3, the main issue here is not the legal framework itself but the efficient (more timely interventions, quicker and more open decision processes) and effective (effects-based approach in assessing cases, protection of competition rather than of competitors) implementation of regulation to the benefit of consumers.

Second the NCCP must include an *efficient policy for the adoption and control of regulations* (section 4.4.2). That is, it should promote actions, policies, and institutions that would reduce unnecessary and excessive regulation (which often becomes a source of corruption) and would repeal legislation which hinders market entry and exit. We return to this in more detail below and propose a concrete action plan.

Third the NCCP must further the development and enhancement of *competition advocacy*. By this we mean that its members should study and promote the benefits of competition for growth and social welfare, so that the competitive spirit and culture will permeate deeply the Greek economy and society.

The absence of competition advocacy in Greece has been one of the reasons why there is no effective competition in many product markets. In the last three years, however, the HCC has intensified its efforts, and according to Loukas (2014), its activities have "revolved around four key themes those of (a) liberalization of professional services (b) legislative distortions mostly affecting retail and food supply chains (c) Greece's Competition Assessment Project[18] and (d) the publication of competition compliance and awareness guides, primarily addressed to trade associations, as well as procurement/contract awarding public authorities." To be sure, the structural reforms advocated by HCC in the context of these activities are, as we have stressed above and as Loukas (2014) also notes, essential for Greece becoming competitive in international markets and entering a sustainable growth path.

4.4.2 Policy for the Adoption and Control of Regulations

A comprehensive policy for the adoption and control of regulations should aim at improving the production of regulations and reducing the regulatory burden. Measures should be taken to:

- remove existing regulations which are not necessary and hamper growth;
- allow new regulations to be adopted only as a last resort;
- reduce the number of new regulations;
- improve the design and ex post assessment quality of new regulations;
- reduce the cost for firms and citizens; and
- improve the way in which regulations are implemented and monitored.

The organizational and decision-making structure required to implement such a policy could be set up as follows[19]:

An Executive Committee for Better Regulation (ECBR) could be established as a governmental committee that assists regulation-makers (in the ministries, etc.) and evaluates possible alternatives to the adoption of new regulations—such as self-regulatory solutions or solutions with less regulation. Such an ECBR could be assisted by a Strategic Group on Better Regulation that would be chaired by the director of the ECBR and would include representatives of nongovernmental organizations or social partners (e.g., the Hellenic Federation of Enterprises), the workforce, consumers, and the government.[20]

Before proposing a new regulation, a Ministry would have to take into account the views of the ECBR; it would be obliged to produce, either on its own or with the help of independent consultants, a Regulatory Impact Assessment Study of the proposed regulation and then send the proposal along with the study to the ECBR and the Reducing Regulation Committee, a subcommittee of the *Cabinet*. One of the main responsibilities of the ECBR would be to examine the proposal, ensure that it is feasible, and advise the Reducing Regulation Committee on whether the proposal should be implemented, amended, or rejected. The evaluation by the ECBR would be based on detailed instructions and recommendations issued by the ECBR. The final decision concerning the adoption of a regulation would be taken by the Reducing Regulation Committee. In the United Kingdom, for example, the Regulatory Policy Committee has been since 2012 an independent advisory non departmental public body funded by the Ministry for Business Innovation and Skills.

We should add that the Greek ECBR would have powers that combine those of the Regulatory Policy Committee in the United Kingdom with at least some powers of the Australian Productivity Committee, and it would replace the existing Greek Competitiveness Council. Specifically we propose that the Greek ECBR take on the following responsibilities:

• Reduce the existing regulatory burden by eliminating or revising existing regulations. The government would need to legislate and implement a regulatory framework with clear deadlines, systematic monitoring, and an ex post assessment of its progress, along with a strong communications strategy.

• Monitor the performance of government departments through annual reports that assess the effectiveness of improvements in the regulatory environment and in other essential government services, such as justice, education, and health care.

• Establish a complaint office for nonobservance of the competitive neutrality principle. This office would receive and evaluate complaints and also inform the Reducing Regulation Commission, and thus the *Cabinet*, of instances where the independent administrative authorities or other government departments act in a way that is incompatible with the competitive neutrality principle.

In conjunction with the establishment of the ECBR, two important rules should be adopted: the *one-in one-out* (OIOO) rule and sunset clauses. The OIOO rule requires that new primary or secondary legislation that adds costs to firms or other organizations can be enacted only when existing regulation of equivalent value (in terms of contribution to firms' costs) is removed. The regulations required for the implementation of EU obligations would be outside the scope of the OIOO rule, except for gold-plating regulatory obligations from the European Union that would result in the removal of an equivalent regulation. The introduction of the OIOO rule means that policy makers would have to account for the net cost to firms and other organizations of every new regulation and would have to seek early on in the policy-making process a corresponding regulatory measure that could be removed.

Sunset clauses (provisions) are a legal tool that provides for a law or a regulation to expire after a certain period of time. At the end of its predetermined lifespan, a regulation can be terminated or updated. Sunset clauses would force the government to periodically assess and justify the regulatory burden, and improve its legislation. In cases where a ministry does not wish to terminate a regulation, it has the opportunity to renew or modernize it. Sunset clauses are used to ensure that the regulations that are no longer useful are deleted and that the necessary regulations are up to date. They also help in identifying regulations that can be abolished so to meet the OIOO rule.

4.5   Regulation of Network Industries: Two Instructive Case Studies—Telecommunications versus Energy

This section provides a description and comparison of recent developments, including regulatory ones, in telecommunications and energy. We have chosen these two sectors both because of their importance for other sectors of the economy (e.g., tourism, energy-intensive manufacturing sectors, public sector) and because they provide an interesting contrast between two regulatory paradigms. In telecommunications, we have witnessed the implementation of a rather prescriptive EU model that combines liberalization with appropriate regulation. In energy, we have instead witnessed the application of a more discretionary regulatory model that follows central rules to a lesser extent and involves more uncertainty.

4.5.1   Telecommunications—Holding Back Economic Growth?

The rapid evolution of technologies has shaken up the telecommunications sector over the last two decades. Telecommunications services were traditionally delivered to households and businesses through fixed (wireline) technologies, by vertically integrated, often government owned, and largely monopolistic operators. This was necessary as the important objective of achieving nationwide delivery of communications services required substantial investments to roll out the national wireline infrastructure. The significant fixed costs enabled the industries involved to function as natural monopolies. The arrival of mobile (wireless) technologies in the late 1980s and their evolution has transformed the telecommunications sector, with most consumers using both fixed and mobile technologies to access and consume communications services—including both traditional voice services and Internet services. Unlike fixed/ wireline markets, mobile markets have evolved into competitive markets, with typically three to four mobile operators, reflecting the rapid growth in demand for mobile communications services combined with relatively lower costs of rolling out a national infrastructure.

The central regulatory tasks have thus been to (1) enable sustainable competition to thrive in national fixed telecommunications markets, which in Europe has been done by encouraging entry based on providing access to the uncontestable parts of the supply chain (i.e., the access network of the vertically integrated incumbents), and (2) facilitate the national/local adoption of both fixed and mobile technological innovation and related services. In light of the rapid and ongoing growth in the Internet economy, and the associated economic and productivity improvements, a key policy objective for the telecommunications sector in all countries has been how to facilitate and encourage the development of higher speed/higher capacity (broadband) Internet access.

The liberalization of Greece's fixed telecommunications market was delayed relative to that in most other EU countries. Greece has also been slow in adopting the latest technologies. High-speed fixed broadband[21] services were only launched in November 2012 after a long period of regulatory review; in fact Greece was the last EU country to clear the spectrum band necessary for use of high-speed mobile broadband services, and one of the last countries in the European Union to award the spectrum in 2014.

Despite the delays, liberalization has been associated with improved outcomes for consumers. New firms have entered the fixed line market, and competitive markets for the provision of mobile services developed during the 1990s and early 2000s. While technological evolution, including the technological fusion between IT and Telecoms, has been a key driver of improved efficiency in the telecommunications sector,[22] competition among mobile network operators has played an important role in passing such gains to consumers.[23] Mobile sector prices in Greece declined by 31 percent between 1999 and 2010 compared to a 43 percent increase in consumer price inflation.[24]

Although there is competition in the provision of both fixed and mobile telecommunications services, the development of the broadband infrastructure and services in Greece lags that in other countries. Broadband take-up in Greece has been slow, and the ultra-high-speed broadband take-up particularly low. The relatively low take-up of broadband services has had implications for the productive capacity of the economy, as broadband is considered to be an important enabler of GDP and productivity growth.[25] This section therefore focuses on the development of broadband in Greece. We review the current state of the broadband sector, and then present a short-term policy proposal to encourage the take-up of (basic) broadband. We finally consider longer term policy options.

The Greek Broadband Sector   Greece's (basic) broadband penetration rate has persistently lagged that in the European Union.[26] Broadband take-up in Greece in 2013 was lower than in all Western European countries, with the household penetration rate being 56 percent against an EU average of 79 percent.[27] The situation is similar in terms of mobile broadband take-up.[28] The penetration rate in Greece in 2013 was 38 percent and second lowest in the European Union, whose average exceeded 60 percent.

Greece's worse performance relative to other EU countries is not only a reflection of its lower GDP per capita. A recent econometric analysis that controls for GDP per capita as well as for other factors that could affect the take-up of broadband[29] (population density, urbanization, and educational levels) reveals that Greece lags in penetration and broadband speeds compared to what would be expected given its lower level of income. Figure 4.7 shows the actual and expected take-up of fixed broadband in Greece. The gap between actual and expected levels has averaged around 15 percentage points since 2009. In terms of prices of fixed broadband services, the evidence suggests that prices in Greece are at the EU average for broadband services, of 12 to 30 Mbps, but are above the EU average for superfast broadband services, 30 to 100 Mbps.[30]

Effect of Broadband Take-up on Economic Performance   There has been a significant amount of research on the relationship between broadband diffusion and economic growth. The bulk of the evidence suggests that broadband take-up has a positive impact on economic growth, and enables:[31]

1. more speed, accessibility, and quality of information flows,

2. more efficient business management,

3. more market transparency and lower barriers to entry, and

4. faster diffusion of innovations.

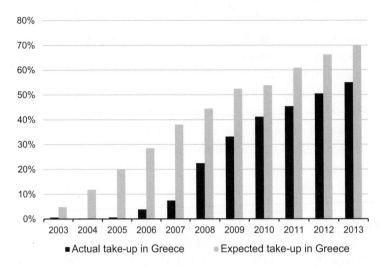

Figure 4.7
Broadband penetration, actual and expected
Source: European Commission and Frontier Economics analysis

A recent study summarizing the research on the relationship between broadband and economic growth[32] has suggested a "critical mass" effect to the impact of broadband take-up on GDP growth by providing evidence of a range of increasing returns. In particular, the study found broadband to have a higher productivity impact on sectors with relatively higher transaction costs (e.g., financial services) and high labor intensity (e.g., tourism). In terms of empirical evidence, three earlier studies sought to estimate the magnitude of the effect that broadband has on economic output. Czernich et al. (2011) estimated a 10 percent increase in broadband penetration to raise per capita GDP growth rates by 0.9 to 1.5 percentage points. Qiang and Rossotto (2009) estimated a 10 percent increase in broadband penetration to add 1.21 percentage points of GDP growth in high-income countries, and 1.38 percentage points in middle- to low-income countries. Koutroumpis (2009) found a 10 percent increase in broadband penetration to be associated with a 0.25 percentage increase in GDP growth.[33] Overall, there is strong evidence that investment in broadband services can contribute significantly to economic growth.

Short-Term Policy Considerations: Stimulating Broadband Take-up in Greece through Tax Policy   Governments have considered a range of policies to promote the growth of broadband take-up,[34] with the focus in developed economies being on promoting *higher* speed broadband take-up. As we noted above, however, Greece lags significantly behind in terms of even *basic* broadband take-up. Given the connection between economic growth and broadband take-up, insufficient broadband take-up is constraining Greece's economic growth.

Policy makers should address this problem and find ways to raise the take-up of basic broadband services to levels at least as high as the EU average. Moreover, since broadband is based on consumers' experience with it, such that consumers are likely to appreciate its full value as they get accustomed to using it, a good short-term policy to increase broadband take-up should take into account longer-term positive impacts.[35]

The main instrument that can be used to stimulate demand in the short term is price.[36] We therefore consider next a taxation policy based on the pricing of broadband services: a reduction in VAT on broadband services from the standard rate of 23 to 13 percent. We model a number of effects of a VAT reduction in order to estimate the net cost of such a policy:

• Take-up of broadband increase.[37]
• VAT revenues decline.[38]
• Wider impacts of increase in broadband on the productive capacity of broadband services,[39] which would raise output and hence taxation revenue.

Table 4.1 shows the impacts[40] of these factors over a three-year period. Note that when the policy is directed only at new subscribers, there is a higher increase in tax intake, as is to be expected.

Our analysis suggests that a VAT cut on broadband services can generate tax revenue and stimulate growth. Designing a scheme that can target current nonsubscribers only

Table 4.1

NPV tax cost of a three-year VAT cut (million euros)

	VAT cut applies to all subscribers	VAT cut applies to new subscribers
Direct effect on VAT	−222.6	−47.5
Increase on general taxation as a result of increased economic output	560.26	560.26
Net effect on taxes	337.66	512.76

Note: Model assumes that VAT is cut from 23 to 13 percent and the VAT cut is 100 percent passed through to retail prices. NPV is based on a social time preference discount rate of 3.5 percent (used by the UK Government's *HM Treasury Green Book*). We assume that the churn rate is 9 percent, but that a VAT cut targeted at "new subscribers" doubles the churn to 18 percent.

will generate tax revenue even if the impact on growth were to be a fraction of the estimated effect.

Longer Term Policy Considerations: Stimulating Basic Broadband Demand without Price Interventions The objectives of policy over the medium term should be to (1) close the gap in the use of broadband between Greece and the rest of the European Union, (2) provide a strong and predictable regulatory framework that supports competition and investments in broadband infrastructure, and (3) incentivize gradual investment in ultra-fast broadband infrastructure (i.e., fiber to the home or building—FTTH/B).

In relation to item 1, surveys of non-users of Internet services have indicated that there are three types of barriers to Internet adoption and use. In order of relevance: non-users do not see the relevance of the Internet to their lives ("not needed"),[41] non-users do not have the skills to use the Internet ("lack of skills"), and non-users cannot afford the equipment and/or telecommunications connection charges required to use the Internet.[42] Therefore measures should be taken to identify low user groups (e.g., elderly and low socioeconomic groups) and to teach e-skills to members of these groups. Although the evidence is limited as to the quantitative impact of such outreach efforts[43] in Greece and elsewhere,[44] policies that encourage the supply of native-language Internet-based applications and services could increase demand for the Internet; policies that enable access to and use of the mobile Internet could further give non-users a good way to build skills and confidence.[45]

In relation to item 2, mobile networks are expected to play a key role in delivering superfast broadband speeds.[46] In the absence of a second fixed infrastructure, facilitating competition between fixed and mobile broadband networks should support the objective of making superfast broadband services cheaper and more widely available. We recommend that the Greek government considers clearing the new sub-1 GHz spectrum (700 Mhz) band for the mobile Internet. Competition in fixed superfast broadband should also be supported.[47]

In relation to item 3, though the case for FTTH/B investment may be currently uncertain in Greece, such investments will be required in the longer term to maintain economic competitiveness and the delivery of public and other services.[48] In the absence of significant government funds that could be used to support FTTH/B rollout, policy intervention should consider the facilitation of "co-investment," whereby all operators in the Greek telecommunications market are provided with incentives to contribute to the necessary investment funds (we note that Vodafone and WIND have recently announced plans for a joint roll-out of FTTH infrastructure).

4.5.2   Energy—A Muddle[49] in Need of Substantial Reforms[50]

Objectives of the Third European Energy Package   The slow development of the Greek energy sector relative to that in other European countries and the sector's muddled future prospects can only be understood if set against the rapidly changing global and European environment. Important events at the global and European level in recent years have been the introduction of new fuels such as shale gas, the rapid growth in renewable energy sources (RES), large-scale changes on the global energy balance, and, most important in Europe, the implementation of the ambitious Third Energy Package.[51]

The main objectives of the Third Energy Package are[52] as follows:

• Strengthen the overall framework for a competitive internal European energy market, develop a common market design (the *target model*) for all member states, to achieve and promote market coupling—broadly, cross-border capacity trading.
• Facilitate cross-border trade and investment in energy, as well as regional cooperation, and achieve a higher utilization factor of the infrastructure such as the electrical interconnections.
• Separate effectively production and supply, which could be competitive, from transmission networks, which have natural monopoly characteristics (unbundling).
• Ensure the effectiveness and independence of national regulatory authorities (NRAs) and achieve greater market transparency on network operation and supply.
• Increase solidarity among the EU member states and promote consumer rights and their protection, in particular for vulnerable customer groups.
• Organize the cooperation at the EU level of NRAs (the ACER), and of electricity and gas transmission system operators (TSOs).[53]

The primary objective of the EU target model is to enhance cooperation among the TSOs and develop common market rules for all member states. This is expected to facilitate efficient use of installed or future infrastructure of electricity and natural gas systems across Europe and create the necessary market size for the development of supplementary markets (reserves, ancillary services). The resulting unbundled energy, capacity, and reserve products are expected to reduce uncertainty, promote investment decisions, and attract private funding, thus enhancing the security of supply and enabling more competition under stronger environmental restrictions.

The implementation of the target model in Greece calls for substantial structural and other reforms of the current market organization. We next describe the current state of the Greek energy market, and then discuss the required reforms.

Recent Developments and the Current Situation in Greece   The main features of the Greek electricity and natural gas markets in recent years are the following:[54]

• The "liberalized" parts of energy markets[55] have been and are still dominated in terms of market share by public monopolies (in production and in supply)—specifically, the Public Power Corporation (PPC[56]) controls[57] both production and supply in the electricity market (as can be seen in figure 4.8) and the Public Gas Corporation (DEPA) controls supply in natural gas.

• Electricity production suffers from serious cost asymmetries. PPC is the only firm using low-cost fuels for generation[58]—specifically, lignite and water, while its competitors rely on natural gas—something that, despite of the existence of the wholesale market in the form of a mandatory pool, makes it difficult to beat PPC's advantage at the retail level. Currently the market structure is highly concentrated, with cost asymmetries in electricity generation (and therefore lack of effective competition) and contractual obligations for importing natural gas from Russia (through the monopolist wholesaler) that were assumed over ten years ago.[59] These factors are inhibiting effective market liberalization and development and any cross-country market integration.

• Market liberalization and efficient regulatory enforcement have been impeded by the existence of too many decision centers. This has been particularly due to the Greek government's capacity as the majority shareholder of both PPC and DEPA.[60] The government is often displacing the National Regulatory Authority (RAE) in such matters as formulating the price structure to be applied to the different consumer groups (low-, medium-, and high-load customers).

• Price regulation, which is ongoing,[61] has been disastrous for the productive efficiency of PPC. Retail prices are set to cover the company's reported costs (also called "cost-plus regulation"), and there are no incentives to reduce costs. Moreover the access to lignite, a relatively cheap but finite energy source, has kept the domestic retail prices in Greece relatively low[62]—easing the pressure to identify and achieve cost efficiencies in the monopoly industries of the supply chain (i.e., in energy transmission and distribution).

• Electricity in the wholesale market has relied on the mandatory pool that obligates all producers and importers to make available each day, to a centralized pool administrator (LAGIE), whatever energy they wish to inject to the system and at specific prices. This information is used to determine the subsequent day's wholesale price (the system marginal price) based on the similarly expressed demand for energy. Originally the main intent of the mandatory pool was to facilitate or induce entry of new producers in the Greek electricity market, and indeed about ten years ago it did enable the gradual entry

a.

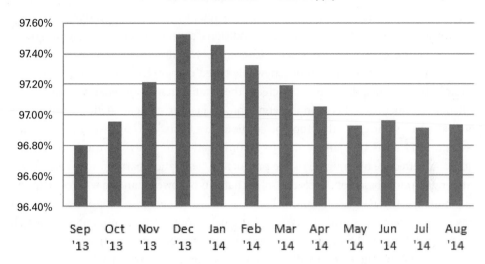

b.

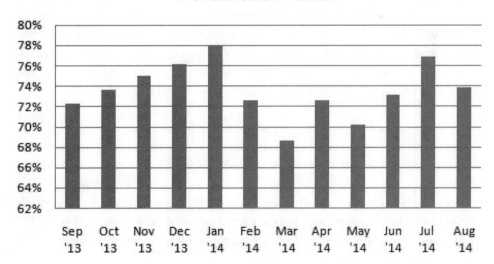

Figure 4.8
PPC market share in retail supply (a) and production (b)
Source: LAGIE

of three new independent producers operating gas stations. However, these benefits are now outweighed by substantial distortions associated with the market's operation. In particular, the cost-recovery mechanism allows relatively high-cost producers to operate, without taking a loss and under *all* conditions, simply by selling wholesale to the pool, a feature that is not conducive to efficiency.[63] Moreover substantial subsidies are available for the generation of renewable-based energy. These subsidies have been induced by the global initiative to increase the share of renewable energy sources.[64]

• Retail competition between energy producers or independent suppliers is nonexistent—some entry that took place about five to six years ago was not sustained beyond 2011. This was largely due to a combination of delays in the implementation of an effective opening up of the production/generation part of the market, regulated retail prices based on PPC's cost-plus that can be lower than the wholesale (pool) prices at which independent suppliers can purchase energy, the economic crisis that has reduced demand substantially,[65] and the behaviour of the dominant PPC, which led to limitations in the incentives of new entrants to compete effectively in the retail market.[66] PPC has now returned to a market share of 97 percent in the residential electricity retail market.

To lessen these problems in the Greek energy markets, we recommend a number of policy measures that are both structural (privatization/breakup of the PPC) and regulatory in nature. As we describe below, the first priority should be the removal of cost-plus regulation of retail prices and the introduction of a type of NOME (Nouvelle Organisation du Marche de l'Electricite) regulation for securing access by other producers and suppliers to the low-cost energy sources currently controlled by PPC.

Policy Priorities for Reform   As noted above, a top policy priority is that the Greek Energy Regulator (RAE) prepares the market rules to meet the EU target model requirements and implements the model. More specifically, Greek policy makers and the regulator should aim to change gradually the fuel mix so to reduce the cost asymmetries between producers that are a result of PPC's legacy as a public monopoly and owner of essentially all relatively cheap energy sources in Greece. They should focus on developing the natural gas supply options, with alternative natural gas supply links, and promoting investment in energy efficiency.[67]

For the implementation of the target model and the development of a more efficient and competitive energy market in Greece, a number of reforms should be undertaken:

1. *Restructure the wholesale electricity market to remove the distortions in its operation, as discussed above.*   In the short to medium run, the market could rely principally, as

it has in many other European and non-European countries, on a non-mandatory, bid-based, centralized spot market. The trading mechanism could be a discriminatory or a uniform-price auction. The market should be designed in a way that the existing capacity is used more efficiently and the current distortions are removed.[68] In the medium to long run, and with the right incentives for productive capacity and long-term investment put in place, we expect that Greece will converge to the European norm[69] whereby the majority of transactions are conducted by over-the-counter (OTC) bilateral contracts. Bilateral contracts would therefore be mandatory for all agents who participate in the NOME-type regulation, described below,[70] opening up retail entry and strengthening competition.

2. *Increase competition among existing producers by encouraging the entry of potential new market players and therefore reducing the risk of large price increases that could follow the removal of direct retail price regulation.*   Structural measures, whereby the low-cost lignite power stations of the PPC are privatized, could be effective in raising competition among existing firms, but could be considered at best a long-term solution as it has been impossible for many years to bridge the gap between the proposals of PPC's main shareholder (the government) and those of potential buyers. The privatization of part of the PPC (and creation of a private "small" PPC) is a viable alternative structure that has been proposed by some parties but is not currently on the policy agenda.[71]

3. *Provide rights of access to third parties/producers that currently operate high-cost gas stations and also to independent suppliers at a cost-oriented (benchmarked) price to the low-cost (lignite and hydro) capacity of PPC.*   This is a measure similar to that originally implemented in France in 2011 (NOME-type regulation) whereby the rights to access the low-cost nuclear power capacity of EDF were given to a number of competitors—with EDF controlling through its nuclear power capacity about 85 percent of production in France.[72]

   The introduction of a NOME-type regulation in Greece could, if properly executed, create a more symmetric market structure in terms of costs and capacities. Indeed a recent study by Courcoubetis et al. (2013) found that in a totally liberalized market operating either through a centralized uniform price wholesale market auction or through bilateral (OTC) contracts, this regulation can lower equilibrium prices in low- and medium-demand states, enabling third-party producers to increase their market share, their profits (which must be significant for new investment), and their retail presence.

4. *Replace the current cost-plus regulatory controls on prices for transmission and distribution with mechanisms that can provide stronger cost minimization incentives, such as multiple-year price controls.*[73]

5. *Reform the capacity assurance mechanism.* The current mechanism compensates with no distinction all the available thermal units without considering which units are needed in the long run. This often creates the wrong incentives for potential future investors. There is presently an ongoing discussion on reforming the capacity assurance mechanism, and it is important, in the context of this discussion, that the Greek TSO (ADMIE) has set long-term targets for the development of the system, provides estimates of the installed capacity that needs to be compensated, and defines which are the most flexible units that are necessary given the RES penetration in order to send the right investment or disinvestment signals.

It is worth noting here that these proposed reforms, especially the introduction of a NOME-type regulation, would have a beneficial impact in reducing the energy costs of the large energy-intensive industries in Greece. This is a key precondition for Greek firms to become competitive in international markets, in the wake of the unprecedented economic crisis that started in 2009, especially since their rivals abroad typically have access to lower cost energy. Under NOME these firms could purchase low-cost lignite energy in auctions directly or otherwise via a common wholesale market auction.[74]

6. *Raise the efficiency in the management of RES production. In this regard secure adequate financing and, most important, manage its impacts on market competition.* In the last few years incentives (through guaranteed high prices) to invest in RES have been responsible for exerting an upward pressure on retail prices. There is renewed thinking in Europe on re-visiting the policies in order to lower CO_2 emissions while maintaining competitive energy costs. Greece should adapt its policy accordingly—especially in terms of continuing to provide incentives for *more* investment in expensive RES.

7. *Improve the capability of the energy regulator.* The energy regulator has to undertake the challenging tasks of designing network price controls, retail price controls (with the regulator deciding the period of phase out, triggers for phasing out, basis of price controls), price controls for the capacity release, and any other regulated tariffs in a way that does not undermine investment incentives and also the implementation of measures that will secure the growth of more competition in the market.

4.6   Concluding Remarks

The deep economic crisis that started in Greece in 2009 was a long time coming. Virtually every international index of competitiveness indicated that the economy was suffering along many dimensions: high obstacles to entrepreneurship and investment, extensive state control, heavy and inefficient regulations, corruption, and lack of effective competition. An article in *Newsweek*[75] described Greece as a country that is "unique in its dysfunctionality" and as "the most wasteful and corrupt Western nation." Another article noted that Greeks "behave as a collection of atomized particles, each of which has grown accustomed to pursuing its own interest at the expense of the common good." [76]

Nevertheless, in the midst of the most serious fiscal crisis that Greece has ever experienced, the Greek government has already undertaken a concerted effort "to change these facts" and has "started with the abolition of some of the strict regulations in various sectors of the economy that are for the first time being freed up to competition." OECD named Greece as a "champion in terms of reforms" for 2012.[77] All international indicators are now showing a reversal of the previous negative trend for Greece. The effort and the achievements so far are unprecedented and impressive. Of course, despite the significant progress, there remains much room for improvement before Greece can regain its international competitiveness. Important structural changes are still needed to reform and privatize public enterprises, liberalize product and service markets, remove unnecessary and distortive regulations, and strengthen independent sectoral regulatory bodies. These reforms are critical for the productive potential of the economy. Simultaneously, a long-term strategy could be launched in the form of a coherent National Competition and Competitiveness Policy that would create the conditions for innovative and sustainable growth. No doubt, we are moving in the right direction, but we do need to do more.[78]

Notes

1. We have benefited from discussions with Dimitris Vayanos and Nikos Vettas and from comments of the participants at the Workshop on Reforming the Greek Economy, Athens, May 27 to 28, 2013, in which a preliminary version of the paper was presented. We are also grateful to Galateia Makri for excellent research assistance. Katsoulacos acknowledges research support from the Bank of Greece, the Hellenic Federation of Enterprises, and the Greek Ministry's of Education Program "Excellence in Research (ARISTEIA)," Research Grant 2591 (CoLEG).

2. The sectors are food processing, retail trade, building materials, and tourism.

3. See OECD (2014, p. 3).

4. For more detailed discussion, see Katsoulacos and Makri (2013).

5. Various components of these indicators are based on "soft data," collected from question-naires reflecting the respondents' attitudes and opinions. Hence these indicators incorporate a great deal of subjectivity, which might not be fully comparable across countries. But there is a common pattern that emerges from the evolution of these indicators, and this is what we focus on.

6. Note that the number of countries included in the report varies from year to year (the average number is approximately 133 countries), so any time series comparisons should be viewed cautiously. Changes in the number of countries could affect Greece's position in the ranking. If a more competitive country (even of lower income) drops out of the sample, the position of Greece will improve. Greece's position will instead deteriorate if such a country is introduced in the sample. Furthermore entry or exit of a country less competitive then Greece would not affect Greece's position, given that the ranking here reflects the absolute position of the country and not its percentile rank. Nevertheless, these indexes are widely used, and with the trend for Greece being so clear and strong, these other factors are likely to be only secondary.

7. Equally important is the fact that the state has a big presence in various product markets through state-owned (or controlled) firms. The state has proved to be an inefficient producer and has distorted healthy competition. This has led to a call for a large-scale program of privatizations, a topic covered in another chapter of this book.

8. To be fair, not all these decisions are new regulations. A number of them are simply adminis-trative decisions that tend to stay constant over time. Yet, the sheer number of decisions provides a good picture of the administrative burden.

9. Two excellent examples are the recent ex post policy evaluations for environmental licensing and transportation from the Hellenic Federation of Enterprises.

10. The first major amendment took place in 1995, and was followed by amendments in 2000, 2005, and 2011.

11. An economic analysis of competition in oligopolistic markets was recently applied in a case concerning abuse of dominance by a major multinational producer in the food industry (Pepsico/ Tasty). The firm was alleged to be abusive by the HCC on the basis of its high market share but without any attempt to link its alleged behavior to any detrimental effects on competition and consumer welfare. Indeed, over the period of the alleged oligopolistic practices, the market share of the firm had not strengthened or declined and its prices were falling despite increasing costs of raw materials.

12. Effects-based (or *economics-based*) assessment procedures have been used for many years in the United States, Canada, Australia, England, Ireland (the term often used is *rule-of-reason*), and more recently adopted and used by the European Commission and many EU countries. It is generally assumed that such procedures lead to fewer type I and type II decision errors by

authorities and that they also have beneficial deterrent effects (see also Katsoulacos and Ulph 2009). The importance of relying on sound economic analysis has often been stressed by OECD. For example, in its recent report evaluating the Russian competition authority that has in the last few years become the largest authority in the world, the OECD makes as its top recommendation that the authority must "improve the quality of economic analysis and its application to competition enforcement throughout the competition authority and in support of improved judicial decisions" (OECD 2013).

13. It is worth noting that this kind of legal formalism is typical of the approach followed more generally by the public administration in Greece. This approach is particularly reprehensible because, as stated in a recent report by the OECD (2011a), it is the cause of much of the enormous corruption in Greece.

14. In fact there has never been a president of the Commission who is an economist (unlike in many other European countries). As a result important issues, which are basically economic, are examined and evaluated by legal experts and the final decisions are based on legal experts' opinions alone even when the recommendation of economists point to different directions and conclusions. It should be noted that the position of a chief economist in the HCC is allowed under the new (2011) competition law, but the position still remains empty. We make these comments not to imply that we underrate the importance of the group of economists in the Commission but that there should be more economists trained at the highest (PhD) level, more investment in the continual development of their expertise through educational opportunities, and more input of these economists in decision-making.

15. Not including alternate members.

16. In one such case concerning an important industrial sector, a decision is being under consideration for about six years.

17. Indeed it ranked 92nd, in the latest 2013–14 report, as shown in figure 4.3. Nevertheless, it should be noted that there *are* signs of an improvement in enforcement procedures in the last two or three years. Efforts have been made to reduce delays and to process an increasing number of cases.

18. An OECD-managed project, in partnership with the HCC, which aimed at identifying rules and regulations that may hinder competition and prevent the proper functioning of markets (see OECD 2014).

19. Our proposal combines features of the existing British and Australian institutional structures that are responsible for controlling and potentially abolishing existing regulations and for monitoring the adoption of new regulations to make sure that they are necessary and proportional to the need that they are supposed to address.

20. The structure proposed in this paragraph and that immediately after, follows closely the British model that went through extensive review and reforms as late as 2012.

21. Called VDSL (very high bit rate digital subscriber line).

22. In a recent study for the Global Special Mobile Association (GSMA 2014) on single wholesale networks in mobile communications, technological advances through mobile spectrum efficiency were estimated to increase the capacity available by around 25 percent annually.

23. In the same 2014 study for the GSMA, it was estimated that competition between mobile networks resulted in the 3G take-up being 17 percent higher than in countries where mobile services were offered monopolistically.

24. See Athens University of Economics and Business (2011), Department of Management Science and Technology and ICAP, *Ανανέωση Μεθοδολογίας για τον Υπολογισμό του Δείκτη Τιμών Καταναλωτή του Κλάδου της Κινητής Τηλεφωνίας*.

25. See OECD (2011b), and references therein, and also ITU (2012).

26. A review of the factors that are hindering wider use of broadband among individuals, firms, and the government can be found in the study by Troulos, Demian, and Tsakanikas (2012).

27. Eurostat, Households, Level of Internet access, see http://appsso.eurostat.ec.europa.eu/nui/show.do?dataset=isoc_ci_in_h.

28. European Commission (2014, slide 24).

29. Frontier Economics (2014).

30. European Commission (2014, slide 26).

31. See Czernich et al. (2011), Koutroumpis (2009), and Qiang and Rossotto (2009).

32. See ITU (2012).

33. These estimates concern the average level of broadband penetration in the sample of the countries included in the analysis. As the studies cover a number of years when broadband penetration was growing, the average would be expected to be lower than the level of broadband penetration in Greece.

34. Section 7 of the ITU study provides a good description. Greece has also adopted recently a policy under the EU funded program of digital Αλληλεγγύη (solidarity)—however, eligibility was limited (up to 290,000 households), and was of limited duration (one year).

35. As consumers and SMEs realize the benefits of basic broadband, they will likely want to upgrade their computing and other technologies and demand services that require higher bandwidth.

36. Factors such as computer literacy, availability of information/services, and availability of content (e.g., movies, games, advanced information services) are expected to affect the demand for broadband (see ITU 2012, sec. 7.5, and Troulos, Demian, and Tsakanikas 2012). Policies to stimulate demand by the development of such factors will have an impact in the longer term.

37. We based our estimates of own price elasticity of demand on the midpoint of two relatively recent estimates. We have assumed an elasticity of –0.71 which is the midpoint of –0.44 (Rosston et al. 2010) and 0.97 (Cardona et al. 2009).

38. We consider first-order VAT effects, that is, lower VAT revenues from "existing" broadband subscribers (or subscribers who would have taken up broadband at the preexisting VAT rates), and increased broadband VAT revenues from "new" broadband subscribers partially offset by the lower VAT from "new" broadband subscribers switching from higher VAT products. We then consider second-order VAT effects, that is, higher VAT from existing consumers who receive an income "windfall" as a result of the VAT reduction. Provided that a proportion of this increase is spent rather than saved, VAT revenues will increase accordingly.

39. Our analysis uses estimates derived from Czernich et al. (2011) that relate broadband penetration to economic growth in order to calculate the increase in GDP that can be attributed to the policy. Czernich et al. report a low and a high estimate, of which a midpoint is taken for the main cases. They find that the GDP effect of broadband penetration is immediate, so lags are not incorporated into the model.

40. The full results and assumptions can be found in Frontier Economics (2014).

41. According to the 2009 Ofcom survey (see Ofcom 2009), among those who responded *Not needed* as the main barrier to Internet use, their "knowledge of the Internet was low," with 95 percent professing little or no knowledge.

42. In studies examining the relative significance of the different factors, price ranks below relevance/skills (e.g., see the summary in Troulos, Demian, and Tsakanikas 2012). Policies to stimulate demand other than price reductions are also important.

43. See Hauge and Prieger (2009).

44. A problem is that often such schemes do not include explicitly quantified targets.

45. In the survey undertaken by Ofcom (2009), on the question of facilitating Internet use and adoption, 72 percent of those who said they intended to get the Internet at home over the next six months were already Internet users outside the home. People who regularly use the Internet at work or at school are likely to get the Internet at home. The study by Troulos, Demian, and Tsakanikas (2012) provides a summary of some other measures from a survey of Greek businesses and consumers.

46. Deployment of fourth-generation technology would deliver download speeds of up to 100 Mbps.

47. Local loop unbundling has been a success in Greece, but the government should ensure that OTE's downstream rivals are provided access to its VDSL network at prices that sustain the level of the existing copper-based competition, while maintaining OTE's incentives to roll out its VDSL network.

48. The EU digital agenda target for 2020 is for 50 percent of the member states to subscribe to broadband with speeds of over 100 Mbps.

49. The confused and troubling present situation in the Greek energy market persists even though the Greek Regulatory Authority for Energy (RAE) has in recent years suggested many

necessary reforms, as will be discussed in this section. In brief, this is due to too many decision centers with conflicting objectives attempting to influence policy.

50. We would like to thank Miltos Aslanoglou and George Stamoulis for very useful comments on an earlier version of this section and Anastasios Mastrapas and Ioannis Psarros, recent postgraduates of the Economics Department for comments and excellent research assistance in preparing this section.

51. The Third Energy Package is a legislative package for an internal gas and electricity market that is intended to further open up the gas and electricity markets in the European Union. The Directive was adopted by the European Parliament and the Council of the European Union in July 2009 and has been in effect since September 3, 2009.

52. For a summary, see Aslanoglou (2013, p. 3); Aslanoglou is vice-chairman of the Greek RAE. See also CRESSE (2013). The target model provides for four levels of transactions: day-ahead markets (coupling of markets, uniform pricing), intraday markets (regional markets), balancing markets (operated by the TSOs), and forward markets (based on cross-border trading activity).

53. TSOs are entrusted with transporting energy in the form of electrical power (or natural gas) from generation plants (or after receiving it from producers) over the electrical grid (or via pipeline) to local distribution operators.

54. The markets for electricity and natural gas are distinct though linked. This is because for the final user of energy, electricity and natural gas can be substitutes, and also because natural gas can be used for the production of electricity.

55. We focus on the monopoly of production and supply (both wholesale and retail), and exclude the natural monopoly of transmission and distribution.

56. At the present time the state is still PPC's majority shareholder. Over the last few months there have been government announcements about privatizing PPC and creating a "small PPC" in which the state would not be the majority shareholder.

57. PPC shares exceed, on average, 70 percent in production and are close to 100 percent (97 percent in 2014) in retail supply, as shown in figure 4.8. DEPA essentially controls 100 percent of the supply of natural gas.

58. There is no precise estimate of the cost gap between lignite and natural gas generation. PPC's customers estimate it at about 40 euro/MWh (given a cost of 35 euro/MWh for lignite and 75 euro/MWh for gas—though PPC insists that lignite cost is 57 euro/MWh).

59. PPC's competitors rely on a high-price supplier (Gazprom) for their natural gas needs. Clearly, it is not just Greece that is paying high prices, and consequently DGCOMP has confronted Gazprom for abuse of its dominant position with excessive gas prices to its European customers.

60. DEPA is in the process of been privatized too and considering an offer from an Azeri company called SOCAR.

61. The formal *ex ante* retail price regulation by RAE was to have been terminated on July 1, 2013. However, the government, as the majority shareholder, has retained the right to continue to set prices. RAE, of course, can set price ceilings and regulate *ex post* excessive pricing on the basis of Competition Law.

62. Between 2011 and 2013 household electricity prices were below the EU28 average though gas prices were among the highest (see Eurostat Energy Prices).

63. For an extensive summary, see Courcoubetis et al. (2012).

64. Environmental factors have mandated the development of renewable energy sources, though they are more expensive. The supply of energy from these sources now takes priority in the operation of the mandatory pool system.

65. The drop in demand and the massive expansion of the system to include renewable energy sources (RES) have generated an overcapacity problem. Of course, the reforms discussed below would be desirable even in the absence of the significant drop in demand.

66. For a detailed analysis, see Courcoubetis et al. (2012).

67. These are the stated objectives of the Greek energy regulator (e.g., see Aslanoglou 2013). As Aslanoglou notes, the current organization of the Greek electricity wholesale market does not allow for the efficient coupling with neighboring markets, that is, it cannot support the implementation of the target model requirements.

68. Uniform price auctions have been used extensively in the United States and in the Scandinavian countries; the best example of the application of discriminatory auctions is that of United Kingdom in the last 13 years or so. The advantages and disadvantages of these two alternative auction designs have been discussed extensively in the literature, both in general and specifically in the context of electricity markets, for example, by Fabra et al. (2006). Of course, a restructuring of the wholesale market will not on its own produce the desirable effects if it is not undertaken in conjunction with the other reforms mentioned below.

69. See, for example, Pototschnig (2012).

70. This is, indeed, a critical point in the EU-ECB-IMF proposals for reforming the Greek energy market, and an argument in support of NOME-type regulation in Greece.

71. The proposal by the previous New Democracy-PASOK government to create a "small (privatized) PPC" that would own a part of PPC's lignite capacity would reduce the risk of significant price increases when the market is effectively deregulated (something that has not yet happened, as we mentioned before), provided that the creation of a small PPC led to competition between two independent cost-symmetric producers operating lignite stations. This could render unnecessary the introduction of NOME-type regulatory measures discussed below. The change in government following the national election of 25 January 2015 has removed this proposal from the policy agenda at least for the foreseeable future.

72. It is important to note that the situation in Greece differs from that of France. While EDF produces essentially with its nuclear power stations, PPC in Greece has a more balanced capacity portfolio, 55 percent of which is accounted for by low-cost lignite stations. For a review of the arguments for and against the NOME regulation see the report of Courcoubetis et al. (2012). No decisions have yet been taken concerning the fraction of lignite capacity to which there will be access through this regulation if/when it is implemented.

73. A consultation issued in December 2013, led to a decision (340/2014) in June 2014 on the principles governing the regulation of IPTO after privatization—regardless of its ownership. High-level principles were established for the interim period 2015–2017, and signals were provided on the enduring arrangements that will apply from 2018 onward. A key feature of the proposals is that the current cost-plus price regulatory regime will be replaced by a multi year revenue cap regime. The enduring arrangements that were envisioned involve the introduction of incentives to improve efficiency by outperforming the targets set, and incentives to improve Greece's quality of service performance, under the four-year price control cycles.

74. This has indeed been a major issue behind the motivation for introducing a NOME-type regulation in Greece.

75. See *Newsweek*, "How Europe's new goals will pay off," December 24, 2010.

76. See *Vanity Fair*, "Beware of Greeks bearing bonds," October 1, 2010.

77. See *Kathimerini*, "OECD praises reforms in Greece," February 15, 2013.

78. We effectively finalized our chapter at the beginning of 2015. Since then Greece has experienced two national elections, a referendum, and the imposition of capital controls. Previous reform efforts have been slowed or halted, and as a result the country has started to slip again in international competitiveness indicators (e.g., Greece moved down five places to 86th position in the 2016 Global Competitiveness report). It remains to be seen if this reversal is temporary and if structural changes will continue with renewed impetus.

References

Aghion, P., N. Bloom, R. Blundell, R. Griffith, and P. Howitt. 2005. Competition and innovation: An inverted-U relationship. *Quarterly Journal of Economics* 120 (2): 701–728.

Aslanoglou, M. 2013. Electricity market reform in Greece: No time to waste. Presentation at the CRESSE Annual Conference: Special Policy Lecture on Energy Markets. Available at http://www.cresse.info/.

Athens University of Economics and Business. 2011. Ανανέωση Μεθοδολογίας για τον Υπολογισμό του Δείκτη Τιμών Καταναλωτή του Κλάδου της Κινητής Τηλεφωνίας (Update of the methodology for the calculation of the consumer price index for the mobile telecommunications sector). Department of Management Science and Technology, and ICAP, February.

Blanchard, O. 2004. The economic future of Europe. *Journal of Economic Perspectives* 18 (4): 3–26.

Blanchflower, D., and S. Machin. 1996. Product market competition wages and productivity: International evidence from establishment-level data. [GENES issue] *Annales d'Economie et de Statistique* 41–42:219–253.

Bloom, N., C. Genakos, R. Sadun, and J. Van Reenen. 2012. Management practices across firms and countries. *Academy of Management Perspectives* 26 (1): 12–33.

Bloom, N., M. Draca, and J. Van Reenen. 2016. Trade induced technical change: The impact of Chinese imports on innovation, diffusion and productivity. *Review of Economic Studies* 83 (1): 87–117.

Blundell, R., R. Griffiths, and J. Van Reenen. 1999. Market share, market value and innovation in a panel of British manufacturing firms. *Review of Economic Studies* 66 (3): 529–54.

Buccirossi, P., L. Ciari, T. Duso, G. Spagnolo, and C. Vitale. 2011. Measuring the deterrence effect of competition policy: The competition policy indices. *Journal of Competition Law and Economics* 7: 165–204.

Cardona, Mélisande, Anton Schwarz, B. Burcin Yurtoglu, and Christine Zulehner. 2009. Demand estimation and market definition for broadband Internet services. *Journal of Regulatory Economics* 35 (1): 70–95.

Courcoubetis, K., Y. Katsoulacos, and G. Stamoulis. 2012. Issues of regulation in relation to the Greek wholesale electricity market in view of the reforms required in order to implement the target model (in Greek). Report prepared for RAE, July 2012. (Short version published as "Implications for the Greek electricity market of third-party access to the low-cost production of PPC" in *Essays in Applied Economics and Finance*, edited by Y. Katsoulacos, Athens: AUEB Publications, 2013 (in Greek)).

Courcoubetis K., Y. Katsoulacos, and G. Stamoulis. 2013. The optimal design of a NOME-type regulation in Greece. Report prepared for RAE (in English), September 2013, available from the authors on request.

CRESSE. 2013. Annual Conference: Special Policy Lecture on Energy Markets. Available at http://www.cresse.info/.

Czernich, N., O. Falck, T. Kretschmer, and L. Woessman. 2011. Broadband infrastructure and economic growth. *Economic Journal* 121 (552): 505–32.

European Commission. 2014. Broadband markets, digital agenda scoreboard. Brussels.

Fabra, N., N.-H. M. von der Fehr, and N. H. Harbord. 2006. Designing electricity auctions. *Rand Journal of Economics* 37:23–46.

Frontier Economics. 2014. Broadband take-up and economic growth in Greece. Mimeo (available on request). London.

Genakos, C., P. Koutroumpis, and M. Pagliero. 2014. The impact of markup regulation on prices. Discussion paper 10243. CEPR, Washington, DC.

GSMA. 2014. Assessing the case for single wholesale networks in mobile communications. GSMA Europe, London.

Hauge, J. A., and J. E. Prieger. 2009. Demand-side programs to stimulate adoption of broadband: What works? Working paper. http://papers.ssrn.com/sol3/papers.cfm?abstract_id=1492342.

IOBE. 2014a. Assessing the macroeconomic impact of structural reforms in Greece. Policy paper. IOBE Foundation for Economic and Industrial Research, Athens.

IOBE. 2014b. State of play of liberalization and remaining barriers in professions and services in engineering, technical and related sectors in Greece. Policy paper. IOBE Foundation for Economic and Industrial Research, Athens.

IOBE. 2014c. State of play of liberalization and remaining barriers in professions and services. Policy paper. IOBE Foundation for Economic and Industrial Research, Athens.

ITU. 2012. *The Impact of Broadband on the Economy: Research to Date and Policy Issues*. Geneva.

Katsoulacos, Y., and G. Makri. 2013. Greece's competitiveness and regulatory burden: Towards a national competition and competitiveness policy. Report funded by the Hellenic Federation of Enterprises (SEV), Athens.

Katsoulacos, Y., and D. Ulph. 2009. Optimal legal standards for competition policy. *Journal of Industrial Economics* 57 (3): 410–37.

Koutroumpis, P. 2009. The economic impact of broadband on growth: A simultaneous approach. *Telecommunications Policy* 33: 471–85.

Loukas D. 2014. Greece: Diversifying and expanding advocacy efforts and outreach activities in view of the ongoing financial crisis. *CPI Antitrust Chronicle* (August): 1.

Nickell, S. 1996. Competition and corporate performance. *Journal of Political Economy* 104: 724–46.

Nicoletti, G., S. Scarpetta, and O. Boylaud. 1999. Summary indicators of product market regulation with an extension to employment protection legislation. Working paper 226. OECD Economics Department, Paris.

OECD. 2001. *Regulatory Reform in Greece*. Paris: OECD Reviews of Regulatory Reform.

OECD. 2009a. *Indicators of Regulatory Management Systems*. Paris: Regulatory Policy

OECD. 2011a. *Greece: Functional Review of the Central Administration in Greece*. Paris: OECD Economic Surveys.

OECD. 2011b. *National Broadband Plans: The Economic Effects of Broadband Access*. Paris: OECD.

OECD. 2013. Recommendations for future action by the Russian authorities to improve competition law, policy and practice. Report prepared by OECD Competition Committee, Paris.

OECD. 2014. *OECD Competition Assessment Reviews: Greece*. Paris: OECD.

Ofcom. 2009. Accessing the Internet at home. Research document. http://stakeholders.ofcom .org.uk/binaries/research/telecoms-research/bbathome.pdf.

Pototschnig, A. 2012. Electricity markets: The wholesale electricity market. Florence School of Regulation, Robert Schuman Centre for Advanced Studies. European University Institute, San Domenico di Fiesole, Italy.

Qiang, C., and C. Rossotto. 2009. Economic impacts of broadband. In *Information and Communication for Development Extending Reach and Increasing Impact.* Washington, DC: World Bank, ch. 3.

Rosston, G. L., S. J. Savage, and D. M. Waldman. 2010. Household demand for broadband Internet in 2010. *B.E. Journal of Economic Analysis and Policy* 10 (1).

Sala-i-Martín, X., and E. V. Artadi. 2004. The global competitiveness index. *The Global Competitiveness Report 2004–2005.* Hampshire: Palgrave Macmillan, 51–80.

Scarpetta, S., and T. Tressel. 2002. Productivity and convergence in a panel of OECD industries: Do regulations and institutions matter? Working paper 342. OECD Economics Department, Paris.

Troulos, C., E. Demian, and A. Tsakanikas. 2012. *Making the Internet Thrive in Greece.* Athens: IOBE.

Van Wijnbergen, S., and A. J. Venables. 1993. Location choice. Discussion paper dp0177, Centre for Economic Performance, LSE.

World Economic Forum. *The Global Competitiveness Reports 2001–14.* Cologny, Switzerland: WEF.

5   Privatizations: Auction and Market Design during a Crisis[1]

Vasiliki Skreta

5.1   Introduction

Privatizations are one of the central pillars of Greece's adjustment program. They have been viewed as essential partly because the public sector in Greece is large and inefficient. Figure 5.1 provides evidence on the size of the public sector: in 2008 Greece was ranked second among all OECD countries in terms of state control and public ownership of productive assets.

The large size of the public sector is associated with high inefficiencies. The national rail company—TRAINOSE—was among the most inefficient rail companies in the OECD (Oum and Yu 1994). Its restructuring in 2010 and 2011 cost 1.4 billion euros to taxpayers. The national airline—Olympic Airways—received 41 million euros of state aid in 2002 alone, which was given to the airline as part of an unsuccessful restructuring. Greece's main port, Piraeus, was operating so inefficiently that following the sale of part of the port to the Chinese company COSCO, output more than tripled over three years (2010 to 2012). For comparison, output increased by only 20 percent in the other Greek ports, which were state run, during the same period.

Privatizing state assets can lead to large efficiency gains through better management and de-politicization, increasing productivity both in the privatized firms and throughout the economy. It can also bring much needed investment and hence promote economic growth. Such investment would not be possible from public funds given Greece's financial situation. An additional benefit to privatizing state assets is that this would help reduce the public debt.

Privatizations taking place in periods of crisis can be pivotal for the economic prosperity of a country. On one hand, a well-designed and executed privatization program can generate funds and can function as a vehicle toward growth and prosperity as it did in Chile (see Gutierrez, Serra, and Fischer 2003) and in other countries. On the other hand, a poorly designed and executed program may unjustifiably enrich few

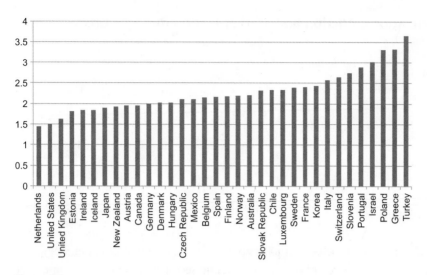

Figure 5.1
State control and public ownership (2008). The index takes values from 0 to 6, with 0 corresponding to least state involvement
Source: OECD (2013) Product Market Regulation Database

well-connected individuals and create "oligarchs" as happened in Russia (see Roland 2008) and in Mexico.

Badly designed and executed privatizations are undesirable not only because the sale does not generate revenue for the state but also because the high prices and lack of competition that may prevail after privatization inhibit economic growth in other sectors as well. For example, assigning monopoly rights for telecommunications to Carlos Slim in Mexico not only created one of the richest men in the world but, more important, the high prices for telecommunications that have prevailed post-privatization have inhibited Mexico's growth (see Acemoglu and Robinson 2012). Poorly allocated public assets create distortions through other channels as well: because few "connected" businesspeople benefit, the status quo is strengthened. Those are often the interests that block the adoption and implementation of beneficial reforms and perpetuate a vicious circle of excessive market power, rent extraction, increasing inequality and slow growth.

The initial target of Greece's privatization program was to sell 50 billion euros of assets in the period 2011 to 2015. As of December 2014, however, only 7.7 billion were raised, and subsequent targets stood at 11 billion by 2016, 22 billion by 2020, and 45 billion in the long term. Moreover the 7.7 billion figure included some privatizations for which agreements with the buyers had not been finalized and funds had not been disbursed. Therefore the target of 50 billion during 2011 to 2015 was missed by a wide margin.

The target was undershot in part because of the way the privatization process was run, but the main causes are deeper and more systemic (e.g., see Vettas 2015). Greece experienced a massive decline in investment during the crisis: investment ranged between 20 and 25 percent of GDP from 2000 to 2009 but fell to 11 percent of (the already much lower) GDP in 2013 and 2014. The picture becomes even bleaker when considering foreign direct investment (FDI). FDI in Greece during 2000 to 2008 was only about 1 percent of GDP, well below the OECD average. It declined further to 0.66 percent of GDP in 2009 to 2013. The corresponding figure for Portugal is 2.5 percent, for Spain 2.1 percent, and for Germany 1.1 percent. Given Greece's chronic difficulty to attract FDI, and the decline of even domestic investment during the crisis, it is not surprising that Greece's privatization program yielded weak results. Some of the key challenges of Greece's privatization program, analyzed in this chapter, are closely related to the reasons behind the chronically low FDI.

This chapter has three main goals. One goal is to give an account of privatizations in Greece, both before and during the crisis. This is done in section 5.2, and section 5.3 then analyzes the challenges of Greece's privatization program. A second goal of the chapter is to offer a framework to evaluate the costs and benefits of privatizations, based both on theory and on empirical evidence. This is done in section 5.4. The large volume of empirical evidence reviewed in that section indicates that privatizations raise output and productivity significantly, while the effects on prices and investment are less clear-cut. A third goal of the chapter is to provide insights from economic theory on how privatizations should be best organized, such as whether to sell or to lease an asset, whether to sell all or part of the asset, or how to structure the selling procedure. This is done in section 5.5. Section 5.6 draws implications for the design of Greece's privatization program, and section 5.7 concludes.

5.2 Privatizations in Greece

5.2.1 Privatizations before the Crisis

Greece raised roughly 31 billion euros from privatizations between January 1991 and June 2011, right before the privatization agency was established. This is a significant amount when compared to the 7.7 billion euros raised from July 2011 to December 2014. Assets that were privatized before the crisis included banks, manufacturing companies, telecommunications companies, parts of electric and water utilities, and rights to operate the main port. Most transactions consisted of sales of a percentage of shares. Roughly half were private sales (PS) and half public offerings (PO). Table 5.1 lists the main sales (above 100 mil euros) that took place between January 1991 and June 2011.[2]

Unfortunately, only few studies attempt to systematically evaluate the impact that pre-crisis privatizations had on the productivity of Greek firms. One reason might be that the main privatizations were very gradual and partial. The state either retained direct control or remained indirectly involved, for example, in dealing with labor union demands (Pagoulatos 2005; Antoniades 1997). Pagoulatos and Zahariadis (2011) document how costly and lengthy it was for the Greek state to deal with the demands of the OTE (the former state telecommunication monopoly) labor union. They find that despite the long tensions, the overall OTE privatization improved efficiency and reliability.[3]

5.2.2   Privatizations during the Crisis

With privatizations as one of the main tasks of the adjustment program, Greece was asked to form an independent privatization agency to run the large-scale privatization program professionally, efficiently, and without political intervention. In response to this request, the Greek government formed the Hellenic Republic Asset Development Fund—HRADF.[4] As of December 2014, HRADF's portfolio consisted of 10 corporate assets, 22 infrastructure assets, and 1,000 real estate properties. According to the HRADF December 2014 Progress Report, the total value of the transactions that HRADF performed since its inception was 7.7 billion euros, out of which 3.1 billion had been received.

The privatization process during the crisis has had successes and failures. On the negative side, revenues were well below target and perhaps some of the assets could have attracted more bidders and higher prices. On the positive side, there has been progress in organizing the assets that could be sold, in setting up rules and procedures, and in selling some important assets. The Fund's main achievements were:

Evaluation of properties   More than 80,000 properties have been initially accessed, and 1,000 have been transferred to HRADF. The effort of evaluating 80,000 properties has been immense, as Greece's land registry is not comprehensive and up to date.

Regulatory and legal reforms   At HRADF's initiative, more than 100 regulatory, administrative, and technical barriers that were slowing down privatizations have been lifted.

Table 5.1

Company name	Industry	Year	Price (€ mil)	Sales (%)	Type of sale
Heracles General Cement Co SA	Manufacturing	1992	599.20	69.8	PS
Chandris	Transportation Industry	1992	186.03	NA	PS
Elefsis Shipyards SA	Manufacturing	1992	347.70	100	PS
OTE (Hellenic Telecom Organization)	Telecommunications	1996	400.81	7.6	PO
OTE (Hellenic Telecom Organization)	Telecommunications	1997	1045.42	12.4	PO
OTE (Hellenic Telecom Organization)	Telecommunications	1998	371.98	3.5	PO
Hellenic Petroleum	Petroleum industry	1998	253.66	23	PO
OTE (Hellenic Telecom Organization)	Telecommunications	1998	948.31	15	PO
National Bank of Greece SA	Finance and real estate industry	1999	514.66	4	PO
Athens Paper Mill SA	Manufacturing	1999	111.62	100	PS
OTE (Hellenic Telecom Organization)	Telecommunications	1999	910.83	14.1	PO
National Bank of Greece SA	Finance and real estate industry	1999	281.75	2	PO
Hellenic Duty Free Shops	Trade industry	1999	161.07	25	PS
Hellenic Industrial Development Bank SA	Finance and real estate industry	1999	370.21	25	PO
Hellenic Petroleum	Petroleum industry	1999	426.11	11.5	PS
EYDAP S.A.	Utilities	1999	196.17	25	PO
Hellenic Petroleum	Petroleum industry	2000	330.21	15	PO
CosmOTE	Telecommunications	2000	375.42	11.02	PO
Agricultural Bank of Greece	Finance and real estate industry	2000	279.80	7	PO
Public Power Corporation SA	Utilities	2001	364.35	15.09	PO
OTE (Hellenic Telecom Organization)	Telecommunications	2002	583.96	8	PO
Opap	Services industry	2002	407.32	19	PO
Public Power Corporation SA	Utilities	2002	301.28	13.2	PO
Hellenic Petroleum	Petroleum industry	2003	357.36	16.65	PS
Opap	Services industry	2003	660.79	24.6	PO
National Bank of Greece SA	Finance and real estate industry	2003	536.80	11	PO

Table 5.1 (continued)

Company name	Industry	Year	Price (€ mil)	Sales (%)	Type of sale
Public Power Corporation SA	Utilities	2003	664.42	15.7	PO
General Hellenic Bank	Finance and real estate industry	2004	143.82	50.01	PS
Hellenic Petroleum	Petroleum Industry	2004	220.57	8.21	PS
National Bank of Greece SA	Finance and real estate industry	2004	674.84	7.46	PO
Opap	Services industry	2005	1412.54	16.4	PO
OTE (Hellenic Telecom Organization)	Telecommunications	2005	964.50	10	PO
Agricultural Bank of Greece	Finance and real estate industry	2006	391.88	7.23	PO
Postal Savings Bank	Finance and real estate industry	2006	737.66	35	PO
Emporiki Bank	Finance and real estate industry	2006	2078.00	36.56	PS
OTE (Hellenic Telecom Organization)	Telecommunications	2007	1382.23	10.7	PO
Greek Postal Savings Bank	Finance and real estate industry	2007	652.14	20	PO
OTE (Hellenic Telecom Organization)	Telecommunications	2008	636.24	3	PS
Port Of Piraeus (35-year concession)	Transportation industry	2008	3999.74	100	PS
Olympic Airlines	Transportation industry	2009	237.45	100	PS
OTE MTS Holding BV	Telecommunications	2009	233.34	100	PS
OTE (Hellenic Telecom Organization)	Telecommunications	2009	903.16	5	PS
Alpha Bank	Finance and real estate industry	2009	1259.60	Preferred Shares	PS
Hellenic Postbank	Finance and real estate industry	2011	280.26	Preferred Shares	PS
Attica Bank	Finance and real estate industry	2011	126.50	Preferred Shares	PS
OTE SA	Telecommunications	2011	544.20	10	PS
Agricultural Bank of Greece	Finance and real estate industry	2011	1653.85	NA	PO

eAuctions   An electronic auction marketplace http://www.e-publicrealestate.gr/ for medium and small real estate assets has been designed and launched.

Transactions   Table 5.2 summarizes the main sales that have taken place as of December 2014. The data in the table come from the December 2014 report of HRADF.[5]

5.3   Challenges of Greece's Privatization Program

The performance of Greece's privatization program must be evaluated against the backdrop of chronically low FDI and of a sharp decline in investment during the crisis. Some of the challenges of Greece's privatization program, listed below, are closely related to the reasons behind the low FDI.

Regulatory and legal complexity   The complexity and inconsistency of Greece's regulatory and legal framework has been a significant obstacle to selling state assets (and to attracting FDI more generally). The assets slated for privatization and managed by HRADF fall into two main categories: (1) firms that operate in partially regulated markets, such as energy, transport, and gambling, and (2) real estate. In both market sectors, investors face complicated and potentially conflicting laws and regulations. Verifying compliance to the regulations is made more difficult because of the inefficiencies in the Greek public administration. Resolving disputes is also costly because of the delays in the Greek justice system. (The public administration and the justice system are reviewed in chapters 12, 14, and 15 of this book.) These factors deter all investors, and especially foreign investors who are less familiar with the idiosyncrasies of doing business in Greece. As a result it is natural that much of the real interest for the assets being privatized would tend to come from well-established domestic incumbents. Entry by new or foreign investors, however, can often yield the largest benefits: it can bring more competition and hence low prices to consumers, as well as more innovation and higher product quality.

Rent-seeking and corruption   Barriers to the entry of new or foreign investors can be created by domestic incumbents. In fact incumbents do have an incentive to lobby for conditions that discourage entry by new players so that they can acquire state assets at low prices. These effects are likely to be important in Greece given the high level of corruption. For example, according to Transparency International, perceptions of corruption were higher in Greece than in any other EU member state in 2012. Moreover there are often close ties between business, media, and politicians, as documented in an extensive report by Reuters, authored by Grey and Kyriakidou (2012). Problems related

Table 5.2

Company name	Industry	Year	Price (€ mil)	Received (€ mil)	Sale terms
OTE (Hellenic Telecom Organization)	Telecommunications	2011–2012	392	392	10% sold
Opap VLT license	Services industry	2011–2012	560	560	10-year license
Game licenses	Game licenses	2011–2012	375	375	
Radio frequencies	Telecommunications	2011–2012	381	317	
International broadcasting center	Real estate	2013	81	81	90-year lease
State lottery license	Game licenses	2013	770	190	12-year license
Opap	Services industry	2013	712	625	33% sold
DESFA	Gas	2013	400	0	66% sold
Astir Vouliagmenis	Real estate	2013	400	0	
Sale and leaseback of 28 buildings	Real estate	2014	261	261	
Afandou Rhodes	Real estate	2014	42	0	
Horse-betting license	Game licenses	2014	40	0	
Hellinikon	Real estate	2014	915	0	99-year lease 100% sold
Radio frequencies rights (800 MHz / 2600 MHz)	Telecommunications	2014	380	0	
Regional airports	Transportation industry	2014	1234		40-year concession
Other assets, including real estate properties		2013-2014	190	131	

to these complications may be related to the unusually large number of resignations of senior HRADF officials.[6]

Imperfect land registry and environmental concerns   Many assets to be privatized are land and real estate. A large fraction of these properties do not have clean ownership titles so selling them is a legally complex and lengthy process. In addition, appropriate regulations must be in place to ensure that the acquirers of the Greek properties respect the environment and the country's natural beauty.

Monopolies for sale (water, electricity, ports)   Some state-owned enterprises (SOE) for sale are natural monopolies, which are difficult to regulate. Greece has agreed to privatize its electric utility, as well as water and sewage utilities in the main urban areas. As California's experience illustrates (see US Congressional Budget Office 2001; Leopold 2002; Huffington 2001), electric utilities can find ingenious ways to collude, working around the regulations, and this can lead to high prices and low quality of service. Privatizations of water utilities in Bolivia and other South American countries also led to high prices in some cases (Harris 2003).

Weak macroeconomic conditions   Greece has gone through a deep recession and there is high macroeconomic uncertainty. The stock market has collapsed and its value as of October 2016 was close to one-fourth of the pre-crisis level. Real estate prices have fallen by more than a third and few transactions are taking place. There is significant political uncertainty and even currency uncertainty. Moreover the recent re-nationalizations of foreign-owned properties by Argentina (see Bronstein 2012) and other countries are likely to make foreign investors nervous.

Short institutional memory   Greece has had five governments since the crisis started. Because key posts in ministries and other government agencies are manned by appointees of the incumbent party, the frequent changes of ministers and other key officials make it difficult for the privatization agency to progress swiftly, as there is short institutional memory.

5.4   Background on Privatizations

In this section I propose a general framework to evaluate the costs and benefits of privatizations. I draw from academic research, both theoretical and empirical.

5.4.1   Objectives of Privatizations

What determines a good privatization design and whether privatizations are desirable in the first place are the specified objectives. The usual objectives of privatization programs (see Mahoobi 2003) are as follows:

1. Reduce budget deficits and debt.

2. Attract investment.

3. Improve productive efficiency of state-owned enterprises (SOEs).

4. Introduce competition into hitherto monopolistic sectors of the economy.

5. Develop capital markets.

To achieve the first goal, assets must be sold at high prices—the *revenue goal*. The state must additionally refrain from subsidizing firms post-privatization directly or indirectly (e.g., by assigning government contracts without a competition process). To attract investment and to improve productivity, assets must be allocated to those who can maximize their value—the *efficiency goal*. The introduction of competition and the development of capital markets are goals shared with other institutional reforms that often accompany large-scale privatization programs. They are often referred to as *post-sale market performance goals*.

Balancing all three goals may not be easy, as they can be, to some extent, conflicting. For example, a post-sale competitive market that lowers the expected profits can lower the buyer's willingness to pay to acquire the asset. Fortunately, revenue and efficiency often go in hand in hand. In section 5.5, I describe selling procedures that can achieve the highest possible expected profit from sales and are efficient as well.

5.4.2 Why Privatize?

One could argue that privatizations are not the only way to raise revenue. For example, revenue could be increased by raising taxes. The productivity of state-owned firms could be improved by tying the compensation of employees to the firm's performance. Opponents to privatizations often raise concerns that privatizations increase unemployment and are socially unjust. Sappington and Stiglitz (1987) suggest that, at least, in theory ownership is irrelevant. The extensive theoretical and empirical literature on privatizations is an indication that privatizations are a highly debated and ideologically charged topic.[7]

Ultimately, whether privatizations are a blessing or a curse is an empirical question. The comparative study by Brown, Earle, and Telegdy (2006) of privatizations in Hungary, Romania, Russia, and Ukraine is eye-opening in that it shows precisely that there is no easy way to pinpoint whether or not privatizations will turn out to be welfare-improving. Clean empirical answers are hard to obtain because privatized firms are often in better shape compared to the SOEs that the state has difficulty selling. Still, since many countries have privatized extensively, there is a large body of empirical evidence that overall provides solid support in favor of privatizations. Below I review some of the empirical evidence.[8] I start with two large case studies that document the benefits in quality, prices, investment, and employment of privatizing utilities (electricity and water). I then provide broader evidence on the effects of privatizations.

5.4.3   Lessons from Past Privatizations
Empirical Findings I: Case Studies on Utilities

Study 1   Andres, Foster, and Guash (2006) analyze the impact of privatization on the performance of 116 electric utilities in 10 Latin American countries using two different methodologies: The first methodology compares averages during three periods: (1) a "pure public" period, consisting of the three years before the announcement of each privatization, (2) a "transition" period, starting from the announcement and ending one year after the privatization was awarded, and (3) a "pure private" period, consisting of the three years after the transition period. The second methodology builds a full-fledged econometric model. Andres, Foster, and Guash find that changes in ownership generate significant improvements in labor productivity, efficiency, and product/service quality, and that most of those changes occur during the transition period. In particular:

Output   Connections to the electric grid increased by 20.2 percent from the pure public period to the transition period, and by 16.7 percent from the transition period to the pure private period. The result remains even after taking into account that a positive trend in connections would exist in the absence of a change in ownership.

Number of employees   Most electric utilities in the sample were oversized in personnel, and reductions took place even before the privatizations. The average annual personnel reduction was 6.6 percent during the pure public period and 9.9 percent during the transition period. The total reduction was 38.1 percent.

Labor productivity   Connections per employee and output per employee grew annually by 18.4 and 20.3 percent, respectively, during the transition period. Both quantities grew by 5.5 percent annually during the pure private period.

Efficiency   The average annual reduction in distributional losses was 5.5 percent during the transition period. During the pure public and pure private periods, the average annual reduction was 0.6 percent and –1.3 percent, respectively.

Quality (duration and frequency of interruptions per consumer)   Both the duration and frequency of the interruptions fell during the transition period. The average annual improvement during the transition period was 9.8 percent for duration and 10.6 percent for frequency.

Prices   Prices increased significantly before the transition period, with annual growth of 9.3 percent and 10.2 percent for prices in dollars and real local currency, respectively. According to the authors, this may have been because governments sought to make the companies more attractive to investors by better aligning prices with costs and ensuring that companies do not make losses. Prices in dollars fell after privatization but increased moderately in local currency.

Study 2 Gassner, Popov, and Pushak (2009) analyze the impact of privatization on the performance of water and electric utilities using a data set of more than 1,200 utilities in 71 developing and transition economies. They find that privatizations increased labor productivity and operational efficiency, with the privatized companies outperforming a set of comparable companies that remained state-owned and operated.

Performance gains In comparing average annual values pre- and post-privatization, they establish:

- A 12 percent increase in residential connections for water utilities.
- A 54 percent increase in residential connections per worker for water utilities and a 29 percent increase for electricity distribution companies.
- A 19 percent increase in residential coverage for sanitation services.
- An 18 percent increase in water sold per worker (following the introduction of concession contracts) and a 32 percent increase in electricity sold per worker.
- A 45 percent increase in bill collection rates in electricity.
- An 11 percent reduction in distribution losses for electricity and a 41 percent increase in the number of hours of daily water service.

Staff reductions On average, employment fell by 24 percent in electricity and by 22 percent in water.

No clear investment gains For company sales, investment per worker increased. For company leases and concessions (i.e., long-term lease contracts under which the acquirer is expected to carry out investments), there is no conclusive evidence that investment increased. The authors note that this lack of investment raises concerns about the long-term sustainability of the operational improvements achieved.

No systematic change in prices Except for electricity concessions, the study finds no evidence of a systematic change in residential prices. The result might also explain the lack of public or private investment.

Summary The two case studies indicate that privatizations of utilities have unambiguous positive effects on output and quality. Employment in the privatized firms decreases, and this causes even larger increases in productivity per worker. The effect on investment is ambiguous. Prices may increase when the firms are prepared for privatization, possibly because governments seek to align prices with costs, but there is no systematic price change otherwise.

Empirical Findings II: Broader Evidence

Impact on Corporate Productivity and Performance Megginson and Netter (2001) survey empirical studies on nontransition economies over different periods of time. They conclude that there is general agreement that privatization increases output, productivity (of each employee), profitability, and investment. An earlier study by Ramamurti (1997) on the restructuring and privatization of Ferrocarilla Argentinos, Argentina's national railroad, finds a 370 percent improvement in productivity. In 1990 Argentine railroad services were expanded and improved, and delivered at lower cost to consumers. In particular, operating subsidies by the state were largely eliminated.

D'Souza and Megginson (1999) document average gains in the productivity of newly privatized firms between 10 to 25 percent, when comparing the last three years before privatization to the first three years after privatization. Boubkari and Cosset (1998) document a 25 percent average increase in productivity, and Megginson, Nash, and van Randenborgh (1994) document a 11 percent average increase in productivity.

Impact on Capital Market Development Privatizations have had a significant impact on the development of capital markets. Capital markets' development is important because it leads to better allocation of capital in the economy, improved macroeconomic performance, and more and better-paid jobs (see Dudley and Hubbard 2004). Boutchkova and Megginson (2000) find that large public offerings of privatized companies are associated with rapid growth of market capitalization as a proportion of GDP. In Portugal, Japan, the United Kingdom, Germany, France, and Italy, privatized and partially privatized companies are the highest valued companies and comprise a large share of total market capitalization.

Employment The empirical evidence on the impact of privatization on employment suggests ambiguous effects that vary greatly by sector (Megginson and Netter 2001; Mahoobi 2003). In the Ramamurti (1997) study of Ferrocarilla Argentinos, there was a 78.7 percent decline in railway employment (from 92,000 to 19,682). Bozec and Laurin (2001) compare productivity and profitability of two large Canadian rail carriers, before and after the 1995 privatization of Canadian National (CN). Both firms reduced numbers of workers after 1992. CN's employment declined more (34 percent decline) and average productivity almost doubled (97 percent increase). D'Souza and

Megginson (1999) examine the effects of privatization of 78 firms from 10 developing and 15 developed countries over the period 1990 to 1994 and find significant drops in employment.

The overall evidence on privatization and job losses is mixed: three studies document significant *increases* in employment following privatizations (Galal et al.1994; Megginson, Nash, and van Randenborgh 1994; Boubakri and Cosset 1998), two find insignificant changes (Macquieira and Zurita 1996; D'Souza and Megginson 1999); and another five studies document significant—sometimes massive—employment declines (Ramamurti 1997; La Porta and López-de-Silanes 1999; Bozec and Laurin 2001; D'Souza and Megginson 1999; Boardman, Laurin, and Vining 2002). According to Megginson and Netter (2001), whether privatizations increase or decrease employment depends on whether the privatized firms' sales increase enough after privatization to offset the dramatically higher levels of each worker's productivity,

Social Justice   Birdsall and Nellis (2002) review the growing, though uneven, literature on the distributional effects of privatization. They note: "The distributional impacts of privatization cannot be simply predicted. But the effects on equity depend on at least three factors: initial conditions in each case, the sale event, and the post-privatization political and economic environment." They continue: "Privatization appears to have worsened the distribution of assets and income at least in the short run. This has been observed more in transition economies than in Latin America. This effect seems to be less clear for utilities such as electricity and telecommunications where privatization may have increased access by the poor than in the case of banks and natural resource companies."

Fiscal Objectives   For Greece, as well as for most OECD countries, fiscal objectives are important. Governments aim to reduce deficits and debt and to generate revenues. Barnett (2000) finds that privatization proceeds tend to be transferred to the budget and saved, and that privatizations seem to have a positive link to improvements in the macro environment. The National Economic Research Associates (NERA) in 1996 examined 31 privatized infrastructure companies and found that the revenues from sale of shares, corporate tax receipts, interest and debt repayments, and dividends received from the government's residual shareholdings contributed to government finances.

These results clearly suggest that privatizations can have an overall positive impact. In the following section I highlight the ingredients of successful privatizations.

5.4.4   Lessons from Past Privatizations: Ingredients of Success and Failures

The large past experience of privatizations suggests the main elements of successful ones:[9]

1. *Transparency*   There should be nothing private about privatizations.

2. *Accountability and de-politicization*   Government authorities in charge of running the privatization process should be accountable. There should be independent and thorough oversight of the privatization authorities, the investment banks, and even the auditing companies involved in the privatization process. The risks of collusion and conflicts of interests between these entities and potential buyers are large and real. Moreover the governance and the structure of the privatization activities must be such that it prevents interference by politicians and interest groups.

3. *Good design of the selling procedure*   This is essential and elaborated on in section 5.5.

4. *Identify suitable buyers*   Large firms have the ability and finances to carry out large investments (Frydmane et al. 1999). Foreign buyers are preferred because they are less susceptible to capture by politicians and other local interests.

5. *Sequencing*   Mahoobi (2003) suggests that selling first more desirable assets helps built market confidence and signals political commitment to the privatization process.

6. *Thoughtful post-sale regulatory framework*   A strong regulatory framework is critical for the privatization of natural monopolies. Chapter 4 (on product markets) reviews product-market regulation in Greece, including in the telecommunications and energy sectors, which have natural monopoly features.

5.5   How to Privatize?

A well-designed privatization program not only raises funds for the state but ensures that the post-sale market brings consumers good services at reasonable prices and that firms have sufficient revenue to make investments. In other words, good privatization design amounts to good *auction/sale design* as well as good *market design* and *post-sale regulation*.

There are a number of important decisions to be made regarding how to privatize an asset to achieve the goals of revenue, efficiency, and post-sale market performance. Each of these goals is essential for the success of the privatization program. Fortunately, we can draw important and robust lessons both from past experiences, as well as from the academic literature. Below I list the main decisions to be made and the corresponding recommendations.

5.5.1 Decisions before the Sale: Type of Transfer

A first consideration is the type of transfer: is the contract to be for a permanent sale of an asset or for a temporary lease or concession? In the event of a lease or a concession, the government has to decide on the duration of the contract. Leases and concessions are particularly attractive at times of crisis because the government does not need to sell the assets at overly low prices and can renegotiate the terms when the economy improves. For this reason the contracts must not be too long. Yet they must be long enough to incentivize buyers to undertake investments.

Another decision to be made is whether to sell the entire firm as one piece, or to sell a fraction to one buyer and keep the rest as public, or to break up the firm into many parts and sell the parts to different buyers. The answer depends primarily on the weight that the government assigns to post-sale market competition and the importance of post-sale investments: if there is risk of excessive market power post-privatization, then academic research suggests that it is best to break up the firm into many parts sold to different buyers and to reduce barriers to entry (see Anton and Yao 1989, 1992; Dana and Spier 1994; Gong, Li, and McAfee 2012; Anton, Brusco, and Lopomo 2010).

Regardless of whether an asset is sold as a whole or in parts, or whether permanent ownership rights or a concession contract is employed, good planning of the transfer process is crucial both for revenue and efficiency. I turn to this topic next.

5.5.2 Decisions at the Sale: Auction Design

Should the ownership rights be transferred through an auction or via negotiations? In an auction, what should be the rules? If shares of an asset are for sale, should all units be sold at the same price (uniform price auction) or at different prices (discriminatory pricing)? Other decisions concern the timing of the auction—should it be simultaneous or sequential—and whether the bids should be sealed or open. Simultaneous and sealed-bid auctions are good when there is relatively less uncertainty about the value of the asset, there are few bidders, and less fear of collusion. Sequential open call-out auctions can help information aggregation about the asset value and thus may ultimately lead to higher sale prices—the linkage principle (Milgrom and Weber (1982))—but there is risk that bidders may exploit the open format to coordinate and collude as happened in the first generation US spectrum auctions.

I now discuss which selling procedures are profit maximizing among all possible sales types. There is often the debate about whether auctions or one-on-one negotiations are better in terms of generating a higher sale price, which is one of the key goals of a well-designed privatization program. An influential paper by Bulow and Klemperer (1996) shows that auctions generally generate more profit for the seller than negotiations do.[10] In other words, even the world's best negotiator is worse than an auction: competition among bidders is more effective in making buyers bid higher to win. If one is worried about how to design the auction rules (since it requires skills and knowledge to design the auction that is best in terms of profitability), Bulow and Klemperer say not to worry: a simple auction without reserve prices and $N + 1$ bidders is more profitable in expectation than any auction (even the profit-maximizing auction) with N bidders. Hence competition from each additional buyer is, on average, more effective than the most sophisticated auction design!

What about efficiency in assigning the asset to the buyer that can put it in the best use? As it turns out, revenue and efficiency go hand in hand: under mild assumptions,[11] standard auctions are efficient in the sense that the winner of the auction is the buyer with the highest willingness to pay. The lesson is clear: *To maximize revenue and efficiency, run an auction with many buyers.*

Entry Costs   Bulow and Klemperer's (1996) result assumes that entry at the auction is costless; that is, the process of assessing the value of an asset and of preparing a bid does not require any resources. In reality, however, preparing a bid to buy an asset is costly and time-consuming. Bulow and Klemperer (2009) analyze the case of costly entry and compare the revenue raised by auctions and by sequential negotiations (whereby the seller negotiates with potential buyers in sequence). They show that revenue is always smaller under sequential negotiations because preemptive bids (high early bids) discourage entry. Gazprom's high early bid for DEPA (Greece's gas company), which was ultimately withdrawn, might have had that effect.

Investment and Uncertain Cash Flows   The preceding results are based on the assumption that it is not possible to contract on the revenues that an asset generates post-sale. Firms, however, generate verifiable cash flows, and buyers can agree with the government at the time of sale on a split of post-sale cash flows. DeMarzo, Kremer, and Skrzypacz (2005) and Skrzypacz (2013) compare the selling procedures in such circumstances,[12] and find that auctions with contingent payments, where the successful bidder can agree with the seller on a split of post-sale cash flows, always generate more revenue than auctions with flat payments. Contingent payments can take, for example, the form of equity participation by the government. If the buyer is not entitled to the full cash flows post-sale, he might have less incentive to invest. This can, however, be addressed with an appropriate design of the contingent payment. Overall, auctions with contingent payments may be attractive when privatizing during weak macroeconomic conditions (as is the case currently in Greece), since some of the payments can be deferred to the future and be made contingent on the asset's full profitability and stock market price.

5.5.3   Decisions after the Sale: Regulation and Market Design

There are a number of important decisions as to what happens after the asset's sale. These decisions affect consumer welfare, as well as the investment incentives and the profits of the buyer. Expectations about these decisions affect the bidders' willingness to pay for the asset during the sale phase.

Commitment to the Sale It must be clear to potential buyers that there is full commitment to the terms of the sale (or of the lease or concession contract). This can be achieved through the formal legal status of the transaction and through achieving consensus with the public and with the political parties during the sale. Commitment can be jeopardized by interest groups (e.g., large local businesses and labor unions) and political parties. For example, in several instances in Greece, political parties have threatened to reverse certain privatizations with the argument that the assets were given away too cheaply and/or consumers' interests were at risk. Such threats signal lack of commitment to the process. This can ultimately translate to low proceeds, since fear that the process may be reversed discourages serious investors from acquiring ownership.

Governance and Incentives The main argument in favor of privatizations is the de-politicization and improved governance of the privatized assets. It is important that the privatized firms are free from direct or indirect interference by politicians and interest groups. The large resources spent by the Greek state to satisfy the demands of OTE's partisan labor union, and the cost that this imposed on the company post-privatization, illustrates how interest groups can prevent efficient functioning even post-privatization.[13]

Post-sale Price and Quality Regulation Price regulation and pro-competitive policies are crucial. If a state-owned enterprise (SOE) is broken into many parts prior to its privatization, post-sale competition and consumer welfare will be higher but the sale price is likely to be lower overall. Selling the company as one unit may yield a higher sale price, but this may come at the expense of economywide productivity and growth, especially if the firm supplies an important input (e.g., electricity) in the economy.

Summing up, all the aforementioned decisions are important in determining revenue and efficiency. Auction rules really matter for revenue, as Klemperer (2002a) nicely documents in auctions of 3G licenses in Europe, especially in the presence of *weak competition* or when suspicions are roused as to possible bidder *collusion*.[14] At the same time, bidders' valuations (buyers' willingness to pay) are *endogenous*, and depend on the type of sale in phase 1 and on buyers' expectations about the phase 3 post-sale circumstances. I now proceed to apply these lessons in order to provide an (early) assessment and proposals for reform.

5.6 Lessons and Policy Recommendations

Bulow and Klemperer's (1996) work, as well as the studies that build on it, suggest that regardless of the specific decisions relating to the three phases explored above, what is central for maximal revenue generation and the integrity of the privatization process is the presence of *many interested buyers* with *high willingness to pay*. Yet one of the main challenges of privatizing during a crisis is weak demand: the number of interested buyers is smaller than usual and buyers have a lower willingness to pay. Weak demand can lead to "fire sales" (a sale at an extremely discounted price) if privatizations must take place quickly and the procedure is poorly designed. Thus under these circumstances the key is to maximize entry and willingness to pay. Ultimately, even a perfectly designed process is doomed to fail if governance and supporting institutions are weak. In what follows I offer recommendations for reform to achieve the following goals:

1. Improve governance
2. Increase value of assets
3. Promote entry
4. Improve auction design

5.6.1 Improving Governance

As I noted earlier, one of the terms Greece had to agree to in exchange for receiving bailout funds was to set up an independent privatization agency, the HRADF. Transparency and accountability were viewed as essential for the good functioning of HRADF. While senior staff at HRADF have immunity,[15] sales are to go through many layers of external approvals: the Council of Experts, the Court of Auditors, the Hellenic Parliament, and the European Union.

Despite the safeguards in place, concerns have been voiced (e.g., in an IMF 2014 report) that politicians and other interest groups try to intervene with HRADF's processes and decisions. This goes back to rent-seeking behaviors and the close relationship of the press, businesspeople, and political parties mentioned in section 5.3. The main recommendations here are as follow:

Political party finances   Political parties and individual politicians should be required to fully disclose their income sources and business involvements.[16] Ideally this law should apply retroactively so as to uncover any past members of the government who might have been involved in businesses or with individuals acquiring government assets through the privatization process.

Disclosure rules   All entities in the privatization process (investment bankers, accounting firms, lawyers) should be required to fully disclose potential conflicts of interest. For example, if a company is hired as an independent evaluator of an asset, it should not be hired by potential buyers as well.

Eliminate political interference and simplify process   In a 2014 report, the IMF hinted that interference by politicians and other interest groups was causing delays and preventing HRADF from taking necessary actions that would maximize asset value and facilitate the sales. It notes (IMF 2014) that:

Although the HRADF owns a majority stake in most of its assets, it lacks effective control over their boards and management and is thus not able to ensure the companies are following policies conducive to privatization (e.g., avoiding entrance into long-term contracts or implementing restructuring plans to reduce costs and improve value to bidders).

It continues:

While the HRADF is in charge of privatizing assets, many of the actions needed to conclude sales are the responsibility of the Greek State. Examples include issuance of Ministerial Decisions, submission of legislation to parliament, and setting up well-functioning regulatory bodies for network industries. Delays in completing such actions have contributed to the slower-than-projected pace of asset sales.

5.6.2   Increasing the Value of Assets

In addition to attracting many buyers, the privatization authority should undertake steps to maximize the value of the assets for sale:

Disclose detailed information   Potential buyers must have easy access to as much information as possible about the asset for sale (even if is not good) and the timing and rules of the sale. The privatization authority can prepare detailed brochures (easily available in electronic format) that present each asset and at the same time should provide all relevant information (as to a firm's debt, receivables, etc.) to avoid post-sale complaints. As Milgrom and Weber (1982) first showed, when buyers' willingness to pay is positively correlated (signals are affiliated in a statistical sense), the seller can generate more revenue by disclosing all known information.

Bundle assets with business plans/access to local know-how   Doing business in Greece is complicated. For example, to run a hotel successfully, it helps to be familiar with the culture of the region and even to be in good terms with the local priest! However, those with the local know-how often lack financing. A privatization agency could therefore set up double-competitions so that venture capitalists, businesses, or banks can bid for the asset and the business/development plan of their choice. This could attract entry that would not come otherwise. Consider, for example, venture capitalists who want to diversify their portfolio with high-risk, high-return investments, but who lack the local knowledge as to how to develop the asset. Such entities would not want to participate at an auction of a hotel or a local airport, but might be willing to finance the purchase of the hotel bundled with the best business plan submitted by entrepreneurs familiar with local idiosyncrasies. Such competitions not only could attract financing by foreign investors but could also be advantageous for idle local talent.

Bundle assets with agreements with other entities   Let us take the example of a former "Xenia" Hotel.[17] Say that the hotel is put up for sale. The hotel would be more valuable if it could operate also as an assisted-living facility throughout the year. Wealthy pensioners from colder climates would enjoy spending the winter months on a Greek island where the winter is mild and mostly sunny. For these pensioners, easy access to good medical care would be crucial. So if the privatization agency bundles the sale of the hotel with an arrangement with the local health center to provide health services to residents for a fee, that could not only raise the sale price of the hotel but also generate revenue through the sale of health care services and benefit the local economy during the winter months when many islands are underpopulated.

Strategize   It can be worthwhile to think about the strategic aspects of each sale. Firms may be willing to pay more to prevent a competitor from acquiring a particular asset (see Jehiel, Moldovanu, and Stacchetti 1996; Figueroa and Skreta 2009).

5.6.3 Promoting Entry

Make sales known   Generating publicity in business circles and the press is crucial. How many people interested in buying a house or land in Greece know there exists an auction site https://www.e-publicrealestate.gr/? This website should be better promoted. The assets for sale should be more fully described—and more pictures would be useful. The format should be similar to what professional real estate agents use, and in addition to the eAuction site, the properties could be listed on the websites of major international real estate firms throughout Europe, the Americas, Asia, and so on. The privatization agency could even leverage social media such as videos of assets on You-Tube and also ads on Tweeter and Facebook platforms. Those links are easy to use and can reach interested buyers all over in the world.

Help bidders assess the value of assets   For assets where entry is costly, as it is with state-owned enterprises, entry could be facilitated by offering free independent valuations and access to free legal help (e.g., summaries and translations of the relevant laws).

Rely on professional intermediaries   A privatization agency might partner with professional intermediaries, such as real estate brokers and investment banks, to find buyers. Each package of real estate for sale could even be offered by different real estate agencies in other countries (as happens with UK private property sales). The agency that provides access to the buyer who acquires the asset would then get the commission. Since intermediaries would be paid only if the transaction takes place through them, using many such agencies would induce competition for the commission and would enlarge the pool of buyers. Moreover the benefit of access to more buyers should compensate for the commission fee that the state would pay to the successful intermediary, as the findings of Bulow and Klemperer (1996) suggest.

Full transparency of bidder qualification process   Criteria used to qualify bidders should be explained in detail. Opaqueness can falsely suggest that there are not many interested buyers, and this can drive down the price.

5.6.4   Improving Auction Design

Provide more clarity on timing and rules   The auction rules and the timing of the sale should be described precisely. At the moment this information is scattered throughout several press releases on HRADF's website, and the exact timing of the auction from the phase of initial indications of interest to final closing date is often unclear.

Disclose information thoughtfully   Disclosure about bidders' willingness to pay—their indications of interest—should be thoughtfully designed. So far HRADF announces them. For instance, announcing a high monetary indication of interest can act preemptively and reduce entry; then after competition is eliminated, the real bid can be much lower. As mentioned earlier, this could have happened in the case of DEPA where Gazprom was said to be offering around 950 million euros, more than 300 million euros higher than the second highest bidder. Sadly, this high bid was later withdrawn. The preemptive role of such "jump bids" is investigated in Avery (1998). It might be best to not disclose to bidders what the others are willing to pay for another reason: these public announcements can also facilitate collusion. Thus, even though Milgrom and Weber's work gives a good argument in favor of disclosing all available information about *the asset for sale*, this is not necessarily the case anymore when it comes to information concerning other bidders' willingness to pay.

Set a suitable reserve price   The reserve price should adequately reflect the value of the asset. A higher reserve price might be helpful for real estate assets sold on https://www.e-publicrealestate.gr/. In many of the transactions the sale price was at, or close to, the reserve price. This suggests a low level of competition. For firms traded in the stock market, the reserve price should probably not be lower than the firms' market valuation. The buyers getting a large fraction of the shares are also buying control, for which they should pay.

The privatization of OPAP, the Greek Organisation of Football Prognostics S.A, is a case in point.[18] In August 2013 an agreement was reached to sell a 33 percent stake at the firm to Emma Delta. The agreed price was 6.19 euros per share, while the minimum share price during all of August 2013 was 6.76 euros. On October 11, 2013, the day the sale closed, OPAP's shares were trading at 9.13 euros, and Emma Delta's 33 percent stake was valued by the market at nearly one billion euros. Yet the Greek state received only 652 million euros from the sale, 30 million of which would be paid over ten years. Taking into account private benefits of control that the 33 percent stake would have conferred to Emma Delta, it seems that the Greek state could have extracted a higher price and could have set a higher reserve price.

5.7 Concluding Remarks

A large body of empirical evidence indicates that privatizations tend to increase significantly output and productivity, while also raising revenue for the state. Greece's recent experience with the sale of Piraeus harbor illustrates dramatically the beneficial effects of privatizations. However, privatizations must be well designed and well run. This chapter has identified some key principles that privatization agencies should observe.

Successful privatizations processes are transparent, resist pressures from politicians and interest groups (businesses, labor unions), and are carried out by privatization agencies that are professional and accountable. To maximize proceeds from the sale, privatization agencies must attract qualified buyers and undertake steps to maximize their willingness to pay. Proper advertising and information disclosure about the assets, as well as a suitable design of the auction mechanism, are important for achieving these goals. The auction rules must be clear and an appropriate reserve price must be set. To ensure efficient post-sale market performance, the appropriate regulations and pro-competitive policies must be adopted.

So far the results of the Greek privatization program have been mixed, with privatization proceeds below target but with some nontrivial progress in terms of organizing the assets that can be sold, in setting up rules the procedures, and in selling some major assets. The government privatization agency also pushed, and in many cases succeeded, in obtaining commitments for significant post-sale investments.

Appendix A: Case Study of the Effects of OTE's privatization (Pagoulatos and Zahariadis 2011)

Pagoulatos and Zahariadis (2011) study the impact of privatizations by examining the country's flagship privatization project, the gradual privatization of the Hellenic Telecommunications Organization (OTE). They investigate how weak regulation and troubled labor relations affected OTE's performance.

Decreasing state ownership had a significant positive effect on most indicators of performance. Productivity increased, and so did the quality of service. In particular, the number of technical faults decreased and network reliability improved. Yet profitability appeared to be unaffected by the transition to private ownership.

The study also documents that privatization increased political involvement prima facie. But, as privatization progressed, labor tensions subsided. This was partly because the government "bought" union acquiescence through generous benefit packages. This was shrewd politics in the short run but saddled OTE with high labor costs over time that, ultimately, burdened taxpayers.

There are many lessons and observations to draw from this study: The labor union caused significant troubles to the privatization process and disproportionally burdened OTE's wage bill compared to other similar companies.[19] The government's inability to ignore the union's pressures was ultimately costly for consumers and taxpayers. Regulation and competitive forces were key in providing correct incentives that led to the post-privatization improved service and market performance.

Appendix B: The Post-2010 Bailout Privatization Agency—The Hellenic Republic Asset Development Fund (HRADF)

In response to the demands of running a large-scale privatization program professionally and efficiently, the Greek government formed the HRADF—Greece's privatization agency. The Fund was established on July 1, 2011 (L. 3986/2011), as an independent body in order to coordinate Greece's privatization efforts following the 2010 and 2011 bailouts.[20] The goal was to restrict government intervention in the privatization process and to ensure that the process would be managed by professionals. The old privatization process under Law 3049/2002 was abandoned. The Fund is a corporation and the Hellenic Republic is its sole shareholder with a share capital of 30m euros. Most public assets for sale are part of HRADF's portfolio (the assets transferred by the government are not part of HRADF's capital).[21] The Fund is governed by private law and is not a public entity.

B.1 HRADF: Organizational Structure

The Board of Directors of HRADF consists of five members appointed by the General Assembly for a three-year term. The eurozone and the European Commission each appoint an independent observer. The Board is supposed to have the absolute authority on privatization decisions. In principle, the CEO is fully responsible for the operation of the Fund and introduces the privatizations to the Board for decision-making. The CEO and the Board have legal immunity with respect to privatization-related decisions. The flat organizational structure facilitates speedy decision-making, while the state-of-the art management systems and experienced staff contribute to good decision-making.[22] The structure of HRADF is depicted in the HRADF May 2013 report.[23] The Fund publishes quarterly reports, has internal regulations, internal and external auditors, and is subject to Parliamentary monitoring.

B.2 HRADF: Stated Vision

The Hellenic Republic privatization scheme is the largest declared divestment program in the world. Its goal is to attract international capital flows to restart the Greek economy and to fuel economic growth. HRADF seeks to base its efforts on three pillars: *clarity of purpose, transparency of process, and speed*. The Fund posts information on its website, in order to provide full information and transparency. Its view is nicely summarized on its website:

Privatizations provide both direct and indirect benefits to the country and the society as a whole. Not only they will have significant financial benefits, as their proceedings will help to reduce the public debt burden, but they will also attract much needed investments to re-launch the Greek economy, benefiting the society and touching the everyday life of the citizens.

Stated goals of HRADF's Program:[24]

Direct Maximize the proceeds to the Hellenic Republic. Reach the goal of raising total proceeds of 50 billion euros as stipulated in the Medium Term Fiscal Strategy Plan (MTFS) (this initial quite ambitious target, has been repeatedly revised: 11 billion by

2016 and 22 billion by the end of 2020). Generate public revenue both through sales and through increased economic activity.

Indirect Promote competition as well as efficiency and productivity in the economy. Bring value and create new jobs by introducing international know-how and best practices and by attracting further investments, thus enabling higher growth rates through multiplier effects. Create better living conditions for local communities.

B.3   The Privatization Process of HRADF

Most of the assets contained in the medium-term plan have been transferred to the Fund, while other assets which the Hellenic Republic has decided to develop or sell will also be transferred. Any asset transferred to the Fund is to be sold or developed. The return of any asset back to the state is not allowed.

Prior to each sale, the Fund approves the Asset Development Plan which is reviewed every six months. To develop the plan, the Fund takes into account the expected revenue from each privatization, its long-term benefits, and the complexity and initial state of each project. The Board of Directors takes into account the opinion of the Council of Experts, which, however, is not binding. The Council of Experts has seven members, among whom four are appointed by the Board and three by the Troika. For a decision to be adopted a simple majority of the Board members is required. The Council of Experts opinion reflects its majority. The Board takes into account the input of the independent evaluator. Upon the adoption of a decision by the Board on a privatization, the contract is submitted to the Audit Office for a pre-contract audit. On average, a privatization process lasts from 9 up to 15 months, from the beginning of the procedure up to the deposit of the consideration with the Fund. The privatization process followed by HRADF[25] is described in Law 3869/2011 and in the May 2013 HRADF report. The fund undertakes reforms such as setting up the regulatory framework, as in the case of marinas, energy, ports, railways, and so forth, and clearing the ownership titles as in the case of real estate.

Notes

1. I am thankful to the book's editors for constructive feedback. I greatly benefited from conversations with Takis Athanasopoulos, Stelios Stavridis, and Andreas Tapranztis. Ernesto Dal Bo offered valuable perspectives based on his experience with Argentina's privatization program. Francisco Espinosa, Ilari Juhana Paasivirta, and Zhen Zhou provided excellent research assistance

at the initial stages of the project, and Apostolis Pavlou and Katerina Nikalexi did the same at the later stages.

2. See privatization barometer http://www.privatizationbarometer.net/database.php.

3. Since OTE's privatization is one of the main ones that took place before the crisis, we summarize the key findings of Pagoulatos and Zahariadis in appendix A.

4. Appendix B describes the governance structure, objectives, and processes followed by the HRADF as of March 2015.

5. For some of the most recent privatizations listed in table 5.2, agreements with the buyers had not been finalized as of December 2014, and funds had not been disbursed. Hence the final amounts in some cases may be different from those in table 5.2.

6. Among others, Spyros Pollalis, former CEO of Hellenikon, resigned from that position allegedly because he did not agree with the valuation method and decisions relating to the privatization of Hellenikon; two heads of the privatization agency resigned within six months in 2013; the privatization agency's representative at the Port of Pireaus resigned in July 2014 after a "friendly" arrangement with COSCO essentially sidestepped the privatization agency's competition. Since its inception, the head of HRADF has changed, on average, more than once a year.

7. Boycko, Shleifer, and Vishny (1996), Vickers and Yarrow (1988), and Roland (2008) offer comprehensive and interesting perspectives.

8. For further details, see the surveys of Megginson and Netter (2001), Mahoobi (2003), Sheshinski and López-Calva (2003), Clarke, Cull, and Shirley (2005), Megginson (2005), Guriev and Megginson (2007), Chong and López-de-Silanes (2004), and Estrin et al. (2009).

9. Megginson and Netter (2001), Mahoobi (2003).

10. They assume that there are N risk-neutral buyers. The number of buyers is exogenous and fixed. Buyer i observes a signal t_i about the asset value and buyer i's valuation for the asset (maximum willingness to pay) is $v_i(T)$, where $T = (t_1, \ldots, t_N)$. Signals can be statistically correlated.

11. See Maskin (1992).

12. Those papers assume that the asset requires an initial investment and generates a verifiable cash flow that can differ across buyers. Moreover, buyers observe private information, are risk-neutral, and their total number is exogenous and fixed.

13. See Pagoulatos and Zahariadis (2011) for an excellent account of costs of labor disputes associated with OTE's privatization.

14. See also Klemperer (2002b).

15. Granting immunity to the heads of the privatization agency is probably useful. Otherwise, no rational person would have been willing to risk a false accusation, especially given the politically charged climate on the topic and the fact that justice moves very slowly.

16. The Greek Parliament voted on such a law in June 2014, but much depends on its implementation and enforcement.

17. "Xenia" is a hotel in the chain of state-owned hotels that were built at excellent locations at the most attractive areas throughout Greece but subsequently saw their value decline, primarily because of poor management.

18. OPAP is a company that operates numerical lottery and sports betting games in Greece. It is Europe's largest betting firm.

19. Until 2006 when a large-scale voluntary personnel exit was implemented, OTE's wage bill totaled 33 percent of the company's revenues, compared to the 22 percent average levels for other European national telecom companies. For a detailed account of the labor disputes associated with OTE's privatization and their associated costs, see Pagoulatos and Zahariadis (2011).

20. For an excellent summary of what has been accomplished so far by HRADF, see HRADF (2013).

21. For a complete and up-to-date list of HRADF's portfolio, see http://www.hradf.com/en/portfolio.

22. The Fund is staffed with experienced and highly qualified professionals from the banking, consulting, and legal sectors and is assisted by a Council of Experts that employs experienced international advisors for each project.

23. See http://www.hradf.com/sites/default/files/attachments/20130530-ADP_May2013-en.pdf.

24. See http://www.hradf.com/sites/default/files/attachments/20130530-ADP_May2013-en.pdf.

25. See http://www.hradf.com/sites/default/files/attachments/20130530-ADP_May2013-en.pdf.

References

Acemoglu, D., and J. A. Robinson. 2012. *Why Nations Fail: The Origins of Power, Prosperity, and Poverty*. New York: Crown.

Andres, L., V. Foster, and J. L. Guash. 2006. The impact of privatization on the performance of the infrastructure sector: The case of electricity distribution in Latin American countries. Working paper 3936. World Bank.

Anton, J. J., and D. A. Yao. 1989. Split awards, procurement, and innovation. *RAND Journal of Economics* 20 (4): 538–552.

Anton, J. J., and D. A. Yao. 1992. Coordination in split award auctions. *Quarterly Journal of Economics* 107 (2): 681–707.

Anton, J. J., S. Brusco, and G. Lopomo. 2010. Split-award procurement auctions with uncertain scale economies: Theory and data. *Games and Economic Behavior* 69 (1): 24–41.

Antoniades, E. 1997. Privatization in Greece: 1993 to the present: Its impact on the economy, the society, and the polity. http://www.hri.org/por/Summer97/story2.html.

Avery, C. 1998. Strategic jump bidding in English auctions. *Review of Economic Studies* 65 (2): 185–210.

Barnett, S. 2000. Evidence on the fiscal and macroeconomic impact of privatization. Working paper. IMF.

Birdsall, N., and J. Nellis. 2002. Winners and losers: Assessing the distributional Impacts of privatization. Working paper 6. Center for Global Development.

Boardman, A. E., C. Laurin, and A. R. Vining. 2002. Privatization in Canada: Operating and stock price performance with international comparisons. *Canadian Journal of Administrative Sciences* 19: 137–54.

Boubakri, N., and J. C. Cosset. 1998. The financial and operating performance of newly-privatized firms: Evidence from developing countries. *Journal of Finance* 53: 1081–1110.

Boutchkova, M. K., and W. L. Megginson. 2000. Privatization and the rise of global capital markets. Working paper 53. FEEM.

Boycko, M., A. Shleifer, and R. W. Vishny. 1996. A theory of privatization. *Economic Journal* 106 (435): 309–19.

Bozec, Y., and C. Laurin. 2001. Privatization and Productivity Improvement: The Case of Canadian National. *Transportation Research Part E, Logistics and Transportation Review* 37: 355–74.

Bronstein, H. 2012. Argentina nationalizes oil company YPF. Reuters. May 3.

Brown, J. D., J. S. Earle, and A. Telegdy. 2006. The productivity effects of privatization: Longitudinal estimates from Hungary, Romania, Russia, and Ukraine. *Journal of Political Economy* 114 (1): 61–99.

Bulow, J., and P. Klemperer. 1996. Auctions versus negotiations. *American Economic Review* 86 (1): 180–94.

Bulow, J., and P. Klemperer. 2009. Why do sellers (usually) prefer auctions? *American Economic Review* 99 (4): 1544–75.

Chong, A., and F. López-de-Silanes. 2004. Privatization in Latin America: What does the evidence say? *Journal of Lacea Economia* (Latin American and Caribbean Economic Association) 4 (2): 37-111.

Clarke, G. R. G., R. Cull, and M. M. Shirley. 2005. Bank privatization in developing countries: A summary of lessons and findings. *Journal of Banking and Finance* 29 (8–9): 1905–1930.

Dana, J., Jr., and K. E. Spier. 1994. Designing a private industry: Government auctions with endogenous market structure. *Journal of Public Economics* 53 (1): 127–47.

DeMarzo, P. M., I. Kremer, and A. Skrzypacz. 2005. Bidding with securities: Auctions and security design. *American Economic Review* 95 (4): 936–59.

D'Souza, J., and W. Megginson. 1999. The financial and operating performance of newly privatized Firms in the 1990s. *Journal of Finance* 54:1397–1438.

Dudley, W., and G. Hubbard. 2004. How capital markets enhance economic performance and facilitate job creation. Working paper. Global Markets Institute, Goldman Sachs.

Figueroa, N., and V. Skreta. 2009. The role of optimal threats in auction design. *Journal of Economic Theory* 144 (2): 884–97.

Frydman, R., C. Gray, M. Hessel, and A. Rapaczynski. 1999. When does privatization work? The impact of private ownership on corporate performance in the transition economies. *Quarterly Journal of Economics* 114 (4): 1153–91.

Galal, A., L. Jones, P. Tandon, and I. Vogelsang. 1994. *Welfare Consequences of Selling Public Enterprises*. New York: Oxford University Press.

Gassner, K., A. Popov, and N. Pushak. 2009. *Does Private Sector Participation Improve Performance in Electricity and Water Distribution?* Washington, DC: World Bank.

Gong, J., J. Li, and R. P. McAfee. 2012. Split-award auctions with investment. *Journal of Public Economics* 96: 188–97.

Grey, S., and D. Kyriakidou. 17 December 2012. *Special Report: Greece's triangle of power*. Reuters. December 17.

Guriev, S., and W. Megginson. 2007. *Privatization: What Have We Learned?* ABCDE. Washington, DC: World Bank.

Gutierrez, R., P. Serra, and R. Fischer. 2003. The effects of privatization on firms and on social welfare: The Chilean case. Technical report. Inter-American Development Bank, Research Department.

Harris, C. 2003. Private participation in infrastructure in developing countries – Trends, impacts, and policy lessons. Working paper 5. World Bank.

HRADF, Hellenic Republic Asset Development Fund. December 2014. Progress Report. Technical Report. May.

Huffington, A. 2001. Gov. Davis and the failure of power California's energy. *Salon.com*.

IMF. 2014. Greece. Country report 14/151. IMF

Jehiel, P., B. Moldovanu, and E. Stacchetti. 1996. How (not) to sell nuclear weapons. *American Economic Review* 86 (4): 814–29.

Klemperer, P. 2002a. How (not) to run auctions: The European 3G telecom auctions. *European Economic Review* 46 (4–5): 829–845.

Klemperer, P. 2002b. What really matters in auction design. *Journal of Economic Perspectives* 16 (1):169–189.

La Porta, R., and F. López-de-Silanes. 1999. The benefits of privatization: Evidence from Mexico. *Quarterly Journal of Economics* 114: 1193–1242.

Leopold, J. 2002. Enron linked to California blackouts: Traders said manipulation began energy crisis. *Wall Street Journal*, May 16.

Mahoobi, L. 2003. *Privatizing State-Owned Enterprises: An Overview of Policies and Practices in OECD Countries*, vol. 961. Paris: OECD.

Maquieira, R., and Zurita, S. 1996. Privatizaciones en Chile: Eficiencia y Políticas Financieras. *Estudios de Administración* 3 (2): 1–36.

Maskin, E. 1992. *Auctions and Privatization*. Tübingen: J.C.B. Mohr Publisher.

Megginson, W., R. Nash, and M. van Randenborgh. 1994. The financial and operating performance of newly privatized firms: An international empirical analysis. *Journal of Finance* 49: 403–52.

Megginson, W. L., and J. M. Netter. 2001. From state to market: A survey of empirical studies on privatization. *Journal of Economic Literature* 39 (2): 321–89.

Megginson, W. 2005. *The Financial Economics of Privatization*. New York: Oxford University Press.

Milgrom, P. R., and R. J. Weber. 1982. A theory of auctions and competitive bidding. *Econometrica* 50(5): 1089–1122.

Oum, T., and C. Yu. 1994. Economic efficiency of railways and implications for public policy. *Journal of Transport Economics and Policy* 28 (2): 121–38.

Pagoulatos, G. 2005. The politics of privatization: Redrawing the public-private boundary. *West European Politics* 28 (2): 358–80.

Pagoulatos, G., and N. Zahariadis. 2011. Politics, labor, regulation, and performance: Lessons from the privatization of OTE. GreeSE paper 46. London: Hellenic Observatory, European Institute.

Ramamurti, R. 1997. Testing the limits of privatization: Argentine railroads. *World Development* 25 (12): 1973–93.

Roland, G. 2008. *Privatization: Successes and Failures*. New York: Columbia University Press.

Sappington, D. E. M., and J. E. Stiglitz. 1987. Privatization, information and incentives. *Journal of Policy Analysis and Management* 6 (4): 567–85.

Sheshinski, E., and L. F. López-Calva. 2003. Privatization and its benefits: Theory and evidence. *CESifo Economic Studies* 49 (3): 429–59.

Skrzypacz, A. 2013. Auctions with contingent payments: An overview. *International Journal of Industrial Organization* 31: 666–75.

Transparency International. 2012. *Corruption Perceptions Index*. Berlin.

US Congressional Budget Office. 2001. *Causes and lessons of the California electricity crisis*. Discussion paper 26. CBO.

Vettas, N. 2015. Privatizations. *Kathimerini* (special edition), January 4.

Vickers, J., and G. K. Yarrow. 1988. *Privatization: An Economic Analysis*, vol. 18. Cambridge: MIT Press.

6 Labor Market Regulation and Reform in Greece[1]

Antigone Lyberaki, Costas Meghir, and Daphne Nicolitsas

6.1 Introduction

A well-functioning labor market is central for the welfare of individuals and for ensuring entrepreneurship capable of adapting to a rapidly changing world. In fact, if the labor market does not operate well, job creation will be stifled and the main source of income for most people, namely a good job, will be less accessible and more uncertain. The performance of the Greek labor market since 2010 has been dire, with unprecedented levels of unemployment overall and even more so for youth; it is no exaggeration to expect a lost decade for most young people, with long-term consequences for their standard of living. Although much of this is due to the massive effect of the crisis, it is likely that the institutional and regulatory framework governing the labor market did not do much to mitigate the impact of the financial cum sovereign crisis and probably exacerbated it. Indeed labor market outcomes prior to the crisis were also poor, characterized by low female participation rates, low rates of reallocation from declining to growing sectors, and low productivity per hour worked.

We start by documenting basic features of the Greek labor market before the crisis. These features suggest problems and reveal important differences compared to well-performing economies. We then describe the regulations that we believe to be the most responsible for some of the longer term problems of the Greek economy and chart the way some of these have changed as a result of the recent reform program.

Our discussion focuses mainly on employment protection regulation, restrictions to pay, including minimum wage laws, overtime premiums, collective bargaining procedures, as well as working time flexibility and the tax wedge.[2] These are in fact the features of the regulatory framework that are most discussed in general.[3]

One of the difficulties with charting a reform program for the labor market is that under certain circumstances some regulation can be beneficial, while at the same time excessive regulation will be harmful. We present the arguments for and against regulation as they have developed over the recent years in economic theory, as well as some relevant empirical evidence. We then link this discussion with the situation in Greece. We argue that while evidence points to the possible need for some regulation, the extent and breadth of it has to be carefully assessed. Indeed, given the state of knowledge, we believe that the onus should be on those who advocate regulation to prove its benefit and define its scope in any specific circumstance. The default should be no regulation, beyond a framework for health and safety at work and robust protection against discrimination.[4] However, lack of regulation in the labor market should not imply lack of insurance and basic protection for individuals. We believe that labor market deregulation should be accompanied by welfare reform that provides wage subsidies for the low paid and contributory unemployment insurance for those who were laid off and are seeking work. This will allow the combination of a flexible and adaptable labor market with appropriate levels of social insurance and income support for the low paid.

In what follows, section 6.2 describes the labor market in the run up to the crisis; section 6.3 presents the main labor market regulations in place at that time; section 6.4 reviews the theory and empirical evidence of the effects of labor market regulation; section 6.5 discusses the reforms that have been implemented since the beginning of the crisis; section 6.6 concludes.

6.2   Labor Market Outcomes prior to the Crisis

We offer a quick tour of the Greek labor market before the crisis. In Greece the activity rate, that is, the ratio of the labor force (sum of employed and unemployed looking for work) to the working age population, was 67 percent in 2007, making it around 3.5 percentage points (pp) below the OECD average. That is to say, 33 percent of the working age population was inactive in Greece compared to around 29.5 percent in the OECD.

Out of those active in the labor market around 92 percent were employed, with the remaining 8 percent of the labor force being unemployed. The ratio of the number of employed to the working age population, the employment rate, stood at 61.4 percent in Greece and 66.5 percent in the OECD. However, if we compare employment rates in terms of full-time equivalents then, due to the limited use of part-time work and a high share of self-employment, employment rates are higher in Greece. Indeed average hours per worker in Greece are longer and the use of part-time work is limited.[5]

The main issue is that certain demographic groups are absent from the labor market while others are over represented. Low participation and low employment rates are concentrated among specific demographic groups: specifically the young aged 15 to

24, men aged 55 to 64, and women at prime working age (25 to 54) have the lowest participation rates (31.1, 43.9, and 69.1 percent, respectively). However, activity and employment rates of men at prime working age are higher in Greece (94.6 and 90.1 percent, respectively) than on average in the OECD (92.2 and 87.9 percent). In effect the labor market shows clear signs of segmentation by gender and age (see Burtless 2001).

The share of self-employed in Greece is the highest among all the OECD countries in figure 6.1. The self-employed, include employers, own-account workers, members of producers' cooperatives, and unpaid family workers. Individuals in the family group category do not have formal contracts to receive fixed incomes at regular intervals, but they share in the income generated by the family enterprise. In Greece the percentage of family workers is significantly higher than in all other EU28 countries with the exception of Romania. While self-employment could be thought of a source of dynamism, the high share of self-employment has potential negative implications for productivity (Blanchflower 2000, 2004; Pagano and Schivardi 2003) due to lost economies of scale in production and limited access to capital.

Figure 6.2 compares the percentage of individuals working part-time in manufacturing, retail and wholesale trade, hotels and restaurants, and transport and communication across EU countries in 2007. The average rate of part-time work (ratio of individuals working part-time to all individuals in employment) in the hotels and restaurants sector, where part-time employment is easy to organize, stood at 27.8 percent in the European Union, ranging from 67.2 percent in the Netherlands to 3.1 percent in Slovakia (figure 6.2). Greece stood at the very low end of the scale, higher only than Slovakia, Croatia, Hungary, the Czech Republic, and Portugal. The low share of part-time employment would not be an issue if participation rates were higher. In view, however, of the low participation rates of the young and prime-age women, and to the extent that these groups would be willing to take up part-time jobs,[6] the absence of part-time jobs seems to be limiting opportunities for employment.

Another distinctive feature of the Greek labor market is the extremely low labor mobility.[7] Figure 6.3 presents data, averaged over the period 2000 to 2005, on annual worker reallocation rates. Worker reallocation is defined here as the sum of hiring and separation rates and is an indicator of the flexibility of the labor market and its ability to adapt to shocks. The hiring rate is calculated as the number of individuals hired in year t over the individuals employed in year $(t - 1)$.[8] Similarly the separation rate is defined as the number of separations in year t over the individuals employed in year $(t - 1)$. According to figure 6.3, Denmark, the United States, Spain, Finland, and the

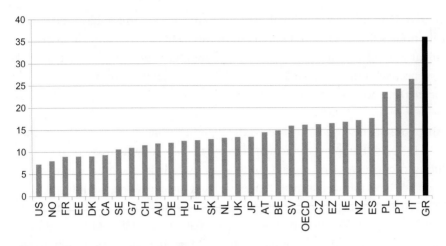

Figure 6.1
Share of self-employed in civilian employment in 2007
Source: OECD Labor force statistics database (extracted August 31, 2014)

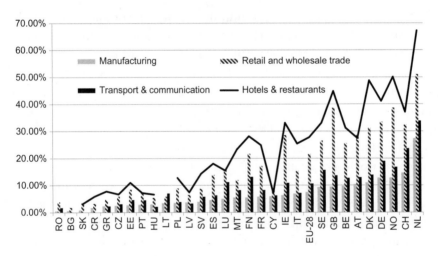

Figure 6.2
Part-time employment as percentage of the total employment in 2007
Source: Eurostat

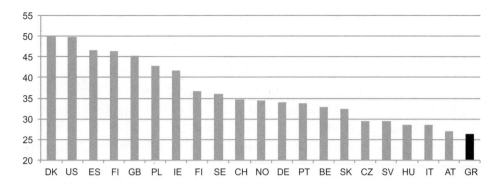

Figure 6.3
Worker reallocation rates in 2005
Source: OECD, *Employment Outlook* (2009, ch. 2)

United Kingdom have among the highest worker reallocation rates while Greece has the lowest worker reallocation rate with Austria and Italy coming close.

As the European Commission (2009) illustrates, low worker reallocation in Greece is due to very low hiring and separation rates—signs of an indolent economy. More up to date information by the ECB (2012) supports this view. Low mobility is also related to a high long-term unemployment rate.

Unemployment rates in Greece historically appear to be relatively low. However, this is in part due to high emigration rates in the 1960s and 1970s to industrialized countries, among them the United States, Canada, Australia, and Germany (Iordano-glou 2008). In the 1980s, despite the significant growth slowdown, unemployment continued to be low. This was to a large extent the result of an expansion in public sector employment. Between 1980 and 1989 employment in nonmarket services, namely public administration, education, health, and social work, increased at an annual average rate of around 3.8 percent. The corresponding figure for market services was 0.5 percent.

In the 1990s the improvement in annual growth rates, especially in the second half of the decade, was accompanied by a sizable increase in the labor force (through migration inflows and higher female participation; see Lyberaki 2011) and a rise in the unemployment rate. Immigrant flows were such that it is estimated that by the mid-2000s immigrants represented around 10 percent of the workforce (Iordanoglou 2008; Lianos 2003). The unemployment rate stabilized at around 9 to 10 percent in the first half of the 2000s and started to decline only post-2006. With the onset of the crisis, the unemployment rate increased dramatically, reaching 27 percent in 2013 and stood at around 23 percent in the second quarter of 2016.

Figure 6.4 presents the unemployment rate in Greece and in the G7, illustrating the absence of cyclical changes. Figure 6.5 further emphasizes the smoothness of the unemployment rate in Greece by plotting that series together with the growth rate. A conspicuous feature of the data is the limited correlation in the short-term changes of the two series until 2008. While the long-term trends are correlated, the unemployment rate series appears much smoother than the growth rate series, even though the latter has been smoothed (three-year average).

The share of long-term unemployed (those out of work for more than a year) among the unemployed in 2007 was 49.7 percent and much higher than the EZ average, which stood at an already high 43.5 percent. This high share of long-term unemployed reveals a sclerotic market, even in comparison to its EZ counterparts, which are highly regulated in many countries. The implication is a low re-employment chance for those losing their job.

Wages in the Greek labor market do not seem to adjust easily to changing market conditions and to varying circumstances across sectors.[9] Factors underlying such rigidity are probably the generous wage setting in the public sector; the complicated bargaining structure with multiple layers of bargaining concerning wages at many levels (not just the minimum); and the automatic extension of collective arrangements to firms not party to the negotiations. These institutions, discussed later in this chapter, were probably responsible for the declining hourly productivity, which at the start of the crisis stood at 70 percent of the EU average.

Over the period 1996 to 2007 the ratio of the national minimum to the median wage in Greece stood at around 0.5, toward the upper end compared to other EU and OECD countries suggesting that the minimum wage bites. Evidence from the 2006 Structure of Earnings Survey (SES) suggests that the sectoral minima are also binding.

Evidence on a binding minimum wage has also been found in a survey on wage and price-setting practices conducted by the Bank of Greece before the outbreak of the crisis (late 2007 and early 2008).[10] Survey responses show that in around half of the firms in the sample over 60 percent of the workforce is paid at the base wage of the sectoral or occupational agreement that applies. If the minimum wage were not binding, one would expect a lower concentration at that level reflecting different skills and responsibilities. Micro-level evidence and arguments in support of the hypothesis that the minimum wage is binding are also provided by Anagnostopoulos and Siebert (2012). According to their findings, in a number of firms individuals are paid below

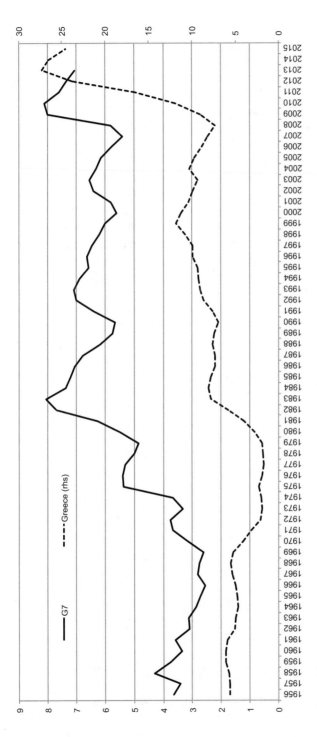

Figure 6.4
Unemployment rate in Greece and in the G7, 1956 to 2015
Source: OECD, Annual Labor Force Statistics database

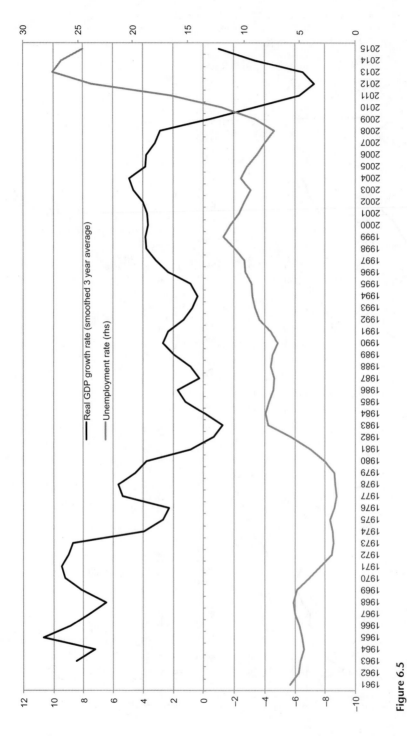

Figure 6.5
Unemployment rate and the growth rate in Greece, 1961 to 2015
Source: OECD, Stat database

the minimum; this indicates both some noncompliance and that the minimum is binding.

The survey of the Bank of Greece further indicates that employment flexibility seems to outweigh wage flexibility in the event of a shock. Firms reply that in a hypothetical scenario of a permanent slowdown in demand for their product, unskilled workers (on fixed-term and indefinite length contracts) are more likely to be made redundant. Freezing wages, containing wage increases, or adjusting working time are the less likely rated alternatives.[11] In 2009 average wages continued to increase despite the increase in the unemployment rate suggesting that the replies to (what was at the time of the survey) a hypothetical scenario might not be far removed from practice.

The labor market we portray above is characterized by low productivity, low mobility, low female participation, rigid wages, large amounts of informal self-employed workers, and high and persistent unemployment. Some of these features are obviously detrimental to well-being: low productivity implies that the cost of goods and services produced in Greece will be higher, putting the country at a disadvantage relative to foreign producers, and thus giving rise to large trade deficits (since the currency cannot depreciate), larger external debt to finance such deficits, and, of course, lower standards of living. High long-term unemployment implies that people get detached from the labor market; they lose their skills with consequences for both their current and future financial position and living standards. Moreover, when youth are unemployed, this has long-term adverse consequences for their careers. Low mobility is an indication of a slow adjustment of the economy to new international economic fundamentals and slow reallocation of labor to its most productive uses; this relates both to long-term unemployment and to low productivity.

A low participation rate (i.e., meaning people not working or looking for work) in itself may not reflect a malaise: there is no inherent reason why people should prefer to work instead of staying at home and enjoying free time. However, low participation may also reflect a shortage of labor market opportunities, such that people become discouraged from even trying to obtain a job. A particularly problematic area in Greece is the low female participation, as documented above, reflecting low opportunity for women to reach their potential and to develop their careers. This may be due to the lack of positions for part-time work, which as we explain below is effectively penalized in Greece; it may also be due to the absence of adequate childcare opportunities, preventing women with children from working and those without from developing full careers, since they anticipate employment to be inconsistent with nurturing a family. Ironically, what leads to the low provision and expensive childcare may be exactly the same labor market rigidities that we will document below; this is because labor market inflexibility makes the provision of services more expensive, restricting or even closing down some market activity.

The other features discussed are also problematic. High levels of informal family firms are associated with low productivity. This is true as small family firms do not exploit economies of scale (i.e., lowering costs by becoming larger) and do not invest in new cutting-edge technologies or hire highly trained experts.[12] But informality is effectively promoted because of the rigid institutional framework and the bureaucracy surrounding the operations of formal firms. Labor market regulation as described in this chapter is a large part of this problem.

Finally, rigid wages can cause unemployment and prevent the economy from adapting to new economic realities, such as the huge shock resulting from the combination of the Greek debt crisis and the international financial crisis. The United Kingdom and Greece are interesting contrasts in this respect: the former suffered one of the largest shocks due to the financial crisis but, given its flexible labor market and more generally its well-functioning institutions, managed to come through this with lower costs than Greece in terms of output and employment. The role of wage flexibility was key in the UK case as shown in Blundell et al. (2014).

The features of the Greek labor market discussed above are likely the result of dysfunctional institutions, as we discuss next.

6.3   Labor Market Institutions in Greece prior to the Crisis

We describe in this section the basic institutional features of the Greek labor market. We argue that most of the labor market outcomes documented above have their roots in these institutions. Ultimately a more accurate link between the outcomes and the institutional structure requires more rigorous empirical work.

Compared to labor market institutions in most advanced OECD countries, the Greek labor market prior to the crisis was characterized by stricter employment protection regulation, limited working time flexibility, multi-layer bargaining systems, and a high tax wedge (the difference between what an employer pays and what a worker gets after taxes). Additionally legal practice operated in a restrictive direction, treating as abuse of prerogative every change in labor contracts instigated by the employer. That was the case even though the needs of the firm might have dictated the changes in question. An often cited example is that if a firm needed to relocate geographically, the employer might be expected to provide employment in the original location though such employment might have ceased to exist.

6.3.1 Employment Protection

The OECD measures the stringency of employment protection legislation (EPL) based on the rigidities in adjusting employment. It has constructed two EPL indexes, both of which concern regular (i.e., not fixed-term) employment contracts. The first EPL index is the equally weighted average of three sub-indexes (in italics in table 6.1) measuring (1) the procedural costs of individual dismissals (need to explain reasons of dismissal in writing, need to notify a third party, need to wait for authorization from the third party, delay between the decision of the employer and the notification of the employee), (2) the required length of notice and the size of the severance pay, and (3) the costs of individual dismissals in the case of no-fault dismissals (definition of justified dismissal, length of trial period, compensation following unfair dismissal, possibility of reinstatement, maximum length of time to make a claim of unfair dismissal). The second EPL index includes a fourth sub-index that measures the costs of collective dismissals.[13]

Prior to the crisis (in 2007), EPL was somewhat stricter in Greece than on average in other OECD countries. This was true of both EPL indexes (rows labeled EPL on regular contracts, and EPL on regular contracts including the difficulty of collective dismissals, in table 6.1). Comparisons with the OECD are made for convenience without implying that the "average" OECD country should be the desired target.

Table 6.1 compares the values of the first EPL index for Greece with the values for Sweden, Denmark, Finland, Belgium, the United Kingdom, the United States, and the OECD average. The sub-indexes (in italics), and the items these are made of, take values between 0 and 6, increasing in strictness of the legislation. The sub-indexes and the indexes are the weighted average of the items listed in the table. The sub-indexes and indexes in bold indicate that these items take a higher value for Greece than the OECD average.

Legislation in Greece was, until recently, stricter than the OECD average, much stricter than in the United States and the United Kingdom but about as strict as in Sweden and Finland. While legislation in Greece was stricter than the OECD average in the aspects measured by all three sub-indexes, it is mainly the second sub-index (row B) that was much more restrictive in Greece. The length of the notice period the employer was required to give to the employee and the size of the severance payment in relation to the length of tenure were, in general, both higher in Greece than in the OECD on average. Only the notice period for employees with 9 months of tenure was somewhat shorter in Greece than in the OECD on average. In this regard a number of features stand out in table 6.1. First is the length of notice period given to employees with 20 years of tenure (row 5); note that this is (at 15 months) much longer than the OECD average and longer than in all other countries in the table with the exception of

Table 6.1
Employment protection legislation on regular contracts in 2007

Item	Greece	Sweden	Denmark	Finland	Belgium	United Kingdom	United States	OECD
1. Notification procedures	**4.0**	4.0	4.0	3.5	2.0	2.5	0.5	3.1
2. Delay involved before notice can start	1.0	2.0	2.0	2.0	2.0	0.0	0.0	1.3
A. *Procedural inconvenience*	**2.5**	3.0	3.0	2.8	2.0	1.3	0.3	2.2
3. Length of notice period at 9 months of tenure	2.0	3.0	5.0	2.0	6.0	1.0	0.0	3.1
4. Length of notice period at 4 years of tenure	**3.0**	5.0	5.0	2.0	5.0	2.0	0.0	2.7
5. Length of notice period at 20 years of tenure	**4.0**	3.0	2.0	3.0	6.0	2.0	0.0	1.7
6. Severance pay at 9 months of tenure	**1.0**	0.0	0.0	0.0	0.0	0.0	0.0	0.6
7. Severance pay at 4 years of tenure	**2.0**	0.0	0.0	0.0	0.0	1.0	0.0	1.7
8. Severance pay at 20 years of tenure	**2.0**	0.0	1.0	0.0	0.0	1.0	0.0	1.5
B. *Notice and severance pay for no-fault individual dismissal*	**2.2**	1.6	1.9	1.0	2.4	1.1	0.0	1.8
9. Definition of justified or unfair dismissal	1.0	4.0	0.0	4.0	0.0	0.0	0.0	1.9
10. Length of trial period	**6.0**	3.0	3.0	4.0	4.0	2.0		4.0
11. Compensation following unfair dismissal		6.0	1.0	3.0	0.0	1.0		1.9

Table 6.1 (continued)

Item	Greece	Sweden	Denmark	Finland	Belgium	United Kingdom	United States	OECD
12. Possibility of reinstatement following unfair dismissal	**4.0**	0.0	2.0	0.0	0.0	2.0	1.0	2.5
13. Maximum time to make a claim of unfair dismissal	2.0	2.0	0.0	6.0	5.0	2.0	4.0	2.2
C. *Difficulty of individual dismissals*	**2.6**	3.0	1.2	3.4	1.8	1.4	1.0	2.5
I. EPL on regular contracts	**2.4**	2.5	2.0	2.4	2.1	1.2	0.4	2.2
14. Definition of collective dismissal	**6.0**	6.0	4.5	4.5	4.5	3.0	1.5	4.4
15. Additional notification requirements for collective dismissals	3.0	3.0	3.0	0.0	6.0	4.5	6.0	3.7
16. Additional delays involved before notice can start for collective dismissals	1.0	1.0	1.0	2.0	4.0	4.0	4.0	1.8
17. Other special costs to employers of collective dismissals	**3.0**	0.0	3.0	0.0	6.0	0.0	0.0	1.7
18. Difficulty of collective dismissals	**3.3**	2.5	2.9	1.6	5.1	2.9	2.9	2.9
II. EPL on regular contracts including the difficulty of collective dismissals	**2.7**	2.5	2.3	2.2	2.9	1.7	1.1	2.4

Source: OECD Indicators of Employment Protection

Belgium. The second fact is that the severance pay (rows 6–8) at all tenures (1 month, 2 months, and 15 months of pay) is much higher in Greece than in the OECD on average and higher as well than in all the countries presented in the table.

Turning to the second EPL index, the sub-indexes for Greece again take a higher value than in the OECD on average (row C-II of table 6.1). The reason is that the definition of a collective dismissal is narrower in Greece (row 14). Dismissals that exceed 4 employees in firms with 20 to 200 employees, or 2 to 3 percent of the workforce in larger companies, required prior authorization by the Ministry of Labor.[14] The item "Other special costs to employers of collective dismissals" (row 17) is also more restrictive for Greece than in the OECD on average.

Labor legislation in Greece is always interpreted in a way that protects the weaker party; in labor disputes this is invariably interpreted to mean the employee. When combined with article 281 of the Civil Code on "Abuse of Prerogative," this means that exercising managerial prerogative is treated by the courts as an abuse of power. Both sides know that, should courts be called to judge cases of individual or collective redundancies, they are almost certain to reach a verdict against the employer on the ground of abuse of power. This strengthens employees' power and discourages attempts by the employer to initiate contract termination. In practice, this means that other reasons are sought and redundancies are either greatly delayed or eventually abandoned. So, in theory, employers have a right, but in practice, they have limited ability to exercise their right.

6.3.2 Working Hours

Working hours were likewise subject to a number of restrictions. While some of these regulations may be considered reasonable precautions for health and safety, regulations are enforced rigidly in all sectors without due consideration of the nature of the business (e.g., seasonal service provider)[15] or the willingness of the employee herself to opt out of the general legislation. Moreover the implementation of these regulations involves large amounts of red tape.

Premiums for overtime work were high. In manufacturing, for example, wages were doubled if overtime hours exceeded 30 hours per semester.[16] In effect overtime had become prohibitively expensive.

Part-time employment was not a popular option for private sector employers, since the cost was not pro rata with the hours worked. Instead, if an employee worked fewer than 4 hours daily there was a premium of 7.5 percent over the hourly wage that the employee would have received if working full time. Moreover any time in excess of the hours agreed on a daily basis was paid at a 10 percent premium. Part-time employment in central government and local authorities was prohibited. Finally, for individuals paid on a presumptive rather than an actual wage (mainly employees who depend more on tips than a salary), the employer had to pay social security contributions on the basis of the presumptive criterion set out by law, which does not vary according to the number of hours worked (Sabethai 2000). While the presumed level of pay was generally much lower than the actual pay, it is the fact that there was no differentiation according to the hours of work that made employers reluctant to use part-time work. Averaging of working time over periods longer than a week (annualization of working time if the period over which working time is averaged is a year) as an alternative means of working-time flexibility was legislated in the mid-1990s. Annualization, however, never took off, probably because of the red tape associated with it.

6.3.3   Collective Bargaining and Minimum Wage-Setting Procedures

Starting in 1990 the minimum wage and daily wage could be freely bargained between employer associations and trade unions with no government involvement (bargained minimum wage). The minimum wage was adjusted for years of experience and marital status. Agreements setting the minimum wage typically had a duration of two years. Although there was no automatic wage indexation, expected inflation was taken into account with retroactive correction if inflation turned out higher than expected. While private and public sector wage negotiations were separate, agreements for public sector wage increases often served as a benchmark for the private sector.

Negotiations between employer and employee organizations at the aggregate level for the national minimum basic wage were followed by bargaining at three further layers: sector, occupation, and firm. Each layer could only provide for better terms than the immediately prior level. Sectoral agreements were extended, by ministerial decree, to all firms and employees of a sector if the employers' association party to the agreement employed over 51 percent of employees in the sector even though this criterion was difficult to ascertain. There is indeed a general impression that employers were inadequately represented in wage negotiations.[17]

Once legal practice encroached on pay determination, it was not limited to minimum protection but extended to all types of remuneration. By the principle of "equal treatment," an employer that voluntarily grants any benefit to one employee creates the legal right for all other workers to be granted the same benefit. Thus, here too, legal practice served to buttress labor rigidity and limit the use of pay as an incentive.

Remuneration practices in the public sector created an environment conducive to burgeoning wage costs. Changes (that is increases) in basic wages of central government employees were determined annually in the budget and ratified by law. Pay scales were closely linked to years of service and little or no consideration was paid to actual performance (Kanellopoulos 2004). Effort to put more weight on professional qualifications, rather than demographic features (e.g., family status) as was the case in the latter half of the 1980s, started in the early 1990s (OECD 1991). Despite the adoption of uniform increases in base wages across a spectrum of central government employees, earnings across ministries differed significantly as ministers established a number of allowances for their own employees.

The pay conditions in state-owned enterprises were considerably more favorable than in the central government. The evidence suggests that conditional on worker productivity characteristics (e.g., age and education) pay in the public sector was between 20 and 35 percent higher than in the private sector (Papapetrou 2003; Kanellopoulos 1997; Kioulafas et al. 1991; Christopoulou and Monastiriotis 2015). The superior terms and conditions of employment in the public sector brought a blow to the private sector, and unavailability and cost of workers had a negative impact on private firms' ability to compete internationally.

Layoffs in the wider public sector were almost impossible because employees enjoyed permanent status. Even when the law clearly favored termination, the investigation of claims was handled so as to avoid layoffs, and in instances where disciplinary charges were levied, the investigation would take so long that the worker could retire in the meantime. In disciplinary boards, workers' representatives were invariably opposed to termination of contracts.

Mobility between, and even within, ministries was met with resistance. Starting in the mid-1990s, hiring was, in principle, regulated through ASEP (the Supreme Council for Personnel Selection) with the aim to promote the selection of government personnel mainly on merit. For a number of years ASEP followed strict rules in the number of permanent staff that could be hired (1 person hired for every 5 departures). However, the government bypassed this system to expand the public sector by mostly hiring employees on fixed-term contracts that were renewed multiple times, effectively transforming fixed-term contracts into indefinite-length contracts.

6.3.4 Tax Wedge

The tax wedge is here defined as the sum of the income tax (net of cash benefits) and employee and employer contributions as a percentage of labor costs for the employer. This is effectively the percentage difference between what labor costs to the employer and what workers obtain in disposable income. Figure 6.6 depicts the level of the tax wedge in Greece for a married individual with two children in a one-earner family earning the average wage. In 2013 Greece has the highest tax wedge (44.5 compared to 41.6

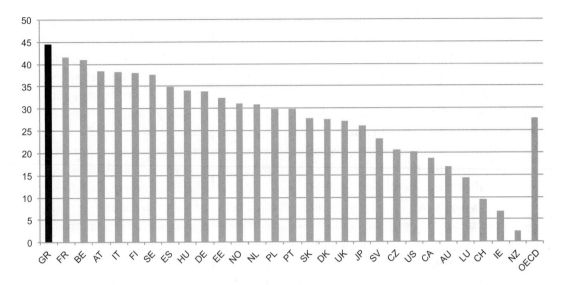

Figure 6.6
Family total tax wedge in 2013
Source: OECD, *Economic Outlook* (2013)

percent in France with the second highest tax wedge) due to high employer contribution rates (28.6 percent when the OECD EU21 average stands at 15.7 percent) and high employee contribution rates (16.5 percent).

6.3.5 Unemployment Benefit Replacement Rate

The labor market in Greece emphasized protection of employment and minimum wages. As already mentioned in section 6.2, unemployment was historically low either because of emigration or because the public sector acted as an employer of last resort. It was thus never considered particularly important to design a robust unemployment insurance (UI) program. Of course, promoting labor market flexibility would require a design of well-functioning UI and a welfare system that would insure workers from large income losses in periods of unemployment, for reasons affecting them alone or in response to large economic shocks that reallocate labor from one sector to another.

6.4 Labor Market Institutions: Theory and Empirical Evidence

To understand the implications of labor market regulation, it is important to use a theoretical framework that lays out clearly the assumptions and defines explicitly how regulation affects the workings of the labor market. It is also important to examine whether the conclusions of the theory are supported by empirical evidence, and what the evidence indicates in those instances where the theoretical conclusions are not clear-cut. In our discussion we will focus on firing restrictions and on minimum wages.

The basic model in economics is that of perfect competition. The key assumptions in this model for our context are that workers can easily locate jobs and can see any existing pay differences that arise for workers with similar skills to their own. Moreover neither firms nor workers (e.g., via unions) have any market power in the labor market. This means that the forces of competition ensure that firms cannot pay workers less than what they contribute to production and in turn that workers cannot force firms to pay more than the workers contribute. Additionally workers are assumed either not to care about risk or to have access to suitable (formal or informal) markets to protect themselves from unexpected fluctuations in earnings.

Under these admittedly strong assumptions almost any restriction on employment relationships mandated by law will be detrimental to employment, output, and aggregate social welfare. Take, for example, a law that makes it expensive to fire workers by making employers go through complicated bureaucratic processes or even pay fines. At first this might seem good for employment, since firms will reduce the number of workers they lay off in bad times, thus attenuating the effects of cyclical downturns. However, firms will anticipate these costs when hiring workers; for them this translates to higher labor costs because they know that eventually they will need to adjust the workforce downward. Consequently they will hire fewer workers in the first place. Overall employment and output produced will thus decline. Moreover the economy will take longer to adjust to reallocation shocks, whereby some sectors decline and others grow. When such reallocation shocks take place, it is desirable for workers to move rapidly from the declining to the growing sector. Firing regulations will prevent this.

Finally, strict labor market regulations can encourage firms to evade them, and thus to become part of the informal economy. In itself this may sound innocuous and indeed beneficial, since this looks like a way to evade some of the effects of undue regulation. However, informal firms tend to be smaller and invest less so as to avoid detection. In so doing, they will lose advantage from possible economies of scale and will not be at the forefront of technology. The result will be a reduction of growth in the economy and a decline in job creation.

Another form of regulation is severance pay, which is an amount often related to salary and length of tenure that is paid to workers who are laid off. There is a lot of debate about the potential detrimental effects of such compensation. Interestingly, in an unregulated world, severance pay has no detrimental effect on employment at least ex ante (Lazear 1990). This is because severance pay is essentially deferred compensation, in that it is pay that the worker will receive in the future with some probability (i.e., if they are laid off). The wage paid to the worker can adjust downward to take into account this future payment, neutralizing its effect on average pay over the tenure of the worker with the firm. Of course, this presupposes that wages are flexible downward and hence that there are no minimum wages. If wages are not flexible downward, severance payments can have important detrimental effects because they raise the cost of labor and thus reduce employment.

While these arguments are intuitive, the pure competitive model is almost certainly wrong. It may act as a useful benchmark and a default position in the absence of reliable information on the labor market. Thus, for a deeper and more complete understanding, we must consider the implications of regulations in the context of labor markets that are imperfect.

The obvious imperfection that takes us away from the perfect competition paradigm are search frictions, namely the fact that it takes time and effort to locate jobs and that workers may not even have knowledge of all the diverse pay opportunities available for their skills and occupation. The implications of search frictions have been investigated for some time now, with one of the first studies being that of McCall (1970). Since then a number of researchers including Burdett, Mortensen, and Pissarides have studied the implications of such a realistic alternative to the competitive model, leading to the Nobel prize winning work of Mortensen and Pissarides (1994) and the equally important work of Burdett and Mortensen (1998), and subsequently of many others.

Beyond search frictions there are other relevant imperfections. For example, individuals might have to choose between full-time work and no work, or more generally, part-time jobs may not be available in some occupations because of technological reasons.

Of course, the key question is the extent to which such frictions affect the conclusions of the benchmark, perfect competition, model in a substantive way that would change our view of policy. In other words, we need to know whether in the presence of the frictions and imperfections described above employment protection regulation is still detrimental or indeed if it can be used to counteract the ill effects of frictions.

Theory offers ambiguous implications and ultimately only empirical evidence based on high-quality data can answer these questions. For example, the model of Mortensen and Pissarides implies that restricting the ability of firms to fire workers can actually increase employment because firms hold on to workers even when they are no longer productive in their original position.[18] However, one needs to interpret this result carefully: by holding on to these workers, firms prevent workers from being reallocated to new, more productive activities. This result is reminiscent of pre-crisis Greece: relatively low unemployment but low productivity per hour worked.

A related point is that the employment rate on its own should not be used as a criterion for overall well-being. Getting a lot of people to work in low-quality jobs in order to lower unemployment is not necessarily better than a world where fewer people are working at any point in time in high-quality jobs and producing overall more, though the unemployed wait longer for the better jobs. Some more examples of instances where employment regulation can increase employment but not improve welfare are provided by Bentolila and Bertola (1990) and Garibaldi and Violante (2005). Employment protection legislation can have the additional negative effect of hindering firms' access to finance as banks are reluctant to fund firms operating under external restrictions (Hart and Moore 1994). The low mobility rates in Greece may well be a symptom of employment protection, which in turn reflects the inability of the economy to adjust to changing economic circumstances. We return to this issue below, but first we discuss minimum wages.

In most countries, minimum wages define the statutory minimum that any worker can receive—usually on an hourly basis. In some countries, the minimum wage may vary by occupation and age, with frequent exemptions added for youth.

Within the competitive paradigm, minimum wages can only reduce employment and output. The argument is simple: in a competitive labor market all workers are paid their marginal product, meaning what they contribute to production. A minimum wage would imply that workers whose marginal product is below that level would be loss making for the firm. Hence, if a worker has to be paid more than she/he can produce (because her/his skills are low), then that worker will not be hired. But in this way minimum wages will translate into permanent unemployment for the lowest skill workers. To get a better and more nuanced understanding of how minimum wages operate, we again consider the implications of the search models introduced above.

Particularly useful insights are offered by the model of Burdett and Mortensen (1998). Workers search for jobs, and when they meet an interested employer, they are offered work at some fixed wage. A key implication in the BM model is that firms have market power in the labor market, and as a result they can pay workers less than they are worth in terms of their productivity. This is because workers can only see one job at a time. When workers meet an employer, their option is to accept the job at the posted wage and thus start earning a wage immediately or remain unemployed and continue searching for an alternative job. This will mean spending more time with lower (if any) income (e.g., unemployment benefits) while waiting for another opportunity. Thus they have to give up income to spend time looking for a better job. This makes them willing to tolerate being underpaid, at least to an extent. As a result the firm appropriates part of the workers' productivity, making "nonnormal profits" (as economists call them). In the competitive model this cannot happen. Profits in the competitive model are just the normal return to capital, meaning the contribution of capital to production. Now suppose that some workers are willing to work at the wage corresponding to their productivity but not at a much lower wage. This implies that in the absence of the minimum wage, they will remain unemployed longer waiting for a suitable wage offer. However, a carefully set minimum wage can induce them to take a job that would have otherwise underpaid them. Firms will still want to hire so long as they earn at least the return to capital—the absence of abnormal profits does not drive them out of business. This will reduce unemployment and increase production and hence welfare.

Beyond this argument there are even more subtle reasons as to why minimum wages can be beneficial. In all cases, however, the emphasis should be on a *carefully set* minimum wage. If it is set too high, the minimum wage will lead to lower employment and lower output. Finding the balance is inherently difficult and even more so in a climate where the various vested interests (e.g., unions of workers and employers) are engaged in a tug of war. It is always important to remember that employed workers are a majority and that they are likely to push for higher wages at the expense of the unemployed, even if a few of their own ranks lose their jobs. So while, in theory, minimum wages can be beneficial, finding a process for setting them at an appropriate level is likely to be fraught with difficulty. In our view, under these circumstances it is likely that having no minimum wage while supporting low earnings with wage subsidies and tax credits is the wiser policy.

Minimum wages are usually set by law, such as in the United States. However, in some countries, including Sweden, Germany, and Greece until recently, minimum wages were the result of collective bargaining. It is not always clear how this process affects the relationship of the minimum wage to productivity. One might think that in a country with good industrial relations, such a process could lead to a consensus between employers and employee organizations such that the minimum wage takes into account competitiveness and productivity. However, in countries where confrontation is the order of the day (as it is in Greece), the result of this process may not internalize the economic conditions adequately and may do so even less than a government-set statutory minimum wage. Issues relating to this form of wage setting are discussed in Boeri (2012).

There are other potentially positive effects of regulation, such as encouraging workers who feel more secure in their jobs to acquire suitable skills or build teams (see Hashimoto 1990). However, this creates a protected group of "insiders" with enhanced bargaining power who may push wages up, increasing the costs to the firm (see Emerson 1988). It could also lead to regulation avoidance by incentivizing other forms of contracts (e.g., fixed-term contracts). Altogether this could lead to increased costs and a slowdown in productivity growth (see Dolado et al. 2011). These authors go on to argue that targeted deregulation (e.g., exempting the young from employment protection) could have important beneficial effects.

Beyond restrictions on layoffs and minimum wages, regulation often touches on other aspects of the work relationship. Important examples are restrictions on overtime and overtime pay and more generally on hours of work. Working hours are restricted in different ways and for different purposes. Some restrictions have been justified on the basis of health and safety. However, hours' restrictions have also been used as a means of increasing employment. Such measures have been applied in France, but they are based on the fallacy of a fixed number of tasks and have not proved to be successful (see Crépon and Kramarz 2002).

Finally, most labor markets include regulations aimed at ensuring health and safety, preventing discrimination, and targeting protection to specific groups, such as pregnant women and mothers with newborn babies. Such regulations are critical for protecting basic human rights. This has become even more so the case in the modern open economies because competition from jurisdictions without such safeguards will put cost-cutting pressure on firms, leading to the erosion of such basic protection. However, it is also possible to overregulate, putting undue burden on firms and increasing costs and thus the unemployment of the very groups meant to be protected.[19]

Beyond minimum wages and employment protection, there are other institutions and features of the economy that can impact the performance of the labor market, among these the system of wage bargaining, the tax system, and the welfare system. Specifically, centralized bargaining is less able to take into account sectoral shifts in demand and may inhibit the adjustment of the economy.[20] The tax system creates a wedge between what firms have to pay to hire workers and what workers actually receive in disposable income. Raising the wedge lowers employment.[21] All these institutional features are important, to be sure, but we do not elaborate more here because our focus is on employment protection regulation.

Where does this leave us? Theoretically, labor market regulation can improve the operation of the labor market when there are search frictions or other imperfections. However, the extent of regulation that could achieve such beneficial results is generally hard to establish. Overregulation will be almost certainly detrimental (Boeri and van Ours 2013). Ultimately resolving the impact of regulation is an empirical matter. The issue is not just qualitative (good/bad), but clearly we care about the size of the impacts, whether they be beneficial or detrimental.

Empirical research has used both microeconomic and aggregate macroeconomic data to evaluate the impact of various regulations. Findings based on aggregate macroeconomic data do not yield clear-cut conclusions on how regulations affect employment, unemployment, and productivity (Abraham and Houseman 1994). This is not surprising because it is hard to distinguish the effects of introducing or removing regulation from other events that may be simultaneously affecting the labor market. Studies based on microeconomic data (individual) and analyzing the effects of specific reforms ("natural experiments") provide instead some clear-cut conclusions.

Heckman and Pagés (2004), using data from a number of countries in Latin America, show that job security legislation increases unemployment and also increases inequality. Kugler (2004) looks at the impact of a reform lowering severance payments in Colombia in 1990. She finds that the reform contributed to increased transition rates into and out of unemployment and to an expansion of the formal labor market, especially for larger firms. Overall the reform led to a fall in the unemployment rate of around 1.5 percentage points. Mondino and Montoya (2004) and Saaverda and Torero (2004) using data from Argentina and Peru find that increased job security is associated with lower employment, somewhat lower remuneration and higher hours of work (Argentina), while employment adjustment becomes possible once labor regulation is relaxed (Peru). Further evidence on the impact of employment protection is provided indirectly by Acemoglu and Angrist (2001), who investigate the effect of the introduction of the Americans with Disabilities Act (ADA), which restricts firing disabled workers. They find that this well-intentioned legislation reduced hiring rates of the disabled and has had no impact on firing rates. The mechanism of the effect is through an increase in the accommodation costs for the disabled. Thus the overall picture emerging from a number of empirical studies from around the world is that job security or employment protection legislation increases unemployment and may also increase inequality. In situations where women and young people perform poorly in the labor market, such regulations work against the improvement of their position.

Indirect evidence on the potential of a deregulated labor market is provided by the performance of the UK labor market in the aftermath of the financial crisis, which hit that country particularly hard. Unemployment in the United Kingdom did not increase by much and certainly much less than in some of the other

European countries. Blundell et al. (2014) attribute the low unemployment rate to wage flexibility.[22]

A number of studies have also sought to isolate the effects of minimum wages in practice. One of the most prominent such studies is that of Card and Krueger (1994). The result of this analysis is that there was no discernible change on employment from an increase in the minimum wage, confirming the idea that large employers of unskilled workers, such as McDonalds, may have some market power the effect of which could be mitigated by increasing minimum wages. Although Card and Krueger's conclusions are considered controversial by some (e.g., see Hamermesh 1995), there is an emerging consensus that low minimum wages do not have large negative effects on employment. Whether they are also beneficial remains unclear. However, there is broad agreement that there should be no minimum wage for youth: this may either cut them off from employment opportunities or, for those who can get jobs at the higher wage level, draw them away from completing their education.

Many economists have tried to use theoretical models to infer appropriate levels of minimum wages based on circumstances and data in specific countries. One such study by Flinn (2000) concluded that the minimum wage should be around $10 an hour in the United States, when currently it is $7.25. Yet his model does not take into account that workers are not locked into the wage they obtain but can look for alternative jobs while working. Using a more general model, Lise, Meghir, and Robin (2016) conclude, again with US microeconomic data, that there should be no minimum wage. In terms of the way minimum wages are set, Boeri (2012) provides evidence to suggest that minimum wages that result from a bargaining process between employer and employee organizations are higher than statutory minimum wages set unilaterally by the government. In this sense centralized wage bargaining determining minimum wages can be more harmful in practice, possibly because unions do not have much of an incentive to take into account the plight of the unemployed, while the government does.

In the absence of hard evidence on the level at which the minimum wage should be set, policy needs to exercise extreme caution. Even if increasing the minimum wage by small amounts may lead to improved pay and employment, large increases can be detrimental for both workers and firms. A good solution for setting minimum wages has been found in the United Kingdom where wages are set following the recommendations of an independent Low Pay Commission (Low Pay Commission Annual Reports 2000–2014), where firms, workers, and academics are all represented and act independently of government. Setting minimum wages out of line of the Low Pay Commission (LPC) would be unjustified and damaging to politicians. Thus, whatever the ultimate merits of minimum wages are, it is important to take into account their effect in the hands of politicians, and to create institutions that protect the labor market from abuse by all those concerned (including government ministers).

When implementing labor market regulation, it is also important to think of it in a broader context of social insurance and redistribution and ask whether such regulation is the best way of achieving these aims. For instance, the minimum wage is just one way of supporting the incomes of the working poor and may not be that effective. While empirical studies in the United States have shown that raising the minimum wage can raise incomes of low-skilled workers at a low cost in terms of unemployment, we need to ask whether the benefits are well targeted and whether other ways of raising incomes, such as tax credits, can be more effective. In recent work MaCurdy (2015) argued that minimum wages are particularly badly targeted. On one hand, firms that hire minimum wage workers tend to offer products consumed by the poor (e.g., fast foods) or low-quality services (e.g., elderly care homes for pensioners). As minimum wages are increased, these products and services are likely to increase in price. Other forms of assistance may also have price effects but may be distributed over a wider variety of goods rather than being concentrated on goods consumed by the poor. An additional consideration is that a large fraction of minimum wage workers are young students often living at home with their relatively well-off parents and whose eventual incomes over their working lives will be quite high. Thus, at least based on US data, minimum wages are badly targeted. By contrast, tax credits, which offer wage subsidies to those workers with low earnings, are a much more reasonable solution because eligibility is based on household income. Moreover tax credits have the distinct advantage of not affecting firms directly. Last, there is an issue of transparency: minimum wages are not costless; they can cause unemployment, a reduction in profits (reducing incomes of those who own firms), and/or an increase in product prices. Yet their costs are hidden from society, whereas other forms of direct redistribution, such as tax credits, have benefits and costs that are visible and transparent. We make this argument not because we do not support raising the incomes of the poor but because minimum wages are a blunt instrument with quite a lot of uncertainty about their positive effects.

The theoretical conclusions and empirical evidence summarized above suggest that even though certain restrictions on labor market operations may be well-intended, their effects are not always in the desired directions. Restrictions seem, in general, to reduce employment creation. The level at which bargaining occurs is also important.

6.5   Labor Market Reform since the Onset of the Crisis

6.5.1   Overview

From the comparative evidence we presented in section 6.3, it is clear that, on average, the regulation of the Greek labor market was stricter and more pervasive than in other OECD countries. Comparative outcomes on labor market performance in section 6.2 also showed that the performance of the Greek labor market was worse than in many other European countries. The theory that we summarized in section 6.4 provides a framework that connects the two.

When the crisis broke out the failings of the various markets came into sharp focus and reforms were proposed to impart efficiency and induce growth. Many commentators believed that although the crisis was manifestly a sovereign debt crisis, the long-term solution would come from institutional changes that would restore entrepreneurship and competitiveness. Labor market reform became a centerpiece of the reform program. In this section we review what has been achieved in Greece in this regard.

The labor market reform took place in three phases. The first phase started in 2010 and lasted until early 2012. Policy makers faced the measures proposed by the Troika almost with disbelief and political economy considerations delayed the implementation of reforms. During this phase there was little effort to reform wage-setting institutions, and measures concerning wages were instead aimed at reducing the fiscal burden (e.g. reduction of public sector pay). The main labor market reforms that took place during the first phase concerned firing restrictions (some reduction in severance pay and in the threshold for collective dismissals). The second phase, starting in early 2012 and lasting until the end of 2014, saw reforms of wage-setting institutions and further easing of firing restrictions. During the third phase, dating from the beginning of 2015 and following the change in government, policy makers have been in a mode of introspection contemplating the reversal of certain of the changes that took place during the second phase.

6.5.2   Wage Cuts

Some of the measures taken from 2010 on were measures of urgent policy action rather than reforms: the reduction of public sector pay (in order to improve public finances) and the cut in the national bargained minimum wage (in order to restore competitiveness) are the prime examples. In February 2012 the national minimum wage was reduced by 22 percent for workers over 25 years of age and by 32 percent for those under that age. Minimum wages will remain frozen at this level until the end of any financial assistance programs. Seniority payments awarded automatically on the basis of the number of years of experience had to be suspended until the unemployment rate dropped below 10 percent (in the second quarter of 2016 the unemployment rate stood at around 23 percent). Collective agreements already in force for three years or longer were automatically terminated. Fallback positions in the event that no new agreement was signed within three months from expiration of the previous agreement had to be drawn up, reducing the remuneration package to very specific components (basic wage and four specific allowances).[23]

Between 2010 and 2015 wages declined both in the private and in the public sector. According to national accounts data, per employee salaries declined by a little over 24 percent (20.8 percent) in nominal (real) terms in the economy as a whole and by 31.5 percent (28.6 percent) in the nonmarket services (public administration, education, and health services). Here it should be noted that public sector pay for medium-skilled jobs was well above equivalent jobs in the private sector—witness the number of individuals taking part in competitions for public sector jobs and the evidence alluded to in the previous section as to a premium between 20 and 35 percent of earnings in the public sector—as the public sector was seen as a win-win situation for low- and middle-level skilled workers: even better employment protection and higher pay. Thus the decline in public sector pay served both to reduce the public deficit and to redress the balance with the private sector (14.2 percent of the decline in public sector pay was due to the abolition of the 13th and the 14th monthly payments, though these continue to be paid in the private sector).

6.5.3   Structural Reforms

The structural reforms that have taken place in the Greek labor market have wide scope and are affecting the most categories of employees. The main reforms introduced concern the procedure for determining the minimum wage, the introduction of a subminimum wage for youths, the elimination of the extension mechanism of sectoral-level collective agreements, a relaxation of employment protection legislation, and a slight reduction in employer and employee social security contributions.[24]

Legislation in 2012 and 2013 provided that at the end of any financial assistance program, the minimum wage—achieved as a result of collective bargaining between employers and employees—would be replaced by a statutory minimum wage, which was to be unilaterally set by the government following consultations with social partners and labor market experts.[25]

To encourage firm-level agreements between workers and employers (as opposed to national collective bargaining that is often divorced from the prevailing conditions in the sectors or firms), two important further changes were introduced during the second phase of reforms. First, preconditions for organized employee representation at the workplace were simplified and the restriction on the minimum size of a firm for a firm level agreement was removed. Second, provisions were set for firms to opt out of sectoral-level agreements, since these no longer define a floor for the outcome of firm-level bargaining. In effect this implies that any extension of a sectoral-level agreement would become irrelevant.

Measures to reduce the segmentation between private and public sector remuneration included not only the larger reduction in wages in the public sector relative to the private sector but also the introduction of productivity related payments and the adoption of a unified wage grid across public agencies, which should increase mobility within the public sector. The appointment of top civil servants has been streamlined with the introduction of criteria of merit and competence and the participation of the independent entity for the recruitment of public servants (ASEP). Public sector pay for executive professional positions, however, remains lower than for professionals in the private sector, and this may be starving the public sector from high-quality human resources.

Employment protection measures have also been relaxed as the procedures for individual dismissals have become lighter (lower procedural burden and less costly). The probationary period, during which dismissed individuals receive no severance pay, has been extended from 2 months to 1 year. The notice periods for dismissals have been reduced to a maximum of 4 months from a maximum of 6 months. Severance pay has been reduced to a maximum of 12 months for those with 28 years of service compared to 24 months prior to the reform. As a result of these changes the OECD EPL index on individual dismissals for Greece now stands at the OECD average.

The threshold for collective dismissals was raised in 2010.[26] Prior to the reform, in firms with 20 to 200 employees, dismissals of 5 employees or more during a month were classified as collective. For firms with over 200 employees the threshold was 2 percent of employees. The reforms have altered these thresholds. For firms with 20 employees, 30 percent of the workforce can be dismissed without the action being considered a collective dismissal. This is a change from 20 percent previously. For firms with 50 employees, the threshold was increased from 8 to 12 percent; for firms with 100 employees, the threshold was increased from 4 to 6 percent; and for firms with 150 employees from around 3 to 4 percent. For firms with over 150 employees, the threshold was raised from 2 to 5 percent with a maximum of 30 individuals (as prescribed by an EU Directive). The decision on collective dismissals above each threshold rests with the Ministry of Labor and could lead to potential conflicts of interest: the Minister of Labor may be concerned with short-term and direct electoral issues and may not wish to take into account the economic health of the enterprise concerned, although this may be a self-defeating strategy if the company eventually becomes less competitive and is driven to closure.[27] Employment protection legislation on fixed-term contracts has also been relaxed somewhat by extending the number of renewals of fixed-term contracts or temporary work agency assignments prior to declaring the relationship one of a permanent nature.

While the unemployment benefit replacement rate is very low in Greece and the duration over which the benefit is being paid is rather short, further conditions for eligibility have been introduced that are linked both to job search intensity (although it is unclear how this will be monitored) and to the length of time over which the individual has received the benefit in the past 4 years so as to avoid abuse by individuals employed in seasonal jobs. In September 2016 only about 16 percent of those registered (35 percent of those registered for less than 12 months) with OAED (the manpower employment agency) receive a benefit.[28] This is due both to the fact that in order to claim benefit, one must have worked for at least 125 days in the last 14 months prior to claiming the benefit and that the regular unemployment benefit can only be received for a maximum of 12 months. The registered unemployed are in turn around three quarters of the number of ILO unemployed.

The combination of the ongoing crisis together with the legislated changes led inevitably to a reduction in the number of sectoral agreements (from 163 in 2008 to 12 in 2015; see Recommendations Experts Group 2016) and an increase in the number of firm-level agreements (see below for exact figures). Moreover, as of 2017, the minimum wage will be set by the government following consultation with the social partners. These developments have led to the general perception that collective bargaining is prohibited and therefore needs to be reinstated. This is the climate that has marked the third phase of labor market reforms.

Social partners had turned early on to the ILO claiming that such abolition of collective bargaining is against international conventions. Ever since the second adjustment program, there was a provision that the wage setting framework in Greece should be reviewed against international best practices. The provision was repeated in the third adjustment program (July 2015) and the review eventually took place in spring 2016 and published the following September. The group of experts that undertook the review met with the social partners before drawing up their conclusions. The main issues on which experts made their recommendations were, first, the institutional setting of the minimum wage and, second, the extent to which firm-level bargaining could underbid the sectoral agreement.

The report clarified that both the model in which the social partners negotiate over the minimum wage and the model in which the social partners are consulted by the government that finally sets the minimum wage were in line with ILO conventions. However, some part of the experts group (the economists) argued in favor of a statutory minimum wage as this would be more consistent with the overall macroeconomic and distributional policies followed by the government. The remaining experts claim that no model of minimum wage setting is more efficient but recommend the negotiated minimum wage on the ground that this is routed in the Greek industrial relations tradition. This is despite the fact that some experts appear to imply that the pre-crisis collective bargaining arrangements did not ensure adequate representation of employers and employees.

Agreement among the experts exists for the need to have a subminimum wage, although there is disagreement regarding the criterion (age or work experience) on which this should be based. The report also reaches no agreement on whether sectoral level agreements should provide an absolute floor for all other agreements. Certain experts argue in favor of subsidiarity according to which the agreement reached at a level closer to the workers should prevail. The remaining experts support the favorability principle according to which higher level agreements have precedence over lower level agreements.

We end this section with a summary of some of the observed labor market outcomes through the crisis and the reform process. Some of the changes we document may be the result of the reforms. However, the reform program and its implementation came too late to have had a substantive effect. Moreover, given that the prevailing political uncertainty and hesitation to reform led to a prolongation of the crisis, it is difficult to associate the outcomes in the labor market with the reforms. This discussion is thus not meant to be an evaluation of the impact of the reform process but rather a description of how the crisis affected work opportunities.[29]

Figure 6.7 summarizes labor market outcomes (employment rate, unemployment rate, and compensation per employee) since 2001. The massive destruction of jobs that has taken place is clear. What is also apparent is a delay in the adjustment of wages despite the fact that employment declined significantly. Once wages started falling, the rate of decline of employment seems to have moderated, and the unemployment rate seems to have stabilized albeit at a very high level.

Evidence on the number of firm-level collective agreements signed in the last couple of years shows an increase from around 200 per year before 2010 to (a peak of) approximately 1000 in 2012. After 2012 the number of firm-level agreements declined somewhat and is estimated to have been around 450 in 2013 and around 300 in each

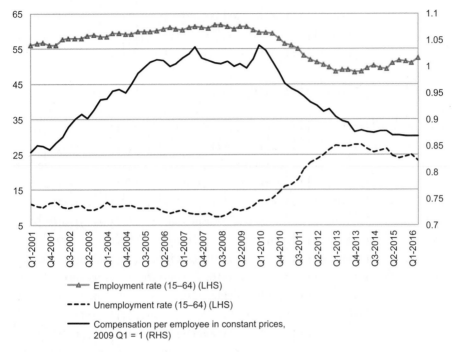

Figure 6.7
Labor market outcomes 2001 to 2016
Sources: ELSTAT, National Accounts data; OECD, Employment Database

of the following years up to 2016—still higher than pre-2010. Most of these agreements have one-year duration. Flexible forms of employment have become more widespread; the percentage of part-time employment among private sector employees more than doubled from 6.4 percent in 2007 (Q1) to 15.7 percent in 2016 (Q1). Job search has intensified, as witnessed from the replies on the methods used for finding a job, and job mobility has increased.

The Greek reforms have been broad and have affected many aspects of the labor market. However, there is a piecemeal feeling about the whole process rather than a clear and coherent direction. For example, the complex collective dismissal rules and the way they affect firms of different sizes is likely to create distortions in the growth of firms (e.g., see Garicano et al. 2016). Moreover it is hard to even think how the overlay on regulations relating to hours, dismissals, wages, and so forth, interact. It would be simpler to focus on what is important, which is the creation of jobs, the avoidance of in-work poverty, and a reasonable protection against unemployment. These goals are easier to achieve by abolishing all regulations relating to dismissals, and introducing a public wage subsidy program, such as tax credits, and a contributory unemployment insurance system. From that benchmark we can consider whether a minimum wage would be beneficial and the level of protection against discrimination.

6.6 Concluding Remarks: Going Forward

Greece has made reluctant moves toward a more deregulated labor market. The emphasis has been on modernizing remuneration policies in the public sector, reforming the way the minimum wage is set, and moving away from multi-layered collective bargaining. There has also been some reform activity relating to firing and severance payments. Yet severance payments continue to be higher than in other EU countries, on average. Moreover the threshold for collective dismissals is still lower than in other EU countries and a firm's decision can still be vetoed by the Ministry of Labor. A lot more needs to be done to reach the point where the labor market is sufficiently deregulated to promote inward investment and growth. Despite these changes in the right direction, labor market regulation is still considered by Greek policy makers as a tool to further social inclusion and as a pillar of the welfare state. While some regulatory intervention may be called for in certain circumstances, it should no longer be viewed as part of the welfare system but as a mechanism for promoting entrepreneurship and opportunity for all. Next to such a deregulated labor market there should be a robust system of social insurance protecting workers from the consequences of unemployment and even low pay.

Thus there is an alternative vision to the one that dominates Greek policy thinking. That is one where the labor market is deregulated and where the government offers suitable public insurance. In this alternative world the only regulations in place will relate to health and safety at work and to antidiscrimination laws ensuring equal opportunities for all independently of gender, race, and sexual orientation as well as protection from unfair dismissal. The few regulations in place would be enforced with rigor by suitable employment tribunals that would operate swiftly and efficiently. Beyond that, employers would choose whom to hire, when, and for how long, and they would pay an agreed wage. Employment terms would be governed by a privately agreed contract, subject, of course, to the minimal protections against discrimination or unhealthy environments.

Such a labor market would promote employment and growth, as the costs of hiring workers would be lowered. It would also allow workers to be reallocated easily from failing sectors to growing ones. However, it would also imply unacceptably low levels of insurance and a degree of insecurity, only mitigated by the greater ease of finding new jobs. This is why at the same time that the labor market is deregulated, a well-designed welfare system must be put in place for both the unemployed and those working.

The welfare system would consist of two key elements. First, there would be a contributory unemployment insurance (UI) system, which would cover a reasonable proportion of lost earnings (up to a ceiling) for a fixed period of time (e.g., six to nine months). This would provide some protection against job loss and would cushion consumption during the period of job search. Ideally this should be funded by workers' contributions. It is also important for incentive purposes that it does have a limited duration. The key point is though that the existence of a well-structured and efficient UI system would make it socially much less costly to reallocate labor and to allow firms to concentrate on managing efficiently their business.

The second element of the welfare system would replace the minimum wage and at the same time would ensure reasonable standards of living for the lower paid/lower skilled workers. This would be a tax-credit or negative income tax system. In this case low incomes would be supplemented by a proportional benefit as with the US earned income tax credit or the UK family tax credit. The rate of supplementation could be as high as 40 percent, which would mean that low earnings would be supplemented by 40 percent from the government (a negative 40 percent tax). Beyond a specific level of assistance to be determined according to the generosity of the system, the negative tax would become zero (so the benefit would not increase further). Finally, beyond a particular level of earnings, the benefit would have to be withdrawn gradually (otherwise all individuals independently of how well off they were would benefit) by the tax rate becoming positive. In large firms, the system could be administered through the payroll automatically and offset against taxes withheld for higher earnings employees—this would be ideal as the employee would receive the benefit immediately eliminating the need to file a claim. If the benefit ends up being too high, it could be taxed away at the end of the year through the tax return. For smaller employers, the government would have to credit them in advance with the benefit so as not to generate liquidity problems. Detailed implications of such as system are given in chapter 10 on taxes in this volume.

While implementation is, of course, key to the success of such a program, at this stage the most important point is not to lose sight of the principles involved. In this suggested system firms are allowed to manage their businesses without interference (other than basic regulation mentioned above). The government then becomes responsible for social insurance, as it really should. Moreover the costs of such social insurance are clear and transparent for every citizen to see and inspect through the democratic system.

The alternative system of supporting workers through employment protection and other labor market regulations (as appears to be the accepted view and practice in Greece) suffers from three key disadvantages. First, employment protection is costly in a major way because it stifles investment and growth. Second, it targets the wrong people, by making it harder for low-skilled workers to be employed. And third, it imposes nontransparent costs that cannot be scrutinized easily via the democratic system.

We have already argued that some regulation may be beneficial, at least in theory because labor markets are imperfect. However, we have also argued that finding the right level of regulation is a very difficult balancing act, and if implemented incorrectly, regulation can do more harm than good. Getting it right, and in particular, insulating the system from populist politicians all too eager to satisfy one or the other constituency is hard and should be viewed as an impediment to sensible levels of regulation. All in all, it is better to offer support and insurance through the more transparent welfare system than to create a rigid labor market that prevents growth.

Notes

1. We thank Manolis Galenianos and Dimitri Vayanos for extensive comments. Costas Meghir benefited from funding by the Cowles foundation and the ISPS at Yale.

2. The tax wedge is the difference between employer's cost and what the worker receives, which is after various taxes are withdrawn.

3. See Blanchard et al. (2013), Holmlund (2013), Boeri (2011), Saint-Paul (2002), and Blau and Kahn (1999).

4. By discrimination, we mean actions that treat people differently on the basis of their gender, race, religion, or sexual orientation. Any such practices should be rigorously prevented.

5. However, the self-employed may be distorting the real picture because they tend to declare themselves full-time workers, which may or may not reflect reality—typically self-employed hours are poorly measured.

6. The use of part-time employment for women has to be viewed in connection with the availability or otherwise of childcare facilities. The absence of such services at a reasonable cost implies that mothers might not be available (willing) to take up part-time jobs.

7. The implications of limited reallocation of resources on productivity and output growth has been well documented; see Martin and Scarpetta (2012) and the references therein.

8. Hirings include individuals who moved into employment from inactivity or unemployment as well as individuals employed both in t and in $(t - 1)$ but having been with their current employer for less than 12 months (see OECD 2009, annex 2.A1).

9. See Blundell et al. (2014) for a discussion of the important role that wage flexibility played in keeping unemployment low in the United Kingdom during the 2007 financial crisis and the Great Recession that followed.

10. The survey is part of an ESCB/eurosystem research initiative on wage and price setting procedures (the Wage Dynamics Network, WDN). Details of the survey at European level can be found in Druant et al. (2012); details on the survey for Greece are included in Nicolitsas (2016).

11. See Bank of Greece (2013, tab. III.7, p. 41), *Monetary Policy Report 2012–13*, Bank of Greece publications.

12. See Meghir, Narita, and Robin (2015) for empirical evidence on the detrimental effects of informality.

13. The first three sub-indexes are now weighted by 5/7 while the final item is weighted by 2/7.

14. For firms with over 200 employees the threshold was set between 2 and 3 percent, depending on a Ministerial decision renewed every semester, and up to 30 individuals. The upper limit of 30 individuals is consistent with an EU Directive.

15. For example, two consecutive days of rest are required even for employees in enterprises working only 5 to 6 months a year.

16. As a comparison, note that in France the annual quota is set at 220 hours (Cahuc and Carcillo 2011).

17. In the price- and wage-setting survey conducted by the Bank of Greece, mentioned above, most firms, when asked whether they participated directly or indirectly in the negotiations for the minimum base wage (national, sectoral, occupational), replied negatively.

18. Ljungqvist (2002) considers four alternative models with frictions: the original McCall search model, two versions of the Mortensen–Pissarides model, which differ in the way the surplus produced from the match is divided between workers and firms, and a model where the friction originates in indivisibility of labor time (employment lotteries). He calibrates these models to the US labor market data and examines the effects of firing costs within each context. The firing cost takes the form of a tax, which is then returned to all individuals in terms of a lump sum, regardless of their labor market status.

19. For the case of Greece in this domain, see Lyberaki (2010).

20. See Calmfors and Driffill (1988) and Calmfors (1993).

21. Nickell (2004) in his survey of the empirical literature shows that a 10 percentage point rise in the tax wedge (defined as the sum of the payroll tax rate, income tax rate, and consumption tax rate) reduces labor input by somewhere between 1 and 3 percent of the population of working age.

22. The United Kingdom does have minimum wages, although these are quite low and did not prevent wages from adjusting. Obviously the impact of minimum wages depends on their level.

23. The impact of the fallback position on negotiations is discussed by Moene (1988) and Manning (1993), among others.

24. Employer social security contributions stood at 27.46 percent in November 2012, were reduced to 24.56 percent in July 2014, but were increased again to 25.06 percent in June 2016. Employee social security contributions stood at 16.5 percent in November 2012, were reduced slightly to 15.50 percent in July 2015, but were increased again to 16 percent in June 2016.

25. By "social partners," we mean representatives of management and labor that participate in collective wage negotiations. For the national minimum wage this involves the following parties: the Hellenic Federation of Enterprises (SEV), the Hellenic Confederation of Professionals, Craftsmen and Merchants (GSEVEE), the Hellenic Confederation of Commerce and Entrepreneurship (ESEE), the Greek Tourism Confederation (SETE) on the employers' side (as nationally representative employers' associations), and the General Confederation of Greek Workers (GSEE), the highest-level trade union body, on the labor side.

26. The threshold is set in absolute values for firms with fewer than 150 employees, with the same threshold level applying to a whole range of firm sizes.

27. In 2015 the Minister of Labor used the authority given by the law and rejected a restructuring plan by AGET Iraklis SA involving dismissals. AGET Iraklis SA took the case to the (Greek) Council of State claiming that the provision was not compatible with Directive 98/59/EC. The Council of State has in turn referred the case to the European Court of Justice. The Court decision will impact on the continuation or otherwise of the need for Ministerial approval.

28. Of the registered unemployed in September 2016, 55 percent have been unemployed for over 12 months.

29. Tagkalakis (2015) looks at the transition rates into and out of unemployment during the Greek crisis and finds that following the reforms in 2012 the inflow rate into unemployment declined while the outflow rate from unemployment increased. His results show, however, also a slight outward movement in the Beveridge curve reflecting the structural changes taking place in production.

References

Abraham, K. G., and S. N. Houseman. 1994. Does employment protection inhibit labor market flexibility? Lessons from Germany, France, and Belgium. In *Social Protection versus Economic Flexibility: Is there a Trade-off?* ed. R. M. Blank. Chicago: University of Chicago Press.

Acemoglu, D., and J. D. Angrist. 2001. Consequences of employment protection? The case of the Americans with Disabilities Act. *Journal of Political Economy* 109 (5): 915–57.

Anagnostopoulos, A., and S. W. Siebert. 2012. The impact of Greek labour market regulation on temporary and family employment: Evidence from a new survey. Discussion paper 6504. IZA, Bonn.

Bank of Greece. 2013. *Monetary Policy Report 2012–13*. Athens: Bank of Greece Publications.

Bentolila, S., and G. Bertola. 1990. Firing costs and labor demand: How bad is eurosclerosis? *Review of Economic Studies* 57 (3): 381–402.

Blanchard, O., F. Jaumotte, and P. Loungani. 2013. *Labor market policies and IMF advice in advanced economies during the Great Recession. Staff discussion notes 13/02*. IMF.

Blanchflower, D. G. 2000. Self-employment in OECD countries. *Labour Economics* 7 (5): 471–505.

Blanchflower, D. G. 2004. Self-employment: More may not be better. *Swedish Economic Policy Review* 11 (2): 15–74.

Blau, F. D., and L. M. Kahn. 1999. Institutions and laws in the labor market. In *Handbook of Labor Economics, vol. 3A*, ed. O. Ashenfelter and D. E. Card, 1399–1461. Amsterdam: Elsevier.

Blundell, R., C. Crawford, and W. Jin. 2014. What can wages and employment tell us about the UK's productivity puzzle. *Economic Journal 124 (576): 377-407*.

Boeri, T. 2011. Institutional reforms and dualism in European labour markets. In *Handbook for Labor Economics*, ed. O. Ashenfelter and D. Card, 1173–1236. Amsterdam: Elsevier.

Boeri, T. 2012. Setting the minimum wage. *Labour Economics* 19 (3): 281–90.

Boeri, T., and J. van Ours. 2013. *The Economics of Imperfect Labor Markets*, 2nd ed. Princeton: Princeton University Press.

Burdett, K., and D. Mortensen. 1998. Wage differentials, employer size, and unemployment. *International Economic Review* 39: 257–73.

Burtless, G. 2001. The Greek labor market. In *Greece's Economic Performance and Prospects*, ed. R. C. Bryant, N. Garganas and G. Tavlas, 453–98. Athens/Washington DC: Bank of Greece/Brookings Institution.

Cahuc, P., and S. Carcillo. 2011. The detaxation of overtime hours: Lessons from the French experiment. Discussion paper 5439. IZA, Bonn.

Calmfors, L., and J. Driffill. 1998. Bargaining structure, corporatism, and macroeconomic performance. *Economic Policy* 3 (6): 13–61.

Calmfors, L. 1993. Centralisation of wage bargaining and macroeconomic performance: A survey. *OECD Economic Studies* 21: 162–91.

Card, D., and A. B. Krueger. 1994. Minimum wages and employment: A case study of the fast-food industry in New Jersey and Pennsylvania. *American Economic Review* 84 (4): 772–93.

Christopoulou, R., and V. Monastiriotis. 2015. Public-private wage duality during the Greek crisis. *Oxford Economic Papers* 68 (1): 174–196.

Crépon, B., and F. Kramarz. 2002. Employed 40 hours or not-employed 39: Lessons from the 1982 mandatory reduction of the workweek. *Journal of Political Economy* 110 (6): 1355–89.

Dolado, J. J., S. Ortigueira, and R. Stucchi. 2011. Does dual employment protection affect TFP? Evidence from Spanish manufacturing firms. Discussion paper 8763. CEPR.

Druant, M. S., G. Fabiani, A. Kezdi, F. Lamo, R. Martins, and R. Sabbatini. 2012. How are firms' wages and prices linked: Survey evidence for Europe. *Labour Economics* 19 (5): 772–82.

ECB. 2012. Euro Area Labour Markets and the Crisis. Occasional Paper 138.

Emerson, M. 1988. Regulation or deregulation of the labor market: Policy regimes for the recruitment and dismissal of employees in the industrialized countries. *European Economic Review* 32: 775–817.

European Commission. 2009. *Employment in Europe 2009*. Luxembourg: Office for Official Publications of the European Communities.

Flinn, C. 2000. Interpreting minimum wage effects on wage distributions: A cautionary tale. Economic research report 08. New York University.

Garibaldi, P., and G. L. Violante. 2005. The employment effects of severance payments with wage rigidities. *Economic Journal* 115 (506): 799–832.

Garicano, L., C. LeLarge, and J. Van Reenen. 2016. Firm size distortions and the productivity distribution: Evidence from France. *American Economic Review*, forthcoming.

Hamermesh, D. S. 1995. Comment on myth and measurement: The new economics of the minimum wage: What a wonderful world this would be. *Industrial and Labor Relations Review* 48 (4): 835–38.

Hart, O., and J. Moore. 1994. A theory of debt based on the inalienability of human capital. *Quarterly Journal of Economics* 109 (4): 841–79.

Hashimoto, M. 1990. Employment and wage systems in Japan and their implications for productivity. In *Paying for Productivity*, ed. A. S. Blinder, 245–294. Washington, DC: Brookings Institution.

Heckman, J. J. and C. Pagés. Introduction. In *Law and Employment: Lessons from Latin America and the Caribbean*, ed. J. J. Heckman and C. Pagés, 1–108. Chicago: Chicago University Press.

Holmlund, B. 2013. What do labor market institutions do? Discussion paper 7809. IZA.

Iordanoglou, C. 2008. *The Greek Economy in the "Longue Durée": 1954–2005*. Athens: Polis Publishers.

Kanellopoulos, C. N. 1997. Public-private wage differentials in Greece. *Applied Economics* 29 (8): 1023–32.

Kanellopoulos, C. N. 2004. Labour market: Institutional framework and employment-unemployment. In *Essays in Economic Analysis*, ed. T. Lianos, 327–46. Athens: Papazisis. (in Greek)

Kioulafas, K., G. Donatos, and G. Michailidis. 1991. Public and private sector wage differentials in Greece. *International Journal of Manpower* 12 (3): 9–14.

Kugler, A. 2004. The effect of job security regulations on labor market flexibility. Evidence from the Colombian labor market reform. In *Law and Employment: Lessons from Latin America and the Caribbean*, ed. J. J. Heckman and C. Pagés, 183–228. Chicago: Chicago University Press.

Lazear, E. 1990. Job security provisions and employment. *Quarterly Journal of Economics* 105 (3): 699–726.

Lianos, Th. 2003. *Contemporary Migration to Greece: An Economic Analysis*. Athens: Centre of Economic Planning and Research. (in Greek)

Lise, J., C. Meghir, and J. M. Robin. 2016. Mismatch, sorting and wage dynamics. *Review of Economic Dynamics* 19: 63-87.

Ljungqvist, L. 2002. How do lay-off costs affect employment? *Economic Journal* 112 (482): 829–53.

Low Pay Commission Annual Reports. 2000–2014. https://www.gov.uk/government/collections/national-minimum-wage-low-pay-commission-reports.

Lyberaki, A. 2010. The record of gender policies in Greece 1980–2010: Legal form and economic substance. GreeSE Paper 36. Hellenic Observatory Papers on Greece and Southeast Europe. LSE.

Lyberaki, A. 2011. Migrant women, care work, and women's employment in Greece. *Feminist Economics* 17 (3): 103–31.

MaCurdy. 2015. How effective is the minimum wage at supporting the poor. *Journal of Political Economy* 123 (2): 497–545.

Manning, A. 1993. A Dynamic Model of Union Power, Wages and Employment. *Scandinavian Journal of Economics* 95 (2): 175–93.

Martin, J. P., and S. Scarpetta. 2012. Setting it right: Employment protection, labour reallocation and productivity. *De Economist* 160 (2): 89–116.

McCall, J. 1970. Economics of information and job search. *Quarterly Journal of Economics* 84: 113–26.

Meghir, C., R. Narita, and J. M. Robin. 2015. Wages and informality in developing countries. *American Economic Review* 105 (4): 1509–46.

Moene, K. O. 1988. Unions' threats and wage determination. *Economic Journal* 98 (391): 471–83.

Mondino, G., and S. Montoya. 2004. The effects of labor market regulations on employment decisions by firms. Empirical evidence for Argentina. In *Law and Employment: Lessons from Latin America and the Caribbean*, ed. J. J. Heckman and C. Pagés, 351–400. Chicago: Chicago University Press.

Mortensen, D., and C. Pissarides. 1994. Job creation and job destruction in the theory of unemployment. *Review of Economic Studies* 61 (3): 397–415.

Nickell, S. J. 2004. Employment and taxes. Discussion paper 634. Centre for Economic Performance.

Nicolitsas, D. 2016. Price setting practices in Greece: Evidence from a small-scale firm-level survey. *Bulletin of Economic Research* 68 (4): 367–382.

OECD. 1991. *OECD Economic Surveys: Greece.* Paris: OECD Publishing.

OECD. 2009. *Employment Outlook.* Paris: OECD Publishing.

OECD. 2011. Taxation and employment. *OECD Tax Policy Studies* 21. Paris: OECD Publishing.

OECD. 2013. *Economic Outlook, vol. 94.* Paris: OECD Publishing.

Pagano, P., and F. Schivardi. 2003. Firm size distribution and growth. *Scandinavian Journal of Economics* 105 (2): 255–274.

Papapetrou, E. 2003. Wage differentials between the public and the private sector in Greece. *Economic Bulletin* 21. Bank of Greece.

Recommendation Experts Group. 2016. Review of Greek Labour Market Institutions. http://www.ypakp.gr/uploads/docs/9946.pdf.

Saaverda, J., and M. Torero. 2004. Labor market reforms and their impact over formal labor demand and job market turnover. The case of Peru. In *Law and Employment: Lessons from Latin America and the Caribbean*, ed. J. J. Heckman and C. Pagés, 131–82. Chicago: Chicago University Press.

Sabethai, I. 2000. The Greek labour market: Features, problems and policies. *Economic Bulletin 16.* Bank of Greece.

Saint-Paul, G. 2002. The political economy of employment protection. *Journal of Political Economy* 110 (3): 672–701.

Tagkalakis, A. 2016. Unemployment dynamics and the Beveridge curve in Greece. *IZA Journal of European Labor Studies* 5 (13): 1–34.

7 Financial Development and the Credit Cycle in Greece[1]

Michael Haliassos, Gikas Hardouvelis, Margarita Tsoutsoura, and Dimitri Vayanos

7.1 Introduction and Summary

Much of the policy attention since the Greek crisis erupted in 2009 has concerned the financial system. Greek banks realized large losses on their holdings of Greek government bonds because of Greece's sovereign default. The banks also saw the fraction of their nonperforming loans (NPLs) to the private sector increase dramatically because of the sharp economic contraction. Restoring the banks to solvency required a large-scale recapitalization, which took place mostly with public funds in 2013, but with increasing participation by private investors in 2014. The negotiation between the SYRIZA-ANEL government elected in January 2015 and the Troika ended with a bank run and the imposition of capital controls in the summer of 2015. A further recapitalization was made necessary by these developments.

Decisive measures were not only necessary in recapitalizing banks, but also in improving the legal framework pertaining to bankruptcy and debt restructuring. Bankruptcy laws were revised repeatedly to facilitate the resolution of nonperforming loans (NPLs) to households and firms. The dramatic increase in NPLs during the crisis reflected a drastic deterioration of households' and firms' finances brought about by the economic contraction. Households and firms were further hit through the effects that the crisis had on banks: loans became hard to obtain and deposits were no longer viewed as safe.

In this chapter we review these developments. We also place them in a broader context by evaluating (1) the long-term performance of Greece's financial system in comparison to other countries and (2) the credit boom-and-bust cycle that Greece has experienced since euro entry. The perspective we offer on the developments since the crisis brings us to suggest some desirable policy options going forward.

In section 7.2, we provide a panorama of the Greek financial system: the types of financial institutions operating in Greece and their relative size, the asset holdings of

Greek households, and the capital structures of Greek firms. A consistent theme that emerges from our findings is that compared to other eurozone countries, as well as to the United Kingdom and the United States, risks in the Greek economy are not well insured or diversified. In particular, financial intermediation is largely dominated by banks, with the insurance and mutual-fund sectors being much smaller than in the other countries. Moreover households hold their wealth in housing and bank deposits to a larger extent than in the other countries, with stocks, bonds, mutual funds, and voluntary pensions playing a minor role, and firms rely more on large shareholders and employ more leverage than in the other countries.

Limited diversification raises the cost of equity capital for firms and is an impediment to long-term growth. Moreover, because it drives up corporate leverage, it can make the economy more vulnerable to shocks. We argue that a natural explanation for limited diversification is weak investor protection and the lack of trust that it breeds. At the same time, factors such as lack of financial literacy, tax disincentives, and limited entry by foreign financial institutions that could promote competition and financial innovation may also be playing an important role.

In section 7.3, we review Greece's credit boom-and-bust cycle since euro entry. We separate the bust into (1) the period from the beginning of the global financial crisis in August 2007 to the beginning of the sovereign debt crisis in October 2009 and (2) the period since October 2009. This allows us to look more deeply into the bank–sovereign loop, and to better isolate the effects that were transmitted to banks from the sovereign government's default and those that originated within banks. Greece's sovereign default caused all Greek banks to become insolvent because of their large positions in Greek government bonds. At the same time, the rapid growth in private sector credit since euro entry had left the banks exposed to the deterioration in global funding conditions, such as the one experienced in 2007 and 2008. This risk exposure appears to have been higher for Greek banks than for the average EZ bank, and caused significant funding difficulties for Greek firms even before the sovereign crisis started.

In sections 7.4 and 7.5, we discuss challenges facing the Greek financial system and possible policies to address them. The main challenge for the short and medium run is to recover from the credit crunch by reducing the debt burdens of households and firms, and ensuring that banks provide an adequate flow of credit to the economy. While some of the required interventions may be at the macroeconomic level and involve actions by the European Central Bank (ECB), we focus on interventions that are more microeconomic and are available to Greek policy makers.

An important set of interventions concerns the judicial procedures governing bankruptcy and debt restructuring, both for firms and for households. The laws in place and their practical applications generate significant inefficiencies, especially the idling of productive assets. These inefficiencies mattered less during the credit boom, but they must now be addressed. A second set of interventions concern the incentives and capacity within the banking system to resolve NPLs.

Coming to the longer run, an important challenge is to further the development of capital markets so that risks are better diversified, equity financing becomes cheaper, and the economy becomes less vulnerable to shocks. Strengthening investor protection laws and their practical application is an important part of the solution. Interventions are required both at the level of the justice system, covered extensively in chapter 12 in this volume, and at the level of financial regulators.

Stronger investor protection will help develop the capital-markets side of the financial system, but attention is also needed on the banking side. As is well known from academic research, state control of banks results in bad lending decisions, corruption, and rent seeking. Hence, clear boundaries must be kept between banks and the state, especially given that the state has become a large shareholder in the banks following the recapitalizations. Encouraging entry by foreign financial institutions should be an important policy priority as well, given the evidence that such entry promotes competition, financial innovation, and better regulation.

7.2   Panorama of the Greek Financial System

In this section we compare the Greek financial system with that in other EZ countries, the United Kingdom, and the United States. In some of the comparisons, we employ only a subset of the above countries because of data limitations. In section 7.2.1, we describe the types of financial institutions operating in Greece, and their relative size. In section 7.2.2, we describe the asset holdings of Greek households, and in section 7.2.3, we describe the capital structures of Greek firms. The main takeaways from the evidence are as follows:

1. Greece's financial system is smaller (as fraction of GDP) than in all comparison countries.

2. Greece's financial system is dominated by banks to a larger extent than in all comparison countries, with the exception of Cyprus. Other types of financial institutions, such as insurance companies and investment funds, play only a minor role in financial intermediation.

3. The wealth of Greek households is held in real assets, such as real estate and private businesses, to a larger extent than in all comparison countries. Hence financial

assets, such as bank deposits, bonds, and stocks, account for a smaller fraction of wealth than in all comparison countries, and thus provide a smaller liquid buffer to smooth out drops in consumption during recessions.

4. The financial assets of Greek households are held in bank deposits to a larger extent than in all comparison countries. This is consistent with the small size of insurance companies and investment funds.

5. Greek firms are dominated by large shareholders to a greater extent than in all comparison countries. This result holds both on average and when controlling for firm size, that is, comparing firms of the same size.

6. Greek firms are more levered, in that they have a larger ratio of debt to equity than in all comparison countries. Again, this result holds both on average and when controlling for firm size.

A consistent theme from these findings is that risks in the Greek economy are not well insured or diversified. This is reflected in the small size of insurance companies, which are the very institutions designed to insure risks. It is also reflected in the limited holdings of stocks and mutual funds by households, the small size of investment funds, and the dominance of large shareholders in firms: all these findings show that households hold only limited equity stakes in firms, and firm risk is not well diversified. The larger ratio of debt to equity in firms' capital structures is an additional indication of this phenomenon.

Limited diversification is harmful at the household level because individuals remain overly exposed to risks affecting their income level, property value, or health status. Because of limited diversification at the firm level, firms have a higher cost of raising equity capital and hence are less able to invest and create jobs. The higher cost of equity capital can drive up corporate leverage, making the economy more vulnerable to shocks.

The extent of diversification and the size of a country's financial system are indicators of the country's level of financial development. A large body of research has shown that financial development promotes economic growth.[2] Our results suggest that financial development in Greece lags that in the comparison countries. Hence boosting financial development should be an important long-term goal for economic policy in Greece.

Factors hindering financial development include weak investor protection and lack of financial literacy. In sections 7.2.2 and 7.2.3, we examine how these and other factors can account for the evidence that we report. In section 7.5, we propose some policy remedies.

7.2.1   Financial Institutions

Figure 7.1 describes the aggregate size of different types of financial institutions in Greece, and compares them with those of other EZ countries, the United Kingdom, and the United States. The types of institutions considered are credit institutions (mainly banks), insurance companies, pension funds, and investment funds (mainly mutual funds and hedge funds). We report data on the aggregate assets held by each type of institution in each country as a percentage of the country's gross domestic product (GDP). The data for credit institutions, insurance companies, and investment funds are from 2012. For pension funds we report data from 2010, which is the latest year available. Pre-crisis data from 2008, which is the earliest year for which data on insurance companies and investment funds are available, present a similar picture.

The aggregate assets held by Greek financial institutions of all four types are 190.1 percent of Greek GDP. The average across the EZ is 404.8 percent, and the corresponding numbers for the United Kingdom and the United States are 777.7 and 298.7 percent, respectively. The aggregate size of Greek financial institutions as percent of GDP

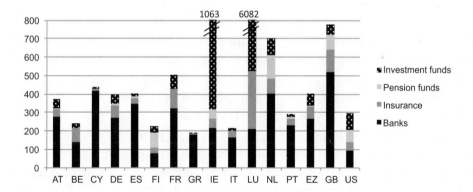

Figure 7.1

Assets held by financial institutions as percentage of GDP. The data for credit institutions come from the ECB in the case of EZ countries, from the Bank of England in the case of the United Kingdom, and from the Federal Deposit Insurance Corporation in the case of the United States. The data for insurance companies come from the ECB in the case of EZ countries, with the exception of Cyprus, Ireland, and Portugal. For these countries, as well as for the United Kingdom and the United States, the data come from local industry bodies. The data for pension funds come from the World Bank's Global Financial Development Database. Pension fund data for Cyprus are missing. The data for investment funds come from the European Fund and Asset Management Association (EFAMA). The data for credit institutions, insurance companies, and investment funds are as of 2012, and for pension funds are as of 2010. EZ averages are computed by dividing EZ assets by EZ GDP.

is smaller than in all comparison countries. Thus the Greek financial system is small in an aggregate sense. Next in size after Greece come Italy (215 percent) and Finland (224.5 percent).

A more complete comparison between Greece and the other countries can be performed by breaking down assets by type of financial institution. Assets of Greek banks are 178.6 percent of GDP. The average across the EZ is 266.6 percent, and the corresponding numbers for the United Kingdom and the United States are 519.2 and 92.5 percent, respectively. The aggregate size of Greek banks as percent of GDP is thus smaller than the EZ average, but assets of Greek banks are a larger percentage of GDP than in Finland (77.2 percent), the United States (92.5 percent), Belgium (138.42 percent), and Italy (166.1 percent).

The gap between Greece and the comparison countries becomes much wider when considering institutions other than banks, namely insurance companies, pension funds, and investment funds. The aggregate assets of these institutions as percent of GDP are 11.5 percent in Greece, while the average across the EZ is 138.2 percent, and the corresponding numbers for the United Kingdom and the United States are 258.6 and 206.2 percent, respectively.

The previous observations suggest that the Greek financial system is dominated by banks to a larger extent than in the comparison countries. Banks indeed account for 93.9 percent of financial-system assets in Greece (taking the financial system to consist of the four types of institutions considered in this section), while the average across the EZ is 70.5 percent, and the corresponding numbers for the United Kingdom and the United States are 66.8 and 31 percent, respectively. The only country for which banks are more dominant than in Greece is Cyprus, where 95.4 percent of financial-system assets are held within banks. Next in order come Spain (87.2 percent), Portugal (79.9 percent), and Italy (77.3 percent). Since assets of investment funds and pension funds are mainly stocks and bonds, which are traded in capital markets, figure 7.1 confirms the preponderance of banks relative to capital markets in Europe and the converse phenomenon in the United States.

As a matter of fact Greece's investment fund sector is not only the smallest than in all countries in figure 7.1 (3.5 percent of GDP in Greece, compared to 9.8 percent in Cyprus, 12.6 percent in Italy, 14.4 percent in Portugal, 14.6 percent in Spain, and 42.6 percent EZ average) but is also comparable to that of European countries with lower GDP per capita, such as Romania (2.8 percent) and Turkey (3.9 percent).

Some of the services performed by insurance companies and investment funds could be performed within banks. Hence banks could, in principle, substitute effectively for a small insurance and investment fund sector. Figure 7.2 shows, however, that Greek

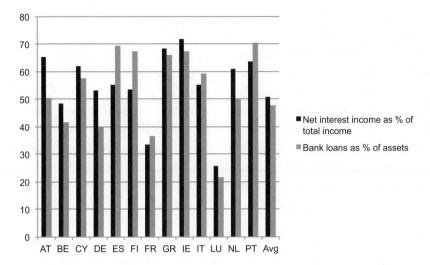

Figure 7.2
Bank assets and income structure. The data come from the ECB and are as of 2007. The average is computed by aggregating numerator and denominator across the countries in the figure and dividing.

banks focus on traditional deposit-taking and lending to a larger extent than many of their EZ counterparts. The figure plots two measures of banks' activities. First is the fraction of income earned from the interest-rate differential between loans and deposits. Second is the fraction of assets that are loans. Both fractions would be equal to one if banks engage only in deposit-taking and lending, and smaller than one if banks engage in additional activities such as insurance and asset management. We report pre-crisis figures, as of 2007. More recent data give a similar picture.

Greek banks derived 68.4 percent of their income from traditional deposit-taking and lending in 2007. The average across all comparison countries was 51.0 percent, and Greece ranked second after Ireland (71.9 percent). The loans of Greek banks were 66 percent of their total assets. The average across all comparison countries was 47.9 percent, and Greece ranked fifth after Portugal (70.5 percent), Spain (69.3 percent), Finland (67.4 percent), and Ireland (67.3 percent).

7.2.2 Households

We next report evidence on the asset holdings of Greek households, and compare with other EZ countries. This evidence comes from the Household Finances and Consumption Survey (HFCS), undertaken under the auspices of the ECB in 2009 to 2011. (The data for Greece were collected during 2009, some months before the start of the EZ sovereign crisis.)

Figure 7.3 plots the breakdown of households' financial assets across various categories. These categories do not include direct holdings of cash, which the HFCS does not record. Greek households hold a larger fraction of their financial wealth in bank deposits than in all comparison countries. The fraction is 80.7 percent for Greece, while the average across all comparison countries is 50.2 percent, and the second highest fraction is 70.6 percent for Portugal. Holdings of mutual funds are very low (2.5 percent), consistent with the small size of the investment fund sector (figure 7.1), and so are direct holdings in bonds and stocks. Investment in voluntary pensions is also very low (7.7 percent), consistent with small size of the insurance sector (figure 7.1), which offers such products.

Figure 7.4 plots households' financial assets as a fraction of their total assets. Wealth not invested in financial assets is held in real assets. Real assets consist predominantly of real estate. Also included are private businesses, which constitute a larger share of real assets for the wealthiest households.

Greek households invest a smaller fraction of their wealth in financial assets than in all comparison countries. The fraction is 7 percent for Greece, while the average across all comparison countries is 15.6 percent. Cyprus is the second lowest (8.1 percent), followed by Italy (10 percent) and Spain (10.3 percent). Greek households hold the vast majority of their wealth in real assets.

Investment in real assets is illiquid, especially at times of crisis, and highly undiversified. Hence figure 7.4 suggests that Greek households suffer the most from under-diversification among their EZ counterparts.[3]

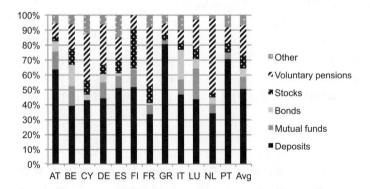

Figure 7.3
Breakdown of households' financial assets. The data come from the HFCS, undertaken under the auspices of the ECB during the period 2009 to 2011. The average is a simple average across the countries in the figure.

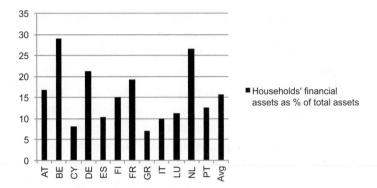

Figure 7.4
Households' financial assets as percentage of total assets. The data come from the HFCS, undertaken under the auspices of the ECB during the period 2009 to 2011. The average is a simple average across the countries in the figure.

We next explore possible explanations for why Greek households hold few financial assets and why these assets are held mainly in bank deposits and not in mutual funds, stocks, bonds, and retirement-related products offered by insurance companies. Such explanations could also help account for the relative underdevelopment of the Greek insurance and investment fund sectors.

One possible explanation is weak investor protection and the lack of trust that it breeds. Greek households avoid stocks, mutual funds, and insurance products because they are concerned about being exposed to fraud. Lack of trust is emphasized in the literature on financial development as a key factor limiting households' participation in the stock market (e.g., Guiso, Sapienza, and Zingales 2008), and could be a consequence of weak investor protection (e.g., La Porta et al. 1998, 2000). Measures of investor protection are indeed lower for Greece than for most of the comparison countries. For example, the World Bank *Doing Business* report computes indexes measuring the legal rights of shareholders ("protection of minority investors"), the legal rights of creditors (sub-index of "getting credit"), and the efficiency of courts ("enforcing contracts"). According to the 2015 report, Greece ranked 62nd out of 189 countries, and below all comparison countries in figure 7.1 except Finland, Netherlands, and Luxembourg, for shareholder rights. It ranked 124th, and below all comparison countries except Luxembourg, Netherlands, Italy, and Portugal, for creditor rights. More troublingly, it ranked 155th, and below all comparison countries, for the efficiency of courts. Hence, while investor protection laws are not the weakest among the comparison countries, the difficulty of enforcing these laws compounds the problem significantly. These issues are analyzed in greater detail in chapter 12 on the justice system in this volume.

The scores in the *Doing Business* report are a useful indicator of weak investor protection. An additional indicator is the many incidences of alleged or confirmed financial wrongdoing. For example, the Greek stock market experienced a severe boom and crash episode during the period 1997 to 2002, and this was accompanied by many alleged incidences of financial fraud and market manipulation. Some of these cases have been taken to the courts, and the majority of those are still pending. It is natural to suppose that such allegations and the lack of trust they have created have contributed to the pronounced reluctance of Greek households to participate in the stock market, as illustrated by their low stock holdings compared to other EZ countries.[4]

Financial wrongdoing has also occurred in the insurance and asset management sectors. For example, in September 2009, the insurance regulator shut down the second largest insurance group in Greece (Aspis) because of insufficient capital and mismanagement. This followed a well-publicized scandal that broke out in 2007 about state pension funds buying complicated structured bond products from brokerage firms at prices significantly above market values.

More recently there have been cases of financial wrongdoing in the banking sector. For example, in October 2011, the central bank of Greece (Bank of Greece, BoG) shut down Proton Bank. Its main shareholder has been jailed since then because of alleged loans of 700 million euros to companies that he controlled. In January 2013 charges were brought against the management of state-controlled Postal Bank because of improper loans exceeding 400 million euros to connected entrepreneurs.

A possibly complementary explanation for the asset-holding patterns of Greek households is lack of financial literacy. Greek households might, in large part, lack familiarity with stocks and mutual funds, and might feel more secure holding their wealth in bank deposits and in the house they live in. According to the measure of financial literacy reported in the IMD *World Competitiveness Yearbook*, Greece lies below the EZ average, but above France, Spain, Italy, and Portugal (Jappelli 2010).

Factors other than weak investor protection and lack of financial literacy might also be at play. For example, the preference of Greek households for real estate may have been the result of their having lived through decades of high and variable inflation prior to euro entry: real estate protects against unexpected inflation, unlike bank deposits and nominal bonds. As another example, the structure of Greece's pay-as-you-go pensions system (analyzed in depth in chapter 11 on pensions in this volume) may have been an important driver of households' limited investment in voluntary pensions. Greece's pensions system provides no incentives for households to save in private pensions, and in fact until 2014 there were tax disincentives: voluntary pension contributions could only be made from after-tax income and taxes were also collected when the pension was paid. By contrast, in several other countries, including the United States, contributions are made from before-tax income and taxes are collected only when the pension is paid. Hence, taxes are deferred rather than being levied twice as in Greece, and households also benefit from being assigned to a lower tax bracket in retirement than in working life. The absence of tax incentives for private pensions in Greece and the small participation by households in such investments are particularly problematic given that the Greek pension system faces serious issues of sustainability.

The factors considered so far are all demand-side: they influence households' demand for financial products. Supply-side factors, affecting the supply of financial products, might also have been important. One such factor is the limited entry by foreign financial institutions. The literature on financial development has shown that entry by foreign banks tends to increase the efficiency of the domestic banking sector (e.g., Clarke et al. 2002; Levine 2002), and this can promote financial innovation and better financial products.[5] Because of its weak institutional environment, Greece suffers from low foreign direct investment, and the financial sector is no exception. As Honohan (1999) points out, the liberalization of the Greek banking sector that started in the late 1980s spurred entry by new players, but these were mainly domestic private banks, with foreign presence remaining small. Presence by foreign banks increased somewhat post–euro entry, although the share of banking system assets owned by foreign banks is well below the EU average.[6]

7.2.3   Firms

We next report evidence on the capital structures of Greek firms, and compare with France, Germany, Italy, Spain, and the United Kingdom. This evidence is consistent with the household evidence presented in section 7.2.2. We elaborate on their relationship and the broader economic implications at the end of this section.

Our data on firms come from the Amadeus database. Amadeus reports data on individual firms, which we aggregate at the country level. We consider only five comparison countries to keep the data exercise manageable. We also consider only publicly listed firms because data on these firms are more complete, and we exclude financial firms and utilities because their capital structures differ systematically from those of other firms. As of 2012, the sample of all firms in Amadeus that meet our criteria includes 317 firms from France, 306 from Germany, 146 from Greece, 148 from Italy, 87 from Spain, and 781 from the United Kingdom.

Figure 7.5 plots the percent of firms' equity held by the three largest shareholders as of 2012. When this measure is high, most of the equity is held by a few entities (individuals or other firms), and small shareholders are less important.

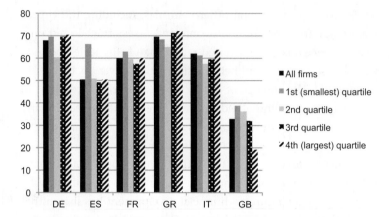

Figure 7.5
Percentage of firms' equity held by the three largest shareholders. The data come from the Amadeus database and are as of 2012. The sample includes the publicly listed firms in each country and excludes financials and utilities. The values reported are medians.

Greek firms are dominated by large shareholders to a greater extent than in all comparison countries. The largest three shareholders hold 69.5 percent of the equity of the median Greek firm. Germany comes second with 67.8 percent, followed by Italy with 61.9 percent, France with 59.8 percent, Spain with 50.6 percent, and the United Kingdom with 32.8 percent. The difference between Greece and the other countries is not driven by the smaller average size of Greek firms. This can be seen by sorting the full universe of firms into four groups (quartiles) according to the size of their assets, identifying the subgroup of firms within each group that belong to each country, and computing values for the median firm in each subgroup. Greece comes at the top of every size quartile except for the quartile of the smallest firms. Thus the smaller average size of Greek firms is not driving the ranking. The evidence is instead consistent with wealthy individuals holding controlling blocks of shares in large firms.

Figure 7.6 plots firms' leverage during the period 2004 to 2012. Leverage is computed in book value terms, by dividing the book value of debt by the book value of assets, and is expressed as a percentage.

Greek firms use more debt in their capital structure than in all comparison countries. For example, debt accounted for 34.3 percent of the assets of the median Greek firm in 2008. Spain came second with 33.7 percent, followed by Italy with 21.5 percent, the United Kingdom with 17.2 percent, France with 12.1 percent, and Germany with 11.5 percent. Greece comes first and with a wider margin in all other years as well, both pre-crisis and during the crisis. It also comes first when breaking the data into size

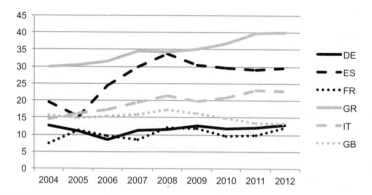

Figure 7.6
Firms' book leverage. The data come from the Amadeus database and cover the period 2004 to 2012. The sample includes the publicly listed firms in each country and it excludes financials and utilities. Leverage is computed by dividing the book value of debt by the book value of assets, and is expressed as a percent. The values reported are medians.

quartiles, with the exception of the quartile of the smallest firms where Spain comes first in some years.

The evidence on the capital structures of Greek firms is consistent with the household evidence presented in section 7.2.2. To elaborate on their relationship and the broader economic implications, we return to two key explanations for the household evidence: weak investor protection and lack of financial literacy. For concreteness, we revisit both explanations in the context of a stylized example of a firm that wants to raise funds for an investment project that costs 1.2 m (1.2 million) and will return a cash flow of 1 m or 2 m with equal probabilities. To keep things simple, we assume that investors are risk neutral. Therefore, if the firm could credibly promise to investors the entire cash flow from the project, it could raise $0.5 * 1$ m $+ 0.5 * 2$ m $= 1.5$ m, and would have enough funds to undertake the project.

Suppose next that because of weak investor protection, the firm's managers can divert all the cash flow above 1 m (i.e., 1 m if the cash flow is 2 m, and zero otherwise). Then only 1 m can be promised to investors. Hence the firm can only raise 1 m from them and cannot undertake the project.

One way for the firm to raise enough funds and undertake the project is to find one or more large shareholders who could monitor the firm's managers and reduce the cash flow that they can divert. Large shareholders could have better incentives to monitor than small shareholders because of their larger stake in the firm. Suppose, for example, that in the presence of large shareholders, managers are able to divert only 0.5 m instead of 1 m. Then the firm could raise $0.5 * 1$ m $+ 0.5 * 1.5$ m $= 1.25$ m, and would have enough funds to undertake the project. Alternatively, the firm could go to a bank that could also exercise monitoring and thus issue debt with face value 1.5 m.

Our stylized example illustrates the consequences of weak investor protection: reduced participation by small shareholders, increased participation by large shareholders, and higher leverage. These fit exactly the evidence that we report for Greece.[7] Note that weak investor protection also results in a higher cost of equity capital, and possibly lower investment.

The consequences of lack of financial literacy are broadly similar to those of weak investor protection. Suppose, in the context of our stylized example, that investors are uncertain about the return of securities issued by the firm and assume the worst-case scenario, that is, 1 m cash flow. Thus, in the presence of such investors, the firm could only raise 1 m and could not undertake the project. The firm might seek instead financing from more sophisticated investors or from banks. If sophisticated investors are also large, then lack of financial literacy (in the form assumed in this example) would generate the type of evidence that we report for Greece.[8]

Weak investor protection and lack of financial literacy imply not only a higher cost of equity capital but also financial fragility. This is because of the higher leverage. Figure 7.6 shows that Greek firms entered the crisis with more debt than their counterparts in the comparison countries and hence were less able to withstand declines in their earnings and asset values. Moreover leverage during the crisis increased for Greek firms, to 40 percent in 2012, while it remained roughly constant for the firms in the other countries. Hence the crisis generated more indebtedness and possible financial distress. (Figure 7.16 in section 7.4 further illustrates this point by showing that the interest coverage ratio, defined as the ratio of earnings to interest payments on debt, decreased dramatically during the crisis for Greek firms, to levels much smaller than in the comparison countries.) The higher leverage of Greek firms was, of course, not the only factor contributing to financial distress during the crisis. Yet a lower cost of equity capital and higher use of equity financing could have softened the effects of the crisis on Greek firms.

7.3   The Credit Boom and Crunch

Greece experienced a large credit boom that started shortly before euro entry, and after a period of financial liberalization, and that ended in 2008. The boom was followed by a severe credit crunch. In this section we present evidence on this credit cycle, and compare with other EZ countries. We focus mainly on the banking system but consider also the corporate sector. Some of the characteristics of the credit cycle are linked to the long-run features of the Greek financial system described in section 7.2. Our discussion of leverage at the end of that section suggests such a link.

7.3.1 Financial Liberalization and the Credit Boom

Greece embarked in a significant program of financial liberalization starting in the late 1980s. Until that time the state and the central bank (BoG) had significant influence over the setting of interest rates and the allocation of credit in the economy. Moreover state-controlled banks accounted for the vast majority of loans and deposits. State control of the banking system resulted in a significant misallocation of credit. This misallocation was evidenced by the large fraction of nonperforming loans held by the state-controlled banks: many of these loans had been effectively directed by the government toward state-controlled or other politically connected firms. The costs of state control of the banking system have been documented by a sizable academic literature.[9] Honohan (1999) provides an account more specific to Greece, and compares its financial liberalization experience to that of Portugal.

Financial liberalization aimed at creating a more market-driven system, and it followed similar steps to those undertaken earlier by other EU countries. Restrictions on lending rates and deposit rates were removed during the period 1987 to 1993. Exchange controls were lifted in 1994. The independence of the BoG from the state was strengthened in 1997. Some state-controlled banks were privatized during the 1990s and the privately controlled banking sector grew, partly because of entry by new players. State-controlled banks accounted for about 60 percent of deposits in 1998, down from 79 percent in 1993 and 88 percent in 1985. The new private banks were mostly Greek owned, and foreign presence remained small. More foreign entry and reduction of state ownership occurred in the years following the adoption of the euro and before the crisis.

During the period 1998 to 2008, Greece experienced rapid economic growth. Its GDP grew faster than all countries in figure 7.1 except from Cyprus, Ireland, Luxembourg, and Spain. The economic boom was accompanied, and to an extent caused, by a credit boom.[10] Figure 7.7 plots the loans of Greek banks to Greek households, corporations (excluding banks), and the government, as a fraction of GDP, from 1998 onward.

Total credit increased from 71.6 percent of GDP in 1998 to 122.8 percent in 2008. The rate of increase was particularly rapid after 2004—total credit in that year was 86.2 percent of GDP.

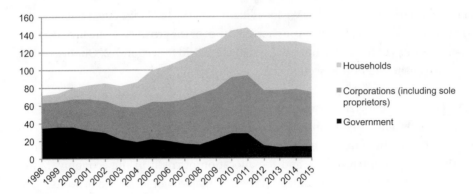

Figure 7.7
Bank loans as percentage of GDP in Greece, by category. The data come from the Bank of Greece
(BoG), are monthly and sampled in December, and cover the period 1998 to 2015.

As figure 7.7 shows, the increase in total credit between 1998 and 2008 resulted from
two opposite trends. First, loans to the government decreased, as the adoption of the
euro made it easier for the Greek government to borrow abroad. This effect, however,
was more than compensated by an increase in loans to the private sector. The increase
in private sector loans was especially pronounced for loans to households, namely consumer loans and housing loans.

Figure 7.8 compares the credit boom for Greece to that in Ireland, Italy, Portugal,
and Spain. We refer to these countries collectively as GIIPS.

Private sector loans as percent of GDP were lower in Greece than in all other GIIPS
countries, both in 1998 and in 2008. The gap became smaller, however, toward the
end of the credit boom. In 1998, Greece stood at 43.4 percent of the EZ average and at
42.4 percent of the average among the other GIIPS countries. In 2008, the corresponding figures were 74 and 53.4 percent. Greece's catching up can be seen more starkly by
computing the growth of private sector credit between 1998 and 2008. Growth was
higher in Greece than in all other GIIPS countries.

The growth in private credit was, to an extent, a natural consequence of the financial reforms that took place in the 1990s. For example, consumer credit was limited in
the 1990s but grew rapidly as quantity restrictions were gradually lifted. Lifting these
restrictions allowed the market for household credit in Greece to develop and reach a
size closer to EZ levels.

Figure 7.9 corroborates the convergence of household credit in Greece to EZ levels.
It plots two measures of household indebtedness, reported in the Household Finances
and Consumption Survey (HFCS): debt-service-to-income ratio, and loan-to-value

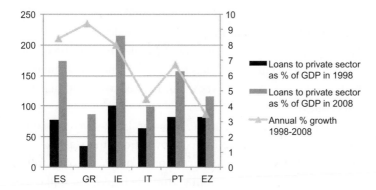

Figure 7.8
Credit boom in Greece, Ireland, Italy, Portugal, and Spain. The data come from the ECB, are monthly, and are sampled in December. The units for private sector loans as percentage of GDP are in the left-hand side *y*-axis, and the units for percentage growth are in the right-hand side *y*-axis. The EZ average is computed by dividing EZ loans by EZ GDP.

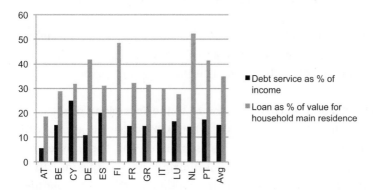

Figure 7.9
Household indebtedness. The data come from the HFCS, undertaken under the auspices of the ECB in 2009 to 2011. The debt-service-to-income ratio is missing for Finland. The average is a simple average across the countries in the figure.

ratio for the households' main residence. The two measures are 14.7 and 32.4 percent, respectively, for Greece, and their averages across all comparison countries are 15.2 and 34.7 percent. The indebtedness of Greek households was thus not out of line with that of their EZ counterparts.

The credit boom turned into a crunch starting in late 2008. As in other EZ countries, the crunch involved a bank-sovereign loop. Solvency problems of the Greek state spilled over to Greek banks by reducing the value of (1) the banks' portfolio of Greek government bonds and (2) the guarantees that the state had provided for bank loans and deposits. Conversely, solvency problems of Greek banks spilled over to the Greek state because (1) the state had to recapitalize the banks and provide them with guarantees, and (2) a drop in bank lending caused a slowdown in the economy and hence a decline in the state's tax revenues.

An analysis of the credit crunch should examine how the bank-sovereign loop manifested itself in Greece. Was the loop mainly a spillover from the state to the banks; that is, did the problems that Greek banks encountered originate solely from the state? Or did some of the problems originate from within the banks and spill over to the state?

Complete answers to the above questions require data and analysis that are beyond the scope of this chapter. Yet, we provide some suggestive pieces of evidence. We organize our analysis by dividing the crisis period into two phases: the global financial crisis (August 2007 to September 2009) and the EZ sovereign crisis (October 2009 onward). We identify the beginning of the EZ sovereign crisis with October 2009 because of the Greek elections and the subsequent announcement by the new government that the deficit was much larger than the previous estimate.[11] Dividing the crisis into the two phases allows us to separate the spillover effects of the bank-sovereign loop, since spillovers from the state to the banks mainly occurred during the second phase.

7.3.2   First Phase of the Credit Crunch: From Lehman to the Sovereign Crisis

The global financial crisis started in August 2007, when BNP Paribas suspended withdrawals from three of its hedge funds exposed to US subprime loans. The crisis reached its peak in October 2008, with the bankruptcy of Lehman Brothers. In figure 7.10 we compare how the crisis affected Greek banks and their counterparts in other countries. We plot the value of a stock market index composed from banks around the world and an index composed by Greek banks. We normalize both indexes to 100 in January 2004, and plot their values during the subsequent period.

Between the beginning of August 2007 and the end of September 2009, the Greek index dropped by 46.9 percent, while the global index dropped by 45.8 percent. Therefore the global financial crisis had almost the same impact on Greek banks as on the average bank around the world. At the same time Greek banks were more sensitive than the average bank to intermediate ups and downs during the crisis: they experienced a larger drop from August 2007 until the Lehman bankruptcy, and a larger rise from that event until September 2009. As we show later in this section, this excess sensitivity was reflected in the behavior of deposit rates and lending in the real economy.[12]

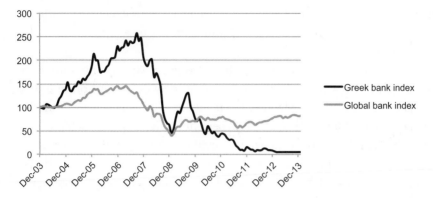

Figure 7.10

Performance of a Greek bank index and a global bank index. The global bank index is FTSE All-World Banks F3AWB3E, and the Greek bank index is FTSE Greece Banks F3GRB3L(PI). The data come from Datastream.

The excess sensitivity of Greek banks to movements in the global bank index suggests that they were exposed to more risks and hence were more vulnerable to a global economic slowdown than the average bank. Moreover this effect is shown on data before the sovereign crisis started, and hence it does not represent a spillover from the state to the banks. Greek banks could have reduced their risks by employing less leverage, and in that sense their leverage would have been too high relative to their risks. This is consistent with the high leverage of Greek firms (computed by excluding financial firms), shown in figure 7.5.[13]

We next examine the channels through which the global financial crisis could have affected Greek banks. The crisis would have had an effect through a solvency channel or a liquidity channel. The solvency channel is that banks incurred losses on assets whose value was reduced during the crisis, such as US subprime bonds. The liquidity channel is that even banks that did not incur losses had difficulty financing themselves in the interbank market, which was impaired by the crisis. The two channels are related: liquidity problems can turn into solvency problems as lack of financing reduces asset values.

Distinguishing between the two channels is difficult without detailed data on the banks' asset holdings. Yet, a suggestive piece of evidence is that from August 2007 to December 2007, the Greek bank index rose (by 3 percent) while most other national indexes dropped. (The global bank index dropped by 14.6 percent.) During that stage of the crisis, the concern was primarily about US subprime exposure. Hence the rise of the Greek index suggests that Greek banks were not holding US subprime products, consistent with anecdotal evidence. The global financial crisis could have affected Greek banks primarily through the liquidity channel, that is, by a difficulty in rolling over interbank loans.

Figure 7.11 plots the liability structure of the aggregate of Greek banks during the period 2000 to 2015. Greek banks had become increasingly dependent on interbank loans in the later stage of the credit boom. Interbank loans were 11.9 percent of total liabilities on average in 2000 to 2006, and 17.5 percent during 2007 and 2008.

That Greek banks might have experienced significant funding difficulties in the interbank market is consistent with the behavior of the rates that they were offering to attract customer deposits. With funding in the interbank market becoming scarcer, one would expect that banks would compete more aggressively for customer deposits—and this is exactly what happened.

Figure 7.12 plots the deposit rate in the GIIPS countries and Cyprus from January 2007 onward. We express these rates net of the average deposit rate across the EZ. In the period around the Lehman bankruptcy, the deposit rate in Greece increased sharply relative to the EZ average. The peak is the circled area in figure 7.12. This sharp movement suggests that Greek banks experienced funding difficulties as the global financial crisis deepened, and more so than banks in other EZ countries. The only other countries that experienced a sharp increase in the deposit rate were Cyprus and Italy.

The funding difficulties of Greek banks appear to have spilled over to the real economy as early as the first half of 2009. This can be seen in the "Access to Finance" Flash Eurobarometer survey, conducted by the European Commission and the ECB. This

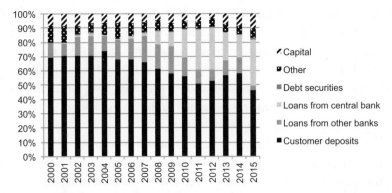

Figure 7.11
Liability structure of Greek financial institutions. The data come from the BoG, are monthly and sampled in December, and cover the period 1998 to 2015.

Figure 7.12
Deposit rates in the GIIPS countries and Cyprus relative to the EZ average. The data come from the ECB. We use the series "deposits up to one year new business," except for Ireland where that series is not available and we use instead "deposits of all maturities." The EZ average is the ECB-reported series.

survey concerns small and medium-size firms. In the 2009 edition of the survey, which was carried out in June to July 2009, 39 percent of Greek firms replied that their most pressing problem was access to finance (p. 28). This was by far the highest percentage in the EU; the second highest was 23 percent for Spain. By contrast, in the earlier edition of the survey, which was published in 2005, the percentage of Greek firms reporting that access to loans was easy or very easy was the fourth highest in the EZ (p. 37). Thus the credit cycle in Greece appears to have started going in reverse in early to mid-2009, before the sovereign crisis started. Further corroborating evidence is that the growth in private credit during 2009 collapsed to zero, down from 15.9 percent in 2008.

An economic slowdown caused by a drop in bank lending is one of the bank-to-state spillover channels of the bank-sovereign loop. A second such channel is that the state incurs a cost to recapitalize banks and provide them with guarantees. That channel was also at play in Greece, but to a lesser extent than in many other countries. The

Greek government passed a law in December 2008 that provided three types of support to the banks: (1) banks were offered the right to sell preferred shares to the state in exchange for acquiring government bonds, (2) banks were offered state guarantees on their interbank loans, and (3) banks were offered government bonds that they could use as collateral for interbank loans. These measures amounted for 5 billion, 15 billion, and 8 billion euros, respectively, and hence for a total of 28 billion euros. Figure 7.13 plots state support to the banking sector as percent of GDP for Greece as well as other EZ countries and the United Kingdom. Approved state support to Greek banks in 2008 was 12 percent of GDP. This ratio is relatively low when compared to an average of 36.1 percent across all comparison countries. (The latter average drops to 21.2 percent when Ireland is excluded as an outlier.)

The main conclusions from our analysis of the first phase of the credit crunch are (1) the global financial crisis had a significant impact on Greek banks, mainly through an impaired access to funding, and (2) the funding problems of Greek banks spilled over into the real economy and helped set the credit cycle into reverse.

7.3.3   Second Phase of the Credit Crunch: The Sovereign Crisis

The sovereign crisis hit Greek banks harder than their counterparts in most other EZ countries. This section focuses on the period that led to the first—and

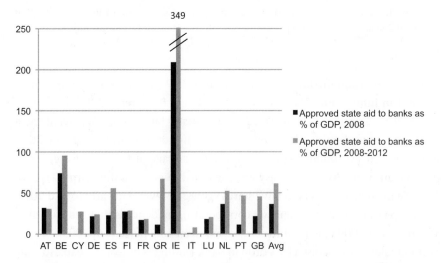

Figure 7.13
State aid to banks as percent of GDP. The data come from the European Commission. The average is a simple average across the countries in the figure.

largest—recapitalization of Greek banks. That recapitalization was completed in June 2013. Section 7.3.4 describes and evaluates the first recapitalization as well as a second recapitalization that took place in April and May 2014. Section 7.3.5 focuses on the period following the SYRIZA-ANEL election in January 2015. During that period a bank run took place, followed by the imposition of capital controls and a third recapitalization.

Between the beginning of October 2009 and the end of February 2013, the Greek bank index lost 94.9 percent of its value, while the EZ index lost 44.4 percent. The largest drops occurred for Cyprus (95 percent), Greece, and Ireland (94.2 percent), followed by Portugal (77.7 percent), and Italy (62 percent).[14]

The sovereign crisis affected Greek banks mainly through the solvency channel: the default (PSI) by the Greek state reduced dramatically the value of Greek government bonds held by the banks. Solvency problems generated liquidity problems: banks faced difficulties financing themselves in the market for retail deposits, as the guarantee by the government lost its value, and in the interbank market. These solvency and liquidity problems reflect state-to-bank spillover channels of the bank-sovereign loop.

Figure 7.11 illustrates the liquidity problems of Greek banks. Interbank loans dropped from 18.7 percent of total liabilities in 2009 to 7.5 percent in 2012, and customer deposits dropped from 58.1 to 53.2 percent. The resulting funding needs were covered by loans from the ECB. These loans were administered either directly from the ECB, with a low interest rate and stringent collateral requirements, or indirectly via the BoG as emergency liquidity assistance (ELA), with a significantly higher interest rate and less stringent collateral requirements that included state guarantees. Central bank loans increased from 10.3 percent of total liabilities in 2009 to 29.3 percent in 2012. These trends reversed somewhat in 2013 and 2014 but became even more pronounced in 2015.

The liquidity problems of Greek banks were reflected in the rates that the banks have been offering to attract customer deposits. As figure 7.12 shows, deposit rates in Greece increased significantly since early 2010, and were 150 to 200 basis points (i.e., 1.5–2 percent) higher than the EZ average during 2011 to 2012.

The solvency problems that Greek banks experienced during the sovereign crisis are summarized in table 7.1. For now we focus on the aggregate numbers, which are in the last row, and turn to the numbers for individual banks later in this section.

The aggregate core equity tier 1 (CET1) capital in the Greek banking sector was 22.1 billion euros as of December 2011. Greek banks experienced total losses of 37.7 billion in their holdings of Greek government bonds and other loans to the Greek state. To meet these losses, they had set aside provisions of 5.8 billion. Thus the banks'

Table 7.1
Calculation of the capital needs of Greek banks

	CET1 capital, 12/2011	PSI loss	Provisions for PSI, 06/2011	Credit loss projections	Loan loss reserves, 06/2011	Capital generation	Target CET1 capital, 12/2014	Capital needs
NBG	7.29	-11.74	1.65	-8.37	5.39	4.68	8.66	9.76
Eurobank	3.52	-5.78	0.83	-8.23	3.51	2.90	2.60	5.84
Alpha	4.53	-4.79	0.67	-8.49	3.12	2.43	2.03	4.57
Piraeus	2.62	-5.91	1.01	-6.28	2.57	1.08	2.41	7.34
Emporiki	1.46	-0.59	0.07	-6.35	3.97	0.11	1.15	2.48
ATEbank	0.38	-4.33	0.84	-3.38	2.34	0.47	1.23	4.92
Postbank	0.56	-3.44	0.57	-1.48	1.28	-0.32	0.90	3.74
Millennium	0.47	-0.14	0.00	-0.64	0.21	-0.08	0.23	0.40
Geniki	0.37	-0.29	0.07	-1.55	1.31	-0.04	0.15	0.28
Attica	0.37	-0.14	0.05	-0.71	0.27	0.02	0.25	0.40
Probank	0.28	-0.30	0.06	-0.46	0.17	0.15	0.18	0.28
New Proton	0.06	-0.22	0.05	-0.48	0.37	0.03	0.12	0.31
FBB	0.15	-0.05	0.00	-0.29	0.17	-0.03	0.12	0.17
Panellinia	0.08	-0.03	0.00	-0.12	0.05	-0.03	0.04	0.08
Total	22.12	-37.73	5.86	-46.83	24.73	11.38	20.06	40.54

Source: Data from table I.1 of the Report on the Recapitalization and Restructuring of the Greek Banking Sector, published by the BoG in December 2012.

Note: For each row, the quantities in the first seven columns add up to the capital needs in the last column. The following quantities are reported in the first seven columns: (1) core equity tier 1 capital as of December 2011, (2) losses on Greek government bonds and other loans to the Greek state during the PSI, (3) provisions that banks had set aside to meet these losses, (4) projected losses in private sector loans, (5) provisions that banks had set aside to meet these losses, (6) projected addition to capital due to earnings during the period 2012 to 2014, (7) target core equity tier 1 capital as of December 2014.

net-of-provision losses from Greece's sovereign default were 31.9 billion. These losses wiped out completely the capital of the banks, and made it negative. In addition there were projected losses on private sector loans, due to the recession in Greece. These losses were 22.1 billion, net of provisions (losses were 46.8 billion and provisions were 24.7 billion).

Table 7.1 makes it clear that Greece's sovereign default bankrupted its banking system. Default generated direct losses of 37.7 billion on the banks' government bond and loan portfolio, which net of the 5.8 billion of provisions exceeded the banks' capital of 22.1 billion. Default also accounted indirectly for some of the projected losses of 46.8 billion on the banks' private sector loan portfolio because it amplified the recession in Greece.

Greek banks could, in principle, have avoided default by holding fewer Greek government bonds. Figure 7.14 compares the exposure of Greek banks to Greek government bonds to the exposure of banks in other eurozone countries to their own domestic government bonds. These exposures are calculated as of December 2010, based on the stress tests that the European Banking Authority (EBA) conducted at that time and reported in July 2011.

As of 2010 Greek banks held 98 percent of their EZ government bond portfolio in Greek government bonds. This percentage was higher than in all comparison countries, and hence the government bond portfolio of Greek banks was the most "home biased." Whether this implies a large exposure to domestic bonds depends also on the

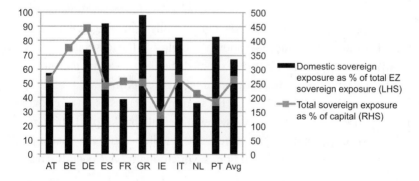

Figure 7.14
Holdings of government bonds by domestic banks. The data are from the 2010 EBA stress tests, as reported in chart 5 and table 1 in Merler and Pisani-Ferry (2012). The units for domestic sovereign exposure as percent of total EZ sovereign exposure are in the left-hand side y-axis, and the units for total sovereign exposure as percent of capital are in the right-hand side y-axis. The average is a simple average across the countries in the figure.

size of the government bond portfolio as a fraction of capital. This was 255 percent in Greece as of 2010, close to an average of 264 percent across all comparison countries. Adjusting for the size of the government bond portfolio, the exposure of Greek banks to domestic bonds was the second highest in the figure, after Germany, with Spain and Italy coming next.

Why did Greek banks have a large exposure to Greek government bonds, an exposure that eventually made them bankrupt? And why did this exposure increase during 2009 and 2010, as figure 7.7 indicates?[15]

One explanation for the large domestic exposure of Greek banks is that these were pressured by the government to buy its bonds. Moreover this pressure became stronger during the crisis, when the government had greater difficulty financing itself. According to the government pressure explanation, domestic exposure should be larger for state-controlled banks than for privately controlled banks, since the government has larger influence on the former. Using table II.1 in the *Recapitalization Report* of the Bank of Greece, we can confirm that this is indeed the case: holdings of Greek government bonds and other loans to the Greek state were 303 percent of capital for the aggregate of state-controlled banks (National Bank of Greece, ATE Bank, Postbank) and 171 percent for the aggregate of privately controlled banks (Eurobank, Alpha Bank, Piraeus, Emporiki, Millenium, Geniki, Attica, Probank, Proton, FBB, Panellinia). Thus government pressure would have made the Greek banking system—which was prone to funding crises, as shown in section 7.3.2—even more crisis prone and government dependent.[16]

The losses on Greek government bonds and the projected losses on private sector loans rendered the Greek banking system insolvent not only on aggregate but also at the level of each individual bank. Indeed, as shown in table 7.1, the losses net of provisions for each bank (sum of columns 2 to 5) exceeded the bank's capital (column 1), even after taking into account projected future profitability (column 6).

The main conclusions from our analysis in this section are (1) losses on Greek government bonds and loans due to Greece's sovereign default bankrupted the Greek banking system, and (2) Greek banks suffered from the default because they had a particularly large position in Greek government bonds, which might have been the result of government pressure.

7.3.4 First and Second Recapitalizations

Because Greek banks became insolvent during the sovereign crisis, public intervention was needed. Public intervention toward insolvent banks generally takes one of three forms:

• *Liquidation* The bank is shut down immediately and its assets are eventually sold off. The proceeds are used, possibly together with public funds, to pay depositors and other debtholders.

• *Resolution* The bank is typically split into two parts, a "good bank" and a "bad bank." The good bank includes the deposits and other debt obligations, some of the assets, and public funds. Bank depositors thus continue being served. The good bank is sold off immediately to an existing bank, or exists temporarily as a "bridge" bank before being eventually sold off. The bad bank includes the remainder of the assets, typically the low-quality ones, namely the bad loans. These assets are eventually sold off and the proceeds go to the taxpayer.

• *Recapitalization* The bank receives an injection of funds, possibly including public funds, and continues its operations.

In principle, each of liquidation, resolution, and recapitalization can be implemented with a haircut on depositors and other debtholders. In the case of Greek banks, a haircut was viewed as destabilizing and was ruled out (although it was implemented later on for Cypriot banks). Because depositors and other debtholders did not take any losses, and because their claims were larger than bank assets (since banks were insolvent), any of the three forms of intervention would have required use of public funds. Public funds came in the form of a 50 billion euro loan from EZ countries.

Liquidation of Greek banks was ruled out, possibly because of its disruptive effects on depositors and other banks. (Reimbursement of deposits and settlement of claims to other banks can take a significant amount of time.) The two forms of public intervention that were employed were resolution and recapitalization. Before describing their actual implementation, we analyze two policies that were not implemented. Our analysis of these policies is stylized. Yet, it helps frame the issues and serves as background for some of the material in section 7.4.

The first policy is an across-the-board recapitalization: all banks would be recapitalized and sold off to new private owners. An estimate of the minimum required level of public funds can be computed based on the BoG data presented in table 7.1. According to the BoG, a recapitalization of the Greek banking system had to bring it to a capital level of 20 billion so that regulatory requirements (Basel capital ratios) could be met. Moreover this necessitated a capital injection of 40.5 billion. Since banks would be 100 percent privately owned post-recapitalization under our assumed policy, the maximum amount that private investors would pay is 20 billion, that is, the value of the banks' new capital. The remainder, $40.5 - 20 = 20.5$ billion, which was required to plug the gap between bank deposits and other debt obligations, on one hand, and bank assets, on the other, could only come from public funds. Note that public funds were required even though the recapitalized banks would be 100 percent owned by private investors. Put differently, the state had to realize a loss of 20.5 billion so that private investors would break even. The only alternative to a loss by the state was to impose a haircut on depositors and other debtholders.

The 20.5 billion of required public funds is only an estimated minimum level because 20 billion overestimates the funds that could be raised privately. Indeed the value of bank assets was highly uncertain, so private investors would require a discount from the 20 billion as compensation for bearing risk. One way that the state could reduce the risk borne by private investors, and hence extract a higher price from selling the banks to them, would be to offer a guarantee. For example, it could cap aggregate losses of investors to 10 billion.

The second policy is an across-the-board resolution: all banks would be resolved, their bad loans would be transferred to a bad bank, and the good banks would be sold off to new private owners. Resolution has two advantages over recapitalization. First, by taking the bad loans out of the balance sheet of the good banks, uncertainty about the good banks' assets is reduced, and so is the discount required by private investors to buy the good banks. Second, the bad bank may have better incentives to maximize the value of the bad loans, and be better equipped to do so, for reasons explained in section 7.4.

A drawback of resolution relative to recapitalization is that more public funds are required. This is because funds must be found to replace the bad loans in the good banks' balance sheet. If, for example, the value of the bad loans net of losses is 40 billion, then 40 billion would be needed, and that would be in addition to the 20.5 billion required to make the good banks solvent. The state would, of course, earn a return on its 40 billion when the bad loans would be gradually sold off. Alternatively, the state could minimize its contribution to the 40 billion by selling 100 percent of the bad bank to private investors outright (and private investors would then gradually sell off the bad loans to others). As with recapitalization, however, a discount would be required because of the uncertainty surrounding the value of the bad loans. Moreover the discount would be larger than under recapitalization because the scope for losses is larger: the investment at stake is equal to the value of the bad loans (40 billion in our example), which exceeds bank capital (20 billion).

That resolution requires more public funds than recapitalization can also be understood by observing that taking the bad loans out of the good banks' balance sheet makes these banks safer for depositors. This is a transfer to depositors, which must be covered by the taxpayer.

The higher cost of resolution over recapitalization was an important reason why resolution was not used in a wide scale in Greece, in contrast to Ireland and Spain.[17] The chosen policy was instead to recapitalize the large four banks and resolve most of the remaining ones. The large four banks were Alpha Bank, Eurobank, National Bank of Greece (NBG), and Piraeus Bank. The agreed procedure for recapitalizing them was that the state and private investors would buy shares in the recapitalized entities, but private investors would receive additionally warrants for each share that they bought. Warrants are rights to buy additional shares at a prespecified "exercise" price. These rights are valuable because of the possibility that the share price increases above the exercise price. An additional feature of the recapitalization procedure was that if private investors could buy 10 percent or more of the shares in a bank, then they could exert full control, except for major decisions such as capital increases and mergers. The process had to be completed by June 2013.

The introduction of warrants allowed private investors to enter the recapitalization in better terms than the state. As argued earlier, a state subsidy to private investors was necessary because the banks were insolvent. To illustrate this point with a simple example, suppose that private investors contribute 1 billion worth of shares in a recapitalization of a bank and receive a subsidy worth 0.5 billion by the state, such as through warrants. Suppose also that the state contributes 9 billion. The total capital raised is 10 billion and private investors own 10 percent of the bank. If prior to the recapitalization the bank's deposits and other debt obligations exceeded assets by X billion, then the bank would be worth $10 - X$ billion after the recapitalization, and the total gain of private investors would be 10 percent $* (10 - X) + 0.5 - 1$, that is, their stake in the bank, plus the subsidy, minus the amount they invested. If $X = 5$, whereby the bank was under water by 5 billion prior to the recapitalization, then private investors just break even (despite having received a subsidy). If the bank was underwater by less than 5 billion ($X < 5$), then private investors earn a rent, and if the bank was underwater by more than 5 billion ($X > 5$), then private investors do not enter. The optimal size of the subsidy from the state's viewpoint is such that investors enter but earn zero rent.

Out of the four large banks, three raised more private capital than the required 10 percent: Alpha with 12 percent, NBG with 11.1 percent, and Piraeus with 19.7 percent. Eurobank could not raise the required 10 percent and became fully controlled by the state. The total amount of public funds that were used was 25.5 billion: 4 billion for Alpha, 5.8 billion billion for Eurobank, 8.7 billion for NBG, and 7 billion for Piraeus. The total amount of private capital that was raised was 3.1 billion: 0.6 billion for Alpha, 1.1 billion for NBG, and 1.4 billion for Piraeus. The sum of public plus private capital raised for each bank is the same as the corresponding number in table 7.1.[18,19]

The remaining banks were either recapitalized with private funds (e.g., Attica Bank), or resolved or recapitalized and then transferred to the large four banks—with the process being essentially completed by July 2013. The public funds used for these banks were 13.4 billion. Hence, out of the 50 billion of public funds that were made available, a total of 38.9 billion were used for recapitalization and resolution.

The first recapitalization resulted in a drastic increase in the concentration of the Greek banking system (i.e., fewer banks). Figure 7.15 plots, for all EU countries, the share of banking system assets held by the five largest banks. This is a common measure of banking system concentration. In 2013 the five largest banks in Greece held 94 percent of banking system assets, the highest share among all EU countries, and up from 67.7 percent in 2007. The increase in concentration between 2007 and 2013 was largest in Greece (26.3 percent), followed by Spain (15.2 percent).

The increase in concentration can facilitate bank recapitalization because banks can have higher profit margins and hence higher earnings. Therefore it can serve as a substitute to issuing additional equity. At the same time a concentrated banking sector can

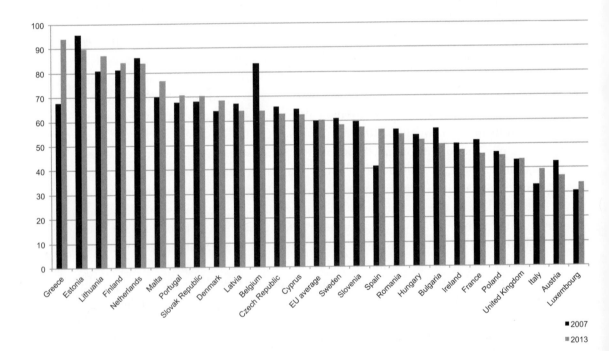

Figure 7.15
Share of banking system assets held by the five largest banks. The data are from the ECB. The EU average is a simple average across the countries in the figure.

have the usual drawbacks of an oligopoly, that is, less competitive prices, less innovation, and political lobbying to prevent entry by outsiders. Given the important risks facing the economy and the banks (risks that became fully apparent in 2015 with the bank run, the capital controls, and the third recapitalization), a policy favoring concentration was sensible.

The consolidation of banking system assets within the large four banks meant that presence by foreign banks was reduced essentially to zero.[20] Entry by foreign banks might have been difficult to achieve given the risks in Greece and the pressure on eurozone banks to de-lever. Yet, the first recapitalization might have been an opportunity to promote such entry, especially given the extensive evidence that entry by foreign banks into a crisis-hit banking system can be beneficial.[21] We should note, however, that entry by strategic long-term investors, which could have some of the same beneficial effects, did occur, especially in the case of Eurobank.

Given the lack of entry and competition, it is possible that the large banks earned rents by absorbing the remaining banks at prices below true value. Such rents would have benefited the private investors who participated in the June 2013 recapitalization. (The rents would have lowered the value of X in the example presented earlier.) At the same time such rents could not have been too large; otherwise, the banks would have been able to attract more private capital in June 2013.

In the spring of 2014, a second recapitalization was required because of increased projected losses on private sector loans. That recapitalization was covered entirely by private funds. The total amount raised across the four large banks was 8.3 billion. Eurobank raised the largest amount, 2.9 billion, and returned to majority private ownership: private investors held a total stake of 64.6 percent, up from almost zero in June 2013. Private investors' stakes in Alpha, NBG, and Piraeus were raised to 30.1, 42.8, and 32.7 percent, respectively.

The first and second recapitalizations were successful in transforming a banking system in which all banks were insolvent into one where banks were solvent and partly owned by private investors. At the same time banks remained fragile and highly vulnerable to a worsening in the economic situation. This can be seen by examining the composition of core equity tier 1 (CET1) capital, and its evolution after the recapitalizations.

In December 2013, the CET1 capital of the four large banks was 26.9 billion. This was comfortably higher than the target in table 7.1, which was 15.7 billion, and indeed the Basel capital ratios of the four banks ranged from 11.2 to 15.9 percent, which are well beyond the minimum 4.5 percent required. Yet these high numbers may provide a false sense of comfort. First, there was a significant risk that losses on private sector loans could exceed the projected values, and hence banks would need to increase provisions by taking away from capital. Second, a significant fraction of CET1 capital was in the form of deferred tax assets (DTA), which reflect projected tax savings from losses that banks realized in the past and could carry forward to apply against future profits. DTA constitute an inferior form of bank capital because they involve uncertain cash flows. Indeed the tax savings inherent in DTA accrue to banks only when they are profitable. Moreover these savings are contingent on the state not modifying the tax code.[22]

In December 2014, the CET1 capital of the four large banks was 28.6 billion. During that year, banks had raised 8.3 billion of new private capital, and increased their DTA by 4.5 billion. Yet the increase in CET1 capital relative to December 2013 was only 1.7 billion (= 28.6 − 26.9), much smaller than 12.8 billion (= 8.3 + 4.5). This was mainly because banks had to increase substantially their provisions against projected losses on private sector loans.

Figure 7.16 summarizes these developments with plots showing the dynamics of CET1 capital, DTA, and provisions for the aggregate of the four large banks.

7.3.5 Bank Run, Capital Controls, and Third Recapitalization

The election of January 2015 brought into power a government formed by the SYRIZA and ANEL parties, both of which had opposed the provisions of the bailout plan. A

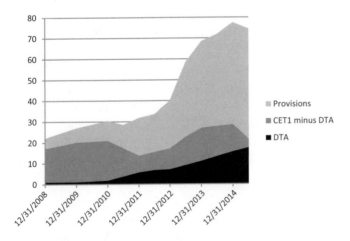

Figure 7.16
Deferred tax assets (DTA), core equity tier 1 (CET1) capital, and provisions aggregated across the four large banks (Alpha, Eurobank, NBG, and Piraeus). The numbers come from banks' balance sheets and are expressed in billion euros. CET1 capital is the sum of the black and dark gray.

lengthy negotiation with the Troika during the first half of 2015 generated uncertainty about whether Greece would continue with the bailout plan or default and exit the euro. That uncertainty drove depositors to withdraw money from banks, and aggregate deposits dropped by 48.6 billion between December 2014 and June 2015. As of June 2015, deposits accounted for 46.2 percent of total bank liabilities, and central bank loans (in the form of ELA or direct ECB loans) accounted for 36.7 percent. For comparison, at the double election of May and June 2012, when deposits had reached their previous minimum, they accounted for 50.1 percent of bank liabilities (a figure that rose to 58.3 percent in December 2014), while central bank loans accounted for 33 percent (a figure that dropped to 15.7 percent in December 2014).

Following the announcement of a referendum to approve a new bailout agreement, on June 28, 2015, there was a renewed flight on deposits. The refusal of the ECB to increase the loan limit (which was already stretched due to the lack of collateral by Greek banks) resulted in the imposition of capital controls and a daily limit of 60 euros for withdrawal of bank deposits.[23]

The deposit flight in the first half of 2015, the imposition of capital controls, and the overall weakening of the economy, increased the projected losses on private sector loans. In response to these developments, the EZ's Single Supervisory Mechanism (SSM) decided to conduct a new asset quality review (AQR) and perform new stress tests specifically for the four large Greek banks, a year after a similar exercise had been conducted by the ECB on all large European banks, and a year before the SSM was due to conduct the second such exercise. The AQR, conducted during the third quarter of 2015, required the four large banks to acknowledge an additional combined capital loss of 9.6 billion relative to the AQR of the previous year. This brought CET1 capital down to 16.2 billion, most of which was in the form of DTA. Banks were required to raise 13.7 billion of new capital, 3.7 billion of which had to come from private investors and conversions of debt into equity, and 10 billion from either private investors or public funds.[24]

Two of the four banks raised all the required capital from private investors. The four banks combined raised 5.3 billion from private investors and converted 2.7 billion of bonds into stocks. Hence approximately 8 billion from the required 13.7 billion were raised from private sources. Later, in early 2016, one of the banks sold its Turkish subsidiary, reducing further the need for state support.

In November 2015, prior to the third recapitalization, existing capital was valued at 0.7 billion. This constituted a large loss for previous private investors, who had invested a total of 11.4 billion in the banks in the first and second recapitalizations. It also constituted a large loss for the state, which had injected 25.5 billion (although about half of that amount was a loss from the outset because it was necessary to bring the banks back to solvency).

After the third recapitalization, the state's stake in the common shares of the four large banks shrank considerably. In October 2016 the state owned 11 percent of Alpha, 2.4 percent of Eurobank, 40.4 percent of NBG, and 26.4 percent of Piraeus. Prior to the third recapitalization, these stakes were 66.3, 35.4, 57.2, and 66.9, respectively.[25]

7.4   Policies for the Short and Medium Run: Dealing with Debt Overhang

In this section we discuss the challenges facing the Greek financial system in the short and medium run, and possible public policies to address them. The main challenge is to recover from the credit crunch; this requires dealing with the high debt levels of households and firms, and ensuring that the banking system provides an adequate flow of credit to the economy.[26] The magnitude of the credit crunch can be seen in figures 7.17 and 7.18. Figure 7.17 plots the interest coverage ratio in the corporate sector. This ratio is computed by dividing corporate earnings by interest payments on debt. We report interest coverage for Greek firms, and compare with France, Germany, Italy, Spain, and the United Kingdom. The set of firms is the same as in section 7.2.3.

An interest coverage ratio that is equal to one means that a firm is generating just enough earnings to make interest payments on its debt. Interest coverage below one

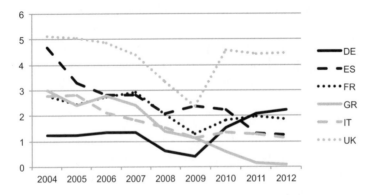

Figure 7.17

Firms' interest coverage ratio. The data come from the Amadeus database and cover the period 2004 to 2012. The sample includes the publicly listed firms in each country, and it excludes financials and utilities. The interest coverage ratio is defined as the ratio of earnings to interest payments on debt. The values reported are medians.

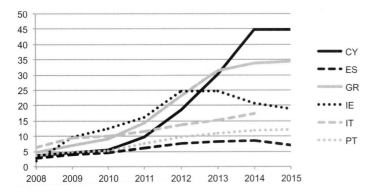

Figure 7.18
Nonperforming loans as percent of the banks' loan portfolio. The data are from the World Bank.

means that earnings are not sufficient and the firm can make interest payments only by taking on additional debt. Figure 7.17 shows that interest coverage for Greece has been significantly smaller than one since 2010. Its value in 2012 was 8 percent, which meant that the median Greek firm generated earnings equal to only 8 percent of the interest payments that it was making. Hence the median Greek firm has been taking on additional debt, consistent with the increase in leverage documented in figure 7.6. Interest coverage has decreased since the beginning of the crisis not only for Greece but also for Italy and Spain. For these countries, however, it has remained above one. Note that for all three countries interest coverage was comfortably above one before 2008.

Figure 7.18 plots nonperforming loans (NPLs) for Greek banks, and compares with Cyprus, Ireland, Italy, Portugal, and Spain. NPLs are plotted as percentage of the loan portfolio of the banks in each country and include both corporate loans and loans to households. Loans are generally classified as nonperforming when payments have not been made for at least three months.

NPLs in Greece were at comparable levels to the other countries in 2008 but increased sharply during the crisis, overtaking all countries except Cyprus from 2013 onward. As of 2015, they accounted for 34.4 percent of all loans (figure 7.18), and the percentage increases above 40 percent when restructured loans are included.[27]

High indebtedness threatens both the financial system and the real economy. If NPLs are not resolved appropriately, a large fraction of productive assets will not be put to their most efficient use and may remain idle. This implies that any growth will be anemic and unemployment will remain high. Moreover lack of appropriate resolution of the NPLs will prevent banks from lending to new and profitable projects, further hindering growth. Lack of growth will in turn worsen the NPL problem, leading to a vicious cycle.

A solution to the NPL problem requires intervention on two fronts: the judicial procedures governing bankruptcy and debt restructuring, and the capacity and incentives within the banking system to resolve NPLs. We consider the two forms of intervention in sections 7.4.1 and 7.4.2, respectively, where we also analyze in greater depth the economic costs imposed by NPLs.

The two forms of intervention that we consider are microeconomic in nature. The NPL problem, however, may also require intervention at the macroeconomic level. The deflation that Greece is experiencing raises the promised payments on loans in real terms, and hence makes loans harder to service. Hence ECB policies to tackle deflation could contribute to reducing the NPL problem in Greece—as well as in other EZ countries with high NPLs. Such policies, however, are outside of the scope of this chapter, which focuses on interventions available to Greek policy makers.

7.4.1 Judicial Procedures for Bankruptcy and Debt Restructuring

Judicial procedures must be designed to render bankruptcy and debt restructuring as efficient as possible. We discuss existing procedures and their shortcomings, distinguishing between firms and households. We do not attempt to be comprehensive, rather, describe what we view as the main issues.[28]

Firms When a firm is unable to repay its debts, two broad outcomes are possible:[29]

• *Liquidation* The firm's assets are sold off. The proceeds are used to pay creditors, as well as any overdue wages to employees and debts to the state. (In what follows, we use the term "creditors" to also refer to employees and the state.)
• *Reorganization* The firm agrees on a reorganization plan with its creditors, and continues to operate. The reorganization plan may involve debt reductions. It can be negotiated before the firm ceases payments to creditors, and can then be ratified by the court. Alternatively, it can be negotiated after cessation of payments, in which case the firm must submit a formal application to the court. During the time that the court considers the application, and until it ratifies the reorganization plan (assuming that it accepts the application), the firm's assets are protected from creditors. If the firm cannot reach an agreement with creditors, then it is liquidated.

The choice between liquidation and reorganization should depend on whether the firm's assets can be put to better use outside or inside the firm. To illustrate this point, we consider a stylized example of a firm that has total debts of 1m (one million) but can generate total income worth only 0.7 m. If other firms are willing to pay 0.9 m to acquire the firm's assets, then liquidation is the better option. If instead they are willing to pay only 0.5 m, then reorganization is better: creditors prefer to keep the firm in operation even though they cannot recover the full 1 m of their debts because the 0.7 m that they earn exceeds the 0.5 m earned under liquidation.

Liquidation in Greece is highly inefficient: the proceeds from selling a firm's assets are significantly smaller than what other firms are willing to pay for the assets. A key source of inefficiency is delay. According to the judicial procedure in place, all the claims of creditors against a firm must be verified before the firm's assets can be sold. Verification can take years because creditors might raise objections against each other's claims. This delay is costly not only because of the forgone output during the verification period but also because lack of use can cause the firm's assets to depreciate and become unsuitable for future use. (This is, for example, the case for buildings.) A second source of inefficiency is that the auction process through which the assets are sold is complicated and opaque. Opacity discourages participation by interested buyers and can benefit well-connected insiders. A third source of inefficiency is that the bankruptcy administrators in charge of selling the assets often have limited experience. Until 2016 they were selected randomly from the local bar association, and hence experience in conducting liquidations was not taken into account.

The inefficiency of the liquidation option makes reorganization more attractive for creditors. To return to the previous example, suppose that other firms are willing to pay 0.9 m to acquire the assets of the bankrupt firm, but 0.35 m is squandered during the liquidation process. Creditors then earn only 0.9 − 0.35 = 0.55 m from liquidation, and hence prefer reorganization.

Shareholders can exploit the inefficiency of the liquidation option to extract significant concessions from creditors. In the context of the previous example, shareholders could push creditors to reduce the debt level to a minimum of 0.55 m, which is the creditors' outside option under liquidation. Shareholders could thus earn a maximum rent of 0.7 − 0.55 = 0.15 m from reorganization, even though their firm is bankrupt. Shareholders could also have an incentive to delay the reorganization process to extract such a rent.

An additional friction in reorganization negotiations, present until 2016, was that employees and the state had seniority over all other creditors; that is, their claims had to be honored in full before honoring any of the claims of the other creditors. This was a friction because in contrast to creditors such as banks, the state has little flexibility to renegotiate its claims and little expertise in designing and monitoring reorganization plans. The same is true to a lesser extent for employees. Because of these considerations, a firm might have been liquidated even when reorganization was more efficient. Indeed, suppose in the context of the previous example that out of the 1 m in debts, 0.75 m are owed to the state and 0.25 m to banks. Suppose also that liquidation yields 0.55 m. If the state has no flexibility to reduce its claim down to 0.7 m, to make a reorganized firm viable, then the firm will be liquidated, yielding only 0.55 m to the state.

Summarizing, a fundamental problem with the judicial procedures governing bankruptcy and debt restructuring is that liquidation is highly inefficient. One consequence of the inefficiency is that shareholders can extract significant rents at the expense of creditors. The seniority of claims to the state and employees was also a problem until 2016 because it was conducive to inefficient liquidation.

Inefficient liquidation aggravates the NPL problem. Indeed efficient resolution of NPLs may require that assets be transferred to other firms that can use them better. If transfers are highly costly, then assets are not put to their best use, causing GDP to remain low and the prospects of distressed firms to remain poor.

Making NPL resolution more efficient has required and still requires a number of public policy interventions targeted to address the shortcomings identified above:

• Modify the judicial procedure to allow prompt sales of assets in a liquidation auction. Any conflicts between creditors can be addressed in a parallel and separate process. Procedures along these lines are followed in a number of countries, including the United Kingdom and the United States. Law 4336/2015, passed in 2015, represents progress in this direction since it has set tighter deadlines for the verifications of creditor claims against a firm,

• Make the auction process through which the assets are sold more transparent, such as electronic auctions. An effort to introduce electronic auctions has been undertaken for assets seized against tax-related debts. Such auctions could be used more broadly.

• Open up the position of bankruptcy administrator to qualified professionals who are not lawyers, such as accountants. In a number of countries, including the United Kingdom and the United States, bankruptcy administrators are often large firms with extensive expertise in the area. Law 4336/2015 has established the profession of bankruptcy administrators in Greece, and has required that registered members of that profession meet certain qualification standards.

• Simplify judicial procedures relating to reorganization. For example, until 2016, a judge needed to decide whether a reorganization plan proposed by a firm was viable before authorizing that it serves as a basis for negotiations between the firm and its creditors. A hearing took four months, and more time was required for a decision. That not only delayed negotiations but also required the judge to make a complicated decision about the viability of a firm under a yet to be implemented reorganization plan. Law 4336/2015 has improved things by granting automatically a short "stay" period during which a reorganization plan could be negotiated between the firm and its creditors and then ratified by the judge. Moving further in this direction by reducing the role of the judge in the bankruptcy process and facilitating instead negotiations between the firm and its creditors, may be beneficial. While in countries such as the United Kingdom and the United States, the judge is free to exercise considerable discretion, judicial discretion in the Greek context is likely to cause delays and unpredictability given the high case load of Greek courts and the limited expertise of many judges on bankruptcy matters.[30]

• Make the seniority of claims of the state and employees more comparable to that of claims of other creditors. In particular, terms agreed with other creditors could automatically extend to the state and employees. Law 4336/2015 represents progress in this direction because it has made claims by secured creditors more senior to those by the state and employees.

Households   When a household is unable to repay its debts, it can apply for protection under the law for over-indebted households (Law 3869/2010 and its subsequent modifications). The law requires that the household first seeks to negotiate debt relief with its creditors out of court. If negotiations do not yield an agreement, then a judge makes a decision. If the household's debts are unsecured, then the household's primary residence is protected (up to a given value), but all other assets can be liquidated to repay the debts. For debts that are secured against the household's primary residence, relief can be granted so that these debts represent no more than 80 percent of the residence value. The exact amounts are up to the judge's discretion and take into account factors such as employment or health status. Until the time that the judge makes a decision, the household's assets are protected from creditors. As of the end of 2014, there were approximately one hundred thousand applications by over-indebted households in the court system.

The law does not constitute a full-fledged personal bankruptcy regime because some types of debts are not covered. For example, debts to the state are excluded, and are effectively given more senior status. At the same time the law has the attractive feature that it allows households to settle their eligible debts and restart with a clean slate. The alternative solution of requiring households to remain in debt until they generate enough new income to repay in full (e.g., as in Spain) could leave them in a perpetual state of debt overhang, with low incentives to generate income.

The practical application of the law has been problematic. A key problem is court delays. Most hearings are scheduled five or more years after the household applies for protection, and some hearings for which applications were made in, for example, 2014, have been scheduled for as late as 2028 (fourteen years after application). Given that household assets are protected from creditors until the hearing, the incentives to apply for protection are strong even for households who can make the debt payments. Such households might hence choose to default strategically. Another problem is that court decisions have been highly variable even across similar cases. This has strengthened incentives to default strategically, and to file in jurisdictions where judges have the reputation of being pro-debtor. Incentives for strategic default have been further strengthened by a ban on liquidations of primary residences even in cases where such liquidations have previously been authorized by the courts.

Strategic default undermines the very existence of the credit market: banks will not lend if they are concerned that even solvent borrowers will not repay. Moreover the losses that banks incur because of strategic default are also borne by taxpayers because the state owns large stakes in the banks. In an attempt to curtail incentives for strategic default, the government modified the law in 2013 to require households to make a small monthly payment, typically around 10 percent of the installment due, until the court hearing. While this measure goes in the right direction, more direct action is needed to reduce court delays and make court decisions more uniform. This is especially so given that court delays have increased dramatically since the beginning of the crisis in 2009.[31]

Reducing court delays will help deal with strategic defaulters. One would want to know also how much debt relief should be granted to those genuinely unable to pay. Court decisions on debt relief have been highly variable and the underlying principles have not been laid out clearly. To illustrate the issues, we consider a stylized example of a household that has taken a mortgage loan of 200K (200 thousand) from a bank for its primary residence but can generate only 40K of total income to repay the loan. If the bank would earn less than 40K by selling the house, then it is in its best interest to not sell the house and reduce the loan to 40K, which the household can repay. If, however, the bank would earn more than 40K by selling the house, should the court allow the house to be sold? And if so, how can the household be protected from becoming homeless?

One way to approach these questions is to determine a minimum housing consumption to which a household should be entitled given its size and possibly other attributes. Suppose that the household in our example is entitled to 60K. Then the bank could be allowed to sell the house, provided that it pays 20K to the household from the liquidation proceeds so that the household could combine with its 40K and access housing worth 60K.[32] The bank would then sell the house if it could get a price greater than 60K. Otherwise, it would reduce the loan to 40K and let the household remain in the house. This solution ensures that the household will not remain homeless while also allowing liquidation to occur if it is the economically efficient option. Liquidation occurs if the price exceeds the maximum of (1) the amount that the household can repay and (2) the household's minimum housing entitlement.

Our stylized example illustrates a principle that is broad and extends beyond housing: a minimum amount of exempt assets can be specified so that only assets in excess of this are made available to lenders. Indeed this is the approach taken in the United States, where responsibility for determining the exempt amount lies with individual states. Using systematic measures of the exempt amount and of collateral values (e.g., house prices) in court decisions can enhance consistency and efficiency. Guidelines ensuring consistency are all the more important given that the sheer volume of bankruptcy cases in a recession makes public protests likely (some such incidents have already occurred), and this can result in partial or inconsistent implementation of the law. Such an outcome would not only be unfair to some distressed households, but could also result in the abandonment of otherwise advisable policies.

7.4.2 Banks

Improving the judicial procedures that govern bankruptcy and debt restructuring is only part of the solution to the NPL problem. Banks must also have the incentives and capacity to use these procedures efficiently. To illustrate the problems that may arise, we return to a stylized example used above, in which a firm has total debts of 1 m, can generate a total income worth only 0.7 m, and its assets can be liquidated for 0.5 m. We also assume that all of the firm's debts are from a single bank. The best option in this example is reorganization, where the bank keeps the firm in operation and reduces its debt down to 0.7 m. The bank might not have the incentives to implement this outcome for three main reasons:

• *"Extend-and-pretend"* The bank may be reluctant to agree to reduce the debt of a firm even if this makes economic sense because by doing so it takes a capital loss. Such a loss could force it to raise new capital (i.e., equity) to meet Basel capital ratios, and this hurts existing shareholders.[33] To avoid having to raise new capital, the bank could choose to "extend-and-pretend," rolling over a firm's debt even if the firm is unable to repay it. The extend-and-pretend problem is more severe for banks that have low capital ratios because they are more likely to be required to raise new capital following losses.

• *Reputational concerns* Reducing down debt can, in some cases, be an admission of a bad lending decision. Hence bank managers may be unwilling to reduce debt, even in the absence of any concerns with capital ratios.

• *State ownership* Because the state has become a large shareholder in the banks following their recapitalization, reducing down debt can expose bank managers to lawsuits for mismanaging public funds. Conviction in those lawsuits carries extremely severe penalties such as life imprisonment. Hence managers may be unwilling to reduce debt, even in the absence of any concerns about capital ratios.

In all three cases the bank in our example could have the incentive to keep rolling over the loan at 1 m and not reduce it to 0.7 m to make the firm viable. The firm would then become a "zombie": it would continue operating despite having a value smaller than its debts. Operating as a zombie is inefficient because the firm would not undertake any new investment, even to maintain its assets. Indeed its shareholders would not invest because all the returns would go to the bank. The firm would eventually have to be liquidated, and at a value possibly much smaller than 0.5 m because of the capital depreciation and the delays. An additional inefficiency caused by zombie lending is that fewer funds are available for profitable new firms.[34]

One solution to the extend-and-pretend problem is to ensure that banks hold adequate provisions against their NPLs, that is, provisions that are based on realistic estimates of NPL losses. In the context of our example, suppose that the regulator forces the bank to take a provision of 0.3 m against the loan to the firm. Taking this provision is an accounting operation that moves 0.3 m from the entry of "capital" in the bank's balance sheet to that of "provisions." Following the regulator's action, the bank has no incentive to keep the loan at 1 m. Indeed, by reducing the loan to 0.7 m, it can recover 0.7 m rather than the smaller amount that it would collect by keeping the firm as a zombie. Moreover it can do so without suffering any reduction to its capital beyond that already imposed by the regulator.

An alternative solution to the extend-and-pretend problem is to transfer the NPLs of all the banks to a "bad bank" whose sole mandate is to resolve them. Assuming that the NPLs are transferred at a price that reflects the amount that can realistically be recovered, the extend-and-pretend problem is solved for the same reason as under the first solution: banks are forced to recognize their capital losses. In the context of our example, the bank would sell the loan to the bad bank at 0.7 m, and hence it would be forced to reduce its capital by 0.3 m. Note that either solution, namely increasing provisions or transferring NPLs to a bad bank, may expose capital deficiencies of the banks and require them to raise new capital. A realistic assessment of capital levels is indeed key to any solution of the extend-and-pretend problem.

An advantage of dealing with NPLs by transferring them to a bad bank is economies of scale. Economies of scale arise because resolving NPLs requires an investment in specialized expertise, which can be amortized over a larger number of loans when these are gathered into a single entity. Economies of scale also arise because many firms and households hold loans from multiple banks. Resolving these loans requires getting all the banks together to share information and agree on concessions that each will make. This process can become more feasible and efficient when the loans are owned by a single entity. Economies of scale could finally arise if the bad bank is expanded to include also debts to the state (e.g., unpaid taxes and social contributions).

An additional advantage of the bad bank solution lies in the incentives to resolve the bad loans. The managers of the bad bank are not "tied" to the lending decisions that led to the NPLs, and reducing down debt does not reflect badly on their reputation. Therefore bad bank managers are more eager to reduce down debt if this makes economic sense, compared to the managers of the bank that made the original loan. A related point is that the managers of the bad bank are more eager to liquidate a firm than the managers of the originator bank. This is both because of the reputational concerns mentioned above and because the originator bank might value the future business that the firm and other connected firms can bring to the bank. In summary, the bad bank has a focused mandate to resolve NPLs efficiently, while for the originator bank efficiency is only one of the objectives.

In addition to the above-noted advantages that concern incentives and efficiency at the microeconomic level, there is an advantage at the macroeconomic level: the bad bank can internalize successfully an economy-wide externality. When a bank resolves its own NPLs, this increases economic activity and benefits other banks by making their NPL problem less severe. The bank in question does not internalize this benefit. A bad bank, however, does because it owns all the NPLs.

A disadvantage of the bad bank solution is that it requires funding because the banks must be compensated for giving away their NPLs. The funds could come from the state or from the private sector. Assuming, for example, that the value of the NPLs is 40 billion, then 40 billion of new funds would be needed. Some of this amount could come from the banks themselves, in the form of debt: the bad bank could issue debt which could be given to the banks as part of the compensation for the NPLs that they would be giving away. The equity of the bad bank, however, cannot come from the banks since the incentive conflicts mentioned above would reappear. The equity would have to come from the state and from new private investors.

Applying either of the above solutions in the Greek context (as of early 2016) is difficult because of the Greek banks' large amount of NPLs relative to their capital levels. While Greek banks have been increasing their provisions against losses on NPLs, and have benefitted from three recapitalizations, their nonprovisioned NPLs exceed significantly their CET1 capital levels.[35] Thus requiring banks to make more realistic provisions would necessitate a fourth recapitalization. Transferring NPLs to a bad bank would not get around this requirement. Given that funds to perform a fourth recapitalization are not likely to be forthcoming (as of 2016), the priority should be to ensure that NPLs return to more manageable levels through the interventions on bankruptcy procedures covered in section 7.4.1 and more importantly through sound economic policies to end the recession. Until this happens, the extend-and-pretend problem is likely to be important and the banks will remain weak. For the banks to strengthen and contribute to the recovery of the real economy, the economy must start to recover first, pulling up the banks in the process.[36]

While a bad bank gathering loans from the four large banks may not be a feasible option in the near future, a smaller bad bank can be created by gathering under the same roof the bad-bank components of all the banks that were resolved during 2012 and 2013. Because separate liquidators were put in place for each bank, it became difficult to realize gains from coordination. In early 2016, however, steps were taken to replace the multiple liquidators by a single one. Such a liquidator could eventually also take over loans from the four large banks and possibly from the state.

The governance of a bad bank should be given careful attention. A state-controlled bad bank would be a disaster, given the extent of corruption and government ineffectiveness in Greece.[37] Such an institution would be subject to extensive political interference, and hence would be managed inefficiently and benefit those with political connections. Moreover the political factors affecting its performance would spill over to the banks if they hold securities in the bad bank. Yet, a bad bank in which private investors hold a controlling equity stake, with appropriate safeguards for the state, could be an attractive policy option.

7.5   Policies for the Longer Run: Furthering Financial Development

To address the longer run challenges facing the Greek financial system, policies are needed that go beyond recovering from the crisis by reducing debt burdens and restoring the flow of credit. The longer run challenges relate mainly to the findings reported in section 7.2. These findings suggest that risk-sharing and diversification in Greece are more limited than in other EZ countries, the United Kingdom, and the United States. Limited diversification leaves households overly exposed to risks, and raises firms' cost of equity capital. A higher cost of equity capital reduces firms' ability to invest and create jobs. It also drives up corporate leverage, making the economy more vulnerable to shocks.

Improving diversification and furthering financial development more broadly, should be an important goal for economic policy in Greece. Section 7.2 suggests that a key cause of the problem is weak investor protection and the lack of trust that it breeds. Investor protection laws in Greece are not the weakest among the comparison countries, although there is significant scope for improvement as section 7.4.1 indicates in the case of bankruptcy laws. The problem is made significantly worse by the difficulty of enforcing the laws, especially the long court delays and the limited expertise of many judges on financial matters such as bankruptcy, market manipulation, and corporate fraud. These shortcomings should be addressed, and chapter 12 on the justice system in this volume offers a number of proposals toward that goal.

Investor protection requires not only an efficient justice system but also strong financial regulators. Financial regulation in Greece is performed by two agencies: the Bank of Greece (BoG), which covers banks and insurance companies (the latter since 2010), and the Hellenic Capital Markets Commission (HCMC), which covers capital markets and mutual funds. The BoG was established in 1927 and the HCMC in 1991. Being the older organization, the BoG is more mature and well resourced. The HCMC's procedures and resourcing are in more need of development, although significant strides have been made in a relatively short period.

A comprehensive review of both organizations was performed by the IMF in its Financial System Stability Assessment (FSSA) report in 2006. Among the recommendations in the report was that the HCMC should be given greater operational independence, be made more accountable, establish better controls for conflicts of interest, and help promote financial literacy.[38]

Strengthening the HCMC's independence and accountability is important, and will help promote the agency's effectiveness and prestige. Concerning operational independence, for example, the HCMC should be allowed to prioritize which cases it will investigate. Currently it is forced to prioritize requests coming from prosecutors, but these requests occasionally concern old or less important cases, and hence the HCMC may lack the resources to focus on more recent market developments. The problem is made worse by HCMC's limited budget, which renders it difficult to attract and retain specialized staff and to employ adequate IT resources. The HCMC should also be given greater authority to levy fines before it refers cases to courts.

Controlling for conflicts of interest is relevant both for the HCMC and the BoG. Regulators should not be making decisions that affect firms for which they worked in the recent past, or where they expect to work at the end of their tenure, or with which they have other links. Such instances have occurred even for past heads of both agencies, and concerns have been raised about the quality of decisions that were made. Requirements that senior staff at both agencies cannot be employed at regulated firms for "cooling-off periods" of a few years after leaving the agencies, cannot have been employed at such firms for periods of similar length before joining the agencies, and cannot hold financial stakes in regulated firms should be enforced vigorously. The appointment process of senior staff at these agencies should also become more transparent and less political. (This is a broader issue that extends to other government agencies as well.) Currently the party in power appoints its favorite candidate as agency head. A more open process in which candidates are approved following a rigorous hearing by a parliamentary committee, and are perhaps preselected by an independent committee of experts, could help ensure that the best qualified candidates are selected.

An important additional factor that contributes to the under-development of the insurance and investment fund sectors is the structure of Greece's pay-as-you-go pension system, which provides no incentives for households to save in private pensions or private life insurance. The Greek pension system is not sustainable in its current form, as it absorbs every year about 10.5 percent of GDP from the state budget compared to an average of only 2.5 percent in the EZ. A reform has been under way since 2010 to make it sustainable. This reform ought to become ambitious and include a separate pillar based on nontaxable individual contributions that could be invested in mutual funds and get taxed when pensions are paid out, similar to the individual retirement accounts (IRA) in the United States. (Chapter 11 on pensions in this volume proposes a multipillar system along these lines.) Generous tax incentives for life insurance policies, possibly with a transparent and well-regulated asset accumulation component, are another important policy that needs to be instituted. Tax incentives for IRA and related savings vehicles are likely to also promote direct participation by households in the stock market and mutual funds, as was the case in the United States. This would promote diversification and hence yield the benefits described in section 7.2.

Concerning the banking system, a key issue is to keep clear boundaries between banks and the state. Following the recapitalizations, the state became a large shareholder in Greek banks (although its stake shrunk considerably during the third recapitalization, as noted in section 7.3.5). The state's shareholdings in the banks are managed by the Hellenic Financial Stability Fund (HFSF), which was the agency that injected public funds (coming in the form of a loan by EZ countries) to help recapitalize the banks.

State ownership of the banks can open the door for interference by local politicians, with negative consequences for the allocation of credit and productivity growth. To guard against these problems, a number of mechanisms have been put in place. Law 4336/2015 has reduced the government's say in the HFSF, giving EZ representatives most of the decision-making power. The same law has required that bank executives or board members have not had a prominent political position in the government for the four years prior to their appointment, and that a number of non-executive board members have not held any position in the Greek banking system for ten years prior to their appointment. Finally, the four large banks are regulated by the Single Supervisory Mechanism (SSM) at the EZ level, and the SSM must approve the banks' senior appointments as well as other key decisions. While some of these measures may be overly strict, such as when capable people with experience in the Greek banking system are excluded from key appointments in the banks, they have significantly reduced interference by local politicians in the banking system. At the same time, it would be important to transfer the banks to full private ownership as soon as circumstances permit (especially when their balance sheets become stronger).

The high concentration of the Greek banking system is an additional issue that should be addressed, although this should be done when the crisis is over. As we argue in section 7.3.4, the benefits of high concentration probably exceed the costs during the crisis, given the important risks facing the economy and the banks. This is likely to reverse, however, when the economy recovers and entry by new players becomes beneficial. It will be important, in particular, to encourage entry by foreign financial institutions. Such entry promotes competition, financial innovation, and better regulation. Greece has been underperforming historically in attracting foreign direct investment in the financial sector (and in other sectors as well) because of its weak institutional environment and the resistance by domestic incumbents. Such investment, however, can bring significant benefits.[39]

Last, the crisis has shown both the appetite for and the lack of a safe asset in Greece. As shown in section 7.2, Greek households are holding their wealth mainly in real estate and bank deposits, probably because they were viewing them as the safest assets. This perception changed dramatically during the crisis. Following an increase in the perceived riskiness of bank deposits due to the state's inability to insure them and to the risk of converting them to a devalued new currency, a significant fraction of deposits left the country, as documented in sections 7.3.2 and 7.3.3. Real estate also ceased to be perceived as safe, as a new real estate tax was imposed and contributed to large declines in house prices. While a loss of aggregate household wealth was unavoidable during the crisis, each individual household should be able to control its own portfolio risk exposure, trading off risk and return. Access to a safe asset will expand the menu of portfolios available to households, and hence will ensure that risk is borne only by those who are willing to bear it (and to be rewarded for that).

Safe assets are available outside Greece, such as German bonds and Swiss bank accounts. These investments, however, are available only to the richest households. Moreover the funds channeled into these investments are not used to finance firms or projects in the Greek economy. Designing safe assets that are both widely accessible in all EZ countries and that channel the savings invested in them also to all countries should be an important policy goal. The ESBies proposal of Brunnermeier et al. (2011, 2017), whereby government debt of all EZ economies is packaged in fixed GDP weights and a senior tranche is extracted to yield a safe asset, has these features. Other initiatives with similar features, and possibly also involving private debt, could be considered as well.[40]

Notes

1. We are grateful to Charles Calomiris, Peter Dalianes, Manolis Galenianos, Luis Garicano, Christos Gortsos, George Katsaros, Louka Katseli, Andreas Koutras, Yannis Manuelides, Giuseppe Nicoletti, Spyros Pagratis, Stavros Panageas, Elias Papaioannou, Stathis Potamitis, Alexandros Rokas, Belen Romana, Ioanna Serafeim, Maral Shamloo, Marina Souyioultzi, Theodoros Stamatiou, and Stavros Thomadakis for their comments and input, and to Dimitris Papadimitriou for research assistance. The views expressed here are our own, and do not necessarily reflect the views of the acknowledged individuals.

2. See, for example, Levine (2005) for a survey. Recent evidence, for example, Cournede and Denk (2015), qualify that view, suggesting a hump-shaped relationship between some measures of financial development and economic growth. That evidence concerns mostly the subsample of advanced economies.

3. We should note, however, that households can also be prone to under-diversification in their holdings of financial assets, such as by investing predominantly in their own country (home bias).

4. The stock market crash might have dissuaded Greek households from investing again in stocks, even in the absence of trust-related issues. Indeed severe stock market downturns have been shown to discourage future participation in the stock market even in countries with stronger investor protection than Greece, such as the United States (Malmendier and Nagel 2011; Ampudia and Ehrmann 2014).

5. The greater development of the investment fund sector in Turkey relative to Greece, despite its lower level of GDP (section 7.2.1), might be due precisely to the larger presence of foreign financial institutions, either directly or through alliances.

6. According to the ECB, the share of banking system assets held by foreign banks in 2007 was 21.8 percent in Greece while the EU average was 46.2 percent. In 2013 these numbers became 1 and 41 percent, respectively. We return to foreign ownership and its dramatic decline during the crisis in section 7.3.4.

7. La Porta et al. (2000) find a link between weak investor protection and the prevalence of large shareholders in a large cross section of countries. The implications from our simple example and the evidence that we report in figure 7.5 are consistent with their results.

8. Weak investor protection and lack of financial literacy yield different predictions concerning the expected return of investing in the firm's stock. Lack of financial literacy (in the form assumed in our example) implies that the expected return is "abnormally" high because investors price the firm's shares assuming the worst-case scenario: investors are willing to pay 1 m for a project from which they will earn expected cash flow 1.5 m. Weak investor protection implies instead that the expected return is fair because investors rationally expect the firms' managers to divert the cash flow: investors are willing to pay 1 m for a project from which they will earn expected cash flow 1 m.

9. For example, La Porta, Lopez-de-Silanes, and Shleifer (2002) show that in countries where state ownership of banks is more extensive, lending decisions are worse, and productivity and GDP grow more slowly. Bertrand, Schoar, and Thesmar (2007) study the deregulation of the French banking system in 1980s, which eliminated state intervention in bank-lending decisions. They find that deregulation raised the cost of capital for poorly performing firms, inducing these firms to restructure or to exit their industries. At the same time more capital was made available for new entrants, and this boosted entry and competition. Overall, deregulation made the allocation of capital more efficient and boosted productivity, consistent with the cross-country findings of LLS. For additional evidence on the costs of state control of banks, see Barth, Caprio, and Levine (2004) and Khwaja and Mian (2005).

10. The IMF 2007 Country Report 07/27 on Greece (p. 9) quantifies the impact of three demand stimuli on Greece's economic growth between 1995 and 2005: private credit, government spending, and EU transfers. According to the report, private credit became the dominant stimulus from 2001 onward.

11. The Greek elections took place on October 4, 2009. On October 19, the Greek Finance Minister announced at the Eurogroup that the deficit was expected to be 12.5 percent, up from the original estimate of 6 percent.

12. Note that the excess sensitivity of Greek banks appears even prior to the crisis: Greek banks experienced a larger rise than the average bank from January 2004 until August 2007. To compare the sensitivity of Greek banks to that of banks in other countries, we use "beta," which is a standard measure of sensitivity employed in finance research. The beta of an asset Y on an asset X is the coefficient of a linear regression of the returns on Y on the returns on X. The beta of the Greek bank index on the global bank index during the period January 2004 to September 2009 and using monthly returns is 1.44. This means that a 1 percent movement in the global index was accompanied on average by a 1.44 percent movement in the Greek index. Among the eleven

countries in figure 7.1 for which we have been able to find FTSE bank indexes (Austria, Belgium, France, Germany, Greece, Ireland, Italy, Portugal, Spain, United Kingdom, United States), Greece has the fourth highest beta, after Ireland (2.59), Belgium (1.64), and Austria (1.62), and is followed by Germany (1.34), France (1.21), the United Kingdom (1.19), the United States (1.16), Italy (1.08), Spain (1.02), and Portugal (0.83). When computing return volatility during the period January 2004 to September 2009 and using monthly returns, Greece ranks fifth with a monthly volatility of 37 percent, after Ireland (78 percent), Austria (46 percent), Belgium (46 percent), and Germany (39 percent), and is followed by the United States (31 percent), France (30 percent), Portugal (29 percent), the United Kingdom (29 percent), Italy (28 percent), and Spain (27 percent). The EZ bank index has beta 1.18 and volatility 23 percent. The figures for Spain are likely to underestimate riskiness because the cajas were not listed in the stock market and hence were not included in the Spanish bank index.

13. Bank leverage is typically measured and regulated based on accounting information. We base our analysis instead on stock market returns. Haldane (2011) argues in favor of the latter approach.

14. The Cyprus index (CYPBANK(PI)) is a non-FTSE index. All other indexes are FTSE.

15. Figure 7.7 shows a steep rise in Greek banks' loans to the Greek government as percentage of GDP between 2008 and 2010. Loans to the government include Greek government bonds.

16. Domestic exposure increased in 2009 to 2010 not only for Greece but also for Ireland, Italy, Portugal, and Spain (table 2 in Merler and Pisani-Ferry 2012). Battistini, Pagano, and Simonelli (2014) argue that an additional explanation to government pressure is that banks were hedging the risk of euro exit: domestic bonds would be redenominated in the new domestic currency under euro exit, but so would bank deposits. A more precise test of the government pressure versus the hedging explanation would require data on domestic bond holdings of individual banks before the crisis.

17. See, for example, the IMF 2013 Country Report No. 13/155 (p. 51) on Greece. An additional reason mentioned by the IMF in the same report is that loans of Greek banks were less homogeneous than those of their Irish and Spanish counterparts, many of which were in real estate. Lack of homogeneity implied fewer economies of scale in forming a bad bank to sell the loans.

18. Piraeus is an exception, as the sum exceeds the number in table 7.1 by 1.1 billion. Piraeus required more capital because it absorbed the Greek branches of the Cypriot banks and the good bank formed after the resolution of ATE Bank.

19. The numbers are from the January to June 2013 report of the Hellenic Financial Stability Fund, the government agency in charge of bank recapitalizations.

20. The share of banking system assets held by domestic banks was 99 percent in Greece as of 2013, up from 78.2 percent in 2007. (Foreign banks Credit Agricole, Millenium, and Societe Generale exited Greece during the crisis by selling their subsidiaries.) As of 2013, Germany and Sweden had a 100 percent share, followed by France, Greece, and Spain with 99 percent, Italy with 94 percent, Portugal with 92 percent, Cyprus with 89 percent, and the United Kingdom

with 84 percent. The EU average was 59 percent. (This is a simple average rather than GDP-weighted.) The data are from the ECB.

21. Calomiris, Klingebiel, and Laeven (2012) report on such evidence from Argentina, Mexico, and other developing countries. According to these authors, entry by foreign banks not only promotes more competition but also puts more pressure on bank regulators to enforce the rules and provide a level playing field. This leads to a virtuous cycle of more competition and better regulation.

22. Revised Basel rules required banks to stop counting most DTA toward CET1 capital. Following similar initiatives in Italy, Spain, and, later, Portugal, the Greek government passed a law in the summer of 2014 allowing Greek banks to convert DTA into deferred tax credit (DTC). DTC was covered by a state guarantee that if banks realized losses in a given year and hence could not use the tax savings, the state would inject the corresponding amount of capital in the banks and would receive equity shares in return. Because of the state obligation, regulators agreed to continue counting DTC-converted DTA towards CET1 capital. Out of 15.6 billion DTA that the four large banks reported in December 2014, 12.8 billion had been converted into DTC. DTC continues to be a major part of banks' capital base in 2016.

23. Capital controls affect primarily cross-border transactions. No limits were imposed on electronic payments or other debit or credit card payments inside the country. Also, later on, the 60 euro daily limit became a 420 euro weekly limit, allowing individuals to withdraw the full amount of 420 euros once a week.

24. Banks had not been required to raise new capital as a result of the AQR of the previous year. More precisely, in the October 2014 ECB static exercise, which utilized the banks' balance sheets at the end of 2013, three of the four large banks needed new capital. Yet, in the dynamic exercise, which took into consideration the net capital-raising actions of 2014 plus the expected bank profitability of the period 2014 to 2016 that had already been approved by DG-Competition, all four large banks were allowed to continue operating in the fourth quarter of 2014 without having to raise new capital.

25. Dependence on the Greek state continued to remain high, however, primarily through the DTC (or DTA) component of equity capital, or through conditional convertible bonds and preferred shares that the state continued to own. In Alpha, 49 percent of equity capital was in the form of DTA as of October 2016. In Eurobank, 68 percent was DTA and another 13 percent was preferred shares (which would expire counting as capital on January 1, 2018). In NBG, 52 percent was DTA and another 21 percent was conditional convertible bonds. In Piraeus, 51 percent was DTA and another 21 percent was conditional convertible bonds. However, the earlier high dependence on state guarantees, whose amount had peaked to over 50 billion euros in 2015, had already declined to less than 5 billion in October 2016.

26. While the discussion in this section focuses on the flow of credit via the banking system, policies could also be designed to channel credit via capital markets. For example, the Athens Stock Exchange has sought to introduce new products to attract foreign investment into Greek firms and projects. Such efforts are especially important given the impaired state of the banks.

27. The rationale of including restructured loans in the NPL calculation is that these loans have a high probability of re-becoming NPLs. In conducting the AQR and stress tests, the SSM examines this latter, stricter ratio, which it calls nonperforming exposure (NPE).

28. For a more comprehensive analysis, see, for example, Potamitis and Rokas (2012) and Potamitis, Kontoulas, and Nounou (2014).

29. We describe outcomes under Greek law, but the description applies to many other countries as well.

30. In the longer term, more emphasis should be given to training judges on bankruptcy matters and related business disciplines such as accounting and finance. It could also be beneficial to create special courts for bankruptcy cases. For a more detailed discussion of these issues, see chapter 12 on the justice system in this volume.

31. For example, according to the World Bank *Doing Business* report, the average time to resolve a simple dispute through the court system in Greece increased from 819 days in 2008 to 1,580 days in 2014. For proposals to reduce court delays, see chapter 12 on the justice system in this volume.

32. If the house can be sold for more than 200K, the household should receive the difference between the sale price and 200K, or 20K, whichever is larger.

33. New capital benefits debtholders because banks are made safer. Since the return on shareholders' investment accrues partly to debtholders, and since new shareholders must break even on their investment, existing shareholders must lose. This is the classic debt-overhang problem (Myers 1977). For a recent analysis of the debt-overhang problem in the context of banks, see Admati and Hellwig (2014).

34. This inefficiency does not arise in our example because the bank's best option is to keep the firm in operation, and this does not release funds to the bank. If, however, the bank's best option were to liquidate the firm (e.g., the firm's assets could be liquidated for 0.9 m instead of 0.5 m), then liquidating the firm would release funds to the bank, but these funds would not be available if the bank kept the firm as a zombie.

35. According to Fitch's pro-forma conservative analysis of November 2015 (Fabo, Iano and Van Lumich 2015), the ratio of nonprovisioned nonperforming exposure (NPE) as of the end of September 2015 to CET1 capital post–October-2015-AQR and post–third-recapitalization was 1.83 when aggregating across the four large banks. Out of 112 billion NPE, 48.8 percent was covered by provisions, while the remaining 51.2 percent was not provisioned. Of course, the ratio of nonprovisioned NPE to CET1 capital does not take into account the recovery value of the loans, which is larger than zero when supporting collateral exists.

36. As of early 2016, fears that Greek banks may soon need an additional recapitalization were widespread and the banks' stock prices tumbled once again together with the stock prices of other European banks. Meanwhile the possibility of a future bail-in, whose framework was put in place and was operational in 2016, was still creeping in the minds of the Greek public. Opinion polls were showing that few Greeks were willing to redeposit in the Greek banking system the cash they withdrew during the crisis years.

37. According to the World Bank's Worldwide Governance Indicators in 2013, Greece scored 26th out of the 28 EU countries on both control of corruption and government effectiveness.

38. The bulk of the recommendations in the IMF FSSA report concerned weaknesses of the insurance regulator, which at the time was a Directorate at the Ministry of Development. These recommendations proved to be prescient in light of the insurance fraud scandal in 2009, following which insurance regulation was handed over to the BoG. The report also highlighted the risks from an absence of a regulator for pension funds. This proved to be prescient as well in light of the pension fund scandal in 2007.

39. Surveys of financial sector executives in Germany suggest that the most important factors in promoting FDI in the financial sector of the European South are high human capital, adequate shareholder protection, and avoidance of policy unpredictability, rather than low wages.

40. The Capital Markets Union, currently being designed, could also provide opportunities for cross-border household investment in financial instruments, not only to the richest and most financially literate segments of the population but also more widely through mutual funds and managed accounts.

References

Admati, A., and M. Hellwig. 2014. *The Bankers' New Clothes: What's Wrong with Banking and What to Do about It*. Princeton: Princeton University Press.

Ampudia, M., and M. Ehrmann. 2014. Macroeconomic experiences and risk taking of euro area households. Working paper. European Central Bank.

Bank of Greece. 2012. Report on the recapitalization and restructuring of the Greek banking sector. Athens.

Barth, J., G. Caprio, and R. Levine. 2004. Bank regulation and supervision: What works best? *Journal of Financial Intermediation* 13:205–248.

Battistini, N., M. Pagano, and S. Simonelli. 2014. Systemic risk, sovereign yields and bank exposures in the euro crisis. *Economic Policy* 29: 203–51.

Bertrand, M., A. Schoar, and D. Thesmar. 2007. Banking deregulation and industry structure: Evidence from the French banking reforms of 1985. *Journal of Finance* 62: 597–628.

Brunnermeier, M., L. Garicano, P. Lane, M. Pagano, R. Reis, T. Santos, D. Thesmar, S. Van Nieuwerburgh, and D. Vayanos. 2011. European Safe Bonds: Working paper. ESBies, Euro-nomics .com.

Brunnermeier, M., S. Langfield, M. Pagano, R. Reis, S. Van Nieuwerburgh, and D. Vayanos. 2017. Forthcoming. ESBies: Safety in the Tranches. *Economic Policy* 32: 175–220.

Calomiris, C., D. Klingebiel, and L. Laeven. 2012. Seven ways to deal with a financial crisis: Cross-country experience and policy implications. *Journal of Applied Corporate Finance* 24: 8–22.

Clarke, G., R. Cull, M.-S. Martinez Peria, and S. Sanchez. 2002. Bank lending to small businesses in Latin America: Does bank origin matter? Working paper. World Bank.

Cournede, B., and O. Denk. 2015. Finance and economic growth in OECD and G20 countries. Working paper 1223. OECD Economics Department.

Fabo, J., F. Iano, and E. Van Lumich. 2015. *Third Greek Bank Recapitalisation: Only First Step towards Restoring Financial Stability.* Fitch Ratings Special Report on Greek banks, November 6.

Guiso, L., P. Sapienza, and L. Zingales. 2008. Trusting the stock market. *Journal of Finance* 63: 2557–2600.

Haldane, A. 2011. Capital discipline. Speech given at the American Economic Association meeting.

Honohan, P. 1999. Consequences for Greece and Portugal of the opening-up of the European banking market. Working paper. World Bank.

International Finance Corporation and World Bank. 2014. *Doing Business 2015.* Washington, DC: World Bank.

International Monetary Fund. 2006. *Greece: Financial System Stability Assessment.* Country Report 06/6. IMF.

International Monetary Fund. 2007. *Greece: Selected Issues.* Country Report 07/27. IMF.

International Monetary Fund. 2013. *Greece: Selected Issues.* Country Report 13/155. IMF.

Jappelli, T. 2010. Financial literacy: An international comparison. *Economic Journal* 120: F429–51.

Khwaja, A., and A. Mian. 2005. Do lenders favor politically connected Firms? Rent provision in an emerging financial market. *Quarterly Journal of Economics* 120: 1371–1411.

La Porta, R., F. Lopez-de-Silanes, and A. Shleifer. 2002. Government ownership of banks. *Journal of Finance* 57: 265–301.

La Porta, R., F. Lopez-de-Silanes, A. Shleifer, and R. Vishny. 1998. Law and finance. *Journal of Political Economy* 106: 1113–55.

La Porta, R., F. Lopez-de-Silanes, A. Shleifer, and R. Vishny. 2000. Investor protection and corporate governance. *Journal of Financial Economics* 58: 3–28.

Levine, R. 2002. Denying foreign bank entry: Implications for bank interest margins. Working paper. Central Bank of Chile.

Levine, R. 2005. Finance and growth: Theory and evidence. In *Handbook of Economic Growth*, ed. P. Aghion and S. Durlauf, 865–934. Amsterdam: Elsevier Science.

Malmendier, U., and S. Nagel. 2011. Depression babies: Do macroeconomic experiences affect risk-taking? *Quarterly Journal of Economics* 126: 373–416.

Merler, S. and J. Pisani-Ferry. 2012. Who is afraid of sovereign bonds? Policy contribution 2012/02. Bruegel Institution.

Myers, S. 1977. Determinants of corporate borrowing. *Journal of Financial Economics* 5: 147–75.

Potamitis, S., and A. Rokas. 2012. A new pre-bankruptcy procedure for Greece. *Journal of Business Law* 3: 235–47.

Potamitis, S., I. Kontoulas, and E. Nounou. 2014. Greece. Getting the deal through. In *Restructuring and Insolvency in 45 Jurisdictions Worldwide*, ed. B. Leonard, 179–89. London: Law Business Research Ltd..

IV Raising Standards in Education and Health

8 Education and the Greek Economy[1]

Nikolaos Vettas

8.1 Introduction

Education affects the economy in Greece, like every other economy, in two main ways. First, expenditure on education services, public and private, accounts for a significant fraction of national income, and therefore a poor design and functioning of the education system leads to an inefficient use of scarce resources and to lower economic welfare. Second, a better education system raises human capital, and thereby increases productivity, both current and future. Especially for economies that in their growth prospects are "caught in the middle," in the sense that they are neither close enough to the technology and innovation frontier nor inexpensive in terms of labor costs, improving the education system may be the key for increasing competitiveness in a sustainable manner. Put more simply, a better-educated labor force allows production to be competitive without resorting to decreasing wages. Moreover productivity depends crucially on the overall quality of institutions (including the justice system, media, and political representation), and institutions tend to function better when citizens are better educated. In parallel, a well-functioning education system is an important condition for social mobility, that is, the ability of those who come from financially struggling and less educated families, to chart out a better life than their parents' if they put in the effort required. Social mobility is a source of dynamism for societies and, by implication, for their production abilities.

The formal structure of the Greek education system does not differ significantly from that of other European countries. However, there are some severe failures in its design and operation, especially in the recent decades, and these have led to serious inefficiencies and mediocre outcomes.

On the positive side, the number of students graduating successfully from the various levels of the Greek education system has been steadily increasing in the recent decades. Greece compares reasonably well in that regard with other countries at a similar level of development. The number of graduating students has been increasing steadily partly because of the high demand for education, stemming from the strong conviction of families that, along with owning a house, their children's education is the best investment they could make in an otherwise volatile environment. Also on the positive side, a significant number of those graduating from the Greek education system pursue advanced studies abroad and have successful professional or academic careers. Statistics (e.g., in the EC bulletin *Education and Training Monitor 2015—Greece*) further suggest that the number of university graduates per capita in Greece is not significantly lower than the EU average despite the fact that Greek public expenditure on education is significantly lower than the EU average. However, a large number of those graduates do not put their skills in use. Unemployment among university graduates in Greece is far higher than in the European Union, on average. Therefore Greece has a significant stock of idle, inert human capital, that, in principle, could be a crucial driver of growth and prosperity if put to proper use.

On the negative side, the average quality of the services provided by the Greek education system appears to be low, with neither the quality of the education institutions themselves nor the average quality of the graduates to be satisfactory, at least as measured in the relevant rankings and international scores. For instance, Greece ranked 24th and 23rd, respectively, out of 31 OECD countries in 2007 in terms of the percentages of the population who had completed secondary and tertiary education. The 2009 PISA tests for 15-year-olds placed Greece 24th for reading, and 27th for mathematics and science, within the same group of 31 counties. Research output by universities also tends to be low, and the relationships between universities and firms are limited. Greece had no university in the top 200 according to the 2007 Shanghai Jiao Tong ranking, while countries with similar population to Greece, such as Belgium and Israel, had three or more universities in the top 150. Overall, the system seems to be underachieving in most of its dimensions.

One may be tempted to attribute Greece's underperformance to the relatively low proportion of its GDP that it spends on education: as of 2005, Greece was spending 4.2 percent of its GDP on education, while the OECD average was 5.8 percent. Yet the OECD-reported expenditure for Greece corresponds almost exclusively to public education and does not include two large out-of-pocket expenditures incurred by Greek households: tuition costs for private tutoring centers (*frontistiria*) to prepare high school students for university entrance exams, and tuition and living costs for university students studying abroad.[2]

The underperformance of the Greek education system is mainly due to poorly designed incentives. An effective evaluation system, explicit or implicit, is lacking at the level of individuals, teams, and organizations, and monetary and other rewards are only loosely (if at all) related to performance. As a consequence incentives to exercise extra effort are weak, and resources are not allocated optimally, that is where they can be most productive, but instead randomly or through a political process that reacts to whoever can apply the heaviest pressure. As an example, the formal evaluation of university units has only started recently but it only operates nominally and without real implications for the evaluated units. Likewise the great majority of teachers and professors are paid directly from the state and their wage is the same for a given rank, without any discrimination that could be based on their abilities or superior performance. Since the link between effort and performance, on one hand, and rewards, on the other, is weak, it is not surprising that the overall results are suboptimal. In this chapter we review this weak system of incentives, how it has been created and why it has proved difficult to change despite some serious reform efforts; we also provide suggestions for improving performance through an appropriate redesign of the incentive system.

The Greek education system suffers additionally from being too centralized, formalistic and dependent on the state, through the Ministry of Education, Research and Religious Affairs (in short, Ministry of Education, in the rest of the chapter).[3] At the primary and secondary levels of education, private schools are in operation alongside public ones, but their structure and curriculum can only marginally deviate from the strict norms set by the Ministry of Education. At the tertiary level of education, private universities or other institutions are not allowed to operate (or, rather, those that do operate are not recognized as universities by the state). The provision that universities have to be public is part of the Greek constitution, and although it has been heavily debated in the last couple of decades, appetite for change is limited. In general, universities are closely controlled by the Ministry of Education in terms of their resources, personnel decisions, admissions criteria and targets, and programs of study. Moreover faculty members and academic units are given only weak incentives for high performance on research and teaching. As we argue later in this chapter, the state's extreme and bureaucratic control on the education system, together with the weak incentives, contribute to the system's underperformance across the board.

With the outbreak of the crisis and the fiscal tightening that followed, the situation has become even worse. Salaries have been severely reduced for all teachers and professors, new hires have been essentially "frozen" since 2009 and budgets for the operation of schools have been sharply cut. Some rationalization through the merging of school units has been attempted but no real progress has been made in the direction of improving incentives. If anything, there has been a regression toward a more centralized system, most emphatically through the *de facto* abolition of an ambitious university reform law that was voted in 2011 and has been systematically dismantled ever since. Overall the performance of the Greek education system before the crisis was mediocre, and the attempts to reform parts of the system during the crisis have mostly been reversed.

A final important point must be stressed here. No education system can prosper in a vacuum. A well-functioning and dynamic labor market that recognizes high ability and rewards it accordingly is instrumental toward providing strong incentives to students to improve their performance and to their teachers and institutions to offer them the best possible education. Yet in Greece the labor market has been hardly operating in this manner. The primary goal of many Greeks has been (until recently) employment in the public sector, and this does not really require a high-quality education but only the relevant formal diplomas or certificates. Moreover, because only a small number of Greek firms are export oriented, innovative, and internationally competitive, the demand to seek and hire the most talented young people has been weak. In this way the low competitiveness of Greek firms and the weak performance of the education system have become mutually enforcing.

In the remainder of this chapter, we discuss some key characteristics of the Greek education system, especially in its relationship to the economy. Section 8.2 presents measures of the system's overall performance, and reviews the literature on the relationship between education and economic growth. Section 8.3 describes the formal structure of the Greek education system and some relevant data on the important "inputs" and "outputs" of the system. Section 8.4 overviews expenditure for education, both public and private, and places it in the broader economic context in Greece. Section 8.5 reviews the main developments since the outbreak of the crisis in 2009 when fiscal tightening caused a significant drop in employment and salaries in public schools and universities, as well as in other public expenditure items. Reforming the structure of the education system, however, was not in any significant way part of the formal adjustment programs. There was an important attempt to reform the university system, with a new law approved in 2011 by a wide parliamentary majority, but in practice, it met significant opposition and obstacles and was essentially blocked; we discuss this case separately, as an example of a necessary and promising reform that essentially failed. Section 8.6 reviews the main weaknesses of the current system and puts forward priority areas for reform and a basic set of recommendations. Section 8.7 concludes.

8.2   Framing the Analysis

8.2.1   Performance Measures

Measuring performance in education can be a controversial matter. Inputs (e.g., number of teachers employed, hours they work, buildings) and costs (salaries, capital investment), as well as outputs (e.g., number of students or graduates at the various education levels) are the usual measures. Yet measuring the quality of inputs (e.g., the quality of teaching and educational materials) and outputs (the skills and incremental knowledge that students obtain at the various education levels) is much harder. In principle, proxies can be used for such measurements, such as the increase in university graduates' average salary subsequent to achieving a certain degree level that leads to the job market, and the research output by university faculty in the form of published papers or patents. For the Greek education system, high-quality official statistics that would cover all dimensions of interest do not exist, at least not in a way that allows for meaningful comparisons across time and across educational units. At the same time, scores and rankings by international organizations, such as the OECD, or independent bodies, provide useful benchmarks.[4]

The recent data generally do not paint a favorable picture of the Greek education system. According to a recent report by the OECD,[5] at least one in four Greek students[6] is unable to locate pieces of information in a text, or carry out routine procedures according to direct instructions, or make a simple connection between information in a text and common everyday knowledge. Likewise, in the 2012 PISA survey, Greece was ranked 39th out of 65 countries in reading, and 41st in mathematics and science. Greece had indeed high percentages of low-performing students.

Student scores in PISA tests are ranked in six levels. Every third Greek student (35.7 percent) scored at the lowest level in mathematics, every fifth (22.6 percent) in reading, and every fourth (25.5 percent) in science, while the respective average frequencies across OECD countries were 23, 18, and 17.8 percent. In contrast, only 0.6 percent of Greek students scored at the highest level in Mathematics, 0.5 percent in reading, and 0.2 percent in science, while the respective average frequencies across OECD countries were 3.3, 1.2, and 1.2 percent. The report points out that low performance in the PISA tests by Greek students is correlated with factors such as the socioeconomic status of the student's family, gender, and enrollment in preschool.

Figure 8.1, which can be produced by averaging the scores across the three subjects, confirms that Greek 15-year-olds score badly in OECD's PISA exams in mathematics, science, and reading. In fact Greek students are consistently the worst performers in Europe[7] in all disciplines tested in the PISA surveys.

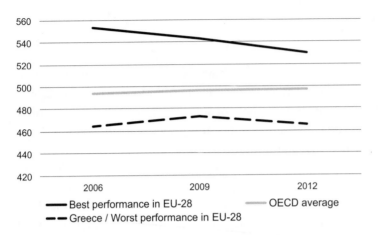

Figure 8.1
PISA overall average of scores of boys and girls in mathematics, reading, and science exams

Greek students perform badly despite being tutored by more teachers than most of their European peers. Indeed, Greece has one of the lowest students per teacher ratio in Europe (figure 8.2). The poor performance of Greek students also cannot be justified by low public funding for education. Although Greek public expenditure on education is below the European average, Greek students perform significantly worse than students in other countries with less funding (figure 8.3). Poor student performance cannot be attributed to underpaid teachers either. Hourly salaries for Greek teachers are close to the European average (figures 8.4 and 8.5). Nevertheless, Greek students do spend significantly less time in class than their European peers (figure 8.6). Interestingly and importantly, Greece also ranks at the bottom among European countries in school autonomy regarding both the curricular content of elective subjects and the choice of school textbooks.[8]

8.2.2   On the Relationship between Education and Economic Growth

Why should we care about the quality of a country's education system from a broader economic perspective? It turns out that education is one of the main drivers of economic growth. A better-educated population tends to be more productive and adapt better to technological change. Moreover the ability of a country to perform well in research and innovation, and to be among the leaders in high added value industry sectors, depends crucially on its education system and, particularly, on the quality of its universities. Numerous studies have attempted to explore, document, and quantify various aspects of the relationship between education and economic performance.

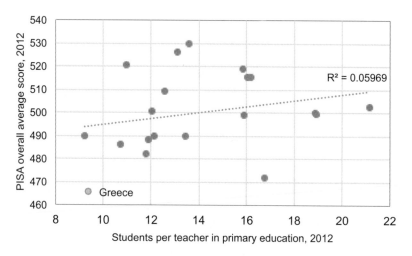

Figure 8.2

PISA average score plotted against the student per teacher ratio

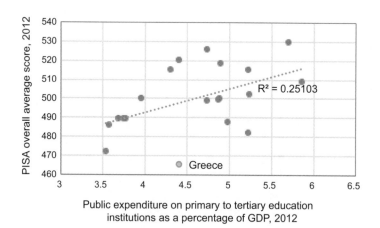

Figure 8.3

PISA average score plotted against the public expenditure on education

The relationship between education and economic growth, in particular, has attracted much attention.

Several studies have documented positive effects of education on growth. Seetanah (2009), for instance, provides empirical evidence that higher enrollment in primary and secondary education is linked with higher growth in African countries.[9] Ciccone and Papaioannou (2009) document that countries with higher initial education levels

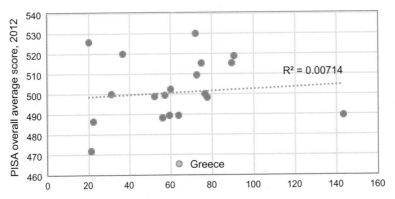

Salary per hour of net contact (teaching) time after 15 years of
experience, lower secondary education, in USD converted using PPPs
for private consumption, 2012

Figure 8.4
PISA average score plotted against teachers' hourly salaries

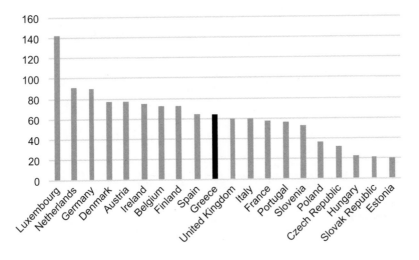

Figure 8.5
Salary per hour of net contact (teaching) time after 15 years of experience, lower secondary education, in USD converted using PPPs for private consumption, 2012

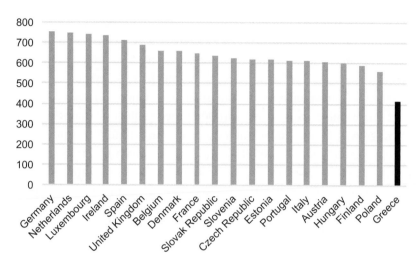

Figure 8.6

Number of teaching hours per year in lower secondary education, 2012

have experienced faster value-added and employment growth in schooling-intensive industries in the 1980s and 1990s. Fleisher et al. (2010) find that secondary and university education positively affect output and productivity growth in China's provinces. Specifically, workers with higher education have higher marginal product and they engage in innovation, increasing total factor productivity.

Gennaioli et al. (2011) provide an empirical analysis of regional data across the world concluding that education is the critical determinant of regional development. Educated entrepreneurs play a crucial role. Similarly Hanushek and Woessmann (2012) find a close relationship between educational achievement and GDP growth across countries. The authors claim that if a country improves the skills of its workforce by about 25 points on a PISA scale, it could expect half a percentage point higher growth rates. Lin (2004) studies tertiary education in Taiwan, measured by years of schooling among employed people, and economic growth over the period 1965 to 2000. The author breaks down tertiary education in four domains (humanities, engineering/science, business/social science, and agricultural sciences) and breaks down output in three sectors (industry, services, and agriculture) to study how each educational domain affects each sector. The author finds that higher education positively affected growth in Taiwan and that engineering and the natural sciences majors played the most prominent role in this process.

At the same time some studies have yielded findings going in the opposite direction. For example, Knight et al. (1993), Benhabib and Spiegel (1994), Islam (1995), Caselli et al. (1996), Hamilton and Monteagudo (1998), and Pritchett (2001) find that human capital is not a significant factor affecting economic growth. Yet subsequent studies have provided strong counterarguments and potential explanations for such counter-intuitive findings. For example, De la Fuente and Doménech (2006) find that schooling does contribute to growth, if one studies the relationship using more carefully compiled datasets. Krueger and Lindahl (2000) find that if one corrects for errors in measuring education, then education has very significant effects on growth, thus refuting previous results of cross-country analyses that showed small effects or no effect. Temple (1999) reports a positive correlation between education and growth in a cross-country dataset and argues that other studies often miss such effects because of a few outlier countries that skew the results. In a subsequent study, Temple (2001) refutes assertions made by some studies that education does not matter much for growth, pointing out that these studies often focus on the effects of changes in schooling, ignoring effects of levels of schooling. The author also notes that such counterintuitive findings often have high standard errors.

More recently Cohen and Soto (2007) compiled a new dataset on years of schooling per country, with reduced measurement errors compared to previous datasets. Using this dataset in standard cross-country growth regressions, they find significant effects of education on growth. Hanushek and Kimko (2000) focus on the quality of human capital, as measured by comparative tests of mathematics and scientific skills, rather than the quantity of human capital, as usually measured by years of schooling, enrollment rates, spending on education, and so forth. They find that the quality of human capital has a consistent, stable, and strong relationship with economic growth. Additionally the authors find that human capital quality causes growth, rather than the other way round.

Some studies point out that primary and secondary education have stronger effects on economic growth than tertiary education. Self and Grabowski (2003) use data for Japan and find that more years of schooling at primary through tertiary education levels lead to higher growth. However, the evidence is weak for secondary and tertiary education. The authors do not find evidence that vocational education creates growth. Similarly Pereira and Aubyn (2009) examine data for Portugal on years of schooling and find that primary and secondary education affect growth but tertiary education does not.[10]

Vandenbussche et al. (2006) hypothesize that skilled human capital, that is, people with tertiary education, is more important for growth in economies close to the technological frontier, which are economies where growth derives from innovation. In economies far from the technological frontier, growth is driven by imitation (adopting technologies developed by others); thus skilled human capital is less important. The authors analyze data from OECD countries and find that their hypothesis is verified. Along the same lines Petrakis and Stamatakis (2002) examine the relationship between human capital and growth across counties and find that the role of primary and secondary education in driving growth seems to be more important in poor counties, whereas growth in OECD countries depends more on tertiary education.

Several studies examine empirically the relationship between education and economic growth in Greece. Following a general trend in the literature mentioned above, many of these studies on Greece stress the importance of primary and secondary education. Asteriou and Agiomirgianakis (2001) find a positive relationship between education in Greece, measured by enrollment rates in primary schools through universities, and GDP per capita. The authors suggest that more education in the first two levels leads to economic growth, while higher growth correlates with higher enrollment in universities.[11] A subsequent contribution by Tsamadias and Prontzas (2012) finds that enrollment in secondary education had a positive effect on growth in Greece over the period 1960 to 2000.

Taking a closer look at the regional economic effects of education, Tsamadias et al. (2010) study human capital, proxied by the educational attainment of the population, and economic variables, at the level of Greek regions in the period 1998 to 2008. The authors find that higher regional human capital causes higher regional GDP and higher disposable incomes. Human capital is strongly correlated with private bank deposits, but the authors suggest higher deposits cause higher human capital, rather than the other way round. The authors find that the stock of human capital among employed people is lower than among the unemployed. The overall average stock of human capital in Greece increased over time, but remains lower than the EZ average, the EU average, and the OECD average.

The effects of tertiary education on economic growth in Greece are also documented in the literature. Pegkas and Tsamadias (2014) examine the relationship between tertiary education, measured by enrollment rates, and GDP per worker in Greece in the period 1960 to 2009. They find that greater enrollment in tertiary education causes more GDP per capita. Solaki (2013) finds a positive relationship between education (proxied both by enrollment rates and spending) and growth over the period 1961 to 2006 in Greece, and suggests that enrollment in tertiary education and public spending on all levels of education cause growth. These effects of tertiary education on growth are all the more notable, in light of the fact that Greek universities appear to be rather cost-inefficient. Aubyn et al. (2009) study tertiary education systems in the European Union, focusing on spending and outcomes. They find that a good quality secondary education system, output-based funding rules, institutions' independent evaluation, and staff policy autonomy are positively related to the efficiency of public spending on universities. They also find that Greek tertiary education is one of the least efficient in the European Union by any measure.

Notably there have also been studies on Greece that have reported results that point in the opposite direction. For instance, Tsamadias and Pegkas (2012) find that secondary education had a negative effect on economic growth in Greece in the period 1981 to 2009. Pegkas (2012), examining the relationship between human capital and growth in Greece in the period 1981 to 2009, does not find any significant effects of years of schooling on output or growth. Likewise Prontzas et al. (2009) find that expenditure on public education (primary through tertiary) had a positive but very low effect on growth in Greece over the period 1960 to 2000. However, these results are overwhelmingly outweighed by the body of evidence suggesting a strong positive relationship between education and economic performance.

8.3   Structure of the Education System in Greece

This chapter describes the formal structure of the Greek education system as well as the regulatory framework within which it operates. It also presents data on the number of students, teachers, and schools or other education units and how these have evolved in recent years.

8.3.1   Structure of the Greek Education System

The education system in Greece consists of three successive levels, namely pre-primary and primary, secondary, and tertiary (figure 8.7). At the first two levels, private schools are in operation alongside public ones. At the third level, only public universities are allowed to operate. All schools (public and private) as well as all universities operate under the authority of the Ministry of Education.

8.3.2   Preprimary Education

Preprimary education is offered by preprimary schools or kindergartens (*Nipiagogeio*), under the supervision of the Ministry of Education. Preprimary education in Greece starts at the age of four, when the children are allowed to enroll in preprimary school, but attendance becomes compulsory at the age of five. Besides preprimary schools there are schools for younger children, namely infant centers (*Vrefonipiakos Stathmos*)

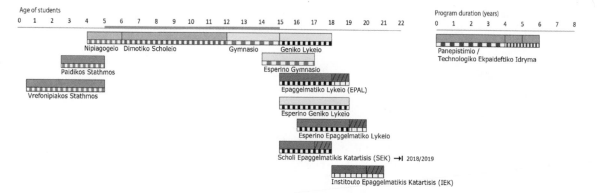

Figure 8.7

Structure of the Greek national education system, 2014–2015

Source: Eurydice Network

and child centers (*Paidikos Stathmos*) that operate under the auspices of local authorities (*Municipalities*). Law 3794/2009 also allows the operation of foreign preprimary schools that can be open not only to foreigners but also to Greek pupils. These foreign schools can follow the Greek curriculum, a foreign curriculum, or both a Greek and a foreign curriculum.

At the beginning of school year 2014–2015, the total number of preprimary schools in operation in Greece was 5,687 (of which 5,088 were public and 599 private), with an enrollment of 162,004 children (92.1 percent in public schools and 7.9 percent in private). These schools employed 13,106 teachers (93 percent in public and 7 percent in private). As table 8.1 indicates, the number of children enrolled in preprimary schools and the number of teachers increased significantly from 2001 to 2014, by 12.5 and 28.4 percent, respectively. However, starting in 2009, the number of schools gradually declined to the 2001 level. The ratio of children per teacher declined from 14.1 in school year 2001–2002 to 12.4 in school year 2014–2015.

The purpose and structure of preprimary education are determined by Law 1566/1985. Presidential Degree 200/1998 dictates the regulatory framework governing preprimary schools, including the admission requirements, the exact daily program, and the curriculum.[12]

Table 8.1

Preprimary education in Greece (start of school year), 2001 to 2014

School year	Children	Teachers	Schools	Children/teacher
2001–2002	144,055	10,211	5,694	14.1
2002–2003	141,010	10,677	5,721	13.2
2003–2004	140,535	10,992	5,722	12.8
2004–2005	141,501	11,276	5,716	12.5
2005–2006	143,401	11,461	5,715	12.5
2006–2007	142,666	11,846	5,763	12.0
2007–2008	148,529	12,343	5,803	12.0
2008–2009	156,629	13,097	5,965	12.0
2009–2010	157,908	13,488	6,103	11.7
2010–2011	165,321	13,496	6,067	12.2
2011–2012	164,790	13,411	5,921	12.3
2012–2013	162,888	13,301	5,823	12.2
2013–2014	165,775	12,719	5,645	13.0
2014–2015	162,004	13,106	5,687	12.4

Source: Hellenic Statistical Authority

8.3.3 Primary Education

Primary education is offered by primary schools (*Dimotiko*). It is compulsory and lasts for six years (with six distinct grades). Enrollment in the first year takes place at the age of six and requires, among other things, a preprimary school "attendance certificate." Public and private primary schools have the same organization, function, and curriculum, and offer equivalent certificates[13]. Their curriculum is prepared by the Educational Policy Institute, is approved by the Ministry of Education, and has to be followed by all teachers in both public and private schools—it can be adjusted to the particular needs of each class, but such adjustments can only be marginal. Pupils who obtain the primary school "leave certificate" are automatically accepted in lower secondary school/ high school (*Gymnasio*).

Primary education is also offered by alternative and parallel structures, such as (1) model experimental primary schools (Law 3966/2011, amended by Law 4327/2015), where new curricula, textbooks and educational approaches are used on an experimental basis; (2) primary schools for special education and training, which offer education to children with special needs; (3) minority primary schools, which cover the needs of Muslim children in the geographical region of Thrace; (4) cross-cultural education primary schools, for pupils who are immigrants, repatriate or Roma, where the curricula are adapted to their special social, cultural, and educational needs; and (5) European education primary schools (Law 3376/2005), for the children of employees of the European Network and Information Security Agency and other EU agencies. The curriculum, timetable, certificates, and all other substantial or formal issues are regulated by Ministerial Decisions. As in the preprimary schools, there exist foreign primary schools with a Greek curriculum, with a foreign curriculum, and with both a Greek and a foreign curriculum.

At the beginning of school year 2014–2015, 629,373 pupils were enrolled to public and private primary schools (590,737 in public schools and 38,636 in private). The number of schools was 4,575 (4,254 public and 321 private), and the number of teachers was 64,323 (94.1 percent in public schools and 5.9 percent in private schools). The ratio of pupils per teacher was 9.8.

According to table 8.2, the number of pupils in primary schools declined from 647,041 in school year 2001–2002, to 629,373 in school year 2014–2015 (–2.7 percent), but the number of teachers increased significantly from 49,842 to 64,323 (29.1 percent). The number of schools decreased significantly from 6,074 in school year 2001–2002 to 4,575 in school year 2014–2015 (–24.7 percent). The ratio of pupils to teachers dropped from 13 in school year 2001–2002 to 9.8 in school year 2014–2015.

The purpose and structure of primary education are determined by Law 1566/1985. Law No. 2525/1997 establishes the function of all-day primary school.[14]

8.3.4 Secondary Education

Compulsory Secondary Education Secondary education consists of two stages, compulsory secondary education and noncompulsory secondary education.

Compulsory secondary education is offered by lower secondary schools/high schools (*Gymnasio*), day or evening (*Esperino Gymnasio*). Lower secondary schools start at the age of 12 and last for three years (with three distinct grades). They constitute the last stage of compulsory education which lasts for nine years in total (six in primary school and three in lower secondary school). As in the case of preprimary and primary schools, both public and private lower secondary schools have the same organization, function, and curriculum and offer equivalent certificates. Their curriculum, approved by the Ministry of Education, is followed by all schools and is adjusted to the particular needs of each class. Students who graduate from a lower secondary school are awarded a "leaving certificate" and can (1) enroll in upper secondary schools/general

Table 8.2
Primary education in Greece (start of school year), 2001 to 2014

School year	Pupils	Teachers	Schools	Pupils/teacher
2001–2002	647,041	49,842	6,074	13.0
2002–2003	647,642	52,788	6,018	12.3
2003–2004	655,369	54,131	5,955	12.1
2004–2005	646,505	56,639	5,870	11.4
2005–2006	639,685	58,376	5,753	11.0
2006–2007	639,083	58,981	5,668	10.8
2007–2008	634,207	59,003	5,590	10.7
2008–2009	635,804	62,502	5,519	10.2
2009–2010	633,406	64,268	5,460	9.9
2010–2011	635,780	65,785	5,377	9.7
2011–2012	633,590	63,592	4,775	10.0
2012–2013	631,834	64,166	4,716	9.8
2013–2014	628,502	63,287	4,665	9.9
2014–2015	629,373	64,323	4,575	9.8

Source: Hellenic Statistical Authority

lyceums (*Geniko Lykeio*) or vocational upper secondary schools (*Epaggelmatiko Lykeio*), (2) enroll in schools of vocational education (*Scholi Eppaggelmatikis Katartisis*) that provide initial vocational education (Law 4186/2013), or (3) join the labor market without specialization.

In addition to lower secondary schools, which are the main provider of compulsory secondary education since they were attended by nearby 98 percent of all students during the period 2001 to 2014, there are a number of alternative and parallel structures:

1. Evening lower secondary schools, for students over fourteen years old who are employed.

2. Lower secondary schools for students with special needs. These offer an additional preliminary noncompulsory year of attendance.

3. Music and art lower secondary schools, for students who wish to follow a career in music and the arts.

4. Special needs vocational lower secondary schools. These schools offer a vocational training program that lasts for five years, and also a program for the completion of nine-year compulsory education.

5. Special needs vocational education and training workshops. Attendance lasts for six years and graduates receive certificates granting 2a level professional rights.

6. Second chance schools, which enable adults to complete their compulsory education.

7. Ecclesiastical lower secondary schools, for students who wish to become clergy or secular executives of the Greek Orthodox Church.

8. Model experimental lower secondary schools, minority lower secondary schools, cross-cultural education lower secondary schools, and European education lower secondary schools, as mentioned above.

Again, as in the case of preprimary and primary schools, there exist foreign lower secondary schools with a Greek curriculum, with a foreign curriculum, and with both a Greek and a foreign curriculum.

According to table 8.3, the number of students in lower secondary schools in school year 2014–2015 reached 311,392 (95.1 percent in public schools, 4.9 percent in private schools, 98.6 percent in day schools, and 1.4 percent in evening schools), the number of teachers was 33,836 (31,768 in public schools and 2,068 in private), and the number of schools was 1,725 (1,633 public and 92 private). From 2001 to 2014 both

Table 8.3

Lower secondary education in Greece in day and evening lower secondary schools (start of school year), 2001 to 2014

School year	Students	Teachers	Schools	Students/teacher
2001–2002	349,397	32,897	1,943	10.6
2002–2003	338,355	35,789	1,919	9.5
2003–2004	331,059	35,636	1,953	9.3
2004–2005	335,548	37,160	1,933	9.0
2005–2006	334,359	37,679	1,969	8.9
2006–2007	342,025	39,250	1,957	8.7
2007–2008	342,605	39,376	1,960	8.7
2008–2009	340,580	41,174	1,967	8.3
2009–2010	335,602	41,865	1,980	8.0
2010–2011	330,800	40,788	1,970	8.1
2011–2012	320,375	39,225	1,857	8.2
2012–2013	315,563	36,853	1,823	8.6
2013–2014	313,227	34,428	1,747	9.1
2014–2015	311,392	33,836	1,725	9.2

Source: Hellenic Statistical Authority

the number of students and the number of schools were reduced, by 10.9 and 11.2 percent, respectively. The number of teachers increased during the period 2001–2009 (from 32,897 in 2001 to 41,865 in 2009) and then decreased by 2015 to nearly the levels of 2001.

The purpose and structure of lower secondary education are determined by Law 1566/1985.[15]

Noncompulsory Secondary Education Noncompulsory secondary education is primarily offered by upper secondary schools or general lyceums (*Geniko Lykeio*) and by vocational upper secondary schools (*Epaggelmatiko Lykeio*). Upper secondary schools can be day or evening. They last for three years and students enrolled in the first year must have the lower secondary school "leaving certificate." Vocational upper secondary schools can also be day or evening. Day vocational upper secondary schools last for three or four years: three years of studies and a one-year "apprenticeship class," which is optional. Evening vocational upper secondary schools last for four years and are targeted to students who are employed or between jobs.

Various types of alternative upper secondary schools exist, such as model experimental upper secondary schools, music and art upper secondary schools, ecclesiastical upper secondary schools, special needs upper secondary schools, minority upper secondary schools, cross-cultural education upper secondary schools, and European education upper secondary schools. There also exist athletic facilitation classes in upper secondary schools, where students specialize in specific sports and are trained by physical education teachers. Finally, there exist foreign upper secondary schools with a Greek curriculum, with a foreign curriculum, and with both a Greek and a foreign curriculum.

According to table 8.4, the number of students in upper secondary schools in school year 2014-2015 reached 239,054 (94.5 percent in public schools and 5.5 percent in private), the number of teachers was 22,827 (21,100 in public schools and 1,727 in private), and the number of schools was 1,269 (1,173 public and 96 private). The number of schools increased from 2002 to 2007 but started to decline in 2008, and in 2014 it reached its 2004 level. Despite the reduction in the number of teachers during the period 2009-2014 by 17.1 percent (from 27.6 to 22.8 thousand) the number of teachers in 2014 is higher than in 2001 by 7.5 percent (21.2 thousand). Finally, the number of students in 2014 is essentially the same as in 2001.

The purpose and structure of upper secondary education is determined by Law 1566/1985. Presidential Degree 60/2006 describes the assessment of students, the length of the school year, and the subjects taught in groups. It also regulates issues related to the diagnostic and the final evaluation of students.[16]

Table 8.4
Upper secondary education in Greece in day and evening upper secondary schools (start of school year), 2001 to 2014

School year	Students	Teachers	Schools	Students/teachers
2001–2002	240,616	21,226	1,306	11.3
2002–2003	238,706	22,325	1,243	10.7
2003–2004	236,765	22,170	1,290	10.7
2004–2005	238,984	23,454	1,313	10.2
2005–2006	235,528	24,470	1,339	9.6
2006–2007	231,098	25,215	1,404	9.2
2007–2008	239,242	25,222	1,375	9.5
2008–2009	240,384	26,548	1,384	9.1
2009–2010	248,927	27,548	1,368	9.0
2010–2011	245,947	26,568	1,375	9.3
2011–2012	248,923	26,275	1,360	9.5
2012–2013	248,251	25,158	1,339	9.9
2013–2014	243,453	23,132	1,302	10.5
2014–2015	239,054	22,827	1,269	10.5

Source: Hellenic Statistical Authority

8.3.5 Postsecondary Nontertiary Education

In accordance with the commitments made in the Medium Term Fiscal Strategy plan 2013–2016, the Greek government should aim to improve the range and the quality of apprenticeship and vocational training and enhance their interconnection with the labor market. Accordingly, Law 4186/2013 allows the operation of nonformal educational institutions that provide training outside the formal education system. These institutions are schools of vocational education (*Scholi Eppaggelmatikis Katartisis*), vocational training institutes (*Institouta Epaggelmatikis Katartisis*), and colleges (*Kollegia*). Vocational training schools can be day or evening and public or private, and they provide initial vocational training to graduates of compulsory education. In day vocational training schools, students attend two grades as well as an "apprenticeship class," for the implementation of their "Workplace Training Program–Workplace Apprenticeship." In evening vocational training schools the duration of studies is increased to four years.[17] Vocational training institutes provide initial and continuing vocational training to graduates of upper secondary schools (*Geniko Lykeio*), vocational upper secondary schools (*Epangelmatiko Lykeio*), or vocational training schools. Attendance lasts for five semesters, and includes four semesters of theoretical and laboratory training and one semester of practical training or apprenticeship. Trainees who successfully complete their studies receive a Vocational Specialization Diploma of Level 4.

Colleges provide nonformal postsecondary, nontertiary education, and they operate on the basis of validation and franchising agreements with higher education institutions from other countries, recognized by the competent state authorities in those countries. The titles issued by colleges may be recognized as vocational qualifications equivalent to higher education titles offered within the Greek education system.

The number of students in vocational education at the start of school year 2014–2015 was 101,213, the number of teachers was 13,680, and the number of schools was 546. The ratio of students to teachers was 7.4 (table 8.5). The number of schools declined by 19.4 percent relative to 2001 (677 schools). This decrease can be explained by the 37.2 percent decline in the number of students during that period (161.2 thousand students in 2001). The number of teachers during the same period declined by 1.5 percent (13,890 in 2001 and 13,680 in 2014).

Table 8.5
Vocational education in Greece in day and evening schools (start of school year), 2001 to 2014

School year	Students	Teachers	Schools	Students/teachers
2001–2002	161,222	13,890	677	11.6
2002–2003	154,139	17,457	684	8.8
2003–2004	144,234	16,128	663	8.9
2004–2005	132,692	16,758	660	7.9
2005–2006	123,436	16,066	660	7.7
2006–2007	107,299	15,785	643	6.8
2007–2008	106,901	14,854	631	7.2
2008–2009	107,191	15,043	626	7.1
2009–2010	110,567	19,042	641	5.8
2010–2011	115,124	19,333	633	6.0
2011–2012	122,353	18,340	628	6.7
2012–2013	124,423	18,195	623	6.8
2013–2014	113,440	15,220	625	7.5
2014–2015	101,213	13,680	546	7.4

Source: Hellenic Statistical Authority
Note: Data refer to vocational upper secondary schools, schools of vocational education, ecclesiastical schools, and vocational schools. The operation of vocational schools ended in school year 2013–2014 and these schools were replaced by schools of vocational education. The remaining vocational schools were abolished during school year 2014–2015.

8.3.6   Tertiary Education

Tertiary education is offered by universities (*Panepistimio*) and technological education institutions (*Technologiko Ekpaideftiko Idryma*). Graduates of general upper secondary schools and of vocational upper secondary schools can enter universities and technological education institutes by participating in a countrywide examination that takes place at the end of each school year and is coordinated by the Ministry of Education.

Studies in Greek universities and technological education institutions are formally divided into three cycles. Completion of a first cycle program requires at least 240 credits and leads to the award of a Bachelor's degree.[18] Completion of a second cycle program leads to the award of a Master's degree. The minimum duration of a second cycle program is one full year, and part of that period is devoted to a dissertation. Part-time second cycle programs must last at least one semester more than full-time programs. Completion of a third cycle program requires at least 30 credits as well as the writing of a doctoral dissertation, and leads to the award of a PhD.

According to table 8.6, during academic year 2014–2015 there were 20 universities in operation in Greece, with a total number of 99 schools, 263 departments, and 10,546 academic staff (professors, associate professors, assistant professors, lecturers, auxiliary teaching staff, research associates, etc.). This corresponds to 527 academic staff and 9,542 students per university, although there is high variance in the size of these institutions. Relative to 2001, the number of departments increased by 11.4 percent (236 in 2001 and 263 in 2014) and the number of students by 16.9 percent (163.3 thousand in 2001 and 190.8 thousand in 2014). These figures include only students within the normal duration of study, which is up to and including the 11th semester; the number of students who exceed the normal duration of study, increased by 80 percent within the same period (118.4 thousand in 2001 and 213.1 thousand in 2014). The data also indicate that a large number of students seek to acquire specialized knowledge and better skills: the number of Master's students increased sharply by 175.5 percent (13.5 thousand in 2001 and 37.3 thousand in 2014) and the number of PhD students increased also very significantly by 84.7 percent (12.5 thousand in 2001 and 23.2 thousand in 2014).

As figure 8.8 shows, the percentage change in the number of academic staff between 2004 and 2009 was greater than the corresponding change in the number of students. During that period the number of academic staff increased by 17.5 percent and the number of students slightly dropped (–0.5 percent). However, after 2010 the number of teaching staff declined rapidly (–13.3 percent) and the number of students rose (+7.4 percent).

Table 8.6

Tertiary education in Greece in universities (start of academic year), 2001 to 2014

Academic year	Universities	Schools	Departments	Teaching staff	Students	Students exceeding 11th semester	Master's students	PhD students
2001–2002	18	53	236	10,708	163,256	118,359	13,538	12,540
2002–2003	19	55	239	11,079	175,597	131,111	15,136	13,816
2003–2004	19	61	243	10,703	172,804	136,873	16,364	13,882
2004–2005	21	64	254	11,347	174,139	145,157	21,799	16,314
2005–2006	21	63	258	11,575	171,967	151,635	23,830	19,100
2006–2007	21	65	261	12,603	171,857	176,761	27,776	20,008
2007–2008	21	64	263	12,871	170,422	182,331	28,443	20,904
2008–2009	21	64	264	13,058	171,882	195,152	30,469	21,404
2009–2010	21	64	267	13,336	173,256	202,261	34,299	23,138
2010–2011	22	63	268	12,162	177,676	194,373	35,570	23,853
2011–2012	22	63	268	11,113	177,296	200,422	36,074	24,142
2012–2013	22	63	268	10,804	178,817	205,957	36,381	23,887
2013–2014	20	99	261	10,009	179,784	206,560	37,014	23,066
2014–2015	20	99	263	10,546	190,835	213,098	37,298	23,156

Source: Hellenic Statistical Authority

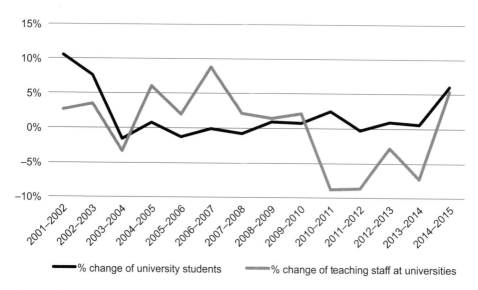

Figure 8.8
Percentage change in number of students and teaching staff in Greek universities, 2001 to 2014
Source: Hellenic Statistical Authority

The ratio of graduating students to the total number of students enrolled rose from 15.5 percent in academic year 2001–2002 to 19.8 percent in academic years 2004–2005 and 2007–2008. After that it fluctuated around 18.1 percent (figure 8.9). The number of graduating students followed a similar pattern: it increased from 25,231 in academic year 2001–2002 to 32,982 in academic year 2013–2014 (+30.7 percent), with the largest number of graduates observed in academic years 2004–2005 (34,489) and 2007–2008 (33,719).

We next turn to the data on technological education institutions. According to table 8.7, at the beginning of academic year 2014–2015 there were 13 such institutions, with a total number of 78 schools, 209 departments, and 4,505 academic staff. The academic staff dropped in number by 62.2 percent during the period 2010 to 2014 (11.9 thousand in 2010 and 4.5 thousand in 2014). The number of students increased significantly during 2001 to 2005 (from 113.1 thousand in 2001 to 147.1 thousand in 2005) before dropping to a lower level (105.9 thousand) in 2014. The number of students who exceeded the normal duration of study increased by 185.1 percent during the period 2001 to 2014 (from 41.1 thousand in 2001 to 117.2 thousand in 2014). The number of Master's students increased by 267.7 percent during the period 2006 to 2014 (from 685 to 2.5 thousand).

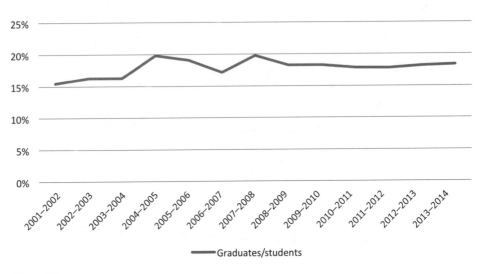

Figure 8.9
Ratio of university graduates to university enrolled students, 2001 to 2014
Source: Hellenic Statistical Authority

The number of academic staff and students (figure 8.10) moved generally in the same direction during 2001 to 2010, but after 2010 there was a large drop in the number of academic staff. During the period 2001 to 2013, the number of students graduating from technological education institutes increased significantly, from 11,451 in academic year 2001–2002 to 19,623 in academic year 2013–2014 (+71.4 percent, figure 8.11). The ratio of graduating students to the total number of students enrolled jumped from 10.2 percent in academic year 2001–2002 to 18.9 percent in academic year 2009–2010. Since then it has fluctuated around 16 percent (figure 8.12).

8.4 Public and Private Expenditure on Education

Expenditure on education in Greece exhibits different characteristics across the public and the private sector. However, there exist significant complementarities between the two. Public expenditure is systematically below the EU average. The gap is more pronounced in primary and secondary education, and may be one of the reasons why Greek pupils underperform in international tests and competitions (section 8.2). Also, in the context of tertiary education, R&D activities do not receive sufficient financial support. Public expenditure is to a large extent capital intensive, focusing less on current operational costs, and certainly not in costs other than salaries. In contrast to public expenditure, the spending of private households is nearly the highest in the

Table 8.7
Tertiary education in Greece in technological education institutions and other higher education institutions except universities (start of academic year), 2001 to 2014

Academic year	Institutions	Schools	Departments	Teaching staff	Students	Students exceeding 11th semester	Master's students
2001–2002	14	68	210	10,652	113,114	41,097	
2002–2003	14	68	210	11,380	129,585	46,346	
2003–2004	14	71	220	11,895	141,184	53,175	
2004–2005	15	73	225	12,454	145,319	65,151	
2005–2006	15	75	230	12,021	147,052	78,558	
2006–2007	15	75	220	11,258	142,254	89,195	685
2007–2008	15	76	227	11,305	128,874	100,441	758
2008–2009	15	76	227	11,313	117,547	108,498	701
2009–2010	15	77	248	11,911	109,830	122,859	694
2010–2011	15	76	249	11,917	128,937	125,221	909
2011–2012	15	77	251	7,507	124,572	112,839	841
2012–2013	15	75	245	6,722	122,077	122,695	689
2013–2014	14	81	206	4,730	121,053	107,478	1,449
2014–2015	13	78	209	4,505	105,926	117,185	2,519

Source: Hellenic Statistical Authority

European Union, and is focused on the levels of education where the government's contribution is relatively low, especially secondary education. Households' expenditures on secondary education are primarily targeted to prepare for the countrywide entrance examination to tertiary education. This examination is challenging, and households' high preparation expenditures reflect their high appreciation for public higher education and the lack of alternatives that lead to comparable employment prospects. The long-standing fiscal consolidation since 2009 took its toll on public and private expenditure on education, though this was less pronounced than in other expenditure categories.

8.4.1 Public Expenditure on Education

On average, total public expenditure on education stood below 4 percent of GDP during 2006 to 2009, more than one percentage point of GDP below the EU average during that period (figure 8.13). Since 2011 public expenditure on education has exceeded

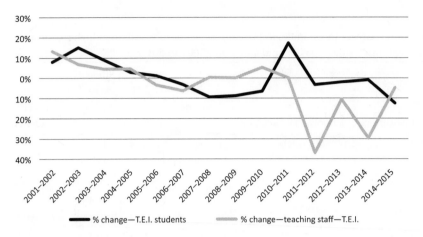

Figure 8.10
Percentage change in number of students and teaching staff in technological education institutions and in other higher education schools excluding universities, 2001 to 2014
Source: Hellenic Statistical Authority

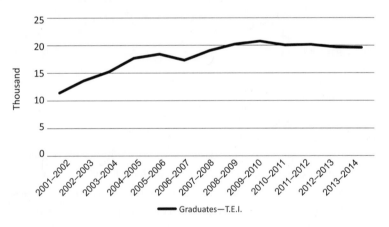

Figure 8.11
Number of TEI graduates, 2001 to 2013
Source: Hellenic Statistical Authority

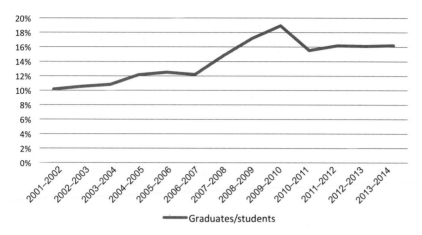

Figure 8.12

Ratio of TEI graduates to TEI enrolled students, 2001 to 2013

Source: Hellenic Statistical Authority

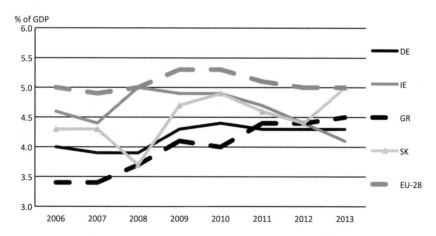

Figure 8.13

General government expenditure on education (percent of GDP). Country codes DE = Germany, GR = Greece, IE = Ireland, SK = Slovakia, EU28 = European Union (consisting of 28 countries). Source: Eurostat

that level, stabilizing close to 4.5 percent of GDP during 2011–2013, with the distance from the EU average narrowing. The increase occurred because GDP dropped faster than public expenditure on education did, and it does not reflect an increase in public expenditure.

A decomposition of the public expenditure on education indicates that the gap between Greece and the EU average is more prominent in secondary education (on average, 1.5 percent of GDP during 2006 to 2013, and 1.9 percent in the European Union), as well as in preprimary and primary education (average spending of 1.3 percent of GDP in Greece, and 1.6 percent in the European Union). Public expenditure on tertiary education amounted to 0.9 percent of GDP during 2006 to 2013, a level slightly exceeding the respective European average (0.8 percent of GDP). However, R&D public expenditure within tertiary education is among the lowest in the European Union (0.31 percent of GDP, instead of 0.48 percent of GDP; figure 8.14).[19]

The relatively low level of public expenditure on education is also reflected on the average annual expenditure per student, for all levels of education combined. Although there exist no relevant data available for Greece after 2005, average annual expenditure per student in Greece at that time was more than 20 percent below the EU average (figure 8.15) and only higher (within the European Union) than in Balkan and some other Eastern European countries.

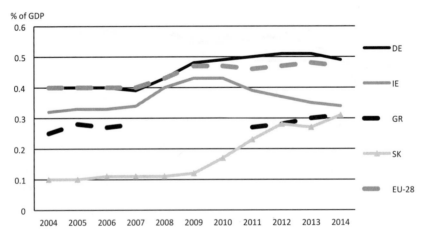

Figure 8.14
Total R&D expenditure within tertiary education (percent of GDP)
Source: Eurostat

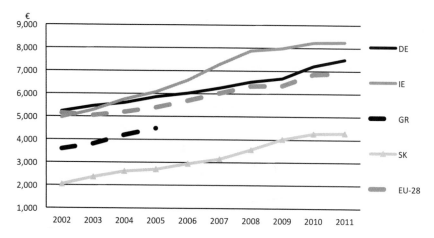

Figure 8.15

Annual expenditure on public educational institutions per pupil/student, for all levels of education combined (in PPS)

Source: Eurostat

Given that public expenditure on education is relatively low, efforts should be made both to increase expenditure and to allocate resources more carefully. Up to 2005, the fraction of public expenditure on education allocated to capital stock building was the highest in the European Union, constantly exceeding 15 percent and more than double the EU average (figure 8.16). Accordingly, the fraction allocated to current expenditure was the lowest in the European Union. Current expenditure is made primarily by salaries. Although the number of teachers and professors employed is not low given the number of students, what contributes toward keeping current expenditure low is a relatively low number of hours worked and not a low hourly rate. A skewed allocation of financial resources toward capital stock building could be attributed to a "catch-up" process with countries that have more and better-equipped educational facilities. However, Greece was not the only country lagging in that respect at that time.

One can isolate some aspects of the Greek education system's underperformance that can be attributed, at least in part, to insufficient funding. A characteristic example is the low number of patent applications by the tertiary education sector in Greece relative to other countries. On average, only 0.5 patent applications per million of active population were submitted annually to the European Patent Office (EPO) between 2002 and 2012 (figure 8.17). The EU average was more than ten times higher (5.2 patents per million of active population). This difference is less pronounced for patents

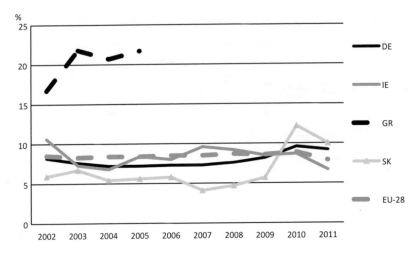

Figure 8.16
Capital expenditure as a percentage of total expenditure in public educational institutions, for all
levels of education combined
Source: Eurostat

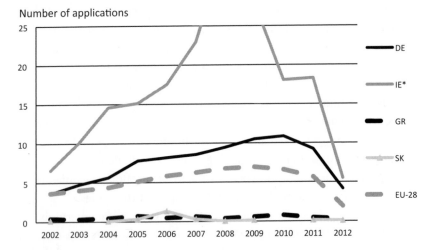

Figure 8.17
Patent applications to the EPO per million of active population, higher education
Source: Eurostat

granted by the US Patent and Trademark Office (0.25 versus 0.83 patents per million of active population).[20]

8.4.2 Household Expenditure on Education

The satisfaction of Greek citizens with their education system appears to be very low (figure 8.18). This unfavorable evaluation may be due partly to the low level of financial aid given by the state to pupils and students. On average, only 5.2 percent of total public expenditure on education was granted as financial aid between 2001 and 2005. This fraction was the third lowest in the European Union, with Poland and Luxembourg ranking below Greece (1.2 and 1.9 percent, respectively) and the EU average being 18.4 percent.[21] Financial aid in Greece has also been on a downward trend, falling to 1.6 percent in 2005 from 5.5 percent in the previous year. The sharp cuts in aid mainly concerned scholarships given to students at the tertiary level of education (from 5.2 percent of total public expenditure on education to 1.4 percent).

The low level of financial support by the state in combination with Greek households' high appreciation for education especially at the tertiary level, are reflected on the private expenditure on education. Between 1994 and 2010 Greek households'

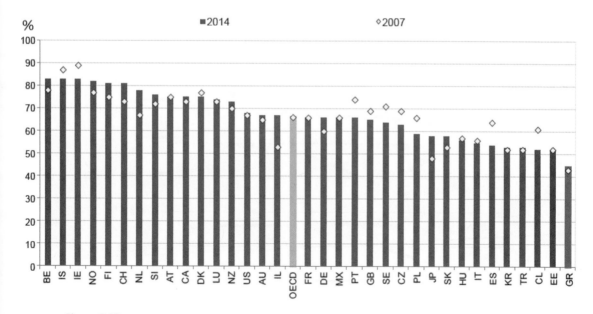

Figure 8.18
Citizens' satisfaction with the education system
Source: Government at a Glance, OECD (2015). Satisfaction assessment based on Gallup World Poll survey results.

expenditure on education as a proportion of total consumption expenditure was the second highest in the European Union, steadily over 2.0 percent (on average 2.5 percent), while the EU average during that period was slightly below 1 percent (0.9 percent, figure 8.19). Half of that expenditure concerns secondary education---mainly payments for tutorials to prepare for the countrywide entrance examination to tertiary education, or for tutorials or specialized private schools to learn foreign languages. We should note, however, that households' direct expenditure on tertiary education (tuition fees) is among the lowest in the European Union (0.2 percent of total consumption expenditure). (This amount does not include housing, water, electricity, and food, as these are classified in other expenditure categories.)

8.5   Education during the Crisis and the Adjustment Programs

This section discusses the main ways in which the Greek education system has been affected since the start of the crisis in 2009 and during the adjustment programs that followed. The adjustment programs, implemented in Greece since 2010, aimed primarily at reducing the deficit. However, to ensure that both the attempted fiscal consolidation and the public debt became sustainable, a wide range of reforms in the modus operandi of ministries, public services, state-owned enterprises, etc, were included in

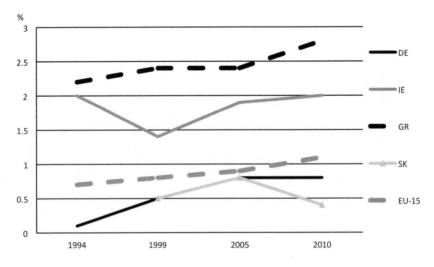

Figure 8.19
Consumption expenditure on education (percent of total consumption expenditure)
Source: Eurostat

the programs, and so were structural reforms in the markets for goods and services. Fiscal adjustment led to expenditure cuts in every government function, including education. Reforms in the education system were not a main focus of the adjustment programs and only played a peripheral role, other than through the overall cost cutting objective in the state budget. Some of the changes that took place during the crisis period included (1) the establishment of a new body for planning a national educational policy, as well as for coordinating and supporting its implementation; (2) the support of vocational education and nonformal education (e.g., colleges); (3) changes in the governance of higher education institutions (HEIs); and (4) the facilitation of collaborations between the research centers of HEIs and the private sector, subject to certain limitations.

The Economic Adjustment Programme for Greece (European Commission 2011a) states the following under the heading "The government intends to rationalize and increase the efficiency and quality of the education system" (p. 42):

The education indicators of Greece lag behind the EU average. Attainment rates are low, and quality issues lead a large number of students to enroll in complementary private classes or, for university students, studying abroad. In the primary and secondary sector, far-reaching reforms are currently being implemented including a revision of curricula, the introduction of teacher evaluation, recurrent training for teachers, an upgrading and extension of all-day schools, improving the quality of technical and vocational education and a reduction in the high drop-out rates. The reform also includes the closure and merger of establishments. This will involve around 30 percent of schools: around 2,000 small schools have already been closed. As for higher education, a law to be adopted shortly envisages changes such as the introduction of governing boards that include non-academic managers; a higher financial autonomy and responsibility of universities; mergers of institutions; student vouchers; and an internationalization of curricula. The government has established an independent taskforce under the OECD's guidance to propose specific policy measures aimed at improving the efficiency and the effectiveness of the sector. The taskforce is expected to present its report by end-June.[22]

The remainder of this section reviews these developments in the education system in more detail.

8.5.1   The Main Trends in the Data

As already mentioned, fiscal consolidation resulted in public expenditure cuts also in education. According to the latest data available, during 2010 to 2013 the cumulative cut in public expenditure on education was higher than for total public expenditure (−15.8 percent versus −12.4 percent).[23] Yet expenditure was not reduced equally in each level of education. Severe cuts were implemented in secondary education (−28.6 percent) and tertiary education (−23.0 percent). Expenditure on these levels accounted for 58.8 percent of total public expenditure on education in 2009. Cuts in preprimary and primary education were less severe (17.9 percent). The smallest cuts were implemented on education expenditure earmarked for R&D (–0.3 percent), while smaller forms of expenditure, such as on subsidiary services to education, rose.[24] R&D comprised only 6.5 percent of total public expenditure on education before the crisis and, as mentioned in section 8.4.1, was already rather limited in comparison to other EU countries.

Expenditure cuts were realized mainly through a reduction in compensation of employees, comprising 81.7 percent of public expenditure on education in 2009. Cumulative cuts up to 2013 amounted to 17.1 percent of the 2009 total wage bill (figure 8.20).[25] A significant fraction of the reduction of the wage bill is accounted for by a drop in the number of teachers and professors employed in the public sector, by 14.8 percent.[26] Gross capital formation in education was reduced during that period by 13 percent, whereas other operational costs were reduced by 18.7 percent. Despite

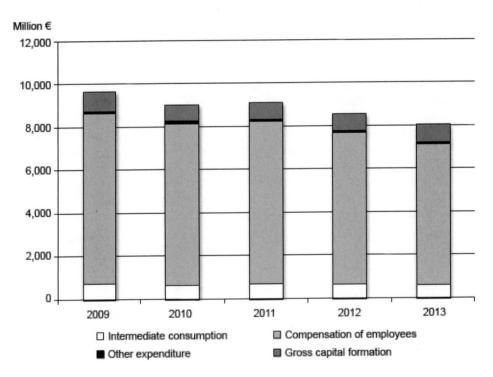

Figure 8.20
Distribution of public expenditure on education per spending category
Source: Eurostat

these cuts, public expenditure on education as a percentage of GDP increased slightly, from 4.0 percent in 2009 to 4.5 percent in 2013, because of the sharp decline in GDP.

Between 2010 and 2014, the total population of students decreased by 1.2 percent (from 1.68 million in 2009 to 1.66 million in 2014). This trend, however, was not uniform across all levels of education. In primary education and in universities enrollment increased, whereas in secondary and vocational education, as well as in technological education institutions (part of tertiary education), enrollment declined. The increase was largest in the number of university students (10.1 percent, from 173.3 thousand students in 2009 to 190.8 thousand in 2014).[27] The decline was instead largest in vocational education (8.1 percent, from 109.9 thousand students to 101 thousand).[28]

8.5.2 The Main Reforms

Education reforms during the Greek adjustment programs were aimed mainly at preparing and implementing a medium-term strategy for education, at boosting vocational training, at promoting the administrative and financial independence of higher education institutions, and at linking academic research with the private sector. Some of the most important recent reforms are summarized below. We should mention, however, that not all legislated reforms have been fully implemented.

An important recent reform was the establishment of the Institute for Educational Policy (IEP) in 2011. The IEP replaced the Pedagogical Institute as the main advisory body supporting the Ministry of Education on issues regarding primary and secondary education and the transition from secondary to tertiary education. The IEP engages in education-related research, and provides scientific and technical support for the planning and implementation of education policy. It also participates in education programs financed by European structural funds, which involve activities such as designing new school curricula, setting up and operating model experimental schools, and developing accessible educational materials for students with disabilities. However, the IEP's progress with such activities has not always been satisfactory.

Another important reform was the establishment of the National Organization for the Certification of Qualifications and Vocational Guidance (NOCQVG). The NOCQVG was created in 2013 through the merger of three existing entities. Its mission is to certify institutions for vocational education, such as professional training institutes, and to carry out objectives set in national and European programs on vocational training. The NOCQVG is also tasked with developing a national qualifications framework for vocational education, along with a credit transfer system, and to implement a lifelong counseling and career guidance program, in cooperation with other public agencies. A national qualifications framework for formal education has already been developed by the NOCQVG, and has been mapped with the European Qualifications Framework. The NOCQVG is a member of the European Credit System for Vocational Education and Training and is the designated Greek agency for transferring academic credits.

Reforms in primary and secondary education included significant changes in the institutional framework for model experimental schools and kindergartens. Law 3966/2011 linked model experimental schools to regular primary and secondary schools, both public and private, facilitating cooperation among them and allowing teachers to train in model experimental schools. The law also introduced a process for the evaluation of both the staff and the overall educational activities in model experimental schools. This was followed by separate legislation regarding the evaluation of teachers in regular primary and secondary schools. Yet no evaluation of education personnel has been implemented in any education level as of the completion of this chapter (late 2016). In April 2015 the Greek government proposed an amendment to Law 3966/2011, which would have changed student selection procedures for model experimental schools in fundamental ways. Under the amendment, students would not be selected based on exams but instead by lottery. This amendment was eventually withdrawn.

A reform in secondary vocational education took place in 2013 through new legislation that changed the organization and operation of vocational education institutions, such as vocational training schools, vocational training institutes, centers for lifelong learning, and other vocational colleges. These institutions operate under a distinct regulatory framework from that governing the formal education system. The new legislation allowed for the establishment of new vocational education institutions, such as the special vocational high schools and the special vocational lyceums. The legislation also provided for the establishment of regional directorates for lifelong learning. These directorates are intended to act as decentralized services of the General Secretariat for Lifelong Learning at the Ministry of Education. However, the regional directorates for lifelong learning are not yet in operation.

8.5.3 Tertiary Education: Law 4009/2011

The most important and visible reform on education during the crisis concerned the universities and other tertiary education institutions. This reform was not required or monitored as part of the adjustment programs but was domestically driven. It followed previous efforts to modernize tertiary education in Greece, a need that has been increasingly recognized in the country since the 1990s.[29] The core of the reform was Law 4009/2011, whose primary goal was to give universities more autonomy to manage their resources.[30] Additional goals and provisions of that law included the following:

• Institute a more robust system for evaluating the performance of each university by an independent authority (which was preexisting but whose role was upgraded) and for upholding quality standards within each university for faculty promotions, and so on.

• Establish modern governing structures within universities by mandating the creation of a university council that would formulate the university's long-run strategy, monitor the rector, and have a significant say over the choice of future rectors and area deans by vetting candidates up for election by the faculty body.

• Eliminate student voting for rectors: that practice had led to collusion between student representatives of political party youths within each university and candidate rectors, with the former extracting concessions from the latter in exchange for their votes and those of their student followers.

• Make it possible for universities to accept private donations for endowed chairs.

• Allow for programs in foreign languages and for the exchange of students.

• Allow for tuition in graduate programs.

• Facilitate visiting and part-time appointments of academics who may also have a part-time appointment abroad.

Key provisions of this law were watered down by subsequent governments. The government that was formed after the September 2015 elections clearly indicated that it wished to overturn most of the main provisions of the law. The law's eventual fate, as well as the overall framework to be adopted in its place, remains quite unclear, although as of the end of 2016 essentially all of the law's key provisions had been eliminated via subsequent pieces of legislation.

The main logic of the law was to loosen the strict and bureaucratic control that the government had on universities and other higher education institutions (HEIs) and to replace it by a form of more autonomous self-governance. Instead of the previous practice, where the Ministry of Education would decide on more-or-less anything important concerning the functioning of HEIs, and where anything not explicitly allowed was essentially prohibited, according to the new framework each HEI would, in principle, set its own set of strategic goals and rules. Executive power within each HEI remained with the rector, along with the senate (which became more flexible than previously). However, and partly so that there could be an element of internal control, replacing the diminished control by the Ministry, a university council was created in each HEI. The council would have the final responsibility for overseeing the functioning of the institution, including the approval of the budget, and would formulate the institution's long-term strategy. It would consist of internal faculty members, elected by their peers, and external members, who would be selected by the internal members following an international open call. Each HEI could self-organize its programs into schools, open new programs across academic departments, collaborate with other academic institutions within the country and abroad, and have greater freedom in raising funds and spending them.

Reducing the students' representation in the administration of each HEI and their power in electing rectors and senate members was also an important change. Students' ability to indirectly control the administration of HEIs, went far beyond anything observed in other European countries. The problem was made worse by the fact that the powers bestowed to students by previous laws were exercised by nonrepresentative groups. Indeed, "regular" students were actually discouraged from participating in the everyday university life and were partly displaced by groups affiliated with political parties. These groups were not interested in bringing the HEIs to the highest possible standards but were instead engaging in rent-seeking activities and in turning students into followers for their political party. At times, this was done in exchange for assuring favors that would indirectly facilitate the students' graduation or bring other such benefits to them. Other times, incidents of violence would erupt, involving either partisan groups of students or even outsiders to the university. These groups typically coexisted with the majority of regular and hard-working students and faculty members, but made their work much more difficult. The 2011 law aimed to limit this problem by restricting students' participation only to areas of administration directly relevant for student issues and establishing limits on the maximum study duration. (Under previous laws, once a student would enter a HEI he/she would never lose his/her student status, unless he/she asked for this, no matter how uninterested in his/her studies he/she might be.) The law gave more power to HEIs, as part of the autonomy given, to prevent violent incidents.

Equally important to giving more autonomy to the HEIs was accountability. After all, these institutions are using public money. Thus, the law provided for a system of evaluation for all academic staff and academic units. This evaluation system would be coordinated at the country level by an independent authority, ΑΔΙΠ. While not part of the law, a next logical step would be that allocations from the state budget would be taking partly into account the performance of the HEIs or even of their academic units.

In practice, the changes in the functioning of the universities that the law was supposed to bring about were met with strong opposition, explicit or implicit, by insiders who stood to lose the high rents that they were extracting under the previous system. Thus, as with most other reforms in education, Law 4009/2011 was only partially implemented. After some initial delays, the implementation had a good start, with faculty members strongly supporting the formation of the university councils and voting in high numbers for their internal members, and with several prominent members of the Greek academic diaspora joining these councils, along with prominent people from within the broader Greek society. However, as a result of both opposition by insiders and a lack of political determination to support the reform at the government level, the law was already getting weak from its 2012 start of implementation.[31] The main provisions that would bring the desired result—more autonomous, outward-looking, and accountable universities—were greatly delayed, derailed, or never implemented. Only the more formalistic of the provisions in the law were applied in practice without much delay, with the process itself taking on the overtones of a bureaucratic exercise. The surrounding environment of deep recession and fiscal tightening certainly did not help either, as funds that would facilitate the transition to a new system, and create incentives, were not available. Overall, the experience from this law has been mixed, but it is apparent that an excellent opportunity has been missed and that regression may occur toward a system that will continue to operate under the strict rule of the Ministry of Education and with weak incentives for high performance.[32]

8.6   Overall Evaluation and Some Recommendations

Any education reform plan has to be carefully designed and executed, so that the resulting system will be stable in its main parameters for a long enough time interval. Frequent and not well thought-out changes in the rules can be extremely disruptive. We next review some of the main problems with the current system and its performance, and sketch some policy recommendations and related ideas.

8.6.1   Some Strengths and Many Weaknesses—Priorities for Improvement and Reform Actions

While the formal structure of the Greek education system does not differ significantly from that in other European countries, the lack of a proper framework of evaluation, incentives, and rewards suggests inadequate attention to students and faculty. The poor performance of the Greek education system is almost a natural consequence of the weak incentives coupled with the heavy government regulation that currently exists at all levels of education. Low and deteriorating PISA scores, low university rankings, and other such measures paint an overall bleak and alarming picture. This is despite some very positive characteristics in Greece when it comes to education: households place high value on education and are willing to spend large percentages of their income on the studies of their children. Moreover students who graduate with high grades from secondary or tertiary education and pursue advanced studies or employment abroad tend to do very well on average. The overall number of university graduates in the population is also rather high.[33]

Yet there is room for much improvement at all levels of the education system. Starting from the preprimary level, not all children currently have access to public services and many of them tend not to get the critical start that will shape positively their character and cognitive abilities in subsequent years.[34] For primary and secondary education, the system is too centralized and bureaucratic, and there are essentially only few degrees of freedom in the curriculum or otherwise, even in private schools. Among other issues, there is not enough recognition that students who are much stronger or much weaker than their peers in some areas may require remedial teaching or should be offered access to advanced courses and special activities, to develop their skills, interests, and character. In fact there is an extreme lack of flexibility in the system. Certain (public) model and experimental schools that have played an important role in past decades are currently being downgraded in importance and their fate remains unknown. There is also a weak and inadequate system of monitoring and incentives at the level of each school unit.

The national examination for entrance to tertiary education is overall a fair one, and with relatively high credibility in Greek society and especially among the students. However, it is quite inflexible (e.g., it does not reward students who may not have certain skills but may compensate through other skills), it does not reward creativity and inquisitiveness, and at least to a certain extent it promotes sterile memorization. It is also extremely inefficient in terms of resources used: a large number of families incur significant expenses to send their children to private tutoring centers in order to increase the chance that they will perform well in the examination and pursue tertiary education. In addition, after these students enter the university departments of their choice it is costly to change their decisions—students thus need to decide at the age of 17 what their studies, and to a large extent career paths, will be.

Technological education institutes (TEI) have been gradually turned into universities of relatively low quality (with few notable exceptions) and have departed from their important and challenging role of producing students with less theoretical education but stronger technological skills that are demanded in the labor market. Overall, the relationship between tertiary education, on the one hand, and private firms and other parts of the real economy, on the other, is extremely weak.

At the university level, and as discussed in section 8.5.3, the most recent reform attempt appears to have been derailed. Universities are public but really operate as divisions of the Education Ministry, and are in many ways run by the government in that the government controls university budgets and the number of students universities enroll. Universities further have little control over their hiring and promotions procedures (and these tend to be quite bureaucratic), selection procedures for students (at least at the undergraduate level), research incentives, and program design. Most important, while there are many universities and their performance differs, there is no mechanism to reward high performers.[35] To be sure, some (public) universities are charging tuition fees for select graduate programs and are competing for top students for these programs. Yet only few such programs draw in foreign students. Private universities are not allowed to operate at all (at least not formally, that is as entities legally recognized as universities; some do operate but under alternative side arrangements).

8.6.2 Looking Forward and Recommendations

Improving the overall performance of the Greek education system should entail primarily two intermediate goals that will eventually work in a complementary manner. The first is to assure that all academic units perform at a level that meets some minimum standards, at par with international benchmarks. The second is to ensure that units (schools, universities, departments) or individuals (teachers, professors, students) who seek excellence will not be inhibited by rules that impose too much uniformity and thereby pull everyone toward the same low level. Once excellence is recognized and rewarded, others will seek to follow in the same direction to the extent of their abilities. For both goals it is important that education units be independent and accountable, following some systematic and transparent evaluation. The autonomy of units should be strengthened. An additional point is that a reform effort should take into account that the country is not a remote "island" and can benefit from being more dynamic and open, in particular, by attracting foreign students and by strengthening its ties with the extensive and prominent academic diaspora. Some general principles that would be beneficial in this context are described below.

Assuring high-quality and affordable (preferably free for all) preprimary education is imperative as it is a key driver of future success. In primary and secondary education, private schools should enjoy considerably more independence. Public schools should also become more independent and, at the same time, more carefully evaluated. Allowing the local communities to be more actively involved, as well as empowering the schools with selecting, evaluating, and rewarding teachers, is important. During the school year, exams with the same questions for students at all schools could help teachers, parents, and students understand their relative performance and monitor the learning outcomes.[36] Secondary education should also gradually become a separate stage of learning and not function primarily as an entry stage to tertiary education. This means, in particular, that the design of the curriculum should be modified, and that universities should be able to select students on the basis of their school performance in addition to national exam scores. Model schools operating at various parts of the country should enable gifted students to make faster progress than their peers.

For universities and other higher education institutions, more autonomy means that they should have the responsibility of essentially all aspects of their operation, including the selection of their students (e.g., departments should be allowed to assign different weights to grades of different courses in the national entrance examination, and to include the general secondary education grade and possibly other criteria). Second, and along with more autonomy, comes the need for systematic evaluations. Universities and their academic departments should be evaluated based on the research output as well as on the quality of their programs. University funding should be allocated following a systematic and strict evaluation procedure: departments that produce cutting-edge research, according to internationally recognized standards, should receive preferential treatment in funding and allocation of new faculty positions. Third, the system should be able to attract and reward highly qualified educators and researchers. As an example, half-year appointments at Greek institutions by faculty at top universities abroad could help reverse the "brain drain" and improve these Greek institutions. Fourth, universities should systematically encourage foreign students to apply both to the undergraduate and graduate programs. A substantial source of students would be the eastern Mediterranean and the Balkans. Fifth, the Open University should be removed from the direct control of the Ministry of Education and become more autonomous, while many of its activities could be transferred to other universities. Last, even if public universities remain the backbone of tertiary education, the prohibition of private and other non-state universities makes no sense and should be abolished.

All these reform initiatives would require careful planning, time, and determination from political leaders, as well as building a wide enough consensus. They cannot work in an otherwise deteriorating economy. A dynamic labor market is much needed to strengthen the education system through a direct labor demand mechanism, and at the same time a stronger education system would facilitate growth and the creation of jobs. The relation works in both directions.[37]

8.7 Conclusion

The education system in Greece has been underperforming in recent decades and delivering mediocre results, at least as measured by scores that allow international comparisons. At the root of this unsatisfactory performance are two interconnected problems. First, the absence of a proper system of incentives: in education, significant progress cannot be made without explicit recognition of merit and a system for rewarding high performance. Second, the heavy dependence on the state, which leads to low flexibility and a poor allocation of resources, along with frequent formalistic changes every time a new government is formed. Additionally, the Greek labor market, reflecting a relatively closed and inward-looking economy, has not been able to offer significant salary compensation to well-trained and productive graduates, and as a result the incentives for maintaining high quality in education services have been low. With these factors combined, we have ideal conditions for an education system with low efficiency and poor quality. This overall negative evaluation comes despite the fact that many bright spots exist and also that Greeks place high value on education and contribute a significant fraction of their household income to it. The underperformance of the education system implies an inefficient use of resources, particularly at a time of fiscal tightening, and undermines future growth prospects. As the education system is one of the main mechanisms ensuring social mobility, its underperformance implies low mobility and a lack of opportunities for children of low income families, with severe economic and social implications.

How can the education system improve in Greece? The current arrangement has produced a "bad equilibrium" in the sense that participants (students, teachers, administrators, and policy makers) have weak incentives for modifying their behavior unless there is a broader and coordinated change in the rules—despite the fact that such a change could increase overall welfare. Moreover changes in the rules of any education system should not be made too frequently, or without enough consensus in society and before studying relevant "best practices" from abroad. Yet it appears that the crisis creates both an opportunity and a need for change. First, assuming that the economy will gradually shift to a new growth model, which would be based on investment, innovation, competition, and exports, there will be gradually increased demand for highly educated people at all levels of the labor force. Second, the ability of the state to fund the education system, as well as the ability of households to make related private expenditures, will remain limited even for several years after the deep recession ends: thus the need for a more cost-effective and efficient system is imperative.

Overall, it is difficult to imagine how Greece can put itself on a path of high and sustainable growth unless it invests in improving its education system. Even ignoring the crisis that has hit the economy hard since 2009, the Greek economy tends to be "caught in the middle" in terms of its growth prospects: it is neither operating at the innovation frontier in enough industries (so that it could be competitive through the production of goods of the highest quality) nor is it offering low wages (so that it could attract global investment that would primarily be seeking easy access to labor services, even if not highly skilled). Since competitiveness has to be improved in any event and rather urgently (after all, Greece's public debt is to a large extent external, and thus cannot become sustainable without a systematic improvement in the country's balance of payments), Greece has only two available options. It must either decisively increase its investment in human capital by improving the education system, and thus increase its innovation capacity, or it can continue operating on a path of gradually declining wages. This choice, certainly, should not be such a difficult one.

Notes

1. I would like to thank warmly, but of course without implicating, Apostolis Dimitropoulos, Alexandros Moustakas, Stavros Panageas, Kostas Peppas, Michalis Vassiliadis, and Dimitri Vayanos for invaluable assistance, comments, suggestions, and insights.

2. Greece is one of the few OECD countries where a system of private tutoring centers has been set up to prepare high school students for university entrance exams. Greece also has one of the largest percentages, among OECD countries, of university students studying abroad: second highest after Ireland as of 2005.

3. According to a 2009 PISA survey, Greece and Turkey scored the lowest in the OECD on measures of schools' autonomy to allocate resources and to set up their curriculum and their assessment methods.

4. In the bulletin *Education and Training Monitor 2015—Greece,* a useful collection of key statistics can be found for spending on education, educational attainment, employment rates of graduates, adult participation in lifelong learning, and other aspects of education in Greece. The bulletin also describes some recent developments in education in Greece, such as the reform in the universities, which was rolled back in 2015.

5. See OECD (2016) on why low-performing students fall behind and how they can be helped.

6. In Greece 41.8 percent of students are low performers in at least one subject, and 15.7 percent are low performers in all subjects, based on the data presented on table 0.2 part 2, on page 19 of the report.

7. Greek students consistently rank last in average PISA score, among the 21 countries both in the EU28 and in the OECD.

8. See Eurydice (2008) on the autonomy and responsibilities of teachers in Europe.

9. An interesting aspect of the effect of schooling on growth is noted by Glaeser (1994). He argues that secondary schooling, apart from its direct economic effects, promotes future schooling growth. More educated parents value education and tend to raise more educated children.

10. Notably the authors also find that increases in human capital cause increases in physical investment.

11. The effect of higher wealth causing more enrollment in tertiary education has also been reported in other countries. For instance, Dănăcică et al. (2010) find that higher GDP per capita in Romania in 1980 to 2008 Granger-causes higher enrollment in tertiary education.

12. Law 2525/1997 established the operation of all-day preprimary schools, and with Law No. 3518/2006 attendance in preprimary schools became compulsory at the age of five. Ministerial Decision 32/190/81670/Γ1/20.07.2007 determines the exact timetable that all-day preprimary schools have to follow.

13. See also Foundation for Economic and Industrial Research (2013) for an analysis of the formal structure of primary and secondary education in Greece. The study presents a comparative analysis of cost per student between private and public schools.

14. Ministerial Decision 12/773/77094/Γ1/28.07.2006 redesigned the timetable of primary schools. Law 3687/2008 regulates personnel and lifelong learning issues as well as issues regarding intercultural education. Ministerial Decision 12/620/61531/Γ1/31.05.2010 redesigned the teaching-education program in all-day primary schools, which operate with a single reformed curriculum.

15. In addition, Law 2525/1997 allowed the foundation of second chance schools, and Law 3848/2010 describes the process of selection of teaching staff and also regulates issues relating to the status and evaluation of teachers in primary and secondary education.

16. Law 3475/2006 also outlines the organization of secondary vocational education, allows for the operation of upper secondary vocational schools and vocational schools, and sets the curriculum and the professional rights of their graduates. The law also renamed the unified lyceums into general lyceums, and regulates issues pertaining to private upper secondary vocational schools. Finally, Law 3848/2010 describes the selection process of teachers in primary and secondary education, and also regulates issues relating to the status and evaluation of teachers in primary and secondary education.

17. Graduates of vocational training schools receive a vocational specialization certification of level 3, while those graduating from the "apprenticeship class," receive a vocational specialization certification of level 4.

18. According to Law 4009/2011, higher education institutions can organize short cycle programs that correspond to no more than 120 credits and lead to a certificate of short cycle training. Such a certificate, however, is not equivalent to a first cycle studies degree.

19. R&D expenditure within higher education is not included in public expenditure on tertiary education.

20. This smaller gap could be attributed to the fact that not all applications to the EPO or to another patent office are granted a patent. In addition, it is probable that, at least when they are first launched, some innovations produced in Europe focus on development and market opportunities within this area and do not target also other markets. In any case, the above data highlight that Greece's lower R&D spending in tertiary education relative to the EU average results in a disproportionately low level of (certified) innovations, possibly in combination with other deficiencies of the domestic higher education system.

21. Eurostat data.

22. The Economic Adjustment Programme for Greece (European Commission 2011b) states on Education (p. 39, 4.3.7) "A new framework law on higher education was approved by Parliament in late August. The law, which gathered a wide political consensus, provides for a radical overhaul of the tertiary education sector, including higher autonomy, but also higher performance-related funding, of universities. The reform has incorporated the recommendations of a report prepared by the OECD-led task force on 'Education Policy Advice for Greece.' The full implementation of the framework law is expected to take two years. The reform of the primary and secondary education sector is under preparation and will also consider the recommendations of the report. Despite ongoing reforms, major challenges remain in the primary and secondary education sector, which include: (i) an excessively centralized governance of the system; (ii) inefficient allocation of resources, with the student/teacher ratio and teachers' working time significantly lower than in other EU countries; (iii) lack of external assessment of schools and teaching and (iv) excessive constraints on private schools."

23. This is at the general government level. All data on public spending are taken from Eurostat.

24. R&D is considered separately according to the classification of the functions of government (COFOG). This classification was defined by the United Nations Statistics Division. It was replicated by Eurostat in the European System of National and Regional Accounts (ESA 2010).

25. The wages of employees in the education sector were cut with Law 4024/2011, which changed wages across the entire public sector except for special payroll regimes. Law 4093/2012, changed special payroll regimes, including that of academic staff.

26. The effect of the crisis on employment, at the various education levels, is discussed in section 8.3.

27. Students up to their eleventh semester of studies.

28. For more details on enrollment trends see section 8.3.

29. Law 3549/2007 was a significant attempt, albeit far from comprehensive or decisive, to correct some of the pathologies of the university system and to modernize it. The roots of many of these pathologies can be traced back to Law 1268/1982, which, despite some initially good intentions at the time for opening up universities to new researchers, in practice weakened

significantly all incentives for high effort and meritocracy. In particular, it allowed partisan student groups to play an excessive role in the day-to-day running the universities, as well as in the election of rectors and other administrators.

30. The law become known in Greece as the "Diamantopoulou law," after Anna Diamantopoulou, the Education Minister who introduced it to the Parliament. A significant part of the background work and design of the law and the underlying coordination was done by Professor Vassilis Papazoglou, in his capacity as Special Secretary for High Education.

31. Some obstacles for the implementation of this law in 2012, and their meaning, are briefly discussed (in Greek) at http://www.kathimerini.gr/729822/opinion/epikairothta/arxeio-monimes-sthles/enas-nomos-h-arxh-toy-teloys

32. http://www.kathimerini.gr/806958/article/epikairothta/ellada/katargeitai-h-diata3h-gia-npid

33. Some studies start from the "bright spots" and identify a nontrivial hidden potential. Kollias and Lambris (2015), for example, argue that research and technological innovation can become the driving force of the Greek economy, and discuss some of the most crucial requirements that have to be met in order for that to happen. The authors note that evidence-based governance and the allocation of public funds on the basis of objective, unbiased valuation of projects, especially regarding funding for research, is urgently needed in Greece.

34. An important body of research has documented that preprimary education can imply important and long-term gains in school success through contributions to children's cognitive abilities. Preprimary education also affects positively children's self-control, class participation, and discipline (e.g., see Barnett 1992; Berlinski, Galiani, and Gertler 2009).

35. An evaluation procedure has been gradually implemented, first only internally, at around 2008, and later also externally. Although perhaps a positive first step, to date this procedure is just a formality without real consequences.

36. This was one of the items in the reform agenda of Education Minister G. Arsenis in 1996 to 2000, but it was met with a wave of heavy protest and demonstrations. One of the areas where the reform succeeded, however, was that teachers in primary and secondary education were hired (in the public system) following a written (ASEP) examination and also considering their grades and other qualifications. This replaced an older system, whereby teachers were hired in strict chronological order based on the year when they graduated from university. See Arsenis (2015) for a detailed description of the events surrounding the reform.

37. Tertiary education can help people develop skills that increase productivity, and highly productive people generate more value and earn more. Yet tertiary education can also be useful as an avenue for rent-seeking. University diplomas may be prerequisites for high-paying, low-effort jobs in the public sector for instance, or for entering closed professions that enjoy privileges. Seeking university diplomas in Greece over the last few decades may have entailed at least some such "rent-seeking."

References

Arsenis, G. 2015. Γιατί δεν έκατσα καλά: Η εμπειρία της εκπαιδευτικής μεταρρύθμισης *1996–2000*. Athens: Gutenberg-Dardanos.

Asteriou, D., and G. M. Agiomirgianakis. 2001. Human capital and economic growth: Time series evidence from Greece. *Journal of Policy Modeling* 23 (5): 481–89.

Aubyn, M. S., A. Pina, F. Garcia, and J. Pais. 2009. *Study on the Efficiency and Effectiveness of Public Spending on Tertiary Education (No 390). Directorate General Economic and Monetary Affairs (DG ECFIN)*. Brussels: European Commission.

Barnett, W. S. 1992. Benefits of compensatory preschool education. *Journal of Human Resources* 27 (2): 279–312.

Benhabib, J., and M. M. Spiegel. 1994. The role of human capital in economic development evidence from aggregate cross-country data. *Journal of Monetary Economics* 34 (2): 143–173.

Berlinski, S., S. Galiani, and P. Gertler. 2009. The effect of pre-primary education on primary school performance. *Journal of Public Economics* 93: 219–34.

Caselli, F., G. Esquivel, and F. Lefort. 1996. Reopening the convergence debate: A new look at cross-country growth empirics. *Journal of Economic Growth* 1 (3): 363–89.

Ciccone, A., and E. Papaioannou. 2009. Human capital, the structure of production, and growth. *Review of Economics and Statistics* 91 (1): 66–82.

Cohen, D., and M. Soto. 2007. Growth and human capital: Good data, good results. *Journal of Economic Growth* 12 (1): 51–76.

Dănăcică, D. E., L. Belaşcu, and L. Ilie. 2010. The interactive causality between higher education and economic growth in Romania. *International Review of Business Research Papers* 6 (4): 491–500.

De la Fuente, A., and R. Doménech. 2006. Human capital in growth regressions: How much difference does data quality make? *Journal of the European Economic Association* 4 (1): 1–36.

European Commission. 2011a. The Economic Adjustment Programme for Greece. Fourth Review. Occasional paper 82. http://ec.europa.eu/economy_finance/publications/occasional_paper/2011/pdf/ocp82_en.pdf.

European Commission. 2011b. Directorate General for Economic and Financial Affairs. The Economic Adjustment Programme for Greece. Fifth Review. Occasional paper 87. http://ec.europa.eu/economy_finance/publications/occasional_paper/2011/pdf/ocp87_en.pdf.

Eurydice. 2008. *Levels of Autonomy and Responsibilities of Teachers in Europe*. Brussels: European Commission, Directorate General for Education and Culture. http://eacea.ec.europa.eu/education/eurydice/documents/thematic_reports/094en.pdf

Fleisher, B., H. Li, and M. Q. Zhao. 2010. Human capital, economic growth, and regional inequality in China. *Journal of Development Economics* 92 (2): 215–31.

Foundation for Economic and Industrial Research. 2013. *Public and Private Education: A Comparative Analysis*. Athens: IOBE.

Gennaioli, N., R. L. Porta, F. Lopez-de-Silanes, and A. Shleifer. 2011. *Human capital and regional development. Working paper 17158*. National Bureau of Economic Research.

Glaeser, E. L. 1994. Why does schooling generate economic growth? *Economics Letters* 44 (3): 333–37.

Hamilton, J. D., and J. Monteagudo. 1998. The augmented Solow model and the productivity slowdown. *Journal of Monetary Economics* 42 (3): 495–509.

Hanushek, E. A., and D. D. Kimko. 2000. Schooling, labor-force quality, and the growth of nations. *American Economic Review* 90 (5):1184–1208.

Hanushek, E. A., and L. Woessmann. 2012. Do better schools lead to more growth? Cognitive skills, economic outcomes, and causation. *Journal of Economic Growth* 17 (4): 267–321.

Islam, N. 1995. Growth empirics: A panel data approach. *Quarterly Journal of Economics* 110 (4): 1127–70.

Knight, M., Loayza, N., and Villanueva, D. 1993. Testing the neoclassical theory of economic growth: A panel data approach. Staff paper 512–541. IMF.

Kollias, George, and John D. Lambris. 2015. A "rule of 3" to revive Greek science, research and innovation. *Nature Immunology* 16: 1206–1208. doi:10.1038/ni.3322.

Krueger, A. B., and M. Lindahl. 2000. *Education for growth: Why and for whom? Working paper 7591*. National Bureau of Economic Research.

Lin, T. C. 2004. The role of higher education in economic development: An empirical study of Taiwan case. *Journal of Asian Economics* 15 (2): 355–71.

OECD. 2016. *Low-Performing Students: Why They Fall Behind and How to Help Them Succeed, PISA*. Paris: OECD.

Pegkas, P. 2012. Educational stock and economic growth. The case of Greece over the period 1981–2009. *Spoudai— Journal of Economics and Business* 62 (1–2): 56–71.

Pegkas, P., and C. Tsamadias. 2014. Does higher education affect economic growth? The case of Greece. *International Economic Journal* 28 (3): 425–44.

Pereira, J., and M. S. Aubyn. 2009. What level of education matters most for growth? Evidence from Portugal. *Economics of Education Review* 28 (1): 67–73.

Petrakis, P. E., and D. Stamatakis. 2002. Growth and educational levels: A comparative analysis. *Economics of Education Review* 21 (5): 513–21.

Pritchett, L. 2001. Where has all the education gone? *World Bank Economic Review* 15 (3): 367–91.

Prontzas, P., C. Tsamadias, and P. Papageorgiou. 2009. Public education expenditures and growth in Greece over the period 1960–2000. *Spoudai— Journal of Economics and Business* 59 (1–2): 125–41.

Seetanah, B. 2009. The economic importance of education: Evidence from Africa using dynamic panel data analysis. *Journal of Applied Econometrics* 12 (1): 137–57.

Self, S., and R. Grabowski. 2003. Education and long-run development in Japan. *Journal of Asian Economics* 14 (4): 565–80.

Solaki, M. 2013. Relationship between education and GDP growth: A bi-variate causality. *International Journal of Economic Practices and Theories* 3 (2): 133–39.

Temple, J. 1999. A positive effect of human capital on growth. *Economics Letters* 65 (1): 131–34.

Temple, J. R. 2001. Generalizations that aren't? Evidence on education and growth. *European Economic Review* 45 (4): 905–18.

Tsamadias, C., and P. Pegkas. 2012. The effect of education on economic growth in Greece over the 1981–2009 period: Does the proxy of human capital affect the estimation? *International Journal of Education Economics and Development* 3 (3): 237–51.

Tsamadias, C., and P. Prontzas. 2012. The effect of education on economic growth in Greece over the 1960–2000 period. *Education Economics* 20 (5): 522–37.

Tsamadias, K., C. Staikouras, and P. Pegkas. 2010. The stock of human capital and the correlations and causal relations between human capital and GDP, disposable income and bank deposits in regions of Greece in the period 1998–2008. Presented at the Europe 2020 conference on The Regional Dimension of the New Strategy. Harokopio University of Athens. http://galaxy.hua.gr/~ctsamad/files/research_proc/pdns2020.pdf.

Vandenbussche, J., P. Aghion, and C. Meghir. 2006. Growth, distance to frontier and composition of human capital. *Journal of Economic Growth* 11 (2): 97–127.

9 Reforming Health Care in Greece: Balancing Fiscal Adjustment with Health Care Needs[1]

Panos Kanavos and Kyriakos Souliotis

9.1 Introduction

It is widely recognized that good health across a population improves quality of life and is essential for economic and social development. While many determinants of good health, such as education, housing, and lifestyle choices, lie outside the realm of health systems, health systems should ensure widespread and timely access to health care services while protecting individuals from financial hardship associated with ill health. To achieve these goals, health policy makers can pursue a number of policy objectives: (1) macroeconomic efficiency, by achieving a desirable level of total health expenditure; (2) microeconomic efficiency, by ensuring that available resources are used in an optimal way; (3) equity in terms of ensuring that patient access is equitable across the population; (4) innovation, by incentivizing research and development in areas with substantial health needs; and (5) financial sustainability, or ensuring that financing of health services is affordable and sustainable.

Whereas the health status of the Greek population has improved significantly over the past few decades, the development of the health care system has suffered from many structural gaps and has not really adhered to the above-noted health policy objectives. Coverage and protection remain partial, though health care costs have increased considerably over the past two decades. Satisfaction with health service delivery remains low compared to most other EU countries. Many citizens prefer to bypass an inefficient publicly funded health system in favor of seeking treatment in private facilities and having to pay out of pocket. The inefficiencies and structural gaps have become more visible with the advent of the economic crisis in 2008 and the requirement for significant fiscal consolidation and structural adjustment.

In writing this chapter, we had two main objectives. First, we sought to highlight the structural gaps and inefficiencies that exist in Greece's health care system as it has developed since the 1980s. Second, we sought to make concrete recommendations in three strategic areas where we feel that intervention is urgently needed to improve on key objectives such as equity, efficiency, responsiveness, and financial sustainability. The three areas concern (1) the financing mechanism of the health care system and the development of contracting and reimbursement mechanisms, (2) the strengthening of primary health care, and (3) the overhaul of pharmaceutical policy. Throughout the chapter we present key performance indicators of Greece's health care system and benchmark against its counterparts in other European countries.

The chapter is organized as follows: Section 9.2 presents a conceptual framework for understanding the main dimensions of health care system design and the relative advantages of different options. Section 9.3 provides an up-to-date assessment of the Greek health care system, based on a number of key performance indicators. Section 9.4 outlines three key priorities for reform in the health care system and provides the rationale for their choice. Section 9.5 discusses how financing reform could be implemented. Section 9.6 puts forward the need for strengthening the primary health care delivery in Greece. Section 9.7 proposes a number of changes in the delivery of pharmaceutical services to improve quality of care and cost effectiveness. Finally, in section 9.8 we draw our main conclusions.

9.2 Conceptual Framework

9.2.1 Financing Health Care

One important dimension of health care system design is how health care services are financed, that is, how the necessary funds are made available. The availability of funds for health care is a fundamental question for all countries. Funding must be available for governments or insurers to be able to provide health services of sufficient quality—namely treatment, prevention, promotion and rehabilitation. For wealthy countries, particularly within the OECD area, a key challenge is to maintain the current levels of health expenditure while responding to the needs of aging populations and to cost pressures brought—in part—by technological advances. Aging populations have implications for both revenues and costs, technological advances have implications for the rate of uptake of new technologies and the rate of dis-investment of older, perhaps less cost-effective technologies.

The financing and provision of health care services can be simplified as an exchange or transfer of resources: patients (the first party) receive health care services from providers (second party), and patients or third parties (governments or insurers) transfer funds to providers. Important considerations in the context of financing health care include (1) revenue collection, (2) fund pooling, and (3) service purchasing.

Revenue Collection   Revenue collection is about who pays, the type of payment made, and who collects it. Funds are collected primarily from the general population of individuals and firms. Key funding mechanisms—particularly in the context of OECD countries—include general taxation, social insurance contributions, private insurance premiums, individual savings, out-of-pocket payments and loans, grants, and donations. Collection agents can be private for-profit, private not-for-profit, or public. Insurer status affects their motivation and incentives, notably whether they act in the interests of shareholders or members. The main methods of revenue collection are as follows:

• Through *general taxation*, taxes can be levied on individuals, households, and firms (direct taxes) or on transactions related to consumption of goods and services (indirect taxes). Direct and indirect taxes can be levied at the national, regional, or local levels. Indirect taxes can be general, such as a value-added tax, or applied to specific goods, such as an excise tax. Taxes can be general or hypothecated—that is, earmarked for a specific area of expenditure. Taxes on harmful products such as tobacco and alcohol are one such option. They reduce consumption, thereby improving health, and increase the resources governments can spend on health.

• *Social health insurance contributions (SHI)* are related to income and are very often shared between the employees and employers. Contributions may also be collected from self-employed people, for whom contributions are calculated based on income or profit declarations (this income may be under-declared in some countries). Contributions on behalf of elderly, unemployed, or disabled individuals may be collected from designated pension, unemployment, or sickness funds, respectively, or paid for from taxes. Social health insurance revenue is generally earmarked for health and collected on behalf of a separate fund. Some social or compulsory insurance contributions are in fact payroll taxes collected by government.

• *Private (voluntary) health insurance (PHI or VHI) premiums* are paid by an individual, shared between the employees and the employer or paid wholly by the employer. Premiums can be individually risk rated, based on an assessment of the probability of an individual requiring health care; community rated, based on an estimate of the risks across a geographically defined population; or group rated, based on an estimate of the risks across all employees in a single firm. The agents collecting private health insurance premiums can be independent private bodies, such as private for-profit insurance companies or private not-for-profit insurance companies and funds. Government may subsidize the cost of private health insurance using tax credits or tax relief.

• *Medical savings accounts (MSA)* are individual savings accounts into which people are either required to, or given incentives to, deposit money. The money must be spent on personal medical expenses. Medical savings accounts are usually combined with high-deductible catastrophic health insurance.

• Through *cost-sharing*, patients may be required to pay part or all of the costs of some types of care in the form of user charges. These charges may be levied as a co-payment (a flat-rate payment for each service), co-insurance (a percentage of the total cost of the service), or a deductible (a ceiling up to which the patient is liable after which the insurer covers the remaining cost). The collection agent is usually the provider, such as a physician, hospital, or pharmacist.

While no country has attained universal coverage by relying principally on voluntary schemes, such as many forms of community health insurance or private commercial health insurance, voluntary health insurance can play a useful role if used in a manner that is explicitly complementary to the compulsory prepaid system. Hence consideration of all sources of funds in an integrated national health financing strategy is essential for progress, particularly in countries that lack the fiscal capacity needed to generate high levels of compulsory prepaid funding.

Fund Pooling   Fund pooling describes the extent to which revenue collected by different individuals and firms (and possibly other sources) is pooled to provide the same health services to all contributors. Pooling thus characterizes the degree of insurance provided by a health care system and the degree of redistribution that takes place across different contributors.

The establishment of a pooling mechanism is a critical precondition for the achievement of universal health coverage. Lack of such a mechanism implies the inability to redistribute resources and target them to those who most need them. Health systems requiring direct out-of-pocket payments from people at the time they need care prevent a significant minority, if not a majority, from accessing services and can result in financial hardship and even impoverishment. Reducing the reliance on direct out-of-pocket payments reduces the financial barriers to access as well as the impoverishing impact of such payments. By contrast, increasing the revenues from prepaid and pooled mechanisms, and using them to cover those in need, is the key element of the broad strategy toward universal health insurance coverage. Countries that have made significant progress on access and financial protection objectives have implemented successfully mandated contributions for people who can afford to pay through taxation, and/or compulsory earmarked contributions for health insurance.

Pooling can take place at different levels. One option is to have a single pool that aims to cover the needs of an entire population. This can be accomplished, for example, when there is a single statutory health insurer, financed by SHI and/or general taxation. An alternative option is to have multiple pools, aiming to cover the needs of specific subgroups within the population. This occurs, for example, when there are multiple insurance funds financed by SHI.

Under a PHI system, funds are pooled between subscribers of the same insurance provider. However, the extent of risk pooling is limited, with actuarial premiums related to an individual's risk. If premiums are community rated, pooling is between high- and low-risk members in the same geographic area. Group rating allows pooling among employees of the same firm.

Under an MSA system, pooling is prevented by keeping funds in individual accounts. MSAs are therefore usually supplemented with catastrophic insurance for very expensive treatments.

User charges are paid at the point of service and are not a form of pooling. The revenue generated by user charges is handled differently depending on how the system is designed. For example, the individual health care provider may retain the money as income. It may be retained at the level of a clinic or hospital and, together with other revenue, may contribute to the cost of maintaining local service provision. If the user charges are surrendered to, or levied by, the insurer or government, they may be used to meet any gap between insurance premium or tax revenue and expenditure.

Summarizing, different forms of revenue collection can be consistent with different degrees of pooling. The relationship between revenue collection and pooling, however, is not straightforward and one to one. For example, under SHI there may be a single or multiple pools depending on whether there is a single or multiple insurers. Pooling choices depend on the selected governance design in the health care system (e.g., single statutory health insurer vs. multiple insurers in the case of SHI, or centralized vs. decentralized tax collection in the case of general taxation model).

Health care systems can differ not only in the extent of pooling but also in the extent to which pooling and revenue collection are *integrated*. In the case of SHI and general taxation, and assuming a single pool, if revenue collection and pooling are *integrated*, the allocation from collection agent to pooling agent is internalized. Examples of this include social health insurance contributions collected by funds and retained by them and, in the case of taxation, national, regional, or local taxes that are collected and retained. If *different agents* carry out the revenue collection and the fund pooling, a mechanism is required to distribute resources from the collection entity to the pool. If there are multiple pools, the allocation is increasingly being adjusted according to the risk profile of the population covered by each pool. This process is referred to as "risk adjustment," and in social health insurance systems with multiple health insurers, such as those prevailing in Germany, Austria, and the Netherlands, it has developed mainly from a concern to prevent adverse selection (van de Ven et al. 1994; Oliver 1999). Within tax-financed systems, such as those prevailing in the United Kingdom, Sweden, and Denmark, risk-adjustment methods have been developed from a concern to ensure equity of access by ensuring a fair allocation of resources to local health authorities based on the needs of the population they cover (Kutzin 2001).

Most European countries have strived to introduce *universal coverage* for health care services since the end of World War II. Based on the WHO definition, universal health coverage "is defined as ensuring that all people can use the promotion, preventive, curative, rehabilitative and palliative health services they need, of sufficient quality to be effective, while also ensuring that the use of these services does not expose the user to financial hardship" (WHO 2015). This definition embodies three interrelated principles: first, equity in access to health services, in the sense that those who need the services should get them, not only those who can pay for them; second, the quality of health services is good enough to improve the health of those receiving services; and third, financial risk protection ensures that the cost of using care does not place people at risk of financial hardship. To a very large extent all European countries have established systems of universal health coverage with varying levels of additional contributions by patients, taking the form of out-of-pocket payments for health services that may not be covered (e.g., restorative dental care), or co-payments, for health care goods and services that are partly covered (e.g., prescription charges) and relate to their use.

In this context, individual countries' path to universal health insurance coverage involves important policy choices and inevitable trade-offs, captured in figure 9.1, which shows the difference between a state of current pooled funds and the outer boundaries, representing universal health insurance coverage. The choices or dilemmas are threefold: first, decisions need to be made on who is covered and how those who are not covered can be included in what the health system offers. Second, decisions need to be made as to which services are covered implying how priorities are set with regards to the benefits package that may apply. Third, it needs to be decided what proportion of the total costs is covered by the health system, essentially outlining a cost-sharing policy and the level of out-of-pocket expenses that insurees will need to pay.

Service Purchasing   Purchasing means "the transfer of pooled resources to service providers on behalf of the population for which the funds were pooled" (Kutzin 2001). A key dimension of purchasing is whether or not the pooling agent is *integrated* with the service providers. Suppose, for example, that the pooling agent is a SHI-financed health

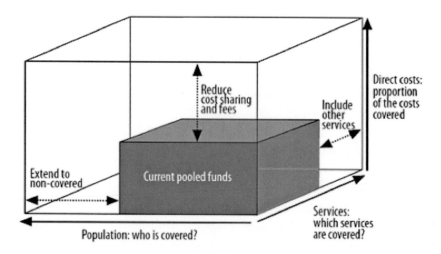

Three dimensions to consider when moving towards universal coverage

Figure 9.1
Three critical dimensions of universal health insurance
Source: WHO

insurer. Integration would mean that the health insurer owns hospitals and has doctors and nurses as its employees. Alternatively, the relationship could be arm's-length, with hospitals being managed independently and being financially autonomous. In an arm's-length relationship, the hospitals would contract with the pooling agent for the provision of health services and the compensation that this entails.

Integration is generally inferior to an arm's-length relationship because it leads to a lack of transparency and inadequate incentives to reduce costs. Indeed, in an arm's-length relationship, hospitals can receive the full benefits from any improvements in efficiency that they generate because they are financially autonomous. By contrast, under integration the lack of financial autonomy implies that accurate performance metrics are hard to construct, and high-powered incentives are not possible. The general trend in OECD countries has been toward creating arm's-length relationships between pooling agents and providers. For example, in France and Germany, providers contract with pooling agents, in a quasi-market setting. In the United Kingdom, hospitals and general practitioner (GP) practices became independently managed after the 1989 reforms.

In some countries, separate agents—rather than the health care system as a whole—purchase services from providers (e.g., Commissioning Care Groups in England purchase services from hospitals); in this case, the resources have to be allocated to those purchasers. Pursuing widely held objectives of equity and efficiency requires allocating resources according to health care need. Capitation is the main method for calculating purchasers' budgets adopted in Europe. However, many health care systems continue to allocate resources based on political negotiation, historical precedent or the lowest bids.

9.2.2 Cost Containment and Efficiency in the Use of Available Resources

Given the amount of collected revenue, health care systems must provide the best possible level of services. For this, it is necessary to make the most efficient use of resources and to minimize waste. Inefficiencies can arise in many areas, for example, in how pharmaceuticals are purchased and used, how hospital admissions are managed, and how health worker capacities and motivation are addressed. The way that health care financing arrangements are organized may also be a source of inefficiency. Above we discussed this issue in the context of the degree of integration between pooling agent and providers. But even within arm's-length relationships, the contracts between pooling agents and providers (e.g., hospitals) are crucial in setting incentives.

In contracts between pooling agents and hospitals (or hospital groups) pre-agreement is often involved for the treatment of and reimbursement corresponding to each diagnosis. Under that arrangement the provider (hospital in this case) supplies the agreed treatment for a given diagnosis and receives the agreed payment. To establish a mutually accepted understanding of what a payment should look like for a given diagnosis, as well as to provide incentives for providers to be more efficient, payments by activity (e.g., *diagnosis-related groups, DRG*) are increasingly being used. If a more expensive treatment is needed for a specific patient with the given diagnosis, then the provider must prove the need to the pooling agent. The DRG arrangement is usually supplemented by a *prospective budget*, which puts a cap on the total reimbursement that will be received by the provider during the contractual period. This acts as an additional safeguard on cost overruns, which may be due to an overuse of expensive treatments. Often reimbursement in integrated (i.e., non–arm's-length) systems is *retrospective* rather than prospective. That is, the provider decides the treatment that it applies to a specific patient and then submits the bill to the pooling agent (with whom it is integrated). However, this can lead to large cost overruns and an abuse of expensive treatments, since cost-control mechanisms are weak or absent.

Contracts between pooling agents and doctors can take many forms. The usual one is *fee-for-service*, under which a provider (doctor in this case) receives a pre-agreed fee for a specific service. Another form of contract is *capitation*, whereby the provider is paid according to the number of prospective patients in the area that he or she is covering, regardless of whether patients use the service.

All contract forms between pooling agents and providers have strengths and weaknesses. Fee-for-service contracts give providers an incentive to overprovide services (e.g., doctors order too many lab tests). Likewise DRG contracts can lead to overprovision of services by hospitals. Monitoring by the pooling agents can keep these tendencies in check. Another mechanism to guard against overprovision is to reduce the payment for a given service if many such services have been ordered during the term of the contract.

Other types of contracts generate incentives for under-provision. This is the case for capitation contracts since the payment—per patient—is fixed and therefore doctors have an incentive to underprovide faced with a fixed budget.

All countries can improve the efficiency of their health systems, thereby releasing resources that could be used to increase the level of coverage. Some of these actions would aim to improve efficiency in a particular area of the health system, such as pharmaceutical procurement (e.g., reducing the cost of off-patent pharmaceuticals through public tenders) or hospital activity (e.g., reducing the length of stay for uncomplicated procedures). Others would address the incentives inherent in the health financing system, in particular, how services are purchased and how providers are paid. Ultimately, improving health system efficiency is bound to increase coverage and therefore promote the objective of equity.

Improvements in efficiency can further be realized by reducing fragmentation in the pooling of funds and purchasing of health services. Reducing fragmentation can cut down on the system's administrative costs.

9.3 An Assessment of the Greek Health Care System and the Need for Structural Changes before the Crisis

Before the economic crisis the Greek health care system underwent considerable expansion (Economou 2010) and experienced significant cost inflation. Total health care costs increased much faster than GDP growth, from just under 6 percent of GDP in 1980 to just over 10 percent in 2008. That increase was in line with developments in other European health systems (figure 9.2). In a similar vein, per capita spending in health care increased sixfold between 1980 and 2008 from about US$500 in purchasing power parity (PPP) terms in 1980 to US$3,000 in 2008, following a similar trend as in other European countries (figure 9.3).

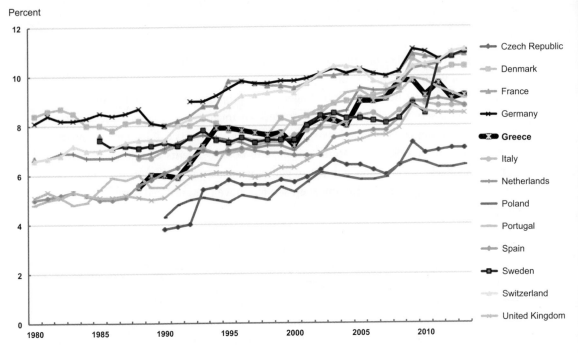

Figure 9.2
Healthcare spending as a percentage of GDP, 1980 to 2013
Source: OECD Health Data (2014)

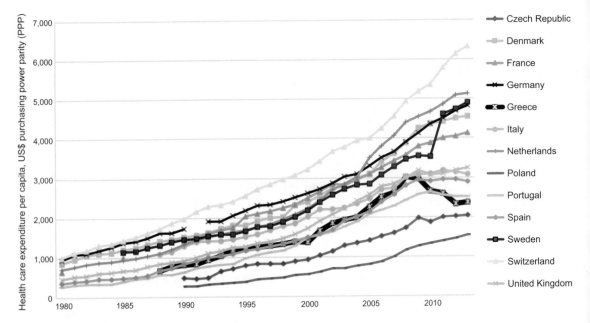

Figure 9.3
Average health care spending per capita, 1980 to 2013 (US$ PPP)
Source: OECD Health Data (2014)

While the increase in health care costs in Greece is comparable to that in other European countries, there is a crucial difference. Unlike in most of the other countries, a significant proportion of the increase in Greece was based on out-of-pocket expenses. The contribution of statutorily funded health spending was limited to just under 60 percent of total health spend in 2008, compared with over 80 percent in most other countries in the European Union. The economic crisis had a significant impact on out-of-pocket spending on health (reduction by 36 percent between 2008 and 2013), while statutory funding also declined but modestly (−4 percent) during the same period. These trends are captured in figure 9.4.

The increase in health care costs in Greece was partly driven by an excessive volume of prescriptions, laboratory tests, and diagnostic procedures. More generally, the government was unable to control volume and the total cost of patient care.

Public pharmaceutical expenditure more than doubled in five years (from 2.4 billion euros in 2004 to 5.3 billion euros in 2009; figure 9.5), and its annual aggregate growth

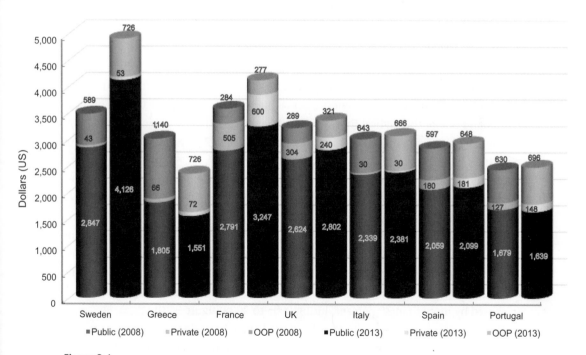

Figure 9.4

Health care spending per capita by source of funding, 2008 and 2013. The data for Spain are from 2012.

Source: OECD Health Data (2014)

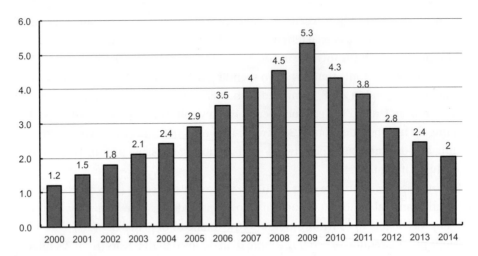

Figure 9.5
Public pharmaceutical expenditures in Greece, 2000 to 2014 (in billion euros). The 2014 figures
are estimates. Rebates to the government have been accounted for.
Source: Foundation for Economic and Industrial Research, General Secretariat for Social Security,
authors' calculations

rate during the period 2000 to 2008 exceeded 11 percent (Kanavos et al. 2011). As a
consequence pharmaceutical spending per capita became the highest in the European
Union and one of the highest in the OECD (US$840 in PPP terms; figure 9.6) in 2009,
and so was the fraction of GDP spent on pharmaceuticals (2.76 percent of GDP in 2009
compared with the OECD average of 1.64 percent; figure 9.7).

Diagnostic care volume increased to become the highest among OECD countries.
This can be seen by two indicators of diagnostic care volume, the number of computed
tomography (CT) scans and the number of magnetic resonance imaging (MRI) scans. In
2013 Greece (together with Italy) had the highest number of MRI and CT scans annually per million inhabitants in the OECD area. The figures for Greece were 24.3 and
35.2 scans, respectively, and they should be contrasted with OECD medians of 9.4 and
17.2 (OECD 2014; figure 9.8 [MRI] and figure 9.9 [CT]). Moreover in-patient care costs
increased by more than 35 percent during 2005 to 2008 (figure 9.10).

Whereas other European countries have implemented a wide array of cost containment and efficiency improvement measures to keep health expenditure in check while
also improving the quality of services provided, this did not happen in Greece. Some
of the reasons have to do with the inefficiencies discussed in section 9.2. For example,

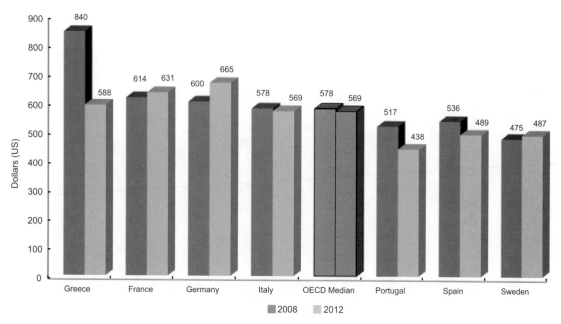

Figure 9.6
Pharmaceutical spending per capita, 2008 and 2012 (US$ PPP). The first column (2008) data for Greece are from 2009.
Source: OECD Health Data (2014)

many public hospitals were integrated with the main (public) insurance providers, and this removed incentives to contain costs and improve efficiency. Cost inflation was particularly important in the private sector, but efficient contracting mechanisms, such as those discussed in section 9.2, were not put in place perhaps due to inertia and low incentives within the public administration. The inefficiencies became evident when control mechanisms and clinical audit processes were first implemented. An example is the civil servants' health care fund (OPAD), where volume of diagnostic tests had doubled between 2005 and 2009 but declined by 40 percent immediately after the introduction of an electronic referral system (Souliotis, Mantzana, and Papageorgiou 2013). Similarly external clinical audits rejected 70 percent of costs for expensive materials used in surgery (Souliotis 2013a).

Additional areas of inefficiency concern the relative inputs of doctors and nurses, and the lack of a focus on primary care. Greece had and continues to have the highest number of practicing doctors per 1,000 inhabitants in the OECD area (6.3/1,000

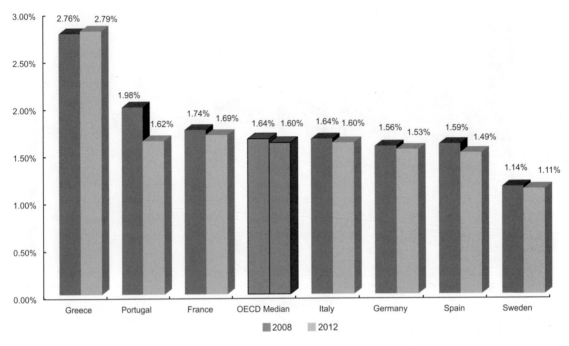

Figure 9.7
Pharmaceutical spending as a percentage of GDP, 2008 and 2012. The first column (2008) data for Greece are from 2009.
Source: OECD Health Data (2014)

inhabitants in 2013, compared with the OECD median of 3.8/1,000 inhabitants; figure 9.11). At the same time the number of nurses per 1,000 inhabitants in Greece was and still remains significantly lower than in most OECD countries (3.6/1,000 inhabitants in Greece compared to 6.1/1,000 inhabitants, which was the OECD median in 2013; figure 9.12). As a result, contrary to what most other European countries are doing increasingly, Greece still relies on expensive labor inputs (doctors) to deliver basic medical care, rather than substituting for less expensive inputs that can deliver the same quality care. Throughout this period the role of the state budget in supporting the delivery of health care has been significant through cash injections into the NHS, aiming to cover hospital deficits that earmarked contributions were unable to cover. These contributions increased substantially during the crisis and reached 32 percent of the social security fund's expenditure in 2012. Additionally the Greek health care system is characterized by a lack of primary care focus, which is having a negative impact

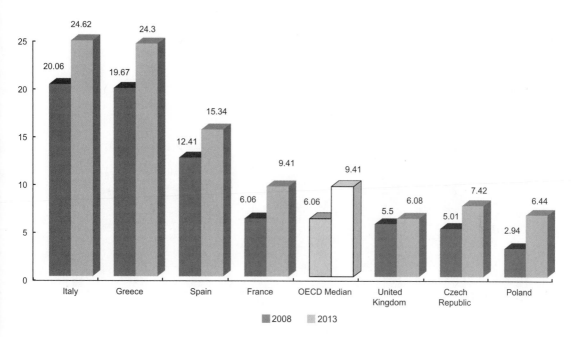

Figure 9.8
Magnetic resonance imaging (MRI) exams per million inhabitants, 2008 and 2013. The first column (2008) data for Spain are from 2010; the second column (2013) data for Italy are from 2012. Source: OECD Health Data (2014)

on the ability of the system to integrate care services and provide care coordination, particularly in chronic care management (Souliotis and Lionis 2004; Lionis et al. 2009). As a result care delivery remains fragmented and disjointed. Such lack of integration has resulted in disparities in access to care (Souliotis and Chrysakis 2007; Athanasakis et al. 2011; Tountas et al. 2011; European Commission 2013; Souliotis 2013b), both geographical and financial.

Since health care spending in Greece as a proportion of GDP is broadly in line with that in other European countries, the inefficiencies in health care provision should manifest themselves in lower quality of the provided services. The high level of out-of-pocket expenses is in and of itself an indicator of low quality, since it indicates that people are under-insured against health risks. Another indicator of low quality is the long waiting times that patients face in public facilities throughout the country. To bypass these waiting times and beat the system, patients incur high out-of-pocket expenses, including informal payments to physicians. Thus low-quality fosters a higher

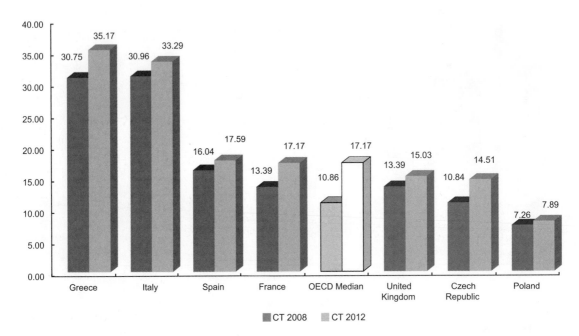

Figure 9.9
Computed tomography scanners (CT) per million inhabitants, 2008 and 2013. The first column (2008) data for Spain are from 2010; the second column (2013) data for Italy are from 2012. Source: OECD Health Data (2014)

reliance on out-of-pocket expenses, feeding a vicious cycle between inefficiency and under-insurance. The low quality is reflected in population surveys. Patient satisfaction from the delivery of health care services is very low in Greece, compared to other EU member states, as shown in a recent Eurobarometer survey (figure 9.13).

On the whole, the Greek health care system until the crisis was highly inefficient, with little ability to control spending and implement reforms to optimize the delivery of care to Greek citizens. Despite a significant amount of money going into health care, patients faced access constraints (European Commission 2013) and had to shoulder high out-of-pocket payments to cover their health care needs. A contracting function did not really exist and providers could not be held accountable for inefficiency, high length of stay, or service overprovision. Clinical guidance—where it existed—on what is both desirable and recommended in clinical practice was not enforced or was observed loosely. The fragmentation of the system into several insurers with some of them practically having ownership of their means of provision (hospitals, doctors) had

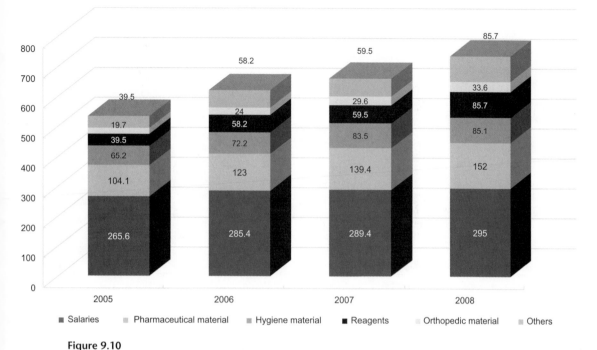

Figure 9.10
Participation of the various cost categories to the daily hospitalization costs in euros (hospitals of First Regional Health Authority, 2005 to 2008)
Source: Center for Health Services Research, Waste in the Public Health System, Athens (2010)

long created a multi-tiered system. In a similar way to other social benefits such as pensions, some professional groups had access to superior benefits, reflecting their superior political power. This created inequities and inefficiencies.

The above-mentioned characteristics underlined the need for structural changes for many years. It was the economic crisis, though, that acted as a pressure point to initiate change. As we explain in section 9.4, one key change was to reduce the fragmentation of the system by unifying all public health insurers under the umbrella of a single fund. Efforts were also made to move away from integration between public insurers and health care providers, and to introduce arm's-length relationships. Attempts to introduce certain elements of efficient contracting, such as DRG payments to hospitals, were made, but while some improvements have taken place, many of the inefficiencies remain. Sections 9.4 and 9.5 elaborate further on these issues and outline priorities for reform going forward.

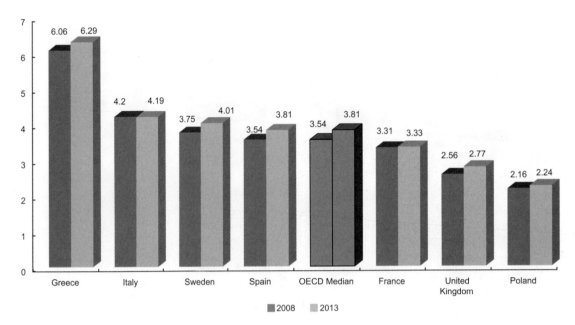

Figure 9.11
Number of practicing physicians per 1,000 inhabitants, 2008 and 2013. The second column
(2013) data for Sweden are from 2012. Data on practicing physicians refer to physicians providing care directly to patients. Data on professionally active physicians refer to physicians working
in the health sector as managers, educators, or researchers (adding another 5 to 10 percent to
number of doctors).
Source: OECD Health Data (2014)

9.4   Key Priorities for Reform and Their Rationale

The previous section highlighted some of the problems and inefficiencies within the
Greek health care system. These have been the subject of academic and policy debate,
resulting in a variety of recommendations about health care reform. The financial crisis deepened the problems and put more pressure on an already inefficient system; for
example, inpatient admissions increased considerably as patients switched from private hospital care to care provided by public hospitals, which are part of the National
Health Service (NHS–ESY). Public hospitals in turn struggled to meet the ever-increasing
demand. Additional problems included, among others, the difficulty of exercising one's
insurance right in primary care and the inability of insurees to pay rising co-payments
for pharmaceutical care, due to cost-shifting policies.

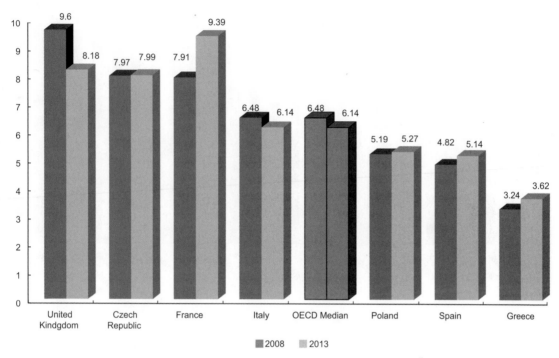

Figure 9.12
Number of nurses per 1,000 inhabitants, 2008 and 2013. The first column (2008) data for Italy are from 2011.
Source: OECD Health Data (2014)

While some reforms have been implemented since the beginning of the crisis, policy making has often focused on short-term pressing issues, and some proposals on more substantial long-run change have not received sufficient attention. In sections 9.5, 9.6, and 9.7 we propose changes in three critical areas of the health care system, seeking the right balance between meeting budget constraints and covering the health needs of the population. These are (1) structural changes in health care financing and contracting mechanisms, (2) strengthening the role of primary care, and (3) re-shaping pharmaceutical policy through a combination of structural and tactical interventions. In the remainder of this section we outline the rationale for these priorities.

9.4.1 The System of Health Care Financing and Contracting in Greece
The change in the financing model is of critical importance for the sustainability of the health system, particularly in a macroeconomic environment characterized by

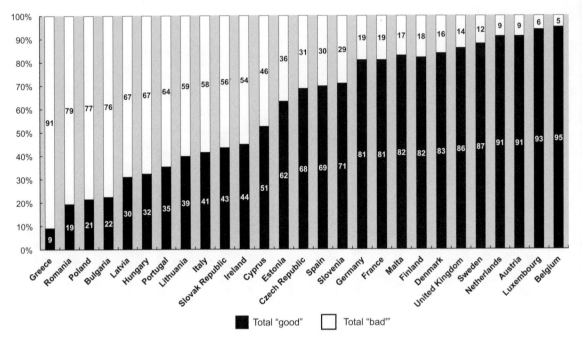

Figure 9.13
Satisfaction with health care provision. Survey results on how Europeans perceive the current health care provisions in their country. Possible answers included: "very good," "rather good," "rather bad," "very bad," "don't know." We compressed positive and negative responses under total "bad" and total "good."
Source: Eurobarometer (2012)

contraction and sluggish growth. The underlying principle is the need to address the problems arising from the coexistence—in almost equal proportions—of the two main pillars of public funding, namely taxes and social insurance contributions. Beyond these, there are additional reform agenda items, such as improving levels of coverage and efficiency and quality of care.

The continuing recession has resulted in the shrinking of tax revenues directed to social policy,[2] while at the same time the capacity of households to fill the gaps in the public financing of health services with their own resources has been exhausted. It is noted that in 2011, in the midst of the severe recession, Greece still held one of the highest positions in the OECD regarding the level of private health expenditure as a percentage of total household expenditure (3.8 vs. 2.9 percent), the vast majority of which was out of pocket. The large size of out-of-pocket expenditures can also be evidenced by the fact that private health care expenditure ranks third and sixth among the different types of expenditures of poor and non-poor households, respectively, in 2012 (Hellenic Statistical Authority 2013). This evidence underscores the extent of under-insurance that is inherent in the Greek health care system. It also indicates that the financing of health care in Greece is regressive, in that the poor bear a larger fraction of the health care costs as a proportion of their income (Mossialos, Allin, and Davaki 2005; Kyriopoulos et al. 2002; Matsaganis et al. 1999).

Adding to these problems is the limited penetration of private insurance (OECD 2013) in the Greek health care market, which covers one of the lowest percentages of the population among OECD countries (12 percent in 2011), as well as the existence, despite the crisis, of informal, under-the-table, transactions in both primary and secondary care (Liaropoulos 2008; Souliotis et al. 2014), which are difficult to capture accurately. Finally, there is no meaningful contracting mechanism for providers to adhere to.

To address all these problems of the Greek health care system, a major reform was implemented in 2010, aiming to reduce its fragmentation and unify all public health insurers and all health insurance contributions under the umbrella of a single fund, the National Health Fund (EOPYY). This created a single fund where funds would follow patients without discriminating on the type of health insurance coverage and regardless of the point of care delivery. This was a major decision and practically followed on the steps of other countries with many health insurers (e.g., Germany). However, this was not enough, and in the contracting mechanism between the single fund and individual providers, there were encountered significant problems of implementation or instances of additional actions to be undertaken. The latter include the establishment of modern funding mechanisms such as DRG in hospital settings that can serve as the basis of a meaningful negotiation between the purchaser of services (EOPYY) and the individual providers (hospitals). Related to that, hospitals need to be independent agencies managing their resources in the context of delivering high-quality care to patients. As a result the legal status of hospitals needs to be reviewed.

9.4.2 The Lack of Effective Primary Health Care

The provision of public primary health care (PHC) is characterized by the parallel operation of two subsystems (NHS and social security). After the administrative intervention that merged the health care provision of the different social security funds under the umbrella of EOPYY, the two subsystems cover nearly the entire population. This new reality suggests, in an obvious way, the feasibility and rationality of forming a single public system of PHC provision with the merging/operation of all public PHC structures (NHS health centers and regional clinics, primary care units of EOPYY, local authority structures, etc.) under a single provider that is responsible for their supervision, operation, and funding. The rationale is clear and relates to improved efficiency, the ability to monitor what is being done, to whom and by whom, the reduction and—possibly—the avoidance of duplications, which are costly and wasteful, as well as care coordination, particularly for chronic diseases. Having a system that retains a gate-keeping function would most certainly promote all these objectives compared with a system that does not (and that has been the case in Greece for a very long time).

9.4.3 The Pharmaceutical Sector

A re-structuring of the way the pharmaceutical market operates should be high on the reform agenda in Greece for a number of reasons. First, despite prices for pharmaceutical products being among the lowest in the European Union, total pharmaceutical expenditure per capita prior to the crisis had grown uncontrollably and was much higher than in most EU member states (figure 9.6), and quite significantly above the OECD median. Similarly Greece spent a much higher share of its GDP on pharmaceuticals than other EU member states (figure 9.7). This cannot be attributed to higher prices of prescription pharmaceuticals in Greece compared with other EU countries; rather, it is a combination of inefficient pricing (low prices for originator, in-patent pharmaceuticals, high prices for generics) and high consumption per capita.

Significant progress has been made since the end of 2009 in terms of overall reduction in public expenditure on pharmaceuticals, as figures 9.6 and 9.7 show. However, one important shortcoming of this rapid downward adjustment is that it was achieved in crude and untargeted manner, through across-the-board price cuts, restrictions on the introduction of new pharmaceuticals, and, ultimately, on their reimbursement by the health care system.[3] In other words, downward adjustment has been achieved through fiscal consolidation without due consideration to efficiency-inducing structural reforms, which are crucial in this context.

Consequently there are concerns that the reduction in expenditure has shifted a significant proportion of expenditure from the public sector to the patient (by increasing out-of-pocket payments). Additionally the need for significant economies to be made on the pharmaceuticals budget has delayed the launch of new therapies into the Greek market. And, last, expenditure reduction has not addressed many of the structural problems in this particular sector, notably, first, a dysfunctional and over-engineered pricing system for originator pharmaceuticals, which results in significant delays in the pricing of new pharmaceuticals; second, the virtual nonexistence of a sustainable reimbursement policy including the overall system of value assessment and the criteria for reimbursement of pharmaceutical products; third, the high-volume issue within the context of prescribing; and, fourth, the issue of appropriateness of care and the introduction, uptake, and monitoring of prescribing guidelines.

These issues clearly highlight the need for intervention on the demand side (particularly prescribing practices as well as prescribing guidance to assist prescribing) but also the need to review the arrangements on the supply side (prices, pricing and coverage system for all prescription pharmaceuticals) and whether these arrangements ensure adequate access to prescription pharmaceuticals by the Greek population. Among the supply-side arrangements that should be reviewed are the regulatory arrangements at the level of the National Drug Agency (EOF) (e.g., timing of approvals, quality assurance of generic pharmaceuticals) and certain arrangements concerning prices and pricing impact on access and availability of essential prescription pharmaceuticals. An issue that also merits significant attention is the complete absence of a modern, reliable, and robust reimbursement system whereby the payer (EOPYY) is able to negotiate with suppliers of pharmaceutical products favorable reimbursement prices on the basis of a series of criteria (additional clinical benefit, budget impact, expected volume, and price-volume agreement, etc.). Linked to these criteria are the incentive structures for health care professionals, as well as of those who administer the system, to ensure that the prescribing and dispensing of prescription pharmaceuticals takes place in a rational and cost-effective manner.

9.5   Reforming Financing and Contracting Mechanisms

The creation of a single fund (EOPYY) was pivotal in changing the way the health care system is financed, but the fund, in itself, may not be enough to ensure financial sustainability and improvements in efficiency. Further reform is needed to create a system that either relies mostly on general tax revenue, rather than social health insurance contributions (SHI).

Given the current circumstances, switching to a system financed out of general taxation rather than SHI may be preferable for a number of reasons. First, the tax base is significantly narrower in social health insurance financing than in general tax financing, as only the employed contribute. Second, there continues to be significant social security contribution evasion or avoidance that amounts to about 20 percent of the total income of social insurance funds (European Industrial Relations Observatory 2004). While the evasion in social security contributions may be close in magnitude to that in income taxes, evasion in consumption (VAT) or property taxes may be less prevalent. Third, the current adverse macroeconomic environment facing the country has resulted in a growing number of uninsured citizens, estimated to be more than

2.5 million. With one in four citizens being uninsured and with the current unemployment rate in excess of 25 percent, it is necessary to disconnect health insurance coverage and entitlements from occupational status and have these replaced with a more redistributive model. Consequently the most sensible choice seems to be the shift toward a tax-based financing model, as should have been implemented in the early 1980s when the Greek NHS (ESY) was established (Liaropoulos 2014). Instead two parallel systems of public financing have been maintained since then, in part resulting in high private payments.

An additional advantage of substituting SHI with general tax revenue is the beneficial effect that this will have on employment. Since firms will be facing a smaller overall cost to employ workers, they will have an incentive to increase employment.

A practical difficulty with switching to a tax-based financing system is the financing gap, as tax revenues will be brought into the system during the next financial year. For the tax-based financing system to be viable, improvements to the efficiency of the tax-collection mechanism will be key. Consequently a transition to a mainly tax-based financing system should be implemented over the longer term (e.g., over a period of five years) to allow for the gradual adjustment in the funding gap. Public funding of health care services should be no less than 6 percent of GDP, a target that was also included in the initial Memorandum of Understanding between Greece and its creditors. As of 2014 public health care spending in Greece has accounted for 5 percent of the GDP, one of the lowest percentages within the OECD (Souliotis 2014).

While the tax-based financing system is proposed as a reasonable choice with regard to financing, a radical reform is also required in the system of contracting for health care services, where an inflexible, inefficient, and outdated model has prevailed. Such a reform should involve appropriate arm's-length relationships between EOPYY and the service providers, as well as an appropriate structure to conduct the contract negotiations. The contracting mechanisms should comply with the general principles sketched in section 9.2.2. National and regional budget ceilings should be imposed, and services should be consumed only within these budgets. Moreover there should be a move away from a purely fee-for-service reimbursement model to one that involves more robust monitoring and audit, and that reimburses services on the basis of criteria such as quality, improved health outcomes, volume, and case mix (severity).

Budget setting should be based on demographic, epidemiological (mortality, morbidity, etc.), and health service utilization criteria at the regional level. This would assume that money would follow the patient, that is, be allocated according to health needs. Regions would have to work backward to allocate resources in an optimal way to meet defined need. That would entail:

• estimation of size and health needs of the reference population and system capacity;
• definition of patient pathways to care, to allow for a structured referral system (Mossialos et al. 2005; Abel Smith et al. 1994);
• reimbursement of providers on the basis of quality and service outcomes, through guidelines and clinical audits;
• incentives to keep the patient in the region (and avoid patient outflows); and
• incentives to implement health promotion and prevention activities.

In addition to the use of quality-related indicators and outcomes would be the use of savings through price-volume agreements achieved with generalized rebates. Such measures are fairer than setting service provision ceilings, which undermine competition in the free privately contracted provider market, as well as deter supplier-induced demand.

Co-payments should also be fundamentally connected to income to remove any inequalities in the distribution of economic burden and to ensure the necessary reallocation in the system. The extent of these co-payments should be associated with (1) total volume of services consumed and (2) income, and should be disassociated from categories of services consumed to avoid favoring specific health care providers. Such measures could be complemented by the introduction of incentives for increased uptake of private insurance, which may further improve patient access to care as well as limit exclusion.

In short, the proposed system is based on the gradual substitution of social insurance contributions by taxation. It also puts forth a novel way to manage state health funds. Specifically, it is proposed that EOPYY become the body solely responsible for the financial management of the health care system. In this framework, EOPYY allocates the entire health care budget to regional health authorities, based on the population to be covered, its health needs, and the service mix. This means that resources will actually follow patients and health care needs, wherever these occur. Such a distribution of funds also provides strong incentives to regional health services to improve their performance, to contain demand within the remit of the region and avert outward patient flows. In this model, providers are reimbursed on the basis of service volume, severity of health need addressed, and quality of services offered, thus instilling fairness and competition in the system, whereas, in primary health care, EOPYY reimburses providers on the basis of a combination of capitation and pay for performance (see figure 9.14).

Finally, we should emphasize that the switch to a general tax funding model in itself is unlikely to resolve two pressing issues: first, the level of out-of-pocket payments in Greece, which are significantly higher than in most EU member states, and second, the

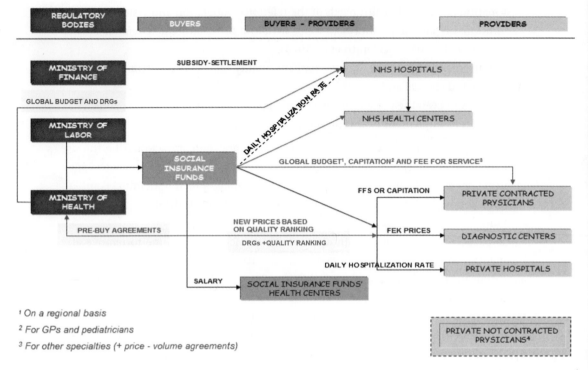

Figure 9.14
Proposed framework for distribution of health funds
Source: Souliotis (2011)

improvements in efficiency and quality of care in the services provided. Both issues are interrelated, as was pointed out in section 9.3. With regard to the former, higher levels of coverage by a tax-funded Greek NHS will only be achieved if a higher portion of tax revenue is channeled toward health care delivery to reduce out-of-pocket payments. If this cannot be achieved over the medium term, then a likely way forward would be for the public system to cover a range of services, including catastrophic coverage, while the remainder could be covered by a form of private insurance. Improvements in efficiency cannot take place simply by reforming the financing mechanism but by also intervening in the models of provision in the ways outlined in this section.

9.6 Establishing and Strengthening Primary Health Care (PHC)

In 2011 over 40 percent of the population sought medical consultations in the private sector, paying out of pocket for the full cost, a reduction in volume of 58 percent compared with 2010, due to financial constraints (NSPH 2012).

Medical consultations constitute the first point of contact of patients with the health care system. The high volume of private consultations for decades reflected the lack of an integrated primary health care system (Souliotis and Lionis 2004). An attempt to address this gap took place in 2004,[4] when it became evident that primary care was mainly provided by the private sector and in a fragmented manner. Until the economic crisis struck, nothing had been implemented. When the crisis hit highlighting barriers to access related to inability to pay for private primary care services, the issue resurfaced in the health care agenda and became a policy priority.

An expert committee, the Scientific Committee for Primary Health Care (2013), re-evaluated the feasibility of introducing a primary health care system that would address fundamental principles such as equal access to health services for all, integrated care and care coordination, orientation of the system toward the individual and their family, and coverage of the uninsured (figure 9.15).

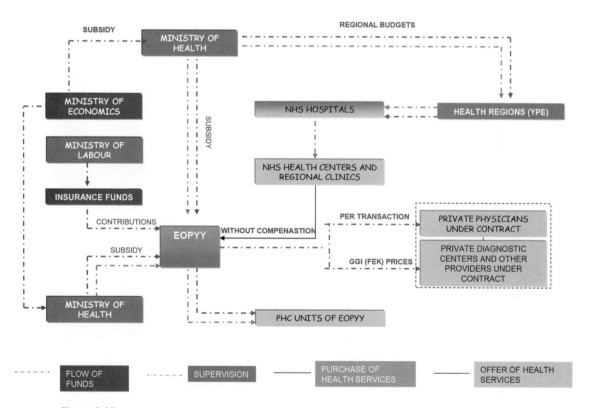

Figure 9.15
Current primary health care structure
Source: Scientific Committee for Primary Health Care (2013)

Beyond these common principles, the committee proposed to expand the scope of primary health care services to include monitoring and evaluation of health indicators for the reference population, implementation of interventions to address such critical issues as risk factors, planning and implementation of prevention programs, and health promotion in the community, as well as dental care, mental illness,[5] and addictions (see figure 9.16).

These developments would presuppose the strengthening of the administrative and organizational capability of the primary care system at regional level. In practical terms, it was proposed that the responsibility for planning, resource allocation, and operation of the system lie with regional health authorities (Ygeionomikes Perifereies, YPE). These authorities should be responsible for entrusting new primary care structures with administrative autonomy, namely concerning their own staff, budget, and outcome targets.

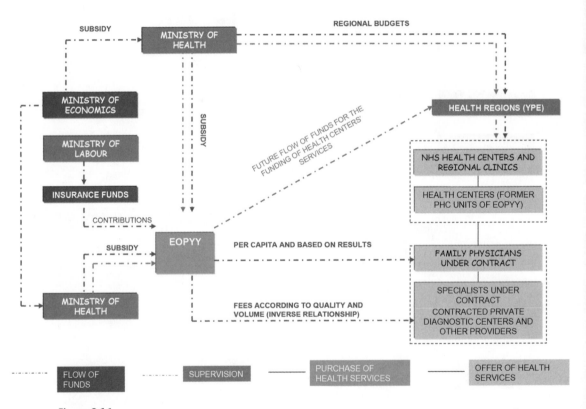

Figure 9.16
Proposed primary health care structure
Source: Scientific Committee for Primary Health Care (2013)

The primary care structures would have the role of family doctor at their core. Family doctors would not necessarily act as gatekeepers, at least in principle, as they could enrich their role with implementation of initiatives related to overall health promotion and disease prevention, patient education, and home care. Their reimbursement scheme would be based on per capita compensation (capitation) and extra payment by results, namely based on the management of multiple comorbidities and a patient case mix, among others. Moreover, to address the seasonality in the demand for PHC services across the country, any unmet need would be covered through contracts with private sector providers. Other initiatives would include the integration of additional health care professionals in primary care, particularly in home care, the development of an action plan for chronic diseases, and the maintenance of personal health records linked to an electronic patient file.

Such recommendations would require 15 percent of total public health expenditure to be invested in primary health care, while the economic crisis had already suppressed that budget to less than 8 percent. This fiscal "limitation" caused a suboptimal legislative intervention (the introduction of PEDY, the Primary National Health Network—Law 4238/2014), which attempted to follow the structural recommendations detailed above but failed due to staff shortages resulting from resignations by medical doctors following the introduction of compulsory and exclusive full-time employment in the NHS. At the same time private sector contractors operate under a restrictive policy of upper ceilings in the sense that they are not allowed to provide services to more insurees once they have reached their target.

These developments raised barriers to accessing care, necessitating higher out-of-pocket payments in a country where household income is shrinking. The obvious implication of such health care barriers is that the health of the population will be adversely affected.

9.7   Restructuring Pharmaceutical Policy

Alongside reforms in financing and contracting mechanisms, and in primary health care, significant reforms need to be undertaken in the pharmaceutical sector. We focus on five priority areas: (1) pricing of prescription pharmaceuticals, (2) reimbursement of prescription pharmaceuticals, (3) prescribing, evidence-based medicine (EBM) and dispensing, (4) cost-sharing, and (5) the need for a National Pharmaceutical Policy (NPP), that is, an overarching strategy that links the policy objectives in the pharmaceutical sector and the stakeholders (institutional as well as other) that are responsible for their implementation. The NPP's objective should be to transform the role of the national authorities and the Ministry of Health from being overly interventionist to being enablers and stewards. In the sections that follow, we discuss the type of interventions that we feel are needed and how an NPP can bring these together under the stewardship of the Ministry of Health.

9.7.1 Pricing of Prescription Pharmaceuticals

While a robust intellectual property framework is necessary to stimulate innovation, it is also important to protect payers and insurers from excessive pharmaceutical expenditures that could limit patient access to life-saving medicines. Various pricing policies have been devised to curb the monopoly power granted to pharmaceutical manufacturers. These policies aim to contain costs in pharmaceutical markets and to improve prescribing quality and efficiency. The current system of pricing prescription pharmaceuticals in Greece is based on external price referencing (EPR) principles, whereby prices from all EU member states are sought with a view to arriving at the average of the three lowest in the basket. The data sources and the actual prices arrived at are often disputed by manufacturers. Moreover the capacity at the National Drugs Agency (EOF) to fulfill the pricing task is low, and it appears there may be lack of appropriate infrastructure, skills, and expertise to provide the necessary support to EOF.

The national pricing policy for pharmaceuticals should provide an effective, stable, predictable, transparent, administratively simple, and sustainable environment for pharmaceutical products, both prescription-only medicines (POM) and medicines available over the counter (OTC). It should also reflect national priorities for and achieve an optimal mix between health and industrial policy objectives placing greater emphasis on the former. Moreover it is important to consider the type and strength of regulation applied to different markets (in-patent, off-patent, over-the-counter, etc.), as well as the operational link between the pricing process and the reimbursement process. In this regard the priorities for reform are twofold: first, to reform and refine the pricing committee that decides on prices of prescription pharmaceuticals, and second, to reform the current system of pricing in order to make it simpler and stable, as well as introduce amendments in legislation for certain types of medicines for which no explicit provisions currently exist.

The role of the pricing committee is of a technical nature, and appropriately it requires the committee to have sufficient capacity, appropriate levels of expertise, and other support to oversee the pricing of all new pharmaceuticals in Greece in a timely fashion and in strict adherence to EU legislation. The framework within which it operates is set in legislation. It will be necessary to better define its terms of reference, membership and composition, governance rules, accountability lines, and support by a secretariat, including in-house capacity for data search, database maintenance, and relations with stakeholders. It will be important to define process, avoid overlap of responsibilities (e.g., between EOF and the MoH) and adhere to the Transparency Directive. Whereas a pricing committee currently exists at the Ministry of Health, supported by technical expertise at EOF, it is important that it acts as a body that is independent of current governmental structures or political intervention in order to increase its effectiveness, responsiveness and efficiency. It will require a sufficient number of technical experts with the competencies necessary to conduct background checks on prices of pharmaceuticals in other European countries that Greece uses as a reference, to maintain databases, and, ultimately, to arrive at prices for all new products entering the domestic market that are not subject to challenges, while at the same time fulfilling its role in a timely fashion and in a credible and robust way.

Another responsibility will be to re-calibrate the current external price referencing (EPR) system used for originator, in-patent pharmaceuticals. Currently pricing is based on the EPR system, which takes prices from a basket comprising all EU member states and settles on the three lowest in the basket. Re-pricing takes place twice annually, but it is almost never the case that pricing bulletins are issued on time. The reasons are that the basket is very large, the frequency of re-pricing is higher than the current system can take, and the number of technical experts to perform these tasks is limited. As a result significant delays in issuing pricing bulletins are common, mistakes made on list prices are frequent, and subsequent political intervention to resolve disputes has become the norm. A simplification of the pricing methodology used, for example, by including only EZ countries in the basket of reference countries would most certainly simplify an already complex administrative process if combined with the increase in the number of experts who can perform these duties. A further item that needs to be considered is to include a legislation processes for the pricing of orphan drugs (for rare diseases) and of biotechnologically derived generics (known as biosimilars), for which little is mentioned in current legislation. Both could result in savings for the Greek taxpayer, as it is not uncommon for expensive products—particularly orphans—to be imported directly, though at a price that is among the highest in Europe.

By intervening in the structure of the pricing committee and by tidying up the legislative gaps identified above, pharmaceuticals may attain a more stable and sustainable pricing environment over the longer term. Simpler and more transparent pricing methodologies for all pharmaceutical products need to be defined that serve the national interest and the overall objectives identified by the Greek government.

9.7.2 Payment (Reimbursement) of Prescription Pharmaceuticals by the Public System

Pharmaceutical reimbursement is an important component of pharmaceutical policy. It requires decisions as to which pharmaceutical products should be covered by the health care system, at what price and with what co-payments, subject to a number of criteria. The notion of reimbursement assumes the existence of a third-party payer or insurer. Currently pharmaceutical reimbursement is under the responsibility of the EOPYY in terms of payments; however, it is the MoH that decides on policy priorities. Unavoidably, there are often disagreements between the two institutions. In itself, this situation is not uncommon based on experiences from other EU member states, particularly former interventionist states in Eastern Europe; nevertheless, the aim should be that reimbursement become the responsibility of the payer, with the MoH having oversight and participation in the process. As such, EOPYY should be given more opportunity initially, and ultimately to take the lead, in setting priorities in reimbursement policy without the direct intervention by the Ministry of Health. The MoH would participate in the decision-making process and offer support to EOPYY in fulfilling this important mission.

Pharmaceutical reimbursement policy in Greece suffers from a number of problems, which, in turn render it incapable of capitalizing on opportunities to optimize the cost of prescription pharmaceuticals it covers. A multitude of committees operate just to assess the extent to which different pharmaceutical products can be reimbursed. Thus pharmaceuticals that are or are not reimbursed through the EOPYY are listed in four formularies (table 9.1), for which a good many committees exist that decide on their

Table 9.1
Current formularies and respective decision-making committees

Formulary	Description of formulary	Decision-making committee
Positive list	Drugs reimbursed by the EOPYY	Positive and Negative List Committee
Negative list	Drugs that can be prescribed but are not reimbursed by the EOPYY (e.g., lifestyle drugs)	Positive and Negative List Committee
OTC list	Products that can be sold only in pharmacies	
High-cost pharmaceutical products list	Drugs that are considered high cost (with a price exceeding €200) and reimbursed by the EOPYY	High-Cost Pharmaceutical Products Committee

inclusion into these formularies. There is an overdependence on administrative rules to determine the "value" of new products, and consequently their reimbursement by the system, rather than a process determining what is value from a Greek perspective. There is no use of modern tools and policy measures, such as health technology assessment (HTA), price-volume agreements, or risk-sharing agreements. This effectively has meant that reimbursement prices are not negotiated with manufacturers on any basis, whether based on clinical benefit assessment or clinical cost-effectiveness. Instead, reimbursement prices are based on list prices (as determined by EPR) minus a compulsory discount (rebate) that is levied on list prices. As the country operates on the basis of a fixed budget (currently at 2 billion euros per annum), excesses on this budget are returned by pharmaceutical companies to the state, retrospectively, a process which is called "the clawback." The discount and the clawback are blunt tools; they can distort performance and hide inefficiencies in certain parts of the market. For example, they penalize manufacturers with a small number of products and high sales as compared with manufacturers with a large number of products and lower sales proportionately. It is also questionable whether they deliver sufficient pecuniary benefits to the insurer. For example, a process of negotiation for a new and expensive pharmaceutical product could achieve a discount between 20 and 60 percent for the insurer.

As a result of the above, whereas list prices in Greece are among the lowest in the European Union, reimbursed prices are among the highest, particularly for high-cost pharmaceuticals, because of the inability of the system to capitalize on negotiation and/or risk-sharing agreements or to pursue an aggressive generics policy in the way that other EU countries do. It is evident that Greece is one of the few countries in the European Union without a robust reimbursement policy enabling health insurance to negotiate reimbursement prices with manufacturers. It is therefore critical that this practice be addressed as a matter of urgency. Improvements can be achieved in a number of areas.

One possible improvement would be to merge the various committees under the umbrella of single committee operating according to one governance structure, with clear rules around responsibility and accountability. This committee would have oversight over the entire pharmaceutical reimbursement policy and would have representation from all institutional stakeholders. Leaving the entire process open to competitive forces is out of the question as reimbursement committees are there to observe national standards and safeguard the public interest. This committee could be served by a number of subcommittees with expertise in particular areas, such as drug coverage subcommittee, appeals subcommittee, alongside a secretariat that would provide support to the committee's overall activities. Specifically, the Negotiation Committee, which was set up in 2014, could be a catalyst by negotiating on behalf of EOPYY reimbursement prices based on a number criteria, including therapeutic benefit, budget impact, and cost effectiveness, while in that process ensuring that it leverages expertise from key stakeholders such as EOF and, of course, EOPYY (figure 9.17). The Negotiation Committee needs to be independent and have an appropriate headcount that is employed on a full-time basis. Only then will it be able to achieve positive results. The Negotiation Committee could be sourced by some of the savings it secures in pricing new pharmaceuticals on behalf of the health care system it serves.

A second main area of improvement concerns the criteria for reimbursement (clinical, economic, fiscal, etc.) and the weight each of these would carry in coverage decisions. Clear rules and criteria for the classification of pharmaceuticals are needed, and in particular, there is a specific need for the use of clinical and cost-effectiveness criteria in decision-making in order to improve the efficiency of the system. Considering that a large number of expensive products are becoming available, the processes of assessing their clinical benefit need to be updated based on the likely impact these products would have on Greek patients. All EU member states have clear and transparent rules and processes of value assessment that stretch beyond administrative criteria. For example, and in regard to new cancer therapies, it is important for the Greek health care system to have a view on whether 2 or 3 months of additional survival offered is

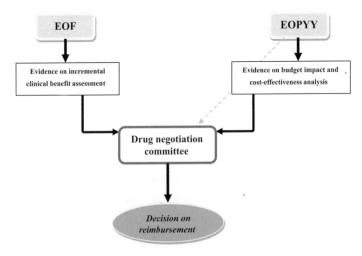

Figure 9.17
Role of the Negotiation Committee in determining reimbursement
Source: Kanavos (2013)

worthwhile for its inclusion into the country's positive list (clinical benefit criterion), rather than including it because the same treatment is on the reimbursement list of another 10 EU member states (administrative criterion). If there is a decision to include it in the positive list, a secondary question would be "at what price" and whether the list price derived from the process of EPR is reflective of the new therapy's value, or whether a discount should be negotiated.

A third main area of improvement would be to adopt a more aggressive generic policy. Nearly three-quarters of all pharmaceutical products that are prescribed in any EU country, including Greece, at any point in time, are off-patent, therefore generic equivalents should be available; these can be both branded and unbranded. The reason that all insurers encourage an aggressive generic policy is because of the significant savings they deliver on pharmaceutical budgets, as the cost of an off-patent product is significantly below that of an on-patent originator. Two conditions are crucial in this respect: first, a high generic penetration (at the expense of the originator) and, second, a low price compared with the originator price at the time of patent expiry. Countries with well-developed generic policies, such as the United Kingdom, Denmark, Germany, the Netherlands, Sweden, and increasingly Spain and France, have achieved rates of generic product penetration in excess of 65 percent on the total number of prescriptions written. The price declines are huge and range from a 60 to 95 percent discount off the originator price at patent expiry (Kanavos 2014). In Greece, however, the figures have been disappointing, with generic pharmaceuticals not exceeding 24 percent of volume and prices of these generics being much higher than in their EU counterparts and ranging between 20 and 40 percent off the originator price. Clearly, there is significant scope for improvement on both fronts.

A fourth main area of improvement concerns tendering processes and, in particular, ensuring that clear rules for these exist as well as an effective and timely appeals process. The notion of timeliness seems to be a very weak point in the Greek system. Often (legislative) intervention is needed in order to expedite the tendering process. Tenders, particularly for off-patent pharmaceuticals, can be instrumental if targeted carefully, in order to achieve much needed price reductions particularly in high-volume markets, such as statins (for the treatment of dyslipidaemia) and ACE inhibitors (for the treatment of hypertension), when prices appear to be sticky downward. Many other European countries have implemented tenders even for pharmaceuticals consumed outside hospitals (e.g., Netherlands, Denmark, Sweden, Germany, Cyprus), and can offer significant insights on how improvements to the current system in Greece can be made.

A fifth area relates to capacity-building on tools such as health technology assessment (HTA), negotiations, price-volume agreements, among others, in order to support the reimbursement process. Negotiations based on clinical- and cost-effectiveness will enhance the efficiency of the system, particularly with regards to new technologies and the prices at which they should become available to the Greek health care system. This requires not only recruiting individuals with the appropriate skill set but an entire HTA process to be set up. Greece is one of the few remaining EU member states (together with Bulgaria and Romania), where there is no HTA process in place. Additionally there is an urgent need to understand and implement new tools that help in negotiations such as price-volume agreements and risk-sharing agreements among others. These priorities for reform suggest that much is needed to take place in Greek reimbursement policy in order for the system to be able to make rational decisions based on available evidence, increase its ability to contain costs and realize savings, and improve efficiency and cost-effectiveness.

9.7.3 Using Evidence-Based Medicine (EBM) in Prescribing and Dispensing

Influencing the prescribing behavior of physicians is crucial in achieving key policy objectives, notably quality, rational drug use, and cost containment. This can be achieved with a combination of financial (e.g., budgets linked to positive incentives or penalties; pay-for-performance rewards, where physicians are rewarded if they meet certain quality targets) and non-financial incentives (clinical practice guidelines, prior authorization, ability to prescribe electronically, among others), none of which existed in Greece prior to the financial crisis. Between 2009 and 2013 a number of positive interventions were introduced, often seen as an imposition to a body of unwilling clinicians. First, a prescribing system based on the molecular (chemical) name of the product (known as INN prescribing),[6] rather than its branded name, was introduced in November 2012 but was further modified in May 2015 to enable prescribing by brand name. Prescribing based on the molecular name of the pharmaceutical product is known to be cost-effective, whereby multiple versions of the same molecule (compound) are available, known as generics. Second, in an attempt to control overprescribing, prescribing targets associated with penalties if exceeded were introduced for individual physicians, which did have an effect, but would need to be further fine-tuned. And, third, a competent electronic prescribing system was introduced in 2011 enabling prescribing to be monitored for the first time in history.

Despite these positive steps, much remains to be done and a number of priority areas seem to be necessary in this component of pharmaceutical policy. Indeed it is critical that policy makers commit themselves to improve system efficiency and exercise better control over costs.

First, it would be important to return to the *status quo ante* concerning generic prescribing (Rx-INN). Allowing physicians to prescribe by brand name particularly in areas where significant savings can be achieved is a regression, not a progression, and is likely to inflate costs for the health care system. Evidence from most EU countries that have implemented mandatory INN prescribing suggests that only through perseverance over a long period of time can this measure deliver savings. In the case of Greece, the political leadership has succumbed to the pressure of the medical profession on this front.

Second, as we outlined above, there is significant need for the development of universal prescribing protocols that will guide prescribing behavior according to treatment pathways (1st-, 2nd-, 3rd-line therapy, etc.) and sub-indications or subpopulations. Such prescribing guidelines or "treatment pathways" could be based on both clinical and economic criteria and could be developed relatively easily by adopting/adjusting the guidelines of other countries with advanced experience (e.g., Sweden, United Kingdom, Germany), in collaboration with domestic medical societies. Both financial and nonfinancial incentives could be considered in this regard, subject to their applicability/feasibility in the Greek context.

Third, there is need for incentives and restraints within the system; these can be both financial and non-financial. For example, it is believed that the current system could change in a direction that non-adherence to prescribing protocols could be linked to non-reimbursement, perhaps through the establishment of contracts between EOPYY and health care providers. Prior authorization (PA), according to which physicians need to gain approval from EOPYY in order to prescribe a particular type of medication, could be a promising tool, among others, for controlling prescribing behavior in specific diagnoses.

Fourth, in assessing the performance of prescribing physicians using the available evidence, EOPYY should closely monitor and audit the available data (i.e., volume and type of prescriptions) through the e-prescribing system; as an additional measure, the details of the prescribing physician outliers could be disseminated among health care professionals or even become publicly available to create peer pressure. Finally, an effective link should exist within the e-prescribing system (if not already in place) that connects the prescriber, pharmacist, and insurer enabling the latter to monitor and audit the performance of physicians and pharmacists in real time.

Fifth, over the longer term, it may be necessary to implement changes in the educational curricula of medical students in order to change prescribing practices as well as enable clinicians manage clinical practices and resources in general. General practitioner (GP) training as an area of focus could be established in medical schools. Although such change is likely to take place in the longer term, discussion on its feasibility and implementation is a short-term issue.

The outcome of this area of specialty will be, among others, the development of clear and explicit evidence-based prescribing protocols, giving rise to an efficient prescribing system whereby physicians prescribe based on clinical cost-effectiveness. Linking protocols to prescribing will be important as this will provide further steering to prescribing physicians. Considering future changes to educational curricula of medical students could also be explored.

9.7.4   Cost-Sharing Policy

Based on the 2013 increases in cost-sharing, EOPYY has now three tiers of co-payment at 0, 10, and 25 percent. The percentage of co-payment is based at either the level of disease category (e.g., 10 percent for specific chronic diseases, 0 percent for life-threatening diseases) or at the individual product level (e.g., 0 percent for "high-cost" pharmaceuticals). Additional co-payments apply through the reference pricing system. As a result the *effective* co-payment for prescription pharmaceuticals exceeds 20 percent. Additionally a clear and transparent cost-sharing policy is missing with different rules and clauses prevailing in different parts of the system.

An explicit, robust, uniform, and clear policy based on clinical, age, and, potentially, socioeconomic criteria for linking different disease categories or individual molecules with different cost-sharing tiers should be selected. Household panel data could be used for setting the exact co-payment levels of the different tiers. Exemptions should also be applied based on additional criteria categories; such categories could relate to both socioeconomic (e.g., age) and burden of disease (e.g., severity, prevalence) criteria.

The result of work under this priority area will be to advise on efficient and fair cost-sharing system, based on epidemiological/clinical, age and, potentially, socioeconomic criteria that will have no adverse effects on affordability and access to medicines.

9.7.5   A Coherent National Pharmaceutical Policy (NPP)

Although there is a consensus among all major stakeholders on what the national overall objectives of pharmaceutical policy should include (e.g., quality of care, universal access, efficiency, health gain maximization), there is currently no explicit policy summarizing the principles and rationale of NPP. It is also important to clarify and set out the role(s) and responsibilities of the key stakeholders in Greece's NPP and to measure performance at different levels by benchmarking against specific targets. As is obvious, there is much need for a policy that outlines Greece's NPP objectives and the roles that the different stakeholders would have in its implementation.

The major stakeholders have long agreed that such a blueprint or "vision" document should be produced, and should explicitly outline the principles and objectives of NPP. The issues addressed would include pricing and reimbursement with regard to quality, safety, and efficacy of pharmaceuticals, but also and more broadly, the prescribing and rational use of pharmaceuticals (e.g., acceptance of generics by prescribers and society, appropriate use of medicines, e-prescribing), dispensing (e.g., generic substitution), cost-sharing options, and national priorities pertaining to clinical use (e.g., antibiotics and importance of antimicrobial resistance), economic/fiscal considerations (e.g., budget impact), or industrial policy (encouraging inward investment in clinical trials; supporting domestic pharmaceutical manufacturing). These broad policy objectives would need to be included in an NPP document according to their relative importance.

The key objectives of a Greek NPP and the role of key stakeholders in it would, of course, be the product of a consensus process. It is to be hoped that the institution of a NPP will signal a re-balancing in Greek health care decision-making. The MoH's role would then be that of a steward in the health care system rather than a clearinghouse of stakeholder interests and pursuits. The MoH will have an oversight and strategic role rather than be a consolidator of rent-seeking behavior and clientelistic relations.

9.8   Challenges for the Near Term

As this chapter shows, the health care system in Greece has many structural gaps and inefficiencies that have been reinforced over decades of lack of attention to pressing fiscal targets. The path to making the changes we propose is far from being straightforward and smooth. Though there is wide consensus as to the causes of the system's collapse and on future options, rational decision-making and proper planning, via a current status analysis, must be followed and include an evaluation of available and feasible alternatives and the evidence-based selection of the most appropriate interventions.

Are Greece's present circumstances amenable to such a planning process? Probably not. The establishment of EOPYY as a national health insurance fund is a striking example of the case at hand—it has so far failed to foresee the readily visible impact of fiscal derailment on health insurance contributions. As a result the newly established organization was called upon to adjust to a budget reduced by 40 percent compared with the *status quo ante*. Accordingly, pharmaceutical policy—as all health policy—has been restricted to one-sided, successive supply-side controls (focus on price freezes or reductions), that have contributed decisively to the rationalization of total pharmaceutical expenditure but not to a sustainable policy tool. This is particularly disheartening because there is plenty of international experience with best practice alternatives that Greece could benefit from, including, among others, the introduction of price-volume and risk-sharing agreements, the implementation of diagnostic and therapeutic protocols as prescribing controls, and incentives to physicians to adjust to global (or regional) budgets and to safeguard quality.

Yet there is hope. The successive reforms of the health sector in Greece over the last few years, especially the establishment of EOPYY as a health insurance monopsony, suggest that the health system is capable of meeting the acceptable norms. Of course, it takes more than an institutional framework to change the way the health care system works: in Greece a sustainable reform would require constant monitoring of system inputs and re-prioritization of interventions, in line with evidence-based needs and practices.

In effect, in Greece we need a shift in mentality and much greater emphasis on data monitoring and reporting, be it data on expenditure, patient registries, or health interventions. This change is the single most important component of health system reform, even more so than any short-term adjustment to fiscal targets, in order to guarantee its long-term financial sustainability and its ability to deliver quality services to the population at an affordable cost.

Notes

1. We are grateful to Anna-Maria Fontrier for excellent research assistance. We are also grateful to the editors for excellent feedback and their support in completing this chapter.

2. In 2011 the costs of social security funds for health services approached 11 billion euros, while the corresponding budget for 2014 does not exceed 6 billion euros.

3. A country's ability to set prices for pharmaceuticals at low enough levels is limited: if price differentials with other countries are significant enough, there may be shortages of pharmaceuticals in low-price countries, and pharmaceutical firms may be reluctant to introduce new therapies in those countries.

4. Legislation to that end was passed in 2004 (Law 3235/2004). However, it was never implemented.

5. WHO recommends managing mental health and addiction treatment in primary care to integrate services, encourage recovery, and re-integration, and also to prevent isolating the professional medical staff and stigmatizing the patient.

6. Otherwise known as prescribed by an international nonproprietary name (Rx-INN).

References

Athanasakis, K., K. Souliotis, E. J. Kyriopoulos, E. Loukidou, P. Kritikou, and J. Kyriopoulos. 2011. Inequalities in access to cancer treatment: An analysis of cross-regional patient mobility in Greece. *Supportive Care in Cancer* 3: 455–66.

Center for Health Services Management and Evaluation. 2012. *System of health accounts* (in Greek). Working paper. University of Athens.

Center for Health Services Research. 2010. *Waste in the public health system* (in Greek). Working paper. University of Athens.

Economou, C. 2010. Greece: Health system review. *Health Systems in Transition* 12 (7): 1–180.

Economou, M., M. Madianos, L. E. Peppou, A. Patelakis, and C. N. Stefanis. 2013. Major depression in the era of economic crisis: A replication of a cross-sectional study across Greece. *Journal of Affective Disorders* 145: 308–14.

Economou, M., M. Madianos, C. Theleritis, L. E. Peppou, and C. N. Stefanis. 2011. Increased suicidality amid economic crisis in Greece. *Lancet* 378:1459.

European Commission. 2010. *Special Eurobarometer Number 315: Social Climate.* Brussels: EC.

European Commission. 2013. *Report on Health Inequalities in the European Union.* Brussels: EC.

Ferrario, A. and P. Kanavos. 2014. Dealing with uncertainty and high prices of new medicines: A comparative analysis of the use of managed entry agreements in Belgium, England, the Netherlands and Sweden. *Social Science and Medicine* 124: 39–47.

Hellenic Statistical Authority. 2013. *Household Budget Survey 2012.* ELSTAT: Piraeus. http://stat.gov .pl/en/topics/living-conditions/living-conditions/household-budget-survey-in-2012,2,7.html.

Kanavos, P. 2013. *Action Plan for the Greek Pharmaceutical Sector.* Brussels: Task Force for Greece.

Kanavos, P. 2014. Measuring performance in off-patent drug markets: A methodological framework and empirical evidence from twelve EU member states. *Health Policy* 118 (2): 229–41.

Kanavos, P., and A.-M. Fontrier. 2017. *The Future of Health Technology Assessment: Evidence from Europe and an Agenda for Policy Action.* Brussels: European Observatory, forthcoming.

Kanavos, P., S. Vandoros, R. Irwin, E. Nicod, and M. Casson, and the Medical Technology Research Group—LSE Health, and London School of Economics and Political Science. 2011. *Differences in Costs of and Access to Pharmaceutical Products in the EU.* Brussels: European Parliament.

Kanavos, P., et al. 2010. *Euro-Observer* 10 (4), December.

Kentikelenis, A., M. Karanikolos, I. Papanicolas, S. Basu, M. McKee, and D. Stuckler. 2011. Health effects of financial crisis: Omens of a Greek tragedy. *Lancet* 378: 1457–58.

Kentikelenis, A., M. Karanikolos, A. Reeves, M. McKee, and D. Stuckler. 2014. Greece's health crisis: From austerity to denialism. *Lancet* 383: 748–53.

Liaropoulos, L. 2014. National Health Insurance: A proposal for reform. In M. Masourakis and C. Gkortsos (eds.), *Competitiveness and Growth: Policy Proposals* (in Greek), 415–33. Athens: Hellenic Bank Association.

Liaropoulos, L., O. Siskou, D. Kaitelidou, M. Theodorou, and T. Katostaras. 2008. Informal payments in public hospital in Greece. *Health Policy (Amsterdam)* 87 (1): 72–81.

Lionis, C., E. Symvoulakis, A. Markaki, C. Vardavas, M. Papadakaki, N. Daniilidou, K. Souliotis, and J. Kyriopoulos. 2009. Integrated primary health care in Greece, a missing issue in the current health policy agenda: A systematic review. *International Journal of Integrated Care* 30 (9): 1–14.

Minas, M., N. Koukosias, E. Zintzaras, K. Kostikas, and K. I. Gourgoulianis. 2010. Prevalence of chronic diseases and morbidity in primary health care in central Greece: An epidemiological study. *BMC Health Services Research* 10: 252.

National School of Public Health. 2012. Health and social insurance. Working paper. September.

OECD. 2010. Product Market Regulation Database. http://www.oecd.org/economy/pmr/.

OECD. 2012. *Economic Outlook*. Paris: OECD.

OECD. 2013. *Health Data*. Paris: OECD.

Panagiotakos, D. B., C. Pitsavos, C. Chrysohoou, I. Skoumas, and C. Stefanadis. 2009. Prevalence and five-year incidence (2001–2006) of cardiovascular disease risk factors in a Greek sample: The ATTICA study. *Hellenic Journal of Cardiology* 50 (5): 388–95.

Primary Health Care Advisory Committee (PHCAC). 2010. Improving access and delivery of primary health care services in New Brunswick. Discussion paper. http://www.gnb.ca/0053/phc/pdf/2011/PrimaryHealthCareDiscussionPaper.pdf.

Psaltopoulou, T., P. Orfanos, A. Naska, D. Lenas, D. Trichopoulos, and A. Trichopoulou. 2004. Prevalence, awareness, treatment and control of hypertension in a general population sample of 26,913 adults in the Greek EPIC study. *International Journal of Epidemiology* 33 (6): 1345–52.

Schneider, F. 2011. Size and development of the shadow economy of 31 European and 5 other OECD Countries from 2003 to 2012: Some new facts. *ShadEcEurope* 31: 1–7.

Scientific Committee for Primary Health Care. 2013. *A Proposal for Reform* (in Greek). Athens.

Souliotis, K. 2011. Proposed framework for distribution of health funds. Cited in the *Proposal of the Independent Expert Committee for the Reform of the Country's National Health Services* (in Greek). Athens.

Souliotis, K. 2013a. *Public Health Insurance in Greece: From the Unthinkable to the Obvious* (in Greek). Athens: Papazisis.

Souliotis, K. 2013b. Increasing health spending whilst widening inequalities: The Greek "paradox" in health policy. In C. Economou (ed.), *Health, Society and Economy: Unequal Relations— Welfare Gaps* (in Greek), 125–44. Athens: Alexandria.

Souliotis, K. 2014. A proposal for the reform of healthcare financing in Greece. Presentation. *Forum for Health Economics and Policy* (October): 11.

Souliotis, K., and M. Chrysakis. 2007. Economic and social inequalities in health and health services, pp 45 – 72. In K. Souliotis (ed.), *Health Policy and Economics: Strategic Planning—Organization and Management—Economic Function—Sectoral Policies* (in Greek). Athens: Papazisis.

Souliotis, K., C. Golna, Y. Tountas, O. Siskou, D. Kaitelidou, and L. Liaropoulos. 2015. Informal payments in the Greek health sector amid the financial crisis: Old habits die last .... *European Journal of Health Economics* 17 (2): 159–70.

Souliotis, K., and C. Lionis. 2004. Creating an integrated health care system in Greece: A primary care perspective. *Journal of Medical Systems* 29 (2): 187–96.

Souliotis, K., V. Mantzana, and M. Papageorgiou. 2013. Transforming public servants' health care organization in Greece through the implementation of an electronic referral project. *Value in Health Regional Issues* 2 (2): 312–18.

Souliotis, K., M. Papageorgiou, A. Politi, D. Ioakeimidis, and P. Sidiropoulos. 2014. Barriers to accessing biologic treatment for rheumatoid arthritis in Greece: The unseen impact of the fiscal crisis—the Health Outcomes Patient Environment (HOPE) study. *Rheumatology International* 34 (1): 25–33.

Starfield, B. 1998. *Primary Care: Balancing Health Needs, Services and Technology*. New York: Oxford University Press.

Tountas, Y., N. Oikonomou, G. Pallikarona, C. Dimitrakaki, C. Tzavara, K. Souliotis, A. Mariolis, E. Pappa, N. Kontodimopoulos, and D. Niakas. 2011. Sociodemographic and socioeconomic determinants of health services utilization in Greece: The Hellas Health I study. *Health Services Management Research* 24 (1): 8–18.

WHO. 2009. Guidelines for the Psychosocially Assisted Pharmacological Treatment of Opioid Dependence. http://www.who.int/substance_abuse/activities/treatment_opioid_dependence/en/index.html.

WHO. 2013. *World Health Statistics*. Geneva: WHO.

WHO. 2015. *Health Financing for Universal Coverage*. Accessed on 30 July 30, 2015. http://www.who.int/health_financing/universal_coverage_definition/en/.

World Economic Forum. 2013. *The Global Competitiveness Report 2012–2013*. Cologny, Switzerland: WEF.

V   Taxation and Public Transfers

10 Tax and Welfare Reform in Greece[1]

Maria Flevotomou, Michael Haliassos, Christos Kotsogiannis, and Costas Meghir

10.1 Introduction

The tax system is an integral part of all modern economies, and together with the array of welfare benefits and transfers, it has a dual role. First, it raises revenue for the various expenditures of the state, such as on health, education, security, defense, and infrastructure. Second, it redistributes income and insures individuals against adverse shocks to their income or employment status. Raising tax revenues can distort the decisions of individuals and firms, affecting their incentives to work and save. For example, income taxes typically reduce individuals' incentives to work, while value-added taxes (VAT) on consumption strengthen their incentives to save. Distortions can also be generated because different types of income or consumption are taxed differently. For example, income from labor is often taxed at a higher rate than income from capital gains, and consumption of certain goods such as housing is often taxed at a lower rate than consumption of other goods. This can create inequities between individuals with the same level of income, and can bias incentives toward certain types of activities. A well-designed tax system should minimize these distortions while also raising the necessary revenues and satisfying society's requirements for equity and social insurance.

There are two main reasons for reforming Greece's tax system. First, the current system is overly complicated and generates many undesirable distortions. Second, there is no systematic welfare system to support the low-paid and the unemployed. A robust welfare system should be a key complement to the market-liberalization reforms advocated in other chapters of this book (e.g., chapter 4 on product markets and chapter 6 on the labor market). For example, liberalizing the labor market by giving firms more flexibility to reduce their labor force when demand for their products is low will make it more attractive for firms to invest and create jobs. Because of the higher flexibility, however, jobs may become less secure and hence workers may be receiving less insurance from firms. The state should provide the missing insurance through the welfare system.

A welfare system should be designed and evaluated jointly with the tax system. This is because means-tested welfare benefits and transfers are, in effect, negative taxes, and what matters are total taxes paid to the state whether they are positive (transfers to the state) or negative (transfers from the state). Total taxes determine the effective marginal tax rate for each level of income, namely the amount of extra disposable income resulting from an extra euro earned. A welfare system can distort decisions in similar ways that a tax system does. For example, suppose that the state offers a benefit to poor individuals, which is withdrawn, euro for euro, when extra income is earned from work. This implies a tax rate of 100 percent for individuals with low incomes, removing incentives to work and leading potentially to welfare dependency. Thus a well-intentioned insurance system may "trap" individuals into poverty.

Distortions can be caused not only by the tax and welfare system but also by its ineffective administration—a consideration of particular importance for Greece. For example, substantial tax evasion shifts the burden of taxation to individuals who are unable or unwilling to evade taxes or have clearly visible forms of income or assets (e.g., a salary in a formal enterprise or real estate) and away from individuals who are self-employed. It also skews economic activity away from large formal firms and from activities that require visible investment and are likely to be associated with growth and new technologies. To reduce opportunities for tax evasion, the tax system should be easy to administer and enforce. It should also be neutral with respect to the sources of income to avoid creating perverse incentives and opening up tax avoidance loopholes.

Our main goal in this chapter is to develop and articulate possible tax and welfare systems for Greece that are significantly simpler and more transparent than the system in place as of 2013, while generating the same overall revenue. We compute revenue through a microsimulation exercise that uses data on the consumption and income of a large cross section of Greek households. We also compute the distributional impacts of each system that we consider, and we analyze the effect that each system has on work incentives. Mainly due to data and time constraints, our analysis is more limited in scope than desired. In particular, the analysis does not consider the taxation of corporations, of capital gains, and of real estate ("property"), with the exception of the emergency property tax established in 2011 and paid via electricity bills. Although our analysis is not fully comprehensive, we believe that the evidence-based approach that we adopt should form the basis for a fruitful discussion on tax and welfare reform in Greece. Such a discussion should take an integrated view of all tax and welfare payments, as we do in this chapter, rather than considering various types of taxes and transfers separately, as is typically the case in practice.

Designing and implementing tax and welfare policies is never easy, but in the midst of a sovereign debt crisis that constrains spending and exhausts the liquid resources of households and firms alike, it is exceptionally difficult. While fiscal consolidation may trump all other considerations under such conditions, Greece needs to focus on designing a tax and welfare system that will support long-term growth and generate an appropriate amount of redistribution and social insurance. In practice, this may mean that some of the measures are implemented gradually.

We show that it is possible to design a tax and welfare system that, once implemented, raises the same revenue as the 2013 system, offers a superior level of social insurance, and is much simpler. The way to achieve these goals is not unique: one could go for a system that is stronger on work incentives but necessarily provides less redistribution to the poor, or alternatively one could choose a system that is weaker on incentives but redistributes more.

As an overall reform program takes hold, and with many disincentives embedded in the current tax system removed, the formal sector will be reinforced, improving compliance. The simplicity and transparency of the systems we propose, together with the broadening of the tax base, will help in that direction.

The structure of this chapter is as follows: Section 10.2 sketches the main features of Greece's current tax system. Section 10.3 presents some key components of a modern tax and welfare system, with particular emphasis on three tax instruments: consumption, income, and real estate taxes. The relative merits of the three instruments are analyzed, including the types of behavior that they induce and the extent to which they are conducive to tax evasion. Section 10.4 evaluates three alternative integrated tax and welfare systems. The parameters of the three systems are chosen so that revenue is the same as under the current system, and the systems are compared in terms of their distributional impacts and their effects on incentives. The exercise is performed using individual household data drawn from the Greek Household Budget Survey of 2012 in combination with the tax and benefit microsimulation model EUROMOD. Section 10.5 compares the three systems, and section 10.6 summarizes and concludes.

10.2   Taxes in Greece

10.2.1   Overview and International Comparisons

The overall tax burden (measured as the ratio of tax revenues to GDP) has fluctuated in recent years, and so have some of its individual components. Table 10.1 shows Greece's

Table 10.1

Total taxes (including social security contributions) as a percentage of GDP, 2000 to 2015

Year	Greece	EU27 (arithmetic average)
2000	34.9	39.8
2001	33.4	39.1
2002	34.6	38.5
2003	33.0	38.6
2004	32.1	38.5
2005	33.5	38.7
2006	32.7	39.1
2007	33.5	39.2
2008	33.7	39.0
2009	32.9	38.4
2010	34.2	38.5
2011	36.1	38.9
2012	38.5	39.6
2013	38.3	40.0
2014	39.0	40.0(p)
2015	39.6	40.0(p)

Source: Eurostat (online data code: gov_10a_taxag); (p) provisional

overall tax burden during the period 2000 to 2015, and compares it to the tax burden in the 27 countries of the European Union. The overall tax burden in Greece declined from 34.9 percent in 2000 to 32.9 percent in 2009, but rose gradually during the crisis and reached 39.6 percent in 2015. It has been consistently below the EU27 average, which was approximately 40 percent during the period 2000 to 2015, although the gap essentially disappeared by 2015.

During the period 2000 to 2015 indirect taxes have played a more prominent role than direct taxes in Greece's public finances. According to EUROSTAT national accounts data, revenues from indirect taxes accounted for 16.2 percent of GDP in 2015 (an increase of 3 percentage points from 2000), whereas revenues from direct taxes accounted for 9.4 percent of GDP in 2015 (a fall of 0.4 percentage points from 2000). In 2015, revenue from direct taxes in Greece was 3.6 percentage points below the EU27 average (9.4 percent as compared to 13.0 percent).

Looking at EUROSTAT derived tax indicators by economic function, the implicit tax rate on labor (defined as the wedge between take-home pay and the cost of labor to the firms) in Greece during the period 2000 to 2011 was consistently below the EU27 average. It stood at around 34.0 percent between 2000 and 2003, and displayed a downward trend since then, reaching 30.9 percent in 2011. It increased significantly in 2012, to 38 percent, 1.8 percentage points above the EU27 average. The tax rate on consumption in Greece was 3.6 percentage points lower than the EU27 weighted average in 2012 (16.2 percent as compared to 19.8 percent, and Greece ranked 26th). This reflects broad application of reduced VAT rates relative to the standard rate.

While the overall tax burden and the implicit tax rate on labor in Greece are similar to other EU countries (and quite high and a problem in themselves), the main problems with the Greek tax system concern the choice of tax base, the complexity (which we demonstrate below), and the low level of tax revenue collection efficiency, as reflected by the significant tax evasion. The causes of tax evasion and its remedies are not the topic of this chapter. However, some of the recommendations made in the chapter, such as the drastic simplification of the system as well as a shift toward consumption taxation may contribute to reducing tax evasion.

10.2.2 The Greek Tax System

The tax system described in this section is the one in place as of 2013. We refer to it as the "current" tax system, although some changes have occurred in subsequent years.

Income Taxes The current income tax system taken as a whole is exceedingly complicated. Over and above a relatively standard income tax system lies an edifice of taxes such as social contributions, taxes on self-employment, and real estate taxes, which make it hard to understand the marginal tax rate that one faces. We now give a brief overview of the current system before we propose and evaluate simpler alternatives. A more detailed description of the personal income tax system for years 2012 and 2013 can be found in appendix C, available at https://mitpress.mit.edu/books/beyond-austerity.

The current income tax code (ITC) is based on the provisions of Law 4110/2013 as enacted in Law 4172/2013 and modified by Law 4223/2013. The ITC defines four broad categories of taxable income: (1) income from employment and pensions, (2) income from business activities (business activities, agricultural activities, freelancers' income, etc.), (3) capital income (interest, dividends, royalties, real estate rental income, etc.), and (4) capital gains income (sale of real estate property, shares, bonds, etc.). The notion of total income is abandoned, with each of the above income categories receiving a different tax treatment as described below.

For income from employment and pensions, the tax schedule depicted in table 10A.3 in appendix C applies. There are three tax brackets, with tax rates ranging from 22 to 42 percent. There is also a tax credit and a small number of exemptions.

The tax credit is for 2,100 euros, and this is given in full to employees and pensioners with annual income of up to 21,000 euros. If the tax liability is below the tax credit of 2,100 euro, then the tax due is zero. For income exceeding 21,000 euros, the tax credit is reduced by 100 euros per 1,000 euros of income above 21,000 euros. Hence the tax credit is 2,100 euros for an individual earning 21,000 euros and zero (= 2,100 − 21 ∗ 100) for an individual earning 42,000 euros. For income exceeding 42,000 euros, the tax credit is zero. Taxpayers are eligible for the tax credit provided that they have collected receipts amounting to 10 percent of their income (up to a maximum amount of 10,500 euros). Alternatively, a tax rate of 22 percent is applied to the shortfall of collected relative to required receipts.

For income from business activities, the applicable tax schedules are presented in table 10A.4 (appendix C). Income earned by professionals and entrepreneurs is taxed at 26 percent up to 50,000 euros and at 33 percent for the excess. A special proviso for start-up businesses applies for the first three years where the marginal tax rate is reduced to 13 percent if gross income is below 10,000 euros. Finally, the new ITC envisaged the taxation of actual profits from agricultural activities at 13 percent (no tax brackets) but this provision was first applied for profits realized in 2014.[2]

Income from business activities is also subject to an occupational tax. The occupational tax stands at 1,000 euros per year for business companies based in towns with over 20,000 residents; 800 euros for business companies based in areas with less than 20,000 residents; 650 euros for the self-employed and sole proprietorships; and 500 euros for those who work as freelancers that issue receipts for services rendered but are effectively wage earners.

For capital income, dividends are taxed at[3] 10 percent, interest at[4] 15 percent and royalties at 20 percent, all at source. Real estate rental income is subject to 10 percent tax up to 12,000 euros and 33 percent for the excess.[5]

The ITC introduces a general rule of taxation at source at 15 percent on capital gains of individuals,[6] replacing a series of special provisions. The capital gains tax levied on property-selling owners is also set to 15 percent. The realized capital gain is deflated based on certain age coefficients, which range from 0.60 to 0.90. The law grants an exemption for capital gains up to 25,000 euros generated from the transfer of a single property that has been held for at least five years. However, individuals who have transferred more than one property in the same five-year period cannot benefit from this exemption. Further the new regime does not apply to capital gains earned by individuals who are commercially engaged in buying and selling or building real estate.

Social Contributions   Both employees and employers pay contributions to social insurance. The main social insurance fund for employees in the private sector is IKA. In 2013, employee contributions were 16.5 percent for white-collar workers and 19.95 percent for blue-collar workers. The corresponding contributions by employers were 27.46 percent and 29.61 percent. Employee contributions are withheld by the employer. The contributions are paid up to a defined maximum monthly wage. The monthly ceiling since January 1, 2013, is 5,543.55 euros.

VAT and Excise Duties   The value added tax is an indirect tax and we often refer to it under the category of consumption taxation. VAT rates have been subject to increases since 2010. The standard rate was raised to 23 percent (up from 19 percent in 2009). The reduced rate—applicable to goods such as fresh food products, some pharmaceuticals and electricity, certain professional services, transport of passengers, and (nonexempt) services by doctors and dentists—was raised to 13 percent in January 2011 (up from 9 percent in 2009). A 6.5 percent rate (previously 4.5 percent and then 5.5 percent) applies to hotel accommodation services, newspapers, periodicals, books, medicines, and vaccines for human medicine. Specific services such as those of lawyers, artists, bailiffs, and also the provision of hospital and medical care services by private entities that were exempted are subject to VAT since July 2010. For the region of the Dodecanese, the Cyclades, and Eastern Aegean islands the rates above are reduced by 30 percent. Excise duties are levied on mineral oils, gasoline, tobacco, alcohol, beer, and wine. Excises on electricity—with the exception of that produced by renewable resources—were introduced in early 2010.

Wealth and Transaction Taxes   In 2010 the special real estate fare (ETAK) was replaced by the large properties tax (FAP). Properties of large value are subject to an annual tax levied at progressive rates ranging from 0.2 to 1 percent. After the reform of July 2011 the exemption threshold for large properties was reduced from 400,000 to 200,000 euros. The highest marginal rate applies to properties valued by the government (cadastral values) above 800,000 euros, while cadastral values below 200,000 euros are tax exempt. Until 2012 real estate with a taxable value exceeding 5 million euros was taxed at 2 percent for the part of value in excess. A real estate transfer tax is in place as well, at rates of 8 percent for the first 20,000 euros and 10 percent for the part of value in excess.

Corporate Taxes   Greece has been cutting the statutory corporate income taxation rate from a high of 40 percent in 2000. Law 3943/2011 set a rate of 20 percent and abolished the distinction between distributed and undistributed profits which was introduced only a year earlier by Law 3842/2010 to apply to profits earned as of January 1, 2011. Law 4110/2013, enacted in January 2013, increased the tax rate to 26 percent from 20 percent. This increase was accompanied by a reduction of the withholding tax rate on profit distributions—approved as of January 1, 2014—from 25 to 10 percent for both dividend distributions and profit capitalizations. The 10 percent tax exhausts any further tax liability. Law 4110/2013 also brought significant changes to the tax regime of partnerships, civil law societies, civil law partnerships, and joint ventures that maintain double-entry accounting books. The tax treatment of those entities became aligned with that of corporations, which meant that the entire amount of their net profits became taxable at the level of the entity (i.e., taxation at the level of the entrepreneur was abolished) and the rate was fixed at 26 percent.

Entities with single-entry books are subject to tax at 26 percent for taxable income up to 50,000 euros and at 33 percent for the excess. A 25 percent rate is applied to partnerships for the proportion corresponding to the legal entity, whereas for the part relating to partners who are individuals the rate is 20 percent. An additional tax of 3 percent is levied on gross income derived from immovable property. This additional tax cannot exceed the tax calculated on the company's income. Companies are subject to real estate taxes, while local taxes are not significant. There is no group taxation; that is, all entities are taxed separately. In general, tax losses may be carried forward for five years. No tax loss carrybacks are allowed. Expenses are deductible only if they are incurred for the purpose of earning income.

10.3   Components of a Modern Tax and Welfare System

As noted in section 10.1, a tax and welfare system should raise the necessary revenue, redistribute income to poorer individuals, provide adequate social insurance, and correct market failures, while also being simple and transparent and minimizing undesirable distortions. In sections 10.3.1 to 10.3.4 we discuss four key components of a tax and welfare system: consumption taxes, income taxes, welfare benefits and social insurance, and real estate taxes. These are distinguished by the tax base: for consumption taxes individual spending forms the base, for income taxes individual earnings and other income form the base, and real estate taxes are based on values of real estate. By combining these three components with a well-designed welfare system, one can design a system that achieves the revenue and redistributive goals required, with minimal distortions.

A modern tax system includes many other taxes such as inheritance taxes, corporation taxes, and payroll taxes. In principle, all these elements of the tax system should be reformed in conjunction with each other. For example, one could consider abolishing payroll taxes and shifting everything to income or consumption tax. This would further simplify the system and make it easier to regulate the desired level of progressivity. Of course, wages would adjust to this change in the medium run, but the change may still have desirable effects, such as reducing informality and tax evasion. In this chapter we do not discuss such more radical reforms, if anything because we do not have the data to simulate the resulting effects.

10.3.1 Consumption Taxes

Consumption taxes refer to systems of taxation whose tax base is the consumption expenditure of individuals, as opposed to their income. In other words, taxes are calculated on the basis of how much people spend rather than on how much they receive in income. There are at least two general ways of implementing a consumption tax.

The first approach is well known and consists of VAT or sales taxes at the point where individuals purchase goods. This has been implemented in various ways, including using different rates on various commodities and exempting others. Indeed there are theoretical justifications for treating different goods differently. However, in practice, the differences and exemptions are based on ad hoc rules that have little or no connection with the theoretical reasons for rates that differ across commodities. The simplest form of VAT or sales taxes is a uniform tax on all consumption goods, including imputed (or actual) housing rents. As we discuss below VAT has a number of advantages particularly in improving enforcement.

The second approach to consumption taxation looks more like a traditional income tax system, with a difference: it deducts net saving from income and taxes the rest. Progressive tax rates are perfectly feasible within this context. Deductible savings may include additional deposits in bank accounts, additional investments in shares and property, and the like. Income includes earnings and redemptions from investments, including withdrawals from bank accounts and sale of real estate and shares. For the purposes of compliance this requires monitoring changes in savings. For example, bank withdrawals or divesting from shares will be treated as income while any savings, such as buying a house or shares, will be deducted from income. With modern technology linking bank and brokerage accounts to the tax authorities, all movements can be easily monitored, as is the case in Norway, for example. Any funds moved abroad, outside the jurisdiction of the Greek state, would be taxed as if they constituted expenditure with an equivalent deduction (not exceeding the tax paid on exit) upon repatriation to Greece. This system in effect taxes all income over the life cycle but defers taxation until consumption takes place. Income from all sources and all types of assets, including dividends, capital gains, salary, self-employment income, and imputed rents are taken into account and treated in exactly the same way with no privileged sources of income. In implementing such a system, the law would define qualifying investments that can be considered savings vehicles.

Both forms of consumption taxation (VAT/sales taxes and deductibility of savings from taxable income) have been implemented in practice to varying degrees. VAT is a legal requirement in the European Union and sales taxes are prevalent in many countries in the world, including the United States. Private pension funds, where individuals can invest before-tax income (i.e., deducted from income for tax purposes) is a step toward consumption taxation because it allows deductions for certain types of income: invested income is exempt from tax, but withdrawals are taxed (e.g., as retirement income). In the United Kingdom there was a time during the labor government of Blair and Brown where there was no limit to how much could be invested in such accounts, effectively implementing a system such as the one described above with the difference that the invested income could only be used after a particular age of retirement.

There are a number of advantages that make consumption taxation attractive relative to income taxation. Because the tax base is extended to all sources of income, it is not possible to avoid taxes by changing the source of income (e.g., from income to capital gains or from salaries to dividends), and hence individuals with different sources of income are treated equally, independently of how they obtain their income. People with different timing of income over the life cycle are also treated equally, and there are stronger incentives to save for periods with low income such as retirement, particularly when the tax system is progressive. On the negative side, consumption taxation does not allow perfect smoothing of taxes because people are taxed more heavily in periods of increased consumption, such as when they have children. We look at these points more in detail in what follows.

Consider first the incentives to save. Suppose that while working the marginal tax rate of an individual is 40 percent because she earns a high income. Suppose her retirement savings lead to a lower income with a marginal tax rate of 20 percent. Then saving while working will allow her to avoid the 40 percent rate and only incur a 20 percent rate later in life, when retired—if consumption is postponed until then. In addition the invested amount benefits from tax-free returns.

The fact that consumption taxation occurs at the point where expenditure takes place also implies that this system preserves the principle of horizontal equity (individuals with equal incomes should be treated equally): individuals who receive the same total life cycle income but spread differently over time are taxed in the same way. This contrasts with progressive income taxation where higher incomes are taxed at higher rates: individuals who receive their life cycle income concentrated over just a few years are treated very differently to those who receive the same amount but spread uniformly over their working lifetime. Consider, for example, two individuals who receive the same total income but one receives it in equal amounts while another receives all of it early in life. Then, with a nonlinear income taxation system where the marginal tax rate increases with the level of income, the second individual pays more tax. This is avoided with consumption taxation because the individual can defer tax until she consumes her income.

An additional important advantage of consumption taxation relative to income taxation is that it makes it easy to treat the various sources of income (salary, dividends, capital gains, self-employment income, etc.) in the same way, without causing unnecessary distortions to investment decisions. This is simply because what is taxed is consumption, regardless of the source of income funding it. On the contrary, income tax codes around the world, and more to the point in Greece, include complicated provisions and varying tax rates for different sources of income, leading to huge opportunities for tax avoidance and unequal treatment of similar individuals. There is no theoretical reason why the income tax code could not treat all sources of income in the same manner. Yet, in practice, this is difficult. For instance, capital gains tax in an income tax system can be highly distortionary because gains are taxed upon realization. Thus, as gains accumulate, individuals get locked into an asset and may make inefficient decisions refraining from readjusting their portfolios to avoid paying a large tax bill. While it would make sense to tax net gains on an accrual basis, this can cause important liquidity problems and difficulties with valuation of such gains. With consumption taxation, the tax will be imposed when capital is used for consumption, leading to a less distortionary tax system in a relatively simple way. Moreover an income tax system may be more open to pressure from vested interests to allow for exemptions or discounts for various sources of income such as capital gains; testimony to this is the complex tax code in the United States, which treats dividend income, long-term capital gains, short-term capital gains, residential property, and salaries all in a different and arbitrary way. Arguably VAT is also open to lobbying that lead to various distortions in the rates but not if it is legislated as a uniform tax rate system.

Consider now the taxation of housing. The key point is that housing offers a flow of consumption services and is a vehicle for saving. Thus, under the logic of consumption taxation, the use of housing services should be taxed, whether the house is owned or rented: actual or imputed rent (i.e., the rent that an owner occupier would have paid had she be renting her residence) would be considered income that is also consumed and hence should be taxed. Moving house in itself would instead not generate a tax liability (e.g., through capital gains tax) but borrowing against the capital of the house, thus releasing capital for consumption purposes, would. Of course, this broadening of the tax base need not imply higher taxation overall but taxes spread evenly over many different activities at much lower rates than currently—in other words, a reduction in distortions that treats some goods and services in a privileged fashion.

VAT and sales taxes are the easiest to implement and most common forms of consumption taxation. They require no tax declaration and from the point of view of the consumer they are obviously simple. A system of VAT and sales taxes may also be preferable for compliance purposes, as we discuss below, both because of its cascade nature (explained later) and because it does not have to rely on income tax declarations. This can allow the authorities to focus on enforcing VAT, in a system with a diminished role for income taxes as we explore later in this chapter. To implement a relatively neutral consumption tax, VAT would be expanded to all consumption goods and services. To the extent that the base could be broadened further to include housing rents and imputed housing rents for owners-occupiers as discussed above, the rate could be lower (see section 10.3.4).[7] In other words, the broader the base, the lower the rate of taxation for everyone. However, this would rely on designing a flexible and fair property valuation system, based on market developments rather than political influence.

One property of a VAT system is that it taxes visitors who consume in Greece as well as locals. This has the advantage to broaden the tax base, but it can make tourism less competitive by effectively increasing prices. Despite our general view that exemptions should be avoided for the purposes of simplicity and transparency, given the importance of tourism for Greece and given the hugely competitive environment of this industry, it may be necessary to reduce the impact of an increased VAT on tourism by exempting foreign residents from paying VAT on hotel bills and more generally on package deals, to the extent allowed by EU laws. This is consistent with the idea that exports are not subject to VAT.

To the extent that broadening the base allows reductions in other taxes, such as payroll taxes, including employer social security contributions, a shift toward consumption taxation may be beneficial for exports at least in the short run: a reduction in such taxes reduces labor costs and therefore the price of exports, while an increase in VAT (which applies to both imported goods and domestic production) will increase the relative domestic consumer price of imports.[8] In the longer run one may expect prices to adjust eliminating this advantage on exports. As usual, policy will have to balance these various considerations.

In the simulations in section 10.4, we can only take into account VAT on standard consumption items as recorded in household budget surveys. Taking into account the effect of broadening the base is important for assessing both the incentive and redistributive aspects of the tax system. However, we are limited in our simulations by the fact that we do not observe enough information to simulate the implications of including imputed rents, although we do include actual rents.

Finally, one of the difficulties that arise when we implement consumption taxation based on a VAT system with a much more limited role for income taxation is the destination nature of VAT taxation: that is, a good is taxed where it is consumed. Income tax, in contrast, is mainly origin based. If individuals earn in Greece during their peak earning years but plan to retire in a low tax jurisdiction later in life, a VAT or residence based consumption tax would allow them to avoid taxes. One way of dealing with this is to charge VAT on all private export of funds and refund VAT on import of funds (up to the amount originally charged).[9] Perhaps this is not the only or the optimal solution, but tax avoidance of this nature is a problem that will have to be addressed in systems of consumption taxation.

A frequent concern about VAT is that it is not progressive in the sense that lower income people pay the same proportion of their income in taxes as the wealthier. In theory, this may be the case particularly if the tax system has no issues of compliance. In practice, VAT has the advantage that all individuals irrespective of income declarations have to pay it. Moreover VAT is blind on the provenance of income. Even those who manage to earn income in what are now tax preferred ways (e.g., capital gains), or indeed those who evade income taxation, have to pay it.[10] So, in practice, VAT may be more progressive than the current income tax system as applied in Greece. Nevertheless, progressivity of a tax and welfare system needs to be judged in its entirety. Thus in a system we discuss below, while a large proportion of revenue is raised through VAT, by introducing welfare support for lower incomes and a higher income tax rate for those in the top 25 percent of the income distribution, the system becomes progressive, with a minimum of complexity.

More generally, as we discussed above, consumption taxation does not have to be exclusively based on VAT, but it can be structured with variable progressive tax rates by applying taxes to income after deducting savings. Thus, in principle, there is nothing to stop the design of a system that is based primarily on consumption taxation and achieves a required level of progressivity.

10.3.2 Income Taxes

Income taxation has been around at least since the nineteenth century. It is a relatively straightforward way of raising revenue, and at the same time regulating the progressivity of the system by applying higher marginal tax rates on higher levels of income.[11] In practice, a key issue with income taxation is defining the tax base and the treatment of the various sources of income such as salaries, capital gains, and dividends. Moreover income can accrue domestically and abroad. Part of the difficulty and complexity of the system consists of deciding whether to tax all forms of income and if so at what rates. For example, in many economies, capital gains are taxed at lower rates and so are dividends. In Greece there was no capital gains tax on real estate until recently and none on shares. Moreover taxation of bank interest is at a low rate, disconnected from the actual tax on other sources of income. Such differential treatment of income sources distorts incentives, allows tax avoidance, and creates unfairness by treating otherwise similar individuals in different ways. It also undermines attempts at redistribution by placing the burden more heavily on those obtaining income from labor rather than capital.

As explained in section 10.3.1, consumption taxation solves many of these problems seamlessly. Yet it is, in principle, possible to extend the base for income taxation and to treat all types of income in the same way. Income from capital gains, dividends, salary, and the like, would be treated in exactly the same way. Ideally capital gains should be taxed on accrual—not realization, to avoid the distortionary lock-in effect resulting from the accumulation of large tax liabilities as a result of gains over time. However, this may be complicated to implement because it causes liquidity problems for individuals, which demonstrates the difficulties of designing an income tax based system. Finally, keeping the logic of broadening the tax base to all sources of income, imputed rents from owner-occupied property, net of mortgage interest, should also count as an income source and be taxed.

If the overall tax burden were kept constant, broadening the tax base would lead to lower income tax rates for all. In this context it would be crucial to include worldwide income into the tax base, since many investments may take place abroad. While investing abroad should be a free choice, it should not be incentivized by the tax system to the detriment of local investment.

10.3.3   Welfare Benefits and Social Insurance

A well-functioning economy requires a well-defined social insurance/welfare benefit system with clear rules and preferably designed to work well alongside the tax system. This provides insurance against low income, ensuring a decent standard of living throughout society. A social insurance/welfare benefit system can also play an extremely important role in an economy with liberalized labor markets: it ensures that people who are in transition between jobs or have low income can obtain adequate financial assistance; it ensures that markets work better, removing any need for the government to interfere with pay and employment decisions of firms.

The welfare system should provide a safety-net support to individuals, without an excessive reduction in work incentives and without causing poverty traps, a situation where the return to work is so low that individuals cannot work themselves out of poverty. Some welfare programs may offer high levels of support, which is then removed euro for euro of extra income accruing to the individual. This removes any incentive to work because increased earnings do not lead to increased take-home pay. As a consequence individuals can become detached from the labor market and depend on welfare even over the long term. On the other hand it is not easy to design systems that offer reasonable protection and at the same time do not distort incentives too much.

One important approach to this issue is to link welfare receipt to work. An example is the earned income tax credit (EITC) used in the United States and a variant thereof applied in the United Kingdom.[12] In the US system individuals receive a benefit (tax credit) that equals a fixed percentage of earnings (40 percent) and starts from the first dollar of income earned until the credit reaches its maximum. The benefit then stays flat at that maximum as earnings continue to rise, until a phase-out threshold. From that point onward the benefit falls by 30 percent with each additional dollar of income until it is phased out completely. Effectively the tax benefit is a subsidy to work for low-paid individuals, but it also generates a tax, higher up the income distribution, over the range of incomes where the benefit is withdrawn. By linking welfare benefits to work the distortion of incentives is much reduced.

The tax credit partially solves the problem of low pay, and indeed it does allow the government to eliminate minimum wages that burden companies, at least provided that the low-skill labor market is competitive, as we discuss later. However, this system does nothing to protect those who are out of work. It may thus be desirable to offer a minimum income guarantee that covers those out of work as well. We discuss this later when we propose possible designs of the tax and welfare system.

In the July 2015 budget George Osborne, the Conservative Chancellor of the Exchequer, moved to abolish tax credits in the United Kingdom and instead raise minimum wages. What is the logic of this move and how does it compare to what we are suggesting here, which is precisely the opposite: tax credits and no minimum wages? If the labor market for low-skill workers is competitive, then minimum wages, if set too high, may reduce employment and create an underclass of very low-skill workers who can never work. They will be forever dependent on welfare benefits without having any attachment to the labor market. With competition, the labor market ensures that workers are paid whatever they are really worth in production, and this is true whatever the subsidy offered. This is one side of the story. However, if the low-skill labor market is not sufficiently competitive, then firms will tend to underpay workers as much as they can afford to without losing their workforce either to unemployment or to other competitors. In this context in-work benefits, such as our suggested EITC, offers an opportunity to firms to shift some of their payroll to government. Consider the following example. Suppose a worker is willing to work for 8 euros per hour but is actually capable of producing 15 euros per hour.[13] Suppose that there is only one firm in existence: then it will pay her 8 euros and keep the difference. In the presence of competition and full information about alternative jobs, however, her wage will eventually be bid up to her full worth, namely 15 euros. Now suppose the government subsidizes the worker by 2 euros per hour (EITC). In the absence of competition the firm will now pay her 6 euros and make 9 euro profit, two of which will be paid by the taxpayer. However, in a perfectly competitive environment her wage will be bid up to 15 euros (because this is what she is worth in production) and she will get to keep the 2 euros in addition. Reality is probably somewhere between the two extremes. If we are to accept some empirical evidence (e.g., Lise, Meghir, and Robin 2015) low-skill labor markets are quite competitive, at least in the United States. The usual response is to combine some reasonable minimum wage with an EITC program. The principle that motivates our approach is to let the private sector compete and produce with as little interference as reasonable and let social policy, insurance and redistribution be carried out by the state. The new British approach is motivated, in part by the belief that the low-skill labor market is not sufficiently competitive and in part by a willingness to reduce the size of the state as well as the opportunities for fraud by falsely claiming benefits. These are serious considerations that cannot be discounted easily.

10.3.4   Real Estate Taxes

We conclude our general discussion of taxation methods with taxes on real estate or "immovable property."[14] These have played an increasing role in Greece, particularly at the time of crisis. Real estate plays two roles: it is an asset that one can invest in, but it also creates a flow of services directly (by living in a house or using a building for production). Taxes on real estate take two forms: taxing the value of the asset and taxing the value of the housing services. Obviously the two are related, since the value of the service is capitalized in the value of the asset.

One might believe that taxing real estate is not subject to the usual distortions that taxation entails because supply remains unaffected. This is true, however, only for a tax that is imposed on all land, is blind to the type of use (residential, industrial, agricultural, nothing), and does not tax the structure itself, since then the tax cannot affect the supply of land. If instead the tax relates to existing structures and their value, it will reduce investment activities and new construction because the returns are lowered—a distortion. On the positive side, real-estate taxes are harder to evade (an issue of considerable relevance for Greece), and perhaps less distortionary than other forms of taxation.[15]

There is a strong argument for taxing residential real estate when it is owner occupied, as when it is used as an investment, such as a rental property. By taxing owner-occupiers, we broaden the tax base, and we remove the distortion between owning and renting a house. For example, there is no rational reason why we should treat differently an individual who occupies his or her own residence versus one who is renting out a property, and then renting some other residence for herself. Thus, whether under a consumption tax system or an income tax system, imputed rents should be taxed unless new structures are taxed upon their first sale. By broadening the tax base in this way, we also improve the progressivity of the tax system, since wealthier individuals tend to be owner-occupiers and own higher value property. (The former source of progressivity is less pronounced in Greece, where real estate ownership is observed from about the 20th percentile of the wealth distribution.)

The logic of taxing the property value is less clear. By taxing rents or imputed rents, we are imposing a tax on the service; if the capital is also taxed, this amounts to double taxation and has little rationale. However, the capital *gain* should be taxed.

In implementing real estate taxation, two issues should be addressed carefully. First, there needs to be an independent authority to decide on valuations to prevent the government from arbitrarily raising revenue by increasing valuations at will, or indeed to avoid following the market when valuations decline, as in Greece over the recent crisis. Second, it is crucial to take into account the liquidity buffers that households possess in order to absorb demands on their resources.[16]

To see this clearly, consider figure 10.1 where we show assets and debts for households ranked by their level of net wealth,[17] from the poorest on the left to the richest on the right. It shows levels of real assets (e.g., houses and plots of land) and of financial assets (e.g., bank accounts or mutual funds), as well as levels of uncollateralized loans

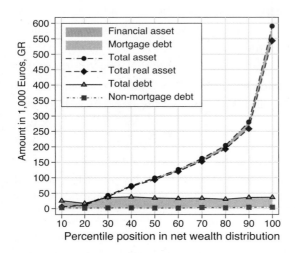

Figure 10.1

Assets and debt by percentile of net wealth

Source: ECB, Household Finance and Consumption Survey, 1st wave

(e.g., consumer loans and credit card debt), and collateralized loans (e.g., mortgages) across the entire distribution.[18] While it is clear that ownership is relevant for all the wealth distribution and, as expected, its value increases with wealth, it is also a fact that liquid assets are a tiny proportion of total assets. Hence emergency measures can cause hardship for households, particularly in the midst of a crisis, where they cannot borrow, and are likely to have reduced housing market values and possibilities to sell. A well-designed and implemented system would be announced well in advance, allowing households to plan for the upcoming liability. Moreover measures should be put in place for deferring taxes (with interest) when individuals have low income (but high housing wealth). For example, accumulated taxes could be payable upon sale of the house or upon death.

In conclusion, real estate taxation should be part of any well-designed tax system. However, methods of valuation and liquidity issues have to be part of a careful and effective design; otherwise, there is a danger of acting rashly and killing the golden goose, by harming the housing market and causing hardship.

10.3.5   Noncompliance

We think of noncompliance as relating both to illegal tax evasion and to complicated forms of legal tax avoidance that were unintended by the legislators and are often due to complex and nontransparent design.

Noncompliance is not simply an issue of revenue shortfall for the government, but it can have additional negative effects. It shifts the tax burden to individuals with sources of income that are easy to monitor, such as salaries in the formal sector. As a result it tends to implicitly subsidize activities that are easy to hide, typically low value-added jobs involving little investment and low technological input. This harms the growth prospects of an economy. Shifting the burden to one part of society through tax evasion also causes a decline in trust in the system and a strong and well-justified feeling of lack of fairness. This undermines social institutions and strengthens the tendency to evade, making tax evasion an "acceptable" activity. It is important to understand that evasion is not only an issue of effective enforcement but is also affected by the design of the tax system and the incentives it creates, as well as by the overall trust in government institutions. An approach that relies purely on enforcement is doomed to failure unless the potential problems arising from the design of the tax system are also addressed.

It is well documented that the Greek income tax system is fraught with problems of collection and evasion. At the start of the crisis Greece collected about 7 percent of GDP in income taxes, while other EU countries with similar tax systems would collect about twice as much (see Meghir, Vayanos, and Vettas 2010). Income underreporting in 2009 was estimated at around 12 percent resulting in a shortfall in personal income tax receipts of 30 percent (Leventi et al. 2013b). Noncompliance of VAT (the main consumption tax in Greece) is also high; estimated to be around 30 percent of VAT in 2006, and significantly higher than the average 9 percent in the EU15 (Keen 2013).

A relevant policy question therefore is whether it is easier to improve compliance when the tax system becomes more reliant on VAT relative to income taxes. We believe that a VAT system may be more conducive to compliance than an income tax system, for reasons that we explain below.

Because VAT is payable where consumption takes place, it is independent of where and how the underlying income was produced. This eliminates a major component of avoidance and evasion, present under income taxation. And, of course, even tax evaders have to consume and hence an increased role for VAT will ensure tax collections take place from those who would otherwise evade.

An additional reason why a VAT system may be more conducive to compliance lies in its cascade nature. Specifically, consider a chain of intermediate producers, leading all the way to the final retail point. Suppose that VAT is 20 percent. The first producer, say, a mine extracting iron ore, sells the product to a steel mill. The mine sells at 120, of which 20 is VAT, and passes the 20 on to the government. The steel mill produces sheets of steel and sells them to manufacturers downstream. The mill sells at 240, of which 40 is VAT. It retains the 20 to cover what it paid to the mine upstream and passes on the remaining 20 to the government. The next producer in line uses the processed steel to make tools and sells them for 300 in retail. The VAT included in that amount is 50. The producer retains 40 to cover what it paid to the steel mill, and passes on 10 to the government. At every level of the production chain, the incentive to evade VAT is low because it is just a tax on value added (i.e., the VAT charged downstream minus the VAT paid upstream). If a producer in the middle of the chain does not charge VAT so as to charge a lower price, then that producer will effectively be unable to reclaim the VAT that it paid to the upstream producer. However, suppose the producer does evade. Then with modern IT, it should be relatively easy to find the evader by matching invoices along the supply chain. If these invoices are matched, then it is harder to evade at any point and the entire chain would need to coordinate so as to evade VAT effectively (see Pomeranz 2015). Enforcement and audits can concentrate at the retail point.

Another source of noncompliance relates to VAT refunds, known as "carousel" fraud: fraudulent businesses could exploit the way VAT is treated within the European Union where the movement of goods between member states is VAT free.

The high level of VAT evasion in Greece may be due to the nature of the Greek economy and not to the VAT system itself. Specifically, the argument made above about the muted incentives to evade and the associated coordination difficulties only works for relatively sophisticated products that involve a chain of suppliers—for example, manufacturing. It works less well when all is produced and sold by, say, a small family-held service company with little or no relationship with upstream suppliers. This is likewise the case of builders, electricians, and small tourist companies. Moreover there is a genuinely large gain to be shared with the consumer if, by not charging VAT, the consumer pays a lower price and the retailer can avoid declaring the sale for income tax purposes, an issue of central importance for small family-run enterprises.[19] This implies that VAT noncompliance is linked to two features: first, the central importance of the income tax system and its low compliance level, and second, the prevalence of small family-run businesses in the service sector. The former is a policy option that we discuss below, while the second is promoted by the huge amount of regulations and bureaucracy of running a business, including labor market regulations among many others. Addressing these issues is likely to reduce noncompliance in important ways.

Further progress in addressing noncompliance can be made through nontax policies, such as reducing cash transactions, which are more difficult to trace, and offering prizes to consumers through lotteries for obtaining and submitting receipts for their taxable transactions. Experience from countries that have implemented the latter policy suggests that this is an effective and low-cost way of reducing noncompliance (Fabbri and Hemels 2013; Fabbri 2013).

In terms of income tax enforcement, there needs to be a combination of a random based and risk assessment based audit system. A number of countries draw tax returns to be audited randomly, with the probability depending on features of the return such as the amounts declared, large changes, and other discrepancies. To avoid corruption, there should be as little direct contact as possible between those being audited and the tax auditors. Increased use of online payment systems for taxes does reduce contact between taxpayers and tax authorities and contribute in this direction.

The systems we suggest in this chapter include welfare programs that depend on the income individuals make. These programs are thus open to manipulation via income misreporting. Welfare fraud is an issue in many countries, including those with advanced and well-functioning tax collection and audit systems such as in the United Kingdom and the United States; hence it is likely even more so to be a problem in Greece. While Greece is repairing its broken tax collection system, the welfare system may have to be more restrictive than otherwise desirable. For example, to qualify for the minimum income, one may have to show that they have worked in the formal sector for some prespecified period of time. If they claim not to be working, they would need to show proof of having been laid off. And, to qualify for the tax credits while employed, one must demonstrate employment in formal firms and submit to audits. Of course, even these requirements offer no guarantee that fraud will not take place, but they make it harder, particularly if audits actually take place. And excluding informal workers from the welfare system may have the added advantage of increasing the incentives toward formality, a central issue in Greece. Of course, this will mean a less broad coverage of social insurance.

Without dealing with the problem of income underreporting and fraud, it will be hard to put in place any well-functioning tax and welfare system that can be seen to be fair and that achieves the stated aims of redistribution and insurance efficiently, while raising the required revenue. There needs to be a buildup of trust toward a system that now is seen as completely one-sided. Tax declarations need to be simple, refunds need to take place immediately, and any actions by the tax authorities should be contestable in courts with the capability of making decisions in a few months (not years as is now the case).

10.4   Three Alternative Tax and Welfare Systems

As we demonstrated in section 10.2, the Greek tax code is exceedingly complex. The objective of this section is to propose and evaluate alternative ways of redesigning the tax code. Our proposed alternatives are much simpler and more transparent, and include an integrated welfare system providing support for the poor. We choose the parameters of each alternative tax system so that revenue, before any behavioral response, is the same as under the current system, and we examine in detail the distributional and incentive implications.

Our analysis is data driven, taking into account the actual demographic and income distribution in the population. In this sense we also demonstrate how the tax reform design should be taking place, using accurate data on the population to understand clearly who are the winners and the losers of any reform. A further step from what is achieved here is to take into account the way individual behavior would change when the tax and welfare system is changed. This is beyond the scope of this chapter.

We compare three systems:

A. A system that is based primarily on consumption taxation, and consists of[20] (1) a large increase in the amount of income that remains untaxed, implying that income tax will be paid only by the richest 25 percent of the population; (2) an increase in the rate of VAT and the VAT base (by taxing all goods and services except for imputed rents) to compensate;[21] (3) one income tax bracket beyond the increased nontaxable allowance to improve progressivity and increase revenue collection, (4) a safety net guaranteed minimum income (GMI) and an earned income tax credit (EITC) subsidizing the earnings of low-paid workers. Since a large proportion of revenue is raised through VAT, we term this the VAT based system.

B. A system that allows for three income tax brackets with two positive income tax rates. This too allows for a guaranteed minimum income (GMI) and an earned income tax credit (EITC) for the low paid. VAT is left as it is currently designed, namely with three different rates and some zero-rated goods. We refer to this system as the income tax based system.

C. A flat income tax system. This allows for one uniform income tax rate payable by all individuals on all their income except for a nontaxable universal transfer per individual. Finally the VAT system is left as is currently designed. We refer to this system as the flat tax system.

Each tax system that we present is integrated with a welfare system. The welfare system in each case implies a different work incentive structure and different amounts of redistribution. In all cases we preserve the social security contributions (although we abolish those relating to health). We treat these social security contributions as a saving, although this is probably a strong assumption given the lack of credibility of the Greek social security. Thus we do not consider their incentive or redistributive effects.

In the first two cases we have opted for a joint system of family taxation. Joint taxation is not an obvious choice—if anything, individuals may wish to keep their financial affairs separate even when married. Moreover joint taxation may cause adverse incentives to the secondary earner, who may be facing high marginal rates as a result of high earnings by the other partner. Indeed in the United Kingdom, taxes are assessed individually; in the United States, there is the option of individual taxation, but generally it is advantageous for married couples to file jointly. Joint taxation becomes natural when integrating the tax and the welfare benefit system: It would be difficult to justify paying benefits to one member of a family (who is a low or zero earner) when, say, the spouse is earning a high level of income. Nevertheless, the United Kingdom has a tax system that is individual based, while the welfare system is assessed at the level of the family.

All tax and welfare systems under consideration overall are budget neutral, when we take into account all their components. Thus there is no revenue change induced by any of the tax proposals, assuming that work behavior and compliance patterns remain the same. This is a simplification, since each system is likely to lead to different work and compliance incentives. The neutrality of the proposed reforms means that they can be implemented without implications on the budget. This is particularly important because we are proposing substantial increases in transfers to the lower income individuals, transfers that would otherwise be quite costly. We also consider the implications of the reforms inducing full compliance in personal income tax.

10.4.1   Considerations for Broader Reform and the Need for a Well-Functioning State

The exercise that is presented here is limited by the available data, and is to an extent illustrative of possible directions. The reform program needs to be broader than what we quantify here, and undoubtedly many of the parameters of our illustrative systems will change when additional considerations are taken into account. We next sketch some of these considerations.

First, we believe that imputed rents (net of mortgage interest) should form part of the income of owner-occupiers. Moreover both rents and imputed rents should form part of consumption and consequently should be subject to VAT. This is an important reform that will make the tax system more equitable and neutral with respect to chosen individual patterns of consumption. However, in the simulations that follow imputed rents are not taken into account because of data limitations. When the base is broadened to include imputed rents, this would allow a decrease in the rate of VAT and/or income taxation. In other words, the rates presented here are *too high* relative to what they should be if the tax base is extended by as much as we believe it should. This will have important distributional implications.

Second, we do not deal with capital gains, which are an important source of income at the top of the income distribution.[22] Here again, we suggest that these sources of income be taxed in exactly the same way as all other sources. Indeed we think that capital gains of all assets *including* residential real estate should be taxed as income, although how this should interact with the taxation of imputed rents requires careful consideration. With a pure consumption tax that also taxed rents and imputed rents there should be no capital gains tax, since all sources of income are taxed in the same way when they generate consumption. Our VAT based system would automatically go a long way toward this. With a partial consumption taxation system the capital gains tax needs to be designed carefully to avoid overtaxing assets, since a large part of the gains are taxed through consumption. These are important and complicated design issues that need to be addressed in a complete overhaul of taxation. However, these design issues, as well as the revenue and distributional implications of capital gains, are not taken into account here. Again, it should be stressed that such broadening of the base *is not intended to increase the level of taxation* but to distribute it more equitably and in less distortionary fashion across all sources of income that individuals generate.

Third, we do not deal with noncompliance of VAT, while in income taxation we allow for some adjustments based on past estimates of evasion by occupational group. Noncompliance, including for VAT, is a major issue with both revenue and distributional implications. One might expect that as the economy is reformed and the informal sector shrinks, compliance will be easier to enforce in all forms of taxation. Nevertheless, noncompliance is a major issue. More generally, it is an inescapable fact that implementing an advanced tax and welfare system and avoiding widespread fraud requires a well-functioning state, which is far from reality in Greece. Consequently reforming the tax code cannot be seen as an isolated exercise but as part and parcel of a modernization of the Greek economy and its state machinery. Just moving to a system like what we suggest here without improving compliance would be pointless and prolong the prevailing fraud.

Finally, a comprehensive reform should consider at the same time the other parts of the tax system, including real estate taxes, capital gains taxes, employers' payroll contributions, which are implicitly a tax on labor, and corporate taxes. Only a complete consideration of the entire tax and welfare system can lead to a well-designed code that achieves the trio of redistribution, good incentive structures, and compliance for a given level of revenue.

We next turn to a brief presentation of our methodology and data, followed by a detailed description of each of our systems and their implications for redistribution and incentives. The precise parameters for each system we consider are presented in appendix A.

10.4.2   Tax–Benefit Microsimulation Model (EUROMOD) and Data Description

In our analysis we combine the Greek section of the European microsimulation model EUROMOD[23] with household level data for the Greek Household Budget Survey of 2012 (HBS). The survey data include original incomes, labor market status, and other characteristics of the individuals and households that responded, to which we then apply the tax and benefit rules in place in order to simulate direct taxes, social insurance contributions, entitlements to most welfare benefits, and unemployment insurance. As there are components of the tax and welfare system that cannot be simulated (e.g., retirement pensions), the relevant parameters are read off the data. EUROMOD has been validated both at the micro and the macro levels and has been tested in several applications.[24]

Microsimulation, in general, and EUROMOD, in particular, enable the analyst to simulate the fiscal and distributional effects of changes in taxes and welfare benefits, taking into account the complex ways in which they interact with each other, something that no direct analysis of actual data can do as well. Our model, however, only provides estimates of first-order distributional effects, ignoring, in particular, incentive effects.

The underlying micro data for Greece, drawn from the 2012 Household Budget Survey (HBS), provide information on the income and consumption expenditure of 8,719 individuals in 3,572 households. We simulated the key characteristics of income taxation, housing taxation, VAT, and welfare benefits for the year 2013. While simulations may be imperfect when, for example, tax rules are too complex to be accurately simulated or when eligibility for welfare benefits depends on income in previous years, the level of detail in the HBS dataset allowed us to simulate complex taxation liabilities and benefit eligibility rules with a satisfactory degree of accuracy.

As is standard practice in microsimulation, updating the model to the year of interest involved two separate steps: simulating tax and benefit policies, as applied in 2013; and simulating changes in underlying incomes, from the data year (2012) to the policy year (2013) (see appendix B.1 for details). With respect to housing taxes, we simulate the emergency property tax (introduced in 2011) affecting owners of commercial or residential property in Greece (see appendix B.2 for details).

Microsimulation models typically treat disposable monetary income as the appropriate income concept for studying the distributional impact of tax and benefit policies. Payments in kind may be important, but these are typically not well observed in the data. Although substantial progress has been made toward incorporating nonmonetary components into EUROMOD (Paulus et al. 2010), the relevant module is not available yet. In view of the above, the provision of private and social benefits in kind (e.g., company-provided motor vehicles as well as publicly funded health care, education, care for the elderly, child care, etc.) is ignored in this chapter.

As we noted earlier, income underreporting is significant in Greece. As a consequence our ignoring tax evasion when estimating the distributional impact of a reform would seriously undermine the validity of our results. Following Matsaganis and Leventi (2013b), we introduced rates of underreporting equal to 5 percent for salaries and wages, 35 percent for self-employment earnings, and 80 percent for farming incomes.[25]

Some benefits are not claimed by people eligible for them, either because they consider the amounts to be too small relative to the effort they need to exert to obtain them or because, quite simply, they are misinformed. This is termed non-take-up of benefits. We allowed for non-take-up of two means-tested benefits: social pension, aimed for persons aged over 67 with insufficient contributions for a social insurance pension, and unemployment assistance for older workers, a small-scale program targeted at the long-term unemployed aged over 45 on low income[26]. The social pension was only assigned to people who declared receipt in the original dataset. The non-take-up rates of unemployment assistance were calculated by comparing administrative data on benefit recipients with the number of those eligible as simulated by EUROMOD. Unemployment assistance was then randomly assigned to the appropriate proportion of eligible recipients in 2013.

Before turning to a discussion of the tax reforms, we briefly describe the welfare system that is an integral part of the first two simulated tax reforms.

10.4.3 Earned Income Tax Credits (EITC) and Minimum Income Guarantee

As briefly touched upon earlier, the EITC is a form of wage subsidy (paid by the government), implemented as a negative tax rate on earnings of individuals who work and earn below a particular amount and a corresponding positive tax rate at higher levels of earnings, to make sure eligibility is limited to lower earning individuals. This encourages low-paid/low-skill individuals to seek employment as the benefit is nil for those with no earnings and it increases as earnings increase before being phased out gradually for sufficiently high earnings. Furthermore the EITC ensures that low-skilled workers receive an acceptable income without the government having to resort to a minimum wage that may discourage firms from employing them, since under the EITC firms do not bear directly the cost of the subsidy. Still, funding the EITC may entail higher taxation among the wealthier and/or lower support for the unemployed. Moreover, since the benefit has to be gradually withdrawn as earnings increase, a higher tax rate is imposed on middle earnings, reducing the incentives to work more hours.

The parameters of the EITC should be chosen carefully so as to ensure that the cost of the program is sustainable and that full-time work is not dis-incentivized with high implicit marginal rates. Such rates arise when the amount of benefit declines fast as earnings increase. For example, suppose that an increase in earnings of 100 euros leads to a decline in the eligible benefit of 70 euros; then the implicit tax rate is 70 percent and this will clearly reduce the incentive to work more.

The EITC system does not provide any support for the unemployed. One way to deal with this deficiency is to offer a means-tested guaranteed minimum income, which is a cash transfer to the unemployed. This could be integrated with the EITC system to reduce the administrative cost of the program and avoid high benefit withdrawal rates and thus low incentives to work. Finally, both the EITC and the guaranteed minimum income could depend on the demographic composition of the household and specifically on the number of children. The amount of support offered particularly for out-of-work singles has to be carefully set so as not to create a culture of living off benefits. In other words the benefit for able-bodied individuals without the responsibility for children should be seen more of as an emergency measure than an amount one can live off in the long term. We discuss various alternatives below.

10.4.4 System A: VAT Based System

The VAT based system aims at shifting the tax base mainly toward consumption. Here we explore how such a system could be designed to include both a welfare component and to be sufficiently progressive, despite relying mainly on indirect taxes. Thus the system we describe here includes three components: an indirect tax based on VAT, an income tax designed to affect only the top quarter of the income distribution, and a welfare system affecting most people below median income. The system is to be revenue neutral with respect to the current system.

In our system, all consumption items are subject to a uniform rate of VAT of 27 percent. This high rate could be reduced substantially (or even the role of income tax could be reduced) once imputed rents (not simulated here) are brought into the tax base. The income tax component is simplified: first, there is only one tax bracket beyond a very high nontaxable allowance, which is set so that only about the top 25 percent of households pay income tax. Lower income households do not pay income tax.

The VAT based system does not depend on the number of children in the household. We only allow the nontaxable allowance to depend on whether the household is a single person or a married couple: a couple has twice the nontaxable allowance of a single person. This effectively means that a couple's both allowances are pooled into one, independently of whether one or both work.[27,28] Support for children is handled through the welfare system together with all other support for lower income groups, thus targeting poverty explicitly, rather than using demographic composition as a proxy for need.

Households receive a guaranteed minimum income (GMI); for example, a couple with one child receives 2,000 euros per annum. This is clearly very low and is meant as minimal cash flow support, the intention being to encourage saving toward self-insurance and to discourage fraud and disincentives to work. In practice, the actual level will have to be debated politically. The GMI is topped with an earnings subsidy (for those in work) at rate s, which we have set at 30 percent. Thus the implied total household income is GMI + (1 + s) * (earnings) until a maximal benefit is achieved. This is 4,400 euros per annum for a household with one child (with 2,400 euros being the EITC). When household before-tax income increases above a certain level (8,100 euros for a couple with one child), the benefit withdrawal starts at a tax rate of 33 percent up to the point where all welfare benefits (GMI and EITC) have been fully withdrawn. This means that as earnings increase by 100 euros the benefit is decreased by 33 euros. For a couple with one child, the level of earnings where all eligibility to benefits is exhausted is 21,433 euros.

Thus benefit eligibility is determined on the basis of pre-benefit income, which means that one benefit does not lead to withdrawal of the other. This design is adopted here to ensure we do not have very high withdrawal rates at the bottom of the income distribution, thus keeping work incentives strong. Once eligibility for benefits is exhausted, the implicit direct tax rate becomes zero and is set at 28 percent only for incomes above the top quartile of the income distribution. The aim of this top tax rate is to help fund the welfare benefits (GMI and EITC) and increase progressivity.

As we discuss below, under full compliance the system can be funded with a lower income tax rate of 13 percent, which demonstrates the huge impact that noncompliance can have on the tax rates that compliers have to pay. In the absence of noncompliance it may make sense to increase the income tax rate so as to improve welfare benefits for the very poor.

A full presentation of the parameters of system A (and the other two tax systems B and C that follow below) can be found in appendix A.

10.4.5 System B: Income Tax Based System[29]

This system is closer in spirit to the current system and more generally to the tax systems in many European countries. It preserves the dependence of income tax on the demographic composition of the household and relies more on income tax than VAT, which is kept to the average rate of 15.2 percent. However, it also integrates a system of welfare transfers to support lower income households and implements numerous simplifications relative to the current tax system.

Relative to the VAT based system, the income tax based system gives greater transfers to the very poor. The GMI is 4,500 euros per annum (couple with one child). This is a substantive increase with respect to the VAT based system, although, in practice, some self-insurance would still be required. The likely downside of the increase in GMI is a reduction in work incentives at the bottom of the income distribution. The GMI is withdrawn at a rate of 80 percent for every euro increase in earnings (100 percent for every euro increase in unearned income). However, overlaid on this is an EITC system with a subsidy rate that now varies depending on the demographic structure of the household, and a maximum benefit amount of 1,350 euros per annum for a couple with one child. The EITC causes the implicit marginal tax rate to decline to 50 percent, which means that as before-tax earnings increase by, say, 1 euro, the effect of overall benefit eligibility (GMI and EITC) is to increase disposable income by 0.50 euro. Once the individual has attained a certain before-tax income level (6,750 euros per annum for a couple with one child), the EITC benefit is withdrawn at a rate of 10 to 23 percent depending on family type (e.g., 15 percent for a couple with one child). When EITC eligibility has been exhausted (i.e., income is high enough for no eligibility to EITC), a simple tax system comes in force with two tax brackets: one at 16 percent and one at 36 percent.[30] If we assume full compliance, these rates can be decreased by 5 percentage points to 11 and 31 percent, respectively. The key feature of this system is the increased generosity to zero or low incomes with a substantially higher GMI. This is funded by a less generous EITC (which only benefits those working). Moreover the amount of benefit has to decline quite fast as income increases.

The income tax based system is a relatively more complex system, and as we will see, it implies worse work incentives in exchange for better support for the poor. It may have the distinct advantage of being easier to implement politically, since it is not such a radical departure from what we have now.

10.4.6   System C: Flat Income Tax with a Universal Benefit[31]

Our "flat tax" system also maintains the existing VAT rates (implying an average VAT rate of 15.2 percent). It makes a universal nontaxable transfer to all individuals differentiated only by whether they are adults or children (2,400 euros per adult if not receiving pension and 1,200 euros per child in our simulations) and imposes a flat tax of 34 percent on everyone on all income over and above the transfer. With full compliance the tax rate would decline to 30 percent. The key advantage of this system is its simplicity. The universal transfer is trivial to administer and the tax authorities can concentrate on compliance with income declarations. Moreover individuals can easily understand the incentives built into the system.

10.5   Tax and Welfare System Comparison

To compare the various systems, it is important to understand how they each affect incentives for work and income redistribution. We start with the notion of incentives, as reflected in the marginal return to working more.

10.5.1   Incentives: The Marginal Return to Work

Consider the concept of the marginal benefit of working an extra hour. This is the increase in real purchasing power, after paying all the direct and indirect taxes, when earning an extra euro. It will depend on the income tax and VAT rates,[32] as well as on the resulting change in welfare benefits. These could increase because of the EITC subsidy, or decrease as eligibility for benefits gradually declines. The marginal increase in disposable income as a result of increases in before-tax income (e.g., from increased work effort) describes the work incentives implicit in the tax and welfare system. The lower the marginal increase, the lower are the incentives to work.

To construct this incentive measure built into the tax and welfare system, we need to combine its various elements. Denote the indirect tax rate (VAT) by t^V, and the marginal tax rate induced by the income tax and the welfare system by t^I. Define $\mathbf{w}$ to be the hourly wage rate and $\mathbf{P}$ an index of prices reflecting cost of living (the price of a "typical" basket of goods). Then the marginal benefit of working an extra hour is given by $(1 - t^I)\mathbf{w}/[(1 + t^V)\mathbf{P}]$. So the relevant marginal tax rate is $1 - (1 - t^I)/(1 + t^V)$. This incentive will differ across the income distribution as the tax rates and welfare benefit eligibility change. We ignore employers' social security contributions. The VAT and the income tax based systems have implicit marginal tax rates that vary with income. This means that the incentives they imply are not the same everywhere. Indeed, over some range, they may encourage people to work more but elsewhere they may discourage work. Here we focus mostly on the lower end and consider incentives to enter the labor market, and to work more, for the low-paid/low-skill individuals.

Take the VAT based tax system. At the lower end of the income distribution, since there is a 30 percent subsidy through the EITC system, the marginal tax rate is $1 - 1.3/1.27 = -0.066$. So the net effect of the benefit system and the VAT is a subsidy of 6.6 percent with respect to an *untaxed* bundle of goods: over this range, increases in earnings increase household income and purchasing power. When the EITC is being withdrawn at a rate of 33 percent, the implicit tax rate becomes $1 - 0.67/1.27 = 0.45$, which implies an overall implicit tax rate of 45 percent. Finally, the top 25 percent of the income distribution are facing an implicit tax rate of $1 - 0.72/1.27 = 0.41$ or 41 percent. This is lower than those receiving EITC in the withdrawal range because the higher income people are receiving no welfare benefits.

The income tax based system, for a couple with one child, has a marginal tax rate of 50 percent for income at the lower end (because of the way the GMI is withdrawn). Currently the VAT rates vary depending on the goods being taxed; the average basket of goods is taxed at a rate of about 15 percent, which we use in our subsequent calculations. Given this, the implicit tax rate for low incomes becomes $1 - 0.5/1.15 = 0.56$ or 56 percent; that is a 100 euro increase in earnings leads to 44 euro increase in purchasing power. For the range of incomes where all the GMI has been withdrawn but the household still has EITC eligibility, the implicit tax rate becomes $1 - (1 + 0.3)/1.15 = -13$ percent (i.e., a subsidy of 13 percent) before EITC withdrawal starts and $1 - (1 - 0.15)/1.15 = 26$ percent beyond that point and until EITC exhaustion. The implicit marginal rates following the exhaustion of eligibility for benefits are $1 - (1 - 0.16)/1.15 = 27$ percent followed by a higher rate of $1 - (1 - 0.36)/1.15 = 44$ percent.

Finally, the flat tax has just one implicit rate across the income distribution.[33] Accounting for the average VAT rate currently in force, this is 43 percent. In other words, throughout the income distribution, an increase of one euro in income leads to 0.57 euro increase in purchasing power.

On the basis of this comparison the VAT based tax system is the strongest in terms of work incentives at the low end of the income distribution: with respect to a consumption basket valued at producer prices, low-income individuals are facing effectively a 6.6 percent subsidy, once we take into account the effect of the EITC. This is because the EITC subsidy rate more than compensates for the high rate of VAT. The other two systems have much higher implicit marginal tax rates at the lower end, with the income tax based system implying a marginal rate of 56 percent at the lowest end and the flat tax 43 percent throughout. The result of this may be increased welfare dependency. However, the latter two systems offer more income support at the lower end.[34] Hence there is a clear trade-off between incentive effects and redistribution.

These features of the three welfare systems are summarized in figure 10.2, for a broad range of incomes, and in figure 10.3, for low incomes. Each curve depicts how each system converts before-tax income to disposable income, that is, after-tax and benefit income, accounting for VAT (by dividing after-tax and welfare income by 1+ the average VAT rate) so as to compare like with like across systems with different VAT rates.[35] We also include a 45-degree line, to show the net transfers to the individual (or household): if disposable income is above the 45-degree line, then the individual is a net receiver of government transfers (e.g., EITC or GMI benefits), and if instead disposable

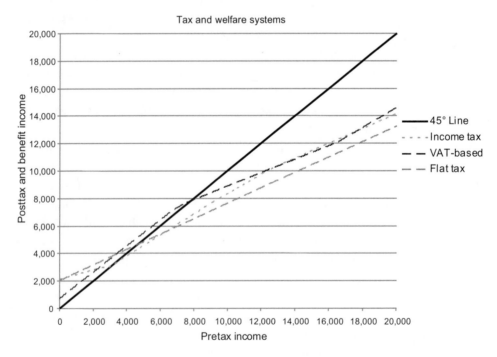

Figure 10.2
Three tax and welfare systems

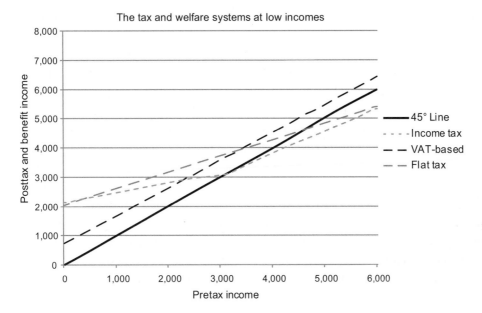

Figure 10.3
Three tax and welfare systems at low incomes

income is below the 45-degree line, then the individual is paying tax. The slope of the disposable income line shows the extent to which a marginal increase in income is taxed or subsidized, with a slope less than 45 degrees representing a positive marginal tax rate and a slope higher than 45 degrees representing a subsidy, which is due to the EITC (negative marginal tax rate).

In these figures we can see the basic differences across the three systems: in contrast to the income tax based system and the flat tax system, the VAT based system preserves the strongest incentive for work at the lower end of the income distribution because the slope of the line converting before-tax income to disposable income is steeper, and indeed steeper than the 45-degree line (albeit only marginally so because of the high VAT rate). This comes at the cost of less income support at the bottom. The trade-off is more evident in figure 10.3, which focuses on the lower range of incomes and clearly shows that the income tax based system (with the parameters chosen here) and the flat tax system provide a much stronger support for the poor. In contrast, our VAT based system (again, as designed here) provides a much stronger return to work at the lower end. This kind of trade-off is always going to be present and society will have to make a choice. Of course, an extra factor in this choice will be the total income produced from work as a result of the selected system: encouraging work will increase the revenue to the state. This will be the result of the behavioral effects of the tax and welfare system, as we discuss below.

As a point of caution, it should be mentioned that some of the gains in revenue obtained from the VAT based system (which allows for a low income tax rate) are due to the assumption that VAT has no compliance issues. Thus, by shifting the tax base from income to VAT, we have artificially reduced the impact of noncompliance on taxes collected. In part, we believe that the VAT based system has better compliance incentives, for reasons explained in section 10.3.5. This belief is partly based on the fact that as the economy is reformed growth will come from the formal sector, where VAT noncompliance is likely to be less of an issue. However, if we did account for VAT noncompliance we would suggest that the sensible policy would be to increase the income tax rate (incident on the top 25 percent of incomes) to compensate, leaving incentives at the bottom of the distribution unchanged from what we presented here. Thus, while we would be collecting more revenue from higher incomes, the discussion relating to the lower part of the income distribution would remain unchanged.

10.5.2 Redistribution

The three alternative systems were designed to be budget neutral relative to the current system. Hence, in principle they cost nothing to implement, other than the administrative process. They differ in the structure of work incentives they induce, as discussed already, and in their redistributive properties. In this section we compare the distributions of disposable income induced by each of the three tax and welfare systems that we propose. We also compare with the current system. In everything we do henceforth we use income per equivalent adult using the OECD equivalence scales.

We use three inequality measures for disposable income: the standard deviation of the level of disposable income, the Gini coefficient, and the difference between the 80th percentile (i.e., 20 percent below the wealthiest household) and the 20th percentile (i.e. 20 percent above the poorest household). We label the latter measure P80–P20.

Inequality Measures   To make the systems comparable despite the different VAT rates, our measure of disposable income accounts for VAT by subtracting a predicted VAT amount based on observed consumption bundles. This does result in some negative disposable incomes at the lower end where either misreporting or low earnings may account for the low before-tax income but higher consumption, presumably funded by nonreported income or borrowing. We leave the numbers as they are, and we note that a more complete system would evaluate the distributional consequences over the life cycle, which would account for borrowing and saving.

Table 10.2 illustrates that no matter how we measure inequality (standard deviation, Gini, or P80–P20), the flat tax system implies the lowest inequality, followed by the income tax based system and then the VAT based system. Inequality under the VAT based system is comparable to that under the current system. Thus, when combined with other parts of the tax and welfare system, indirect taxes need not increase inequality. This result is robust to allowing for noncompliance if, as we suggest, any revenue shortfall is made up by increasing the single tax rate. Finally, we expect improvements in inequality once we allow for a broadening of the tax base to include imputed rents in the VAT tax base.

The extent to which the systems differ will relate to the treatment of the very low-income individuals. Indeed, as we saw earlier, the GMI is much more generous in the income tax and flat tax systems (at the expense of incentives). To address this difference, we also present the difference in disposable income between the median household and the 5th percentile (P50–P5 in table 10.2). In fact all three systems reduce inequality at the lower end relative to the current system. Among the three systems we propose, the flat tax system lowers inequality at the bottom the most, next comes the income tax based system, followed by the VAT based system, where the decrease is only marginal. These facts reflect the improved support for the low-income households by the three systems as well as the differing incentive structures at the bottom: the VAT based system leads to more rapid increases of disposable income as earnings increase, allowing for stronger work incentives—this is, of course, at the cost of some income support. However, the VAT based system achieves this objective without a worsening the welfare of those at the bottom vis-à-vis the current system.

Table 10.2
Effects of alternative tax systems on inequality

Disposable income	Current system	Income tax based system	VAT tax based system	Flat tax
Standard deviation	6,099	5,377	5,930	5,258
P80–P20	8,054	7,363	8,064	6,037
P50–P5	7,150	5,027	7,050	4,351
Gini	0.468	0.408	0.481	0.381
Mean equivalized income	6,646	6,648	6,589	6,432

Note: Income in euros per year; all income measures are per equivalent adult. Mean household income is 16,200 before taxes and transfers and 11,001 after taxes and transfers.

We show more detail on the after-tax distribution of income in figure 10.4 in which we compare the disposable income in each of the three systems to the current one across the income distribution. For this purpose we use a histogram, where each cluster of bars corresponds to a decile of before-tax income.[36] The height of bars corresponds to the difference in disposable income (under each tax system) from that of the current system.

Figure 10.4 shows the similarities among the three systems from a pure distributional perspective. Yet there are some interesting differences at the tails. First, the flat tax and the income tax based systems are more generous for those in the lowest 10 percent of the before-tax income distribution. The flat tax system is the most redistributive, increasing income substantially at the lowest 20 percent. Second, the VAT based system redistributes from the middle part of the distribution to the top decile. Last, the flat tax system taxes the middle and the top of the income distribution more heavily than the other two, with implications for work incentives.

What, of course, remains to be considered are the behavioral effects of the reforms; these may well lead to changes in employment and hours worked as well as to compliance, leading to different redistributive and revenue effects and adding an important component in the comparison between the various systems. We discuss these effects later in this section.

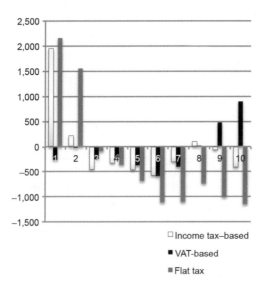

Figure 10.4
Changes in disposable income by decile of gross equivalized income for the three tax and welfare systems, relative to the current system

The three systems treat the various demographic groups differently. In particular, the income tax based system allows the tax parameters to differ by household demographic composition, the VAT based system only allows welfare benefits to depend on household composition, and the flat tax provides a minimum income for each person but otherwise does not distinguish among household types. We explore the impact for each demographic group in table 10.3 where we present the effect of the tax and welfare systems on disposable income (per equivalent adult) and inequality for the various demographic groups, allowing also for the effects of VAT.

The largest demographic groups consist of singles with no children and couples with and without children. We see that among the three systems, the flat tax system favors couples with children relative to those without, as might be expected from its design. The VAT based system is favorable to couples with no children. In terms of inequality the VAT based system implies more or less the same inequality relative to the current system, but with some demographic groups witnessing a decrease and others an increase. The other two systems lower inequality for all groups.

Table 10.3
Impacts of the three tax and welfare systems on income distribution by demographic group

	Percent of population	Before-tax income per equiv. adult		Current	Income tax based	VAT based	Flat tax
Single, no children	47%	9,446	Average	6,318	6,433	6,080	5,848
			Gini	0.546	0.446	0.527	0.440
Single, 1 child	2.1%	9,186	Average	6,479	6,294	6,113	6,341
			Gini	0.358	0.342	0.381	0.319
Single, 2+ children	1.0%	6,227	Average	4,325	4,008	3,547	4,820
			Gini	0.468	0.450	0.495	0.317
Couple with no children	29.5%	13,022	Average	8,001	7,618	8,139	7,129
			Gini	0.338	0.327	0.358	0.321
Couple, 1 child	8.8%	11,781	Average	7,443	6,822	7,046	7,440
			Gini	0.400	0.376	0.395	0.324
Couple, 2+ children	11.3%	9,492	Average	5,329	5,579	5,406	6,461
			Gini	0.477	0.432	0.461	0.334

Note: Income in euros per year; all income measures are per equivalent adult. Gini refers to equivalized income.

Full Compliance   The distributional effects for our three proposed systems, under full compliance on income tax, are presented in figure 10.5. When we assume full compliance, we keep the budget balance fixed and reduce tax rates. The distributional implications of full compliance will additionally depend on how we choose to redistribute the extra revenue generated from the enlarged income tax base. To achieve revenue neutrality for the income tax based system, both income tax rates are reduced by 5 percentage points. For the VAT based system, the single income tax rate is reduced from 28 percent to 13 percent and the flat tax in our third system is reduced from 34 to 30 percent. Figure 10.5 shows how the income distribution (when equivalized) would change for each system, relative to the current system. The differences in percentages are small, although there is an overall effect of a reduction in taxes. The notable difference is that under the flat tax system the disposable income of the population up to the 30th percentile (based on before-tax income) improves. Then, under full compliance and with the specific choices, if we impose revenue neutrality, inequality remains unchanged for the income tax based system, it increases from a Gini of 0.481

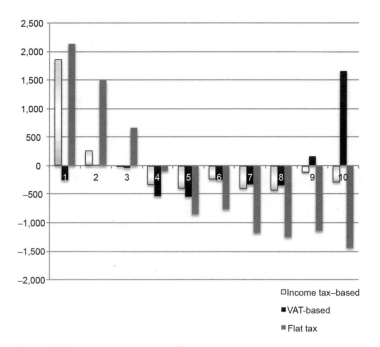

Figure 10.5
Changes in disposable income by decile of gross equivalized income for the three tax and welfare systems under full compliance, relative to the current system

to a Gini of 0.492 for the VAT based system, and declines from 0.381 to 0.377 for the flat tax system.

To be sure, once full or improved compliance is achieved, there will be many options for improving the tax and welfare systems, balancing better redistribution and incentives. For example, the minimum income guarantee and the EITC subsidy rates could both be increased in the VAT based system. This would reduce poverty and improve work incentives at the lower end of the pay distribution.

10.5.3 Behavioral Effects, Tax Incidence, and General Equilibrium

So far in our discussion of incentives and redistribution under alternative direct and indirect tax scenarios, we have ignored the behavioral effects. In response to changes in taxes and welfare benefits, individuals will change their work and consumption behavior. These changes will have distributional impacts as well as impacts on total revenue, requiring changes in the parameters of the tax and welfare system so as to achieve the actual targets. For example, if individuals are incentivized to work more as a result of the EITC system, income will increase at the lower end of the distribution. This is bound to reduce inequality and generate revenue, which can be used to improve the tax and welfare system. Below are three issues that were sidestepped by our not looking at behavioral effects:

• *VAT and goods prices* When we change indirect taxation individuals change their consumption and savings behavior. If indirect taxation increases overall, everything else being equal, individuals will have a lower incentive to work and a higher incentive to save. They will also restructure their consumption basket buying goods that have now become relatively cheaper (because goods that were previously taxed at a lower rate have now become more expensive, assuming a higher uniform VAT rate). However, another important effect that can have substantial impact on outcomes is that, depending on the overall elasticity of demand and supply, the prices of goods may change. If the goods market is fully competitive (which means there is no market power or monopolies) and goods are tradable internationally, then the increase in VAT will not affect producer prices but be passed on to the consumer in increased prices. This is because producers can always sell to the international market, and thus they have no incentive to reduce prices in the local market. This is the assumption we have been making when evaluating the distributional and incentive effects of VAT reforms above. However, if goods are non-tradable (internationally), as is the case with many services, and the domestic market is not sufficiently competitive, producers will absorb part of the increase in VAT and will lower the price so that the tax increase is shared between consumers and producers. The implication is that increasing VAT will not translate one to one on prices, and hence the actual effects on the outcomes we consider will be muted relative to the results of our simulations. How much is an empirical question.

• *EITC and incentives to work*   The EITC is a subsidy to work. It will increase the incentive to work vis-à-vis a world with no such subsidy. Increased earnings potential at the lower end of the income distribution will induce people into work or and incentivize individuals to move from informal to formal jobs. However, there are other complex effects to consider concerning incentives. First, the way the system is structured may create incentives for some people who used to work a lot to now work less. Moreover, because the benefit is assessed on a family basis, the marginal incentive to return to work for a secondary earner may decline. The balance of these effects needs to be assessed empirically. However, research in both the United States and the United Kingdom indicates that EITC increases work quite substantially for single parents, without considerable negative side effects.[37]

• *EITC and wages*   We mentioned in section 10.4.3 that if the labor market for low-skill workers is not sufficiently competitive, firms can reduce wages for EITC recipients, thus capturing part of this subsidy and blunting its effect. This is the argument for minimum wages, as an attempt to prevent firms from doing so. However, empirical work in the United Kingdom has shown that employers do not absorb any of the EITC (see Shephard 2012). Presumably this is because search frictions among unskilled workers are not that important, implying that if employers attempt to absorb part of the benefit by offering lower wages, workers may find better alternatives. The other reason employers may not be able to capture part of the subsidy is that they would need to discriminate between those workers eligible for EITC and those who are not. This would lead to complications and legal issues, making the capture of the subsidy a costly exercise. Finally, EITC may have the effect of inducing workers to seek employment in the formal sector, since otherwise they would not be able to claim the benefit unless they can prove they work in a formal job. For a country like Greece with the preponderance of small low-tech family firms in the informal sector, such a move could have substantial effects on growth (e.g., see LaPorta and Schleifer 2008; Meghir, Narita, and Robin 2015). In general, the reform of the tax system as well as reductions in regulation (see chapter 4 on product markets) could have a double dividend in that they would increase investment in the formal sector and lead to higher paying jobs. The improved employment opportunities would in turn incentivize workers to move to the formal sector and obtain better jobs and better protection and insurance.

10.6   Concluding Remarks

A well-designed tax and welfare system is at the heart of a modern economy. Taxes need to be raised to fund various activities of the state such as health, education, defense, infrastructure projects, and the like, and for redistribution and social insurance purposes. A well-designed system can help fight poverty and provide work incentives. However, there are many ways of designing a tax system, and they differ in fundamental ways in relation to the effect they have on the economy.

In this chapter we characterized three tax and welfare systems that are transparent and simple to understand and implement. Simple and transparent systems allow people to plan better, and are likely to improve trust and thus compliance. It is also easier to understand the work incentives that such systems generate and to avoid highly distortionary taxation.

The three tax and welfare systems that we studied include elements of other systems either in existence or considered internationally. We determined the implied incentives from the three systems and the way they would redistribute income in Greece under the restrictive assumption of no changes in behavior. It is clear that each system has its merits and drawbacks and thus will appeal to some people more than to others. One important conclusion is that it is relatively straightforward to simplify the current system, while preserving revenue. We also show quite explicitly, that a consumption tax system based on increasing VAT generates no more inequality than the current system, while at the same time taking 75 percent of people out of the income tax system and leading to important simplifications. Moreover we expect improvements in inequality and/or incentives if the tax base is broadened to include imputed rents and capital gains, all without increasing the overall tax burden. We also showed how two other systems (the income tax based and the flat tax) can improve inequality substantially. Each system does come at the cost of a deterioration of work incentives relative to the VAT based system.

Ultimately the choice of system is social and political. We have illustrated some of the trade-offs involved. However, this choice should be based on facts rather than speculation. All too often in many countries, including Greece, reforms are based on unfounded assumptions regarding their effects or on expediency and for revenue purposes only. Here we have illustrated how data can be used to analyze the differences between systems and show with some degree of accuracy who may gain and who may lose from a particular system. While a more detailed analysis is beyond the scope of this chapter, it is possible with available data. Such an analysis should be standard in the design of public policy.

Appendix A: Parameters of Proposed Tax and Welfare Systems

Common departures from current system:
Personal income tax system radically revised*
Additional tax on rental income abolished
Solidarity contributions and self-employed and liberal professions' contributions abolished (but not pensioners' solidarity contributions)
Employees' and self-employed individuals' health social insurance contributions abolished
All benefits abolished, except for unemployment insurance, pensions and the social pension; replaced by basic income and earned income subsidy*
*Details below

	System A: VAT-based system	System B: Income tax–based system	System C: Flat tax system
Demographic group notation s_i= single with i dependent children c_j=couple with j dependent children			
Personal income tax			
Tax unit	Joint spouse	Joint spouse	Individual
Exemptions	Unemployment insurance, social pension and basic income		
Tax allowances	Social insurance contributions and pensioners' solidarity contributions		
Tax base	Taxable income includes reported employment and self-employment income, other market income (received by children in the Household Budget Survey), income from rent, private transfers received, disability pensions, main and supplementary old age pensions, minor old age pensions, orphans' and widows' pensions. The tax base is defined as taxable income minus the various tax allowances described above.		

Appendix A (continued)

Income tax	System A: VAT based system	System B: Income tax based system	System C: Flat tax system

System A: VAT based system

Tax base	Tax rate (%)	Full compliance
0–T	0	0
>T	27.7	12.7

Where

	T
s0	15500
s1	15500
s2+	15500
c0	31000
c1	31000
c2+	31000

System B: Income tax based system

Tax base	Tax rate (%)	Full compliance
0–GMI	0	0
GMI–U	0 (earnings), 16.4 (other income)	0 (earnings), 11.4 (other income)
U–T	16.4	11.4
>T	36.4	31.4

Where

	GMI	U	T
s0	2500	8750	12500
s1	3250	11375	16250
s2+	4000	14000	20000
c0	3750	13125	18750
c1	4500	15750	22500
c2+	5250	18375	26250

System C: Flat tax system

Tax base	Tax rate (%)	Full compliance
0+	34.1	30.2

Appendix A (continued)

Tax credits	System A: VAT based system	System B: Income tax based system	System C: Flat tax system
		(see below)	

System B: Income tax based system

Tax base	EITC
0–L	min(maxEITC, s * Earnings),
L–U	EITC at L – w * (Taxable income – L)
>U	0

Earned income tax credit (EITC)

where s=subsidy rate

w=withdrawal rate

maxEITC= maximum EITC

L= lower earnings threshold; EITC withdrawal starts

U=upper earnings threshold; EITC eligibility ends

	s	w	maxEITC	L	U
s0	20%	10%	500	3750	8750
s1	30%	17%	1100	4875	11375
s2+	40%	23%	1850	6000	14000
c0	20%	10%	750	5625	13125
c1	30%	15%	1350	6750	15750
c2+	40%	20%	2100	7875	18375

Appendix A (continued)

	Reform	Baseline (6.5%, 13%, and 23%)
VAT	Uniform 27% on all goods	
Basic income	*(Basic income formula, see below)*	*(Baseline formula, see below)* / Universal transfer €100 per month to all children aged 0-17; €200 per month to all persons aged 18+ if not receiving a pension; otherwise €0

Basic income (Reform):

Tax base	Basic income
0–L	GMI+ min(maxEITC, s * Earnings)
L–U	GMI+ (EITC at L) – w * (Taxable income – L)
>U	0

where
s=subsidy rate=30%
w=withdrawal rate=33%
maxEITC= maximum EITC
L= lower earnings threshold; benefit withdrawal starts
U=upper earnings threshold; benefit is zero

	GMI	maxEITC	L	U
s0	500	1000	5000	9545
s1	1500	1200	5400	13582
s2+	2000	1300	5500	15500
c0	1000	2000	7500	16591
c1	2000	2400	8100	21433
c2+	2500	2800	9000	25061

Baseline (Disposable income – 20% * Earnings):

GMI– (Disposable income – 20% * Earnings)

where

	GMI
s0	2500
s1	3250
s2+	4000
c0	3750
c1	4500
c2+	5250

Appendix B: EUROMOD

B.1   Updating

In order to update incomes to 2013, we disaggregated earnings growth by occupational category and then applied the procedure described in Leventi et al. (2014). Workers in dependent employment were divided into four categories: civil servants, public utility workers, banking employees, and workers in the (nonbanking) private sector. Specific updating factors, based on Bank of Greece estimates, were applied to account for earnings growth of employees by category in 2012 to 2013. However, farmers' earnings were updated on the basis of data on gross value added by industry. As regards self-employment, given that no reliable information on earnings was available for the period of interest, we assumed that they moved in tandem with average incomes in the entire economy.

For indirect taxation, comprising both value added tax (VAT) and excise duties, we applied the methodology established in Decoster et al. (2010). The core strategy underlying the simulation of indirect taxes with EUROMOD is the translation of tax legislation in Greece in 2013 into tax rates for the classification of individual consumption by purpose (COICOP) expenditure aggregates. Given that in the HBS we observe household expenditure at consumer prices, whereas most of the indirect tax legislation is expressed in terms of producer prices, the departure point of the analysis is the relationship that links consumer to producer prices through the different elements of the tax system. Indirect tax liabilities paid on individual commodities are summed over to obtain the tax liability for a commodity aggregate, and expenditures on individual commodities are summed over accordingly to obtain each household's expenditure and hence indirect tax liabilities. In order to update VAT and excise duties to the policy year (2013), we adjusted consumer prices using the harmonized consumer price index (the HCPI fell by 0.9 percent in 2012 to 2013).

B.2   Simulation of Emergency Property Tax

The amount of the emergency property tax, varying from 3 to 16 euros per square meter, depends on the size and the cadastral value of the building. A specific factor varying from 1 to 1.25 according to the age of the building is also applicable (Property tax = Tax rate × Square meters × Age factor). A reduced rate of 0.50 euro per square meter applies to certain vulnerable categories (i.e., people with more than three children with taxable income less than 30,000 euros per year or people suffering from disability over 67 percent). The long-term unemployed or recipients of unemployment benefit for more than six months, with family income not exceeding 12,000 euros per year (plus 4,000 euros for every dependent child) are exempted from the tax. In this chapter, the tax rates per square meter that we used were the average rates for urban and rural/ semi-rural areas according to a large tax data sample provided by the Greek authorities (i.e., 5.3 euros per square meter for those residing in urban areas and 3.7 euros per square meter for those residing in rural/semi-rural areas). For more information, see Leventi and Matsaganis (2013a).

Notes

1. Parts of this chapter were developed with the help of Manos Matsaganis, who offered his expertise and valuable comments. We thank Dimitri Vayanos, Maria Vergou, Basil Manessiotis, Emmanuel Saez, Cathal O'Donoghue, Francesco Figari, Chryssa Leventi, and Kostas Manios for comments and advice throughout this study. We also thank George Douros from EL.STAT. for his help with the Greek Household Budget Survey, and participants in the Athens workshop that launched this book. Costas Meghir thanks the Cowles foundation and the ISPS for financial support. The views expressed in this chapter are those of the authors and do not reflect those of the Bank of Greece.

2. Prior to that, agricultural income has been taxed on a presumptive basis using farmed acres and crops.

3. Dividends from listed companies are not aggregated with the rest of income. Following the application of corporation tax on the entire set of profits a further 10 percent is deducted at source before distribution. No further tax is paid (or refunded) once this is received by the individual. Thus dividends are taxed independently of the level of income of the individual and do not affect her marginal tax rate.

4. Interest payments made by nonresidents are subject to tax withholding of 20 percent if the beneficiary is an individual and of 33 percent if the beneficiary is a legal entity.

5. These tax rates have increased since then.

6. The new provisions do not apply to legal entities, where every capital gain is simply considered as business income.

7. Note that there is an equivalence to taxing imputed rents or just taxing the sale of new built houses. So the tax system should not include both. Taxing imputed rents may be harder administratively, but it does have the advantage that the tax adjusts to changes in the valuation of the property.

8. For empirical evidence, see de Mooij and Keen (2013).

9. Thus, someone who exports 100,000 euros of accumulated and untaxed savings pays VAT as the euros are spent domestically. Reimporting these euros (or a fraction thereof) would generate a VAT refund.

10. We discuss VAT evasion below.

11. The optimal marginal income tax structure, as function of income, has been shown to be U-shaped, with high marginal taxes at the bottom, high at the top, and low at the middle of the income distribution (Diamond 1998; Saez 2001). This is because at the bottom of the distribution, where incomes are low, the high marginal tax rates are the result of means testing, in the sense of a gradual phasing out of cash transfers (negative income taxes); this is optimal because it ensures that redistribution is targeted to those with the lowest incomes. In turn, this allows lower marginal tax rates across the board and smaller overall tax distortions. For individuals at the middle of the income distribution, the marginal tax rates should be lower because there are typically many of this group, so the aggregate distortionary effect of high marginal rates in this range would be very costly. At the top of the distribution, the optimal marginal tax rate should increase again, as there are typically a small number of individuals at that income level, so the redistributive gains dominate the efficiency loss.

12. The evidence suggest that in the United States and the United Kingdom these programs had a positive net effect on employment, and in particular, for single women with children; see Hotz and Scholz (2003), Eissa and Hoynes (2006), Immervoll and Pearson (2009), and Blundell et al. (2013).

13. Her reservation wage is then 8 euros per hour and her productivity is 15 euros per hour.

14. In practice, real estate taxes encompass a variety of levies on the use, ownership, and transfer of property; whether land or residential properties, these obviously include land and the housing structures built on it.

15. OECD (2008, 2010) establishes a "tax and growth" ranking, with taxes on immovable property being the least distortive in terms of reducing GDP per capita—followed by consumption taxes, income taxes, and corporate income taxes.

16. Among the austerity measures adopted by the government in the recent fiscal crisis, real estate was used extensively to collect tax revenue, mainly through two taxes on ownership: (1) the emergency property tax paid on electricity-supplied buildings via electricity bills and (2) the real estate tax paid on buildings and land if their cadastral value exceeded 200,000 euros and up to 400,000 euros. This measure was adopted in order to expedite tax collections, but it had ripple effects throughout the economy: electricity bills in arrears caused liquidity problems for the electricity distribution company, as well as practical problems between renters and owners, as renters typically were receiving electricity bills with taxes owed by the owners.

17. Net wealth is defined as the difference between all household assets, financial and real, taken together, and all forms of debt, collateralized and uncollateralized.

18. The data are drawn from the new eurozone survey coordinated by the European Central Bank, namely the survey on Household Finances and Consumption (HFCS). The Greek data were

collected during the three months before the breakout of the crisis in September 2009 and released by the ECB in March 2013.

19. This statement needs to be qualified because even formal longer chains of producers can evade by overstating the cost of inputs and understating sales. Hence the statement assumes that in more formal complex production chains, compliance can be enforced better by matching the invoices across the chain.

20. The benefits of shifting to a consumption tax based system originate in the Meade Report (1978) and are reiterated in the Mirrlees Report (2011). The specific structure we are examining here comes from Michael Graetz, Professor of Law at Columbia University, who discussed this point in a talk presented at Yale University during the US presidential election campaign of 2012.

21. Ideally we would also tax housing services, namely imputed rent for owners. Such an approach would simplify real estate taxation and would lead to an overall reduction in tax rates. There are, of course, practical difficulties because rents have to be imputed fairly and by an independent body. From our perspective, we do not have the appropriate data to simulate the effects of such an extension. In the present simulations we do impose VAT on actual rents but not on imputed ones. This is a shortcoming that remains to be addressed.

22. Dividends, along with interest, are assumed to be taxed at 15 percent in the simulations.

23. EUROMOD version G1.0+ is employed. For more information about EUROMOD, see https://www.euromod.ac.uk/.

24. For a comprehensive overview, see Sutherland and Figari (2013), and for a recent application for Greece, see Matsaganis and Leventi (2013a).

25. For more information on the methodology, see Matsaganis et al. (2012). Artavanis et al. (2016) find that in 2009 evaded income (for the self-employed) was 28 billion euros. Interestingly, this implies that, at the tax rate of 40 percent, the forgone tax revenue accounts for 31 percent of the budget deficit in 2009.

26. Since 2014 workers aged 22 to 66 years may be eligible for unemployment assistance.

27. Note, however, that the proposed system still makes marriage more attractive for a couple than mere cohabitation. In a marriage, if a partner does not work, the other person effectively can claim twice the allowance. In the case of an unmarried couple, the married nonworking partner's deduction would be lost. One solution to this distortion may be for government to treat cohabiting couples as married.

28. Again, with regard to cohabitation versus marriage, ideally, cohabiting couples could file taxes as married couples to avoid further distortions. But this will depend on other aspects of institutional reform in Greece.

29. This system was proposed by Manos Matsaganis.

30. Note that the 16 percent tax rate applies also before EITC eligibility is exhausted for non-earned income. See appendix A.

31. We thank Manos Matsaganis for suggesting, and elaborating on, the elements of this tax system.

32. When VAT increases, prices will rise. This is equivalent to earnings declining by the same rate as that of the price increase. In practice, prices tend to rise by less than the increase in VAT because some of the VAT increase can be absorbed by producers.

33. We assume here that the same basket of goods is consumed throughout the income distribution.

34. We should note that incentivizing work may be as distortionary and inefficient as disincentivizing work from the perspective of individual welfare. In all cases the efficiency effects of a tax system need to be assessed against alternatives in attempting a similar redistribution.

35. More precisely, disposable income is defined as before-tax income net of income tax, the emergency property tax, VAT, social insurance contributions and pensioners' solidarity contributions.

36. The first set of bars shows the disposable income after all taxes and benefits for those with a before-tax and benefit income in the bottom 10 percent. The second set of bars relates to those with before-tax and benefit income above the lowest 10 percent and below the lowest 20 percent, and so forth.

37. See Blundell et al. (2013), Breweret al. (2006), and Eissa and Hoynes (2006).

References

Artavanis, N., A. Morse, and M. Tsoutsoura. 2016. Measuring income tax evasion using bank credit: Evidence from Greece. *Quarterly Journal of Economics* 131 (2): 739–98.

Atkinson, A. B., and J. E. Stiglitz. 1976. The design of tax structure: Direct versus indirect taxation. *Journal of Public Economics* 6: 55–75.

Bastani, S., S. Blomquist, and J. Pirttila. 2013. How should commodities be taxed? A counterargument to the recommendation in the Mirrlees Review. Working paper 4240. CESIfo. Ludwig Maximilians University.

Blundell, R., M. Dias, C. Meghir, and J. Shaw. 2013. Female labour supply, human capital and welfare reform. Working paper 19007. NBER.

Boadway, R., M. Marchand, and P. Pestieau. 1994. Towards a theory of the direct-indirect tax mix. *Journal of Public Economics* 55: 71–88.

Brewer, M., A. Duncan, A. Shepard, and M. Suarez. 2006. Did working families' tax credit work? The impact of in-work support on labour supply in Great Britain. *Labour Economics* 13 (6): 699–720.

Cabral, M., and C. Hoxby. 2012. The hated property tax: Salience, tax rates, and tax revolts. Working paper 18514. NBER.

Christiansen, V. A. 1984. Which commodity tax rates should supplement the income tax? *Journal of Public Economics* 24: 195–220.

Deaton, A. 1979. Optimally uniform commodity taxes. *Economics Letters* 2: 357–61.

Decoster, A., J. Loughrey, C. O'Donoghue, and D. Verwerft. 2010. How regressive are indirect taxes? A microsimulation analysis for five European countries. *Journal of Policy Analysis and Management* 29 (2): 326.

Diamond, P., and E. Saez. 2011. 'The case for a progressive tax: From basic research to policy recommendations. *Journal of Economic Perspectives* 25 (4): 165–90.

Eissa, N., and H. Hoynes. 2006. The hours of work response of married couples: Taxes and the earned income tax credit. In *Tax Policy and Labor Market Performance*, Jonas Agell and Peter Birch Sorensen (eds.). Cambridge: MIT Press.

Fabbri, M., and S. Hemels. 2013. Do you want a receipt?' Combating VAT and sales tax evasion with lottery tickets: Involving customers (March 4, 2013). http://ssrn.com/abstract=2232249.

Fabbri, M. 2013. Shaping tax norms through lotteries (May 14, 2013). http://ssrn.com/abstract=2202189.

Hotz, J., and J. Scholz. 2003. The earned income tax credit. In *Means-Tested Transfer Programs in the United States*, R. Moffitt (ed.), 141–97. Chicago: University of Chicago Press.

Immervoll, H., and M. Pearson. 2009. A good time for making work pay? Taking stock of in-work benefits and related measures across the OECD. Social, Employment, and Migration Working paper 81. OECD.

Johansson, A., C. Heady, J. Arnold, B. Brys, and L. Vartia. 2008. Tax and economic growth. Working paper 620. OECD.

Kaplow, L. 2006. On the undesirability of commodity taxation even when income taxation is not optimal. *Journal of Public Economics* 90: 1235–50.

Keen, M. 2013. The anatomy of the VAT. Working paper 13/111. IMF.

La Porta, Rafael, and Andrei Shleifer. 2008. The unofficial economy and economic development. *Brookings Papers on Economic Activity* (Fall): 2008.

Laroque, G. 2005. Indirect taxation is superfluous under separability and taste homogeneity: A simple proof. *Economics Letters* 87: 141–44.

Leventi, C., A. Karakitsios, M. Matsaganis, and P. Tsakloglou. 2014. EUROMOD Country Report: Greece 2009–2013. https://www.iser.essex.ac.uk/files/euromod/country-reports/Year5/CR_EL_Y5_May2014_FINAL_29052014.pdf.

Leventi, C., and M. Matsaganis. 2013a. Distributional implications of the crisis in Greece in 2009–2012. Working paper EM 14/13. Microsimulation Unit. University of Essex. https://www .iser.essex.ac.uk/research/publications/working-papers/euromod /.

Leventi, C., M. Matsaganis, and M. Flevotomou. 2013b. Distributional implications of tax evasion and the crisis in Greece. Working paper EM 17/13. Microsimulation Unit. University of Essex. https://www.iser.essex.ac.uk/research/publications/working-papers/euromod/.

Matsaganis, M., and C. Leventi. 2013a. The distributional impact of the Greek crisis in 2010. *Fiscal Studies* 34 (1): 83–108.

Matsaganis, M., and C. Leventi. 2013b. Distributional implications of tax evasion in Greece. Newsletter 2/2012. Policy Analysis Research Unit. Athens University of Economics and Business. http://www.paru.gr/index.php?lang=en&page=newsletters/2012_2.

Matsaganis, M., C. Leventi, and M. Flevotomou. 2012. The crisis and tax evasion in Greece: What are the distributional implications? *CESifo Forum* 13 (2): 26–32.

Meade Report. 1978. *The Structure and Reform of Direct Taxation. Report of a committee chaired by J. E. Meade*. New South Wales: Allen and Unwin.

Meghir, C., R. Narita, and J. M. Robin. 2015. Informality and wages in developing countries. *American Economic Review* 105 (4): 1509–1546.

Meghir, C., D. Vayanos, and N. Vettas. 2010. The economic crisis in Greece: a time of reform and opportunity. http://greekeconomistsforreform.com/wp-content/uploads/Reform.pdf.

Mieszkowski, P. 1972. The property tax: An excise tax or a profits tax? *Journal of Public Economics* 1: 73–96.

Mirrlees, J. 1971. An exploration in the theory of optimum income taxation. *Review of Economic Studies* 38: 175–208.

Mirrlees Review. 2011. *Tax by Design*, J. Mirrlees, S. Adam, T. Besley, R. Blundell, S. Bond, R. Chote, M. Gammie, P. Johnson, G. Myles, and J. Poterba (eds.). New York: Oxford University Press.

Norregaard, J. 2013. Taxing immovable property. Working paper 13/129. IMF.

OECD. 2010. Tax policy reform and economic growth. *Tax Policy Studies* 20.

Paulus, A., H. Sutherland, and P. Tsakloglou. 2010. The distributional impact of in-kind public benefits in European countries. *Journal of Policy Analysis and Management* 29 (2): 243–66.

Piketty, T., and E. Saez. 2012. Optimal labor income taxation. In *Handbook of Public Economics*, vol. 5, A. Auerbach, R. Chetty, M. Feldstein, and E. Saez (eds.). Amsterdam: Elsevier.

Pomeranz, D. 2015. No taxation without information: Deterrence and enforcement in the value added tax. *American Economic Review* 105 (8): 2539–69.

Saez, E. 2001. Using elasticities to derive optimal income tax rates. *Review of Economic Studies* 68 (1): 205–29.

Saez, E. 2002. Optimal income transfer programs: Intensive versus extensive labor supply responses. *Quarterly Journal of Economics* 117: 1039–73.

Shephard, A. 2012. Equilibrium search and tax credit reform. Mimeo. University of Pennsylvania.

Sutherland, H., and F. Figari. 2013. EUROMOD: The European Union tax-benefit microsimulation model. *International Journal of Microsimulation* 6 (1): 10–12.

Tiebout, C. 1956. A pure theory of local expenditures. *Journal of Political Economy* 64: 416–24.

11 Pensions: Arresting a Race to the Bottom

Stavros Panageas and Platon Tinios

11.1 Introduction: Plain Sailing?

Reforming pensions has been on the cards in Greece for half a century (Tinios 2012b). Yet, with the exception of measures passed in 1992, in 2010 the country was still waiting for meaningful change. Thus no one was surprised that the first reform in the first Memorandum of Understanding (MoU) agenda was that of pensions.

The IMF characterized it, in its first report in August 2010, as a "landmark pension reform, which is far-reaching by international standards" (IMF 2010), and three years later, "as one of the main achievements of the program" (IMF 2013). Similarly, the EU Aging Working group in its 2012 report concurred that viability had been conclusively dealt with: Greece showed the largest improvement in the burden of pensions forecast for 2060 of any EU country (EPC 2012).

Notwithstanding these appreciative statements, pensions since 2010 have remained a key locus for concern. Individual pensioners hearing the triumphal official declarations may wonder how viability is consistent with ten consecutive cuts of their own pensions since 2010 (Tinios 2013). Despite the reforms, fiscal overruns in pension systems and pension providers persist as major short-term threats to the budget. Pension expenditures rise as more people seek refuge from the labor market, while at the same time, despite efforts to curb evasion, the contribution base appears to be dissolving. Firms complain vociferously of non-wage costs impinging on their ability to operate and compete.

The official response to those paradoxes—up to early 2015—could be paraphrased as "No need to worry. The major decisions are behind us. From now on, tinkering is sufficient." In this way the general route was affirmed; only teething problems remain. The outlook was for plain sailing. This complacency was replaced in January 2015 by an alternate reading by the SYRIZA government, which appeared, initially at least, to reject out of hand all changes since 2010, in favor of returning to the pre-reform 2009 situation as a sort of "promised land." (See Tinios 2015b on developments in 2015.) Both expectations were spectacularly disproved when pensions were, once again, the primary concern and most pressing task of the *third* bailout period from July 2015 to the passage of a new pension reform law in May 2016.

This chapter argues for a more balanced and nuanced reading: reforms provided only partial fixes. While dealing with the very long term, pensions during the crisis operated perversely. Early retirements led to cost overruns, which were made up by large and repeated cuts in pensions of all pensioners. This dealt a major blow to the (already shaky) credibility of the pension promise, encouraging further evasion and setting in motion a vicious circle. The pension system, while remaining a charge on competitiveness and a drain on public finances, is no longer trusted to deliver old-age income security—the reason for public pensions *in the first place*. Our verdict on the 2010 pension agenda was that it did not go *far enough*—that it was, essentially, only *"half* a reform." Its forced completion in 2016 will only serve to underline the short-comings of an approach that persists on relying exclusively on the state for old-age protection.

If *half* a reform sets off a vicious circle, the outlook may not be for plain sailing, but for a race to the bottom. This could be addressed, we argue, by completing the reform in a more thoroughgoing manner and making participants feel that a fresh start has been made. A new system should *both* serve individual needs for old-age income protection *and* inflict lower costs on production. We will argue that a reform bringing elements of prefunding can correct the overweening ambition of the public pension system and answer convincingly the challenges faced today.

We build up our case by appealing to first principles—both of the functions of pensions and the structure of the systems that provide them. By explaining in section 11.2 the options and dilemmas faced by pensions generally, we shed light on why Greek pensions present special difficulties. Section 11.3 examines our key contention that reforms since 2010 have not disposed of pension problems, but in some respects seem to have made them worse. Key to this is that, even in the very long term, pensions will be provided by the state and will have to be financed exclusively by future generations of workers. Section 11.4 outlines a reform that brings in elements of prefunding as well as providers other than the state—a public-private partnership based on clear rules and demarcation of responsibility. We sketch an explicit multipillar pension system, similar to that introduced in many European countries, which can establish a stronger link between contributions and pensions, hence acting as a smaller tax on labor, while also focusing the state's role more squarely to addressing poverty in old age. Section 5 deals with the transition period, which is thought to be the Achilles' heel of pension reform because of the "double payment contention"—meaning the transitional generation will have to both finance their own and their parents' pensions. We propose a solution to the transition problem that spreads the costs of transition across all future generations. A calibrated overlapping-generations model in appendix B shows that the switch to the new system could realize gains of the order of 8 percent of GDP even during the transition period. The final sections of the chapter highlight some problem areas and issues that must not be left to chance. Economic analysis can spot obstacles on the way, and adapt ideas from an increasingly richer international toolbox. Our key message is that technicalities are obstacles that can be overcome and should not be seen as trump cards preventing the exercise of fundamental choice. Appendix A provides an outline of pension developments in the troubled year 2015—the period of negotiation, the third bailout, and the lead-in to the new reform bill in May 2016.

11.2   How to Organize Pensions to Safeguard Peace of Mind: Options and Dilemmas

11.2.1   Pensions and Old-Age Security

Pensions exist in order to "buy peace of mind" to help the aged or infirm maintain their standard of living at a time when their earning capacity is limited. Pensions are in reality a kind of game facilitating income redistribution between and within generations, with each type of redistribution addressing different kinds of risk. Players in the pensions game can be individuals, families, occupational groups, or society at large in the guise of the state. The potential complexity could be an asset, through widening the field of choice; however, it could also prove a liability, if systems are subverted by individual groups, occupations, or even generations that can secure larger benefits at the expense of others.

The development of old-age protection over time has been characterized by two trends. First was a trend toward greater collective provision (Mackenzie 2010), which can combine risk pooling with an active redistributive role. Second was a tendency to clarify the roles played by the various institutional actors involved. Transparency allows the various types of redistribution to be separately identified, and the pension promise to be managed more efficiently. Into this structure the state entered as a potential provider (frequently of a pension "floor") but also as the system coordinator and regulator. In managing the pension promise, the state applies four "levers" that determine *both* the overall weight of pensions *and* how that weight is distributed across society:

1. *Size of the overall pension promise relative to the size of production (GDP)*   This depends on the number of pensioners, how long pensions are paid for (the age at retirement), and the size of pensions relative to the working-age incomes (the replacement rate).

These three numbers determine how much needs to be subtracted from the consumption of producers for retirement benefits—a key macroeconomic distributional issue.

2. *Mode by which pensions are financed* Pensions may be financed *either* directly from the generation currently working—known as pay-as-you-go (PAYG) financing—*or* pensions may be paid from a stock of funds accumulated in advance by the retired generation—prefunding. However, an individual can draw pensions from both sources in separate tranches (sometimes called "pillars"). Financing is a key equity consideration, since it determines the extent to which each generation bears the macroeconomic costs caused by the retirement of its members.

3. *Extent of reciprocity in finance—or how closely benefits are linked to contributions* Systems of social insurance typically link benefits closely to contributions, while social welfare assigns benefits on the basis of need. Reciprocity may result automatically as a consequence of the mode of financing, or may result as a by-product of how pension entitlements are built up from contributions.[1] Notional defined contribution systems (NDC), for example, are financed by PAYG but calculate individual entitlements by mimicking prefunding—crediting notional individual accounts with contributions and calculating pensions as annuities resulting from the accumulated funds.

4. *Extent of redistribution taking place within generations—in the sense of favoring particular classes of individuals over and above their entitlement based on reciprocity* This cross-subsidization may favor "socially deserving" categories such as widows, mothers of young children, the unemployed, war veterans; it may extend to entire occupational categories such as farmers.[2]

Managing pensions is fraught with difficulties. Unless great care is taken, the system can be "hijacked" by one group at the expense of other groups. This can happen directly through explicit subsidies or grants. It can also happen due to departures from reciprocity (e.g., special privileges). It can even result if groups break away from a general system[3] in order to take advantage of favorable conditions, such as a rise in employment. While disaffiliation due to more adventitious employment could, at first, be thought to be sensible, it contravenes the operating logic of a PAYG system: in such a system the key parameter is the overall, society-wide ratio of workers over pensioners. If one group faces a favorable ratio, it follows that another group must face a *less* favorable one. In contrast, prefunding can separate redistribution between and within generations, as higher pensions must ultimately reflect a greater pension pot. It can also guard against cross-subsidization between occupations.

Contributor perceptions matter a great deal. Benefits linked closely to contributions—what we call reciprocity—make social insurance akin to a voluntarily chosen insurance contract. In such a contract, the premiums are seen as inseparably linked to benefits. Severing this link, through lack of reciprocity, risks contributions being perceived as a tax on labor. Similarly benefits could be understood by some as politically motivated handouts, unrelated to individual effort. Such perceptions magnify the economic distortions caused by both contributions and benefits. Well-run pension systems emphasize the link with contributions, and provide explicit justification in the way of general rules for any social policy related departures from reciprocity. This attempt at transparency highlights the difference between a system governed by arbitrary interventions and one applying clear-cut rules. Pension systems are ultimately systems of information handling, implying careful record keeping and smooth operation. As Barr and Diamond (2010) make clear, whether a system is well or badly run is of more importance than whether it is public or private.

11.2.2 Thinking of Pensions by Means of Pillars

Total pension income can be made of three components, each of which corresponds to a different "pillar of support." Each of the three pillars is assigned a role, and the system operates so that the different pillars act in a complementary manner.[4] The three pillars correspond to different kinds of solidarities.[5] First-pillar pensions are public, corresponding to *collective* societal solidarity, underwritten and managed by the state. The redistribution is both within and between generations. Second-pillar pensions arise out of the employment relationship and may redistribute *within* occupational groups; they correspond to occupational solidarity, where the social partners may play key roles. The third pension pillar relies on individually negotiated provision, such as life insurance, in the context of life-cycle savings; it is, in this sense, solidarity between stages of life.[6]

Of the three pillars, the state pillar can redistribute *within* generations in ways that avoid occupational cross-subsidies. Thus, in the absence of dedicated instruments, pensions can play a second-best role in social policy. In underdeveloped financial systems, such as those pertaining in Greece when the pension system was being built up, the size of the non-state pillars is constrained by financial capacity. Given the lack of sophistication of financial systems in Greece in the 1960s and 1970s, there was no realistic alternative to a state pension system. Where financial underdevelopment is not an issue, the preferred size of the state pillar may depend on the intergenerational redistribution desired, as well as on the extent of correction deemed necessary to supplement individuals' choices (e.g., for those who save "too little").

As economies develop, financial sophistication advances, prosperity grows, and social policy matures, we may expect the "optimum" size of the state pillar to fall over time. We will certainly be surprised to see the persistence of corner solutions—where all provisions are concentrated in a single pillar. Nevertheless, perceptions do often lag behind reality: opposition in Greece to players other than the state in pension provision is often justified by distrust of the financial sector, or is phrased as a general defense of social policy. Both positions may be premised on a priori misperceptions, about modern finance or about the infeasibility of social policy instruments other than pensions.

Yet such perceptions are arguably anachronistic and generate what political scientists term "path dependence" (Pierson 2000). For example, Greek public discussions often used to rule out any suggestion of a multipillar framework. This sidesteps discussion about the problems of relying exclusively on a monolithic source for pensions. It also avoids mention of the benefits of relying on a wider base: the ability to spread demographic risk more widely, or the advantages of not being locked in a "one-size-fits-all" pension policy.

Likewise multipillar systems, through clear assignment, can add transparency and limit the possibility of "playing the system" to benefit some individuals and groups at the expense of others. Two conditions, however, are *sine qua non*: First, public systems using PAYG finance should be based on uniform general rules; otherwise, some sectors will benefit at the expense of others. Second, occupational systems should be based on prefunding (a pension pot). Such systems deal automatically with job mobility, as the pension pot moves with the worker. Prefunding also limits one occupation from paying for another, as would be the case in a PAYG system when one occupation systematically retires at a younger age.

When state pension systems were originally set up, they often replaced preexisting PAYG systems. In the postwar climate, redistribution in favor of the older generation was also seen as an important consideration. As aging increasingly replaced this solicitude with worries about future sustainability and public contingent liabilities, the built-in generosity of pension systems was questioned (OECD 1988), and pension reforms were once again placed on the agenda. Early on "path dependence" was perceived as an endemic threat; institutions could acquire a life of their own and vested interests could block reform or steer it toward their own benefit. Nevertheless, after a slow start in the 1980s, the pace of pension system reform picked up, with the result that by 2010 those countries that had *not* rebased their system to include non-state pillars were in a clear minority, at least in the European Union (see Commission of the European Communities 2012), as shown in figure 11.1.

Contribution of private pension schemes varies across the EU

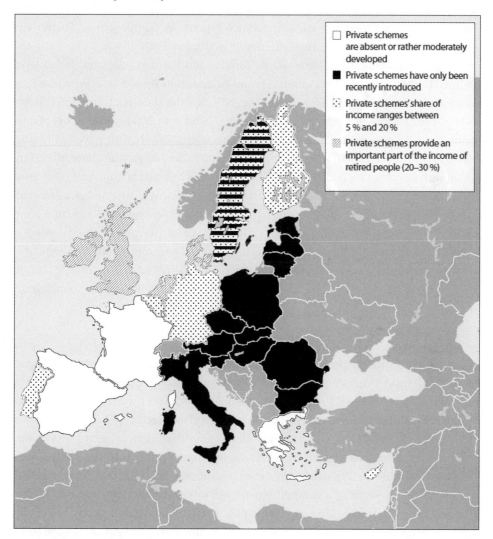

Figure 11.1
Spread of the introduction of private pension schemes in the European Union, 2010
Source: European Commission (2010)

A large number of variants exist internationally that take a general multipillar framework (Bonoli and Shinkawa 2005; Barr and Diamond 2010). We find variants of multipillar systems replacing social insurance systems in Europe, where Switzerland was the first to introduce a formal multipillar system in 1988. It was successfully followed by Denmark and the Netherlands. Sweden was the first to introduce Notional Defined Contributions in 1995 and has found emulators in Poland and elsewhere. Italy proceeded on a multipillar reform based on NDC for the state pillar in 1995 (known as the "Dini reforms"). Germany's own "Riester" reform in 2004, while not explicitly going the NDC way shares many of its key characteristics. The Antipodes (Australia, New Zealand) have experimented widely with means testing for the state pillar combined with annuities for occupational pensions. Other selected features can be gleaned from elsewhere: Canada, the United States (401k pensions), Latin America (recognition bonds), and Asia (provident funds). International experience does not only point to positive lessons but also negative ones. Argentina and Hungary both proceeded to multipillar reform only to reverse course later, as the state appropriated accumulated private reserves. The pension policy toolbox is thus far fuller than many (at least in Greece) think it is; eclectic utilization of system elements can be adapted to match the needs of Greece.

11.2.3 The Greek Pension System: A Mechanism for Disaster

If one examines the history of pension insurance in Greece, it is governance capacity that is most obviously deficient. The pension system is constructed around the main pension provider IKA (Foundation for Social Insurance), with responsibility for the social insurance of employees chiefly of the private sector. IKA was founded in 1934 and re-founded post war in 1951. At the time the financial sector was reeling from the effects of state default in the 1930s and hyperinflation in the 1940s, while postwar conditions necessitated major intergenerational transfers. IKA, as its contemporary US Social Security, exhibited what were in the 1930s state-of-the-art design features: a foundation on insurance principles, PAYG financing, a progressive benefits scale favoring lower pensions, an ambition to be the chief provider of old-age social protection.

Unlike the United States, social insurance in Greece faltered on two flaws: The first such were problems in governance and implementation. Two examples will suffice. A unique social security number is an indispensable tool for a social insurance system, as it allows the tracking of individuals' careers and pension claims. Such a number was operational in the United States within three years; in Greece it was legislated in detail in 1992 and started being used only after 2009. Regular actuarial reviews are important as early warning devices. In Greece the obligation to table such reviews was repeatedly legislated, and universally ignored. Governance shortcomings greatly magnified the impact of the second flaw: As in the United States, the original plan foresaw IKA operating as the unchallenged sole provider by fully incorporating preexisting PAYG funds. However, reaction by unions and employers, led to a compromise where IKA tolerated the parallel existence of other occupational PAYG funds, which were allowed to persist, supposedly to ease the transition.[7]

The second flaw is fragmentation. Seventy-five years after the decision to consolidate pensions, old-age income protection is still characterized by the existence of three "tranches" of state-provided benefits. Everyone is entitled to a "primary pension." For private employees this is mostly, though not exclusively, supplied by IKA, which supplies around 70 to 80 percent replacement for a full 35-year career. Farmers have their own primary pension fund (OGA) as do the self-employed (OAEE). Employees are additionally covered by compulsory "auxiliary funds"; these are more specialized by occupation and supply a further 20 percent (or so) replacement. Though all pension providers (both primary and auxiliary) were financed by PAYG, they are commonly understood by their members *as if* they operated on a prefunded basis. The third tranche is provided by separation funds paying out one-off lump sums on retirement to a minority of the population, who are overwhelmingly associated with the public sector. In recent years there has been a trend toward institutional consolidation, limiting both the number of primary funds (currently down to under ten), and auxiliary funds (currently in the teens). However, this is more apparent than real, as consolidation is often limited to the "name plate in the entrance"; the new amalgamated fund can preserve within itself differentiation both in contributions and entitlements in perpetuity.

The decision to tolerate fragmentation and to abandon the principle of equal treatment in PAYG systems was tantamount to giving a nod in the direction of cross-subsidizing parts of the population. This fragmentation, coupled with a judicious absence of information, meant that pension provisions could be used to introduce, maintain, and disguise sectoral privileges. This institutional framework encouraged defensive attitudes and attitudes highly resistant to change (O'Donnel and Tinios 2003). In retrospect, fragmentation was responsible for four key shortcomings that have plagued the system since its inception (Börsch-Supan and Tinios 2001; Tinios 2010):

• Fragmentation was used as a mechanism in the political economy of securing privileges. Lobbying for embedded privileges, earmarked taxes, special retirement ages, and other privileges were practiced with great aplomb. Over time this bred further fragmentation, both by the creation of new funds[8] and by securing different insurance terms *within* larger funds (e.g., IKA). Fragmentation is thus understated by the number of institutions available, as there is as much heterogeneity within as between institutions. For example, in IKA what is held to be "the rule" for retirement ages is followed only by 15 percent of recent retirees; 85 percent retire earlier, citing one of a multitude of exceptions. Despite the legal complexity, in economic terms all funds were indistinguishable: They were mandatory, governed by law, state-run, and financed by PAYG. Their separate existence, however, allowed individuals and groups to "play the system." The combination of primary and auxiliary pension could easily lead to earnings replacement exceeding 100 percent. In those cases where revenue was insufficient, it was sometimes politically easier to endow funds with earmarked taxes in order to ensure their continued independence as institutions.[9]

• Fragmentation also removed constraints on increasing expenditure on a micro level. So long as an occupational group could pay for its own pensions by shifting the cost to others, there was little to limit its ambitions for higher pensions. Particular groups who had secured open-ended guarantees took the lead in pension generosity; in the civil service and in banks total pensions rose to well above 100 percent of final salary. Pension ages for specific groups fell as they vied to be included in the "heavy and hazardous occupations list," or to negotiate separate old-age pension ages—some comically low. While the average person probably did not retire especially early, there was a large privileged minority in the public sector who retired well before their 50s (Tinios 2010). Given that pension privileges were concentrated among better-off workers, the pension system as a whole operated to increase inequality—despite its justification as social policy.

• Ever since the inflation of the 1970s and 1980s, pension increases were decoupled from pension providers' income, the shortfall being made up by government grants. The sudden increase of the minimum pension in the early 1980s resulted in two-thirds of IKA pensioners being entitled to the same amount, regardless of their contribution histories. Thus a majority of IKA members receive a pension unrelated to their contributions. This makes nonsense of the supposedly insurance basis and serves as a dramatic incentive to evade contributions. So high minimum pensions both increase expenditure and limit revenue. Starting with IKA, ballooning deficits of pension providers, and the need to provide grants to finance them (equivalent in 2007 to a third of total pension expenditure), became an increasingly important determinant of the overall deficit of the government, and of its borrowing needs.

• Discussions on the need to reform the system were invariably stalled, as differences about redistribution *within* generations (the privileges of particular sectors) were conflated with the general issue of needing to rebase redistribution *between* generations. As a result reforms were piecemeal and consistently fell below needs. System generosity, originally justified by the special needs of the first postwar generation, was retained and even increased. In consequence the pension system was seriously in deficit from the 1980s, well before aging struck. It thus has to cope with an aging problem ("the issues of the 21st century") while "the issues of the 20th century" are still pending (Tinios 2012b; EBEA 2016).

The upshot of these considerations was a dysfunctional pension system, a true "microfoundation of disaster" (Lyberaki and Tinios 2012). Being in a perennial state of reform, it nurtured constant uncertainty as to the exact content of the promises being handed out. Indecision on pensions had wider implications. Other social expenditure was crowded out. The "rebasing of social protection" away from the family, which was necessary to build a social safety net, remained merely a stated wish—in contrast to what happened in other EU Mediterranean countries from the mid-1990s (Lyberaki and Tinios 2014). Similarly pensions from the 2000s became the "sacred cow" of Greek political economy, galvanizing opposition to the reformist agenda and thus blocking wider structural change (Featherstone and Papadimitriou 2008).[10]

11.3   The Challenge: How to Stop a Race to the Bottom?

Greece entered the bailout period with a pension system universally acknowledged as in need of reform: it was fulfilling its social role badly; it added to public deficits and undermined productive efficiency. The Greek pension system had five key failings.[11] It was:

1. *Costly*   In 2007 pensions absorbed more than 12 percent of GDP (OECD 2007), the second highest percentage in the European Union after Italy.[12]

2. *Under severe demographic threat*   According to government projections, Greece expected the highest additional pension expenditure of any EU country in 2060, almost double compared to 2010. In contrast, Italy, which had implemented the "Dini" reforms in 1996, was actually able to show a fall in expenditure (EPC 2009, 2012).

3. *Economically inefficient*   Pensions bore a weak link to contributions. Contributions were hence perceived as a labor tax, and incentives for contribution evasion were large. Moreover a multitude of pension regimes led to a patchwork of cross-subsidization, typically aiding the public sector and other sheltered sectors. Contributions were high in manufacturing and hence constituted a permanent burden to

competitiveness, which was shouldered by the private sector and exports.[13] (Börsch-Supan and Tinios 2001; Tinios 2014).

4. *Socially ineffective*   Official reports admit that "poverty is gray in color," in the sense that the risk of poverty in Greece was overwhelmingly concentrated in the population over 65 years of age, despite the high expenditure on pensions (Lyberaki, Tinios, and Georgiadis 2010; Tinios 2010).[14]

5. *Resistant to change*   At least since 1990 the pension system was undergoing a perennial "reform by installments" (Tinios 2005; Triantafyllou 2006; Featherstone and Papadimitriou 2008); partial reforms took place in 1990, 1992, 1998, 2002, and 2008. This increased uncertainty, and retained pension reform as a permanent thorn in the political economy of the country.

The combination of the five "woes" *should* have made pension reform a win-win proposition, combining economic efficiency with equity, while tackling the looming issue of population aging. That meaningful reform was postponed is proof that the pension system had been "subverted" to support sectional interests; it was those interests that, time and again, blocked change.

It was thus left to the MoU to fill the gap, with the July 2010 pension reform, the first piece of legislation following the loan agreement. The simple argument of "there is no alternative" served as justification, allowing the internal political establishment to "wash its hands," by citing external compulsion by the Troika (Tinios 2015a). This stance simplified PR (public relations) but stoked up legitimization problems.

11.3.1   Features of the Post-bailout Greek Pension Reforms

Whatever its origins, the preamble of the pension law L3863/2010 stated boldly that "our objective is to change the system radically" (Parliament 2010). There is general agreement that the law is far more drastic than its predecessors. In describing the system, we must be careful to distinguish between long-term "steady-state" provisions setting up new pension arrangements and medium-term implementation effects that would operate in the decade after the law was passed. These two types of effects frequently operated in opposing directions. Pension legislation was added in at least four further laws between 2010 and 2014. A summary of these developments is as follows (for details, see OECD 2011; Matsaganis 2011; Tinios 2010):

1. *A "new" state pension system for the very long term*   (a) *Pension calculation.* The previous system was to be replaced by a new system of pension calculation, timed to start in 2015. Each pensioner would be entitled to a pension from the public system which would come in two parts: A flat-rate "basic pension" of approximately

360 euros, together with a proportional part linked to the number of years of contributions.[15] If careers remain as short as at the time when the law was passed (around 25 years' contributions), the new system would prove less generous. However, should careers match those in the rest of the EU (around 40 years), replacement rates would be equivalent to current ones (figure 11.2).[16] (b) *Gradual introduction.* The new system was to spread very gradually, in the sense that it was to be implemented for the first time in 2015, after which date it would be applied on a *pro rata* basis. In other words, a retiree in 2015 with 30 years' contribution, out of which two in the new system, should receive 2/30ths of his pension by use

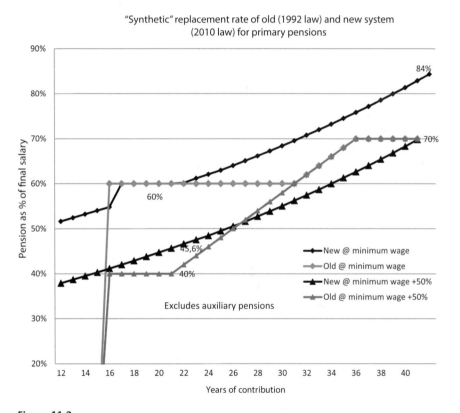

Figure 11.2
Simulation of replacement rates of the old and new pension systems, for different career lengths. Auxiliary pensions are not included. Pensions evaluated at different years of contributions for individuals paid through their lives at (a) the minimum wage and (b) minimum plus 50 percent.
Source: Tinios (2013, app. 2)

of the new system and 28/30ths by the old system. The spread of the system was to be extremely slow; for the duration of the crisis individuals would be faced with the old system. (c) *Retirement ages*. For those distant from retirement, their retirement age would increase very rapidly in a step fashion and at different speeds for different individuals, occupations or cohorts, affecting especially women younger than 30. A subsequent law in 2012 further increased retirement ages to 67, without a period of transition.[17]

2. *Fund consolidation for primary pensions*   The law abolished a large number of providers incorporating them into a single primary pension provider—IKA ETAM. However, the consolidations were largely cosmetic (in the sense that preexisting differences in contribution rates, retirement ages, and pension entitlements were preserved within the larger funds). A notable exception was the new hire of civil servants, who are insured since 2013 in the private sector fund (IKA) on an equal basis to private employees. Thus, while the steady state became less generous across the board by implementing uniform rules for new periods of work across providers, cross-subsidies due to fragmentation were retained in the long transition period. A strange feature is that differences in contribution rates were retained, despite accrual rates for *new* rights being equalized after 2013. Contributors are thus in the paradoxical position of paying different amounts for the same insurance coverage, depending on what their original pension provider had been,[18] "*Effective* fund consolidation" remained as one of the items still outstanding in 2015.

3. *Extensive "grandfathering"*   Grandfathering measures protected those close to retirement during what was characterized as the transition phase. So rights to lower retirement ages and higher replacement rates were largely preserved for people close to 50 years of age. This allowed the government to legislate for later retirement in the steady state, at the same time as vigorously pursuing early retirement during the crisis, especially among women (Lyberaki and Tinios 2012).[19] For example, those close to retirement age in 2010 were allowed to "buy in" up to 7 years' extra contributions to facilitate exit. In a similar development, a "technical" detail meant earlier retirement for mothers by up to 5 years.[20] Many individuals thus saw their retirement ages effectively *reduced*. Though no projections were ever released, these measures largely exempted all those retiring by 2020.

4. *Preannouncement of future retrenchment*   Many changes were preannounced. Such were an overhaul of the "heavy and unhygienic occupations" system, a clamp down on fraudulent invalidity and survivors' pensions, and other governance improvements. Emphasis would once again be placed on curbing contribution evasion. The

contribution of these changes to the fiscal situation of the system remains uncertain. The way hairdressers are treated in the reform of the "heavy occupations" is indicative of the general medium term issues: *New* hairdressers are, since 2012, no longer entitled to retiring 5 years early as a "heavy occupations." However, those with more than 10 years tenure retain that right. In this way the government could claim that the iconic case of hairdressers is no longer privileged; however, all hairdressers who were to retire for the next 15 or more years will do so 5 years earlier than other workers. In this, as in other cases, public finance savings were postponed to the distant future.

5. *Rebasing of auxiliary pensions to take place by 2015*   The 2010 reform only dealt with primary pensions. It hived off auxiliary pensions by arguing that they were inherently different, notably by explicitly ruling out any guarantee on behalf of the state. Subsequent legislation in 2012 (rather wishfully) attempted to treat them as self-sustaining independent occupational pension systems, based on individual accounts and operating on a version of a notional defined contribution system.[21] Should there appear a shortfall of revenue, financial equilibrium would have to be achieved by across-the-board percentage cuts affecting all pensions. Interestingly, there is no converse provision—pensions can only *fall* but not rise. The stability of the system may be in question (Zampelis 2013). The decision not to bankroll auxiliary pensions led to cuts that were difficult to justify or to explain, with the result that the future of the new arrangements is itself controversial. Many measures had not been completed or were suspended pending discussion with the Troika. As a result, four years after the reform, it was still difficult to definitively characterize the position and function of auxiliary pensions in overall system architecture.[22]

The criticism often voiced is that the Greek austerity program is directly due to the implementation of a "neoliberal agenda" (e.g., Busch et al. 2013). Such an agenda—at least in its Latin American variant—included privatization of pensions as a central feature (e.g., Diamond and Valdes-Pietro 1994). Similarly European reforms since the 1990s all included the strengthening of non-state pensions (Tompson 2009; Tinios 2012c). By contrast, the Greek reform conspicuously failed to move in any direction encouraging non-state provision. It did *not* challenge the central role of public pensions, and maintained PAYG as the sole mode of finance. Despite some innovative features, it is a reform that has clearly chosen continuity over systemic change. The new system is better seen as part of a defensive strategy to contain change rather than a bold attempt to use pension policy as part of the overall adjustment necessitated by the crisis.

Other features of the reform can be cited to support the position that the 2010 reform is less bold than it is made out to be:

• *Is the new system for the steady state less generous than the old?*   The replacement rate of the new system will lead to lower pensions only if the current low number of contribution years is maintained, namely if contribution evasion remains at its current high levels indefinitely (Tinios 2013). If, as is reasonable for the decades to 2060, career length converges to European norms—which are well above 35 or 40 years—then simple calculations (figure 11.2) simulating old and new provisions show that the new primary pensions system leads to *higher* replacement rates (except perhaps for the very affluent).[23] For a full career of 40 years, once auxiliary pensions are factored in, replacement rates will remain close to 100 percent. If this is so, the new system leaves very little room for income to be supplemented from sources outside the state, even in the distant future.

• *Do the ambitions the state assigns to its own system remain imperial?*   In the sense that it persists in denying any role to occupational or private provision for income replacement for the coming two generations to 2060, the state does remain imperial. Financing pensions is expected to remain an exclusive charge on the public purse, complicating long-term fiscal planning.

Grandfathering and other provisions make clear that the targeting of the 2010 reform was the very long term. The IMF *ex post* review concedes that the reform, despite addressing pension sustainability, "addressed only *long-term* structural imbalances" (IMF 2013, p. 38). This left entirely open what was to happen in the decade to 2020, the crucial years of adjustment to post–MoU reality. We can see this by comparing the official expenditure projections submitted to the EU Aging Working Group (AWG) in 2009 (before the reform) with those submitted in late 2010 (published in 2012) that incorporate the effects of the reform. Indeed in the AWG 2012 the reduction of the pensions as percent of GDP is by far the largest in the European Union—a fall of 9.5 percent in 2060. Figure 11.3 compares the two projections to show that the effect of the law (despite pension cuts) only begins to be noticeable well *after* 2020.

The situation is *more* critical for the medium term and the transition period. In the period 2010 to 2015 retirement was taking place under the old system. We have seen that the law encouraged early retirement especially among women; this could be due to a belief that it is more important to shelter male family "breadwinners," as well as a misplaced belief that less work for older workers means more work for the younger unemployed.[24] The law also encouraged early retirement because pensions for those close to retirement age were barely affected. Pension deficits from 2010

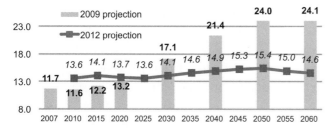

Figure 11.3

Comparing official pre- and post-reform projections, 2009 and 2012

Source: Tinios (2013, app. 1)

onward consistently overshot targets, due to greater demand for pensions but also due to a faster than expected reduction in contribution revenue. Revenue shortfalls concentrated in those areas where contributors had greater discretion and where liquidity issues were more pressing (small businesses, the self-employed, farmers).[25]

This design fault in the pension reform was the starting point for a vicious circle that severely undermines trust in pensions as a whole. As the short- and medium-term effects in net cash flows were not foreseen, and the impact of grandfathering was underestimated, fiscal underperformance became endemic. It was added to a similar underperformance due to the late or inadequate implementation of structural measures (e.g., cutting back on pension entitlements or reducing the size of the public sector) with (hoped for) fiscal implications built into the medium-term or annual programs. As these programs could not be amended (the amount of bailout finance had been fixed *ab initio* and was invariant), other sources of budget finance had to be found to compensate for the losses.[26]

Indeed the overall progress of the bailout in Greece cannot be understood without factoring in these regular, yet completely unforeseen, "unintended consequences" (Tinios 2015a). What this meant in terms of budget execution was that, as expenditure overruns could not be financed by borrowing, they had to be counterbalanced by extraordinary measures to make up for losses. So the overall budget targets were met, but the *actual* program was far removed from that originally planned. In particular, structural measures were replaced willy-nilly by extraordinary taxation levies and across-the-board cuts. The most notorious fiscal example was the imposition of an extraordinary levy on income of homeowners using information in electricity bills in September 2011, as the only way to meet the 2011 borrowing target.

Pensions-in-payment (i.e., current pensions paid out of existing commitments, some to individuals well into their 80s) were a tempting target for this process. Pensions are the largest single public expenditure item; they are paid to groups who have exited the labor market and whose protests, for that reason, are less disruptive than those of others. As a consequence, after the government had solemnly declared that "pensions were safe for a generation," it went ahead to cut pensions in payment on *ten* separate occasions between 2010 and mid-2013. The IMF in its ex post review (IMF 2013) politely acknowledges this issue, by stating that medium-term fiscal issues were solved by "eliminating pension bonuses" (*sic*); however, in all cases the pensions that were cut were calculated based on a consistent application of the pension rules that were still in force.

These repeated raids on pensions-in-payment led to cuts in the gross amount of some pensions of around half (figure 11.4). Interestingly, farmers' basic pensions (paid without the precondition of contributions) were *increased* by 9 percent, at the same time as larger pensions of the civil service were reduced by 48 percent and those of IKA by up to 44 percent. However, the bulk of non–farm sector pensions (including beneficiaries of the minimum pension) were only hit by the abolition of the 13th and 14th pension in 2013, amounting to a reduction of 14 percent.[27] Given that GDP per capita had fallen by 26 percent since 2008 and that private sector earnings were down by about a third, low-income pensioners were relatively more fortunate than low-wage workers; the rush to retirement is partly due to this fact. Confusion was increased by politicians and the media citing the *maximum* cuts (40 percent), which affected pensions over 2,000 euros per month, fewer than one in twenty pensioners, as characterizing *all* pensions.

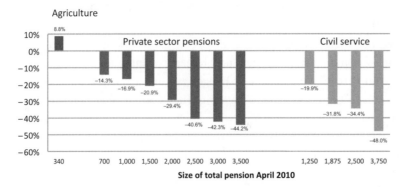

Figure 11.4
Cumulative drops of different types of pensions, 2010 to February 2013
Source: Tinios (2013)

Nevertheless, it is significant that no justification was ever offered for the extent of the cuts and their distribution across the pensioner population. In each subsequent episode the governments were concerned to point out that care had been taken to protect lower pensions. No calculation was ever published showing the *cumulative* effect of directing the brunt of retrenchment to the same group of individuals (as that of figure 11.4). Nor was any algorithm or underlying principle justifying the locus or extents of the cuts ever offered, let alone a justification of terming all such expenditure "pension bonuses." Finally, the same cuts were also applied to *new* pensions being issued, while governments were studiously vague about whether they were there to stay; even the *names* of cuts stressed the notion of "solidarity" and their extraordinary nature and were obviously designed to keep hopes alive that losses would, somehow, be recouped in the future.[28]

It is indicative of policy deliberation taking place in post–MoU Greece that the budgetary impact of these apparently not programmed, yet seemingly permanent, interventions was never made public or discussed. This applies *a fortiori* to their impact on long-term magnitudes and on system viability. For instance, the authorities had officially communicated to the European Union (EPC 2012) that long-term pension viability was assured on the basis of measures taken in 2010. When two years later the retirement age was *further* raised by two more years to 67, the impact this had on long-term magnitudes was never mentioned. Discussion of pensions appears to be condemned to take place in permanent fog.

One cannot overemphasize the importance of *ex post* cuts of this scale to pensions. In order for pensions to play their role as old-age income security, it is usually taken as axiomatic that once an award is made, the pension amount cannot be cut.[29] As no justification was ever given in Greece for the incidence or extent of the cuts, insecurity was entrenched. If pensions of 85-year-olds can be cut without justification and no warning, then any other cut is conceivable. A number of plausible reasons could have been offered for the cuts: retrospective adjustments imposed due to delays in pension reform, as a claw-back of pension increases received in the previous years, or even as redressing pension inequities. Yet, in an effort to pin an unpopular decision on the Troika, no explanation was ever sought or offered. In this way the paradoxical consequence of this blame avoidance was to "take the bottom out of the pension promise."

The cuts amount to an acknowledged inability to perform the functions (old-age income security), for which the system was set up in the first place. This could lead to a vicious circle—a pernicious race to the bottom where the reneging on commitments justifies and fuels disintermediation, which then leads to a shrinking of the contribution base. This, in turn, may necessitate further cuts, which push the system further along its downward spin.

The reneging of promises is evident in both the individual and the economywide scale. For those young enough to plan their life, it may mean a disincentive to participate and a reinforcement of the existing tendency to abandon the system. For those caught out, pensioners and those close to retirement, it must mean considerable hardship—in the form of sudden and abrupt falls in consumption. Higher pensions suffered the most; they were high most often because of long contribution histories and high contributions. In contrast, minimum pensions, which were the reward to career-long contribution evasion, were least affected (Tinios 2010). The social insurance character of the system thus suffered a heavy blow. Paying pension contributions will appear to the individual more and more like a tax on labor unrelated to any *quid pro quo*. The 2010 reform's declared attempt to boost reciprocity was thus largely neutralized. There will thus be increasing polarization between those with a full career in sectors where contributions cannot be evaded and those, such as the self-employed or employees of small businesses, who choose to avoid contributions where they can.

Taking a macro point of view and examining how the state pension system relates to the economy, we still have a system which is "too big." If collection of contributions has to rely increasingly on compulsion (because contributions bear only a weak link to future pensions), then it will affect the economy much as a tax on labor, which (unlike other taxes) is fully reflected in the price of exports. The pensions system's efficiency cost will thus be greater. Figure 11.2 shows that the public pensions system still aims at a replacement close to 100 percent (primary + auxiliary) of total remuneration for a full career of 40 years. This is large, even by European standards. Public pensions will hence carry on absorbing a large fraction of total production.[30]

The dysfunctional situations of the past—the primacy of pension claims on the distribution of income and the crowding-out of other social expenditure—are likely to return.[31] It is possible that the medium-term issues—disintermediation, encouragement of early retirement in the crisis, grandfathering—will *never* allow the system to graduate to the steady state anticipated in the long-term pension projections.[32]

11.3.2   Have Reforms since 2010 Addressed the Greek Pension Problem?

It is certainly true that the old habits of problem denial returned with a vengeance. Under the MoU, November 2014 was the time to review developments and to assess the need for corrections. However, all political parties decided that it was best that no discussions on pensions take place. The government parties claimed that the decisions taken in 2010 were more than sufficient; apart from technical details that do not involve major decisions, no one needed to worry. In order not to stoke discussion, the flow of data about the system was stemmed and information limited to press leaks. SYRIZA, then in opposition, was more complacent; they would have preferred to roll back the changes and return to 2009. A new round of social dialogue, scheduled for autumn 2015, would have had to start from scratch.

In the event, problem denial of this size proved infeasible. *New* pensions changes were forced by the necessity of completing a third bailout in the dramatic summer of 2015. Urgent measures in August 2015 to halt early retirement were followed by a lengthy and fraught process culminating to a *new* pension reform bill in May 2016.

Pension reform ushered in the first bailout in 2010. Paradoxically, *correcting* that reform with a succession of laws was the first and most difficult task of the third bailout in 2015 and 2016. Appendix A, written at the end of 2016, outlines how the 2016 legislation completed the vision initiated in 2010.

The conflicting views, the dearth of statistics, and the repeated and forced changes only reinforce the position of this chapter that enough is known to motivate the search for the new pension equilibrium. This should be in the direction of spreading risk away from the state and among all actors in society. The next section proceeds to outline such a new arrangement.

11.4   A Risk-Spreading Cooperative Solution in Outline

The reform we are advocating must be consonant with and complementary to the overall reform process the country needs. This implies a number of things as to both the ends of the reform and the means to be employed.

As far as *ends* are concerned, the first consideration is that the pension reform should support (and not undermine) economic recovery. It should help adjust the *overall* public sector size to post-crisis fiscal realities—notably in long-term national debt sustainability. We cannot ignore that public pensions constitute a large and rising part of general government expenditure. Second, it should provide a definitive resolution of the "pension problem." This means that it should remove pensions as an issue around which opposition to economic policy rallies. Third, it should restore trust to the system and reaffirm its organizing principles. For younger contributors, it should re-establish a credible link to contributions. For older contributors, it should offer a different type of reassurance—that cuts to pensions have reached their maximum and that in this way system promises can, once again, be taken seriously. This translates to providing a convincing quantitative justification (in the form of an algorithm) for the pension cuts that have already taken place. This justification must be based on ideas of horizontal and vertical justice and should be applied retrospectively to the cuts since 2010; it should provide a bridge between aggregate magnitudes and the way these are shared out among individuals.[33]

As for *means,* the key idea is to call for a partnership between the state, individuals, and firms. If the state were to concentrate on poverty prevention, in the context of clearly assigned roles, then for the majority of contributors there will appear a clear link between contributions and individual pension benefits. Paying in to the pension system will cease to be viewed as a labor tax but will rediscover a role as a means toward individual betterment. A clear link between individual pension contributions and finance of the real economy will also stress the interdependence between social expenditure and the real economy. A mixed system, as contrasted to the current monolithic system, will allow individuals and the private sector (through occupational solidarity, individual saving and more work) to finance, and to be *seen* to finance, a greater share of the overall benefits they will themselves draw as pensions. In other words, the reform will encourage a kind of public-private partnership to meet the costs of aging. It will do so through the restoration of incentives and through new structures for cooperation and joint resolution of problems.

This overall adjustment will be based on two key margins. The first concerns pension system design. By providing incentives for more affluent individuals (or occupations) to finance and bear the risk for a greater share of their own retirement, public monies can be concentrated in areas of greater need (poorer individuals, interrupted careers, insufficient entitlements). In such a way, by drawing pensioner guarantees from two (or more) separate directions, risk is dispersed, as compared to a system that relies exclusively on the state. Rather than the state subsidizing and guaranteeing all pensions, it would concentrate its efforts on poorer individuals. Distinguishing between redistribution and income replacement can combine a focus on poverty with a stronger link between contributions and pensions.

The second margin concerns the expansion of employment, through positive incentives for participating in the labor force and working for more years. Lengthening the actual period of contributions may act as a fourth pillar of the pension system.[34] This would prolong active life at the individual contribution level. In Greece, it would further mean increasing women's labor participation from its current low state to the levels encountered in Northern Europe, namely from 56 percent participation to closer to 80 percent (Tinios 2010). Enabling more child care services would raise women's labor participation and thus, by their permanent addition to the pension system's contributions, go around the problem of inadequate pensions for women in old age.[35]

Such a pension design could be considered a 3-1/2 pillar system. The current system that depends exclusively on the state would be replaced by a system where total income replacement comes from three different sources and means of finance. Below we provide a sketch of the system's "architecture," and leave the full discussion of the problem areas to section 11.5. Yet such details as the relative size of pillars, the exact replacement rate of each, the extent of state subsidy, and the speed of transition still remain open. They will take shape at public forums as a menu is deliberated.

11.4.1   First Pillar

The *first pillar* pertains to public pensions. These are pensions financed and provided by government agencies on a PAYG basis. Public pensions will be two-tier. They will offer replacement of between 30 and 50 percent—that is, a little over half of today's public pensions. This range is similar to the share of public pensions in systems such as those of the Netherlands and Denmark, and it will include meaningful interactions with the other pillars. Reduced expenditure on public pensions will be accompanied by substantial reductions in the contribution rate (currently at least 26 percentage points) and will likely replace *both* primary and supplementary pensions. It may even be that the two components will be merged: a means-tested pension collectable at the age of 67 and a notional defined contribution (NDC) pension for the remaining years (Holzman and Palmer 2006). The means-tested pension would be designed to alleviate old-age poverty and to serve as a safety net, replacing the current system for the uninsured with a minimal pension. Notional defined contribution systems, as in Sweden and Italy, finance current pensions from current contributions; individual pensions, though, are rationalized based on the contributions made to an individual (notional) account. The amount collected in an individual's account then has to finance that individual's entire retirement period; the individual decides when to retire taking into account that later retirement yields a higher pension. The NDC pension may be collected after the age of (say) 63 and will be completely neutral with regard to postponing retirement. On the supply of pensions, *all* current old-age providers will be replaced by a single state provider. All separate social insurance contributions and collection systems will be replaced by a single system that collects contributions. This may be collected as part of income tax, as in the United States, or may (at least initially) be collected by a single institution integrated with a bank payment system.[36]

11.4.2   Second Pillar

The *second pillar* will make occupational pensions mandatory based on a defined, pre-funded contribution. The funds will collect assets, invest them, and pay annuities to the members, additional to the public pensions of the first pillar. Membership will be compulsory by occupation, with a minimum contribution rate of 3 to 5 percent. These pensions will thus admit any petition by an occupational group to raise pensions more than the amount guaranteed by the first pillar. The main feature of this design is that it will include a provision to gradually eliminate "privileges" by folding their cost into new funds, as will be discussed in the next section. Auxiliary and separation funds properties will help finance higher entitlements of previously privileged sectors, a concept that was implemented in Italy. It may be possible for individuals to opt out of stakeholder pensions and to direct their contributions to third-pillar pensions, as already introduced in the United Kingdom.

11.4.3 Third Pillar

The *third pillar* refers to individually tailored provisions, akin to personal savings. As we mentioned earlier, the 2010 reform abruptly changed public entitlements. Consequently only younger participants will have the time to substitute private savings to make up for the losses. Unfortunately, the time available to today's 40-year-olds is not sufficient, and they face the prospect of entering old age with grossly inadequate pensions. The third pillar will play the critical role of enabling those with unsteady employment to accumulate finances to partially make up for the gaps.[37] The third pillar will thus allow individuals whose careers do not follow conventional paths (e.g., expatriates, occupationally migrant workers) to fashion their own provisions for old age. It is for these reasons that an argument can be made for privileged tax treatment of third-pillar contributions, as is common in many countries including the United States.

11.4.4 Third and a Half Pillar

The *third and a half pillar* will be a conscious attempt to integrate greater participation in the workforce and longer careers into the system's design. The expansion of work periods could take different forms: delaying retirement for the employed, increasing employment opportunities for working mothers, and even luring recent pensioners back to the labor market with new flexible types of labor contracts. The possibility of "re-contracting retirement" would be an opportunity for baby boomers (primarily women) who retired during the 2010 crisis to return to the labor force, and avoid the prospect of spending their remaining lives on very low pensions. Many such pensioners regret what was in many instances a rash decision (as may become more evident when the recovery sets off), and bringing the retired back to the labor market will be a net gain.

The new proposed system must meet a number of requirements, which will also differentiate it from the current approach:

• *A fast transition* The 2010 law foresaw a very gradual, *pro rata,* spread of the new system. In that system the old arrangements dominate until well into the second half of the 2020s. A faster transition should aim to bring forward the date in which the first pension calculated fully under new rules is issued. It is unavoidable that *current* pensioners cannot fully join the new arrangements; they should receive, however, new guarantees supported by actuarial studies. All those born after, say, 1985, should enter fully in the steady state from the first day. Intermediate generations should be allowed to choose, and there should be incentives to encourage a faster switch. Such may be "recognition bonds" for those who want to transfer to the new system, giving the possibility of buying in to the new system. The part of the system that remains under PAYG does not pose major problems; current contributions would still pay for current pensions. A problem arises for that part of the new system that is prefunded; in that case 'new' contributions will not be available to finance 'old' pensions, as they are earmarked to finance future pension liabilities. The part of second pillar pensions guaranteed by recognition bonds must remain a charge on the current working generation. That is the well-known "double-payment contention," whereby the last generation of a PAYG system has to finance both their own and their parents' pension. Though this problem is not insurmountable, it introduces a trade-off between the size of the new prefunded pillar and containing the costs to the public purse. Section 5 analyzes the transition period in greater detail, including the double-contention issue.

• *Need for new institutions* A social policy institute is needed to collect and collate all information from old funds. It must be responsible for system governance and will take over social policy and social planning, a role now dispersed among a number of actors. The new second and third pillar pensions need to be supervised by a new body. Finally, there must be a major investment in financial literacy. A switch from today's paternalistic structure where all major decisions are taken centrally by the state to a situation where the individual takes control of key decisions, presupposes that individuals are in a position to take advantage of such freedoms.

However it may be, the policy toolbox is much fuller than is generally thought in Greece. It is remarkable that past proposals that were made received little attention. For instance, the use of recognition bonds to speed up transition to prefunding was already advocated by Tinios (1995), while the Spraos report (1997) and Börsch-Supan and Tinios (2001) sketch the transition to a multipillar system. Nektarios's writings on such a reform stretch over a decade (Nektarios 1996, 2008, 2012). Zampelis (1998) has also been an early advocate for a systemic transition. Karavitis's (2011) position is well argued, while the Bank of Greece (2013) is, apparently, a late convert to the cause. Xafa and Tinios (2014) flesh out a proposal to replace all pensions with a fixed monthly payment of 700 euros for everyone over 67; this was to be financed by a retirement age increase and by existing government grants. Their proposal would have allowed all contributions to be abolished and all pension fund employees who collect contributions to be redeployed. The third bailout saw increased interest in a multipillar system: The Athens Chamber of Commerce and Industry published a report in late 2015 (EBEA 2016). A report in October 2015 of a Committee of Sages appointed by the Minister of Labor argued openly for such a system; its recommendation was quickly shelved, however (Ministry of Labor Committee 2015).

As the crisis evolved, and many dire warnings became reality; radical proposals that had been dismissed before the crisis started to appear feasible and even desirable. One of the advantages of the rapid deterioration and disappearance of trust in the pension system has been that the population may be more willing to consider alternatives. When a return to the pre-crisis status quo is accepted as impossible, radical but economically sensible alternatives appear preferable to the arbitrariness and rapid shifts of current practices. Reform discussions enter a more productive phase.

11.5   Is the Transition Period the Achilles' Heel of Multipillar Reforms?

Multipillar systems do, however, have an Achilles' heel, in the form of the transition period. Indeed the problems that could arise during the transition have often been used as the main argument to halt discussion in its tracks. The main problem is the *double-payment contention*: during the transition, individuals of working age will have to pay both for their own and for their parents' pensions.

Appendix B examines this issue in detail and goes so far as to calibrate a macroeconomic model that features a transition. The argument is summarized in this section. The bottom line is encouraging: *there is no theoretical basis to argue against a transition to a multipillar system.*

In a nutshell, the transition problem can be reduced to the intentionally extreme and stylized argument: if the PAYG system is abandoned overnight, who will provide for the current retirees, whose livelihood depends on the contributions made by the current workers?

The simple approach would be to put all the burden on current workers: in such a scenario the current workers would have to keep on making contributions to provide for the current old and additionally save to fund their own retirement (since from now on the system will be fully funded, so that the current workers cannot count on receiving contributions from future workers). We *do not accept* such an approach. It would place a disproportionate burden on the current generation of workers and would stall GDP growth.

We consider an alternative approach to the transition problem: The current retirees receive "recognition bonds." To ensure that they do not suffer any losses, we require explicitly that these bonds be of equal value to the payouts the retirees would obtain from the current PAYG system. The current workers are no longer required to make social security contributions. The government, however, raises taxes (in perpetuity) to pay interest on the recognition bonds.

Intuitively, by this means, the government achieves several objectives simultaneously. First, it allocates the burden of providing for the current retirees across all generations (rather than a single one). Second, it requires no increase in external borrowing, since the recognition bonds are held by domestic retirees. (Indeed "recognition" bonds should not even be thought as conventional debt, but rather as recognition of a liability to the current retirees, which exists anyway.) Third, this proposal enhances current workers' incentives to save and work, since they internalize the benefits of their labor more fully.

An open question, of course, remains as to whether the taxes needed to service the recognition bonds end up annihilating the benefits of a transition. To address this question fully, we need to consider an explicit macroeconomic model. We undertake this task in appendix B. Specifically we solve a standard, two-period, deterministic, overlapping generations model, such as that used to analyze the way in which one generation finances the pensions of its predecessor in a stylized PAYG system. In the model, competitive consumers supply labor to competitive firms. Wages and interest rates are set so that markets clear. To be conservative, we consider a closed economy, so that by construction, all debt (or change in national debt) must be held by domestic residents. Alternatively phrased, we exclude any possibility of cross-border financing.

Using the model, we first study a PAYG system under which current workers' contributions are directed to current retirees. We then study the transition to a prefunded system, with simultaneous usage of recognition bonds, as we stated above. We examine a full rather than a partial transition to prefunding—in other words a complete abolition of the first pillar and its replacement by the second and the third. We do not advocate such an extreme solution, but we analyze it to make our point more simply and forcefully.

We study the transition to prefunding in two different cases. In the first case, which we use as a benchmark, *labor is supplied inelastically, so higher labor taxes do not reduce the employment level*. We show that in this case, allocations and welfare of all generations are left unchanged during and after the transition to a prefunded system. This result is useful because it shows that it is possible to achieve a transition to a prefunded system without lowering the welfare of *any* generation—contrary to a common misperception that individuals will experience financial loss because of such a transition.

We then turn to the more realistic case where labor is supplied elastically, so labor taxes reduce the employment level. We treat social security contributions as labor taxes: this is an especially adequate assumption for Greece, where the constantly changing rules of the retirement system along with the pervasive contribution evasion essentially annihilate any reciprocity of the social security system. (Besides acting as labor taxes, social security contributions also distort intertemporal saving decisions.)

When labor supply is elastic, the transition to a fully funded system is strictly beneficial. The intuition is as follows. Suppose that the current old receive pension Y. In the PAYG system, the current young have to pay them Y, and that amount has to be raised through distortionary labor taxes, which reduce employment. The same holds for the young next period, and so on. With recognition bonds, the pension Y of the current old will be financed only partly through labor taxes: the current young pay $rY/(1 + r)$ in taxes, where r denotes the interest rate, and the remainder $Y/(1 + r)$ is collected through their purchases of recognition bonds. Recognition bonds pay Y when the current young become old, and this covers that generation's pension. In turn the government makes the payment Y on the bonds by raising taxes $rY/(1 + r)$ on the new young and by issuing new bonds worth $Y/(1 + r)$, which are purchased by the new young, and so on. Because labor taxes are smaller under the new system, employment and GDP are higher.

We assess the magnitude of these effects through a calibration exercise.[38] Depending on the assumptions that we make on the capital share, the Frisch elasticity of labor supply, trend growth, and so on, we obtain substantial gains in GDP. In our base-case scenario the benefits amount to a 7.68 percent increase in GDP during the transition period. In table 11.1 in appendix B we also report output gains when we perturb the baseline parameters in various directions, and show that for any reasonable calibration we obtain nontrivial GDP gains ranging from 2.88 to 11.5 percent.

Our model is likely to underestimate the benefits of moving to a prefunded system. This is because we assume, for tractability, representative workers who work for only one period. This means that labor supply in our model adjusts only at the intensive margin (increase/decrease of work hours per unit of time) and not at the extensive margin (participation/retirement decisions). In reality, both margins are relevant and the mechanisms that we describe would apply to both. Moreover a substantial fraction of the benefits of moving to a prefunded system is likely to arise from the extensive margin (i.e., longer working lives). This is because a prefunded system is better tailored to lead to optimal, individual-specific retirement decisions. In other words, individuals in such a system will be encouraged to work more and to retire later.

The conclusion we draw is the following: the transition problem can appear difficult to solve. However, there exists a relatively straightforward way to deal with it successfully, without raising external debt or making further cuts to existing retirement benefits.

Having addressed the theoretical objections, we next turn to the more pragmatic problems. There is the concern that issuance of recognition bonds will breach the Maastricht Treaty limits on national debt; thus, unless changes are made to that legal document, a shift to prefunding is ruled out. However, even in our thought experiment, though the stock of debt will be larger, the capacity to service it will also rise; the rise in debt is in essence different from the kind of obligation the treaty was mindful to avoid. Intuitively, what this reform does is to make explicit an obligation to future pensioners, which was previously implicit and contingent. It does not add to societal obligations but only makes them more transparent.

The transition in Greece would also have to deal with the practical issue of the fate of auxiliary funds and other special arrangements. The higher generosity in the case of independent funds was met by outside guarantees (the state or oligopolistic employers), while internal differentiation was borne by the less fortunate contributors. Currently most privileges are retained through grandfathering. However, the logic of recognition bonds can be adapted to deal with the phased withdrawal of the privileges. A similar issue was faced by auxiliary funds in enterprises, which had to adopt International Financial Reporting Standards (IFRS) in the early 2000s (Tinios 2011). IFRS required employers to prefund the totality of Defined Benefit pensions, even if those had hitherto been ignored.[39] A scheme implemented in 2005 for commercial banks (and subsequently adapted in Portugal) was to divide pensions in two. Those corresponding to general entitlements were retained by IKA, but the part *exceeding* "general entitlements" was actuarially costed and prefunded by the employer to a new fund.[40] This scheme could be adapted to deal with privileges in the new system, treating them as a "stranded cost": the cost of privileges could motivate negotiations as to how to split their financing among employers, workers, pensioners, and possibly the state (insofar as the privileges were originally guaranteed[41]). Privileges based on different behavior of occupational groups (e.g., later retirement for the professions) could justify their retention on a permanent basis. In this way previously privileged groups could be seen to be rising to their responsibilities, while heterogeneity could be justified through appeal to general principles of equitable burden sharing.

11.6   The Way Ahead: Signposting Four Problem Areas

One of the lessons that reformers have learned over the years is not to underestimate problems in implementing reform projects. Indeed this is precisely where economists can help the most. Problems should be charted and guidance should be provided. We next highlight four problem areas in the context of our proposed reform.

11.6.1   Problem Area I: Characterizing the Starting Point

Have post–MoU cuts already paved the way to a system change? We have seen that the highest pensions have already been reduced far from their purported values (up to 50 percent) and that retirement ages were increased to 67. While the abruptness and the lack of justification of the cuts have exerted a pernicious effect, to expect them to be restored is completely unrealistic. At the same time, the cuts remain to be justified. Moreover a floor beyond which pensions cannot fall should be found and defined in a convincing manner. This action is the key for confidence, and may well be the factor that convinces many people to endorse a new system.

The Supreme Court (Council of the State) had ruled that pension cuts up to 2012 were constitutional. However, it decided in March 2015 that those imposed *after* 2013 were insufficiently justified and hence were unconstitutional. Implementation of this decision is still pending in 2016. How to obey the court ruling without endangering public finances is one of the balancing acts of the third bailout program. (see appendix A; EBEA 2016).

Timing, and how that is related to the crisis, is another big issue. We must take onboard that setting up prefunding will follow a major destruction of asset values, whether these be bonds, real estate, or any other real assets such as small businesses. While the political risk of a future government raid (as in Argentina or Hungary) cannot be ruled out, coming in at the bottom of a rising market could imply the possibility of gains.[42]

Last, the inadequacies of data after 2010 have been mentioned. Characterizing the starting point would necessitate being able to track changes since 2010 and being very clear about the relative contribution of demographic factors, medium-term reform impacts and short-term crisis effects.

11.6.2 Problem Area II: Savings—Can Greece Save Enough?

Greeks have been used to heavy doses of paternalism in pensions. Though individual provision (through life insurance) has always been available, few have taken it up. Private coverage is seen as competitive to public provision (Tinios and Poupakis 2013). So relying on individual provision will encounter major obstacles. A big obstacle is understanding complex financial relations—by which we mean financial literacy. Can we "nudge households" in the right direction? A Greek reform must factor in the small family businesses, as well as the fact that Greek families plan at the household level—as the prevalence of gifts *inter vivos* proves. This is the kind of field where insights from behavioral economics can help (see Clark et al. 2012).

The supply side of savings must also be a source of concern. Is the financial sector in a position to offer the services and products needed? In Greece annuities are almost unknown.[43] But even across the European Union (barring the United Kingdom) financial services are expensive and stand in the way of private savings being able to compete with public pensions on an even playing field (Becker 2012). Though demand on a large scale will help with the provision of services, the transition would be smoother if there are initiatives preparing the supply side to respond.

11.6.3 Problem Area III: Fine-Tuning the Reform to Greek Idiosyncrasies

Greece has a number of idiosyncrasies that *could* enable reform to bypass its bottlenecks. The reform should be designed taking these idiosyncrasies into account. Three examples may suffice.

First, it is well known that Greek households, especially those with people over 50 years of age, have high holdings of illiquid real estate (European Central Bank 2013; Nektarios and Georgiadis 2009) and low holdings of financial and other assets. Households' illiquid assets could be used to help speed up the transition to the new system, and they could lessen the abruptness of changing entitlements for cohorts "caught out" by the latest reforms. In particular, households could be enticed to trade real estate holdings for pension rights. Households rich in property but with few contributions could use a variant of "reverse mortgages" to "purchase pension rights" using real estate as collateral—transforming illiquid real estate into an annuity (or perhaps even rights for long-term care—as is increasingly the case in the United States; see Nektarios 2012).[44] This proposal could set in motion an orderly run down of real estate holdings. It might prevent a housing market meltdown, which could occur when aging cohorts liquidate their holdings to pay for property taxes and their sustenance during retirement years.

Second, early retirement that appeared as a short-term solution during the crisis is only accruing problems for the future, both for system viability and for pension adequacy. There is overwhelming evidence that early retirement took off after 2010.[45] If this is combined with a tendency on the part of immigrants to return to their countries of origin, it is possible that the recovery may falter due to the labor shortages that result. An ordered "recall" of early retirements can be a major source of pension funding for the medium term. For example, in exchange for (part of) the pension being suspended, the possibility of "re-contracting" could be offered. This would reduce the pension bill in the medium term as well as offer an experienced source of labor when workers are in short supply.

Third, the contribution base needs to be reconsidered. At the moment, the contribution base for employees is the payroll, and for the self-employed and farmers contributions are based on "classes," which are arbitrary minimum amounts not related to any notion of ability to pay. Thus the system is labyrinthine and encourages contribution evasion on the part of small businesses and the self-employed. This so-called system of classes was traditionally justified as a second-best solution to problems of collecting contributions and estimating taxable capacity. The latter is, presumably, much less of a problem after six years' of improving tax administration. Thus the arguments for moving toward ad valorem contributions for the self-employed and farmers based on income declarations are far stronger. This strengthens the overall case for moving from payroll to income[46] as the basis for social insurance contributions, using the income tax infrastructure to collect the taxes. Such a consolidation would mean that government employees entrusted with contribution collection could be redirected elsewhere, and thus permit a major reduction in the government payroll. It also will do much to cut compliance costs on the part of businesses. The change in the distribution of social insurance payments could help the traded sectors as well by encouraging solidarity among different population groups.[47]

11.6.4   Problem Area IV: Governance and Implementation Issues

A pension reform contains a host of measures whose implementation may not be taken for granted. For example, stating the importance of means testing is easy—it allows for "social leveraging" by directing scarce public funds where they will have greater social benefit. Establishing who will be the beneficiary, ensuring that this does not inflict undue violence to incentives, and preventing fraud are all matters that demand governance capacity. Australia and New Zealand are two countries that rely on means testing to an extent far greater than other EU countries, combined with extensive private annuities (Bateman et al. 2001). It is possible that an antipodean-style discretionary system could be more attuned to the Greek situation than the European variants, so it should warrant further study.

However, there are a host of other administrative and governance preconditions, on which the success of the reform will be ultimately based: What will happen to pension fund employees? Will there be competitiveness gains for enterprises (compliance costs, transparency) and gains in labor mobility? Will insurance companies (currently severely circumscribed) be allowed a role in occupational provision? What kind of second-pillar provision can cover the large SME sector?[48] Simply enumerating the issues underlines the point that any reform must be carefully considered and tailored to the precise needs of the country; simply lifting a successful model from abroad will not do.

11.7   The Process: The *What, Who, How* Questions

Past attempts at pension reform in Greece all came to naught because they failed to communicate their intentions and to convince Greek people of the benefits of change. As a result pension reform became hostage to path dependence and languished for a very long time. The question of explaining and convincing must be seen as an integral part of a reform, and not as a simple PR enterprise to be completed as an afterthought.

The pension discussion in early 2015 is indicative of the problems. The new coalition government was united in its opposition to all changes implemented since 2010, which it interpreted as emblematic of the ills of Troika intervention. The relevant ministers are on record as intending to suspend the new method of pension calculation, preventing further rises in pension ages, restoring most (if not all) pension retrenchment, and rolling back changes in auxiliary funds. In doing so, they seem to be have been oblivious to the underlying demographic challenges, the preexisting deficit issues, as well as the fact that the country's GDP has shrunk by a quarter since 2008. Thus the complacency of the departing government was replaced by a kind of autism by the new one. The net result was to deepen confusion and uncertainty even further. The about-turn in the summer of 2015 preceding the third bailout was too abrupt and insufficiently justified not to make matters even worse.

This observation underlines the urgency of the project described in this chapter: *how* to undertake an overview of the state and prospects of pensions starting from first principles. A thorough investigation of the Greek government's most important long-term contingent liability should accompany and inform any discussions on the sustainability of the public debt.

There are indeed a number of features that could comprise an information pack that should accompany a pension discussion, to illustrate both the benefits of reform and the drawbacks of non-reform. Such an information pack should, at a minimum, contain data derived from three technical exercises: new sustainability figures to incorporate the effect of the crisis on employment and factor in the impacts of reforms, including the pension reductions; a detailed medium term cash flow projection to 2020; and last, microsimulations illustrating the impacts of both reform and non-reform to individuals.

There only remains one question, which is *who* will prepare, argue for, and promote the reform?[49] Pension reforms in Greece are subject to a version of the Prisoners' Dilemma. All agree that preparatory work should be started; no one wants to be seen to take the first step, especially if that involves preparing unpopular measures.

Taking the possible actors in turn, we know that governments have manifestly and repeatedly failed, political parties are ignored or maligned, no think tank has risked taking up pensions seriously, and social partners see the technical preparation of a pension reform as simply another move in a bargaining process. Pension reform is certainly beyond external institutions' political remit. Of course, it is more than a single individual can attempt (or perhaps be trusted with).

In querying who can take the first step for pension reform, we have come full circle. In the complex political economy of post-crisis Greece, we have reached an impasse: the search of an identity for the instigator apparently reached the null set.

And yet, arguing from first principles, we must conclude that the task of preparing a pension reform *should* be both doable and could be made laudable. It is, after all, clearly a win-win change.

Appendix A: Completing an Incomplete Reform: Pensions in 2015[50]

A.1   Completion of a "Half-Reform"

The second adjustment program was to end in December 2014, with pension changes at a critical juncture. The authorities had to prepare and submit in November 2014 a report assessing the pension situation, the implementation of reforms and the possible need for corrective action, something like a mid-term review of the overall reform. That report was never submitted, nor made public. Instead, the country proceeded to elections, with the pension issue apparently still open.

The narrative of this book documented that such a review was more than essential: Changes since 2010 were extensive for *younger* participants. However, the situation faced by the rest, namely by pensioners and by workers facing retirement was far less clear-cut. The evident desire of the authorities to protect incumbents had proved infeasible, necessitating repeated cuts of pensions in payment. These cuts were portrayed as due to the crisis and not linked to internal issues of the pension system. Partly due to that lack of justification, cuts imposed after 2012 were deemed unconstitutional by the Supreme Court in early 2015.

The pension system in 2014 thus appeared divided in two halves: (1) A well-defined system for the younger generation, but one that would only be widely applied after 2030. (2) A highly unstable and uncertain framework for the *older* generation, namely for those retiring in the period to 2030, but also for current pensioners. Viability appeared to have been secured only for the very long term. Budgets from 2015 to well into the 2020s appeared doomed to suffer from twin ills: expenditure overruns, chiefly through early retirement, and revenue shortfalls, chiefly through increasing contribution evasion. The immediate and continued cash problems meant that current pensioners could have expected more cuts in future. In the meantime pension expenditure as a percentage of GDT had risen to 17 percent in 2013, the highest level of the EU (OECD 2016) and was expected to rise further.

What at the end of the second bailout, was, evidently, only *"half* a reform" was in urgent need for completion. That was the first task of the *third* bailout.

A.2 Negotiation and the Third Program

The new anti-austerity government came in office in late January 2015 committed to renegotiate many aspects of adjustment. Rolling back the pensions changes, after a social dialogue to start after negotiations with the lenders, was a clear part of their election platform. In consequence the implementation of the 2010 pension laws scheduled to take place in January 2015 was put on hold. This affected new pension awards from January, which meant that no "new system" pensions were ever issued.

The *third* adjustment program in August 2015 placed the completion of the pension reform project high on the agenda. Urgent action to end early retirement was the focus of the prior actions preceding the new, third, bailout. Minimum retirement ages were increased so that all separate ages would converge by 2022 to 67 years for a full pension. This involved steep increases in eligibility ages for all those previously protected, who had not *already* retired by August 2015. In order to eliminate incentives to retire early, access to minimum pensions was blocked to all *new* retirees aged less than 67. Pensioners' health care contributions were increased to bring them into line with employees.

The MoU (Parliament 2015) stressed "the need for social justice and fairness, both across and within generations," placing pensions on center stage. Foremost among the objectives in the social field, are "Pension reforms … to remove exemptions and end early retirement." Pension changes were to be legislated by October 2015. Action was required in areas left aside in 2010, such as organizational change, contribution and revenue harmonization and phasing out of privileges. The authorities were also obliged to propose measures to compensate for the Supreme Court ruling on pension cuts of March 2015.

Crucially, the MoU allowed the authorities to propose parametric measures of equivalent effect, "provided that they are submitted during the design phase and are quantifiable." The Minister of Labor took up the challenge. Though the report of the Ministry Committee formed for this purpose (Ministry Committee, October 2015) was deemed too radical, the Ministry made public the Greek government's proposals in January 2016; these proposals were under discussion for the first months of 2016. A new pension reform law (L4387/2016) was finally passed in May 2016.

A.3 Completing the Reform: The Logic of the 2016 Reform

The emphasis on pensions in the run-up to the third adjustment program signaled a concern that the situation was unsustainable—that the "half-reform," should, in one way or another, be completed. As changes affecting the younger generation were extensive, measures focused on those previously protected—namely people who would retire in the 2020s. The reform attempted to preserve the generosity of the system and finance it through higher contribution revenue. The law stipulated three types of consolidation:

1. *Consolidation across generations* The law extended conditions similar to those legislated in 2010 to *all* participants (rather than only the young ones). New pensions from 2016 were to be calculated as if participants had always been part of the new system. The stipulation of the 2010 law that only time since 2011 would be subject to the new arrangements and that pensions should be a *pro rata* combination of old and new provisions, was scrapped. Additionally pensions of *existing* pensioners were to be recalculated using the new rules by 2018. Though the government has stated that any excess over current pensions will be honored, there are already (as of late 2016) suggestions that such a course is not feasible and older pensions will have to be brought in line with new pensions. Applying common calculation rules for all participants, old and new, meets some of the generational fairness objections raised;

however, it will also lead to major falls relative to expectations, which will become apparent as the process of recalculation proceeds.

2. *Consolidation across occupational groups* All people and all categories of earned income are to contribute on the basis of declared income using the *employees'* contribution rate structures (a maximum of 38.5 percent). This means exceptionally high contribution rises for the self-employed and farmers; the increased revenue is to be used to prevent further cuts in employees' pensions in the short term. Implementation of the new rules is set to begin in early 2017 and many crucial details are yet to be decided. This change implies extending the kind of social protection enjoyed by wage employees to all more flexible forms of employment relations; this entails a massive increase in the ambition of insurance cover and a corresponding increase in costs. Many groups object to this as a case of over-insurance, while the impact of these changes in the incentives for evasion and on competitiveness has still to be factored in.

3. *Consolidation across all providers of primary pensions*   All preexisting bodies are to be merged into a single provider EFKA, operating as a single organization. The economies of scale involved should mean than almost 50 percent of employees of pension providers can be redeployed. The merger involves significant organizational challenges of which unifying management and information systems is only one. Only a few weeks before the new body is to operate, the exact mechanics of its formation and operation remain opaque.

If the changes above are fully implemented, the Greek system will have changed from one of the most fragmented to one of the most rigid and uniform systems in Europe. It will apply common rules across all generations and types of employment allowing few exceptions, while it will aim for a level of protection that is very high by international standards. It will do so with a minimum of warning and preparation. Many groups whose treatment is to change radically from 2017, such as the self-employed, appear to be unaware of the extent of the changes in store and what these could mean about how they plan their lives. As attempts are made to implement the new rules, and the exact nature and extent of the changes are made progressively clearer, the dissatisfaction with the system is unlikely to abate.

As time goes on, these problems are likely to be joined by a realization of the system's shortcomings in meeting the microeconomic design standards of a modern pension system. Indeed, the problems of a unitary, monolithic state system heavy on redistribution weigh more when the proposals are generalized across all generations and modes of working. The argument for a fresh start will only become stronger.

A.4 Timeline of Pension Reform, 1934 to 2018

Phase	Date	Description
Prehistory	1934	Law founding IKA on social insurance lines. A compromise permits fragmentation.
	1950–1970	Re-founding and expansion of system. First IKA deficit 1958.
Ineffectual combating of deficits leads to the crisis	1980s	Deficits become endemic. Stabilization program 1985–1987 fails to include structural reform. Government grants to pension providers introduced.
	1990–1992	Two major reform bills under ND government. "New" system introduced for post 1992 labor market entrants. Last contribution increase.
	1997	"Spraos Committee" shocks by suggesting that system will collapse by 2007. Ignored on the ground that the pension system is supported by the state.
	2001	Greek entry into the eurozone. Reform attempt by PASOK Minister T. Giannitsis withdrawn after protests.
	2008	Reform under ND government; "cursory" consolidation.
Undeclared crisis	2008	Financial crisis begins. First year of negative growth in Greece. Government declares "Greece is buttressed against the crisis."
	Oct. 2009	New PASOK government. "Greek statistics" episode ushers in the Greek crisis
First program	June 2010	First bailout agreed. First pension cut in May.
	July 2010	Pension Law 3863/10 is first bailout law. New system for the young generation; increase in pension ages to 65; incumbents protected.
	2011	Various implementation laws, including disability, heavy and hazardous occupations Early retirement builds up.
Second program	2012	Second bailout. PSI cuts privately held debt. Reserves of some pension funds also hit.
	2012	Supreme Court decision declares pension cuts to 2012 constitutional
	2012	Further rises of retirement ages to 67. Major cuts in pensions. Law governing auxiliary pensions introduces "zero deficit clause."
	2014	Zero deficit clause leads to 5.2 percent cuts across-the-board cut to auxiliary pensions
	Nov. 2014	Obligation by government to review and to suggest corrective action ignored
	Jan. 2015	ND/PASOK government neglects to issue first "new pensions."

Phase	Date	Description
Third program	Jan. 2015	Election of SYRIZA anti-austerity government committed to overturn pension changes, make up for cuts, and start afresh. All implementations placed on hold
	March 2015	Supreme Court ruling that all pension cuts *after* 2012 are unconstitutional, for being insufficiently justified.
	June 2015	Government only has enough cash to *either* pay pensions *or* to pay back the IMF. Chooses to pay pensions
	July 2015	Referendum called. EU insistence to abolish the low pension safety net cited as reason. EU president insists Commission misrepresented.
	July 2015	Decision to proceed to third adjustment program despite referendum result.
	July 2015	Prior actions passed increasing retirement ages drastically to apply immediately and increasing pensioners' health insurance contributions.
	Aug. 2015	Third MoU voted with cross-party support. Key requirement to deal with generational justice. Detailed pension reform needed by October 2015.
	Sept. 2015	Elections won by SYRIZA; same coalition as before
	Oct. 2015	Government-appointed "Committee of Sages" issues report calling for a "new social contract" and a fresh start. Government distances itself from the report
	Jan. 2016	Government proposals unveiled. 170-page document, not accompanied by quantification. Negotiations with the institutions and with domestic bodies
	May 2016	Law 4387/16 passed generalizing post 2010 changes to the entire population. Implementation begins.
	Jan. 2017	New pension body to be operational. New pension contribution rates for self-employed begin
???	Dec. 2018	End of transition period for full implementation of 2016 pension reform End of third adjustment program.

Appendix B: Analytic Framework for a Fully Financed System

In this appendix we use a simple analytical framework to study the impact of shifting from a PAYG system to a prefunded (or fully funded) system. Purely for analytical simplicity, we analyze and quantify the gains from a complete change in the way the system is financed. With this exercise we (1) illustrate the analytical arguments in favor of such a policy and (2) provide a quantitative estimate of the efficiency gains associated with a fully funded system. To be clear, the multipillar policy proposal that we describe in the text does not entail or envisage a full move to a fully funded system. However, as a matter of analytical convenience, and to better isolate both the theoretical reasoning and the quantitative benefits of switching to a fully funded system, we refrain from modeling all aspects of the policy we propose.

The appendix is organized in steps. First, we set up the analytical framework and discuss some basic features of PAYG systems, assuming that contributions are raised in a completely nondistortionary manner. In particular, we illustrate how a PAYG system reduces capital accumulation and welfare in steady state.

Then we discuss the major problem of shifting from a PAYG to a fully funded system, the so-called transition problem. We consider a policy that solves this problem by having the government issue (domestically held) special-purpose bonds. The amount of the bond issuance is determined so that retirees continue to receive the same pension as under the existing PAYG system. Furthermore the bonds are bought by the current young as a vehicle for their savings. We perform this exercise assuming that Greece is a closed economy and so any new debt issuance must be domestically held. This is a conservative assumption which ensures that any additional government borrowing must be financed by the additional savings of the young.

We first study the case where taxes are nondistortionary. We show that a transition from a PAYG to a fully funded system, accompanied by the issuance of the aforementioned special-purpose bonds, does not alter allocations or welfare.

We next introduce distortionary taxation. Under the assumption that the current system acts as a distortionary tax on labor, we evaluate again a transition from a PAYG to a fully funded system with simultaneous domestic debt issuance as described above. We show that moving to the new system produces nontrivial gains, without affecting the welfare of the current retirees.

B.1   Analytic Framework and Some Elementary Results

This basic model helps provide a first-pass comparison between PAYG and fully funded systems. The spirit of the exercise in this section is to analyze the impact of the introduction of a PAYG system in the long run (steady state).

We use a two-period OLG framework to quantify the effects. An OLG framework with multiple overlapping generations would allow more accurate computations, but at the cost of greater opacity. Since the goal of this chapter is to provide a qualitative explanation for the source of the benefits and a quantitative order of magnitude, the simpler structure of a two-period OLG framework is particularly well suited.

Specifically, we assume that individuals live for two periods. In the first period, they are referred to as "young," and in the second period as "old." We use the superscripts y, o to refer to these two periods of life. We assume that individuals have logarithmic preferences over consumption and a discount rate β. The assumption of logarithmic preferences is inessential for the theoretical results; the main motivation for using a logarithmic specification is that it facilitates analytically tractable expressions.

As in the typical OLG model, the young earn labor income, a fraction of which they save to finance their consumption when old. When old they simply consume their accumulated assets. Population grows at the rate n, in the sense that $N_{t+1}^y = (1+n)N_t^y$.

The young use their savings to accumulate government bonds and private capital. Competitive firms produce output by utilizing a Cobb–Douglas production function $Y_t = K_t^\alpha \left(A_t N_t^y h_t\right)^{1-\alpha}$, where K_t is capital, N_t^y is labor, h_t refers to hours of work, and A_t is labor-augmenting technological change. Firms are competitive and hire capital and labor in competitive markets by paying the rental rates r_t and w_t, respectively. Labor is provided inelastically, so that $h_t = \bar{h}$. (We relax this assumption later.)

Besides private savings, we also assume the presence of a pure pay-as-you-go system that gives current retirees a total benefit $P_t^o = \pi A_t N_t^y$, financed by a lump-sum transfer from the current young. The parameter π is used in the calibration to control the magnitude of pensions as a share of labor income. Finally, we assume an exogenous rate of labor augmenting growth $A_{t+1} = A_t (1+g)$.

We start by computing the decentralized market equilibrium in this model. It is easiest to start by introducing an additional element of notation. Throughout, we agree that lowercase letters refer to the ratio of the respective aggregate quantity divided by the stochastic trend $A_t N_t^y$. For instance,

$$y_t = \frac{Y_t}{A_t N_t^y}, \ k_t = \frac{K_t}{A_t N_t^y}.$$

With these conventions, we start by noting that an individual's Euler equation implies the following savings relationship:

$$\frac{1}{\frac{W_t}{N_t^y} - \frac{S_t}{N_t^y} - \frac{P_t^o}{N_t^y}} = \beta(1+r_t)\frac{1}{\frac{S_t}{N_t^y}(1+r_t) + \frac{P_{t+1}^o}{N_t^y}} \, , \tag{1}$$

where S_t denotes aggregate savings, and W_t aggregate labor income.

Equation (1) states that the marginal utility of per-capita consumption when young should equal the discounted marginal utility of per-capita consumption when old times the gross rate of return. Upon multiplying both sides of (1) by A_t and re-arranging, we arrive at

$$\frac{1}{w_t - s_t - \pi} = \beta(1+r)\frac{1}{s_t(1+r) + \pi(1+g)(1+n)} \tag{2}$$

Profit maximization of firms implies that

$$W_t = (1-\alpha)Y_t \Rightarrow w_t \bar{h} = (1-\alpha)k_t^\alpha \bar{h}^{1-\alpha}, \tag{3}$$

and that

$$r_t K_t = \alpha Y_t \Rightarrow r_t = \alpha\left(\frac{y_t}{k_t}\right) = \alpha k_t^{\alpha-1}\bar{h}^{1-\alpha}. \tag{4}$$

Market clearing of the goods and assets markets implies that aggregate savings need to equal next period's capital stock:

$$S_t = K_{t+1} \Rightarrow s_t = (1+g)(1+n)k_{t+1}. \tag{5}$$

Substituting equations (5), (4), and (3) into (2) and re-arranging gives the first-order difference equation:

$$k_{t+1} = \frac{1}{(1+g)(1+n)}\frac{\beta}{1+\beta}\left[(1-\alpha)k_t^\alpha \bar{h}^{1-\alpha} - \pi - \frac{\pi(1+g)(1+n)}{\beta(1+\alpha k_t^{\alpha-1}\bar{h}^{1-\alpha})}\right] \tag{6}$$

Imposing the steady-state condition $k_{t+1} = k_t = \bar{k}$ gives an algebraic equation that allows us to solve for the steady-state capital stock per unit of labor efficiency units. Applying the implicit function theorem yields

$$\left.\frac{d\bar{k}}{d\pi}\right|_{\pi=0} = -\frac{1 + \frac{(1+g)(1+n)}{\beta(1+\alpha\bar{k}^{\alpha-1}\bar{h}^{1-\alpha})}}{\frac{1}{(1+g)(1+n)}\frac{\beta}{1+\beta}\alpha(1-\alpha)\bar{k}^{\alpha-1}\bar{h}^{1-\alpha}} < 0.$$

Simply put, the introduction of a PAYG system leads to a reduction of the steady-state value of $\bar{k}$. A lower value of $\bar{k}$ implies lower steady-state wages. Therefore an increase in π (the parameter controlling the magnitude of pensions) decreases steady-state welfare whenever the steady-state value of r satisfies

$$1 + r > (1+g)(1+n). \tag{7}$$

This is the intuitive and well-known Aaron–Samuelson condition. Whenever the rate of return on a private account exceeds the "effective rate" of return that an individual obtains from her contributions in the PAYG system, the steady-state welfare is lowered. It is straightforward to solve for $\bar{k}$, and hence r from equation (6), so that we can see whether for the assumed primitive parameters (7) holds. For instance, it is possible to show that around $\pi = 0$, condition (7) holds as long as α is not too small. However, and more important for our purposes, condition (7) does hold empirically in the case of Greece. Indeed the magnitude of the gap between the rate of return on private savings and the effective return on PAYG contributions is substantial, implying that further increases in contribution rates would have significantly negative effects on welfare.

Before proceeding, we must caution the reader in interpreting the results of this section. The fact that increases in π can lower steady-state welfare should not be misunderstood as a statement that a decrease in π makes all generations better off. To be sure, the first generation, which receives benefits from the young without contributing to the social security system, is clearly better off when π increases.

B.2   The Transition Problem

The key takeaways from the previous discussion are that (1) a PAYG system crowds out private savings and hence capital accumulation and that (2) steady-state welfare is reduced by a PAYG system, provided that (as is the case in the data) the (effective) return on contributions is inferior to the prevailing rate of interest on private investments.

More fundamentally, comparing the effects of different systems on the steady state is similar to comparing trains before one puts them on the rails. Once a given train has been set in motion, changing trains is no longer trivial. This metaphor is particularly applicable to social security systems where a "cold turkey" transition to a fully funded retirement system would bring up the problem of how to provide for the current old. This section addresses precisely this issue.

Specifically, if we switched cold turkey to a fully funded system, current workers would stop contributing to the PAYG system, which is how current retirees are being

supported. This problem is particularly serious because current retirees did not anticipate this transition when they were workers contributing to the social security system
and hence would not have saved privately enough for their retirement.

To address this problem, we introduce domestic government debt, in the form of
"recognition bonds" given to current retirees. Specifically, we perform the following
exercise: We assume that there exists some $\bar{\pi}$ that was inherited from the past. At the
time of the reform (e.g., time zero) the government issues recognition bonds equal
to $B_0 = \bar{\pi} A_0 N_0^y$. The government uses the proceeds to pay the old generation that is
alive at time zero. These bonds are bought by the current young, who are no longer
subject to PAYG contributions and hence can use their additional disposable income
to purchase these bonds. (The simultaneous increase in domestic savings and bond
issuance is a key feature of the exercise, which makes recognition bonds a special class
of debt—quite distinct economically from conventional government debt.) From that
point onward, the government determines lump-sum taxes on all future generations
so as to keep $b_t = B_t / A_t N_t^y$ constant at $b_t = \bar{\pi}$. To determine the tax amounts that are
required to achieve that, we start by postulating the government budget constraint

$$B_{t+1} = (1 + r_t) B_t - T_{t+1},$$

where T_{t+1} are the total taxes raised in period $t + 1$. Dividing both sides by $A_{t+1} N_{t+1}^y$ gives

$$b_{t+1} = \frac{1 + r_t}{(1 + g)(1 + n)} b_t - \tau_{t+1},$$

where $\tau_{t+1} = T_{t+1} / A_{t+1} N_{t+1}^y$. Setting $b_{t+1} = b_t = \bar{\pi}$ and re-arranging gives

$$\tau_{t+1} = \left[\frac{1 + r_t}{(1 + g)(1 + n)} - 1 \right] \bar{\pi}.$$

The government collects the taxes in a lump-sum fashion during the old age of each
individual, starting with the generation that is young at time zero. The respective intertemporal optimization conditions now take the following form:

$$\frac{1}{w_t - s_t} = \beta(1 + r_t) \frac{1}{s_t(1 + r_t) - (1 + g)(1 + n)\tau_{t+1}}, \tag{8}$$

and the market-clearing equation (5) becomes

$$S_t = B_t + K_{t+1} \Rightarrow s_t = \bar{\pi} + (1 + g)(1 + n)k_{t+1}.$$

Equations (3) and (4) remain unchanged.

We next define $\hat{s}_t = s_t - \bar{\pi}$, so that $\hat{s}_t = \hat{s}_t + \bar{\pi}$ and rewrite (8) as

$$\frac{1}{w_t - \hat{s}_t - \overline{\pi}} = \beta(1 + r_t)\frac{1}{\hat{s}_t(1 + r_t) + (1 + g)(1 + n)\overline{\pi}} \tag{9}$$

and

$$\hat{s}_t = (1 + g)(1 + n)k_{t+1} \tag{10}$$

A comparison of (9) and (10) with (2) and (5) shows that if one transitions to a fully funded system, while raising government debt in the form of recognition bonds to compensate the current retirees, the resulting allocations are equivalent to those that would be obtained under a PAYG system with unchanged contribution rates. In short, the transition to a fully funded system can be managed in a way as to leave intertemporal allocations unchanged.

B.3 Social Security Contributions as Distortionary Taxes

The social security system is not financed in a nondistortionary way; instead, social security contributions are similar to labor taxes, especially in Greece. Social security contributions are distortionary because they bear only a weak link with eventual pensions. In particular, the erratic, repeated, and unpredictable pension cuts make it hard for an individual to perceive a credible link between her contributions and her eventual pension. Additionally widespread contribution evasion puts a disproportionate burden on the law-abiding workers who end up subsidizing welfare payments to the evaders.

Motivated by these facts, in this section we take the distortionary nature of social security contributions into consideration and repeat our analysis of a PAYG system, assuming an endogenous labor supply. The main additions to our previous analysis are that (1) labor supply is endogenous and that (2) social security contributions are financed by labor taxes levied on workers. (Allowing separate contribution rates for workers and employers would call for more notation, without changing our analysis.) Specifically, we assume a labor disutility function of the form $\kappa(h^\eta/\eta)$ that is separable from the utility of consumption.[51] h denotes the hours supplied by the representative worker, while production is given by $Y_t = K_t^a(A_tL_t)^{1-\alpha}$, where L_t denotes the total units of employed labor. Taxes imply that firms pay a wage rate ω_t, while workers receive $(1 - \tau_t)\omega_t$. Each period the tax is determined so that the contributions equal the pensions $\tau_tW_t = P_t$, where $W_t = \omega_tL_t$ denotes the total wage bill in the economy. Clearing of the labor market requires $L_t = N_t^y h_t$. With these assumptions, we obtain the following first-order condition for labor supply:

$$(1-\tau_t)\omega_t = \kappa\left(\frac{W_t}{N_t^\gamma} - \frac{S_t}{N_t^\gamma} - \frac{P_t}{N_t^\gamma}\right)h_t^{\eta-1}$$

Multiplying both sides of the equation above by h_t, dividing by A_t, and utilizing the fact that $\tau_t W_t = P_t$ results in

$$w_t - \pi = \kappa(w_t - s_t - \pi)h_t^\eta. \tag{11}$$

An individual's intertemporal optimality condition is unchanged. Therefore we can re-arrange equation (11) to find

$$w_t - s_t - \pi = \left(\frac{1}{1+\beta}\right)\left[w_t - \pi\left(1 - \frac{(1+n)(1+g)}{1+r}\right)\right]. \tag{12}$$

Combining (11) with (12) results in

$$\frac{w_t - \pi}{w_t - \pi\left(1 - \frac{(1+n)(1+g)}{1+r_t}\right)} = \kappa\left(\frac{1}{1+\beta}\right)h_t^\eta. \tag{13}$$

To determine h_t, we apply the firm's optimality condition

$$\omega_t L_t = (1-\alpha)Y_t \Rightarrow w_t = (1-\alpha)k_t^\alpha h_t^{1-\alpha}. \tag{14}$$

Then, combining (13) with (14) allows us to obtain an equation for labor input h_t as a function of the capital stock k_t and the rate of return r_t:

$$\frac{(1-\alpha)k_t^\alpha h_t^{1-\alpha} - \pi}{(1-\alpha)k_t^\alpha h_t^{1-\alpha} - \pi\left(1 - \frac{(1+n)(1+g)}{1+r_t}\right)} = \kappa\left(\frac{1}{1+\beta}\right)h_t^\eta. \tag{15}$$

We will denote the solution of (15) as $h_t(k_t, r_t; \pi)$. Since $r_t = \alpha k_t^{\alpha-1}h_t^{1-\alpha}$, we can write more simply $h_t(k_t; \pi)$. With this observation the dynamics of the capital stock are given by

$$k_{t+1} = \frac{1}{(1+g)(1+n)}\frac{\beta}{1+\beta}\left[(1-\alpha)k_t^\alpha[h(k_t;\pi)]^{1-\alpha} - \frac{\pi(1+g)(1+n)}{\beta(1+\alpha k_t^{\alpha-1}h(k_t;\pi)^{1-\alpha})} - \pi\right]. \tag{16}$$

Note that equation (16) is identical to equation (6) with the main difference that the hours h are now endogenous and determined by equation (15). Setting $k_{t+1} = k_t$ allows us to solve for the steady-state value of k. These values (and the associated values for consumption, etc.) will serve as the point of reference for our analysis.

B.4   The Full Policy Experiment

Here we re-evaluate the proposal to shift to a fully financed system, while raising domestic debt to solve the transition problem. Specifically, we assume that at time zero, the government announces that it will cease transfers to future retirees. At that same time the government issues recognition bonds B_t (domestic debt) equal to the value of pensions promised to *existing* retirees $(\pi A_0 N_0^y)$. From that point onward, the government raises taxes on the young through distortionary labor taxation so as to maintain the de-trended debt $b_t = B_t/A_t N_t^y$ constant. To determine the de-trended tax revenue that will achieve that, we start with an equation for the de-trended debt dynamics:

$$b_{t+1} = (1+\hat{r}_t)(b_t - \hat{\tau}_t), \tag{17}$$

where $\hat{\tau}_t = T_t/A_t N_t^y$ is the de-trended tax revenue and $1+\hat{r}_t \equiv (1+r_t)/(1+g)(1+n)$. To ensure that $b_t = \pi$ for all t, $\hat{\tau}_t$ must equal

$$\hat{\tau}_t = \frac{\hat{r}_t}{1+\hat{r}_t}\pi. \tag{18}$$

Following similar steps to those we used in equation (11), we can write the first-order condition for labor supply as

$$w_t - \hat{\tau}_t = \kappa(w_t - s_t - \hat{\tau}_t)h_t^\eta. \tag{19}$$

From the Euler equation, we can infer that an agent's consumption when young is

$$w_t - s_t - \hat{\tau}_t = \left(\frac{1}{1+\beta}\right)[w_t - \hat{\tau}_t]. \tag{20}$$

Equations (19) and (20) then imply that

$$1 = \frac{\kappa}{1+\beta}h_t^\eta. \tag{21}$$

Comparing equations (13) with (21) shows us that work hours h_t are now higher. To determine the dynamics of capital accumulation, we use the market-clearing condition $S_t = B_t - T_t + K_{t+1}$, which—after de-trending—is equivalent to

$$s_t = b_t - \hat{\tau}_t + (1+g)(1+n)k_{t+1}.$$

Proceeding in a fashion similar to section 2 we define $\hat{s}_t \equiv s_t - (b_t - \hat{\tau}_t)$. Then the market clearing condition becomes $\hat{s}_t = (1+g)(1+n)k_{t+1}$ while an investor's Euler equation is

$$\frac{1}{w_t - s_t - \hat{\tau}_t} = \beta(1+r_t)\frac{1}{s_t(1+r_t)} \ . \tag{22}$$

Using the definition of $\hat{s}_t$, the definition of $\hat{r}_t$, equations (18), (17), and the fact that $b_t = \pi$, we can rewrite equation (22) as

$$\frac{1}{w_t - \hat{s}_t - \pi} = \beta(1+r_t)\frac{1}{\hat{s}_t(1+r_t) + \pi(1+g)(1+n)}, \tag{23}$$

which is identical to equation (2), with s_t replaced by $\hat{s}_t$. Hence, by an argument similar to that in section B.2, the dynamics of the capital stock are unchanged and given by equation (16), with the important exception that now the hours worked are higher and given by (21).

B.5   A Calibration Exercise

To obtain a quantitative order of magnitude of the likely benefits of a transition, we next turn to a calibration exercise. We specify parameters to match empirical moments of Greek data and then perform simulations to quantify the benefits of a transition.

We calibrate the parameters of the model with the Greek economy in mind. We take $1 - \alpha = 0.6$ to be conservative in our calculations. We choose $\pi/w = 0.26$, motivated by current employer and employee contribution rates. For the sum of population and productivity growth we assume that the sum of these two quantities increase at a rate of 1 percent. Clearly, there is substantial uncertainty about this figure. Finally, we choose β so as to match a (real) annual interest rate of 4 percent. One should keep in mind that the "period" inside the model corresponds to 30 years, so it is prudent to enter an interest rate that is likely to be representative of this long haul. An implication of the fact that the "period" corresponds to 30 years is that annual interest rates need to be converted to 30-year rates of return. Even though inside the model, we assume that consumption, pensions, and the like, occur at the beginning of the period, it is appropriate to think of them more as flows that occur over the entire period. With that in mind, letting $(1+r)$ denote the 30-year return, and $\bar{r}$ the continuously compounded rate of return, we set r so that

$$(1+r) = \int_0^T \frac{1}{T}e^{\bar{r}(T-s)}ds.$$

We make similar imputations to arrive at $(1+g)(1+n)$. Last, we set $\eta = 1.5$, which implies a Frisch elasticity of labor supply equal to 2. This choice is popular in the macroeconomics literature, and since we are calibrating a macro model with adjustment both in the intensive and the extensive margin, we want to use the large values that are typically used in macro studies rather than the smaller numbers used in micro studies.

Having determined the parameters to match these targets, we can now compute the benefits of a transition to a fully financed system. Again, to be conservative, we focus exclusively on the immediate impact of the reform on output, not the steady-state gains.

To compute the immediate impact on output, we let h_t denote the hours under the status quo and h_t^* the hours worked under the transition proposal. Equations (21) and (13) imply that

$$\Delta \log h_t \equiv \log h_t^* - \log h_t = -\frac{1}{\eta} \log \left(\frac{\frac{w_t}{\pi} - 1}{\frac{w_t}{\pi} - \left(1 - \frac{(1+n)(1+g)}{1+r_t}\right)} \right),$$

and therefore the GDP change is $(1-\alpha)\Delta \log h_t$.

The baseline scenario assumes a real continuously compounded interest rate of 4 percent and trend growth of 1 percent for a 30-year period. The other parameter constellations reflect parameter assumptions whereby we modify these assumptions (one at a time). In table 11.1 the results are reported in the column "percentage GDP change." The gains range from 2.88 to 11.5 percent, depending on assumptions, with the base-case scenario producing benefits of the order of magnitude of 7.68 percent of GDP. We would like to emphasize that in computing these gains, we made the (strong) simplifying assumptions that Greece is to remain perpetually a closed economy and that the current cohort of retirees should not be affected by the change. Despite these rather strong assumptions, we find that the proposed reform would be associated with nontrivial output gains.

Table 11.A1
Results of the calibration exercise

Parameters	Percentage GDP change
Baseline	7.68
Interest rate = 5%	6.50
Trend growth = 2%	8.89
Frisch elasticity of labor supply = 1	2.88
Frisch elasticity of labor supply = 4	11.50
Capital share = 0.2	10.20
Capital share = 0.5	6.40

Notes

1. This affects how pensions treat risk. Defined benefit (or "final salary") schemes favor the beneficiary by specifying the pension as a function of the salary at the end of an individual's career; defined contribution (or accumulation) schemes favor the system guarantor by limiting pensions to annuities paid out of the accumulated funds.

2. Insofar as pension systems operate as insurance, the existence of minimum pensions could be seen as a kind of insurance against being unlucky in one's occupation.

3. PAYG depends on society-wide solidarity. Disaffiliating is equivalent to a group declaring they want no part of general solidarity, meaning they are a kind of insurance island.

4. Competitive relations between the pillars could undermine the pension promises given by each and hence end up undermining trust in the entire system.

5. This numbering scheme for pillars corresponds to practice in Europe. World Bank practice (e.g., World Bank 1994) distinguishes between the two public pillars: one for poverty prevention and one for income replacement. The European terminology conflates these two into a single public pillar, partly due to difficulty in separating the two functions.

6. European countries stress as mandatory the second pillar's occupational provision, unlike the United States where occupational pensions tend to be voluntary. This possibly reflects a corporatist tradition, plus a desire to involve unions and employers in constructive relationships.

7. See Tinios (2012b). The fate of preexisting funds was the issue that led to the fall of *two* governments of the center-left.

8. A favorite fragmenting mechanism was to set up new "auxiliary" funds to provide for additional income replacement. These funds were mandatory and financed by PAYG; in essence they were little different from the primary funds they were supposed to supplement. Setting up a new compulsory auxiliary fund could allow occupations whose primary funds were in deficit to expand expenditures for as long as the new funds were still new—that is, had more contributors than pensioners.

9. Micromanagement of the pension promise (e.g., resolving contradictions, expediting procedures) remains a significant part of the clientelistic operation of the Greek state. Control over these "favors" is a prize that is not easily surrendered.

10. The vocal opposition to the (withdrawn) 2001 pension reform bill is widely considered to have undermined other reform efforts.

11. The five failings were mentioned by the 2002 EU Joint Report on Pension Strategy (ECE 2003; Tinios 2010); they have only worsened over time.

12. Since the crisis, pensions as percentages of GDP have soared, reflecting early retirements as well as a fall of a quarter in the denominator, rising to almost 17 percent of GDP. Figures are reported for 2007 to exclude crisis-related effects.

13. Non-wage costs do not stop at social insurance contributions, which can rise to 50.7 percent in total. They include compliance costs as well as the impact of general taxation needed to finance government grants, which account for a third of pension expenditure.

14. Data subsequent to 2005 show a rapid decline in the poverty rate of the over 65 population relative to the overall population (Mitrakos and Tsakloglou 2012). That relative poverty rate fell further during the crisis, as other incomes fell faster than pensions.

15. The proportionality factor is somewhat smaller for larger pension amounts, making the calculation more complex.

16. A feature of the new system is that it retains the old system's minimum pension, in addition to the flat rate basic pension.

17. It is interesting that no estimate of the impact of the second increase in retirement ages was ever offered.

18. Differences of generosity between providers are thus left as a "stranded cost."

19. These provisions were used in lieu of redundancies to facilitate the shrinking of the public sector.

20. Mothers of underage children were entitled to retire at 50—a theoretical right for the majority, as children would have ceased to be underage by the time their mother reached 50. After 2010 whether a child is underage is judged after the mother has worked for 20 years. So the right to retire at 50 for a woman who started work at 20 will be judged when she is 40 rather than 10 years later. At that time the "underage child" for whose benefit the early pension is granted may well be as old as 30.

21. The choice of NDC was to limit cross-subsidization between occupations. Some government employees had replacement rates in excess of 60 percent, while others had less than 20 percent. Retrospective application of NDC would retain only differences corresponding to greater contributions. A subsequent change in 2014 reneged on this, legislating that NDC would only start in 2014. In this way frugal occupations pay for profligate ones.

22. Many provisions remain to be tested in the courts, where they could be challenged as to their retroactive character (see Katroungalos and Morfakidis 2011).

23. This effect is due to the fixed EUR 360 component that every pensioner is entitled to in the new system—thus initiating a more progressive replacement schedule. Paradoxically, the new system retains additionally the old system of minimum pensions.

24. This is an example of the "lump of labor fallacy," where there is a fixed amount of work and more jobs for some means fewer jobs for others. Authoritative rebuttals have existed for 150 years. Employing more workers increases total output, and this can make everyone better off.

25. The precise magnitude of these effects cannot be gauged as the flow of information on the pension system essentially stopped after the bailout. Though information was supplied to the Troika, the publication of even basic statistical information—such as the annual Social

Budget—was discontinued. Comment thus has to rely on what finds its way to the public domain. A further issue is delays in processing pension awards; in 2014 tens of thousands were outstanding, so the cash expenditure underestimated true outlays on an accrual basis.

26. This mechanism could partly lie behind the controversy around fiscal multipliers; projected expenditures entailed a different set of measures from those finally employed.

27. As part of the first bailout package in 2010, these had been replaced by fixed amounts that were abolished in August 2012.

28. Pension quarterly receipts received by all pensioners itemize all cuts individually. In pension payment statistics it is unclear whether pre- or post-cut pensions are being counted (Ministry of Labor 2013).

29. In countries implementing crisis-related adjustment, such as Latvia and Romania, reductions of pensions were found to be unconstitutional by their Constitutional Courts (ESCR 2010; BBC 2010). In Portugal the Constitutional Court ruled that the abolition of holiday bonuses selectively for pensioners violated the principle of equal sharing of burdens (Petroglou 2012).

30. The new system calculates replacement using a career average; this might lead to a reduction in actual replacement rates, the extent of which is open to question.

31. Since pensioners' electoral weight is bound to increase, decreasing the pension share will be harder in future. Tinios (2003) has estimated that with the age of the median voter set to rise by 10 years between 2000 and 2040, pensioners will form an absolute majority of voters in 2033.

32. IMF (2013) acknowledges that "implementation risks remain."

33. The same aggregate impact might result from different apportioning of adjustments to individuals, depending on the considerations the algorithm will reflect.

34. The Geneva Association of Insurance economists in fact calls working longer a fourth pillar of the pension systems—in the sense that it can help support more expenditures (Geneva Association 2012).

35. Greece has one of the largest gender gaps in pensions in the European Union (see Betti et al. 2015).

36. It is important that all current state or quasi-state bodies be folded in the new system. This will include all primary funds and all supplementary funds. Separation funds as organizations can join the new provider, yet their contribution rates and property can be added to the second or third pillar—as has notably happened with the Dini reform in Italy.

37. More orderly accounting of real estate holdings would, of course, have beneficial effects on the housing market.

38. A consumption tax distorts labor supply but not intertemporal allocation decisions. Hence its overall effect on consumers' labor supply (in our model) is less distortionary than social security contributions, which can distort both margins.

39. Firms such as banks claim that they were providing pensions in lieu of the state, so they are entitled to handle their accounting obligations on a PAYG basis—meaning ignore anything but current obligations.

40. See Tinios (2011). The idea was first broached in the Spraos Committee 1997.

41. This methodology could sort out the possible legal problems that may arise from challenging the unilateral abrogation of state guarantees that could be held to have existed under the previous system.

42. Recognition bonds could complicate matters here. If they are issued during a crisis, they are likely to offer high yields, and the cost to the state of issuing them could be high.

43. The Greek word for annuities (ράντα, from the French *rente*) is not recognized even by financial market specialists.

44. The illiquidity of real estate holdings is a broader problem. The problem can be partly addressed by changes in the legal and town planning status of properties, as well as by changes in taxation, such as the reduction or abolition of transaction taxes which severely limit the size of the real estate market.

45. In the United States, the incentives have been going in the opposite direction. Coil and Levine (2009) find that on balance the recession has led to an exodus from the labor market.

46. There could be some smoothing of income or exemptions of some kinds of income from the payment of contributions (e.g., rents).

47. Broadening the contributions base will make a big impact on categories of income previously nearly exempt—such as second jobs and farming income.

48. A larger "third pillar" might be UK-style "stakeholder funds," allowing the self-employed to opt out of occupational funds.

49. This is often termed the *Spraos question*. John Spraos in 1997 had the courage to speak out and say that pension reform was overdue. The entire political system converged to accuse him of saying in public what everyone was whispering in private. As a result all reform preparations stalled (see Featherstone et al. 2001).

50. The role of reforms of social policy is outlined in Tinios (2015).

51. Given that the utility of consumption is logarithmic, we can specify the utility for leisure in a separable way, while preserving balanced growth properties.

References

Bank of Greece, 2013. Monetary Policy 2012–2013. Report of the Governor. Athens.

Barr, N., and P. A. Diamond. 2010. *Pension Reform: A Short Guide.* New York: Oxford University Press.

Bateman, H., G. Kingston, and J. Piggott. 2001. *Forced Saving: Mandating Private Retirement Incomes.* Cambridge, UK: Cambridge University Press.

BBC. 2010. Romania pension cuts ruled illegal. http://www.bbc.co.uk/news/10421118.

Becker, G. 2012. The insurance industry's role in addressing longevity funding issues: opportunities and limitations. In P. M. Liedtke and K. U. Schwartz, eds., *Addressing the Challenge of Global Ageing—Funding Issues and Insurance Solutions.* The Geneva Reports, Risk and Insurance Research, vol. 6. Geneva. https://www.genevaassociation.org/media/201020/ga-2012-geneva_report%5B6%5D.pdf.

Betti, G., F. Bettio, T. Georgiadis, and P. Tinios. 2015. *Unequal Aging in Europe: Women's Independence and Pensions.* London: Palgrave Macmillan.

Boeri, T., A. Börsch-Supan, and G. Tabellini. 2005. How would you like to reform your pension system? The opinions of German and Italian citizens. In R. Brooks and A. Razin, eds., *Social Security Reform: Financial and Political Issues in International Perspective,* 333–52. Cambridge, UK: Cambridge University Press.

Bonoli, G., and T. Shinkawa. 2005. Population ageing and the logics of pension reform in Western Europe, East Asia and North America. In G. Bonoli and T. Shinkawa, eds., *Ageing and Pension Reform around the World. Evidence from Eleven Countries,* 1–23. Cheltenham, UK: Edward Elgar.

Börsch-Supan, A., and P. Tinios. 2001. The Greek pensions system: Strategic framework for reform. In R. C. Bryant, N. Garganas, and G. S. Tavlas, eds., *Greece's Economic Performance and Prospects,* 361–443. Washington, DC: Bank of Greece and Brookings Institution.

Busch, K., C. Hermann, K. Hinrichs, and T. Scholten. 2013. *Euro Crisis, Austerity Policy and the European Social Model: How Crisis Policies in Southern Europe Threaten the EU's Social Dimension.* Berlin: Friedrich Ebert Stiftung.

Clark, G. L., K. Strauss, and J. Knox-Hayes. 2012. *Saving for Retirement: Intention, Context and Behaviour.* Oxford: Oxford University Press.

Coil, C., and P. B. Levine. 2009. The market crash and mass layoffs: How the current economic crisis can affect retirement. Working paper 15395. NBER.

Commission of the European Communities. 2012. Pension adequacy in the European Union 2010–2050. Report prepared jointly by the Directorate-General for Employment, Social Affairs and Inclusion of the European Commission and the Social Protection Committee. http://ec.europa.eu/social/BlobServlet?docId=7805&langId=en.

Diamond, P., and S. Valdés-Prieto. 1994. Social security. In B. Bosworth, R. Dornbusch, and R. Laban, eds., *The Chilean Economy: Policy Lessons and Challenges,* 257–320. Washington, DC: Brookings Institution.

EBEA (Athens Chamber of Commerce and Industry). 2016. The social insurance problem in the 21st century: A need of rethinking for a fresh start. http://www.acci.gr/acci/Portals/0/Announcements/Pr/MeletiAsfalistikou.pdf.

Economic Policy Committee (EPC). 2009. Ageing report: Economic and budgetary projections for the EU-27 member states (2008–2060). *European Economy*, 2. http://ec.europa.eu/economy_finance/publications/publication14992_en.pdf.

Economic Policy Committee (EPC). 2012, 2012 Ageing report: Economic and budgetary projections for the EU-27 member states (2010–2060). *European Economy*, 2. http://ec.europa.eu/economy_finance/publications/european_economy/2012/pdf/ee-2012-2_en.pdf.

ESCR case law database. 2010. Latvian "Case No. 2009-43-01 on compliance of the first part of section 3 of State Pensions. In ESCR net 2014. http://www.escr-net.org/docs/i/1285934.

European Central Bank. 2013. The Eurosystem Household Finance and Consumption Survey: Results from the first wave. Statistics paper series, April 2. Brussels.

European Commission. 2010. Private pension schemes: Their role in adequate and sustainable pensions, p. 9. https://www.scribd.com/document/31131925/European-Commission-Private-pensions-schemes-their-role-in-adequate-and-sustainable-pensions.

Featherstone, K., and D. Papadimitriou. 2008. *The Limits of Europeanisation: Reform Capacity and Public Policy in Greece. Palgrave Studies in European Union Politics*. Basingstoke: Palgrave Macmillan.

Featherstone, K., G. Kazamias, and D. Papadimitriou. 2001. The limits of external empowerment: EMU, technocracy and the reform of the Greek pension system. *Political Studies* 49 (3): 462–80.

Holzmann, R., and E. Palmer, eds. 2006. *Pension Reform: Issues and Prospects for Non-financial Defined Contribution (NDC) Schemes*. Washington, DC: World Bank.

International Monetary Fund (IMF). 2003. *Adequate and Sustainable Pensions. Joint report on pensions with the European Commission*. Washington, DC: IMF.

International Monetary Fund (IMF). 2010. *Staff report on request for stand-by arrangement. Country report 10/110*. Greece: IMF.

International Monetary Fund (IMF). 2013. Greece: Ex post evaluation of exceptional access under the 2010 stand-by arrangement. Country report 13/186. IMF.

Katroungalos, G., and C. Morfakidis. 2011. Law in books and law in action: Uncertainty in the implementation of social insurance law after the pension reform of 2010–2011. *Epitheorisis Dikaiou Koinonikis Asfaliseos* 9 (628): 657–71.

Lyberaki, A., P. Tinios, and T. Georgiadis. 2010. Multidimensional poverty in Greece: A deep, persistent grey? *South Eastern European Journal of Economics* 8 (1): 87–110.

Lyberaki, A., and P. Tinios. 2012. Labour and pensions in the Greek crisis: The microfoundations of disaster. *Südosteuropa. Zeitschrift für Politik und Gesellschaft* 60 (3): 363–86.

Lyberaki, A., and P. Tinios. 2014. The informal welfare state and the family: Invisible actors in the Greek drama. *Political Studies Review* 12:193–208.

Mackenzie, G. A. 2010. *The Decline of the Traditional Pension: A Comparative Study of Threats to Retirement Security*. Cambridge: Cambridge University Press.

Matsaganis, M. 2011. *Social Policy in Hard Times: Financial Crisis, Fiscal Austerity and Social Protection*. Athens: Kritiki.

Ministry of Labour. 2013. Unified system of control and payment of pensions "helios." http://www.idika.gr/files/4th_ekthesi_HLIOS_SEPTEMBER.pdf.

Ministry of Labour Committee. 2015. Towards a new social contract for pensions, October (in Greek). http://www.tovima.gr/files/1/2015/10/po.pdf.

Mitchell, O. S., and S. P. Zeldes. 1996. Social security privatization: A structure for analysis. *American Economic Review* 86 (2): 363–67.

Mitrakos, T., and P. Tsakloglou. 2012. Inequality, poverty and material well-being: From 1974 to the current crisis. In *Bank of Greece, Social Policy and Social Cohesion in Greece under Conditions of Economic Crisis* (in Greek), 173–215. Athens: Bank of Greece.

Nektarios, M. 1996. *Social Insurance in Greece*. Athens: Forum.

Nektarios, M. 2008. *Pension Reform with Consensus and Transparency*. Athens: Papazisis.

Nektarios, M. 2012. Greece: The NDC paradigm as a framework for a sustainable pension system. In R. Holzmann, E. Palmer, and D. Robalino, eds., *Non-financial Defined Contribution Pension Schemes in a Changing Pension World: Progress, Lessons and Implementation*, vol. 1, 259–77. Washington, DC: World Bank.

Nektarios, M., and T. Georgiadis. 2009. The aged in Europe: Ownership and value of net assets. In *Life 50+, Health, Ageing and Pensions in Greece and in Europe, 329–46*, ed. A. Lyberaki, P. Tinios and A. Philalithis. Athens: Kritiki.

O'Donnell, O., and P. Tinios. 2003. The politics of pension reform: Lessons from public attitudes in Greece. *Political Studies* 51:262–281.

OECD. 1988. Reforming public pensions. Social policy study 5. Paris.

OECD. 2007. *Economic Surveys: Greece*. Paris: OECD.

OECD. 2011. *Economic Surveys: Greece*. Paris: OECD.

OECD. 2016. *Economic Surveys: Greece*. Paris: OECD.

Parliament. 2010. Law 3863, preamble. http://www.parliament.gr.

Parliament. 2015. Greece Memorandum of Understanding for a Three-Year ESM Programme (Law 4336/15). http://online.wsj.com/public/resources/documents/greecedoc.pdf.

Petroglou, A. 2012. The constitutionality of pension cuts in periods of financial crisis, according to the Council of State and the Portuguese constitutional court. *Epitheorisis Dikaiou Koinonikis Asfaliseos* 6 (637): 900–907.

Pierson, P. 2000. Increasing returns, path dependence, and the study of politics. *American Political Science Review* 94 (2): 251–67.

Spraos Committee (Committee for the Examination Economic Policy in the Long Term). 1997. *Economy and Pensions: A Contribution to the Social Dialogue*. Athens: National Bank of Greece. http://www.antigonelyberaki.gr/index.php/en/pics-from-recent-reading/item/26 1-έκθεση-σπράου-για-το-ασφαλιστικό.

Stergiou, A., and T. Sakellaropoulos, eds. 2011. *The Pension Reform: Findings, Proposals, Articles*. Athens: Dionikos.

Tinios, P., and S. Poupakis. 2013. "Knowledge is power": Public attitudes and the stalling of pension reform in Greece. *Journal of Population Ageing* 6 (4): 247–67.

Tinios, P. 2003. *Growth with Solidarity: A Blueprint for Pensions in the New Century*. Athens: Papazisis.

Tinios, P. 2005. Pension reform in Greece: Reform by instalments—A blocked process? *West European Politics* 28: 402–409.

Tinios, P. 2010. *The Pension Problem: A Method to Decipher* (in Greek). Athens: Kritiki.

Tinios, P. 2011. Accounting standards as catalysts for pension reform: Greek pensions and the public/private boundary. *Journal of European Social Policy* 21 (2): 164–77.

Tinios, P. 2012b. The pensions merry-go-round: End of a cycle? In S. Kalyvas, G. Pagoulatos, and H. Tsoukas, eds., *From Stagnation to Forced Adjustment: Reforms in Greece 1974–2010*, 117–32. London: Hurst.

Tinios, P. 2012c, forthcoming. The Lisbon agenda and its value added for pension reform. In P. Copeland and D. Papadimitriou, eds., *Ten Years of the Lisbon Agenda*. London: Palgrave Macmillan.

Tinios, P. 2013. Pensions and the economy after the Memorandum of Understanding: towards a strategy spreading risk. ELIAMEP Crisis observatory Research Publication 1. ELIAMEP. http://crisisobs.gr/wp-content/uploads/2013/03/Ερευνητικό-Κείμενο_1_Π.Τήνιος2.pdf.

Tinios, P. 2014. Social insurance and competitiveness: A neglected link. In M. Massourakis, ed., *Hellenic Bank Association*, 139–53. Athens: HBA.

Tinios, P. 2015a. "Off-the-shelf reforms" and their blind spots: Pensions in post-memorandum Greece. In R. Gerodimos and G. Karyotis, eds., *The Politics of Extreme Austerity: Greece beyond the Crisis*, 66–76. London: Palgrave Macmillan.

Tinios, P. 2015b. Employment and social developments in Greece. DG for Internal Policies. European Parliament, October 2015. http://www.europarl.europa.eu/RegData/etudes/STUD/2015/563468/IPOL_STU(2015)563468_EN.pdf.

Tompson, W. with R. Price. 2009. *The Political Economy of Reform: Lessons from Pensions, Product Markets and Labour Markets in Ten OECD Countries*. Paris: OECD.

Triantafyllou, P. 2006. Greece: Political competition in a majoritarian system. In E. M. Immergut, K. M. Anderson, and I.Schulze, eds., *The Handbook of West European Pension Politics*, 97–149. Oxford: Oxford University Press.

World Bank. 1994. *Averting the Old Age Crisis: Policies to Protect the Old and Promote Growth.* Washington, DC: World Bank.

Xafa, M., and P. Tinios. 2014. The choice in pensions: A cul de sac or a fresh start? *Athens Review of Books*, May, pp. 11–15. http://athensreviewofbooks.com/?p=1086.

Zampelis, P. 1998. *For a New Model of Social Insurance*. Athens: Mimeo.

Zampelis, P. 2013. The new calculation of Auxiliary pensions of ETEA and separation payments of provident funds. *Epitheorisis Dikaiou Koinonikon Asfaliseon.*

VI   Law and Order and Public Administration

12   The Greek Justice System: Collapse and Reform[1]

Elias Papaioannou and Stavroula Karatza

12.1   Introduction

When the Greek crisis started unfolding in 2009, the focus of international media, investors, and policy makers was on the huge stock of government debt and the rising fiscal deficit. Most policy makers and commentators viewed the Greek crisis as the outcome of fiscal profligacy that started when Greece joined the eurozone and accelerated after the 2004 Athens Olympic Games. In line with this view, the emergency program of financial assistance that was agreed between Greece and its lenders, the International Monetary Fund, the European Union, and the European Central Bank, the so-called Troika, considered the Greek problem primarily as fiscal in nature. While fiscal adjustment clearly had to be a part of the economic stabilization program, structural reforms were equally urgent. The Greek crisis had its roots in deep institutional failures.[2] In this chapter we focus on a key institution, the justice system.

The Greek justice system has been a drag to the business environment and to sustainable growth. Not only has legal inefficiency been a contributing factor to the loss of competitiveness that preceded the crisis, but the formalism and rigidity of the system are major contributing factors to the severity and duration of the crisis.[3] The prevalent injustice is a major reason for the loss of legitimacy of Greek institutions and the public's feeling that the political-economic system is unfair, favoring a small oligarchy.

There is no settled definition of what counts as the "justice system" or a "legal system." Thus in this chapter we focus on the set of institutions directly entrusted with administering civil and administrative justice and the laws protecting property, shareholders, and creditors.

As of end-2015 there were 253,325 cases pending in administrative courts. For 157,783 of those cases, the date for the first hearing had not been set. And hearings for cases filed at the First-Instance Administrative Courts of Athens were being listed for 2020. The situation in civil courts was not much better. If a claim were filed in

December 2015 at the First-Instance Civil Court in Athens, it would be heard in September 2018 at the earliest (for claims between 20,000 to 250,000 euros) and in January 2018 (for claims exceeded 250,000 euros). The conditions on penal courts are no better, as important felonies have been pending in courts for a decade. It is common for a trial to start after the maximum (18-month) period of custody has elapsed. Suspects for serious crimes and felonies, including terrorism, murder, and drug trafficking, have been released from custody if their trials have not been completed in 18 months.

Figure 12.1 illustrates one of the key points in this chapter. The graphs plot an index of legal quality capturing the strength of investors' rights (data sourced from the World Bank) against the typical proxy of development, the (log) of real per capita gross national income (GNI). The data are plotted for 2008, just before the crisis started, 2012, and 2015. There is a clear-cut positive correlation between legal institutions and development across the world in all three periods. Economically successful countries offer, on average, superior protection to investors and have more efficient legal systems.

Greece is an outlier, especially in 2008: the Greek legal system was offering investors poor protection against expropriation from firm insiders (managers and key shareholders, who often tunnel firm assets to personal firms and accounts), compared to its (relatively) high level of income per capita. Investor protection in Greece was comparable to that in Costa Rica, Gabon, and Jordan, while Greece's level of development was similar to that in South Korea, Israel, and New Zealand, countries with sound property rights protection and well-functioning judiciaries. And while the gap between economic and legal development was present also in other crisis-hit EZ countries (Italy, Spain, Portugal), it was the highest in Greece. (Using various proxy measures of rule of law, bureaucratic efficiency, graft, and state capacity, Papaioannou 2015 shows that institutional quality deteriorated in all countries of the EZ periphery since the inception of the euro.) The gap was still present in Greece in 2012 and it only narrowed in 2015. Sadly this happened mostly because of the sizable drop of output (between 2008 and 2015 output per capita fell by more than 25 percent) rather than institutional advancement.

A major deficiency of the economic adjustment program that was followed in Greece during the crisis has been its narrow focus on fiscal stabilization and the relative neglect of wider institutional reforms. And while reforming labor and product markets and social security has been part of both the initial (in spring 2010) and the subsequent (in 2012 and in 2015) Memorandum of Understanding (MoU), little attention was paid to the rule of law, the legal system and the judiciary (e.g., see Eleftheriadis 2014). In fact many of the reforms in the judiciary (implemented mostly

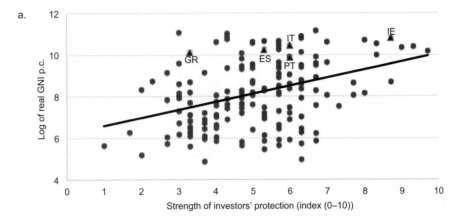

Figure 12.1a

Investor protection and economic development: Unconditional relationship in 2008

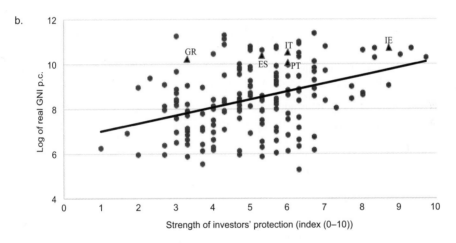

Figure 12.1b

Investor protection and economic development: Unconditional relationship in 2012

over 2010 to 2013) were initiated by local authorities rather than foreign experts and advisers. And Greece's foreign partners did not push Greek authorities to stay on the reform path, when the latter abandoned reforming efforts (in 2014 and especially after 2015). At the same time the economic crisis has made things worse, as the demand for judicial/legal services has increased (due to rising bankruptcies, nonperforming loans, and higher litigation) and judges and attorneys have been on back-to-back strikes that have further slowed down judicial process. Despite some progress and reforms

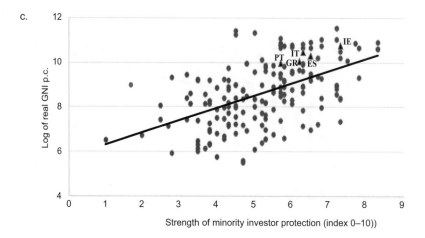

Figure 12.1c

Investor protection and economic development: Unconditional relationship in 2015

(discussed below), delays have increased, and steadily Greece is becoming a lawless society. To make things worse, over the past years there have been many accusations in the media of political and big-business interference in courts and corruption. Trust in the system has plummeted.

Greece needs a multidimensional, massive redesign of the legal system that includes abolishing unnecessary formalism by drastically reforming civil, penal, and administrative procedures, legislating and implementing efficient management practices in courts, investing in information technology (at the beginning of the crisis most judges did not use personal computers and even today the penetration of IT is small to moderate), and dealing decisively with the large case backlog. The strong evidence of a link between the quality of legal institutions and economic development suggests that this institutional reform is one of the most essential (Acemoglu, Johnson, and Robinson 2005; La Porta et al. 1997, 1998; Acemoglu and Robinson 2012).

This chapter is organized as follows: In section 12.2, we place our analysis in the broader context of institutional economics. In section 12.3, we use various international measures of legal efficiency to provide an empirical account of the Greek justice and legal system. In section 12.4, we present a radical and innovative proposal to deal with case backlog and discuss its financing. In section 12.5, we detail reforms in ten areas; these reforms can have an impact if implemented *jointly* with our radical proposal for dealing with the backlog. In section 12.6, we list additional reforms and discuss some successful interventions that should be strengthened. Section 12.7 summarizes.

12.2 Legal Institutions and Development

In its 2014 EU Justice Scoreboard the European Commission stated that "high quality institutions are a determinant of economic performance ..." and that "predictable, timely and enforceable justice decisions are important structural components of an attractive business environment" (European Commission 2014, p. 4). This statement summarizes much recent research. La Porta et al. (1997, 1998), Djankov et al. (2003), and Djankov, McLeish, and Shliefer (2007) constructed quantitative proxies of shareholder and creditor protection, bankruptcy procedures, and other legal system features for a large number of countries (see also Dakolias 1999 for an early attempt) and studied the interconnection between legal institutions and economic well-being. The academic literature has focused on two aspects of legal institutions: legislative quality (*de jure*) and court efficiency and delays (*de facto*). Besides compiling quantitative proxies of these aspects, the literature has tried (1) moving beyond correlations and establishing causal relationships, (2) detecting the channels of influence, and (3) identifying the factors shaping legal institutions (e.g., related to social features, trust, family ties, religion, legal origin).[4] The first set of studies showed that the quality of legal and property rights institutions correlate strongly with various aspects of economic efficiency, such as access to bank credit, investment, and entrepreneurial activity (e.g., La Porta et al. 1997; Djankov et al. 2003).

Figure 12.2 summarizes the main channels linking legal institutions with economic well-being.

12.2.1 Domestic and Foreign Private Investment

A direct negative consequence of a dysfunctional judicial process is to lower external finance. In countries with poor investor protection and slow judicial practices, stock markets are, on average, less developed and less liquid, bank credit is constrained, and loans come with shorter maturities and higher interest rates.[5] Firm size is also inversely related to the quality of the legal system, as inefficient legislation and court delays impede firms form growing (Demirgüç-Kunt and Maksimovic 1998; Laeven and Woodruff 2007). As finance is a "nexus of incomplete contracts" (Shleifer and Vishny 1997) a well-functioning legal and court system is needed to quickly and efficiently resolve disputes that may emerge. High interest costs and frictions in external finance are particularly harmful for young entrepreneurs who usually lack the necessary capital or collateral to obtain a loan.[6] Research shows that venture capital investment is low in countries with slow and inefficient courts.[7] In line with this evidence, there are few private equity and venture capital firms in Greece.

Mechanisms

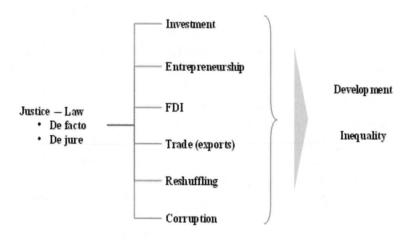

Figure 12.2
Legal institutions and development mechanisms

Poor investor protection and slow judicial practices are key impediments to foreign investors, who usually lack the necessary connections to bypass the hurdles. Empirical work shows that the quality of legal institutions is more important for attracting foreign capital, than education, infrastructure, and market size (e.g., Alfaro, Kalemli-Ozcan, and Volosovyc 2008; Papaioannou 2009). In line with this body of research, there has been little foreign direct investment in Greece over the past years, and in the few instances of large foreign investment deals, there were local middlemen who facilitated the process, helping foreign investors bypass red tape and deal with the necessary permits and licenses.

12.2.2 Entrepreneurship, Trade, and Creative Destruction

The high cost of capital is particularly harmful for entrepreneurship and employment in high-tech skill-intensive sectors that usually lack collateral and thus depend strongly on external sources of finance (Rajan and Zingales 1998). It is also harmful for productivity growth because it prevents the economy from re-allocating quickly productive resources toward sectors with high potential (Ciccone and Papaioannou 2006, 2007; Fisman and Love 2007). Ciccone and Papaioannou (2006, 2007) develop a multi-sector multi-country general equilibrium model in which legal inefficiency and other frictions to financial intermediation impede new investment in sectors with globally expanding demand, such as biotechnology, information technology, and energy. Thus the economy is stuck in traditional sectors that face increasing global competition from low-labor cost producers. Moreover the limited reallocation that takes place— is driven by incumbents who, via connections, bypass legal barriers and obtain cheaper finance. This in turn leads to less innovation, higher prices (inflation), and lower quality goods. Both features seem to apply to Greece. Greek banks during the booming years financed traditional sectors, such as real estate, government agencies (and parties), and utilities and there was little—if any—financing of high-tech sectors. Most lending was directed to incumbents, and usually in the oligopolistic sectors.

The frictions that emerge from the inefficient legal system are especially harmful for exports (e.g., Nunn 2007; Levchenko 2007). In line with the established link between legal efficiency and success on global export markets, Greek exports have been a small percent of GDP. And during the boom years (1995 to 2007) Greek banks allocated few funds to export-oriented firms.

12.2.3 Corruption

Legal inefficiency goes in tandem with corruption. Obscure legislation allows bureaucrats, administrators, and even judges to accept illegal payments. Only a small fraction of allegations end up in courts, and when this happens, loopholes and never-ending procedures allow corrupt officials to escape imprisonment. This fuels people's perception of injustice, destroys civic capital, and lowers trust. Conflicting laws and numerous entry barriers fuel a decentralized system of corruption, where entrepreneurs have to bribe numerous bureaucrats, and administrators. Decentralized corruption is more harmful than centralized corruption systems (Shleifer and Vishny 1993). Greece fits this paradigm well.

12.2.4 Inequality

The negative effects of injustice go well beyond economic efficiency. Theoretical work and case studies reveal that legal inefficiency is associated with increased inequality. Loopholes, legal uncertainty, and a slow judicial process allow the elite and their political cronies to escape the law (by buying judges and politicians). A Greek prosecutor eloquently summarized the situation: "Who is in jail in Greece? The poor and those who lack connections."[8] Moreover the numerous legal and civil procedure formalities impede entrepreneurial activity, magnifying income inequality. Therefore legal inefficiency leads to the worst type of inequality, the one emerging from lack of opportunity (e.g., Glaeser, Scheinkman, and Shleifer 2003).

12.3   The Greek Legal System: A Comparative Assessment

In this section we provide an analysis of the Greek legal system using comparative indicators reflecting the formalism, quality, and speed of the resolution mechanisms using cross-country data from World Bank's *Doing Business Project* and the 2014 and 2016 European Justice Scoreboard (European Commission 2014, 2016).[9]

12.3.1   Investor Protection

In table 12.1 we report Greece's score on (*de jure*) indexes measuring how well the legal system protects investors. We report these indexes for 2008 (in panel a), just before the crisis started, 2012 (panel b), and 2015 (panel c). The indexes for 2008 and 2012 are not fully comparable to the 2015 one as the World Bank has changed is methodology for measuring investor protection. For comparability the table reports the mean values across the world (excluding Greece), the eurozone (excluding Greece), and the four World Bank income groups.

Shareholder Protection   The shareholder protection index (column 1 in table 12.1) measures the "strength of minority shareholder protection against directors' misuse of corporate assets for personal gain." It captures three characteristics:

1. Transparency of related-party transactions (disclosure rights, column 2).
2. Liability of managers, directors, and dominant shareholders for self-dealing transactions (director liability, column 3).
3. Ability of non-controlling shareholders to sue officers and directors for misconduct (shareholder suits, column 4).

All measures range from 0 to 10, where higher values indicate a better legal environment protecting shareholders.

In 2008 Greece scored 3.0 on the composite index of shareholder protection, ranking 170 out of 211 countries (world average was 4.86). Greece had the lowest score among all EZ countries and scored considerably lower than the other crisis-hit countries in the European periphery. Greece's score was lower than even that of the low-income group of countries (consisting mainly of young democracies and autocracies in Africa and Asia). Greece's score was particularly low on disclosure requirements for related-party transactions. That problem became more apparent during the crisis, as reflected by the charges filed by criminal prosecutors against many influential business people and bank managers for related-party transactions and tunneling activities. An example is the collapse of Proton Bank. According to the reports by the bank regulator (Bank of

Table 12.1

Investor protection

		Shareholders rights				Creditors rights
	Observed	Composite index	Disclosure index	Anti-director rights	Suits rights	Legal rights
		(1)	(2)	(3)	(4)	(5)
Panel a: 2008						
Greece		3	1	3	5	4
World (excl. GRC)	211	4.86	4.89	4.17	5.54	5.22
Euro area (excl. GRC)	18	5.65	5.88	4.75	6.31	6.13
High income (excl. GRC)	66	5.80	5.78	5.35	6.27	6.33
Upper middle income	55	4.94	4.83	4.44	5.58	5.29
Lower middle income	61	4.23	4.16	3.33	5.22	4.69
Low income	29	3.91	4.54	2.75	4.43	3.64
Panel b: 2012						
Greece		3.3	1	4	5	4
World (excl. GRC)	211	5.11	5.22	4.49	5.63	5.85
Euro area (excl. GRC)	18	5.75	5.94	4.83	6.44	6.06
High income (excl. GRC)	66	5.85	5.88	5.34	6.33	6.50
Upper middle income	55	5.38	5.27	5.19	5.67	5.54
Lower middle income	61	4.51	4.57	3.54	5.43	5.54
Low income	29	4.18	4.96	3.18	4.39	5.57
Panel c: 2015						
Greece		6.2	7	4	5	3
World (excl. GRC)	211	5.28	5.72	4.70	6.09	5.26
Euro area (excl. GRC)	18	6.10	6.06	4.89	6.72	4.94
High income (excl. GRC)	66	5.98	6.11	5.49	6.92	5.45
Upper middle income	55	5.36	5.75	5.13	5.87	5.15
Lower middle income	61	5.02	5.44	4.18	5.84	5.15
Low income	29	4.07	5.38	3.17	5.10	5.31

Source: World Bank Doing Business Project

Greece) and the prosecution, close to 700 million euros were lent to firms related to the bank's main shareholder without any disclosure and without any internal controls. The government had to bail out Proton Bank at a cost exceeding one billion euros.

Greece's ranking improved considerably during the crisis thanks to a series of reforms in the period 2010 to 2014. In 2015 Greece ranked 47 on the revised index of shareholder protection, a noteworthy improvement. The improvement was limited during the initial crisis years (table 12.1, panel b) but more rapid in later years (table 12.1, panel c). Greece has improved the legal tools that shareholders can employ to defend themselves against expropriation by directors and managers. At the same time, no major reform has taken place on raising disclosure requirements from company insiders regarding self-dealing transactions.

Creditors' Rights and Bankruptcy   The creditor protection index (column 5 in table 12.1) measures the "degree to which collateral and bankruptcy laws protect the rights of borrowers and lenders." In 2008 Greece's score on the creditor rights index was 4. This placed the country at the 97th position.

Greece's poor performance on protecting creditors can be seen more directly by looking at measures related to insolvency. As figure 12.3a shows, a typical insolvency in Greece in 2008 was expected to take two years, the highest across EZ member counties at the time (Latvia, Lithuania, and Slovakia had not joined the eurozone). As figure 12.3b shows, the recovery rate for creditors was less than 50 cents on the euro, again the lowest (with Luxembourg) across the eurozone at the time.[10]

Potamitis (2014) eloquently summarizes the Greek public's perception of Greek insolvency laws: "insolvency and recovery proceedings betray a stunning lack of purpose combined with excessive formalism: Bankruptcy is so complex and involves so many players (many of whom lack valuable claims) that it ends up as a black hole where whatever goes in nearly never comes out. The procedural complexity of pre-insolvency proceedings entails tremendous delays. Procedural protections are easily abused by holdouts thereby frustrating the statutory goal of encouraging pre-insolvency turnarounds" (see also Potamitis and Psaltis 2013; Potamitis and Rokas 2012).

Despite various amendments to the insolvency code over the past few years, the situation remains unsatisfactory. In 2015 a typical insolvency in Greece was expected to take 3.5 years, almost double the time in 2008. Moreover the process has become less efficient, as the estimated recovery rates have fallen to 34.9 cents on the euro, the lowest among all 19 EZ countries. The combination of "zombie" firms with undercapitalized banks impedes creative destruction and the reshuffling of capital and labor to young, innovative firms.

a.

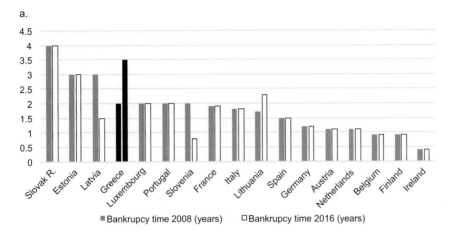

Figure 12.3a
Bankruptcy time across EZ countries

b.

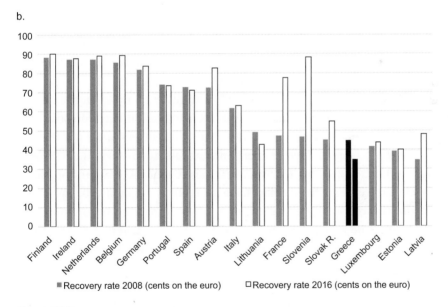

Figure 12.3b
Recovery rate in bankruptcy across EZ countries

12.3.2   Legal Enforcement

A further key feature of legal systems is court efficiency.[11] In table 12.2 we compare Greece to other countries on three aspects of contract enforcement: the number of days it takes to file a claim, obtain judgment, and enforce it (column 1), the number of steps that are required (column 2), and the attorney, court and enforcement costs as a share of the claim value (column 3) for a dispute regarding a commercial claim that equals 200 percent of per capita GDP (approximately 40,000 to 50,000 euros for Greece). As before, we report data for 2008, 2012, and 2015.

In 2008 it took more than two years to resolve a relatively straightforward dispute (819 days) that, on average, the rest of the world resolved in 620 days. The comparison with other EZ countries was even starker, as there plaintiffs needed 507 days. Court delays were sizable in other European crisis-hit countries (around 500 days in Ireland, Spain, and Portugal) and especially in Italy (1,000 days). Legal formalism, as reflected in the number of steps required to enforce a simple contract, was similar in Greece as in other countries (39) though somewhat higher than the EZ average (31.5).

Sadly and despite some incremental steps in speeding the process, things have become worse during the crisis (table 12.2, panels b and c). The latest World Bank data suggest that the resolution time for a simple dispute was approximately 1,580 days at the end of 2015, more than twice the world average (631 days) and almost three times more than in the high-income group of countries (532 days).

We can further explore how Greece compares with other countries on the disposition time of court cases using information from the European Justice Scoreboard (EJS 2013), which reports various statistics on the functioning and resources of court systems across Europe. [12] Table 12.3, panel a, presents the case disposition time in 2009 to 2010 for various types of disputes. On average, it took roughly 500 days to complete a legal dispute in Greece, while the median value for EU27 was around 150 days. While we lack data for Greece for 2014 and 2015, things seem to have been worsening over time, since in 2012, the time needed to resolve disputes increased to 700. The differences are especially pronounced on administrative courts, as it takes years to resolve cases.

Table 12.3, panel b, sheds some light on this increase. The clearance rate in Greek courts is low (around 0.8 and in some cases even lower), thus over time the workload of Greek courts gets higher as new cases add to the stock of former pending cases.

In figure 12.4a and b we tabulate incoming and pending litigation cases in civil-commercial courts and administrative courts in the early crisis years. The numbers are significantly larger than the EZ average. The big difference is in the number of pending cases in administrative courts, which is four to five times larger than in other EZ

Table 12.2

Court efficiency

		Contract enforcement		
	Obs.	Calendar days	Procedures	Cost (% claim)
Panel a: 2008				
Greece		819	39	14.40
World (exc. GRC)	211	619.64	37.48	34.59
Euro area (excl. GRC)	18	525.13	31.19	18.61
High income (excl. GRC)	66	512.15	34.78	20.97
Upper middle income	55	626.46	37.96	29.90
Lower middle income	61	697.59	38.98	40.45
Low income	29	687.39	39.57	62.19
Panel b: 2012				
Greece		1,100	39	14.40
World (exc. GRC)	211	621.86	37.47	34.95
Euro area (excl. GRC)	18	555.94	31.72	20.46
High income (excl. GRC)	66	539.71	34.75	21.71
Upper middle income	55	617.81	37.73	29.80
Lower middle income	61	687.70	39.31	40.88
Low income	29	678.04	39.29	62.41
Panel c: 2016				
Greece		1,580		14.40
World (exc. GRC)	211	631.13		34.44
Euro area (excl. GRC)	18	579.28		20.21
High income (excl. GRC)	66	532.89		22.19
Upper middle income	55	609.92		29.36
Lower middle income	61	742.84		43.79
Low income	29	659.97		52.27

Source: World Bank Doing Business Project

Table 12.3

Case disposition time

	First instance			Second instance		
	Total	Civil and commercial litigation	Administrative law	Total	Civil and commercial litigation	Administrative law
Panel A: Case disposition time (in days)						
Greece	510	190	2003	520	298	1048
EU27 (median)	147	216	205	156	206	362
Panel B: Case clearance rate						
Greece	0.79	0.79	0.80	0.74	0.78	0.66
EU27 (median)	1.00	1.00	1.00	1.00	1.00	1.00

Source: European Justice Scoreboard (2013)

countries. The various reports of the EJS suggest that across the European Union the conditions in administrative courts are the worst in Greece, alongside Malta and Cyprus. According to the latest (2016) EJS, the backlog in Greece's administrative courts is the highest among all EZ countries. EJS (2016) reports that 3.1 cases per 100 inhabitants were pending in Greek administrative courts in the end of 2014, compared to approximately 1 in Cyprus, 0.4 in Spain, Netherlands, and Finland, and 0.8 in Germany.

There are many factors behind the severe delays in administrative courts. First, there is no alternative to litigation. Second, until very recently, similar tax disputes (of the same individual/firm) occurring in different fiscal years had to be the subject of separate claims requiring separate hearings. Third, legislation, especially regarding taxation, keeps changing and often tax authorities are uncertain about the law that applies to each case. Fourth, the constant change of ministers and key administrators makes executive orders problematic, either because of inconsistencies (e.g., contradicting legislation) or because of improper staffing. Fifth, as the law on public contracts is complex, formalistic, and without clear guidelines, firms often challenge the decisions of the contracting authority (Bernitsas 2014). Sixth, public authorities often push firms and individuals to the administrative court system in order to delay payment. Finally, negotiated settlements between state agencies and firms are not allowed, and the interest cost for state agencies (τόκος υπερημερίας) is smaller than the actual time value for money.

a.

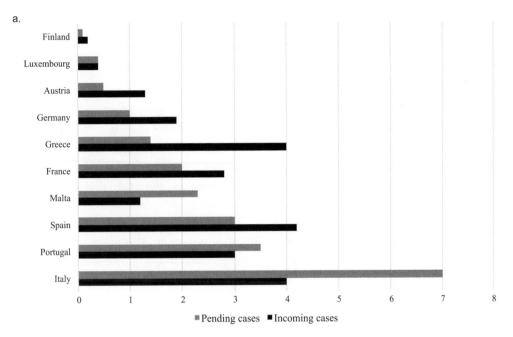

Figure 12.4a
Incoming and pending litigation cases per 100 inhabitants in civil courts in 2010

b.

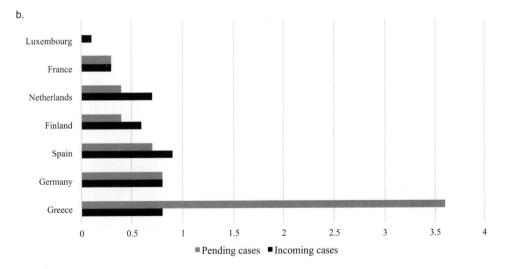

Figure 12.4b
Incoming and pending litigation cases per 100 inhabitants in administrative courts in 2010

The problem in administrative courts is so severe that the Council of Europe and the European Court of Human Rights have roundly condemned Greek authorities for the massive delays. The Committee of Ministers of the Council of Europe argued in 2007 that there has been a persistent violation of human rights on account of court delays and the absence of any remedy against them. In unusually undiplomatic language the Committee spoke of the "gravity of the systemic problem at the basis of the violations" of the right to a fair trial. Three years later the European Court of Human Rights issued another resounding condemnation.[13] The problem is even more general, as Greece has been found by international judicial bodies to violate human rights in other areas such as asylum and abuses of immigrants. Things became worse with the crisis as the constant strikes of lawyers, attorneys, and notaries contributed to the delays. There have even been rumors that opposing salary cuts, judges were also on a "silent strike."

The inefficiency and delays of the Greek justice system are also manifest on issues related to competition, antitrust, dominant position, and market power abuse. The latest EJS (2016) suggests that average delays over 2012, 2013, and 2014 have exceeded 1,000 days, double the time in other EU jurisdictions. The 2016 statistics further suggest that the average length of judicial review cases against decisions of national competition authorities is the highest in Greece, Denmark, and the Czech Republic, among all EU jurisdictions.

12.3.3   Resources and Efficiency

We next review the resources made available to Greek courts to understand whether the long delays reflect lack of financing and personnel or whether the problem stems from low productivity, arising from the misallocation of resources, mismanagement, lack of incentives, and so on.

Expenditure   Figure 12.5a and b plots the total budgeted amounts allocated to all courts in Greece and other EU countries in 2010 in per capita terms and as a share of total public expenditure, respectively. Greece spent 454,066,828 euros. (This amount does not include the cost of public prosecutions or legal aid.) The average expenditure per capita in Greece is 40.1 euros, similar to the EU27 average (median) of 41.7 euros (39.6 euros).

However, an independent report of the European Commission for the Efficiency of Justice (CEPEJ), commissioned by the Council of Europe, which employs a broader definition of expenditures that includes expenses on public prosecution, legal aid, and the costs of the Court of Auditors (*Ελεγκτικό Συνέδριο*), suggests that the Greek justice system was relatively underfinanced. According to their 2010 estimates, the total

a.

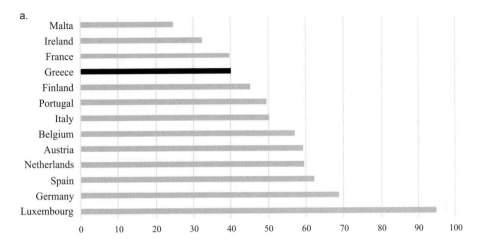

Figure 12.5a
Court budgets per inhabitant in 2010

b.

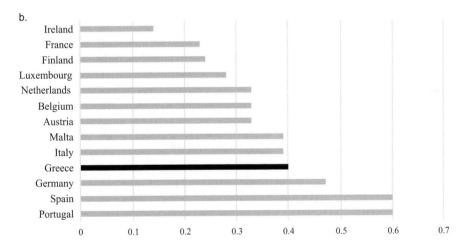

Figure 12.5b
Court budgets as a share of public expenditures in 2010

annual approved public budget for the Greek justice system that year was 632,472,911 euros. This amount is somewhat smaller than that of Portugal (700 million euros) and significantly smaller than that of Belgium (935 million euros), both countries with populations similar to Greece. If one were to also include the budget allocated to the prison system, the total budget increases to 715 million euros for Greece—but Belgium's budget doubles to 1.8 billion euros and Portugal's budget more than doubles to 1.7 billion euros.[14]

The two sources above point out that relative to the other countries, courts in Greece may be moderately underfinanced. While the extent of underfinancing is not severe, it is the allocation of funds that is particularly problematic. The Greek budget is almost exclusively spent on salaries, and there are minimal funds for maintenance, new infrastructure, investment in information technology, and so on. According to the CEPEJ report, the ratio of salaries to overall expenditure of the court system across 29 European states is 66.1 percent, but this ratio in Greece is 95.9.

Employment   There are three types of court personnel across most jurisdictions: full-time professional judges as well as magistrate judges, other judge-like personnel who perform judicial duties, and judicial clerks and assistants (paralegals, interns, secretaries, etc.). We now examine how the Greek justice system compares to other EU systems on these three categories.

Figure 12.6a illustrates that in 2010 Greece had 29.3 full-time professional judges per 100,000 inhabitants.[15] This includes magistrate judges (ειρηνοδίκες) who are full-time in Greece. With the exception of Luxembourg, this was the highest number across the European Union, where the average (median) was 18.9 (17.9).[16] Greece's ranking reverses when other judge-like personnel such as "professional judges sitting in courts on an occasional basis, non-professional judges, and Rechtspfleger for countries (such as Germany and Austria) which have such a category" are added.[17] Because Greece has only full-time judges, it falls below the EU average, as shown in figure 12.6b. In 2010 Greece had 29.3 judges and judge-like personnel per 100,000 inhabitants (same as the number of full-time professional judges), while the mean (median) for the European Union was 45.6 (29.8)

In 2010 Greece had 89 judicial clerks per 100,000 inhabitants in Greece. This is similar to the EU mean and median. Greece appears to be significantly under-resourced in the personnel assisting judges (paralegals, interns, secretaries).

Salaries   In figure 12.7 we examine the pay of Greek judges as compared to their colleagues in the European Union. Both plots show the ratio of first instance professional

a.

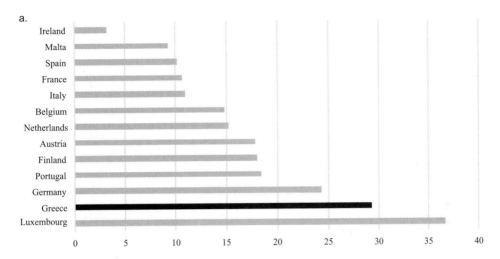

Figure 12.6a

Number of judges per 100,000 inhabitants in 2010

b.

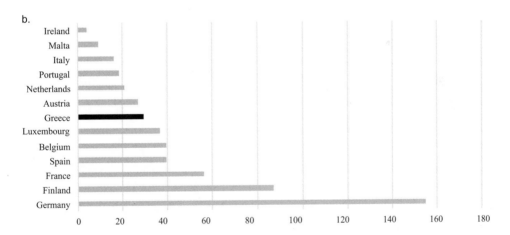

Figure 12.6b

Number of judges and other judge-like personnel in courts per 100,000 inhabitants in 2010

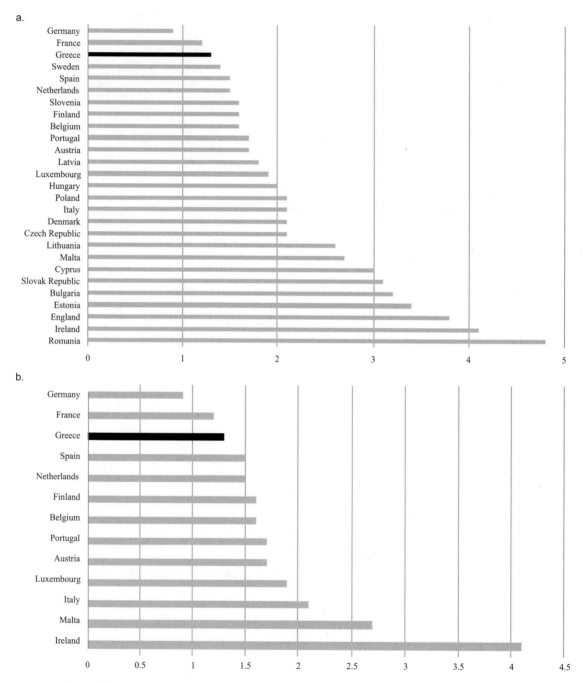

Figure 12.7
First-instance judges' relative wages in 2010

judges' salary to the average gross annual salary (across all occupations). Greek judges are among the lowest paid in the European Union. A similar picture emerges from the CEPEJ report that compares entry-level salaries and salaries at the Supreme Court. The 2010 report puts the gross pay of first-instance Greek judges at 33,000 euros. For comparison, the pay of first-instance judges in Belgium is 62,367 euros, in Austria 47,713 euros, in Cyprus 71,000 euros, in France 41,000 euros, in Italy 50,290 euros, in Portugal 36,000 euros, and in Spain 47,500 euros.[18]

Since salaries (and special allowances) were cut considerably in 2011 and 2012, Greek judges were still among the lowest paid across the European Union. In particular the base monthly salary for a newly appointed judge was reduced from 2,067 euros in 2008 to 1,778 in 2013.[19] The two main supplementary allowances (library allowance, επίδομα βιβλιοθήκης, and allowance for presiding, παραμονής στην έδρα) fell from approximately by 500 and 650 euros to 420 and 460 euros, respectively, lowering the overall compensation by 10 percent (from approximately 3,200–3,300 to 2,600 euros). The annual pay cut was larger as the special allowance for Christmas, Easter, and vacation was almost eliminated for all public sector employees. As appendix table 12A.1 shows, the salary cuts for senior judges were even more pronounced. The base salary for judges sitting in the three supreme courts dropped by 1,000 euros, while allowances fell by 500 euros.[20]

Infrastructure   While the European Justice Scoreboard does not provide information on infrastructure expenses, there are estimates of such expenses in the CEPEJ report. The budget allocated to the maintenance of court buildings in 2010 in Greece was 10,416,000 euros, much smaller than in Belgium where expenses on existing court infrastructure was six times larger at 68,767,000 euros, and Portugal where they were more than three times larger, 38,762,543 euros. The 2010 Greek budget allocated close to 9.4 million euros for new building infrastructure, exactly as much as in Belgium (no data available for Portugal).

ICT (Information, Communications, and Technology)   The European Justice Scoreboard (EJS) reports statistics for ICT infrastructure of courts across the EU, distinguishing between three types:

1. Computer facilities for the work of judges and other legal personnel (word processing, electronic database of jurisprudence, email and Internet connection).

2. Case registration and management systems, such as the case tracking system, court management information system, and financial information system.

3. Systems of electronic communications and information exchange.

For each of these dimensions, the EJS produces a 0–4 index, where higher values indicate a higher degree of computerization. Figure 12.8a plots the values for Greece in each ICT index and the average values for the eurozone. Greece scores very low across all three dimensions.

Let us start with the computer facilities index. The average score for EZ countries is 4, indicating that in all EZ countries *all* judges have basic computer facilities, such as word processing systems, email, and Internet. The score for Greece is 2, reflecting the fact that in many courts judges do not have basic computer facilities. Greece scores poorly on ICT index for case registration and management (1.7), while the EU27 mean (median), excluding Greece, is 3.6 (4). Whereas the electronic filing, registration, and management of cases is a common practice across all EU countries, it is almost absent in Greece. For example in the Second-Instance Administrative Court of Piraeus records and case registration are kept in handwritten catalogs. Although five years have passed since the initiation of the e-Justice system, Greece still scores the lowest (with Belgium) across all EU countries on an index of electronic submission of claims (European Justice Scoreboard 2016). Greece scores very low (0.4 as compared to a mean value of 2.8 for the EU27) also on the third dimension of computerization that captures electronic communications and information exchange between the courts and related agencies.

Figure 12.8b illustrates the aggregate picture emerging from a composite index of ICT in the court system that averages the three (sub) indicators. Greece was by far the worst performer across the eurozone. The ICT index for Greece is 1.3, compared with 2.5 for Belgium (where ICT penetration is, relatively speaking, low compared to the other countries).

The poor state of ICT provision in Greece is also revealed by the CEPEJ report that measures computerization in three related areas. As of 2009, Greece had the lowest score across 29 European countries, which included both advanced and developed countries such as Albania, Ukraine, and Turkey. The European average and median was 50, and Greece's score was 20. Greece also scored the lowest among all EU countries in terms of the two European Commission indicators that measure people's electronic online access to judicial decisions as of December 2015. First-instance and appellate courts decisions are not publicly and easily available, while in almost all other countries at least some decisions of the lower courts are available online.

At the beginning of the crisis the political system had not realized the severity of the problem. This is best illustrated by the annual public budget allocated to court computerization, which in 2010 (according the CEPEJ report) was just 330,000 euros. By comparison Belgium allocated 37.5 million euros and Portugal 10.5 million euros.

a.

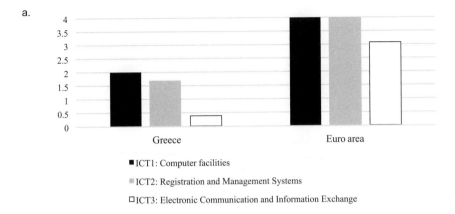

■ICT1: Computer facilities

■ICT2: Registration and Management Systems

□ICT3: Electronic Communication and Information Exchange

Figure 12.8a
ICT practices across courts in EZ countries in 2010

b.

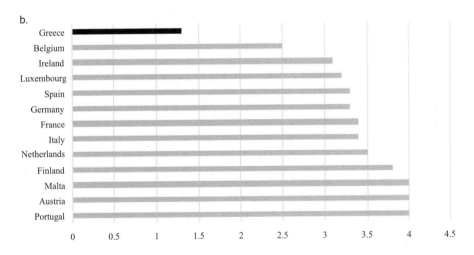

Figure 12.8b
ICT composite index: EZ countries in 2010

CEPEJ estimates that across 29 European countries in 2010, around 3 percent of the court budget was allocated to computerization. In Greece it was less than 0.1 percent.

In 2010 to 2011 the Greek Ministry of Justice initiated the e-Justice system that aimed to bring ICT in courts, speed up the process, and raise accountability. The 2016 European Justice Scoreboard records suggest that there was only a modest improvement, mostly because the administrations of the supreme courts and the Ministry of Justice did not proceed with the initial reforms.

12.3.4   Other Features

Specialized Courts and Tribunals   The EJS gives some information on the organizational structure of the justice system. Figure 12.9a plots the number of first-instance courts per 100,000 inhabitants for Greece (in black bars) and other EZ countries (in gray bars). These statistics reveal that there are more first-instance courts in Greece than in other EU countries: approximately 4 such courts for 100,000 inhabitants in Greece compared with a median of 2 in the European Union.

However, as figure 12.9b illustrates, Greece scores the lowest in the number of specialized courts. This suggests that a structural deficiency of the Greek court system is the lack of specialized courts, where experienced judges settle similar disputes in a timely fashion.

Lawyers   The highly inefficient legal system helps sustain and is sustained by an extremely high number of practicing lawyers (attorneys). According to Pagliero and Timmons (2012) there were 3.389 lawyers per 1000 inhabitants in Greece in 2008, and this was the second-highest ratio in the European Union after Italy (3.574). The EU average was 1.935. Greece also had the highest ratio of legal professionals (3.761) in the European Union, followed by Luxembourg and Italy.[21] The estimates of the EJS are similar (figure 12.10). As of 2010 (2014), Greece had 370 (388) lawyers per 100,000 inhabitants, compared to the EU average/median of around 230 to 250.

The high number of lawyers is sustained partly because of the highly formalistic nature of the legal system. The complexity and obscurity of laws, the constantly changing legislation, the conflicting rulings on similar cases, the lack of bundling of even identical cases, and the court delays, fuel the demand for lawyers.

12.3.5   Political Economy

One may wonder how such a dysfunctional, inefficient, and unjust system continues to exist in a developed democracy. Why does the political system tolerate such an inefficient branch of government? Why does it not respond with proposals and actions of reform? And don't the people protest against such a dysfunctional system? Unfortunately, the political economy is unfavorable, as most stakeholders gain from the status quo. The huge case backlog and the absurd formalism help sustain the large number of lawyers. At the same time the complexity of procedures, the labyrinth of constantly changing legislation, and the partial application of precedent allow connected individuals and firms to get around the system (sometimes with the help of connected lawyers and corrupt judicial personnel).

a.

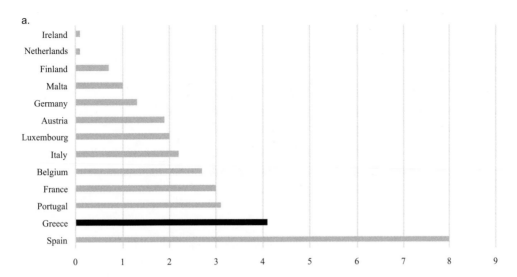

Figure 12.9a

Number of first-instance courts per 100,000 inhabitants

b.

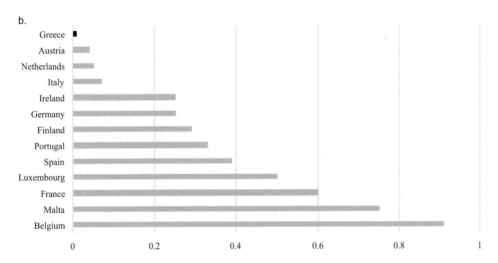

Figure 12.9b

Share of specialized first-instance courts in 2010

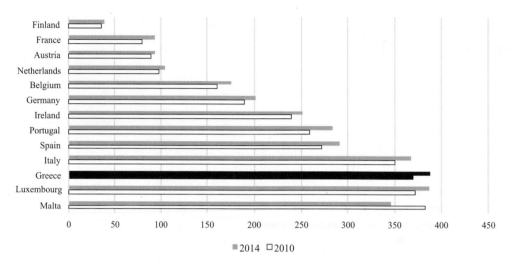

Figure 12.10
Number of lawyers per 100,000 inhabitants across EZ countries

The lack of computerization is beneficial both to judges and prosecutors, as it prevents monitoring, and helps judicial officials conceal misconduct or incompetence. The system is designed in such a way that not even the evaluation and promotion panels, the Supreme Court, or the Ministry of Justice have information on how many times a judge has allowed for adjournments, how many times his/her verdict on first-instance has been overruled by appellate courts, and how long it takes to complete a case. At the same time lawyers gain from the massive delays and lack of computerization by charging for the extra time needed in dealing with paper work and procedure. While there have been a couple of noteworthy efforts to reform, these policies have had moderate (at best) effects. Most important, the key stakeholders (lawyers, judges, clerks) oppose most reforming steps. For example, many opposed even the "model trial" (that helped considerably deal with backlog), and most insiders opposed the small/moderate increase in the cost of appeals. In 2013 to 2014 the whole of the legal profession was on strike, protesting proposed amendments to the Code of Civil Procedure that were aimed at shortening and simplifying civil justice.[22]

12.3.6 Summary

First and foremost, the Greek justice system offers poor protection to shareholders and creditors against managerial entrenchment, tunneling, and even outright theft. Second, Greece has steadily become a state without legal protection, and a regime has begun that can be characterized as "institutionalized injustice." The average time to resolve even simple disputes exceeds four years, while many cases have been pending in courts for more than a decade. And despite some incremental reforms, things have worsened as the crisis has further stressed the already dysfunctional system. Third, the Greek justice system is underfinanced, especially when one nets salaries. Fourth, while the number of full-time professional judges per capita is higher than in other European countries, the number of assisting personnel (paralegals, interns, secretaries) appears to be much lower. Fifth, the composition of the body of judges is itself inefficient. For example, there are is large (and growing) number of Supreme Court judges and high-ranked appellate court judges compared to first-instance judges.[23] There are also few specialized courts. Sixth, the use of information technology is by far the lowest in Europe, lowering productivity and accountability. The inefficiencies of the Greek legal system are partly driven from the malfunctioning of public administration. These conditions have led to a sharp reduction in trust. While before the crisis the Greek people trusted the judiciary (compared to the general level of distrust toward the Parliament, political parties, and Europe), trust has plummeted during the crisis. The issue of distrust toward the legal system and other major institutions (e.g., political parties, members of parliament, European Parliament) is crucial, as it relates both to the intensity of the economic downturn (e.g., Papaioannou 2011, 2013; Algan et al. 2016) and to the reforming process.

12.4 Dealing with Case Backlog

Given the crisis, the squeeze on public finances, and the huge backlog of Greek courts, any reform effort must take place under the strain of exceptional fiscal pressures, low morale, and distrust. For these reasons it is unlikely that moderate reforms, such as the ones implemented as of the writing of this chapter, will have significant impact. Only a radical overhaul with long-term strategic aims is likely to have an effect. We believe that the first priority of reform ought to be to clear the case backlog—without compromising the safeguards of a fair trial. In this section we discuss some commonsense proposals to accomplish this. We outline a plan that consists of four steps, and we present an idea for its financing. Our proposals seek to overcome the rigid organization of courts set out by the Greek Constitution—which heavily regulates judges, judicial personnel, and the organization of courts. We try to respect these restrictions, though some may argue that our ideas may fall foul of the highly prescriptive and detailed constitutional provisions on justice. In next section, where we present our proposals for the next Amendment of the Constitution, we argue that particular emphasis should be given to the articles of the Constitution that pertain to the courts, judges, and prosecutors. We need to stress that neither the current nor the previous Greek administrations, and not even the Troika, have dealt with the case backlog. So while our proposal is far from perfect and complete, no alternatives have been offered.

12.4.1 Recruiting Temporary Magistrates

We believe that the Ministry of Justice should recruit for a three-to-five year period suitably qualified lawyers as temporary magistrates ("justices of the peace," ειρηνοδίκ ες). Recent legislation transferred a sizable portion of cases from first-instance courts to magistrate courts (4055/2012) and anecdotal evidence suggests that this has been beneficial at least in some cases. While the Greek Constitution allows only for full-time permanent judges at higher levels of jurisdiction (article 87 of the Constitution), one could argue that magistrates, who are not trained by the National School of Judges and Prosecutors (Σχολή Δικαστών και Εισαγγελέων), could be exempt from these restrictions. The additional magistrates would be able to process much of the current backlog. After completing their term of office (of 3 to 5 years), these magistrates could either return to private practice or join the judiciary through examinations. (There could be a special procedure/examination for these magistrates entering the School.) Some experts express concerns that such a policy would be deemed "unconstitutional." An alternative option would be to recruit, for a five-year period, lawyers as "judicial assistants." These newly appointed assistants would help judges, by gathering the necessary documents for a case, drafting memos, reviewing legislation, and analyzing precedent.

12.4.2 Recruiting Retired Judges

Retired appeal judges could be recruited for a fixed term of office to deal with the backlog in appellate courts.[24] Since senior judges retire at age 65 to 67, and since the Constitution explicitly recognizes that judges are *"for-life"* (article 88.1), we believe that this proposal does not defile the constitutional prohibition.[25] Retired judges could choose to work on either a full-time or part-time basis; since pensions have fallen considerably, and judges will get paid for their employment (see below for the financing), we believe that a sizable number of retired judges will decide to work at least part-time for some years to complement their income.[26]

If it proves cumbersome to recall retired judges, a (potentially complementary) approach may be to entice judges and prosecutors to continuing their service on a full-time basis for two or more years after their retirement age, with a salary that is significantly higher than the current pension.[27]

12.4.3   Judicial Overtime

The Ministry of Justice could offer monetary incentives to judges and to assisting personnel for overtime, so that the courts could remain open in the evenings, Saturdays (and even Sunday mornings), or during the summer recess. During these periods, cases that are currently scheduled for 2018 to 2022 could be brought forward.[28]

12.4.4   Assisting Personnel

It may be necessary to recruit additional assisting personnel. Greek courts are presently understaffed; so judges are in dire need of assisting staff. Given the fiscal constraints and that the Constitution allows only for permanent full-time judicial personnel in courts, it may be possible, in collaboration with the Troika, to recruit a small number of judicial clerks (a similar exemption was wisely granted for personnel for the Supreme Court of Auditors in 2011).

12.4.5   Financing

To finance these four proposals, we suggest that for a moderate fee an "expedited case process" be created that would offer to plaintiffs the option of moving forward the hearing of their dispute. The fee would be used to cover the pay of court personnel and the recruitment of temporary magistrates (or judicial assistants) and retired judges. A plaintiff, whose case may be currently listed for hearing at a first-instance civil court in mid-2020 could therefore opt to pay a fee of 500 euros (and 1,000 or even more for cases with significant financial stake), so as to bring the hearing forward to some date in a weekend of 2017/8. An alternative plan would be for all parties to share the fee, perhaps agreeing that the losing party will cover it in the end. Since legal costs in Greece are much lower than the average in other EU jurisdictions (see table 12.2), we think that this special fee will be a reasonable burden.

A constitutional issue may arise here, since the Greek Constitution (rightly) says that justice is free and open to all citizens. It might be argued that the introduction of a fast-track process creates unacceptable inequalities. We disagree. This is an urgent response to a crisis. At the moment justice is unavailable to everyone, so the fundamental constitutional right on access to justice is actually void. Our proposal would benefit everyone. It would not take away resources from the justice system nor would it delay any individual access to justice. It instead would create additional resources and free up time for ordinary cases as well. The scheme entails also a positive externality; even parties that will not pay the fee to expedite the hearings will gain as the early resolution of the cases where plaintiffs pay the fee will allow for all cases to be handled faster.

There is also an alternative, complementary, way to finance these reforms. In a draft of this chapter we proposed to finance this scheme using leftover funds from the Hellenic Financial Stability Fund (HFSF) that were earmarked for the banks' recapitalizations in 2012 to 2013. This made sense as many pending cases in civil courts involve the banks and in administrative courts involve state agencies. Unfortunately, this buffer is no longer available (due to actions by the Greek Ministry of Finance in the first semester of 2015). Nevertheless, the government could negotiate with the Troika for special funding.

12.4.6 A Complementary Proposal

The delays in administrative courts are largely driven by the nonpayment of certain debts by the government, state agencies, and municipalities. By some estimates, state's verified outstanding liabilities to construction firms and pharmaceutical firms were close to 5 billion euros as of 2016. Yet the state forces firms to seek payment by getting orders from courts and then utilizes the slow and formalistic legal procedures to delay payment.

The government has the capacity to stop this absurd and costly practice (which has been employed by many Greek administrations). This will be beneficial for all concerned, including the government. Paying up front saves money on court procedures and on the interest that accumulates to the plaintiff at the end of the process. If the government were to pay the verified liabilities in an out-of-court settlement, it could ask plaintiffs to forgo part of their claim (a haircut of 10 to 20 percent seems reasonable, and in the case of pharmaceutical firms this could be higher given the extent of overcharging). This policy would also act as a direct liquidity injection into the market and would be beneficial to all sectors of the economy. The banking system would benefit as well, since firms usually pass their future claims from litigation to banks in exchange for financing. If the state were to immediately reimburse firms, this would also lower illegal side payments and corruption (in the current regime, firms often bribe state officials so as to get priority treatment and be reimbursed first).

12.5 Medium-Run Reforms

One important reason why past reforms had limited impact was their partial and incremental nature. In this section we consider reforms in ten broad areas, and our proposals are complementary.[29] We believe that reforms have to be multi-faceted because it is hard to predict which policies will have the most impact. The Greek government needs to learn from past failures and focus on those policies that seem to be working. Judges, prosecutors, judicial clerks, and lawyers need to be open to reforms, embrace them, and work with the administration. Moreover the public needs to engage and participate in this process.

Presently, the Greek Constitution is rigid and prescriptive. It regulates heavily every aspect of the justice system, including court structure and organization, and the professional status of judges, prosecutors, and clerks. Hence many of our proposals require a constitutional amendment. (Given the sharp deterioration of the parliamentary process during the crisis and the rising populism, the success of a constitutional amendment at this stage may be uncertain.)

12.5.1 Monitoring and Evaluation

An ongoing problem with the Greek justice system is its lack of accountability. Just like many other professional bodies in the public sector, judges are largely immune to external assessment. The monitoring and evaluation process in place for judges is incomplete, anachronistic, and wholly inadequate.[30] Although there have been three amendments in the period 2010 to 2014 to address the lack of accountability, the justice system remains unacceptably ineffective and unaccountable.[31]

The Current System   The process of evaluation and monitoring is entirely internal to the judiciary. This is, in part, mandated by the Constitution, which provides detailed rules about the evaluation of judges and prosecutors. Any comprehensive reform in this area requires therefore a constitutional amendment.[32]

In practice, a judge's inspection works as follows: the inspector (who is *not* randomly matched to the inspected judge) asks the judge to *freely* submit some (usually five) judgments issued either when the judge served in a single-member judicial body (e.g., single-member first-instance court, Μονομελές Πρωτοδικείο) or as a reporting judge (εισηγητής) in a three- or five-member court. The same happens in the case of judges and prosecutors involved in issuing orders (διαταγές); the inspector asks judges to provide five ordinances and proposals of their choice. Out of hundreds of cases that each judge presides over in a year, evaluation is based only on a handful of decisions, all chosen by the inspected judge, rather than by the inspector or at random. Although the law specifies that the inspector should take into account the opinion of the head of the court (προϊστάμενος πρωτοδικείου) and conduct a thorough interview, these are formalities that do not carry much weight. The supervisor then submits an *ad hoc* evaluation

(not based on a template or/and a prearranged method) to the Supreme Judicial Council (Ανώτατο Δικαστικό Συμβούλιο), which is almost always approved without much
discussion or further consultation.

Three key features stand out. First, the roles of judicial supervisory and inspector
councils are diminished. While in the past, the evaluation process was conducted in
a professional manner, today it is just a formality. In very few cases are there any penalties for inappropriate behavior, delays, poor justification of decisions, and the like.
And even in these cases, penalties are trivial. The gradual decline of the Greek justice
system to its current state of collapse was not accompanied by any disciplinary or other
measures focusing on underperforming judges. Such steps have been attempted only
recently.

Second, the current system does not provide incentives for good performance.
Almost all junior (first-instance) judges will follow a career path with promotions up
to the level of president of the Appeal Court (Πρόεδρος Εφετών), whatever they do.
With few exceptions the system of promotions is based simply on seniority, meaning
the number of years served at each level (first-instance courts, appellate courts, and
supreme courts) and the grades in the entrance exams. Even when performance is poor
and this is mentioned in the evaluation report, the judge will still get promoted and
moved to a provincial court as an appellate judge. There is no performance-based pay
for judges and overtime pay is minimal.[33] There is no way to reward efficient judges, or
those particularly gifted, other than by accelerating somewhat their eventually certain
promotions. Moreover, as for other types of public sector employees (e.g., in the army
or the national health system), promotions after ages 60 to 62 are done in order for the
retired judges to receive higher pensions (until recently, pensions were based on the
last year's salary rather than on the average salary over one's career).

With the exception of the appointment of presidents and vice presidents of the
Supreme Courts, neither the Ministry of Justice nor the Parliament nor the president of
the Hellenic Republic has any role on the evaluation of judges. In contrast to the models followed in other countries, where professionals, university professors, and other
stakeholders are part of the evaluation process, there is no lay representation or any
input from outsiders. And while there is some representation of university professors
on the Supreme Disciplinary Council, their role has proved ineffectual. They are the
minority and always follow the recommendation of the judges. While the principle of
the independence of the judiciary is an essential requirement of the rule of law, this is
surely compatible with some external input into the monitoring and accountability of
individual judges, as shown by practice elsewhere.[34]

Recommendations   We believe that reform regarding the monitoring and evaluation of judges (and prosecutors) should include at least the following measures:

1. A constitutional amendment on evaluating judges. The structure, role, and conduct of the Supreme Judicial Council should be redesigned and this Council should not be solely staffed by judges. Members of the Supreme Judicial Council should include both judges and laymen. We propose the following membership rules:

   a. A third of the Supreme Judicial Council's members should be senior judges. The presidents of the Three Supreme Courts and the most senior vice presidents could participate *ex officio*.

   b. Another third of the Supreme Judicial Council's members should be appointed by the president of the Hellenic Republic, following the recommendation of a council of experts. He/she could appoint university professors (in the fields of law, economics, sociology, criminology, etc.), Greek legal scholars from the diaspora, former judges and prosecutors, and other people of similar standing.

   c. The Parliament should appoint the remaining third of the Supreme Judicial Council's members.

2. The Supreme Courts should be required to submit annual reports to Parliament with details on performance (adjournments, clearance rates, delays) for all courts under their supervision, including themselves.[35] Moreover the Supreme Court presidents should present this report before the Parliamentary Committee for Justice.

3. A highly debated issue (even among us) is whether the presidents and vice presidents of the Supreme Courts should be appointed exclusively by the Council of Ministers (the cabinet). Some argue that the cabinet should have no role; yet the problem of the current system is the lack of external checks and balances. A modest feasible reform would endorse the model of the United States on the appointment of federal appellate courts and Supreme Court judges. The government would still put forward the names of the heads of the Supreme Courts, but only after securing broad parliamentary approval (e.g., requiring three-fifths of the members of the relevant parliamentary committee).[36] An alternative mechanism would be to give the role of selecting the chief justices to the president of the Republic, who would appoint on the recommendation of a super majority of the Parliamentary Committee and the government. Other mechanisms could be conceived along these lines.

4. The framework of disciplinary proceedings against Supreme Court judges (πειθαρ χικός έλεγχος), which is currently conducted by the Minister of Justice (article 91.1 of the Constitution), should be modified so as to prevent the direct involvement of the executive. The Minister of Justice should not be able to pursue disciplinary action against Supreme Court judges.

5. The e-Justice program should record the number of adjournments and why they adjourned, the time that a judge takes to release a verdict, as this often exceeds six months (and in some cases a year).[37] Likewise the e-Justice system should record, for each judge, the number of judgments in the first-instance that were overruled in appellate courts. This information should be taken into account in the evaluation of that judge.

6. Currently checks for corruption and bribery involving judges and prosecutors are weak. While judges and prosecutors are required by law to declare their assets, and the means by which they have acquired them (ποθεν έσχες), this is not a genuine check. Indeed, these requirements apply to thousands of public sector employees, and because the relevant inspection bodies are understaffed, the checks are impossible to perform. We think that a process of *random audits* every year would allow for thorough checks on a small randomly chosen number of judges and prosecutors. For example, 1 percent of first-instance judges, 2 percent of appellate judges, and 5 percent of Supreme Court judges could be randomly subjected to a thorough investigation of their financial affairs by professional auditing firms.

7. The evaluation reports of inspectors should be standardized and modernized with an electronic template, so that it would be possible to reach solid statistical conclusions. In fact such a measure has already been legislated (in 2010), but has not been applied because judges are vehemently opposed to it. The inputs used for the evaluation (judgments, decrees, delays) should be selected at random or at the initiative of the inspector and not the inspected judge. The inspector should be assigned to the supervised judge (or prosecutor) via a lottery. Supervisors should come from different jurisdictions, so as to avoid conflicts of interest.

8. To deal with grade inflation, the inspector should evaluate judge's effectiveness both in absolute and in relative terms.

9. The Council of Europe Report on the Judiciary shows that backlogs are smaller and clearance rates higher in jurisdictions where Supreme Court judges have explicit administrative duties on monitoring and promotions.[38] Thus a proposal that should be further developed is to have a division in the Council of State and the Supreme Civil and Penal Court dealing solely with evaluation, promotions,

inspections, and supervision. The division's head will be one of the vice presidents, but most important, this individual could recruit HR specialists to assist the judicial councils by tabulating statistics, organizing the interviews, and so on.

10. While the law allows for filing suit against a judge for erroneous judgment ($\alpha\gamma\omega\gamma\dot{\eta}$ $\kappa\alpha\kappa o\delta\iota\kappa\dot{\iota}\alpha\varsigma$), be it due to incompetence, lack of impartiality, or bribery, there are few known such cases because the law is arcane, complex, and puts a high burden on the plaintiff. After a serious consultation with experts, the Ministry of Justice should put forth a new regime for such trials based on best-practices from other jurisdictions.

12.5.2 Training and Professional Development

Currently all professional judges, except magistrates, receive formal training for eighteen months at the National School of Judges and Prosecutors. The curriculum is narrow and includes various legal subjects. As a result a judge's knowledge of corporate finance, auditing, and accounting is limited. After assuming their duties, their training is minimal. Many (older) judges are not computer literate. These problems are magnified because the curriculum of the local Law Schools is devoted exclusively to legal doctrine and selections of literature in history, politics, and philosophy.[39]

Curriculum We believe that the curriculum of the National School of Judges and Prosecutors should be amended so as to include lectures on the following subjects:

1. *Accounting* Judges should be able to read financial statements and understand balance sheets. The auditing course should include lectures on transfer pricing, as this is a common practice. The School could get guest part-time lectures from local universities and invite practitioners to deliver short customized courses.

2. *Basic principles of auditing* Judges often have to take decisions based on reports by auditing firms; it is vital that they understand the key principles and toolkit of auditing. Since the Institute of Certified Public Accountants of Greece (SOEL) runs training programs (for interns and members of the affiliated firms), judges could attend these courses or alternatively SOEL could develop customized courses for judges.

3. *Fundamentals of corporate finance* At least some judges have to be able to understand the basics of net present value (NPV) and grasp the difference between book-based valuation and mark to market. Adding a mini-course in corporate finance should not be difficult.

4. *Management principles* Judges would benefit from management courses covering human resource management, information technology, organizational structure,

and negotiation. The school should also seek collaboration with judges performing managerial tasks in foreign jurisdictions, so that Greek judges get some hands-on knowledge of best practices.

The National School of Judges and Prosecutors is understaffed and underfinanced. It is a matter of the highest priority that the work of the National School is supported and its resources strengthened. In addition the School should be allowed to seek assistance from large trade unions and employer groups that may be willing to finance some training programs on economic, financial, and labor issues.

Continuing Professional Development The second area involves continuing professional development and the development of specialized skills, at least for some judges. Greece scores low relative to other EU countries on the number of judges participating in continuous training activities (European Justice Scoreboard 2016). The National School of Judges and Prosecutors should develop mini-courses for experienced judges on some key economic issues that have become increasingly important.[40]

Building on recent legislation (article 92, Law 4055/2012),[41] the Ministry of Justice and the Supreme Courts could also arrange for short-term visits to European courts, so as judges dealing with court administration (προϊστάμενοι πρωτοδικείων και εφετείων) familiarize themselves with best practices.[42] Moreover judges who get appointed as court administrators should pass a master class on basic human resource and IT management principles.

IT Training The third area concerns training in information technology. Since many judges and judicial clerks do not use personal computers, the administration should organize short courses on the use of basic software. For example, the Ministry of Justice or the National School of Judges and Prosecutors could team with an IT training company, whose instructors would visit all first- and second-instance courts four times per year (for two to three years) and offer seminars. After the lectures the judges could be evaluated by taking an online test.

12.5.3   Management and Organizational Issues

An area where there is room for drastic improvement is management. There is ample empirical evidence showing that higher quality management (human resources, incentives, and targets) leads to better performance, not only among manufacturing firms but also in areas with significant state involvement, such as hospitals and schools.[43] The court system would benefit from a significant administrative-management reshuffling and reorganization. Besides accountability and human resources, discussed in the previous sections, we believe that the following policies should be part of a reform agenda:

1. The government and the Supreme Courts should redraw the map of courts' jurisdiction, which dates from the era of King Otto in the mid-nineteenth century. In 2012 a successful reorganization program reduced the number of magistrate courts from 301 to 154. A similar reorganization program should take place for other types of courts.

2. Greece has the highest ratio of Supreme Court judges to the total number of judges. Over the past two decades the positions of the vice presidents of the three Supreme Courts have increased. (Currently there are ten vice presidents at the Supreme Civil and Penal Court and ten vice presidents at the Council of State). While it used to be the case that the number of vice presidents was equal to the number of each Court's divisions ($τμήματα$), the number has increased, allegedly because the government wanted to appoint politically friendly judges in the most senior positions (entailing higher status as well as salary and pension increases). After consultation—and ideally with wide consensus in Parliament there should be a redesign of the structure and organization of the three Supreme Courts.

3. Court management should be devolved. Court administrators should be given an annual budget, and at the end of each fiscal year they should submit financial reports (which should be checked by the Council of Auditors). It is impossible for the Ministry of Justice to know the exact needs of each court. Each court should have some discretion over how to spend its budget (net of salaries and major infrastructure).

4. In many European court jurisdictions, there are judicial administrators who oversee management, ICT, personnel, and so on. Introducing managers in courts would be beneficial, especially for the large courts in Athens, Thessaloniki, and Piraeus. This reform will require a Constitutional Amendment as the Constitution and the Code for the Organization of Courts explicitly states that only full-time professional judges should administer courts. So a less radical proposal would be that judges whose duties include court administration should be required to pass a customized program at the National School of Judges and Prosecutors. Such a program would cover IT, human resource management, and best practices from foreign jurisdictions.

5. There should be specialized management offices at the highest courts with the responsibility of monitoring the management and the administration of lower courts. These offices could be overseen by a senior judge who should not have any

other duties. The new senior managers should be adequately supported by IT staff, management, and human resource specialists, as these are the areas where judges lack expertise. This proposal also requires a Constitutional Amendment, as each court has to be self-managed and no intervention from senior judges (and officials) is allowed.[44]

6. The management offices should set specific targets, taking into account courts' resources (infrastructure, degree of computerization, number of judges, and assisting staff) and the needs of each jurisdiction. Based on standardized templates, the chief administrators (or currently, the court chairmen) should produce progress reports, detailing on- and off-target areas. These reports should form the basis for the annual comprehensive report that the three Supreme Courts should submit to the Parliament. These court-specific reports should be available to the public via the web, as this would raise pressure for reform and help identify courts/areas where interventions are needed.

12.5.4 Information and Communications Technology (ICT)

The Greek court system lags considerably in deploying information and communications technology. Introducing information technology should be a top priority. This does not require constitutional amendments, since the government could adopt best practices from abroad. Use of ICT by courts will free up judicial time that is currently spent on manually printing and archiving documents. It will speed the work of judges in providing access to the Internet and specialized online resources on legislation, case law, and academic commentary. Information technology will also allow the productivity of judges to be monitored.

Ongoing Developments The Ministry of Justice initiated in 2011 and 2012 an integrated e-Justice program.[45] This much-needed program had the following key objectives:

1. Install a centralized electronic system for filing, monitoring, and managing cases in all courts to enable electronic submission of lawsuits and the necessary documentation. Pilot programs have been started at first-instance civil courts in Athens, Piraeus, and Thessaloniki, and the electronic submission of lawsuits and the necessary documentation was due to be implemented soon (as of April 2016) at the Council of State and the Court of Auditors. A program for electronic filing of case documents is being expanded in all administrative courts.

2. Develop a public-private partnership to help digitize all transcripts of public hearings, documentation, and verdicts for a comprehensive database of all cases.

This program is still in a design phase although many years have passed since its legislation.

3. Create an electronic national criminal record. This project has already entered a pilot implementation stage. The New Criminal Record will be connected with the Ministry of the Interior and the citizen service centers (KEP).

4. Install a centralized electronic system for prisons. No progress has yet been made, as in many prisons there is not even an electronic registry.

5. Create electronic support for numerous small-scale projects, such as in establishing an online system listing all cases (ηλεκτρονικό πινάκιο).

6. Install a state-of-the-art IT program so that there is electronic management of cases at all stages, and require electronic submission of all documentation (Integrated Case Management System, OSDDY). This project was initiated in 2012, but it was not expected to be implemented in some courts until 2016 (at best).

Moving Forward   The e-Justice program has been initiated and some of its components are now under way. Yet, despite an ambitious start and some immediate successful steps, progress has been moderate, likely due to the chaotic conditions in courts. Some additional steps are necessary:

1. Provide all judges with personal computers (with Internet and electronic libraries access).

2. Hasten the pace of extending the program to all courts, based on the paradigm of first-instance civil courts in Athens, Piraeus, and Thessaloniki, where plaintiffs have already started to submit electronically the case documentation.

3. Assign the archiving and the digitization of outstanding cases to the private sector for a transitional period of five years.

12.5.5   Specialized Courts and Tribunals

Specialized courts and tribunals are set up in many jurisdictions worldwide to concentrate resources in areas where expertise is crucial and where the nature of the case requires the participation of specialists. For example, in England and Wales a system of tribunals provides for a more flexible, quicker, and cheaper procedure, and a less adversarial process on a variety of issues (e.g., immigration, property tax, social security appeals, child custody). Tribunals are judicial bodies and their membership includes judges and laymen. A tribunal's judgment can be challenged before ordinary courts, so there are increased safeguards of fairness. Yet tribunals provide an expedient and cheaper alternative to mainstream litigation. Specialization and division of labor among judges enables the court system to deal with cases more efficiently and achieve higher consistency and predictability.

Current System   Greece has the lowest number of specialized courts and tribunals in the European Union. This reflects the highly formalistic nature of the Greek justice system, where justice is only provided by full-time professional judges. While nowadays there is some de facto specialization at civil courts, it is far from being sufficient.

Recommendations   We believe that the system requires fundamental reform after due consultation and a comprehensive technical preparation. The Constitution should not prohibit the participation of laymen in tribunals, since this is established practice in many European jurisdictions. And a robust national system of flexible specialized tribunals should be created as follows:

1. An Act of Parliament would enable the Ministry of Justice to set up specialized tribunals, on the basis of a general framework that would guarantee independence and provide a stable system of appeal to the ordinary courts after one or two levels of jurisdiction at tribunal level (e.g., in England there are first-tier tribunals and an upper tribunal).

2. The tribunals would be supported by an independent authority that would report annually to the Parliament and the president of the Hellenic Republic. This agency could get a constitutional recognition (Συνταγματικά κατοχυρωμένη Ανεξάρτητη Αρχή).

3. Tribunals should be set up for tax, social security, insolvency, and banking disputes. Tribunals could also be set up in family law and immigration-asylum seeking. The ongoing plans of the Ministry of Justice to establish special family courts staffed with specialized judges and supported by professionals such as psychologists and social workers should be brought forward (and should not be opposed by lawyers and judges).

4. The tribunals could meet in one- or three-member panels. Members could be recruited among retired judges, practicing lawyers, and in some cases lay professionals with expertise in the field. They would be hired by a specialist administrative service serving all tribunals with long-term contracts.

5. Procedure before tribunals would be simpler and more flexible than in the ordinary courts. Tribunals would not normally meet in court buildings. They would be housed in town halls and other public venues.

6. Applicants would be allowed to directly appeal to a civil or an administrative appellate court. The fee for such appeals, which should be considerable, would be deposited to a special account (e.g., at TPD, Ταμείο Παρακαταθηκών και Δανείων), and if the appeal is successful, it would be returned (with interest) to the plaintiff.

12.5.6   Drafting of New Legislation

A key problem with the Greek legal system is that legislation constantly changes, often in unpredictable ways.

Current Practice   The drafting of legislation is a complex process. However, many important pieces of legislation are introduced in irrelevant parliamentary acts in the form of amendments or modifications (*τροπολογίες*). These amendments/modifications are usually introduced at the very last minute (just before the parliamentary vote on the bill), without previous consultation, and then their validity is decided in a quick and unprofessional manner. And while all political parties argue that once in government, they will stop this process, this practice keeps on going and, if anything, has increased in the past three years. Then there is the problem that legislation keeps changing. For example, the New Construction Regulation (Νέος Οικοδομικός Κανονισμός) that was legislated in 2012 was altered four more times in 2013 and 2014 (see Androulakis 2015). Much of this reflects the brief tenure of ministers. For example, over the past five years, in most Ministries the leadership has changed more than five times. Yet another problem is that the drafting of new legislation is done by (usually inexperienced) staff at Ministerial offices rather than by professional law-making committees of experts. Discussion in Parliament does not improve legislation, and if anything, the populist comments and inaccurate media coverage of parliamentary acts are often even more obscure and esoteric compared to the initial draft.

These practices are particularly problematic (though in a milder form) for the legislative preparation committees at the MoJ, which has sought to modernize civil, penal, and administrative procedures, the penal code, and family law, among other things. Currently the drafting of new legislation starts with the MoJ. The MoJ sets up a committee of experts to draft the new legislation. The committee is almost always composed of university professors, current and former judges, representatives of attorney bar associations, and some practitioners. Next the committee submits its draft to the Minister, who after some consultation with the Chairman of the Committee submits the draft to his colleagues at the Council of Ministers and subsequently submits the law to Parliament. But there are at least three problems with the current process. First, membership in drafting committees (*προπαρασκευαστικές νομοθετικές επιτροπές*) is still unpaid even though it involves onerous duties. While usually the committee members work hard under tight deadlines, professionalism dictates that they receive a decent honorarium and have their expenses covered. Second, while in most cases the Minister does not get directly involved in a committee's work, various pressure groups infiltrate and exert significant influence. Third, quite often the draft changes considerably during the discussion in the Cabinet Council or/and the Parliament, and in most cases these changes are not intended to improve the law but rather to nullify its provisions, make it more obscure, and so on.

Proposals   Dealing with the legislation problem requires not only formal interventions but also a change of attitude of the political class. Even the best-intentioned policies will have minimal impact if the people in key administrative positions (Ministries, key state agencies) change every year. We believe that the appointment of members in legislation drafting committees should stay with the MoJ, but has to be accompanied by a consultation with relevant stakeholders and the Parliament. Committees should not be overstaffed with any of the key stakeholders (e.g., judges, representatives of bar associations) so as to avoid conflicts of interest. Committees should include some legal scholars (or other specialists) from the Greek diaspora who can contribute to the adoption of best practices. It may also be useful to include non-legal professionals, such as economists or sociologists, who can bring fresh insights.

Committee members should be paid and their expenses should be covered. This will increase accountability and raise the quality of the legal drafts. Since the drafts will be based on a thorough analysis of a well-paid committee of experts (where no key stakeholder will have a disproportionate voice) it will become harder for the political class to make significant modifications.

12.5.7   Penal System

The Greek MoJ acknowledges openly that the criminal trial system is characterized by "impunity," as some trials of serious felonies take as much as ten years.[46] The Greek penal philosophy is based on severe punishment, almost exclusively imprisonment. There are few provisions on alternatives to imprisonment (e.g., community work), damage restoration, and assisting convicts to integrate again with the society. This problem is especially pronounced for juvenile or young drug addicts.[47] While comparative data are lacking, it seems that the Greek penal system has sentencing laws that are significantly harsher than in other EU jurisdictions. Yet it frequently allows a convicted criminal at first instance to walk free until his or her appeal is heard.

Though this topic deserves more extensive discussion, reform should include at least the following measures[48]:

1. Sentences should be redesigned based on international best practices. For example, punishments for minor crimes (as currently dealt by single-member misdemeanor penal courts) should not be prison sentences but fines and community work. In this regard we endorse the recent steps of the Ministry of Justice to de-criminalize a wide range of minor offenses.

2. Even for serious crimes (κακουργήματα), for which prison sentences should be retained, the emphasis should be on restoring damages and compensating victims. For example, in cases of serious tax fraud or embezzlement of state funds, it is more constructive to seize bank accounts and compensate victims rather than impose absurdly high prison sentences.

3. An interesting proposal is establishing a "criminal conciliation" process for criminal offenses that are prosecuted after a complaint (e.g., media, slander, damage to property). This way there would be the possibility of withdrawing the lawsuit after compensation has been granted.

4. All prisons should be computerized with a centralized IT system. This is vital for the monitoring of inmates and personnel, and to help prosecutors and judges deal with prisoners' "leaves of absence."

5. Greek prisons are overpopulated, understaffed, and lack medical support (as the state cannot even pay visiting doctors), and the infrastructure is on the verge of collapse. The Greek society and political establishment have ignored this issue. These conditions persist despite the harsh and well-justified rulings of the European Court of Human Rights that conditions on Greek prisons violate basic human rights. The MoJ should come up with a comprehensive system of reform that, besides investing on infrastructure (new prison facilities) and recruitment of guards,[49] will promote the electronic monitoring of convicts and review cases where probation orders rather than imprisonments might apply.

6. As has recently been learned, shameful practices persist whereby prisoners convicted for multiple assassinations and terrorism escape by violating rules for temporary "leaves of absence." Hence the MoJ should re-think this practice of allowing prisoners to visit their families for short periods of time. While we do not suggest altogether prohibiting this practice, the safeguards could be enhanced by applying common rules and discretion.

7. The Ministry of Justice should also re-think the current system for custody and detentions by which, for similar disputes and criminal charges, some judicial panels

deem that the defendant should remain in custody while other panels deem that he/she can walk free until the case is heard. Given the massive delays in court hearings, it is not uncommon for defendant to stay in custody for 12 or even 18 months (the maximum period). Our proposal here is mostly to standardize cases and detail in the penal code the cases where custody is mandatory, cases where it should not be, and perhaps some cases where a decision by a council is needed. In this regard it is vital that the MoJ proceed with the electronic monitoring of detainees (via an electronic bracelet).

12.5.8   Legal Uncertainty: Constitutional Review of Statutes

Current System   Another deficiency of the Greek legal system is that it is not uncommon for Greek courts to issue different rulings in almost identical disputes. As in the Greek civil law system, precedent is not mandatory and given the low-quality legislation, judges usually apply different statutory provisions in similar cases. Moreover, since the Greek legal system is formalistic and (until recently) did not allow for case bundling, in many circumstances different courts have been issuing different decisions for similar cases. This was especially a problem in tax courts where an individual's dispute with tax authorities occurring in a different tax year was evaluated by different judges. Then there is the issue of constitutionality. Greece follows a diffuse approach, where every judge evaluates the constitutional basis of every act, statue, or decree that he/she has to apply (article 93, paragraph 4, of the Constitution). This system is old (its origins date back to first Greek Constitutions of 1844 and 1867) and the diffuse check is a key part of the Greek legal culture.[50] While the system worked effectively for many years, and is deemed by many scholars as an important check on potential abuses from the executive, in the past few years it has proved to be dysfunctional. Many policies—that clearly are in the spheres of the executive and the legislature—have been deemed by some judges as un-constitutional. For example, the 200 euros fee for appeals—that was introduced in 2012 in an effort to reduce congestion at appellate courts—has been deemed by a few judges as "un-constitutional." In September 2014, the Council of State ruled that the executive decree that allowed retail shops to be open for six Sundays a year was "unconstitutional," as it prevented people from exercising their "religious rights." Many salary and pension cuts have also been deemed as "unconstitutional," while clearly the domain of fiscal policy lies with the executive.

Recommendations   Dealing with the issue of coordinating the Greek legal system is tricky. One idea may be to establish a Constitutional Court that—like the German example—that would decide on the constitutionality of laws. Yet the diffuse check of constitutionality is part of the Greek legal culture. It symbolizes a democratic ethos that the judiciary should not enforce legal acts going against the core values and principles of the Constitution. Thus our proposals are to strengthen the doctrine of precedent in Greek law. A constitutional amendment could make explicit, what academic lawyers assume already to be the case, that in public law matters, the decisions of higher courts bind the decisions of lower courts. A binding doctrine of precedent in public law will contribute more to legal certainty than any creation of a new, largely politically appointed, Constitutional court. The reasoning and written explanation should be part of the evaluation process of all judges.

1. When a lower court judge deems a law as unconstitutional, then the Councilor of the State (Επίτροπος Επικρατείας) or the Chief Prosecutor of the Supreme Civil and Penal Court (Εισαγγελέας του Αρείου Πάγου) should immediately file an appeal (αναίρεση υπέρ του νόμου), so as any of the Supreme Courts make a ruling in plenary sessions.

2. If any of the three Supreme Courts deem a law as unconstitutional, then the issue should be immediately moved to the Supreme Special Court (Ανώτατο Ειδικό Δικαστήριο) of article 100 of the Hellenic Constitution (where the presidents of all Supreme Courts participate alongside senior civil, penal, and administrative judges).

3. To deal with legal uncertainty—unrelated to constitutionality—we believe that the administrative procedure should make it easier to "bundle cases" as with a model trial.

12.5.9 Adjournments and Case Management

Current System Adjournments waste court time and can cause delays and unfairness. Adjournments can also lead to inefficiencies and to inequities, whereby a delay benefits the wrongdoer. The procedural rules and practices of Greek courts have been remarkably tolerant toward adjournments. For example, civil courts award an adjournment when the claimant's legal team "has not had time to prepare" (something for which in Anglo courts the case would be dismissed). The situation in administrative courts is even worse. Often administrative courts adjourn on their own motion, without giving a reason. It is not uncommon for hearings before the Council of State to be postponed five times. Although after some recent reform, civil procedure rules provide for imposing a fee against the party responsible for the adjournment, judges rarely impose this penalty.

Recent legislation (in 2010, 2011, 2012, and 2013) has placed many statuary restrictions on adjournments (the restrictions have been growing at least since the mid-1990s). The problem is systemic and hence needs a comprehensive overhaul rather than incremental statutory restrictions.[51]

Before we describe our proposals, a caveat is in order. Key to dealing with this problem is to find a solution that induces a change of attitude (mentality) among judges and lawyers. To be sure, it is impossible for any law to make provisions for every possible scenario, as there is always going to be some leeway taken by the judge for granting an adjournment. Nevertheless, when judges abuse their discretion in this regard, their colleagues, based on the internal norms and annual assessments, should impose penalties.

Recommendations   We believe that some rudimentary procedural legislation could be used to compel the court to conform to a set of rules:

1. Pre-hearing "case management conversations" between the judge and legal representatives could be used, whereby the judge issues instructions on the exchange of documents, outlines the phases of the trial, and is apprised of the witnesses to be called. The judge should warn interested parties that their case would be rejected if they disregard their procedural duties.

2. Failure to comply with court orders and deadlines for serving documents should entail penalties and costs for the guilty party, including in the most serious cases, the rejection of a claim.[52]

3. Reasons for adjournment should be documented in court records.

4. Adjourned cases should be returned to the same judge (if he/she is still in the same court). This will save time since the judge will be already familiar with the pleadings, but it could also remove the incentive to adjourn complicated cases. While such a provision was legislated for criminal cases in 2012, for various technical reasons, it was not enforced and then was removed with subsequent legislation (in 2013). Such a provision should be re-introduced for civil, administrative, and penal courts, once the e-Justice project is complemented.

5. Adjournments should be recorded in a judge's file for promotions.

6. Likewise a court's record on adjournments should be made available to the public through the court's website. This will enable the public to compare the efficiency of each court.

7. Penalties should be imposed to plaintiffs who do not submit necessary documentation or are absent for hearings. The Code of Civil Procedure provides that the

court may award legal costs up to 400 euros at the expense of the postponement-requesting party, and this provision should receive mandatory and not optional application. For cases with large financial stakes, the fines could be higher. In any case, the fine should be mandatory and payable immediately.

8. Adjournments (with the sole exception of serious medical reasons) could be suspended for two to three years. The plaintiffs would then be petitioned to either prepare for a hearing or delay indefinitely the case. In the latter instance—which could carry a fine—the hearing should be set at a distant time, so as for plaintiffs to bear the consequences of the cancellation.

12.5.10 Insolvency Law and Bankruptcy

Current System Numerous deficiencies exist in the current bankruptcy process. As identified by Potamitis and Psaltis (2013) and Potamitis (2014), these are as follows:

1. The process gives significant power to shareholders, even when the value of equity is zero. Creditors lacking collateral also have a strong say, even if the firm's assets are barely sufficient to compensate workers, pension funds, and senior creditors.

2. The legislation is extremely formalistic and stakeholders have numerous procedural tools for delaying the process.

3. Judges who lack expertise allow plaintiffs to delay the process by abusing all procedures.

4. The seniority of the state (and social security funds) and the rigidity of state agencies to re-profile their claims (even where secured creditors and workers are willing to lower them) prevents restructuring.

5. The process is very slow, and it is quite common for bankruptcies to last more than ten years.

6. The process is handled by an insolvency administrator (σύνδικος), who often lacks credentials and special knowledge. And though the administrator is supposed to be chosen at random, quite often judges (and bar associations) put in charge "friends" and loyalists. While there have been many allegations of corruption, very few have been reviewed.

Recommendations[53] The crisis has created many "zombie" firms. This has put Greece in desperate need for a modern, business-friendly bankruptcy regime. Given space constraints, we cannot detail here a comprehensive reform of the Greek insolvency law. We outline below, however, some principles on which future legislation should be based. More in-depth discussions of Greek insolvency law and reform proposals can be found in chapter 7 (on the financial system), as well as in Potamitis and Rokas (2012) and Potamitis (2014).

1. Bankruptcy should be moved to specialized courts. Research by Visaria (2009) shows that in India, the introduction of special insolvency tribunals reduced considerably the delinquency and interest rates.

2. Specialized courts could be established for cases involving small financial interests (e.g., annual firm turnover of less than 1 million), separate from those of medium and large corporations. Some such small cases could be dealt by a specialist, and then verified by a judge, provided that an agreement has been reached with the key stakeholders.

3. Specialist practitioners (accountants, consultants, engineers) could be asked to assist judges.

4. The Hellenic Federation of Enterprises (SEV) proposed (in September 2014) the establishment of certified specialized insolvency practitioners (επαγγελματίες εκκαθαριστές).

5. Equity could be sourced for debt. Special reorganization funds could be set up for the converted equity. Re-profiling of social security liabilities and taxes could be a consideration where senior creditors are willing to forgo some portion of their claims.

6. The Household Bankruptcy act (1869/2010) needs to change as there are many loopholes (many debts are excluded) and the process is complex (hearing dates for household debt settlement before Magistrates' Courts in the region of Attica have already reached 2028!).

7. As the current auction system is not transparent, an electronic auction platform is urgently needed. So far this simple solution has been opposed.

12.6   Additional Proposals

Many other areas are in need of reform and policy interventions. In this section we turn to policies in other areas, without going into much detail. We then discuss recent reforms that seem to be working and that should be strengthened.

12.6.1   Other Areas of Reform

Public Prosecution   The comparative data from the Council of Europe's Report on Justice shows that the Greek public prosecution system is severely understaffed. There were 4.8 public prosecutors per 100,000 citizens in Greece in 2010, while the average (median) across 40 European jurisdictions was 10 (11). The public prosecution system shares many of the deficiencies of the court system. Prosecutors have few assistants and clerks. There is little (if any) ICT infrastructure. There is no specialization. And there are few checks and monitoring of judicial procedures. Reform should include the following measures:

1. Recruit sufficient numbers of assistants, paralegals, and experts for prosecutors who deal with complex cases (e.g., economic crime, tax evasion, fuel smuggling). The current effort of the MoJ to create a special body of experts assisting prosecutors goes in the right direction.
2. Strengthen administrative departments that support prosecutors, such as the branch of the police that deals with electronic crime.
3. Re-organize the public prosecution system by centralizing it nation-wide.
4. Set up offices for special prosecution. In 2010, a prosecutor's office was created for economic crime, and in 2012, an anticorruption office was set up. While both offices are still understaffed, they could prove to be quite useful, especially if some deficiencies are addressed. For example, the deputy-prosecutor of the Supreme Civil and Penal Court could chair the economic crime office, and local offices could be established in other cities besides Athens.

Court of Auditors   The Court of Auditors could be strengthened to become the central supervisory institution of the state. Apart from investigating the legality of state contracts and public tenders, the Court of Auditors could conduct thorough checks of the financial statements of all state agencies (municipalities, Ministries, etc.) and political parties. Since the Court of Auditors is an institution with a dual purpose, as both a court agency and a state supervisory agency, it should have the power to impose penalties as it conducts its annual checks. The Court of Auditors could also collaborate with private auditing and consulting firms on an ad hoc basis so as to increase its reach and influence.

Appeals   The Greek justice system is open to appeals, meritorious or not. Practically all trials end up on appeal or even on a second appeal. A more reasonable procedure would create filters. For example, an appeal on matters of law could be assessed first by a single Appeal Court judge. If he/she thinks that an appeal is without merit, it ought not to reach the court. A similar system is adopted in many jurisdictions.[54] Here we should stress that the state agencies are frequent abusers of the appeals system. This reflects the (erroneous) view that the public interest is best served when the state appeals. Dealing with this requires redrafting the code of conduct for public sector employees.

Legal Costs   Greek costs orders are fixed and among the lowest in Europe (and much smaller when compared to other developed countries). They are not an effective deterrent of unnecessary litigation. An important reform would create a new system of costs orders, where cost awards would reflect the true costs and would force the loser to cover them in full. Costs work well as a deterrent of frivolous or vexatious actions and would strengthen alternative dispute resolution mechanisms. Yet, the system does need protection against aggressive parties that seek to intimidate an opponent with exorbitant costs. And likewise a system of costs could be created for administrative cases. These should be a priority in revising the anachronistic provisions of the Code of Civil Procedure (article 189) that severely underestimates legal costs. We believe that the revised article should mandate plaintiffs to submit a detailed table with actual legal costs, along with the relevant receipts and itinerary outlays. The Lawyers Bar Associations could provide tables with a range of legal costs by type of case, so as to avoid abuses and benchmark costs.

Codification and Procedure Simplification   Adding to the complexity of Greek legislation are the adjustments due to Acts of Parliament. These often include lists of entirely unrelated provisions amending the provisions of earlier laws, without the original text being listed. It is essential that such incoherent process of legislation be stopped. An independent body should be formed along the lines of a dedicated Law Commission to advise and plan the codification and legislation. In addition the process of consultation for new legislative proposals, which is currently short (e.g., the consultation process for the new Code of Civil Procedure lasted 21 days, from Friday March 7 to Friday March 28, 2014), should become an essential part of the legislative process.[55]

Standardization   Currently there is very little standardization of lawsuits: lawyers file cases without following a template or some basic norm. In fact, until 2012, it was at the discretion of lawyers to submit an abstract or extended summary of the dispute. In this regard we propose the following:

1. The European Court of Human Rights issues detailed instructions and provides templates to assist persons wishing to make an individual application. It would be useful if Greek courts would standardize their application forms as well. Moreover judges

could standardize the way they frame their decisions. Other areas where case filings and court decisions could be standardized include summary judgments (αιτήσεις για την έκδοση διαταγής πληρωμής και απόδοσης μισθίου), rental disputes, child custodies, and parent-child communications, cases involving indebted households, labor disputes, social allowances, and so on.

2. Judges could compel attorneys to submit standardized synopses of their lawsuits, as this will help categorize cases and allow courts to deal with them in an effective manner. Though Law 4055/2012 (article 41) requires submitting an executive summary, this mandate is not enforced. Even though, by law, the Supreme Courts are required to issue templates and provide guidance, none of this happens. Following the example of foreign courts, the Supreme Courts could provide (via their websites) information materials, specific guidelines, and examples for various cases, as this will minimize instances where a case will be put on file because of the claim being unacceptably vague. Likewise, to lower the number of appeals rejected on grounds of inadequate reasoning, the Supreme Courts could issue manuals to assist judges on drafting judgments.

3. Providing a framework to follow for different administrative documents would help reduce cases of infringement of essential procedural acts (περιπτώσεις παραβάσεως του ουσιώδους τύπου της διαδικασίας) and questioning of the assembly and composition of administrative bodies (συγκρότησης και σύνθεσης διοικητικών οργάνων), for example. While such standardization may seem to be of minor importance, administrative courts are often beseeched by citizens who challenge the validity of administrative decisions due to improper justification, infringement of procedures, and illegal composition of administrative committees.

12.6.2 Enhance Recent Reforms

Over the past five years, the various Greek administrations passed many legislative acts in an effort to improve the system's performance. We believe that all of these steps were in the right direction—though the interaction of increased litigation, reduced funding, and a large backlog has not brought tangible improvements.[56]

Single-Member Courts   A way to deal with the large backlog may be to move cases from multi-member panel courts (Πολυμελές Πρωτοδικεία και Εφετεία) to single-judge courts (Μονομελή Πρωτοδικεία και Ειρηνοδικεία). While there is risk of error when court decisions are based on the judgment of a single individual, it may be worth that risk for cases involving small sums of money.[57] However, the large workload of judges and the lack of clerical support often causes the single-judge court to agree with the recommendation of the judge from the multi-panel court who wrote the "report" (*εισ ηγητής*). In 2010 and 2012 legislation moved many disputes from multi-panel courts to single-member courts to free up judicial resources. While we acknowledge the need for impartiality and a fair trial, given the current conditions and the lack of financing, the Greek system cannot afford having three, five, and even seven-member court panels to decide on many cases. It is clearly a good outcome that the MoJ, at the end of 2014, rejected pressure from judges and attorneys and that the Code of Civil Procedure retained the increased competence of single-member courts (for claims up to 250,000 euros) and single-member Courts of Appeal.

Model Trial   The introduction of model trial into the Greek legal order (with Acts 3900/2010 and 4055/2012) has been a success. Thousands of cases regarding pensions, social security benefits, and allowances have been resolved. The wide application of model trials has the potential to eliminate unnecessary procedural steps and foster party cooperation and dispute resolution outside courts. This new procedure could be strengthened by expanding its application to civil cases. It could also be institutionalized through a constitutional amendment.

Training Lawyers and Paralegals   With recent legislation (Law 4055/2012), courts are allowed for the first time to hire recent law school graduates as interns, so that they do (part of) their training in courts. Anecdotal evidence suggests that this program has been successful, and we thus support expanding this internship training program, as is explicitly encouraged by the new Code of Lawyers (Law 4194/2013). Judges now have the opportunity to get help from law school graduates, and the interns gain much-needed experience. These interns can further work as judicial assistants for one to two years after passing their bar examinations. This is often done in other jurisdictions.

Mediation (*Διαμεσολάβηση*)   At the end of 2014 the MoJ launched an electronic platform for mediation, in accord with Act 3898/2010. This process is cheap, fast, and maintains confidentiality, and it has generated public interest as a way to settle private and commercial disputes. While it is premature to evaluate its effectiveness, we believe that this is a step in the right direction, moving cases outside courts so that lay judges can handle them in a casual (nonformalistic) manner.

12.7   Conclusion

The Greek justice system has been going through an unprecedented crisis. We draw on our experience, anecdotal evidence, and the voluminous literature on law and economics to address its failures. The massive inefficiencies of the justice system have contributed to the severity of the economic downturn, the prolonged recession, and the weak recovery. The justice system's failures are further related to deep structural deficiencies of the political and institutional environment: political interference, cronyism, absurd legal formalism, administrative weaknesses, lack of forward planning, absence of checks and balances, and lack of accountability. These failures provide an inhospitable environment for business, as there is poor protection of investors. Court delays render judicial protection practically nonexistent. Laws are complex, obscure, and constantly changing, especially in regard to taxes. The judiciary has shown little urgency to respond to this crisis. Despite some small reforms over the last few years, the economic crisis has increased massively the volume of incoming cases, and these are brought to courts receiving minimal outlays of public funds. The only working procedures as of the time that this chapter was being completed (April 2016) are interim injunctions and interim orders, while in criminal cases, custody has become a substitute of punishment. In our view Greece has been entering a regime of "institutionalized injustice."

The need for change at all levels is obvious. There is an urgent need to distinguish between, first, an emergency short-term plan to clear the backlog of hundreds of thousands of cases and restore the normal operation of justice, and, second, a larger longterm plan to reform the justice system. Such long-term reform must encompass every aspect of the justice system: the hiring and training of judges, the administration of courts, the infrastructure, the provision of information systems, the accountability of judges to the community, and many more.

The Greek economy will not recover, unless a way is found to reform radically the justice system. The political system's own legitimacy will not be restored until it manages to reform the current system of institutionalized injustice, the most corrosive of its many failures.

Table 12A.1

Gross and net annual salaries of first-instance professional judges and prosecutors at the start of their careers (in euros)

Jurisdiction	Judge's gross salary	Gross salary/ national salary	Judge's net salary	Prosecutor's gross salary	Gross salary / national salary	Prosecutor's net salary
Albania	7,350	1.9	6,231	7,285	1.9	6,323
Andorra	73,877	3.1	69,814	73,877	3.1	69,814
Armenia				5,637	2.2	4,701
Austria	47,713	1.7	30,499	50,653	1.8	31,999
Azerbaijan	11,364	3.0	9,338	5,398	1.4	4,368
Belgium	62,367	1.6	33,925	62,367	1.6	33,925
Bosnia-Herzegovina	22,936	3.1	14,946	22,936	3.1	14,946
Bulgaria	10,230	3.2	9,651	10,230	3.2	9,651
Croatia	30,396	2.4	16,416	30,396	2.4	16,416
Cyprus	71,020	3.0	52,026	32,942	1.4	20,540
Czech Republic	24,324	2.1		19,632	1.7	
Denmark	104,098	2.1		50,540	1.0	
Estonia	31,992	3.4	25,632	15,108	1.6	11,845
Finland	57,250	1.6	40,250	45,048	1.2	33,200
France	40,660	1.2	31,599	40,660	1.2	31,939
Georgia	11,642	3.8	9,313	8,976	3.0	7,188
Germany	41,127	0.9		41,127	0.9	
Greece	**32,704**	**1.3**	**24,300**	**32,704**	**1.3**	**24,300**

Table 12A.1 (continued)

Jurisdiction	Judge's gross salary	Gross salary/ national salary	Judge's net salary	Prosecutor's gross salary	Gross salary / national salary	Prosecutor's net salary
Hungary	18,252	2.0	10,647	16,852	1.8	9,828
Iceland	56,885	1.7		51,769	1.5	
Ireland	147,961	4.1		33,576	0.9	
Italy	50,290	2.1	31,729	50,290	2.1	31,729
Latvia	13,798	1.8	9,292	13,524	1.8	9,180
Lithuania	18,072	2.6	13,728	12,529	1.8	9,522
Luxembourg	78,383	1.9		78,483	1.9	
Malta	38,487	2.7				
Moldova	3,220	1.5	2,572	2,707	1.2	2,122
Monaco	43,271	1.3	41,020	43,271	1.3	41,020
Montenegro	24,142	2.8	14,500	19,947	2.3	13,364
Netherlands	74,000	1.5	43,000	54,036	1.1	32,604
Norway	113,940	2.1	62,035	62,400	1.1	40,000
Poland	20,736	2.1	16,711	20,736	2.1	16,492
Portugal	35,699	1.7		35,699	1.7	
Romania	25,750	4.8	18,062	25,750	4.8	18,062

Table 12A.1 (continued)

Jurisdiction	Judge's gross salary	Gross salary/ national salary	Judge's net salary	Prosecutor's gross salary	Gross salary / national salary	Prosecutor's net salary
Russia	15,988	2.6	13,098	9,594	1.5	8,347
Serbia	13,595	2.5	9,600	13,595	2.5	9,600
Slovakia	28,148	3.1		26,585	2.9	
Slovenia	28,968	1.6	17,521	34,858	1.9	19,901
Spain	47,494	1.5		47,494	1.5	
Sweden	52,587	1.4		52,290	1.4	
Switzerland	126,206	2.2	100,965	106,718	1.9	85,375
FYROM	17,219	2.9	11,451	14,147	2.4	9,535
Turkey	21,137	1.8	16,390	21,137	1.8	16,390
Ukraine	6,120	2.6	4,872	5,232	2.2	4,116
UK-England and Wales	120,998	3.8		33,515	1.1	
UK-Scotland	150,106	5.2		35,154	1.2	26,009
Average	46,056	2.4	25,348	32,831	1.9	20,696
Median	32,704	2.1	16,564	32,704	1.8	16,390

Source: Council of Europe, 2012 Report on the Justice System.

Table 12A.2

Distribution of professional judges

Jurisdiction	First instance (%)	Second instance (%)	Supreme Court (%)
Bulgaria	36	56	8
Monaco	44	14	42
Romania	46	51	3
Hungary	58	39	3
Greece	58	29	13
Czech Republic	61	32	8
Latvia	63	26	10
Slovakia	67	27	6
Norway	67	29	4
Sweden	68	28	4
Poland	68	30	2
Spain	68	30	2
Bosnia and Herzegovina	69	21	10
Ireland	69	25	5
Georgia	70	22	8
Switzerland	70	27	3
France	70	25	5
Ukraine	70	27	3
Azerbaijan	71	23	7
Moldova	72	18	11
Croatia	72	26	2
Estonia	73	19	8
Denmark	73	23	4
Portugal	74	22	4
Germany	75	20	5
Armenia	75	17	8
Serbia	75	24	1
Finland	76	20	4
Netherlands	77	22	2
Slovenia	77	19	4
Albania	77	18	4

Table 12A.2 (continued)

Jurisdiction	First instance (%)	Second instance (%)	Supreme Court (%)
Belgium	79	19	2
Montenegro	80	13	7
Italy	81	15	4
The FYR Macedonia	81	16	4
Lithuania	83	12	5
Austria	85	12	4
Cyprus	88	13	4

Source: Council of Europe, 2012 Report on the Justice System
Note: In Cyprus, the Court of Appeals is also the Supreme Court.

Table 12A.3

Numbers of lawyers and legal professionals in 2008

	Total population	Legal professionals	Legal professionals per 1,000 persons	Lawyers and attorneys	Lawyers per 1,000 persons
Austria	8,318,592	9,901	1.19	5,129	0.617
Belgium	10,666,866	18,686	1.752	15,363	1.44
Cyprus	4,436,401	2,133	0.481	1,781	0.401
Czech Republic	10,381,130	10,204	0.983	8,020	0.773
Denmark	5,475,791	4,786	0.874	5,246	0.958
Estonia	1,340,935	732	0.546	676	0.504
Finland	5,300,484	3,332	0.629	1,810	0.341
France	64,007,193	66,364	1.037	47,765	0.746
Germany	82,217,837	127,781	1.554	146,910	1.787
Greece	11,213,785	42,179	3.761	38,000	3.389
Hungary	10,045,401	12,506	1.245	9,934	0.989
Ireland	4,401,335	9,386	2.133		
Italy	59,619,290	179,479	3.01	213,081	3.574
Latvia	2,270,894	1,949	0.858	1,091	0.48
Lithuania	3,366,357	3,155	0.937	1,590	0.472
Luxemburg	483,799	1,629	3.367	1,318	2.724
Netherlands	16,405,399	27,800	1.695	14,882	0.907
Portugal	10,617,575	14,113	1.329	25,695	2.42
Romania	21,528,627	18,539	0.861	16,998	0.79
Slovak Republic	5,400,998	4,825	0.893	4,595	0.851
Spain	45,283,259	123,114	2.719	154,953	3.422
Sweden	9,182,927	9,186	1	4,503	0.49
United Kingdom	61,191,951	105,380	1.722	155,323	2.538
European Union	453,156,826	797,160	1.759	876,671	1.935

Source: Pagliero and Timmons (2012)

Notes

1. A special thanks goes to Pavlos Elefteriadis for useful comments and critical insights, and we are much obliged to his contribution. We thank Dimitris Vayanos, Kostas Kosmas, George Georgiades, Nikitas Konstantinides, Marina Souyioultzi, Miltiadis Papaioannou, and Stathis Potamitis for useful comments and feedback. A special thanks also goes to Nicolas Kanellopoulos for detailed comments and for elucidating the policies of the Ministry of Justice in 2011 to 2015.

2. Another dimension of the Greek crisis that has received little attention is the role of distrust and of the low levels of civicness and social capital. In this chapter we focus on institutional aspects, the judiciary, courts, and legal institutions; yet institutional performance is clearly linked to cultural issues, related to values, norms and beliefs. On the effect of civic-social capital and trust on institutional and economic performance, see Alesina and Giuliano (2013), Algan and Cahuc (2014), and Guiso, Sapienza, and Zingales (2013). Papaioannou (2011, 2013) discusses the role of distrust and low levels of civic-social capital on the Greek and the European crisis.

3. The IMF has acknowledged that that it under-estimated the weakness of the Greek public administration and the Greek state's inability to enforce laws, and that this has been an important problem with the design of the adjustment program (IMF 2013).

4. Legal quality and court efficiency differ considerably across legal families. Common law countries offer on average superior protection to investors and have relatively fast court systems, whereas countries with a French civil law tradition offer relatively poor protection to investors and have formalistic procedures. Countries with a Germanic civil code tradition and Scandinavian nations lie somewhere in the middle (La Porta et al. 1997, 1998).

5. See Bae and Vidhan (2009) and Laeven and Majinoni (2005). Jappeli, Pagano, and Bianco (2005) show that in Italian provinces with longer trials and large backlogs, bank credit is less widely available than elsewhere. International evidence shows that the depth of mortgage markets is inversely related to costs of mortgage foreclosures and other proxies for judicial inefficiency. Lilienfeld-Toal, Mookherjee and Visaria (2012) show theoretically that if credit supply is inelastic, then improving creditor protection will expand bank credit disproportionally in large firms (as their collateral has higher value) as compared to small firms. Using firm level panel data, they show that an Indian judicial reform that increased banks' ability to recover nonperforming loans had such an impact.

6. See Claessens and Laeven (2003), Ardagna and Lusardi (2008), and Ciccone and Papaioannou (2007).

7. See, among others, Lerner and Schoar (2005) and Desai, Gombers, and Lerner (2007).

8. This expression is attributed to Mr. Vasilios Floridis. "Στην Ελλάδα ποιος είναι φυλακή; Οι φτωχοί και όσοι δεν έχουν ισχυρές διασυνδέσεις" (*Kathimerini*, March 6, 2011).

9. The 2016 European Justice Scoreboard was released in April 2016, when this chapter was being completed. Thus our analysis of the available data is preliminary.

10. Djankov, Hart, McLiesh, and Shleifer (2008) analyze bankruptcy practices in 88 countries. They find a strong association between best practices and income per capita.

11. Using firm-level data from 27 European countries in 2002 and 2005, Safavian and Sharma (2007) find that creditor-friendly laws increase firms' bank financing only in countries with efficient courts. Likewise Ponticelli (2013) finds that in Brazil bankruptcy reform increased access to finance only in areas with efficient courts.

12. The European Commission has released the 2014 edition of the European Justice Scoreboard. There are no major differences relative to the 2013 edition. Where there are differences, we note them.

13. *Vassilios Athanasiou et Autres c. Grèce*, Requête no 50973/08, Judgment of 21.12.2010.

14. Those comparisons should be interpreted with caution, as data for Greece are missing for various categories.

15. This number does not include officials at the Council of State (159) and magistrates (551).

16. The number of judges has declined over the last few years, as there have not been new appointments. The 2016 European Justice Scoreboard reports that in Greece the number of judges per 100,000 inhabitants was 20, which is close to the EU average.

17. Fifteen European countries have a Rechtspfleger system (or a system operating with staff having powers and status close to the Rechtspfleger): Andorra, Austria, Bosnia and Herzegovina, Croatia, Czech Republic, Denmark, Estonia, Germany, Hungary, Ireland, Poland, Slovakia, Slovenia, and Spain.

18. See appendix table 12A.1, which we reproduce from the 2012 CEPEJ report.

19. This was part of a broader pattern of salary and pension cuts that took place between 2010 and 2015. Contrary to what many believe, the cuts were significantly larger for public sector workers and for pensioners collecting higher benefits.

20. In 2013 Greek courts (απόφαση 88/2013 του Μισθοδικείου) ruled that the salary cuts of judges during 2011 and 2012 were at odds with the constitutional provision of judicial independence and the parity of the judiciary with the legislature and the executive. The administration passed legislation (4270/2014) returning judges' salaries to the 2008 levels.

21. Pagliero and Timmons (2012) estimate that there were 38,000 lawyers and 42,179 legal professionals in Greece in 2008. For comparison, in Belgium, the Czech Republic, and Portugal (countries with populations similar to that of Greece), the numbers were less than half, 18,686, 12,506, and 14,134, respectively. The full data are reported in table 12A.3 in the appendix.

22. The protests were justified, however. Although the proposals were reasonable overall, the one that generated the protests concerned witnesses in standard civil trials being not examined in chief, or cross-examined, unless the judge gave specific directions to that effect. It is questionable if this proposal complies with the right to a free trial and article 6 of the ECHR.

23. See table 12A.2 in the appendix for the estimates from the 2010 CEPEJ report. With the exception of Monaco, Greece has the highest ratio of Supreme Court judges to total number of judges (13 percent). And in late 2016 the Greek government announced that the number of Supreme Court judges would further increase.

24. We should emphasize that senior judges (close to retirement) often perform administrative duties; thus postponing retirement may not be as beneficial as recruiting young lawyers to serve as magistrates or judicial assistants.

25. The MoJ considered this option but decided not to proceed, on the basis that the policy would be ruled unconstitutional.

26. According to recent legislation, if a retiree gains income from any kind of work, his/her pension is automatically reduced to a sum that is equal to the base salary. Moreover he/she has to pay social security contributions. This provision is a disincentive for judges (and prosecutors) to continue working, and should be changed.

27. The Council of Europe indicates that judges' retirement ages range from 63 years (in Cyprus) to 72 years (in Ireland).

28. Recently a vocal minority opposed the opening of retail shops on Sundays, so we are aware that this proposal is polemical. Yet we believe that this can be a win-win situation, as judicial clerks and judges can supplement their incomes and many firms and individuals will be helped by their disputes finally reaching settlement.

29. After we completed a first draft of this chapter, the Hellenic Federation of Enterprises (ΣΕΒ) released a report on the Greek justice system detailing a comprehensive set of reforms (October 2014). Many of reforms that we suggest in this chapter are similar to those put forward in that report. Unfortunately, only a few of the reforms were tendered by the Greek government, and in many instances the MoJ has either abandoned or reversed them.

30. According to a report by the Society for Judicial Studies (Εταιρεία Δικαστικών Μελετών; ETDIM 2005), the process of evaluation is ineffective largely due to the large number of evaluations that each evaluator has to oversee.

31. The relevant articles of the Code for Court Organization (Κώδικας Οργανισμού Δικαστηρίων, Law 1756/1988) were amended with acts 3904/2010, 4055/2012, and 4139/2013.

32. According to article 91 of the Constitution, the disciplinary power of judges with a rank of Areopagite (Supreme Court judge) or deputy prosecutor of the Supreme Civil and Penal Court and above, or with equivalent ranks at administrative courts (Council of the State), is exercised by the Supreme Disciplinary Judicial Council (Ανώτατο Δικαστικό Συμβούλιο). The president of the Council of State serves as the council president; the Supreme Disciplinary Council also comprises two vice presidents or councilors from the State Council, two deputy Supreme Court judges or Supreme Court judges, two deputies or councilors from the Court of Audit, and two full-time law professors teaching in one of the country's law schools. For the rest of the judiciary (magistrates, first-instance and appellate court judges and prosecutors), disciplinary power is exercised by councils composed exclusively of judges.

33. The Report of the Council of Europe shows that in approximately half of the jurisdictions there are no bonuses for judges. Bonus schemes for judges are present in the United Kingdom, Switzerland, and Belgium, among others.

34. For example, the Judicial Appointments Commission in the United Kingdom is an independent body that selects candidates for judicial office in courts and tribunals in England and Wales, and for some tribunals in Scotland or Northern Ireland. It consists of fifteen commissioners, only three of whom are appointed by the Judiciary.

35. A similar process applies to Greek independent authorities (Ανεξάρτητες Αρχές).

36. However, given the recent radicalization of Parliament and the evident sharp deterioration in the quality of elected politicians, it is questionable whether this process will improve the current system of appointments or worsen it!

37. The time that a judge takes to release a decision is an essential and important evaluation criterion in the administration of justice internationally. In Greece it was only partially introduced in 2012.

38. We should stress here that contrary to conventional wisdom, the presidents of the Supreme Courts have little power of monitoring, as their role is limited to their participation in the (eleven member) Supreme Judicial Council.

39. Philosophy, history, and ethnics constitute elective courses, so it is common for legal professionals to ignore basic issues in legal philosophy and the historical evolution of legal thinking. Another evident deficiency of the curriculum of the Greek Law Schools is the lack of professional training (e.g., students are not required to attend court sessions).

40. The Code for the Organization of Courts (article 74) includes a provision for the establishment of a Center for Judicial Studies that would organize the professional development of judges, prosecutors, and judicial employees. Such an institute has not been created. Rather than setting up a new institution, we believe that the National School of Judges and Prosecutors should handle the continuing education of court personnel.

41. This legislation allowed judges to get a special leave of absence (for a maximum of five months) to visit foreign national courts, the European Court of Justice, and the European Court of Human Rights. However, this perk has not been widely used (likely due to the huge workload).

42. Chemin (2009b) analyzed the impact of a training program in Pakistan (in 2002) on case management; his analysis reveals large positive effects. He estimates that judges who attended the training disposed 25 percent more cases in the year following their training, as compared to judges who did not attend the training. See also Chemin (2009b, 2012).

43. See Bloom et al. (2014a, 2014) for recent reviews. On the role of management quality on school performance and hospitals, see Bloom et al. (2012, 2014b).

44. Again, the origin of this restrictive constitutional provision is the abuse of power from 1936 to 1974, when there was interference of senior judges in lower court rulings (e.g., Lambrakis case).

45. In contrast to widespread belief that the e-Justice system was initiated by the Troika, it was the MoJ and the Greek government that incorporated this project in the Memorandum of Understanding. The Greek administration in place since 2015 has put the completion of this program high on its agenda.

46. This comes from the introductory paragraph of the draft legislation on the new penal code.

47. Though in 2011 and 2012 the Ministry of Justice had prepared a reform whereby drug-related sentences would treat drug addicts not as criminals but as humans in need of medical help, subsequent legislation did not go as far.

48. The recent drafts of the penal code and the code for penal procedure include some of these provisions.

49. It is unfortunate that the government and the Troika have been unable to agree on the recruitment of guards for the new prison facilities.

50. Greece adopted this system in 1871 and further strengthened it by adding explicit constitutional provisions in 1927 and 1952. Other countries with a diffuse constitutionality check model include Switzerland, Sweden, and Japan. Many other countries follow a polar opposite system, where a Constitutional Court evaluates the constitutional basis of all legal acts. Examples include Germany, Austria, and Belgium.

51. Here are two examples. Act 4055/2012 includes a provision that in the event of a lawyer's abstention, the hearing of the adjourned civil proceeding has to be set within a period of ninety days. However, this is not enforced in practice because of overcrowding. Likewise the provision of the same Act that adjourned penal cases are to be presided over by the same judge has remained void because of the lack of IT infrastructure. Both provisions were removed with Act 4139/2013 (paragraph 4, article 93). Provisions targeting plaintiffs have been more successful. For example, Act 3904/2010 has had some success with the provision that plaintiffs requesting adjournment for serious health conditions should submit a medical record from a hospital. Also Act 4055/2012 has been successful with the provision that in interim measure cases (υποθέσεις ασφαλιστικών μέτρων) the granted interim injunction (προσωρινή διαταγή) is automatically lifted if a plaintiff requests an adjournment of the hearing. The latter Act has been effective in removing the incentive for plaintiffs to postpone hearings.

52. For example, quite often a plaintiff will request an adjournment, despite not having submitted a written proposal twenty days before the hearing, as the Code for Civil Procedure mandates.

53. The October 2014 report of the Hellenic Federation of Enterprises (SEV 2014) also discusses proposals concerning the insolvency law.

54. Recently the administration added appeal filters in tax disputes.

55. According to article 76, paragraph 6, of the Constitution, judicial and administrative codes are to be prepared by specialized committees (set up by specific Acts). The committee's proposals for the code are introduced in the Parliament, which in a plenary session can either approve or reject the code (without being able to make any amendments).

56. Androulakis (2015) finds that case backlogs and new filings fell somewhat after 2012 across most administrative courts. This suggests that the numerous reforms between 2010 and 2012 may have been beneficial.

57. This is a risk that many legal systems are willing to take even for the most important cases. The English legal system relies mostly on single-member courts. The County Courts (for smaller claims) and the High Court (for all other cases) of England and Wales almost always meet as single-member courts.

References

Acemoglu, Daron, Simon Johnson, and James A. Robinson. 2005. Institutions as the fundamental cause of long-run growth? In *The Handbook of Economic Growth*, vol. 1A, ed. Philippe Aghion and Steve Durlauf, 385–472. Amsterdam: North-Holland.

Acemoglu, Daron, and James A. Robinson. 2012. *Why Nations Fail? The Origins of Power, and Prosperity*. New York: Crown.

Alesina, Alberto, and Paola Giuliano. 2013. Culture and institutions. Working paper 19750. NBER.

Alfaro, Laura, Sebnem Kalemli-Ozkan, and Vadym Volosovych. 2008. Why doesn't capital flow from rich to poor countries? An empirical investigation. *Review of Economics and Statistics* 90 (2): 347–68.

Algan, Yann, and Pierre Cahuc. 2014. Trust, institutions and economic development. In *The Handbook of Economic Growth*, ed. Philippe Aghion and Steven Durlauf, 49–120. Amsterdam: North-Holland.

Algan, Yann, Sergei Guriev, Evgenia Passari, and Elias Papaioannou. 2016. *The European trust crisis. Mimeo*. London Business School and Paris School of Economics.

Androulakis, Vasileios. 2015. On-time legal protection in administrative justice (in Greek: Η Επίκαιρη Παροχή Δικαστικής Προστασίας στη Διοικητική Δικαιοσύνη. Μία Συνεχής Αναζήτηση). *Legal Advice* 1:1–26.

Ardagna, Silvia, and Annamaria Lusardi. 2008. Explaining international differences in entrepreneurship: The role of individual characteristics and regulatory constraints. Working paper 14012. NBER.

Bae, Kee-Hog, and Goyal K. Vidhan. 2009. Creditor rights, enforcement, and bank loans. *Journal of Finance* 64 (2): 823–60.

Bernitsas, Panagiotis. 2014. The pathologies of public tenders (in Greek: Οι Παθογένειες κατά την Ανάθεση Έργων). *Kathimerini,* October 26. http://www.kathimerini.gr/789578/article/oikonomia/epixeirhseis/apoyh-oi-pa8ogeneies-kata--thn-ana8esh-ergwn.

Bloom, Nicholas, Christos Genakos, Raffaella Sadun, and John Van Reenen. 2012. Management practices across countries. *Academy of Management Perspectives* 26 (1): 12–33.

Bloom, Nicholas, Renata Lemos, Raffaella Sadun, Daniela Scur, and John Van Reenen. 2014a. The new empirical economics of management. *Journal of the European Economic Association* 12 (4): 835–76.

Bloom, Nicholas, Renata Lemos, Rafaella Sadun, and John Van Reenen. 2014b. Does management matter in schools? Mimeo. Department of Economics, Stanford University.

Bloom, Nicholas, Rafaella Sadun, and John Van Reenen. 2012. Does management matter in healthcare? Mimeo. Department of Economics, Stanford University.

Chemin, Matthieu. 2009a. The impact of the judiciary on entrepreneurship: Evaluation of Pakistan's "Access to Justice" program. *Journal of Public Economics* 93 (1–2): 114–25.

Chemin, Matthieu. 2009b. Do judiciaries matter for development? Evidence from India. *Journal of Comparative Economics* 37 (1): 230–50.

Chemin, Matthieu. 2012. Does court speed shape economic activity? Evidence from a court reform in India. *Journal of Law Economics and Organization* 28 (3): 460–485.

Ciccone, Antonio, and Elias Papaioannou. 2006. Adjustment to target capital, finance, and growth, Discussion paper 5969. CEPR.

Ciccone, Antonio, and Elias Papaioannou. 2007. Red tape and delayed entry. *Journal of the European Economic Association* 5 (2–3): 444–58.

Claessens, Stijn, and Luc Laeven. 2003. Financial development, property rights, and growth. *Journal of Finance* 58 (6): 2401–36.

Dakolias, Maria. 1999. *Court Performance around the World: A Comparative Perspective*. Washington, DC: World Bank.

Demirgüç-Kunt, Asli, and Vojislav Maksimovic. 1998. Law, finance and firm growth. *Journal of Finance* 53 (6): 2107–37.

Desai, Mihir. A., Paul Gompers, and Josh Lerner. 2005. Institutions, capital constraints, and entrepreneurial firm dynamics: Evidence from Europe. NOM working paper 03–59. Harvard.

Djankov, Simeon, Rafael La Porta, Florencio López-de-Silanes, and Andrei Shleifer. 2003. Courts. *Quarterly Journal of Economics* 118 (2): 453–517.

Djankov, Simeon, Caralee McLiesh, and Andrei Shleifer. 2007. Private credit in 129 countries. *Journal of Financial Economics* 84 (2): 299–329.

Djankov, Simeon, Oliver Hart, Caralee McLiesh, and Andrei Shleifer. 2008. Debt enforcement around the world. *Journal of Political Economy* 116 (6): 1105–49.

Drago, Francesco, Roberto Galbiati, and Pietro Vertova. 2011. Prison conditions and recidivism. *American Law and Economics Review* 13 (1): 103–30.

Eleftheriadis, Pavlos. 2008. *Legal Rights*. Oxford: Oxford University Press.

Eleftheriadis, Pavlos. 2014. *The misrule of the few: How the oligarchs ruined Greece. Foreign Affairs.* November/December. https://www.foreignaffairs.com/articles/greece/misrule-few/.

ETDIM (Society for Judicial Studies). 2005. 2005 Report on the Evaluation of Judges.

European Commission. 2013. *The European Justice Scoreboard*. Brussels.

European Commission. 2014. *The European Justice Scoreboard*. Brussels.

European Commission. 2016. *The European Justice Scoreboard*. Brussels.

European Social Survey. 2012. ESS 1–5, European Social Survey Cumulative File. Data file edition 1.1. Norwegian Social Science Data Services, Bergen.

Fisman, Raymond, and Inessa Love. 2007. Financial development and growth in the short and long run. *Journal of the European Economic Association* 5 (2–3): 470–79.

Glaeser, Edward, Jose Scheinkman, and Andrei Shleifer. 2003. The injustice of inequality. *Journal of Monetary Economics: Carnegie-Rochester Series on Public Policy* 50 (1): 199–222.

Guiso, Luigi, Paola Sapienza, and Luigi Zingales. 2011. Civic capital as the missing link. In *The Handbook of Social Economics*, ed. Jess Benhabib, Alberto Bisin, and Matthew O. Jackson. Amsterdam: Elsevier, North-Holland.

Hellenic Federation of Enterprises (SEV). 2014. *Topics Reports. Speeding Justice and Dispute Resolution, a Prerequisite for Investment and Development* (in Greek: Θεματική Μελέτη. Επιτάχυνση της Απονομής Δικαιοσύνης και της Επίλυσης Διαφορών, Προϋπόθεση για τις Επενδύσεις και την Ανάπτυξη). Proposals for Discussion. Observatory for Investment Climate. http://www.sev.org.gr/Uploads/pdf/synopsiEkthesisAponomiDikaiosinis_25914.pdf.

Heston, Alan, Robert Summers and Bettina Aten. 2013. *Penn World Table Version 7.1.* Center for International Comparisons of Production, Income and Prices. University of Pennsylvania.

International Monetary Fund. 2013. Greece: Ex-post evaluation of exceptional access under the 2010 Stand-By Arrangement. Country report 13/156. IMF.

Jappelli, Tulio, Marco Pagano, and Magda Bianco. 2005. Courts and banks: Effects of judicial enforcement on credit markets. *Journal of Money, Credit and Banking* 37 (2): 223–44.

Karatza, Stavroula G. 2013. The New Provisions of Act 4055/2012 for Administrative Case (in Greek: Οι Νέες Ρυθμίσεις του ν. 4055/2012 για την Διοικητική Δίκη). *Constitution*, 965–98.

Laeven, Luc, and Christopher Woodruff. 2007. The quality of the legal system, firm ownership, and firm size. *Review of Economics and Statistics* 89 (4): 601–14.

La Porta, Rafael, Florencio Lopez-de-Silanes, Andrei Shleifer, and Robert Vishny. 1997. Legal determinants of external finance. *Journal of Finance* 53 (1): 1131–50.

La Porta, Rafael, Florencio Lopez-de-Silanes, Andrei Shleifer, and Robert Vishny. 1998. Law and finance. *Journal of Political Economy* 106 (6): 1113–55.

Lerner, Josh, and Antoinette Schoar. 2005. Does legal enforcement affect financial transactions? The contractual channel in private equity. *Quarterly Journal of Economics* 120 (1): 223–46.

Levchenko, Andrei. 2007. Institutional quality and international trade. *Review of Economic Studies* 74 (3): 791–819.

Lilienfeld-Toal, Ulf, Dilip Mookherjee, and Sujata Visaria. 2012. The distributive impact of reforms in credit enforcement: Evidence from Indian debt recovery tribunals. *Econometrica* 80 (2): 497–558.

Nunn, Nathan. 2007. Relationship-specificity, incomplete contracts and the pattern of trade. *Quarterly Journal of Economics* 122 (2): 569–600.

OECD. 2013. *What makes civil justice effective?* Policy note 18. Economics Department, OECD.

Pagliero, Mario and Edward Timmons. 2012. Occupational regulation in the European legal market. *European Journal of Comparative Economics* 10 (2): 243–65.

Papaioannou, Elias. 2009. What drives international financial flows? Politics, institutions and other determinants. *Journal of Development Economics* 88 (2): 269–81.

Papaioannou, E. 2011. Civic capital(ism). TEDxAcademy Talk. https://www.youtube.com/watch?v=S5nth5jlCP0.

Papaioannou, E. 2013. Trust(ing) in Europe? How increased social capital can contribute to economic development. Annual meeting, Helsinki, Finland. Center for European Policy Studies Report.

Papaioannou, E. 2015. Eurozone's original Sin? Nominal rather than institutional convergence. In *The Eurozone Crisis: A Consensus View of the Causes and a Few Possible Solutions*, ed. R. Baldwin and F. Giavazzi. VOX E-book. September.

Paparigopoulos, Xenophon, and Nikolaos Kiriazis. 2010. On speeding-up and improving justice (in Greek: Για την Επι τάχυνση και τη Βελτίωση της Δικαιοσύνης). *To Vima,* May 7. http://www.vimaideon.gr/MS_1804.html.

Ponticelli, Jacopo. 2013. Court enforcement and firm productivity: Evidence from a bankruptcy reform in Brazil. Working paper. Booth School of Business, University of Chicago.

Potamitis, Stathis. 2014. The deficiencies and gaps of bankrupcty law (in Greek: Οι Ανεπάρκειες του Πτωχευτικού Δικαίου). *Kathimerini,* October 26. http://www.kathimerini.gr/789581/article/oikonomia/epixeirhseis/apoyh-oi-aneparkeies--toy-ptwxeytikoy-dikaioy.

Potamitis, Stathis, and Marios Psaltis. 2013. Productive means towards the indebtedness trap (in Greek: Παραγωγικά μέσα στην παγίδα της υπερχρέωσης). *Kathimerini,* December 15. http://www.kathimerini.gr/506326/article/oikonomia/ellhnikh-oikonomia/paragwgika-mesa-sthn-pagida-ths-yperxrewshs.

Potamitis, Stathis, and Alexandros Rokas. 2012. A new pre-bankrupcy procedure for Greece. *Journal of Business Law* 3: 2012.

Rajan, Raghuram, and Luigi Zingales. 1998. Financial dependence and growth. *American Economic Review* 88 (3): 559–86.

Safavian, Mehnaz, and Siddareth Sharma. 2007. When do creditor rights work? *Journal of Comparative Economics* 35 (3): 484–508.

Shleifer, Andrei, and Robert Vishny. 1993. Corruption. *Quarterly Journal of Economics* 108 (3): 599–617.

Shleifer, Andrei, and Robert Vishny. 1997. A survey of corporate governance. *Journal of Finance* 52 (2): 737–83.

World Bank. *Doing Business. Measuring Business Regulation.* http://www.doingbusiness.org/.

13   Thinking about Corruption in Greece[1]

Costas Azariadis and Yannis M. Ioannides

13.1   Introduction

The Great Recession along with the onset of the Greek crisis raised awareness that corruption is an endemic problem in Greece. To start with, the Transparency International Corruption Perceptions Index[2] placed Greece at the bottom of the EU28 countries in 2014, and 99 percent of the Greek respondents in a European Commission Eurobarometer survey in the same year (*EU Anti-Corruption Report* 2014) agree that corruption is still widespread in their country. Data on corruption and other forms of antisocial behavior, collected from extensive surveys and other sources, are summed up in section 2.

Why does Greek society tolerate so much corruption? What can be done to control it? To deal with the first question we look at ideas from economic theory and political science that explain why and how individuals choose to seek bribes and engage in various forms of expropriating income from others. The second question takes us into a review of the policy recommendations made by the European Commission and others seeking to discourage corruption in Greece.

Greek citizens who may experience corruption as an everyday event may naturally think that "corruption is to be tolerated" and that "corruption pays." Why is corruption so widespread? Is there a link between perceptions of corruption and *actual* corruption? We look at these questions in two different ways. One is to think of corruption as a tax on legitimate economic activity, that is, on the wages and capital income earned by productive members of society (see Benhabib and Rustichini 1996). Perceptions of widespread corruption are equivalent to a high corruption tax that steers many citizens away from legitimate work, is informal and unpredictable, and generates "tax revenue" that is privately appropriated. Closely related to corruption is the phenomenon of tax evasion because of two reasons: one, it reportedly involves large-scale bribery of public officials; two, it is another and conceptually related instance of antisocial behavior.

Another way to approach this problem is through the prism of the social interactions literature (Brock and Durlauf 2001; Durlauf and Ioannides 2010; Ioannides 2013, ch. 2). This helps us conceptualize how corrupt practices and widespread tax evasion can emerge when individuals interact within common social settings. In social settings, peer pressure may be significant, and an individual's perception that others do not engage in corrupt practices may provide an incentive for him or her to also not do so. Because of peer pressure, multiple intensities of corruption can be self-confirming. At one extreme, corruption is rare: because others are not corrupt, one is also induced to be not corrupt. Corruption is widespread at the other extreme. There is also an intermediate possibility, suggested by specific models from the social interactions literature, where corruption is moderate. As we explain below, the two extreme outcomes are stable and the intermediate one is not.

Corruption is defined by Transparency International as the "abuse of entrusted power for private gain."[3] We define corruption more broadly to include tax evasion, especially when evasion is aided and abetted by tax officials, reportedly a rampant practice in Greece.[4]

The next section reviews some facts about corruption and tax evasion in Greece as background for the remainder of the chapter. From a pragmatic point of view, the key issue is what can be done about corruption. Growth theory, an established branch of macroeconomics, helps us frame corruption as a tax on income and wealth. Such a tax is borne by all the members of a society, perhaps in varying degrees and given different individuals' exposure to actual corrupt practices. Corrupt individuals benefit from it, but all suffer the consequences of the tax. For example, licensing ineligible individuals to perform professional services in exchange for bribes impacts the entire society via its consumption of substandard services. Society can reduce the burden of this tax by pouring resources into enforcement and deterrence. Hiring more policemen and prosecutors could be a solution and so would be the removal of laws that shield embezzlers of public funds through statutes of limitations or other means. In the case of tax evasion as an instance of corruption, the resulting burden as a tax on those who comply with the tax laws is literal. They are asked to pay more to make up for the shortfall of tax revenue, a burden that also feeds social bitterness. This has been felt with particular acuteness since the onset of the Greek crisis in 2009 through huge tax increases on compliant taxpayers, especially those with incomes that are hard to misreport.

The theory of social interactions gives an alternative: we could fight corruption by changing social perceptions of it. A society is made up of individuals who enter into myriad formal and informal interactions every day. Some of these interactions are exchanges of goods, services or favors, and their social counterparts serve as conduits for exchanges of opinions and information, and for observing personal values and related practices. Based on their observations, individuals adjust their expectations on what they may encounter in the future, and alter their behavior accordingly. Switching from a pattern of widespread corruption to one where corruption is rare requires a small jolt to social norms. This could happen in several ways.

Inducements against corruption include a variety of measures, some of which have been suggested by the European Union, others by Christopher Pissarides and ourselves in op-ed writings. For example, can social media and the web be used constructively in changing attitudes? One example is social media as tools that can "shame" antisocial individuals and public officials.[5] Another is whistleblowing, and independent authorities like the Office of the Ombudsman in Greece.[6] Above all, expectations will depend on how society deals with embezzlement and conflicts of interest by members of the political and labor elites.

13.2   Facts

Information about corruption and, to a lesser extent, about tax evasion comes from recent surveys conducted on behalf of the European Commission, and from regular annual reports by Transparency International. One of these surveys, taken in 2013 and published by the Eurobarometer, measures business attitudes toward corruption. Another is a series of Europe-wide anticorruption reports with annexes for each EU member country.[7] These are particularly helpful because the data, collected from answers to common questionnaires for the years 2005, 2007, 2009, 2011, and 2013, are of uniform quality. But because much of the information collected tends to be somewhat qualitative, these data sources have not received the attention they fully deserve.

Starting from 2005, for the question QC 4.1, "corruption is a major problem in our country," 94 percent of Greek respondents answered affirmatively, more than any other EU country (Eurobarometer 2005, p. 5). In contrast, only 27 percent of Finnish and 24 percent of Danish respondents answered affirmatively. Responses for 2007 are similar, while worse for Greece at 97 percent, and better for Finland and Denmark, at 25 percent and 22 percent (Eurobarometer 2007, p. 4). The situation is roughly unchanged for Greece and Denmark in 2009 (and worse for Finland), and the same is true in 2011 and 2013 (Eurobarometer 2013, p. 20). Table 13.1 summarizes key data for Greece in 2013. We return to the 2013 data by means of an econometric analysis in box 13.1.

Table 13.1

Percentages of business people responding affirmatively as to their awareness of corruption in their countries

	EU	Greece
Tax fraud	42	52
Widespread bribery	23	48
Very widespread corruption	76	99
Daily life affected by corruption	26	63

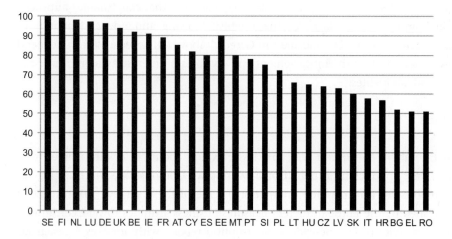

Figure 13.1

Summary rankings for corruption, 2013

Source: EU Anti-Corruption Report (2014), Country Sheet Greece.

The 2013 Eurobarometer data are consistent with information published by Transparency International and by the World Bank in 2013 and 2012, respectively. Transparency International ranks Greece at the bottom of the EU28 for perceived corruption. The World Bank's *Control of Corruption* index ranks Greece at the bottom of the EU 28, together with Romania (see figure 13.1).

At the same time some improvements appear to be taking place. According to Transparency International (2013a), the fraction of Greek households reporting corruption declined from 13.4 percent, in 2009, to 10.4 percent, in 2010, and to 8.2 percent in 2012. The extent in which this decline is related to the crisis is not known, except that it has persisted since its onset. The *Annual Report* for 2012 of the Inspector General for Public Administration (Inspector General of Public Administration 2013) documents

Table 13.2
Prosecutions, indictments, and convictions, 2007 to 2012

Year	2007	2008	2009	2010	2011	2012
Number	302	478	375	432	561	866
Percent	10	16	12	14	19	29

Source: Inspector General of Public Administration, *Annual Report* (2013)

an increased drive, documented in table 13.2, to bring charges and to convict civil servants in Greece.

International agencies point out that Greece has not implemented the OECD Anti-Bribery Convention, which requires lobbyists to register with the government and to report contacts with public officials. The weak finances of Greek mass media, their close relationships with politicians, and the failure of the Greek government to promptly legislate proper use of the electromagnetic spectrum as a state asset or to enforce existing legislation have been blamed as factors that prevent media from exercising their normal mission to expose government corruption or safeguard the public interest (Eleftheriadis 2012).[8] Greek law and constitutional rules require parliamentary approval before prosecutors can investigate or bring to trial any members of Parliament or serving government ministers. Even with such approval, the actions of current or past ministers are protected by statutes of limitations that expire within one year of the alleged misconduct. Malfeasance by politicians or civil servants seldom leads to punishment. A grand total of only 91 civil servants had been dismissed for bribery or corruption from the beginning of 2012 through the middle of 2013 (Inspector General of Public Administration 2014).

Transparency International blames many factors, including some of the above, for the high level of corruption in Greece: dysfunctional democracy, weak rule of law, lack of transparency in the work of the government, influence of political parties on public administration, excessive discretion in the exercise of public authority, legislative complexity, bureaucracy, lack of audits and sanctions, lack of codes of conduct in the public and private sectors, complex mechanisms for identifying corruption, anemic civil society, and inadequate education of citizens in matters of corruption. There are, naturally, a multitude of other factors at work as well, including waste of financial resources, distortion of competition, weak moral codes, a spreading culture of tolerance and fatalism, and prevalence of a system of corrupt legality (Transparency International 2013d, p. 26). This report also outlines the evolving legal framework for combating corruption in Greece.

As we have already mentioned, closely related to corruption is the phenomenon of tax evasion because of two reasons: one, it is reported to involve large-scale bribery of public officials; two, it is another and conceptually related instance of antisocial behavior. What are the facts about tax evasion in Greece?

Using micro data supplied by a large private bank, Artavanis, Morse, and Tsoutsoura (2016) estimate unreported income in 2009 to be at least 10 percent of GDP, and the foregone tax revenues to be 30 percent of the government deficit in that year.[9] Matsaganis, Leventi, and Flevotomou (2012) give alternative estimates based on Greek tax returns and on the EU Survey of Income and Living Standards conducted from 2006 to 2010. They find that 11.8 percent of income was underreported on average in 2006, resulting in a shortfall of tax receipts of 27.8 percent (ibid. p. 27).[10] For the top 1 and 0.1 percent of incomes, their estimates of income underreporting are 24.9 and 30.1 percent, respectively. They also find that self-employed persons report on average only 60 percent of their actual income and farmers only 20 percent.

Income tax evasion in Greece is, not surprisingly, facilitated by its extensive informal sector. Lost tax revenue was estimated at 27.5 percent of GDP on average between 1999 and 2007, higher than any other EU country and higher than the OECD average of 20 percent (Schneider and Buehn 2012). The problem is multifaceted (see IMF 2013). Tax revenue is lost because business activity is not formally declared and registered but operates underground in the shadow economy, because individuals evade taxes, and because tax evaders use legal but often unfair means to escape payment.

Tax avoidance, as distinct from tax evasion, is plausibly due to reliance on ambiguities, loopholes, and convenient self-serving interpretations that help reduce tax obligations. For example, social security contributions are much smaller for self-employed relative to salaried employees, which increases the attractiveness of self-employment and thus affects occupational choice leading to smaller average sizes of business organizations.

Like the income tax, the value-added tax (VAT) is also evaded. Actual VAT collections relative to expected revenues are much lower in Greece compared to the EU average. The same applies for corporate tax collections. The IMF (2013) reports that the VAT gap in Greece in 2006 was 30 percent, compared to an EU average of 12 percent. Income tax and VAT rates in Greece are at the high end among OECD countries. Undisputed tax arrears reached 56 billion euros at the end of 2012, nearly 90 percent of annual revenue collection, more than 60 percent higher than any other EU country except Slovakia. Tax arrears may themselves lead to real tax revenue loss (Tagkalakis 2014).

Audits by the tax authorities tend to focus on bookkeeping formalities rather than assessments of tax liabilities, and are generally not as productive because they use limited third-party information (e.g., access to bank accounts) to detect inconsistencies between declared and actual income and wealth. Despite high nominal penalties for tax evasion, poor management of audits and frequent tax amnesties make it cheaper for taxpayers not to declare tax liabilities even if the taxable income is eventually detected.

Corruption in the delivery of public services along with poor quality and excessive bureaucracy can combine with social permissiveness to sustain tax evasion. Furthermore the glaring inability of the government to pursue tax evasion by particular groups of the population can feed into the public perception of an unfair tax collection system. Salaried employees, who have fewer opportunities to evade audits, are subject to payroll taxes deducted at source and therefore pay more in taxes.

It is natural to wonder about how deeply rooted corruption and tax evasion are in Greece. Economists have sought to understand the origins of antisocial behavior, and their insights might be helpful in thinking about how to combat corruption and tax evasion. Papaioannou (2011) in his "Civic Capital(ism)" TEDx Talk[11] seeks deep causes of the Greek crisis rather than proximate ones. By drawing attention away from the twin deficits, he instead advances the challenging view that the true causes of the crisis are entrenched in the social values and lack of civic capital in Greece. Papaioannou sees the current state of legal institutions, property rights, regulation, and protection of investors as generally weak and not conducive to the modernization of Greece. Another key factor is trust, an essential part of civic or social capital. Many studies show that distrust is negatively correlated with income per capita and positively correlated with corruption.

Algan and Cahuc (2014) offer numerous tabulations of trust-related measures deriving from the World Values Survey and the European Values Survey (1981–2008). The key variable they use is the answer to the question: "Generally speaking, would you say that most people can be trusted or that you need to be very careful in dealing with people?" Trust is recorded as 1, if the respondent answers "Most people can be trusted," and 0, otherwise. The average trust levels over the study period they tabulate (shown in figure 13.2) place Greece below all other EU countries, except for Latvia, Croatia, Malta, Slovenia, Slovakia, Portugal, Romania, and Cyprus, and numerous non-EU countries. Relative to Norway, which ranks highest, and holding individual characteristics constant, the fact of living in Greece rather than Norway reduces trust by 51 percent (ibid., p. 69). Data show that generalized trust is an important contributor to economic growth.

Trust is negatively correlated with the prevalence of labor market regulations (Algan and Cahuc 2014, fig. 2.13, p. 95), and with inequality, as measured by the Gini

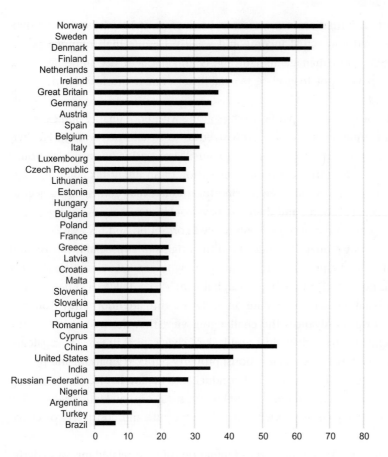

Figure 13.2
Average trust levels in EU and other countries.
Source: Algan and Cahuc (2014, fig. 2.1b)

coefficient (ibid., fig. 2.16), while it is positively correlated with the quality of the legal system (ibid., fig. 2.14), and with life satisfaction (ibid., fig. 2.19).

One question asked of respondents in the Social Values Survey was: "Do you think it can always be justified, never be justified, or something in between to claim government/state benefits to which you have no rights?" Papaioannou (2013, pp. 54–56) shows that Greece is an outlier. While in most countries more than 60 percent of the population believes that people should never claim social benefits that they do not have a right to, in Cyprus, France, and Slovenia more than half of respondents argued that at least in some instances it is justifiable to claim such benefits." For Greece, the only survey available that includes this question is in 2000. It reports that almost 80 percent of the population replied that it was justifiable to get benefits from the state that one is not entitled to.[12]

The provision of public goods requires cooperation to achieve socially beneficial outcomes in the presence of free-rider incentives. Voting, paying taxes, fighting corruption, contributing to public goods, teamwork, common pool resource management, recycling, are just some examples where cooperative behavior pays off. These are frequent situations with the common feature that cooperation leads to a beneficial outcome for an entire group but is jeopardized by selfish incentives to free ride on others' contributions. Below we make further progress along such lines by clarifying that the same fundamentals may be associated with multiple alternative social outcomes, seen as social equilibria.

Herrmann et al. (2008) report results from laboratory experiments with public goods games, focusing on a phenomenon that has been largely neglected: People might punish not only free-riders but cooperators too. For example, in an experimental game that those researchers set up, participants who had been punished in the past for contributing too little might retaliate against cooperators because cooperators are precisely those individuals most likely to punish the free-riding low contributors. The experimental evidence, obtained by these researchers from 16 participant pools with various cultural and economic backgrounds across the world, shows that antisocial punishment of prosocial cooperators is indeed widespread in many participant pools. Societies covered in this study diverge strongly according to several widely used criteria developed by social scientists to characterize collective behavior.[13]

The results are notable. The Athens pool, made up of samples of Panteion University students, scored lowest of all 16 cities in the experiment judged by the mean recorded contributions to the public good over the 10 experiment rounds. At the same time, the Athens pool scored the second highest in terms of mean antisocial retaliation, with average retaliation and average contributions per participant pool being very strongly and significantly negatively correlated across all periods. The authors interpret the findings as suggesting that the quality of the formal law enforcement institutions and informal sanctions are complementary. Informal sanctions might be more effective in sustaining voluntary cooperation when formal law enforcement institutions operate more effectively because antisocial retaliation is lower in these societies. The detrimental effects of antisocial punishment on cooperation (and efficiency) also provide a further explanation why modern societies shun revenge and centralize punishment in the hands of the state. This particular finding involving the Athens subject pools could have been dismissed as unimportant, were it not for the fact that it agrees with a common exhortation used among Greek youths, in high schools and university settings. Advice like "don't spoil the market" is directed at persons who violate current norms of antisocial behavior, and thus helps maintain solidarity with and adherence to commonly agreed rules of antisocial behavior.[14]

It is tempting to interpret the widespread incidence of corruption as an intrinsic Greek characteristic. However, a comparison with Cyprus, a country that is culturally and linguistically very similar to Greece, might suggest otherwise. Cyprus has consistently scored much higher in Transparency International rankings while Greece has been slipping. Furthermore, indirect evidence that cultural origin effects in corruption may be overcome by institutions is reported by Barr and Serra (2010). These authors conducted a bribery lab experiment in the United Kingdom and found that, among undergraduates, they could indeed predict who would act corruptly using as a predictor the level of corruption in their home country. That effect disappeared, however, among graduate students. They replicated their result in 2007 and also found that time spent in the United Kingdom was associated with a decline in the propensity to bribe, although that finding did not explain their inability to predict behavior among graduate students. These authors conclude that while corruption may, in part, be a cultural phenomenon, individuals should not be prejudged by their country of origin.

13.3   Social Equilibria with Antisocial Behavior

Let us think about a typical public policy situation where individual welfare depends on the consumption of a private good, of leisure, and of a public good. Next assume that a government imposes a proportional tax on labor incomes to finance the provision of the public good. To simplify matters, suppose that labor income taxation does not affect labor supply. A benchmark solution occurs when a hypothetical benevolent government sets the income tax rate to achieve maximum social welfare by balancing the loss of individual welfare (when taxes are raised and private consumption falls) against the improvement in social welfare from the higher provision of the public good.

To study the impact of rampant tax evasion, we assume that individuals can ignore with impunity the official tax rate, and in effect set their own tax rates, while recognizing that public good provision has to be financed somehow. Since public goods cannot be financed out of nothing, individuals must decide how much they wish to contribute, assuming a given level of contribution by other taxpayers. Everyone acts in like manner: they all recognize that they stand to benefit from the provision of the public good at some level, and as a result each one of them free rides on everyone else. When individuals decide how much to contribute, each one takes as given, and beyond their control, the amounts they expect others will contribute. The resulting level of the public good financed from the sum total of everyone's contribution would typically be lower than what a benevolent government would choose by extracting mandatory contributions from all citizens, that is, by fully enforcing taxation. This reflects poor social coordination, which in turn leads to an inferior social outcome.

The inferior social outcome becomes a "race to the bottom"; it is the outcome of free riding by each individual contributor who wishes to prevent a wholly undesirable loss of welfare to himself, all along assuming that others will also contribute. The greater the number of other individuals contributing, the less each one will want to share. The individually optimal "voluntary tax rates" sum up to less than what would have been the socially optimal rate. This story is a caricature of a tax system intended only to underscore the consequences of a government's inability to enforce tax compliance on individual citizens. Nonetheless, as a way to think about Greece's tax problem, it is quite a useful one, as we discuss next.

13.3.1 Good and Bad Social Equilibria

Implicit in the description above is the idea that each individual's optimally chosen "own tax rate" is unique, given the behavior of others. This does not have to be true in general, and indeed it is likely not to be in many settings where the social context matters. We return to this in more detail below, but to see it simply, suppose that individuals are conformist, that is, they follow what they *expect* others to do. Then the more similar individuals are in terms of their underlying characteristics, the more likely it is that their expectation of what others are likely to do (which we call social effects here) is decisive in determining individual choice. This in fact generates the possibility of three alternative patterns ("equilibria"). Good intentions to pay one's "fair share" of taxes can be overcome by the impact of bad influences from one's social milieu, that is, by a strong urge to conform to what others are doing. Suppose that social effects are originally weak. That is, few people are prepared to pay substantial contributions toward the public good. As social effects become stronger, initially they-induce (or perhaps encourage) individuals to follow what is developing as the dominant social behavior. Ultimately, the impact of social effects on individual behavior may weaken and vanish, but there will be some "reasonable" norms of behavior that are self-confirming.

This possibility is demonstrated in figure 13.3, where the horizontal axis measures a typical individual's *expectation* of the social outcome and the vertical axis measures an individual's own expected outcome. The three different curves A, B, and C picture different sets of fundamentals. When the expected outcome for an individual coincides with his/her expectation of the social outcome, then society is in what is known as *Nash equilibrium*. This is pictured when the 45-degree line through the origin intersects with the respective curve. A formal derivation of figure 13.3 as well as a full presentation of the model sketched in this section, can be found in this chapter's appendix, available at https://mitpress.mit.edu/books/beyond-austerity.

When individuals are really different, large fractions of the population will experience large differences in the random factors that determine individual choice. Included among those are social effects. That will narrow the scope for self-confirming behavior. Curve A corresponds to the situation where noncompliance is inherently more attractive, relative to an individual's evaluation of the social outcome, and thus noncompliance prevails as the unique social outcome (m^- for curve A is on the negative half-axis). In such a case, marginal improvements in enforcement, either by means of more and possibly random[15] audits and/or larger penalties, can increase the inherent attractiveness of compliance. However, given fundamentals, enforcement needs to be sufficiently powerful to shift the curve to a higher position, like curve B, and if they are drastic enough to shift it to curve C. Similarly curve C corresponds to the situation where compliance is inherently more attractive, relative to an individual's evaluation of the social outcome, and thus compliance prevails as the unique social outcome (m^{**} for curve C is on the positive half-axis).

If individuals are broadly similar, the social effect is more powerful than other determinants. The social effect at first dominates individual attitudes, then becomes proportional to them, and at the end tapers off. This is exactly the analytical setting that allows multiple self-confirming behaviors in socioeconomic systems. The idea is pictured by curve B, figure 13.3, which intersects with the 45-degree line at three points, m^-, m, and m^*. We note that such a situation could indeed be the outcome of stricter enforcement, relative to curve A, but still not strong enough to shift it up to curve C, which is associated with compliance as a unique equilibrium indicated by point m^{**}.

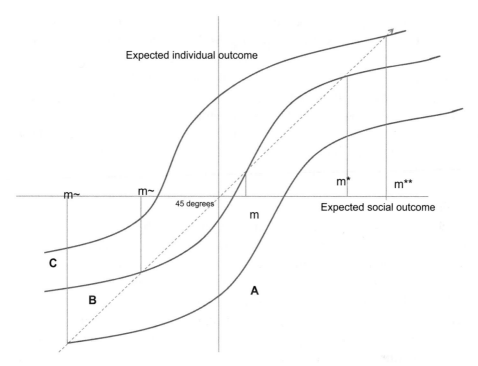

Expected individual outcome

m~   m~   m*   m**

45 degrees   Expected social outcome

m

C

B   A

Figure 13.3
Multiple equilibria in antisocial behavior

We underscore that only drastic enforcement can move the economy from, say, point *m* on curve *B* to point *m*** on curve *C*, that is, from widespread noncompliance to widespread compliance.

This mode of thinking validates, *inter alia,* using perceptions of corruption (which underlies the Transparency International Rankings) as an indicator of actual corruption. In box 13.1 we report an econometric analysis with Eurobarometer data that makes particular use of information on both perceptions and experience of corruption.

So far we have discussed taxation as motivated by the need to finance the provision of public goods. Of course, taxation also finances redistribution and the demand for redistribution is often a justification for larger governments. A number of studies that are of particular relevance to Greece link bigger governments to more corruption, and more corruption in turn raises support for redistributive policies to mitigate the effects of unequal access to returns from corruption across the population. If opportunities to engage in corruption and rent-seeking are unequally distributed in the population, and/or generate wealth that is unequally distributed, a positive feedback from past to present corruption emerges that in turn reinforces the persistence of bigger governments. Alesina and Angeletos (2005) show that under certain conditions multiple steady-state equilibria may exist that are entirely due to the presence of corruption. Thus political support for redistributive policies intended to reduce inequality can bring about more corruption. Corruption begets more corruption through bigger governments, in those settings. At the same time inspection of figure 13.1 suggests that EU countries with big governments and big public sectors do very well in terms of corruption, which implies that other forces are present, such as redistributive policies that do not necessarily discourage work and investment.

13.3.2   Social Effects in Tax Evasion

Individuals' attitudes toward tax evasion are likely shaped by social forces.[16] Hence our understanding of tax evasion[17] is likely to improve our ability to design policy. Yet there is no empirical research with actual data. Existing research studies on the topic use either experimental data, such as Fortin et al. (2007) and Kaplanoglou and Rapanos (2015), or numerical simulations, such as Llacer et al. (2013).

Kaplanoglou and Rapanos (2015), in particular, report results from an experimental study using 350 volunteer subjects, recruited from among undergraduates at the University of Athens who were assigned to four hypothetical settings and instructed accordingly.[18] Their econometric analysis shows that trust increases voluntary compliance, and power (defined as tax authorities' working efficiently and implementing tax laws) increases enforced compliance. Power has no influence on voluntary compliance in the high-trust setting, but high power is associated with lower voluntary compliance in low-trust setting. The authors interpret these findings as suggesting that power of tax authorities is perceived as legitimate in high-trust conditions but as coercive otherwise.

We conclude this section by recalling that when social effects influence individual decisions about tax compliance, they create multiple tax evasion outcomes. Nonlinearity is critical for equilibrium multiplicity and is associated with presence of endogenous social effects. Unfortunately, there have been no empirical studies anywhere with real data that can be brought to bear on the question of social effects in tax compliance, however plausible the presence of such effects might seem.

At the same time we note that positive association of the fundamentals many associate with social trust is quite consistent with this story. Factors that cause trust to improve bring about better social outcomes. Yet such a positive association, as in the studies we discussed earlier, glosses over possibilities that may be fruitfully examined as multiple local equilibria.

13.3.3   Corruption: Measurement and Experience versus Perception

Despite the availability of corruption metrics, it is widely recognized that corruption is very hard to measure. Furthermore perceptions of corruption are often relied upon extensively in discussions of corruption. They form the basis for Transparency International's Annual Corruption Perception Index (CPI) and the World Bank's Control of Corruption Index. This leads to the natural question of how important a factor is the perception of corruption in influencing actual corruption? We find that this question has a natural answer from the theory of social interactions, and one that helps us better understand corruption as a social phenomenon.

Olken (2009) is a particularly significant study, in that it uses empirical evidence on perceptions of corruption and on actual corruption from Indonesia. Olken finds that perceptions of corruption do contain information about actual corruption. Olken and Pande (2012) review the evidence on corruption in developing countries and find robust evidence that corruption responds to standard economic incentives: for example, public officials find alternate strategies to pursue rents when anticorruption drives are in effect. Still, corruption as actually measured (see Olken and Pande 2012, tab. 1) appears to be rather small.

In an effort to bring as much information as possible to bear upon the incidence of corruption in Greece, relative to the other EU countries, Ioannides and Murthy (2014) use micro data from all four cross sections of the Eurobarometer to study the experience of corruption against the perception of corruption across all EU countries. Their ordered logit regression (with the experience of corruption as a dependent variable and perception of corruption as an explanatory variable) takes account of groups of observations associated with different EU countries and allows for a large number of additional explanatory variables based on individual demographics. These variables are defined and more details are given in box 13.1. The perception of corruption is highly significant at the 1 percent level, with a positive coefficient for all four survey years, while controlling for all other variables. This finding suggests that the social effect, as defined by these authors, is important. Admittedly, the Ioannides and Murthy finding does rely on those authors' interpretation of the survey questions. This does not mean that corruption perceptions "cause" corrupt behavior; it is nonetheless evidence of a social effect. The higher the perception of corruption, the higher is the experience of corruption. Quantitatively, for 2005, a one-unit increase in perception of corruption would increase the log odds of experiencing one more instance of corruption by 0.125. The country dummy for Greece is positive and highly significant. This means that, everything else being equal, Greek respondents were more likely to experience corruption. See box 13.1 for more details.

Box 13.1

The Eurobarometer study publishes micro data for 2005, 2007, 2009, 2011, and 2013 (Eurobarometer Data, various years) based on roughly 1,000 observations from each EU country, amounting to a total of 26,856 observations. Ioannides and Murthy (2014) interpret as *perception of corruption* the answer to the following question (2011, QC4): "In (our country), do you think that the giving and the taking of bribes, and the abuse of positions of power for personal gain, are widespread among any of the following?" The categories listed range from police; customs; the judiciary; politicians at the national, regional, and local levels; officials awarding contracts or business and building permits; people working in the public education or the public health sectors; to inspectors in health, construction, food quality, sanitary control, and licensing. Ioannides and Murthy recode the micro data as the sum of affirmative responses under these categories into a categorical variable ranging from 0 to 14. They interpret as *experience of corruption* the following question (2011, QC5): "Over the last 12 months, has anyone (in our country) asked you, or expected you, to pay a bribe for his or her services?" They recode the micro data as a categorical variable, that ranges from 0, if the answer is "No, nobody did," or equal to the sum of individual responses to each of the categories above. Interestingly, those two variables in their raw data form are very weakly correlated: their Spearman correlation coefficient is equal to 0.177. Thus they likely report different information.

Ioannides and Murthy experiment with a number of alternative econometric specifications: one is a Poisson regression because the recoded data is based on counts; a second is an ordered logit regression with the experience of corruption as a dependent variable, and the perception of corruption as an explanatory variable, along with country dummy variables for each of the EU countries. They choose to emphasize the ordered logit regression because, as the online appendix to the present chapter clarifies, its underlying analytics fit better the canonical social interactions approach adopted by this chapter. That is, the ordered logit model expresses analytically very well that the likelihood of experiencing corruption is related to the perception of corruption through the cumulative distribution of the logistic function. The estimation allows for 13 discrete thresholds plus a large number of explanatory variables based on all available individual demographics, such as age ranges, occupational categories, and gender. Regressions were carried out separately for all five survey years and show the following results:

1. The perception of corruption is statistically highly significant, variable, at the 1 percent level, with positive coefficients, while controlling for all other variables. This shows that the social effect is important.

2. The higher the perception of corruption, the higher the experience of corruption. In particular, the estimated coefficients for perception of corruption are 0.114, 0.0895, 0.0724, and 0.0677, respectively, for 2005, 2007, 2009, and 2011, all significant at the 1 percent level. Quantitatively, for 2005, a one unit increase in perception of corruption would increase the log odds of experiencing one more instance of corruption by 0.125.

Box 13.1 (continued)

3. The country dummy for Greece is positive and significant at less than 1 percent for all samples except 2007 and 2009, when it is significant at 5 percent.

4. Among the various EU countries, and for 2013, the country dummy is also positive and significant (in addition to Greece) for Austria, Czech Republic, Estonia, Hungary, Latvia, Lithuania, Poland, Slovakia, Bulgaria, Romania, and Croatia. It is negative and significant for Great Britain and Sweden, and it is insignificant for all other countries.

5. The estimated country dummy for Greece is the second smallest among those that are significant. Among the other countries, the largest coefficient is for Lithuania followed by Romania. There is, however, variation among the countries over the four different survey years.

In order to help mitigate possible criticism of this formulation, namely that it might be that experience of corruption causes perception of corruption, Ioannides and Murthy (2014) also regress perception of corruption against experience of corruption. The estimated coefficient of experience of corruption is also very significant; those for the other regressors are not as intuitively appealing, and the overall fit is slightly inferior. The interpretation of such a regression is, however, akin to social learning, and thus provides support for the notion of social effect. Although those two variables are weakly correlated, the more corruption citizens experience the greater the perception of its importance. We hasten to add that one should not attempt to interpret the coefficients of the dummy variables indicating specific countries as implying that the larger the coefficient, the higher is the experience of corruption unconditionally. Instead, the interpretation is conditional on the values of all other explanatory variables. The effect of the perception of corruption is in fact very different across the EU countries, when regressions are run with country-specific data separately. We feel that these estimates provide a tentative justification for the significance of social influences on corruption.

13.3.4 Industrial Organization of Corruption in Greece and Its Implications[19]

Our analysis so far has addressed corruption primarily by means of microeconomic tools. We have looked at how individuals make decisions in a social context and how individual responses can be consistent with society-wide alternative patterns of widespread, moderate, or rare corruption. Government policy can interfere with individual decisions and thus avert antisocial outcomes, a possibility that is easiest to contemplate in the context of tax evasion. As the online appendix to this chapter shows, sufficiently vigorous enforcement by high probabilities of audits and/or larger penalties for noncompliance can induce the typical individual, and thus a social group, to move toward full compliance.

Improving tax compliance in practice requires honest behavior by the tax collection administration as well: employees at several hierarchical layers of bureaucracy may be exposed to similar temptations for dishonest behavior as individual taxpayers. In view of at least anecdotal evidence of corruption by tax authorities in Greece,[20] anticorruption policies must address the "industrial organization" of corruption, a term due to Shleifer and Vishny (1993). A similar problem occurs with requesting permits or licenses, where several layers of a particular public sector branch must sign off on a particular authorization, making an individual vulnerable to requests for bribes and quid pro quos, or other forms of rent-seeking. Thus, for an individual dealing with the Greek public sector, all levels of the respective bureaucracy must sign off, creating a complementarity among all those steps. In countries like Greece, the public sector does not only generate delays and excess-permitting costs but also provides many opportunities for corrupt behavior. It is necessary to stamp out all of the opportunities in every hierarchy of decision making in order to create an effective administration. Thus fighting corruption can be combined with reforming the organizational structure of the public sector by reducing its bureaucratic structure and simplifying its provision of services. At the same time we know from Shleifer and Vishny (1993) and Aghion et al. (2010) that government regulation is strongly correlated with distrust. Improving social trust along with simplifying government regulations will likely help make the public sector less conducive to corrupt behavior.

Policies aimed at stamping out corruption must recognize the incidence of corruption in a modern society. There are instances of large-scale corruption involving bribes and other forms of rent-seeking associated with politicians in charge of major public sector procurements, like defense equipment purchases and public works contracting. Any legal system would treat such instances of corruption differently from petty "decentralized" corruption affecting individual citizens dealing with the public sector. Of course, when practiced extensively, the private and social costs of petty corruption add up to serious macro consequences, and must be dealt with. Other instances of decentralized corruption are accommodated by cooperative social values and can be pervasive. For example, public servants in personnel recruitment positions have unlimited ways to favor relatives, friends, and acquaintances.[21] In many societies, and arguably in Greece too, it is culturally and socially acceptable to trade meritocracy for favoritism. This results in a culture of permissiveness. Such practices cannot be easily stamped out by means of specific policies and instead require long-run efforts through the educational system, to be complemented by the efforts of parents and all institutions involved in shaping the value systems of younger generations.[22]

In important ways the clientelistic nature of the Greek political system plays a big role in maintaining decentralized petty corruption. That is, by granting favors of different sorts within their bailiwicks (e.g., public sector jobs, favoritism in access to social benefits, special grandfathering deals, and exclusive or even fraudulent loan guarantees) corrupt politicians help ensure their own survival. There exists a socially decentralized demand for corruption transmitted via the political system, met by the wholesale supply and facilitation of corruption at the top. Such a symbiotic relationship is best highlighted by the famously crude pronouncement (and book by the same name) by former Deputy Prime Minister Theodore Pangalos, *Together We Looted Everything* (Pangalos 2012). However crudely cynical and self-serving, especially since it is from such a long-standing and prominent PASOK politician, that phrasing is quite apt: it does prompt questions about how Greek civil society instills values and moral fundamentals in political life. If antisocial behavior in the form of corrupt practices is deeply ingrained and entangled with the political system, via interactions between citizens and politicians, then even the most draconian punishment of offending politicians will not go far enough in eliminating antisocial behavior.[23]

13.4 Corruption and Growth

13.4.1 Fiscal Deficits and Corruption

Corruption affects a country's government spending through several channels. First, a given amount of public expenditure delivers less in terms of goods and services. Welfare fraud, lack of transparency, and kickbacks in awarding public projects stand out and have regularly been mentioned in many countries, including Greece, as leading examples of corruption. Second, corruption in the form of tax evasion lowers the tax yield from standing tax legislation. Corrupt practices in the management of public debt add to the deficit by increasing borrowing costs and interest rate spreads. They may also increase the perceived uncertainty associated with a country's public debt. By increasing the cost of doing business, corruption also lessens competitiveness and thus contributes to external deficits.

In industrialized countries, possible causal links between fiscal deficits and corruption have not been investigated until relatively recently. Kaufmann (2010) is a notable exception. He draws attention to the fact that measures of corruption control like the World Governance Indicators compiled by the World Bank vary widely among EU countries: one standard deviation between Greece and Spain and more than two standard deviations between Greece and Finland. These variations correspond to large differences in fiscal balances, positive for Finland, negative for Spain and even more so for Greece. The coexistence of several channels between corruption, government spending, and taxes leads to a correlation coefficient of 0.52 between corruption control and fiscal balance (Kaufmann 2010). Achury, Koulovatianos, and Tsoukalas (2013) show that among eurozone countries during 1996 to 2010, fiscal balance improves 1 percent per unit increase of the Corruption Perception Index!

Achury, Koulovatianos, and Tsoukalas (2013) also offer a political economy theory of how excessive rent-seeking and noncooperation by rent seekers worsens a country's ability to handle fiscal deficits, and thus exacerbates debt dynamics. The mechanism they highlight is a tragedy-of-the-commons problem leading to a vicious circle of high interest rates and default. If rent-seeking groups are not prepared to cooperate in fiscal governance, then excessive debt issuance is inevitable. Noncooperating rent-seeking groups wish to avail themselves of additional resources earlier, before other groups do so, which amounts to collective "impatience." The greater the number of rent-seeking groups, the greater is the collective impatience. This impatience leads to demands for high interest rates from the nation's creditors and immediate or eventual sovereign default. By increasing the uncertainty about a country's fiscal management as perceived by the markets, corrupt practices fuel a spiral of increasing borrowing spreads and further increases in deficits, very much like self-fulfilling currency crises. Their model implies that to prevent such a dysfunctional outcome in the presence of rent seekers, a country needs to maintain a lower debt-to-GDP ratio.

13.4.2 Institutions and Growth

If corruption is not an inherent attribute in any society, it must be a matter of choice for some or all of its citizens. This trivial syllogism means that Swiss citizens have made a deliberate choice in favor of sound institutions while the citizens of many nations in South Asia, Latin America, and Southern Europe have gone the other way. How societies choose institutions has been a central theme in political economy and economic history since the 1970s (see North 1990; Skaperdas 1992; Acemoglu et al. 2005). Of particular importance in this literature is the social choice of property rights, namely of the fraction of income earned by labor and capital that society chooses to shield from the rapacity of thieves, corrupt officials, and other rent seekers.

To understand what is at stake, consider an economy consisting of many different individuals. Suppose that all of them are equally good at rent seeking (e.g., with gross productivity equal to one unit) but unequal at earning honest income (e.g., gross productivity varies from one-half to two units). How will individuals divide into mutually exclusive groups of workers and rent seekers, that is, between productive activities and corruption? How will voters collectively decide how much to protect property rights?

Firmly enforced property rights in this context function like a tax on the productivity of rent seekers, which reduces revenue from dishonest work. Strong property rights will deter rent seekers from appropriating honestly earned income and, perhaps more important, reduce the attractiveness of rent-seeking as an occupation. On the minus side, good institutions are expensive: they need to be implemented by a judicial system of laws, judges, prosecutors, inspectors, and police who must be paid by taxes levied on honest citizens. Societies seem to face a trade-off between two taxes: the cost of corruption and the cost of enforcement. For any level of property rights, rational individuals will choose the occupation—thieving or honest work—that gives them the highest income. For example, a relatively expensive regime of firm property rights will tax honest work and deliver low corruption and few rent seekers. This choice will appeal to most productive citizens but not to those who have a comparative advantage in rent-seeking. Having many educated citizens raises the chances that society will choose firm property rights over lax ones and good institutions over feeble ones.

What does this mean for the questions asked at the beginning of this subsection? Why have Swiss citizens consistently opted for stronger, and more expensive, institutions than those in other countries? Four reasons seem to be of relevance to the Swiss experience. (1) A large mass of Swiss citizens is sufficiently educated to earn incomes above those of rent seekers. (2) Switzerland is rich enough in capital to the point where relatively labor-intensive rent-seeking does not pay off as well as honest work that is more capital intensive. (3) Expectations of strong property rights discourage rent seekers and raise the fraction of citizens who favor good institutions. (4) Any political bias toward the status quo discourages changes in existing institutions—good or bad. Switzerland benefits from this inertia. Greece suffers from it.

Finally, we need to understand a bit more deeply the importance of civic capital as a self-reinforcing mechanism that steers society toward good outcomes when civic capital exists in abundance, and to poor outcomes when it is in short supply. Civic capital reinforces itself when it influences how well the public expects institutions to work in the future. Will society govern itself by rules that are fair to all or by laws stacked in favor of certain groups? When civic capital is plentiful and institutions treat everyone fairly, citizens will choose honest work over corruption in overwhelming numbers, thereby reducing the corruption tax to insignificance and enhancing the economic attractiveness of honest work. A large amount of this "capital" is a good substitute for strong deterrence against criminals and embezzlers or for an all-out war against corruption. Crime does not pay when civil society is well developed.

At the most basic level, civic capital is a form of shared trust that society will be ruled by transparency, fairness, and peace. From a technical standpoint, civic capital is an *equilibrium selection device*, that is, a set of habits and moral codes that leads societies to select good outcomes over mediocre or bad ones when all three are possible.

An example from public finance is a clear case in point. Governments that wish to raise a given sum in tax revenue have two options: impose a low tax rate that will enlarge their tax base and bring in the desired tax revenue, or choose a high tax rate that shrinks taxable incomes and collects the same revenue. The first outcome is more desirable and feasible if citizens do not evade taxes. The second one is inevitable when they do. Which one prevails depends on civic capital, that is, on what each citizen expects others will do.

13.5 Conclusions and Policy Recommendations

13.5.1 Conclusions

Writing in *The New Yorker*, July 11, 2011, James Surowiecki states:

If a hefty chunk of the population is cheating on its taxes, people who don't (or can't, because of the way their income is reported) feel that they're being abused. The result has been a vicious circle: because tax evasion is so common, people trust the system less, which makes them less willing to pay taxes. And, because so many don't chip in, the government has had to raise taxes on those who do. That only increases the incentive to cheat, since there tends to be a correlation between higher tax rates and higher rates of tax evasion.

Because corruption and tax evasion are so common, civic capital in Greece has contracted to the point where people do not trust the system much, which makes them less willing to behave honestly or pay taxes. A consequence of the government's raising taxes on those who do pay them is a disincentive to continue being honest. Thus tax rates are even higher if we add in the burden of corruption on honest economic activity. High tax rates only increase incentives to cheat still more and evade taxes to a greater extent, which completes the vicious circle but does not stop it.

The essence of the present chapter is that research brings both bad and good news. The bad news is that corruption is rampant in Greece, and with a much higher incidence than in other EU countries. One way to deal with it is by means of zero tolerance and vigorous relentless vigilance. As we now know, the successful criminal prosecution of Former Minister A. Tzochatzopoulos and his accomplices (for fiscally significant abuse of power and bribe-taking) has been particularly welcomed by Greek public opinion. A second way to deal with corruption is to design institutions that encourage honest behavior and facilitate reporting of abuses. The good news from this chapter is that an economic and social equilibrium that is permeated by corrupt practices is not the only possible social outcome. Taste for proper social behavior can be taught and learned, and adverse practices, discussed in this chapter, may be altered by suitable reforms and retraining of public servants. The EU Task Force for Greece is a very good case in point,[24] and so is the Greek Annex of the *EU Anti-Corruption Report*.[25] The latter details a specific legislative agenda to combat antisocial practices in Greece.

In announcing the US District Court verdict in the prosecution of Rod J. Blagojevich, former governor of Illinois, for corruption, US District Court Judge James B. Zagel[26] said before telling Mr. Blagojevich his fate: "The harm here is not measured in the value of property or money, the harm is the erosion of public trust in government."

13.5.2 Policy Recommendations

Governing requires trust. This is true for firms and organizations of all sizes and types. It is also true for every modern state. To restore public trust in the political process, we believe that *Greek citizens will have to witness political events that have never happened in the last fifty years*, in particular severe limits on the privileges of professional politicians, an all-out war on corruption, and fair taxation. Serious political reform, including all of the draconian proposals we list below, requires enormous changes. Those include not only changes in the current law but also constitutional amendments that facilitate prosecuting members of the executive, legislative, and judicial branches of government for embezzlement, for bribery, for tax evasion, and for other forms of illegal enrichment.

The policies we propose below to combat corruption fall into two categories: proposals 1 through 6, which require legislative changes within the existing constitutional framework, and amendments 1 through 3, which need constitutional tinkering. Among the proposals contained in the Greek Annex of the EU Anti-Corruption Report for 2014, we judge the following to be most urgent:

1. Institute legislative protection of whistleblowers.[27]

2. Formalize lobbying and compel lobbyists to register with the Office of the Inspector General of Public Administration and report all contacts with public officials.

3. Require political parties to keep and to publish audited income-and-expense statements, and mandate use of international auditors.

4. Abolish all statutes of limitations on crimes committed by members of Parliament and government ministers.

5. Improve the transparency of public procurement, and the capacity of the Supreme Audit Council to oversee state purchases.

6. Devise and implement strategies to combat fraud in pensions, healthcare, and the tax administration.

Implementing these proposals will be immensely facilitated if citizens come to place a bit more trust in their government. To achieve that, we suggest the following constitutional amendments.

To discourage politics as a lifetime career we propose three amendments:

Amendment 1 Parliament is reduced to 100 members. After a maximum of 12 years of service, members become ineligible for re-election or for any paid or unpaid work in the broader public sector.

We note that the current Greek Constitution does allow for the number of its members to be 200, a limit that could be enacted by means of a law.[28] There is also a fair amount of experience with term limits worldwide, which could be used to bolster the case with the Greek public. Given that the time between elections and the life spans of Greek parliaments have become shorter, term limits should reflect both time in office and the life span of the respective Parliaments.

To combat embezzlement and bribery at high levels, we propose a draconian

Amendment 2

1. Embezzlement, bribery, and other serious misuses of public funds or positions of authority are a high crime for politicians, for labor and business leaders, and for high-level civil servants. Charges of these crimes can be filed with no statute of limitations by any citizen or public prosecutor, and must be adjudicated to a final conclusion within one year by specially constituted administrative courts. Those convicted face mandatory penalties that include loss of pension rights, forfeiture of embezzled wealth, and life imprisonment.

2. The forfeited wealth of convicted embezzlers is shared between the Greek state and citizens who filed charges.

3. Victims of unproved or disproved corruption charges are entitled to compensation from their accusers.

To combat tax evasion, whose arrears amount to 25 percent of Greek public debt as of this writing, we propose the following:

Amendment 3 Major tax evasion is a crime punishable by fines and incarceration. Tax returns of wealthy individuals are audited regularly and randomly by anonymous tax officials.

Draconian measures to be effective require expedient adjudication of cases. This provides additional arguments in favor of critical reforms in the Greek justice system, whose weaknesses are examined in depth in chapter 12. Draconian measures that are legislated but are not truly implemented (including measures mandated by the agreements associated with the Stabilization Program) breed cynicism and are unfortunately a serious problem in Greece, especially since much of the administration of the justice system is not immune to government pressure. Draconian measures, of course, pit the need to confer discretion to elected officials and to protect them against witch-hunting and political party agendas, while they are disposing of their duties, against the checks and balances of a democratic society. Ultimately, improving the ability of the country's legal system underpins the effective administration of effective measures.

Thus fresh approaches must be sought, including empowering independent authorities. The example of Hong Kong, touted by Romer (2010), is a good case in point and argues in favor of the design of a supranational institution to fight corruption, which could operate along the lines of others EU supranational institutions, like the European Court of Auditors and the Office of the European Ombudsman and its national offshoots.[29] An independent supranational authority can also be answerable directly to heads of state.[30] It is our conviction that it would take a very high-level approach beyond the purview of local political control, with EU-level institutions playing a role akin to that of US federal authorities vis-à-vis US states.

With a need for a proper phrasing in terms of constitutional language aside, these three amendments must also be accompanied by concerted efforts to build up civic capital. Our goal is to generate a consensus for changing the entire value system of nihilism and antisocial behavior that parents and schools have allowed to percolate through Greek society. We realize that deep structural changes go against long-held privileges of established interest groups and also against the inertia of the inherited status quo. As we have all learned from experience, investment and material progress are very difficult within the institutional corruption that is so thoroughly ingrained in the Greek body politic.

The key question is the same as it was when the present depression erupted in Greece around 2009: Will public opinion embrace the long-delayed reforms that are essential for the country's survival in the global environment of the 21st century? Or will they stand by and watch the nation slide into the backwater of the Balkans as it did from the 13th to the 18th century?

Notes

1. An earlier version of this chapter was presented before the GreekEconomistsforReform.com Workshop on "Crisis in the Eurozone Periphery and Policy Options for Greece," May 27–28, 2013, Athens. We are grateful to Adair Morse for some useful tabulations with the Artavanis, Morse, and Tsoutsoura data that are referred to herein. We are also grateful to editors C. Meghir,

C. A. Pissarides, N. Vettas, and especially to D. Vayanos; to participants at the workshop; to Anna Hardman, Alexandros Kyrtsis, Manos Matsaganis, Elias Papaioannou, and John Tsitsiklis for very thoughtful comments, and to Andros Kourtellos for help with data.

2. See http://www.transparency.org/cpi2014/results, partial ranking for European Union and Western Europe. Greece shares internationally the same ranking (69) as Bulgaria, Italy, and Romania, which places this group of countries at the bottom among countries in the European Union and Western Europe.

3. Corruption is defined by the Eurobarometer Survey more broadly as "including, offering, giving, requesting and accepting bribes or kickbacks, valuable gifts and important favours, as well as any abuse of power for private gain" (Eurobarometer Data, various years).

4. A particularly egregious practice is the so-called 4:4:2 rule, according to which in dealing with tax liabilities produced by audits, revenue officers authorize a discount of 40 percent, collect 40 percent themselves, and let 20 percent accrue to the Treasury. This practice received notoriety when it was alleged by Professor Diomidis Spinellis, a former tax official during a public presentation at ELIAMEP, Athens. See http://www.tovima.gr/vimamen/guys/article/?aid=447524. We thank Alexandros Kyrtsis for this source.

5. See http://www.bbc.co.uk/news/magazine-20874650. Sites like www.edosafakelaki.org (*edosa fakelaki* is Greek for "I paid a bribe") invite anonymous (and eponymous) reports of corrupt practices, but it is unclear at this point what their impact is likely to be. The site www.ipaidabribe.com was set up by Janaagraha NGO, located in Bangalore, India, as a forum for public awareness on corruption in receiving services from the Indian public sector (see Tanaka 2013).

Encouraging signs do appear from time to time in Greece. The fact that the government's firing of the CEO of the Hellenic Republic Asset Development Fund, apparently for having demonstrated egregious disregard to serious conflict of interest, and the furor it caused in the press, are both hopefully indicative of changing sensibilities, if not attitudes.

6. For an evaluation of this relatively new Greek institution to date, see Ladi (2011).

7. See Eurobarometer Data (various years) and Eurobarometer Survey (2012, 2014).

8. Eleftheriadis (2012) writes in connection with the role of the decline of the press: "Until 1989 radio and television were a government monopoly. After a series of inconclusive court battles, a group of businessmen started broadcasting terrestrial television programmes. They were effectively stealing the frequencies. The government of the day did not react. Eight stations were given 'temporary licences' in 1993. These were renewed in 2007. No permanent regulation has ever been put in place. A senior court ruled in 2010 that the temporary licenses are unconstitutional. The ruling made no difference. … The television stations absorbed the print media. Most of them respect no rules for objectivity or moderation. Owner interference is rampant and blatantly favours selected politicians. The press as a whole is not independent, but guided by large business interests."

The electromagnetic spectrum is supposed, at the Troika's insistence, to have been auctioned off by the Hellenic Republic Asset Development Fund (HRADF). See http://www.hradf.com/el/digital-dividend. As of the time of writing, legislation confirming renewal of temporary licenses was enacted by the Greek Parliament that was dissolved in December 2014. It has been severely criticized as scandalous by the press and, more important, by SYRIZA, the party that won the 2015 parliamentary election. It thus behooves the new government to reconsider the matter urgently.

In 2016 the Greek government passed a law according to which nationwide broadcasting was to be limited to four licenses. An auction did take place, but as of the time of writing, litigation has prevented the implementation of the new law because it was found unconstitutional by the Council of State and a new procedure needs to be followed.

9. Artavanis, Morse, and Tsoutsoura (2016) use micro data for Greek households, provided by a large private bank in Greece, and work on the premise that the bank makes lending decisions based on the bank's assessment of borrowers' true income, instead of what the respondents report. They replicate the bank's models of credit capacity, credit card limits, and mortgage payments to infer the bank's estimate of individuals' true income. This insight suggests a novel approach for estimating tax evasion by the private sector in Greece. Their estimate of a lower bound of 28 billion euros of unreported income for Greece and the associated tax revenue forgone amounts to 31 percent of the deficit for 2009. Principal tax-evading occupations are doctors, engineers, private tutors, accountants, financial service agents, and lawyers. The authors' evidence across different industries suggests that industries with low paper trail and industries that are favored by Parliament members engage in more tax evasion.

Another look at the Artavanis, Morse, and Tsoutsoura data (shared with us privately by Adair Morse) shows a general pattern of greater tax evasion in rural than in urban areas. This is not surprising since more salaried workers live in cities than in rural areas, and thus there are fewer opportunities for tax evasion. Generally, the self-employed have higher tax evasion than wage earners (measured by mean tax-evaded income), higher median untaxed income, and a higher incidence of tax evasion. Their actual income, as imputed by the bank, is 192 percent of what they report to the tax authorities.

10. As estimated by Matsaganis et al., underreporting ranges from 22.9 percent for the lowest decile to 15.9 percent for the highest decile of the income distribution, while reaching a low of 8 percent for the mid deciles.

11. See http://www.youtube.com/watch?v=S5nth5jlCP0.

12. We thank Manos Matsaganis for pointing out to us that tabulations of the 1999 World Values Survey gives a somewhat different and not as stark a picture. The survey asked respondents to rank their attitude to "claiming government benefits to which you are not entitled" on a scale whose values ranged from 1 (never justifiable) to 10 (always justifiable). The average score in Greece was 4.0, compared to 2.1 in Germany. But only 5.1 percent of respondents in Greece responded that cheating on benefits was always justifiable (score 10), and only 26.1 percent that it was more justifiable than unjustifiable (scores 6–10). Those were still far higher than the corresponding scores for Germany, 1.4 and 7.4 percent, respectively.

13. Herrmann et al. (2008) report on the following public goods game played by groups of four members: Each member receives an endowment of 20 tokens. Participants have to decide how many tokens to keep for themselves and how many to contribute to a group project. Each of the

four group members earns 0.4 tokens for each token invested in the project, regardless of whether he or she contributes any. Because the cost of contributing one token in the project is exactly one token whereas the return on that token is only 0.4 tokens, keeping all one's own tokens is always in any participant's material self-interest, regardless of how much the other three group members contribute. Yet, if each group member retains all of his or her tokens, there are no earnings to be shared, whereas each member would earn $0.4 \times 80 = 32$ tokens if each of them invested their entire 20-token endowment.

Two types of experiments, P and N, were conducted and the only difference between the P experiments and the N experiments was that participants in the P experiment could punish fellow group members after they were informed about the others' investments, whereas the N experiments ended after participants were informed about the other group members' contributions. A punishment decision was implemented by assigning the punished member between zero and 10 deduction points. Each deduction point assigned reduced the punished member's earnings by three tokens and cost the punishing member one token. All punishment decisions were made simultaneously. Participants were not informed about who punished them. Punishments were for both low contributors (free riders) as well as high contributors, which the authors label as antisocial punishment.

14. For a definition, see http://www.slang.gr/lemma/show/xalao_tin_piatsa_19179.

15. We thank Elias Papaioannou for bringing to our attention the successful experience of Brazil with random audits. Ferraz and Finan (2008) show that random audits of Brazilian municipalities on their spending of federal transfers, and subsequent disclosure of results to media sources, had significant effects on election outcomes. Using a data set on corruption constructed from the audit reports, they compare the electoral outcomes of municipalities audited before versus after the 2004 elections, with the same levels of reported corruption. They show especially the impacts that the release of the audit outcomes had on incumbents' electoral performance where the electorate was more informed because of presence of local radio stations.

16. See Korobow, Johnson, and Axtell (2007). As they put it, "if in fact most crime does have an element of social interaction as its cause, then it would not be unreasonable to conclude that, since tax evasion is a crime, evasion has social drivers as well."

17. Alm (2012, p. 13) in the latest review of research on tax evasion does discuss briefly works in the "social interactions theory," but he too is stymied by the lack of empirical research.

18. The four fictitious groups were defined as follows: one (two) made up of those who were told they lived in a fictitious country run by a high (alternatively, low) trust government, and three (four) where tax authorities had high (alternatively, low) power to enforce tax laws. All subjects were asked the following questions: "How likely is it that you will fill in your tax return honestly? How much of your yearly income would you declare completely honestly? Generally speaking, tax evasion is never justified, always justified or something in between?" There were additional questions pertaining to individual characteristics (age, income, and gender), which were treated as independent variables.

19. We are grateful for detailed comments and suggestions by Manos Matsaganis, Elias Papaioannou, and John Tsitsiklis that helped us shape this section.

20. See discussion of the so-called 4 : 4 : 2 rule in note 7 above.

21. The Supreme Council for Civil Personnel Selection (ASEP) (https://www.asep.gr/) has been instituted by Law 2190/1994, but it seems that in practice it can, in many instances, be effectively bypassed by the government. We thank Nikos Vettas for this clarification.

22. Lest it be thought that we are involving a maximalist approach here, we wish to direct attention to the consequences of values inculcated at the Greek home, at least as seen via data. The research on distrust shows that a measured distrust index is negatively correlated with the importance parents assign to children's being taught "tolerance and respect" (see Aghion et al. 2010, fig. 28). In fact they show that Greece is an outlier, lowest on tolerance and respect, and highest in distrust.

23. We thank Manos Matsaganis for emphasizing this point.

24. The term for the European Commission's Task Force for Greece is, at the time of writing, not yet renewed and might be allowed to expire. This is unfortunate because here we have a pan-European effort at providing technical assistance to Greece, to which even tiny Iceland, a country one-fortieth of Greece, has contributed. For its latest (and last?) report; see http://europa.eu/rapid/press-release_MEMO-14-495_en.htm.

25. See http://ec.europa.eu/dgs/home-affairs/what-we-do/policies/organized-crime-and-human-trafficking/corruption/anti-corruption-report/docs/2014_acr_greece_chapter_en.pdf.

26. As reported by the *New York Times*, December 8, 2011: http://www.nytimes.com/2011/12/08/us/blagojevich-expresses-remorse-in-courtroom-speech.html.

Mr. Rod Blagojevich was sentenced to 14 years in prison on his 18 corruption counts, that included wire fraud, attempted extortion, conspiracy to solicit bribes and notably trying to sell or trade the US Senate seat that became vacant when US Senator Barack Obama was elected US president in Fall 2008.

27. Transparency International (2013e).

28. We thank Elias Papioannou for bringing this fact to our attention.

29. See Ladi (2011) for an assessment of the Greek case, which is arguably a success.

30. The importance of independent authorities is underscored by Paul Romer (2010) in the case of Hong Kong, which succeeded in stamping out corruption during the waning years of British rule while it was administered by a governor appointed by the British government.

References

Acemoglu, D., S. Johnson, and J. A. Robinson. 2005. Institutions as a fundamental cause of economic growth. In P. Aghion and S. Durlauf, eds., *Handbook of Economic Growth*, 385–472. Amsterdam: Elsevier.

Achury, C., C. Koulovatianos, and J. Tsoukalas. 2013. *Political Economics of External Sovereign Defaults*. Mimeo.

Aghion, P., Y. Algan, P. Cahuc, and A. Shleifer. 2010. Regulation and distrust. *Quarterly Journal of Economics* 125 (3): 1015–49.

Alesina, A., and G.-M. Angeletos. 2005. Fairness and redistribution. *American Economic Review* 95 (4): 960–80.

Algan, Y., and P. Cahuc. 2014. Trust, growth, and well-being: New evidence and policy implications. In P. Aghion and S. N. Durlauf, eds., *Handbook of Economic Growth,* vol. 2A, 49–120. Amsterdam: Elsevier.

Alm, J. 2012. Measuring, explaining, and controlling tax evasion: Lessons from theory, experiments and field studies. *International Tax and Public Finance* 19: 54–77.

Artavanis, N., A. Morse, and M. Tsoutsoura. 2016. Measuring income tax evasion using bank credit: evidence from Greece. *Quarterly Journal of Economics* 131 (2): 739–98.

Barr, A., and D. Serra. 2010. Corruption and culture: An experimental analysis. *Journal of Public Economics* 94: 862–69.

Benhabib, J., and A. Rustichini. 1996. Social conflict and growth. *Journal of Economic Growth* 1: 125–42.

Brock, W. A., and S. N. Durlauf. 2001. Interaction-based models. In J. Heckman and E. Leamer, eds., *Handbook of Econometrics*, vol. 5, 3297–3380. Amsterdam: North-Holland.

Durlauf, S. N., and Y. M. Ioannides. 2010. Social interactions. *Annual Review of Economics* 2: 451–78.

Eleftheriadis, P. 2012. What is wrong with Greece? *Financial Times*, April 24.

EU Anti-Corruption Report. 2014. Brussels. http://ec.europa.eu/dgs/home-affairs/e-library/documents/ policies/organized-crime-and-human-trafficking/corruption/docs/acr_2014_en.pdf.

Eurobarometer Data. Various years. https://dbk.gesis.org/dbksearch/home.asp.

Eurobarometer. 2005. 64.3 http://dx.doi.org/ 10.4232/1.10971.

Eurobarometer. 2007. 68.2 http://dx.doi.org/ 10.4232/1.10986.

Eurobarometer. 2013. 79.1 http://dx.doi.org/ 10.4232/1.11855.

EU Special Eurobarometer Survey. 2012. *Corruption*. Brussels. http://ec.europa.eu/public_opinion/ archives/ebs/ebs_374_en.pdf.

EU Special Eurobarometer Survey. 2014. *Corruption*. Brussels. http://ec.europa.eu/public_opinion/ archives/ebs/ebs_397_en.pdf.

Ferraz, C., and F. Finan. 2008. Exposing corrupt politicians: The effects of Brazil's publicly released audits on electoral outcomes. *Quarterly Journal of Economics* 123: 703–45.

Fortin, B., G. Lacroix, and M.-C. Villeval. 2007. Tax evasion and social interactions. *Journal of Public Economics* 91: 2089–2111.

Herrmann, B., C. Thöni, and S. Gächter. 2008. Antisocial punishment across societies. *Science* 319: 1362.

IMF. 2013. Greece: Selected issues. Country Report 13/155. IMF.

Inspector General of Public Administration. 2013. *Annual Report* (in Greek). http://www.gedd.gr/article_data/Linked_files/105/EktheshGEDD2012.pdf.

Inspector General of Public Administration. 2014. *Annual Report* (in Greek). http://www.gedd.gr/article_data/Linked_files/114/EktheshGEDD2013.pdf.

Ioannides, Y. M. 2013. *From Neighborhoods to Nations: The Economics of Social Interactions*. Princeton: Princeton University Press.

Ioannides, Y. M., and A. Murthy. 2014. Social effects in the experience of corruption using the Eurobarometer Data: 2005–2013. Unpublished manuscript. Available on request.

Kaplanoglou, G., and V. T. Rapanos. 2015. Why do people evade their taxes? New experimental evidence from Greece. *Journal of Behavioral and Experimental Economics* 56: 21–32.

Kaufmann, D. 2010. Can corruption adversely affect public finances in industrialized countries? Brookings Institution. http://www.brookings.edu/research/opinions/2010/04/19-corruption-kaufmann/.

Korobow, A., C. Johnson, and R. Axtell. 2007. An agent-based model of tax compliance with social networks. *National Tax Journal* 60 (3): 589–610.

Ladi, S. 2011. Policy change and soft Europeanization: The transfer of the ombudsman institution to Greece, Cyprus and Malta. *Public Administration* 89 (4): 1643–63.

Llacer, T., F. J. Miguel, J. A. Noguera, and E. Tapia. 2013. An agent-based model of tax compliance: An application to the Spanish case. *Advances in Complex Systems* 16 (4–5): 135007-1--33. doi:10.1142/S0219525913500070.

Matsaganis, M., C. Leventi, and M. Flevotomou. 2012. The crisis and tax evasion in Greece: What are the distributional implications? *CESifo Forum* 13 (2): 26–32.

North, D. C. 1990. *Institutions, Institutional Change and Economic Performance*. New York: Cambridge University Press.

Olken, B. O. 2009. Corruption perceptions vs. corruption reality. *Journal of Public Economics* 93 (7–8): 950–64.

Olken, B. O., and R. Pande. 2012. Corruption in developing countries. *Annual Review of Economics* 4: 479–505.

Pangalos, T. 2012. *We "Ate" It All Together (Ta fagame Oloi Mazi)*. In Greek; e-book (private edition). https://www.viva.gr/tickets/books/ta-fagame-oloi-mazi/.

Papaioannou, E. 2011. Civic capital(ism). TEDx Talk. http://www.youtube.com/watch?v
=S5nth5jlCP0.

Papaioannou, E. 2013. Trust(ing) in Europe. http://www.martenscentre.eu/sites/default/files/
publication-files/civic_capital_web.pdf.

Romer, Paul. 2010. Cutting the corruption tax. http://www.voxeu.org/article/cutting-corruption
-tax-way-out-greece/.

Schneider, F., and A. Buehn. 2012. Shadow economies in highly developed OECD countries:
What are the driving forces? Discussion paper 6891. IZA.

Shleifer, A., and R. W. Vishny. 1993. Corruption. *Quarterly Journal of Economics* 108 (3): 599–617.

Skaperdas, S. 1992. Cooperation, conflict and power in the absence of property rights. *American
Economic Review* 82: 720–39.

Surowiecki, J. 2011. Dodger mania. *The New Yorker*, July 11 and 18. 2011. http://www.newyorker
.com/magazine/2011/07/11/dodger-mania/.

Tagkalakis, A. O. 2014. Tax arrears and VAT revenue performance. *Economic Bulletin* 34 (1):
106–21.

Tanaka, S. 2013. Uncovering the market prices of bribes: The effect of information technology
on corruption in India. Discussion paper. Fletcher School. http://papers.ssrn.com/sol3/papers
.cfm?abstract_id=2327607.

Transparency International. 2013a. *National Integrity System Assessment Greece*. http://www
.transparency.org/whatwedo/pub/nis_greece_2012/.

Transparency International. 2013b. *Less and Cheaper Fakelaki in Greece: The Key Results of 2012
National Survey on Corruption in Greece*. http://www.transparency.org/news/pressrelease/20130307
_less_and_cheaper_fakelaki_in_greece_the_key_results_of_2012_nation/.

Transparency International. 2013c. *National Survey on Corruption in Greece*. Public Issue. http://
www.publicissue.gr/wp-content/uploads/2014/04/NSCG-2013.pdf.

Transparency International. 2013d. *National Integrity System Assessment Greece*. http://www
.transparency.org/whatwedo/publication/nis_greece_2012/.

Transparency International. 2013e. *Alternative to Silence: More Effective Protection and Support for
Whistleblowers in Greece*. http://www.transparency.gr/Uploads/File/TI-G_WB-REPORT_2013.pdf.

14   Public Administration and the Tragic Trident: Understanding the Organizational and Structural Drivers of the Greek Malaise[1]

Michael G. Jacobides

14.1   Why Public Administration Matters So Much in Greece

The crisis that has engulfed Greece since 2010 has many different facets. It has not been brought about purely by macroeconomic mismanagement, but rather it reflects certain fundamental weaknesses in the structure of the Greek economy and state. Those flaws had previously gone undetected partly as the result of Greece's entry into the euro, which provided abundant credit and facilitated growth based on consumption. When the crisis hit, and credit dried up, the underlying challenges of problematic structures and practices came to the fore.

Nowhere is this more evident than in the role of the Greek public administration, which has been a central part of the problem (OECD 2011a). Over a period of several decades, Greece built a Byzantine array of regulations, and a large, centralized, inefficient state apparatus that shaped a concomitant rent-seeking private sector based on state protection and allowed for systematic tax avoidance and rule bending (Featherstone and Papadimitriou 2008). Public administration sits at the hub of these interrelated problems, and it is the foundation of an inefficient, nepotistic political system built on granting favors and privileges for influence. The Troika program's (2010 to 2014) limited success in addressing these issues has also been an important factor in its disappointing performance (Ladi 2014; Featherstone 2015), a topic we consider in section 14.5.

The received wisdom is that the main problem with Greece's public administration is the size of the state. After all, the key challenge facing the country in 2010 was its monumental deficit, which spoke to an urgent need to reduce public expenditure. Yet, while the Greek public sector was certainly large at the onset of the crisis, international comparisons suggest that, measured by the number of employees, the Greek state now falls almost exactly at the mean of OECD countries, as outlined in figure 14.1.

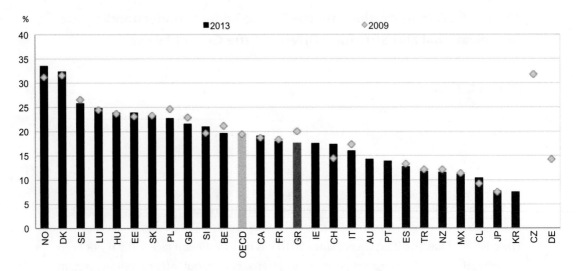

Figure 14.1
Public sector employment (percent of total employment)
Source: Government at a Glance (OECD 2015)

What this figure does not show, though, is the impact that the state has on the economy. The issue isn't only that this figure drastically underrepresents the parts of Greece's GDP that are directly or indirectly affected by the state—including state-controlled private entities. It is mainly that it neglects the "tragic trident" (Jacobides 2012)—that is, the three key ways by which the public administration shapes and debilitates the Greek economy.

First, the public sector has proved to be a poor manager of its own resources, as we document in section 14.3, with disappointing outcomes in terms of health care, education, and social protection. It is in fact a poor custodian of assets, from public land to real assets to endowments. Indeed, until recently, many state assets, and endowments in particular, had not even been fully accounted for. They are often allowed to depreciate, and so they can be plundered by those with connections (see EU DG ECFIN 2011, p. 25; Maglaras 2010, p. 3).

What is more, much of the administration's energy is dissipated on mindless procedural tasks. This disturbing condition was described in a 2011 OECD report, which has provided the most comprehensive review to date. The Greek public administration is not structured so as to create accountability either at the level of the administrative unit or at the level of civil servants. As a result, instead of focusing on how to substantively serve their purpose, civil servants fall back on ossified formalistic rules at every turn, which, after all, are what they are evaluated on. Additionally, the civil service lacks independent senior leadership; it has increasingly relied on an army of advisors to short-lived government ministers to inform its direction. Outlined in section 14.4 are the lack of data, information, and management systems; the remarkably inefficient organizational structures and coordination mechanisms; and the poorly designed and pernicious incentive systems. All constitute key pathologies that drastically limit the public sector's effectiveness. Additionally the inefficient structures and practices in the Finance Ministry have allowed for significant tax evasion, curtailing public revenues and cultivating a sense of social unease with the whole idea of taxpaying. Overall, the underperformance of the public sector has created a vicious cycle of increasingly adversarial relations between the Greek state and its citizens.

Second, the skewed interface between the private and public sectors has damaged Greece's productive tissue. The Greek state had long been a purchaser of services for construction, armaments, technology, and more mundane goods and services. As figure 14.2 shows, prior to the crisis Greece had a higher share of its GDP devoted to such purchases than the OECD average.[2] At one extreme were the procurements of basic goods and services by local authorities; at the other, gold-plated, EU-funded investment projects loosely monitored from afar in terms of their financial stewardship. Both represent substantial economic activity, and use of resources that might be productively employed elsewhere.

The figure, however, underrepresents the state's influence through purchases from organizations and private companies that it controls, where side-payments are often an inherent part of procurement. As table 14.1 documents, the Greek procurement system around 2010 was closed and opaque, leading to both higher costs and/or lower quality for state-procured services, and opportunities for rent-seeking entrepreneurs. The lack of a central procurement website or transparent supplier-selection criteria until 2011—standard practice in other OECD countries—gives a sense of the ample scope for creating privileges and special relationships. While the situation has improved, implementation is still an issue.[3]

Given the incentives and structures at play, Greek initiative, adaptability, and drive has mutated into manifold corruption, both active and passive, as we document in section 14.6. This is despite some effort to redress the balance via IT-enabled solutions—especially the Di@vgeia ("clarity") transparency initiative. Corruption, tax evasion, and distrust of the state have combined to create a vicious circle that is amplified by the political system—though *not* desired by most Greeks. As we argue in section 14.7, the cycle needs to be broken by a top–bottom reorganization of the public sector.

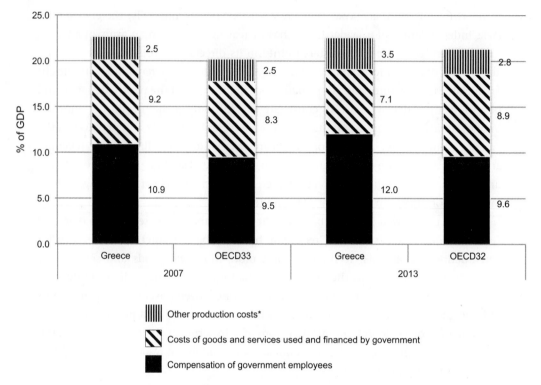

Figure 14.2

Production costs of government-produced and government-funded goods and services (percent of GDP, 2007 and 2013). Consumption of fixed capital (depreciation of capital) and other taxes on production less other subsidies on production.

Source: Government at a Glance (OECD 2015)

Third, the state distorts the functioning of the private sector. Entrepreneurial activity and private investment are deterred by "closed," or regulated, professions that have engendered as local monopolies; a loose competition policy that does not really promote competition; and most important, a bewildering array of regulations. Capricious taxation and unpredictable authorities compound the problem of a malfunctioning justice system, with long delays and inefficient procedures.[4] This is why Greece has been the worst European performer in (among others) the World Economic Forum's competitiveness indexes (WEF 2012), ranking 96th overall, and 111th in terms of institutions—below some sub-Saharan countries.

As table 14.2 documents, there is little concern about the impact of regulation on enterprises, and limited private sector consultation and involvement. This problem

Table 14.1

Transparency in public procurement in Greece, 2010

	Central proc. Center	Contracting entity website	Domestic printed or electronic journal	Other website	Percentage of OECD countries that publish info
Information for potential bidders	No	Yes	No	No	97
Selection and evaluation criteria	No	Yes	No	No	97
Tender documents	No	Yes	No	No	82
Contract award	No	Yes	No	No	100
Justification for award	No	Yes	No	No	59
Tracking procurement spending	No	No	No	No	32

Source: Government at a Glance (OECD 2011b)

Note: Percentages refer to the share of OECD countries that reported publishing information "always" or "sometimes."

was amplified by the Memorandum of Understanding (MoU) between Greece and the Troika, which led to a flurry of legislative activity under extremely tight deadlines in which laws were hastily cobbled together without due consultation or consideration of impact on the everyday conduct of business. Unlike the vast majority of OECD countries, Greece, until recently, did not involve the private sector in developing new regulations, did not track the regulatory burden, and would resolutely ignore the compliance and enforcement issues that might emerge when designing new regulation—preferring instead to rely on an endless and often confusing succession of decrees, clarifications, and circulars to explicate its new laws, rules, and regulations. Also, the complexity and incoherence of the Greek regulatory apparatus has created onerous administrative burdens that impose significant costs on economic activity and seem to indirectly encourage, or at least tolerate, illicit practices. As the comprehensive OECD (2013) study on regulatory burdens confirmed, the Greek economy is disproportionately held back by state involvement.

The pathologies of the public administration both predated the crisis, and partly caused it—but, as we outline in section 14.5, the subsequent response has failed to address them. While public spending was slashed (figure 14.3), this was primarily by means of horizontal salary and pension cuts, and through a significant push for the early retirement of public sector employees: between 2010 and 2014, as the Flow

Table 14.2
Regulatory governance mechanisms, 2008

Functions of the oversight body		Percentage of OECD countries responding "yes"	Greece
Consulted as part of process of developing new regulation	2005	73	No
	2008	82	No
Reports on progress made on reform by individual ministries	2005	43	No
	2008	56	No
Authority of reviewing and monitoring regulatory impacts conducted in individual ministries	2005	43	Yes
	2008	50	Yes
Conducts its own regulatory impact analysis	2005	43	Yes
	2008	47	Yes
Anticipating compliance and enforcement			
Regulatory policy require that issue of securing compliance and enforcement be anticipated when developing new legislation	2005	57	No
	2008	70	No
Guidance for regulators on compliance and enforcement	2005	37	No
	2008	47	No
Existence of policy on risk-based enforcement	2005	NA	NA
	2008	30	No

Source: Government at a Glance (OECD 2011b)

Census of ELSTAT confirms, 55,176 employees (out of a total of 576,856 working in 2014) retired, reducing headcount but maintaining the pressure on public finances through pension benefits. This early retirement program exacted a heavy toll in lost institutional knowledge and memory.

Despite the fact that institutional reform did feature prominently in the MoU, relatively little happened on the ground other than cost-cutting.[5] While Greece got at least some basic tools, such as a register of public servants (in 2013), progress was patchy at best (Ladi 2014; Featherstone 2015). Several of the positive changes undertaken between June 2013 and October 2014 (e.g., the reform of the Civil Servant Code) were halted, and many were even reversed early in 2015. While the current MoU is much more explicit on changing the administration, the proof will be in the pudding. There are grounds to be pessimistic about both the ability and the will to execute (see Jacobides 2015).

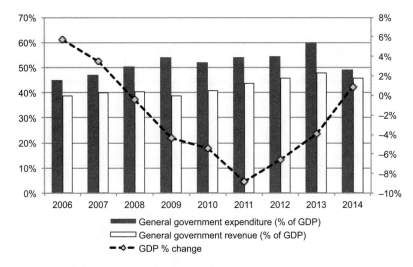

Figure 14.3
General government revenues, expenditures, and economic growth
Sources: OECD.Stat—News release 72/2015; Eurostat, April 21, 2015

In the remainder of this chapter we first review the nature, structure, and evolution of the Greek public administration (the "what," section 14.2), as well as some measures showing its relative underperformance (section 14.3). We next analyze the underlying pathologies (the "how," section 14.4) and the causes of the underperformance (the "why," section 14.6). We also look at what has been done so far to fix the administration (section 14.5) before considering what lies ahead (section 14.7). Chapter 15 further analyzes some of the pathologies concerning the structure of the public administration and the challenges in addressing them.

14.2 Unpacking the Greek Public Administration (the "What")

14.2.1 Background and History
The Greek state as we know it today was constituted in the 1830s. Its blueprint was the heavily centralized Napoleonic system (Peters 2008), but this quickly adapted to preexisting structures and power relationships. The resulting hybrid was an idiosyncratic system with significant distance between formal and informal structures that allowed politicians to exert a powerful influence (Mouzelis 1978; Diamandouros 1994). As Spanou (2008, p. 152) notes:

The overwhelming presence of party-political competition and the weakness of social and economic pressure has allowed the survival of political patronage and prevented the shaping of a professional and independent civil service organisation, such as represented by the Weberian conception of bureaucracy. These factors left their mark on modern state features, such as political centralisation and interference into routine administrative operation. They also account for a general mistrust towards political-administrative institutions on behalf of society governmental structure.

There have been several efforts to reform the public administration (Papoulias and Tsoukas 1998; Pagoulatos 2005). However, they have been fairly localized and incremental, serving to confirm the significant resilience of the state apparatus and its structures (Spanou 2008).

The public sector includes ministries, local government agencies (e.g., municipalities and communities), public legal entities (i.e., entities delegated with public authority and nonprofit objectives, e.g., universities, hospitals, and the IKA social insurance fund), and Independent Administrative Authorities (e.g., Hellenic Competition Commission, Hellenic Telecommunication and Post Authority, Regulatory Authority for Energy), as well as the Parliament and the Bank of Greece (the Central Bank, part of the Eurosystem). For all the state's ostensible commitment to decentralization, most expenses (and tax revenues) are centralized, as figure 14.4 shows, and the much smaller budgets of local authorities mostly go through the central government. That said, municipalities, communities (regions), and prefectures enjoy, at least in principle, both administrative and fiscal independence (Hlepas 1999; Spanou and Sotiropoulos 2011).

14.2.2 Central Government

The Greek public administration depends heavily on political leadership, since it has limited autonomy compared with, say, Whitehall's Permanent Secretaries in the United Kingdom. The internal organization of a ministry consists of political and administrative positions. Political positions include the minister, deputy or vice ministers, and the general and special secretaries. The general secretary is usually responsible for the general organization of the ministry, while special secretaries are in charge of specific policy fields. There are also positions for revocable employees who staff the offices of ministers and secretaries and provide advisory and consultancy services.

The organization of each ministry is set out in a Presidential Decree (PD), which describes the administrative structure (number of entities at each hierarchical level), the allocation of competences among entities (the division of labor), and the number of job posts. As such, organizational structures are fairly rigid, and their change requires

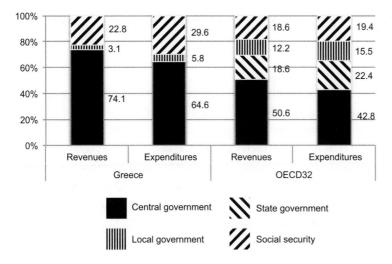

Figure 14.4
Revenues and expenditures by level of government in 2013. No state government level exists in Greece.
Source: Government at a Glance (OECD 2015)

governmental approval and final sign-off from the President of the Republic (the ceremonial head of the Greek state).

In addition to line ministries, there are other entities that perform cross-cutting functions. Overall coordination is performed by four organizations reporting directly to the Prime Minister: General Secretariat for Coordination, General Secretariat of the Prime Minister, General Secretariat of the Government, and General Secretariat for Communication. There are also horizontal functions performed by entities subordinated to ministries: human resources management (General Directorate of Human Resources, in the Ministry of Interior and Administrative Reconstruction) and budgeting (General Accounting Office, in the Ministry of Finance).

14.2.3 Decentralized Administration

Greece has seen an increase in the role of decentralized administration, following the "Kapodistrias" project of 1997 (Hlepas 1999). There are seven regions, with regulatory authority over urban planning, the environment, and energy policies, among other areas. In parallel, decentralized agencies of the ministries (e.g., General Directorate of Public Property and Public Welfare Property, Dispute Resolution Authority of the Ministry of Finance) perform specific policy tasks at local level. Yet there is little true fiscal autonomy, as budgets depend on the central authority, and little independence in practice, since decentralized agencies' decisions have to be in line with the relevant ministry's directions.

14.2.4 Local Self-Government

There are two levels of local self-government. The first consists of 325 municipalities, whose Mayors and Municipal Councilors are elected by direct suffrage for a five-year term. Municipalities were strengthened by the Kapodistrias law of 1997 and reorganized through the Kallikratis project, which clarified the boundaries and transparency of state-dependent entities in the local administration. They now have responsibilities in development; environment and housing; employment, health, and social protection; education and sport; tourism; trade; agriculture and fisheries; economic development; social welfare and cohesion; and environmental protection. Legal entities under private law are also under the supervision of the municipalities, creating problems we will soon review.

The second level of local self-government consists of 13 regions divided according to geospatial, social, and economic criteria. Their authority partly overlaps with that of local and central government.

14.2.5 Other Public Institutions

In addition to government agencies, other institutions—including hospitals and universities—are parts of the state, and form part of the "broader public sector," generally accounted for in the statistics on public sector employees shown in figure 14.1. Their independence and self-governance is established by the constitution and in law—at least in principle. In practice, their independence is severely constrained, as a result of the procedures set out by law. For example, higher education institutions cannot hire or fire employees, set compensation levels, or decide how many students to accept; everything is determined centrally by the Ministry of Education.

14.2.6 Private Legal Entities

The broader public sector includes private legal entities in which the state has a majority shareholding, whose senior managers are appointed by the state, or that receive state subsidies that exceed 50 percent of their annual income.[6] During the 2000s, many entities were also set up by local authorities that undertook significant activities without posting accounts, while drawing on state credit. These were curtailed under the Kallikratis project (and the Rangousis law), though many municipal enterprises, with wide-ranging scope, still exist.[7]

14.2.7 DEKOs (National Companies of Public Interest) and Indirectly Controlled Private Firms

DEKOs are companies that serve the public interest, operating in areas such as utilities, infrastructure, and transport. The state has either full ownership (as in OSE, the train operator; Attiko Metro, the Athens metro provider; EAS, the Greek defense contractor and manufacturer; KEELPNO, the Center for Disease Control; or ERT, the public broadcaster), or partial ownership (as in DEPA, the Public Gas Company; ELPE, the Hellenic Petroleum Company; OLP, the Piraeus Port Authority; or TT, the Greek Postal Bank). Many of these have been in the process of privatization—but success has been limited, and state involvement remains pervasive. DEKOs, while still subject to some constraints (salary caps, public procurement procedures), have historically had much greater flexibility than the "narrow" public sector, and as such were used by politicians as preferential sources to employ party faithful without the controls or limitations inherent in the central or local administration. While DEKOs have evolved considerably, not least as a result of many of them being publically listed, they are not always known for their efficiency and customer friendliness—with, it has to be said, significant variance.

Some major corporates are still under the direct control of the state (e.g., PPC/ΔEH, the public electricity company). Interestingly, banks, which are partly owned by the state, or private organizations where the state has a substantial equity stake yet possibly less control (e.g., OTE, the major fixed and mobile telecommunications company majority-owned by Deutsche Telekom) do not appear in these official figures.[8] Nevertheless, PPC, in particular, has struck a stunning deal with the Greek government, with the state agreeing to subsidize its pension funds to the tune of 600 million euros a year—an arrangement that has not been revisited, despite the crisis. A similar arrangement has been secured by pensioners of OTE, for about 534 million euros a year.[9]

The state also exerts undue influence over financial services. Control is most intrusive in pension funds, where top spots often go to government-friendly managers. However, this represents an advance over the appointment of mere party hacks who tended to get these posts in the 1980s and 1990s. As for the banking sector, especially before the 1990s, control through the political apparatus led to significant distortions of investment and loan decisions. Banks under direct state control, such as Agrotiki and ETBA, were notorious for favoring friends of the government, thus distorting the allocation of capital in the economy. While the situation has improved—partly as a result of companies being listed, and thus shielded from intervention and corruption by regulatory and shareholder pressures, and partly as a result of the industry maturing—influences remain (see chapter 7 on the financial system).

The measurement of the activities of the Greek state has been limited in scope and lax in execution. This has been exacerbated by a chronic lack of data, and a related lack of accountability, which has allowed many state entities to be run on a cash basis right up to the crisis—a challenge that the Troika reform programs tried to tackle, as we explain in section 14.5. To illustrate, the largest hospital in the Balkans, Evangelismos, had not, until 2011, balanced its books, estimated its profit and loss accounts, or produced detailed information—despite a legal obligation to do so from the 1990s on—since payments would be made on a consolidated basis.[10] And although there is now an even clearer requirement for hospitals to publish and provide such data, progress has been patchy, and it is currently unclear whether compliance has caught up with legal and regulatory requirements.[11]

More broadly, the questions of what falls within the boundaries of the state, or how it performs, are not properly addressed—as the Troika controllers discovered, often to their surprise, during the crisis (Featherstone 2015).

14.3   From Structure to Output: Assessing the Efficiency of the Greek Administration

The lack of measures—and, in particular, the near-universal absence of key performance indicators (KPIs)—begs the question of just how well, or poorly, the administration performs. Still, we can obtain some indirect performance measures that map to the Greek state's key roles in the economy.

14.3.1   The State as a Producer, and a Manager of Its Own Resources

While we lack objective measures of how efficiently the Greek state transforms its inputs into outputs, we can consult international comparisons of citizens' satisfaction with key state services. As figure 14.5 shows, by 2015 Greece not only had the lowest satisfaction rates for health care of all OECD countries (with a significant fall from 2014); it also ranked significantly below developing countries such as Indonesia. Greece's performance in international education tests has also declined in the last decade, as have the rankings of its public institutions of higher learning. More broadly, as figure 14.6 shows, Greece had one of the worse indexes of confidence in the national government, with one of the sharpest declines since 2007.

As we discuss in greater detail in the next section, there is increasing evidence that state resources are rarely used to anything like their full potential, as a result of antiquated HR practices and irrational organizational structures. For instance, the Ministry of Education, by far the biggest employer in Greece, only requires secondary school

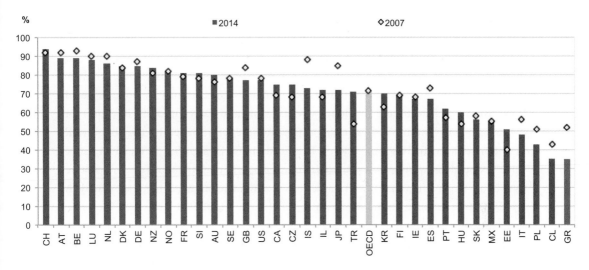

Figure 14.5

Citizens' satisfaction with the health care system. Data for Austria, Finland, Ireland, Norway, Portugal, the Slovak Republic, Slovenia, and Switzerland are for 2006 rather than 2007. Data for Iceland and Luxembourg are for 2008 rather than 2007. Data for Australia, Canada, Chile, Hungary, Iceland, Japan, Korea, China, Latvia, and South Africa are for 2013 rather than 2014.

Source: Government at a Glance (OECD 2015)

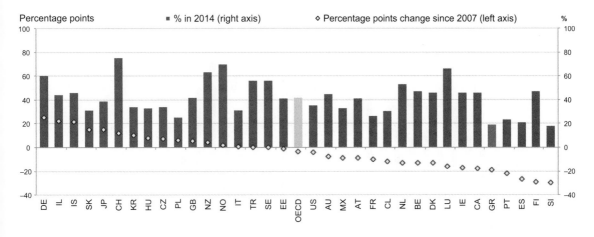

Figure 14.6

Confidence in national government. Data for Chile, Hungary, and Iceland are 2013 rather than 2014.

Source: Government at a Glance (OECD 2015)

teachers to teach approximately 415 hours a year, compared with an OECD mean of 694 hours, as discussed in section 14.5 (OECD 2014).

Tax collection is another can of worms. Tax evasion in Greece is rampant, and considerably higher than in the rest of the European Union and the OECD, contributing to Greece's fiscal woes (Vasardani 2011; Schneider 2015). Contrary to popular belief, tax evasion is not restricted to the rich (Matsaganis and Flevotomou 2010); rather, it cuts across broad swathes of society and is sometimes legitimized by the state's well-intentioned but ill-advised policies.[12] This leads both to significant social injustice, since tax burdens are unequally shared, and to a severe distortion of Greece's productive tissue: larger firms that find it harder to fly under the taxman's radar are disadvantaged vis-à-vis smaller, more elusive, and potentially inefficient firms (see McKinsey and Company 2012).

The administration's inability to increase revenues by organizing its tax-collection arm more effectively is a result of chronic failures and pathologies that we discuss in the next section. An objective way to assess tax-revenue efficiency is to measure the VAT gap (i.e., the shortfall between VAT due and VAT actually collected). As figure 14.7 shows, Greece has the third highest ratio in the European Union, after Latvia and Romania. As the OECD (2011a) report on the administration finds, the focus on formalism and procedures absorbs resources without producing substantive outputs, thus directly reducing what Greek citizens can expect from their state.

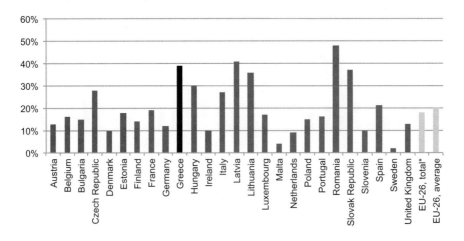

Figure 14.7
VAT gap (as a percentage of VAT theoretical liability), 2011
Source: Study to Quantify and Analyse the VAT Gap in the EU-27 Member States (CASE and CPB 2013) for DG TAXUD, European Commission

14.3.2 The State as a Procurer, and the Creator of a Supply Ecosystem

The impact of the Greek state in terms of shaping a supply ecosystem is hard to assess directly. However, as table 14.1 shows, Greece is very much behind in terms of transparency in public procurement—although e-government initiatives introduced around the onset of the crisis have helped somewhat. The Di@vgeia project, launched in 2010 (Law 3861/2010, later expanded by Law 4210/2013) against significant resistance, required all public or publically controlled entities to publish their decisions, including any procurement decisions, at a dedicated website (diavgeia.gov.gr)—see ΕΚΔΔ (2012).

The culture of accountability was lacking, especially prior to Di@vgeia, as many parts of the central or local government did not have to disclose their finances. More important, even when expense reporting became mandatory, the lack of proper consolidated budgeting, and the inability of central government to impose a system that would allow it to monitor and react to overspending, meant there has historically been limited interest, incentive, or infrastructure to monitor costs. Even now, although data on procurement are becoming available, little headway has been made in consolidating it or assessing the efficiency of state services; only in the last few months have crowd-sourcing initiatives started to complement the limited work on tracking where public money goes and how effectively it is spent.[13]

This, along with the lack of disciplinary procedures to guard against corruption, has allowed the private sector to gorge on "easy money" gained through preferential government access. This can be seen in figure 14.8, which illustrates public perceptions of corruption. Greece has the highest (i.e., worst) score in the European Union, and the second highest, after Mexico, in the OECD (closely followed by Korea and Japan).

14.3.3 The State as Regulator of Private Enterprise

An OECD report of 2013 confirmed the magnitude of the problem with inefficient and excessive regulation in Greece. It identified administrative burdens of 3.28 billion euros and total administrative costs of 4.08 billion euros in 13 key sectors of the Greek economy (OECD 2013). This is in line with a 2007 EU study, which found that bureaucracy cost 15 billion euros, or 6.8 percent of 2007 GDP, against an EU average of 3.5 percent (see Gritzalis et al. 2014).

However, this figure may be misleadingly low for Greece because it only captures the "cost of paperwork" and neglects the many other frictional costs that firms incur in meeting their substantive regulatory obligation—time, resources, and capital equipment (let alone opportunity cost). More important, it ignores all the dynamic costs and

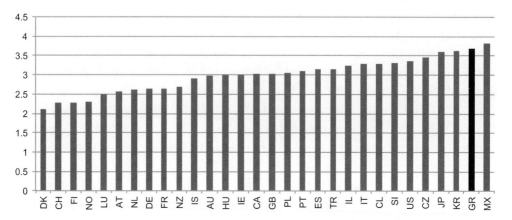

Figure 14.8
Perceptions of corruption. Results from the report on corruption conducted by TNS Opinion and Social at the request of EC Directorate-General Home Affairs. Average perception of corruption across six public institutions: 1 = not at all corrupt, 5 = extremely corrupt.
Source: Economic Surveys: Greece (OECD 2013)

inefficiencies imposed on firms. As such, it underestimates stagnation resulting from the inability of efficient firms to grow, the costs to exit, and barriers to entry imposed by bureaucracy and/or protectionism. While this point holds true in any country, it is *particularly* important in the Greek context, given the state's role in the economy and the inefficiencies of the administration. As table 14.2 shows, the Greek regulatory environment is opaque, and there has been a longstanding problem in terms of the framework provided for private enterprise—as also evidenced by Greece's low ratings for the ease of doing business. To this we should add the fiendishly complicated—and remarkably volatile—tax environment (documented at greater length elsewhere (e.g., see Bank of Greece 2010, p. 5; IMF 2013, p. 32; OECD 2013, p. 2).

Sheer legislative and administrative complexity also causes confusion within the administration itself, calling for "administrative intervention" to clarify matters. In each of the last five years, the Greek Parliament has passed around 120 pieces of legislation, comprising 3,500 pages of laws per annum. However, this represents just 2 percent of the total regulatory production. Subsequently the executive branch generates an avalanche of decrees, clarifying text, and other stipulations delimiting what companies can do.[14] This fragmentation, along with a lack of codification and rationalization, makes doing or growing business legally in Greece very hard. Ironically, growing a business illegally (e.g., adding extra seating space in a restaurant/bar by covering unbuilt areas, or selling contraband a few blocks away from the Ministry of Finance) is apparently remarkably easy, and rendered more likely as a result of administrative failures, as evidenced by the significant "shadow" (i.e., unregulated and untaxed) economy in Greece. According to a cross-country study by Buehn and Schneider (2012), the shadow economy in Greece in the period 1999 to 2010 accounted for around 27 percent of GDP, compared to an OECD average of 20.2 percent (IMF country report, May 21, 2013). Greece also had a sizable amount of undeclared work (see http://ec.europa.eu/europe2020/pdf/themes/07_shadow_economy.pdf).

Administrative complexity has also increased protectionism, both explicitly and indirectly (see chapter 4 on product markets). A host of professions and practices are protected by law, and stipulations for *ad hoc* protectionism are often interspersed in whatever (entirely irrelevant) legislation is currently being introduced, making it hard to even understand the rules. Complexity then begets corruption, as officials at several levels of government can use their judgment on how such complicated stipulations are to be observed by particular businesses or individuals. These problems are amplified by issues with the judiciary, detailed in chapter 12 (on the justice system). According to the 2016 Doing Business Indicators of the World Bank, it takes 1,580 days to enforce a contract in Greece, compared to an OECD average of 539 days.

As a result the latent potential of the Greek economy cannot be realized. The problem isn't just the size of the state but how it operates: specifically, the way it shapes inefficient, potentially corrupt supply chains and hampers the redeployment of productive resources, rewarding rent-seekers who know how to work the system, and individuals and small, probably uncompetitive firms who can hide in the shadow economy. This also inhibits the entry of new types of firms in new markets, hampers larger organizations whose rigorous systems make transgressions more conspicuous, and prevents productive firms from growing with a slew of overregulation.

14.4 From Symptoms to Causes: Understanding *How* the Administration Is Structured

The sobering picture we have painted so far makes it vital to understand the pathologies behind the inefficiencies. To start unraveling the chain of causation, we look inside the "black box" of the administration (which many, including most in the Troika, have so far regarded merely as a cost item), moving from the measurable to the qualitative. Some of these topics are further analyzed in chapter 15.

14.4.1 Demographics of Public Servants and HR Practices
Figure 14.9 reports data on the number of civil servants gathered from the Hellenic Statistical Agency ELSTAT and dating back to 1987. The figure shows that the public sector

population grew from the late 1980s to the late 2000s, with a noticeable acceleration in 2004 to 2007. After the recent crisis hit, civil servant numbers started decreasing, particularly after 2010, when Greece was shut off from the markets and leaned on the Troika, initiating a series of bailout agreements.

It is interesting that especially prior to 2010, evidence on the exact number of civil servants is patchy, leading to diverging estimates, as there had not been an independently verified number of public sector employees. Indeed, at the beginning of the Troika program in 2010, one of the things that became apparent was that Greece did not have a reliable registry of civil servants, as the key ELSTAT numbers provided in figure 14.9 were not fully reliable. To rectify this, the Greek government instituted a web-based civil servant census project. In principle, this was a program to fully account for all public sector employees. In practice, however, the lack of enforcement and controls regarding the participation in census could have counted people who mistakenly believed they were civil service employees (e.g., people working on fixed-term contracts) and undercounted those who refused or were unable to participate. In addition no mechanisms were set in place to update the data fully in real time. Figure 14.9 provides the (still patchy) data from the census project alongside the main ELSTAT results, to provide further calibration on civil servant numbers and also note the lack of transparency of the Greek state even in terms of its own employee population.[15]

The hiring boom of the 1980s and early 1990s distorted the civil service's age distribution. In 2009, 38 percent of central government civil servants were 50 or older, compared to 23 percent in 2000. Almost 60 percent had been working for the government for more than 20 years, although this issue has been attenuated by mass early retirement during the crisis (see chapter 15). Figure 14.10 illustrates.

What this figure does not reflect is the severe mismatch between the skills needed to operate a government and those of public servants. For example, in 2012, out of more than 1,000 employees in the most crucial part of the Secretariat General for Information Technology of the Ministry of Finance (which collects taxes), just *seven* were commissioned to write programming code. This, according to a former Secretary General for IT, was the combined result of personnel misallocation, strategic preference for outsourcing rather than in-house development, and lack of continuous education, as opposed to lack of skills *per se*—suggesting a multi-layered Human Resources (HR) and organizational challenge even in the most sensitive government areas. The issue is that the government has an overabundance of middle managers with no particular practical, managerial, or technical skills, adept at focusing on procedures, rules, and processes, as opposed to outputs. To this, we should add the fact that there are no

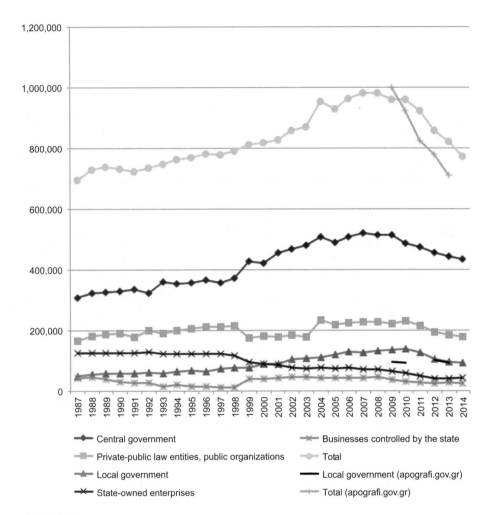

Figure 14.9

Number of civil servants, 1987 to 2014. 1987 to 1997 ELSTAT figures refer to the second quarter, and not the average of the quarters of each year. Apografi figures for local government include only ordinary staff in 2009 to 2010.

Sources: EU DG ECFIN (2011);

ELSTAT Labor Force Survey—Apografi.gov.gr.

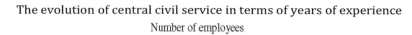

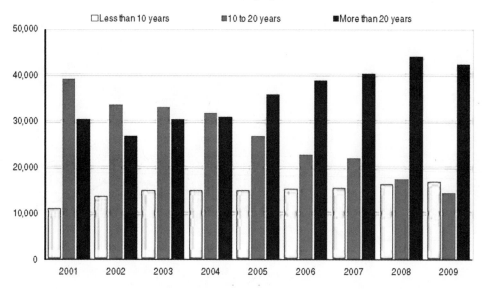

Figure 14.10
Evolution of central civil service in terms of years of experience
Source: Greece: Review of Central Administration (OECD 2011a)

revolving doors between the public and private sectors, making career progression in the public sector insular and rigid, with little scope for renewal. HR practices also play a role. In the narrow public sector (i.e., ministries, local governments, and all entities that operate under public law), public servants are protected under the Constitution of Greece (article 103), which guarantees permanent employment.

Not all public servants enjoy the same pay conditions, and there is significant heterogeneity. This leads, on average, to a more attractive proposition than one might expect, especially in an international context. Figure 14.11 shows that, at least pre-crisis, public sector pay was higher than that of the private sector on a nonadjusted basis.[16]

In terms of the expectations for time worked, the largest employer in Greece, the Ministry of Education, apparently expects of its teachers far less than the OECD average, and the second lowest in all countries surveyed—this against a post-crisis backdrop

■ Government employees as a share of total employees

■ Compensation of government employees as a share of total compensation of employees

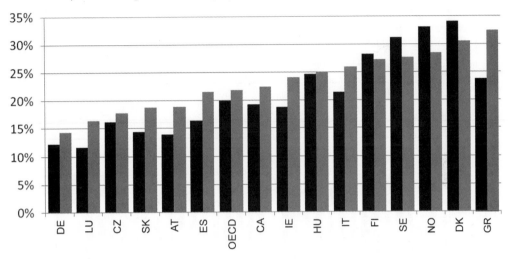

Figure 14.11

General government employees: Share of total employees and compensation as share of total compensation, 2007

Source: Greece at a Glance, Policies for a Sustainable Recovery (OECD 2010)

of teaching-post gaps (figure 14.12).[17] Relatedly, when comparing the private and public sectors *overall,* Greece appears to offer public servants a favorable deal in terms of hours worked, as figure 14.13 suggests.

14.4.2   Incentives, Motivation, and Penalties in the Public Administration

As in other countries, Greek civil servants enjoy greater (mostly, absolute) job security than their private-sector counterparts, but face flatter pay conditions and slower career progression. Yet they differ from other countries in how little their performance affects their careers, and also in terms of the very limited and crude measures used to gauge that performance.

In the narrow public sector, public servants are promoted according to pay and grading schemes defined by law. Performance assessment is mandatory for almost all, and takes the form of annual written feedback from a hierarchical superior within the organization. However, this has become perfunctory, with most ratings being 9 or 10 out of 10. The lack of KPIs has been both a cause and an effect of this system: Only a handful of performance criteria are used, including activities undertaken; values, disciplines,

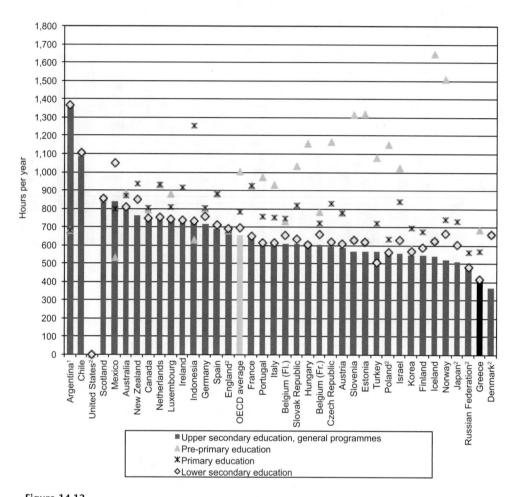

Figure 14.12

Number of teaching hours per year, by level of education, in 2012. Net statutory contact time in public institutions 1; year of reference 2. Actual teaching time countries are ranked in descending order of the number of teaching hours per year in upper secondary education.

Source: Education at a Glance (OECD 2014)

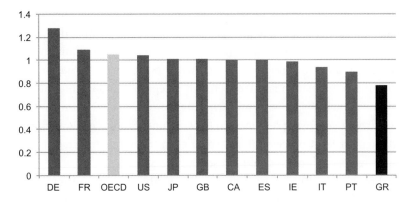

Figure 14.13

Ratio of working hours in government to private sector
Source: Government at a Glance (OECD 2011b)

and inputs; and interpersonal skills. However, as there are no detailed performance criteria, it is virtually impossible to evaluate civil servants, since there is no sense of their expected output (Psarakis and Rigopoulos 2014).

Remuneration is nonnegotiable, since base salary and bonuses are set by an independent examining committee. Promotions among top and middle managers are assessed on years of experience, performance appraisals by line managers, and objective qualifications (e.g., education). While recent legislation is supposed to have introduced some merit-based career progression, in practice there is little evidence this has taken place.

Since the 1980s, the appointment of senior civil servants had become highly politicized, denting the administration's efficiency, nullifying the role of potentially nodal posts (especially General Directors), and promoting party loyalists over competent administrators. Law 3839/2010 (the "Rangousis law") aimed to tackle this, by instituting a Special Council for the selection of senior personnel as part of the ASEP. While the law did pass, the Special Council was never constituted, and old practices remained. Only the law's most transitory arrangements were enacted in practice, illustrating the resilience of the political system's grip on the administration, as well as the power of implementation procedures to defeat even well-intentioned and sensible laws.

Relatedly, disciplinary procedures, especially those related to corruption, had long been rather limited, amplifying the sense of impunity. Especially from the 1980s onwards, a lenient set of rules on corruption was further weakened by weak implementation. Essentially, no corruption was investigated unless there was a specific accusation; and sanctions were hardly more than a slap on the wrist: even for the most serious offenses, the maximum punishment was a demotion by a single administrative grade. Many offenses were written off within only two years. Worse still, the judging panels were appointed by ministers, with no accountability and no requirements in terms of composition, allowing union representatives to move in. As Stavropoulos (2015) explains, this cultivated an ambient sense of acceptance and normalization about corruption and inefficiency, at least until the 2012 reforms. Penal courts, when used, also tended to show surprising lenience, and punishments were generally very light. The long, drawn-out legal process offered cover even to those convicted in the first instance, while the appeal process could last several years.

A 2012 reform (through Law 4057/2012) aimed to abolish this process and get tough on those convicted, and also changed the composition of the judging panels as well as the ability of those convicted to stay in their jobs. Even after the law was passed, however, it took a full year and a new Minister of Administrative Reform and Electronic Governance (ΥΔΜΗΔ/MAREG) for its provisions to be implemented in practice. More important, significant parts of the legislation were overturned by the first SYRIZA government in 2015—despite its professed desire to tackle corruption, as we explain in section 14.5.

The development of the Inspectors-Controllers Body for Public Administration (SEEDD) (Law 2477/1997, www.seedd.gr), and to a lesser extent the creation of the Office of the Ombudsman (www.synigoros.gr), has eased these pressures by creating greater transparency and accountability. However, as SEEDD's recent reports suggest, while accusations of corruption have increased, control percentage has decreased, partly as a result of fewer resources being at the inspectors' disposal.

Finally, political interference has also been an issue, with civil servants proving unable or unwilling to fend off political pressure for fear of receiving unfavorable postings. Conversely, it is considered commonplace to expect political interference in a career in the civil service (Spanou 2008). This makes the state more liable to political pressure.

14.4.3 Organizational Structure, Complexity, and (Lack of) Coordination

To fully understand what drives the inefficiency of the state, we need to understand the inefficiencies of its structure—in terms of both the composition and nature of units, and the ways in which they collaborate.

Starting with the demographic analysis of unit size, as reported in chapter 15, a remarkable 20 percent of departments have a head but no employees! This is because remuneration depends on rank, so if someone is to be paid above a certain level, they must be made a director. To facilitate these promotions, departments proliferate—regardless of duplication, inefficient division of labor, or complicated and even conflicting internal structures (439, on average, in each ministry, as the OECD review attested). Worse still, as more civil servants graduate to managerial positions, a problem arises of "too many heads, not enough hands," as well as "ghost departments" that only exist on paper.

Corroborating these concerns, the analysis of the span of control reveals a steep hierarchical structure, which leads to hierarchical distortions. In 2011 there were, on average, five general secretariats per ministry, two general directorates per general secretariat, six directorates per general directorate, and four departments per directorate (Gritzalis et al. 2014). This is the absolute antithesis of the contemporary ideal of agile, lean government (World Economic Forum 2014).

This problem is compounded by ministries' tendency to build ever more complex structures over time, untroubled by the periodic shakedowns that simplify and streamline private sector firms. Observing Parkinson's law (Parkinson 1958) that "work expands to fill the time available," the Greek administration has proved adept at creating structures, committees, and subcommittees with overlapping responsibilities. Not surprisingly, lines of command and communication are unclear, making coordination *between* these units another major challenge.

To add insult to injury, each new government (i.e., following a reshuffle rather than an election) reconfigures the administration, with politicians appointing party grandees to ministerial and deputy ministerial positions as well as special and general secretariats. This perpetuates an inefficient merry-go-round of responsibilities and authority, and political tensions stymie interdepartmental communication, since the key players are (transient) politicians rather than career civil service managers.

Such structural inflation and complexity is not confined to ministerial departments. Many agencies and public entities were created primarily to accommodate party-political operators. As there are few indications in terms of either output (and, as such, the benefits they create) or cost (direct or indirect), it is hard to assess their value.[18]

14.4.4 Formalism and the Role of So-called "Competences"

Stepping back along the chain of causation brings us to what lies behind this inefficient, malfunctioning, and wasteful edifice. To comprehend it, we must appreciate that it is pervaded by *procedural,* not *substantive* rationality (see March and Simon 1958; Olsen 2006); that is, it only makes sense on its own terms. The Greek state was built, in a path-dependent way, on principles of formalism (Spanou 2008; Spanou and Sotiropoulos 2011). Such an ethos dovetailed nicely with the political economy of clientelism, as appointees would not have to worry about their substantive output.

As the OECD (2011a, p. 27) functional review comments:

All the areas covered by this review—from HR management to budget processes—reflect a massive issue of "legal formalism" which stands in the way of effective and efficient governance. Legal formalism is partly the by-product of a legal system based on civil law, which traditionally emphasizes the need for a comprehensive and detailed structure of laws and regulations to cover all issues. ... Legal formalism also reflects the excessive use of internal administrative processes to frame the work of the administration, so that more attention is paid to these processes than to underlying policy work. ... Legal formalism has generated a culture and legal framework which provides no incentives for initiative on the part of civil servants, discourages any policy actions which are not accompanied by a legal text, privileges the observance (and development) of administrative processes rather than attention to the policy substance of civil service work, and slows down the work of the administration.

Excessive legal formalism is the cause of a range of dysfunctions and inefficiencies, and leads to a kludgy structure that finds it hard to adapt while justifying and maintaining inefficient silos (see chapter 15). It also widens the disconnect between formal structures (e.g., as reflected in organizational charts) and reality, making it harder for citizens and businesses to deal with government (OECD 2011a, pp. 51–52).

This formalism is evident when we look at what the Greek central administration actually produces. As figure 14.14 shows, while most outputs are laws, decrees, and circulars, action plans round down neatly to 0 percent, since they represent a mere 0.1 percent of the total *number* (let alone volume) of articles produced.

A specific issue that vividly illustrates formalism's corrosive effects is the role of "competencies." As the OECD review notes (2011, pp. 50–51), "It is virtually impossible to take a significant policy or administrative decision, at any level of government, if it does not fall within the scope of a legally provided competence." So, when a new need emerges that doesn't *quite* fall within the scope of a preexisting competency, "any change in the organization or competencies of a structure entails the adoption of a new law, presidential decree or ministerial decision .... In other words, a ministerial or high-level reshuffle of responsibilities cannot be carried out until the corresponding legal change has been enacted. But even day-to-day decisions regarding a unit's staff numbers or composition have to conform to the specific provisions of the law."

If competencies were broad enough, this would perhaps be less of an issue. Yet, as figure 14.15 shows, they have actually proliferated and narrowed, leading to ever-greater organizational and administrative complexity and rigidity, and adding an extra layer that clearly slows things down and absorbs disproportionate resources without any clear benefit.

Finally, formalism in HR policies prevents the efficient use of resources. An arch culprit is the principle of "branches," which define what each civil servant is expected to do throughout his or her career. On the supply side, once assigned to a "branch," civil

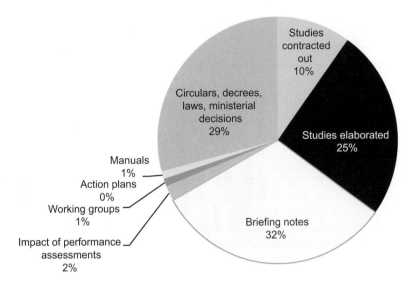

Figure 14.14
Output of general directorates in 2010. Output of the general directorates with executive compe-
tencies, excluding the output of general directorates
Source: Greece: Review of Central Administration (OECD 2011a)

servants are limited in both what they can do and where they can go. On the demand
side, ministries looking to recruit must stick to their own prespecified "branch attributes," rather than sourcing the best people for the job from within the public service.
This means that, even though both the ministry and the civil servant they need might
agree that a posting would be appropriate, the opening could still be in the wrong
branch (i.e., it doesn't match the civil servant's own branch assignment), in which case
the appointment falls through. This leads to substantial inefficiencies and lack of flexibility (OECD 2011a, p. 78).

14.5   Efforts to Change the Administration, before and during the Crisis

Before asking *why* these problems arise, it is instructive to consider one last area of
evidence: efforts to change the administration, and the stumbling blocks they have
encountered. This will allow us to better comprehend the pathologies of the administration by looking into the sources of resistance to change.

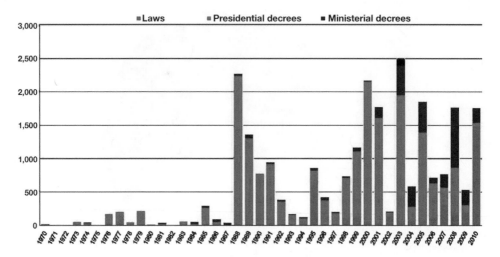

Figure 14.15
Number of government competencies defined through legal texts per year
Source: Greece: Review of Central Administration (OECD 2011a)

14.5.1 Background, and the Unhappy Fate of Pre-crisis Reforms

There have been a number of isolated attempts to effect change—partly to fix particular issues identified within Greece, or by international organizations such as the OECD, and partly as an effort to modernize the Greek state (Spanou 2008). In particular, there have been efforts to privatize, at least partly, key state-owned enterprises (including Olympic Airways, notorious for its excessive losses, plush working conditions, and hiring via political patronage), especially under the 1991 to 1993 New Democracy government. To some extent, this trend resumed after 1997, with the prospect of joining the EMU (Pagoulatos 2005).

Privatization, both as a means to increase public revenue and as a way of replacing ostensibly inefficient structures with presumably more efficient market-driven participants, has been adopted as a target by most Greek governments over the last two decades, yet has progressed extremely slowly. There are success stories, including the deregulation of telephony and the subsequent metamorphosis of former state monopoly OTE from sleepy also-ran to market leader in both fixed-line and mobile telephony, co-owned by Deutsche Telekom (see Pagoulatos and Zahariadis 2011). Also the demise of Olympic Airways, a massive black hole for state funds for decades, eventually allowed Aegean Airlines, a profitable and dynamic competitor, to emerge and eventually take over the remains of the former state monopoly, leading to state revenues from taxes, as opposed to subsidy costs.

Overall, though, there has been significant resistance to privatization. This has been supported by a generalized distrust of "the market," and the view—widely held in the media and by many politicians—that Greece was becoming an "extreme neoliberal economy," when in reality it remains statist and overregulated, with a long arm for the government and its friends. The efforts of the Troika to privatize have been repeatedly faced down, but at least there is now a better register of what the state owns, partly at the insistence of Greece's creditors.

The Greek administration itself has mostly changed in terms of centralization, partly in response to the European Union's emphasis on regions. During the 1990s there was a push toward greater local autonomy, through upgrading the role of regions, creating elected (as opposed to appointed) prefects, and rationalizing municipality structures, which were often merged to create stronger local units (Hlepas 1999; Spanou 2008); the Kapodistrias project (1997) was pivotal in this regard. This also allowed local government to have a say in various policy areas—which has had the side effect of increasing regulatory complexity and compliance burdens, given the poor coordination between central and local government (OECD 2011a, 2013.) Despite the nominal authority of local government, though, neither fiscal authority nor real independence has been granted in practice, leading to concerns of administrative duplication and inefficiency, as well as limited local voice (IMF 2006).[19]

More important, progress on rationalizing the Greek state has been limited to date, with a handful of exceptions in the form of projects such as Kapodistrias, which set up the local authorities; Kallikratis, aimed at rationalizing them (Law 3852/2010); and Di@vgeia, the most important project on transparency in the public sector. Tools that have become known in the literature as "New Public Management" (Lane 2000), which have underpinned the transformation of administrations including those of the United Kingdom (Andrews et al. 2013, Accenture, 2008) and the Netherlands (Jilke et al. 2013), have fallen on stony ground in Greece (Spanou 2008; Ladi 2014; Featherstone 2015). New Public Management focuses on incentives, principal–agent relationships, measurement, and resource allocation on the basis of efficiency—elements that would be familiar to any economist. But its principles of considering citizens as customers, the use of contract providers as alternatives to public employees, focusing on output, and total quality management have proved anathema to Greek unions and the body politic of the administration, not to mention those in the political system (and public service) who feel threatened by them. The alternative "approach" to reforming the administration, dubbed the "Neo-Weberian State" (Pollitt and Bouckaert 2011, pp. 118–19; Featherstone 2015, p. 6), which focuses on the preservation of the state's unique status and culture (and, presumably, power and benefits) but attempts to foment a shift from "bureaucratic rule-following" toward "a professional culture of quality and service," might be more apposite for Greece but probably overestimates the odds of change on the ground.

From the late 1980s on, the Greek administration faced increasing challenges of navigating a more complex economic environment, with greater responsibilities vis-à-vis the European Union, and an economy making increasing use of network industries and sophisticated capital markets. Its response was the trend dubbed "agencification" (Spanou 2008)—that is, the creation of independent entities that helped it meet particular objectives, circumventing the rigid structures and hiring (or salary) limitations of the public sector. These included the Office of the Ombudsman and the Data Protection Agency (created in 1997), the National Broadcasting Council (1989), the Independent Authority for the Selection of Personnel (1994), and other institutions that, among others, helped strengthen accountability and the rule of law (Eleftheriadis 2005, p. 332).

Finally, one of the few important innovations was the institution, in 2000, of "one-stop shops" for handling citizens' requests to the government (known as KEP, or Centers for Citizen Support). This bottom–up initiative achieved significant success, significantly easing people's relationships with the state. It also instilled the idea that citizens should be served by the state, and not just beholden to it. This came at the same time that citizens' rights became codified in law, even though their *de facto* protection remains uncertain.

Overall, reform in the administration was proclaimed more often than it was progressed. For instance, Law 3032/2004 could have facilitated organizational rationalization in the government, as it allowed administrative departments or agencies to set their own goals and evaluate results. Despite being passed, however, it was never implemented, since the steps required for it to work (i.e., creating job profiles, identifying and standardizing procedures, setting up appraisals) were never taken (see chapter 15). Other initiatives withered on the vine due to political opposition: one such was the attempt to link budgetary expenditures to policy areas, attempted with OECD support between 2007 and 2010 and finally abandoned (Bergvall et al. 2008).

14.5.2   Assessing the Progress of Reform under the Troika MoU

While the record of administrative reforms in Greece may appear disheartening—not only before the crisis but also during it—this was not an area neglected by Greece's creditors, and in particular the Troika. As Featherstone (2015) notes, "administrative measures represented approximately 40 percent (282) of the total number of reforms (706) required of Greece under the terms of the two bail-out Memoranda of Understanding

(MoU). Clearly, there was the recognition that reforming the Greek state administration would be crucial to the ability of the country to adapt to the requirements of the Eurozone." It is also important to note that the Troika's emphasis, while it shifted over time (with the increasing understanding of the nature and the magnitude of the program), was distinctly different from that of Greece, and focused on some key areas of deficiency within the country.

Figures 14.16 and 14.17 show the reforms by category. Figure 14.16 illustrates all the reforms that were included in the MoU, and figure 14.17 shows the reforms that were initiated by the Greek state. Comparing and contrasting these two figures is instructive.

The absence of audit and performance from the Greek administration agenda is a clear symptom of the lack of drive for accountability that pervades Greek public service. As Featherstone (2015, p. 9) notes, "the focus of the reforms shows a major shift from the preexisting domestic pattern detailed above. Measures concerned with the audit and performance of the public administration now loomed large on the Troika's radar; indeed, the list of required reforms here was three times the level sustained before their arrival. A further major difference was the attention given to financial management, which became a very prominent concern (consistently in the top three). Performance and delivery, as well as budget discipline, were of central concern to Greece's creditors,

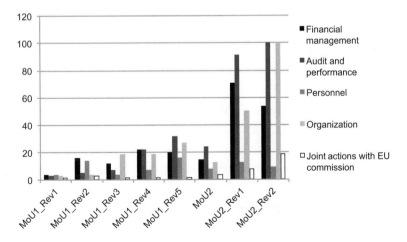

Figure 14.16
Administrative reforms in Greece post–MoU by subject category in 2010 to 2013
Source: Featherstone (2015, p. 9); data from Troika reports differentiated according to the typology proposed by Ongaro (2009).

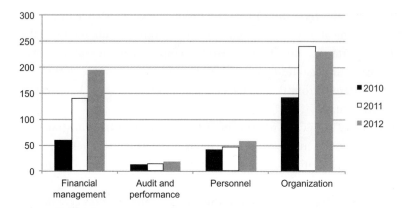

Figure 14.17
Administrative reforms initiated by the Greek government by subject category
Source: Featherstone (2015); data from website of Ministry for Administrative Reform, Greece, and
differentiated according to the typology proposed by Ongaro (2009).

and the differences in the patterns of reform actions are indicative of contrasting
(external and domestic) agendas."[20]

The Troika reform project, as Featherstone (2015, p. 11) notes, was focused on five
pillars, which, if successfully completed, could have transformed the public sector:

1. *Operational improvements*   Increase operational efficiency, enhance the quality of
   available data, better the use of information technology (IT), and coordinate more
   effectively state organizations and parts of the public apparatus.

2. *Governance and political autonomy*   Strengthen the autonomy of key parts of the
   administration against political manipulation and corruption (e.g., in the tax revenue administration).

3. *Managerial rationalization*   Shed posts, introduce performance management, and
   develop a human resources strategy.

4. *Organizational rationalization and accountability*   Review current state provisions in
   certain key areas with the purpose of evaluating performance outcomes in relation
   to resource commitments.

5. *Transparency*   Open up the administration to external review and technical advice
   and support (See European Commission, 2014)

Progress vis-à-vis these objectives has been limited, and focused on critical areas for
Greece's finances—such as tax collection, where the office of a Permanent Secretary
for Public Revenue was instituted—that are intended to be shielded from political
interference.[21]

Beyond taxes, however, only limited progress has been made. The Troika frequently signed off failures to meet structural targets (Ladi 2014), even though it had stood firm on fiscal targets (Jacobides 2012). In practical terms, this meant reducing civil servants' salaries and reducing the workforce through early retirement.[22] Structural issues and reforming the administration might be important on paper, but there was neither the sustained pressure, nor the skill, to see them through. Reforms were undermined by Greek politicians, unions, and others, while those who did want reform neither understood the context fully nor were in a position to invest in making it a success (see Featherstone 2015 for a detailed discussion).

The fact that almost all opposition parties saw the MoU as an "imposition" by "foreign powers" (only to change their views when they came to government) legitimated resistance to change. Politicians of many stripes, as well as the unions (ADEDY, in particular), mobilized resistance around the idea that potential public sector layoffs were an assault on Greek democracy. The fact that this was a crumbling, unsustainable system did not enter the discussion.

Reforms were neither budget nor output focused; they were not directed to results. There was little accountability, and the various strands soon slowed to a crawl—or ground to a halt. To wit, the "Delos" system (created by the government to track the progress of reform and report back to the Troika) didn't focus on the percentage of reforms that were completed, as seen from the perspective of the individual citizen or business. Rather, it focused on administrative steps completed toward a goal—for example, a 99 percent completed reform, as far as the citizen was concerned, would look identical to one that never happened at all. It seemed that the reforms themselves needed reforming before they could achieve reform.

The lack of attention to process management, and the inherent difficulty of the massive reform process, also limited success. Take the civil servant evaluation: given the publically stated need to reduce headcount, civil servants understandably suspected that evaluation would lead to downsizing by the backdoor. Similar concerns were raised about the role of mobility, and this idea too soon became politicized, increasing retrenchment and resistance to change.

One of the key factors holding back reform has been the lack of buy-in (Featherstone 2015). As we know from other cases, including those in Central Europe (Drazen 2002; Haughton 2007), local ownership is a determining factor for the success of a reform project. As Featherstone (2015) notes, in the 2006 EU–Turkey negotiations, Turkey's Prime Minister Erdogan renamed the EU conditions for his country's accession the "Ankara criteria," proclaiming that they were in the national interest anyway (Cengiz and Hoffmann 2013). Whether out of convenience or malice, Greek politicians did the exact inverse—and the reform process, which nominally had supporters across the political spectrum, was duly orphaned.

These issues are illustrated by the sad fate of an important initiative: Law 4048/2012 (on Better Regulation), intended to stem the tide of overregulation. In practice, its provisions—that legislation should consider impacts on business ahead of time—are not met (chapter 15). Likewise the effort to identify administrative burdens was met with concerted resistance. Ostensibly the concern was that launching major projects for the detailed recording, analysis, and reduction of administrative burdens was far too costly and time-consuming.[23]

In this regard the magnitude of legislative change imposed by the MoU led to a notable side effect. Greece had to legislate extensively to meet obligations in the MoU—often using multipurpose, bumper legislation considered to a very tight timetable in Parliament. This *de facto* precluded the conduct of rigorous *ex ante* assessment of regulatory impact, or indeed sufficient consideration of how the laws could be effectively implemented in such an administratively inefficient system. There was no mechanism to ensure that the regulations imposed as a result of the MoU would not actually compound regulatory complexity and bureaucracy, even if they allegedly met their primary reform aims; neither was there any initiative to eliminate older, outdated, and potentially conflicting provisions in prior law or practice.

As for the law on simpler business licensing (Law 3853/2010), it advanced with difficulty, with the government presumably having to consider pressures from vested interests. The General Commercial Register (GEMI),[24] a step toward strengthening the regulatory environment for businesses, has yet to emerge fully from the pilot phase.

14.5.3   Reforming the Public Administration and the Role of MAREG

The role of ownership, as well as leadership, is well illustrated by the impact of a ministerial change in June 2013 in the Ministry of Administrative Reform and Electronic Governance (ΥΔΜΗΔ/MAREG). Following the change of guard, Troika reports began to sound much more upbeat, as targets began to be met. In the European Union, the mood became more positive, leading to some momentum for change, despite significant resistance.

An important element of the June 2013 to December 2014 MAREG activities was to implement the new tighter rules on the civil servants' penal code (Law 4057/2012). Previously even those rare prosecutions that led to a conviction were not considered final until the last appeal was finalized, often six or seven years post-conviction (and possibly well over a decade after the crime). Meanwhile the culprit would receive full benefits, progress unimpeded in their career, and their full pension—with no clawback even if the conviction was finally upheld. This was changed to immediate dismissal after the initial conviction (but with the possibility of reinstatement should an appeal be successful). More important, the law (described in Stavropoulos 2015) provided for a new composition of judging panels, which had to be chaired by a judge and include one representative of the Legal Council of the State, as well as a senior civil servant who would have to come from a *different* ministry than the accused's, after a random draw process organized by the Legal Council of the State to ensure impartiality. This was in sharp contrast with the old system, where the local ADEDY union representative and other ministerial appointees populated the panels. But it met with fierce resistance, and it was only in 2013, with a new MAREG, that it was finally possible to push through implementation. (The previous MAREG had preferred to circumvent the law and stick with the *status quo ante*.) There were also further changes in the nature and magnitude of punishments, as well as in the appeals process, focused on keeping those convicted in the first instance from returning to their jobs—which would raise issues of the guilty covering their tracks.

Yet, while it is important to push for the accountability of civil servants, another important problem is that conscientious public servants should not be unduly accused. (This problem is magnified by the fact that civil servants are not assessed on the substance of their output.) As Stavropoulos (2011) points out, laws 4093/2012, 4111/2013, and 4210/2013 changed the disciplinary procedures against public servants. First, the list of sacking offenses lengthened dramatically to include relatively minor misdemeanors such as abusing equipment belonging to the state or poor timekeeping; and second, the process was moved away from a disciplinary panel to the courts, themselves riddled by serious inefficiencies. This risks unleashing a torrent of abusive claims, as accusations can be made on the flimsiest grounds.

As it turned out, many of the more sensible provisions of the law were reversed in 2015 by the new SYRIZA/ANEL government, which also reinstated members of the Civil Servant Union (ADEDY) in disciplinary boards. The new law also afforded a remarkable *de facto* impunity to union members accused of embezzlement (Stavropoulos 2015, p. 11). The fact that a left-wing government would herald softer sanctions for bribery, embezzlement, or gross negligence as a "democratic reform" indicates the depth of the Greek malaise—and the importance of rent-seeking, to which we will return in the next section.

A more recent illustration with the challenges of administrative transformation came in late 2016 when Greece, responding to another important MoU requirement, belatedly voted for the establishment of a Digital Organizational Blueprint of the Administration. The original staff proposal provided for mandatory declaration of all parts of the public sector, along the lines of the Di@vgeia programme, with severe penalties for those who fail to report their unit, staffing and reporting lines. The Government, however, chose to significantly water down the text and the law that was passed (4440/2016) omitted references to the compulsory and comprehensive character of the Blueprint, and also omitted the references to a historical record that can be followed over time. Instead, it left it to the discretion of the Minister of AREG to specify the way in which this blueprint will be implemented. While valiant efforts are being undertaken to push the Minister of AREG to ensure that this mapping becomes truly compulsory and comprehensive, the implementation details are still unknown at the time of this chapter's writing. There is a risk that yet another opportunity to get some data to streamline the public sector, and to be able to track it and evaluate it, may be lost.

While these developments underscore the role of the Minister of AREG, in addition to the Ministry, we would be amiss not to consider the role of the Troika and in particular the Task Force for Greece (TFGR) during the crisis. A report prepared for the European Commission by Adam Smith International and Alvarez & Marsal (2014) offers a positive assessment, yet others have been more critical noting that change has been limited (Featherstone 2015). Discussions on the ground seem to confirm the latter impression. Neither the TFGR nor the IMF—nor indeed any other institution—had the capacity, manpower, or skill to drive through this massive transformation process, which in the best of all possible cases would have required sustained attention and effort directed by highly skilled and competent leaders (inside) and advisors (outside). There was no real focus on issues of process or understanding of the organizational implications of change management (see Kotter 1996; Fernandez and Rainey 2006; Boston Consulting Group 2012).

14.6   From Proximate to Deeper Causes: Getting to the "Why" of the Greek Administrative Malaise

In many respects the story of the Greek public administration is a textbook case of organizational pathology: a co-dependent ecosystem of powerful vested interests determined to preserve a deteriorating equilibrium. While causes and symptoms often overlap, there are a few clear attributes that seem to be at the root of the malaise.

14.6.1   The Historical Context: The Political Economy of the Failures in Greek Public Administration

First, an aggressive expansionary policy, associated with a rapid increase in public debt, and a wholesale replacement of senior public servants with party officials (a practice that has continued unabated) allowed Greek governments from the 1980s onward to use public appointments as a means of political control. Once this trend had been cemented by PASOK, most other governments followed suit. The few brief exceptions were mostly forced by near-bankruptcy, a more moderate fiscal view (e.g., 1991 to 1993), or the prospect of joining the euro (1996 to 2000).

The boom years saw Greece increasing its indebtedness and allowing its public administration to decline even further, as tax evasion increased and layers of additional cost were added to an already inefficient state apparatus. The ready availability of funding, especially following euro entry, allowed the state to throw money at the administration's problems instead of trying to solve them.

Early warning signals of financial and operational shortcomings were ignored by all concerned. The political system relied on the electorate for support, in return for jobs and favors; politicians and administrators operated within a political economy of vested interests; and public and private sector actors benefited from state largesse, lack of transparency, and limited competition. The power bestowed by political connections to navigate an inefficient bureaucracy suited both politicians and the businesspeople associated with them—as well as other rent-seeking groups, including unions, which secured remarkable privileges for their members. State inefficiency, in other words, became part and parcel of a system that enabled economic and structural inefficiency to grow. Nobody needed or wanted objective measures; rewards flowed to those who could "work the system" (Featherstone and Papadimitriou 2008; IMF 2010).[25]

The challenge is, of course, that the existing system had clear beneficiaries. Whether in the public sector, the political or media system, or the private sector, substantial rent-seeking had combined with inertia—a natural process in any system, especially if it is large and complicated. Rent-seeking wasn't the preserve of wily entrepreneurs or corrupt officials; it became institutionalized, such that *all* groups sought special rights and protections. The problem affected everyone, from unions (e.g., PPC) gaining astonishing benefits for their members, and professional groups such as lawyers and pharmacists being sheltered from competition, to industries such as transport and haulage, where protection and complexity became normalized.

Even when the system started crumbling under its own weight, collective inefficiencies were not enough to drive change. In the words of Niccolo Machiavelli (1947 [1515]), "it must be remembered that there is nothing more difficult to plan, more doubtful of success, nor more dangerous to manage, than the creation of a new system. For the initiator has the enmity of all who would profit by the preservation of the old institutions and merely lukewarm defenders in those who would gain by the new ones."

Those within the system see objective criteria as threats to their power, while the outside beneficiaries of the system (procurers to the state, or other beneficiaries of state largesse and protectionism) have even more to lose from greater transparency. Regrettably, those who would benefit from change have interests that are simply too loose and diffuse to react with equal vigor. The lack of understanding, the lack of true willingness to engage, and the limited progress on reforms documented in the previous section complete this depressing picture.

This downward spiral was further accentuated by the political process, and by the role of the media. In public discussions, it is remarkable how rarely one hears of evaluating a minister's tenure using metrics in their area of competence. Without clear metrics to be evaluated by (e.g., waiting time for operations, learning outcomes for education, crime statistics per area, efficiency of public resource usage), politicians have no reason to press for efficiency in the state apparatus, as it is not their primary target. They have focused instead on media appearances, public pronouncements (as opposed to saying whether their previous pronouncements have been followed through), and finding ways of rewarding loyal party clientele and their own political apparatus. Without a change in the criteria and data by which politicians are evaluated, it would be absurd to expect them to change this system.

Given media ownership by major contractors—part of the system known as *diaploki* (intertwining of the private and public sector)—it is not surprising that Greece has no tradition of investigative journalism, and that the Greek media are deafeningly silent in terms of quantifying and assessing the efficiency of government. By focusing on short-term stories, they deprive their audiences of the evidence and data needed to hold power to account. This has facilitated the survival and resilience of political parties in what is, in essence, a statist economy, with very inefficient centralized economic control. It is remarkable that there has been such scant coverage from the press—and even less from TV and radio channels—of the astonishing and often ghastly evidence that emerges from the MoU progress reports. Rather than unearthing the underlying problems, the media have focused on the ephemera and micropolitical tensions of those "for" and "against" the MoU. This obfuscates what is really happening on the ground, and sustains abstract, vacuous, and frequently hypocritical discussions on "the politics of the memorandum," neoliberalism, or the "attack from market extremists."

14.6.2 Inertia and the Difficulty of Change

The Greek woes, however, are not only due to the unhealthy political economy that has coalesced around these public sector inefficiencies and the rent-seeking opportunities they provide. In the Greek public administration, the *status quo* is preserved by the interaction of inertia, routines, habits, and culture (March and Simon 1958; Olsen 2006).

The substantial inertia in the administration has gifted an alibi to those implicated—and cultivated the widespread popular view of an irrevocably broken system that can never change. However, such unconditional defeatism belies the possibility of progress. The example of KEP (described in section 14.5) gives cause for optimism, and the implementation of the TAXIS system, which allows for online tax submission, has been a boon to both individuals and businesses. Also, for all of their shortcomings, several initiatives over the last few years have managed to improve the way the state operates (Featherstone 2015; Adam Smith International and Alvarez & Marsal 2014). Moreover history suggests that even highly inert systems can change—provided we take the sources of inertia seriously and address them systematically (see Fernandez and Rainey 2006), which is precisely the area of concern in Greece. It is worth emphasizing that there has been precious little effort to understand organizational issues, whether by Greece's politicians or its creditors. Yet there has been growing interest in rethinking the structure of the administration (e.g., Jacobides, Portes, and Vayanos 2011).

This potential for change, though, seems consistently belied by strong forces working against it. The root causes of the administration's problems are both structural and evolutionary. Its structure provides the wrong incentives, hampers well-meaning agents, and channels energies in inefficient ways. The issues are rooted in a longstanding and resilient heritage of formalism, and a battery of processes and routines that can only change gradually. The structure determines what is rewarded—often inefficiency—and what is disregarded, and shapes the administration's evolutionary trajectory and dynamics. Worse, this system is often poorly understood by outsiders, and deliberately misrepresented by insiders who want to preserve it. To change it, piecemeal interventions or fiscal policies alone will prove woefully inadequate. What is needed is a systematic, holistic rethink—not only of where we want to go, but how we get there from where we are today.

14.6.3 The Lack of a Real Reform Agenda and Change Management

Summarizing the literature and the evidence on successful public sector change, Fernandez and Rainey (2006) identify eight factors that drive successful public sector change: ensuring the need, providing a plan, building internal support for change and overcoming organizational resistance, ensuring top management support and commitment, building external support, providing resources, institutionalizing change, and pursuing comprehensive change. It is remarkable that in the case of Greece, other than the establishment of a clear need and endless lip service paid to the idea of reform, almost none of these steps has been taken seriously. Even in the most recent reform efforts, and despite a context of the largest bailout in global history, there was practically no capacity, scant resources (if any), and almost no process management. Unless and until both Greece and, currently, its creditors decide to take this process seriously, and get down to designing a proper change management program, with a keen understanding of the political economy within the administration and across society, and until they endow it with resources and leadership, and incentives to change, little will change in the Greek economy and polity. Conversely, there is a huge potential upside from reorganizing the administration and from changing the way the state interacts with citizens and with businesses. The task is not impossible, and we can surely learn from both successes and failures of similar large-scale change, including in Central Europe, or more recently in the Baltics (Estonia: OECD 2011c; Latvia: World Bank 2013; World Bank 2006). It is encouraging that some of the investors in Greek government debt are starting to push for these reforms, highlighting the turnaround angle (www.mostimportantreform.info).

As we consider how to improve the process and ownership of the change agenda, we must also think carefully about the conditions of the massive current loan arrangement, which are a powerful tool for the Greek public administration over the next few years. They should provide not just a stick but also a carrot that will motivate the country to improve (Drazen 2002). In doing so, capacity support and focused resources are absolutely essential: from combating tax evasion to improving the monitoring of the public sector, from the use of IT to changes in business processes and organizational structure, there is ample room for helping improve the Greek administration, state, and economy, and to address all three points of the "tragic trident" that has punctured Greece's productive potential, sending it into an entirely avoidable tailspin.

14.7   Priorities Looking Ahead

This is a challenging time for governments and public administrations the world over. Social, demographic, economic, and technological changes are transforming our expectations of what a state should provide, and how it should be structured (e.g., World Economic Forum 2011). In this context Greece's antiquated, inefficient state, which has severely restrained its economy and reduced its citizens' quality of life, appears truly remarkable. Clearly, there is a lot to do, and much that should have been done already.

That said, there is reason to believe that this crisis would not be fully wasted. The scale and root causes of the problem are much better understood now than they were a few years ago. Moreover the political process in Greece has run its course; the final set of promises to maintain the status quo was quashed when the SYRIZA/ANEL government signed the MoU in August 2015, agreeing to transform both the country's economy and its administration. New technologies and the possibility of a massive Business Process Redesign could help the Greek state rationalize its structure while taking advantage of the opportunities offered by IT,[26] if only government were bold enough to address not only the symptoms of its decline but also its underlying causes. Of course, against this promise lies the deeply entrenched political economy in the public and private sector and, crucially, in the political class. What can be done to help tilt the balance in favor of reform?

14.7.1 Redesign Performance Measures and Incentives for and in the Administration

The obvious area for improvement is measures of performance and corresponding incentives in the public sector. First, a reform-minded movement must ensure that it provides both a stick and a carrot, in terms of the way that individuals (within units), units (within organizations), and organizations (within the state apparatus) perform. While a few tentative steps have been made, we are far from having even a rudimentary evaluation of effectiveness at each level. As a result good performance is not adequately recognized—not even symbolically. It is important to stress that an appropriate measurement system can exert a positive influence even if it is only loosely linked to compensation; a broad connection between output achieved and career progression, as well as the symbolic impact of recognizing good performance, can have significant effects—even in the absence of direct pecuniary rewards (Perry et al. 2006).

Second, it is important to consider the incentives in place, and the perverse outcomes that they generate. In this regard disciplinary procedures toward civil servants appear deeply flawed, and even some of the recent changes are misdirected. The problem is that real malfeasance (embezzlement, gross negligence, etc.) is written off by statute after an excessively short period of time, and that the legal process for investigating malfeasance renders its punishment inefficient. Unfortunately, rather than improving the policing of inappropriate behavior, extending the statutes of limitation, and speeding up the process or shortening the time for appeals, the emphasis has instead been on cracking down on even the most minor transgressions; that is, the proportionality between the punishment and the crime has been removed (Stavropoulos 2015), while the process remains problematic. Such ostensible "toughening up" can seriously back-fire, since it opens up the possibility of conscientious civil servants being open to abusive claims and lawsuits from those whose interests are threatened.

A balance must be struck. It is important to be tough on abusive behavior by civil servants, and get better at going after those who benefit from it. At the same time, however, it is also important to protect those who are making difficult judgment calls on behalf of the state. The current system, which makes no allowance for performance management, and looks at legal formalism as opposed to substance, perversely favors obstruction and inaction over initiative: civil servants can suffer severe repercussions (including criminal ones) if their handling of a case is deemed to have harmed the state's interests, but almost no penalty if they burden citizens, businesses, and other departments with heaps of onerous bureaucracy. For example, it is common practice for the administration to appeal all legal cases (even hopeless ones) to the highest level, in order to avoid the risk of getting accused of mishandling the state's interests. Similarly, and for the same reasons, prosecutors send all cases to trial (even ones with no merit), increasing the burden for the litigants and the legal system. Changing the upsides and downsides of actions by civil servants will allow them to be much more effective, and may promote bottom–up innovation.

In designing incentive systems, the devil will be in the detail, but it is clear that performance KPIs need to be aggressively pursued, while at the same time considering how to both protect and audit civil servants as substantively as possible. The abuse of lawsuits in Greece, and the intimidation by threat of lawsuit of those trying to perform their duties, should be taken seriously.

More daringly, perhaps, there is a need to challenge taboos including life employ-ment for public servants; such practices, originally intended to protect civil servants from political interference, could be substituted by a greater reliance on the outcome that leaders in the administration are able to achieve.

14.7.2 Impose Transparency and Use the Power of Crowdsourcing

The best defense against abusive lawsuits, inefficient incentives, and people taking advantage of the system is transparency. The growth of Di@vgeia was a crucial devel-opment in this respect; it has already been built on and should be developed further. The recent availability of data, and the creation of repositories such as publicspend-ing.gr, can help expose inappropriate practices, and also identify areas of weakness or strength in the state apparatus. It would further be very helpful for a culture of investigative journalism to take root in Greece, especially in terms of probing the links between politicians, entrepreneurs, and the state, on the basis of the increasingly available data.

To ensure that the administration focuses on outputs, it is crucial to ensure that there be made public whatever KPIs are chosen for each part of the government. They should be visible to all, through a mandatory platform analogous to Di@vgeia, and exist at the level of the unit, the agency, and the ministry, so that each public official, whether appointed or elected, can be assessed on the progress made in their area of responsibility in real time. If Ministries reported the aggregate evolution of metrics in their own areas, so that there can be a focus on how effective ministers and politicians are in terms of their progress, significant change of behavior could ensue. Ministerial and governmental pronouncements and pledges should also be tracked, and their realization checked with data—either centrally, or through collaborative media (e.g., a wiki for public work). This will allow promises to be followed up, and public spending analyzed. As we design the reform process, it is crucial to think about how to co-opt politicians, or make it difficult for those who are part of the old system to remain undetected. This requires engagement with the press and, more plausibly, social pressure and the use of social media.

The effort to push for greater accountability and control (of the administration and politicians alike) will depend on the availability of data. The law passed on December 31, 2014, on making government data public by default (unless there is a reason it should remain private) was a welcome development, provided that it does not perish in practice through implementation failure, as has happened in the past. This should be strengthened further, along with the Di@vgeia project, to help scrutinize the operation of the administration. It is important to *help* groups such as publicspending.gr, transparency.gr, and other bottom–up initiatives aimed at fighting corruption, since they appear to be struggling, or retreating from their original goals.[27]

Finally, transparency should be used to strengthen the leadership of the administration. The recent government appears to be relapsing into old practices of appointing close political allies throughout the administration, which can undermine credibility and morale while reducing operational abilities in critical parts of the state apparatus. The recent record of the Greek government is appalling in this regard, and it is entirely possible that the administration, and even the country, may collapse as a result of its administrative inefficiency and managerial incompetence. It is therefore crucial to end such practices and focus instead on the expansion of open recruitment platforms such as http://www.opengov.gr/en/, where all major public sector posts should be advertised.

With transparency and accountability should also come a change in the compensation structure, where we may want to accept targeted increases, with salary for top posts made commensurate with skill and responsibility—provided that the information and rationale are also made public. Focusing on meritocracy is absolutely crucial, and openness should complement it. Greece could take a leaf out of the City of Chicago's book, which publishes the compensation details of every employee or contractor, to ensure transparency and fairness. Selection processes should be more transparent, candidates' CVs must be public, and we should invite executives from the private sector to help staff the administration, potentially on shorter contracts.

14.7.3   Redesign Organizational Structure and Business Processes

In addition to redesigning KPIs, measures, and incentives at the individual level, there is a great opportunity to drastically rework inefficient, antiquated, formalistic procedures that protect those who are inefficient or even corrupt, with the help of automation, information provision, and a rational business process redesign. There is much scope for improving operational efficiency—though we must measure it both before and afterward, and share our findings too.

Likewise there is much potential in rethinking the basic principles of organization design and HR development. Given the massive inefficiencies and inherent problems in hierarchical organizations, we may want to start by addressing the issues of the centralized control of the state over its ministries and agencies. One could, for instance, give secretary-generals in each ministry the authority to organize their own units as they deem appropriate, rather than needing a Presidential Decree to do so. Senior managers should also be given tools to identify, select, promote, and motivate civil servants. This additional freedom should be combined with accountability in terms of outcomes, and longer contracts for senior positions, through a reactivation of the Rangousis law.

It is important to dispense with long-held practices that are clearly outdated. It is time to throw out "competencies" and bring in *outcomes* and become more flexible in procurement, especially with regard to IT. Public spending should be revisited from a radical perspective, looking at return on investment—for example, by resourcing more areas within the Finance Ministry where skills and capital are needed, deployments could easily pay for themselves within weeks.

More innovative practices could be a concrete tool for forcing organizational adjustment. They might include the potential centralization of back-office processing at different hospitals or local authorities, or other shared services that could be developed throughout the state apparatus. The potential gains from the thoughtful, flexible, and strategic application of IT (as opposed to blind faith in white-elephant mega-projects that are expected to resolve all public needs) can be bundled with organizational and process redesign as part and parcel of the change process.

Success will come more easily once it framed as an opportunity for the civil service, and not just a threat. One should be cognizant of deteriorating pay and conditions, the public discontent with civil servants, and the challenging conditions faced in the administration as we seek not only to curtail poor behavior but also to promote, motivate, excite, and engage those in the service who have the appetite and skill to produce. To do so, innovative practices must be fostered, and it is important to rethink the relationship between the private sector, the public sector, and civic society, as the Redesign Greece initiative (http://www.redesigngreece.gr/) showed was possible.

14.7.4 Focus on Change Management and Ownership of the Transformation Process

Last, but surely not least, it is critical to build a clear, compelling, and unifying narrative with the power to induce buy-in, highlight benefits, and guide the process of change. This massive change-management process cannot be driven by top–down pressure alone; it also depends on bottom–up support. To do so, the challenge must be seen from the perspectives of *all* stakeholders, and the challenge will be to find ways to motivate and coerce them. Continuity should also be promoted in government policies: currently, civil servants view all change initiatives with a deep mistrust tempered with stoicism—since they know full well that in a few months another government will impose yet another set of changes.

As with any program of organizational transformation and change, strong leadership is essential. A few key, determined change agents will need to be identified and empowered. Such strong leaders would ideally have turnaround experience, with an understanding of how to manage complex organizations. They may need to be professionally established, or outside the day-to-day political fray, and as such able to take risks without fearing reprisals. They should create their own teams, where discretion will have to be irrevocably linked to medium-term results.

More generally, strong emphasis should be placed on managing the process of change. One of the key difficulties in Greece is that there has been almost no attention, skill, or resources dedicated to change management. This needs to change if we are to have any hope of a strong outcome, and the conditionalities of the loan agreement should reflect this. Success will also require adequate financial resources and expertise, both inside and outside Greece, to be secured, in order to make change happen.

As we look at managing the change process, it is critical to learn from both international and domestic experience—both failures and successes. We need to engage those outside the administration in this process, but also build institutional capacity to *absorb* knowledge, and use it—as opposed to letting ideas float by. The fate of Greece rests on the efficiency of its implementation.

14.7.5   Coda: Is Any of This Feasible?

Given the mishaps and disheartening trajectory of the public administration so far, the question naturally arises: Is any of the steps above feasible? Or are they just a litany of wishes that is doomed, like many others before it, never to see the light of day?

The answer has to be qualified. On one hand, we face a powerful prehistory and an even stronger political economy, bolstered by entrenched routines and limited skills, that suggest little will change. On the other hand, the political economy that bred this monstrously inefficient system has collapsed. The platform, quite plainly, is on fire. Greece has entered a vicious circle of contraction, increased state involvement, and problem accumulation, which has left the politicians unable to promise jobs to their fans, contracts to their supporters, or even privileges to themselves. Yet poverty and scarcity alone are neither sufficient nor necessary antecedents of such a major change.

The recent MoU, for all its shortcomings, may be useful in this regard. As creditors become more keenly aware of the importance of reforming of the administration, so the external pressure to change grows. While the track record of the Troika has been mixed at best, the existence of an outside imperative for change can provide an important push. This will only be effective, though, when political leadership emerges that dares to address the challenge. To succeed, Greece needs communicators who can state the problem clearly and simply: rouse a new grassroots movement willing to clash with the establishment; a realization among at least part of the business, political, and administrative elite that catastrophe is nigh if Greece does not change; and strong leadership by a new type of politician. It will also need a small, dedicated team, motivated by the desire to change the country.

If this sounds overly idealist, it may be worth looking at the unexpected growth of entrepreneurial ventures throughout Greece, indicating the gradual transformation of a sleepy economy. Of course, change will not be easy; the current crisis is the reflection of deeper societal and moral problems, which coevolved with this inefficient system, and change needs to be pervasive (Doxiadis 2013; Kalyvas et al. 2013; Kostis 2013; Pappas 2015). The old will coexist uncomfortably with the new, and nothing short of a cultural clash is needed to restore the administration, and the country. Greece has seen a number of cycles of growth and institutional failure (Kalyvas 2015). Yet, daunting as these prospects are, change can happen. We are now at a low point, but turnaround is possible, however unlikely it might seem. Provided, that is, that we start with a solid understanding of causes, symptoms, and tools for change.

Notes

1. This chapter was informed by my previous collaboration with Panagiotis Karkatsoulis and my engagement with the Greek public administration, government and Troika in 2012 to 2014, while doing field research and pro bono work with RedesignGreece. Michalis Vassiliadis provided outstanding and dedicated research assistance, and deserves much credit for helping gather and organize the evidence. I would like to thank Yerassimos Yiannopoulos, Diomidis Spinellis, and especially Dimitris Vayanos for detailed comments on several drafts. Tassos Gianitsis, Nikos Vettas, George Pagoulatos, Kevin Featherstone, Haris Theocharis, Dionysis Rigopoulos, Michael Vafopoulos, Stefanos Manos, Nikos Georgiadis, and Aristos Doxiadis provided valuable comments, and Tom Albrighton helped sharpen the text.

2. Note that the increase in the share of GDP devoted to payments of government employees has increased between 2007 and 2013 as a result of the drastic reduction of GDP, as opposed to the increase of the total wage bill, as we explain in section 14.2. Given the sharp increase in unemployment (due to private sector contraction), and the contraction of the economy overall, the relative stability of number of employees was the result of a wave of retirement and pay reduction in the administration.

3. The OECD-MAREG administrative burdens project undertaken during the crisis included public procurement improvements, and helped create the Central Electronic Registry for Public Procurement (CERPP/ΚΗΜΔΗΣ), which is a transparency register and includes additional information such as contract award notices. CERPP was established by Law 4013/2011, and has been operating since February 2013 for all orders above 1,000 euros (OECD 2013, p. 36).

4. As noted in chapter 12 (on the justice system), in 2008, contract enforcement took an average of 819 days in Greece (compared with 620 in the rest of the world, and 506 in the euro area). By 2012, it was taking 1,100 days (as opposed to 620 in the rest of the world and 541 in the euro area).

5. This is not to denigrate the importance of cost-cutting, which can, in principle, be beneficial inasmuch as it removes resources from inefficient structures and imposes budget constraints—and can, as such, have direct and indirect efficiency benefits. It is, however, necessary to point out that rather than cost-cutting, the focus ought to have been, and was clearly not on, rationalizing processes, practices, and structures. Cost-cutting could have been used as a tool to re-engineer the administration and push through reorganization. The reality is that cost-cutting happened without any guiding principle, straining an inefficient system, often depriving it from the resources needed for its efficient operation, let alone redesign.

6. Examples include Enterprise Greece S.A., Hellenic Fund for Entrepreneurship and Development S.A., National Hellenic Research Foundation, Organization of Urban Transportation of Thessaloniki, Hellenic Centre for Disease Control and Prevention, Greek National Opera, and the Athens Concert Hall.

7. For an example, consider ΔΕΠΤΑΗ (Municipal Business of Heracleion, Crete), which carries out activities ranging from running a tourist shop to managing several leisure sites, as well as organizing cultural events. All these are ostensibly for the benefit of the Municipality—yet ΔΕΠΤΑΗ is a private company.

8. Neither OTE (which is more private than public) nor PPC/ΔEH (which is resolutely more public than private) appear on the register, even though the budget includes massive yearly payments to subsidize their pension funds. Yet Hellenic Railways Organisation and its successor Trainose are included. The criteria for inclusion appear to allow significant discretion.

9. These remarkable arrangements, which amount to 1 billion euro annual subsidies to a relatively small group of pensioners in an economy producing 180 billion euros in total, were created when stakes of PPC and OTE were sold to private investors, presumably to compensate employees in terms of the benefits that had been built up until that time. This was done so as to facilitate a "clean slate" privatization without contingent pension liabilities for investors. Interestingly, the proceeds from the privatization have been, to date, eclipsed from the yearly outflows to pensioners, which have yet not been revised. On the history of the legal arrangements leading to the PPC subsidy, see Manos (2015). The subsidy to OTE pensioners can be seen clearly in the Greek State Expenditure Report, under code Ξ2361. See the 2013 Regular Budget expenditure per Ministry, Ministry of Finance (2014, p. 231).

10. For many of these entities, publishing accounts had been mandated, but not observed, for years or even decades. Hospitals, in particular, had to publish accounts from 1993 onwards (Law 2084/1992). However, this law was never properly implemented—showing how, in Greece, administrative procedures can often nullify even well-intentioned laws, and cement inertia and the lack of accountability.

11. As the Second Economic Adjustment Program for Greece (Occasional Papers 148, May 2013, Second Review) notes, "all hospitals implemented double-entry accounting. Out of 89 hospitals: 13 implemented analytical cost accounting, 68 are in the process and 8 do not have the necessary software yet. A report was sent to the Troika regarding January 2013 data. EC requested an action plan and timeline on the introduction of analytical cost accounting in hospitals not yet equipped with it." Interestingly, progress on this front (MoU 2.9.4) was not documented in the third and fourth review of the Memorandum.

12. To give a concrete example, civil servants are prohibited from taking second jobs. Yet the fact remains that, thanks to a fiendishly complicated tax code, many employees of the Ministry of Finance moonlight as accountants in the evenings, helping citizens prepare their returns and navigate this complex system with the help of an inside ally. As all this activity is not officially allowed, it is undeclared, and cements an ethos of accepting tax evasion even among those employed to combat it. Likewise schoolteachers employed by the state are often also employed as

private tutors, and doctors at the National Health System supplement their earnings by bribes that range from the benign "thank you" for an operation, to the more sinister requirement of funds to speed up procedures (socially known and legitimized as *fakelakia*, or "little envelopes"). Stemming this practice has become hard, given the relatively low pay of public sector doctors, and the fact that they are not legally allowed to engage in private work without substantial pay cuts or losing their permanent position in the National Health System.

13. It is encouraging that it has become possible, through a bottom–up platform such as Public-Spending.net (Vafopoulos et al. 2015) and its successor LinkedEconomy.org, to track where public money goes in Greece and compare to other countries. At the same time the lack of a proper system of financial flows and expenses, at least until recently, is remarkable.

14. The years from 1975 to 2005, for instance, have seen 3,430 laws, 20,580 presidential decrees, 114,905 ministerial decisions, 24,010 regional decisions, and 8,575 prefectural decisions.

15. Data on civil servants from ELSTAT are derived from their distribution by tenure status of the business/employer according to the sample-based results of the Labor Force Survey. Thus they are not census information. One needs to exercise caution in interpreting these figures, as we must assume that the data reflect accurate tracking of government entities, which should not be taken for granted. Data from Apografi.gov.gr were initially based on the 2010 census of civil servants. At that time all those paid by the state were asked to electronically submit their data (job position, public service/entity of employment, etc.) to an electronic platform created for this self-reporting procedure. Since 2010, Apografi has been able to track departures, as retirees provided their information on retirement, and new hires were meant to update their information. Finally, data from Apografi.gov.gr regard end-year employment, whereas these from ELSTAT are based on each year's average of quarterly figures.

16. Note that this figure clearly collapses a very heterogeneous population, as in the narrow public service nonpolitical appointees and advisors tend to have lower pay, whereas those in the broader public sector can enjoy remarkable benefits. Also this does not take into account educational and other differences that can explain pay differentials.

17. Note that figure 14.12 may understate the true requirements, as teachers are exempt from the full load when working, such as in a minister's office, or working, on paid time, for their union.

18. The same goes for *ad hoc* advisors, generally appointed on political criteria and often with scant reference to the portfolios involved. At best, advisors with knowledge, desire to make a change, and capacity can help remedy skill gaps in the administration. At worst, they add another layer of complexity, and remove permanent civil servants' incentive to take ownership and accountability for their portfolios, imposing a system-wide cost.

19. There have been calls to transform the government through greater local authority in both establishing the level of taxes, and collecting taxes at the local level—for instance, as in the United Kingdom, the United States, and many European countries. Proposals, such as those aired by former minister Stefanos Manos, have unfortunately fallen on deaf ears.

20. Note that these categories, taken from Featherstone (2015), reflect the template provided by Ongaro. See Ongaro (2009) for further details on each of these categories.

21. Ironically, the first Permanent Secretary was dismissed after the European elections of 2014 by PM Samaras, marking the end of the New Democracy led coalition appetite for reforms, and the eventual collapse of the government and rise to power of SYRIZA.

22. Cuts were heterogeneous within the civil service, with top posts and top salaries being the hardest hit.

23. Likewise Greece established the General Secretariat for Coordination through Law 4109/2013 to improve its government structure. Despite the good intentions, implementation has been lukewarm and coordination remains a challenge.

24. See http://www.businessportal.gr/english/index.html.

25. The root of this malaise goes back in history. Kostis (2013), going back to the functioning of Greece as a province of the Ottoman empire in the eighteenth century, explains the pathologies of the political economy still evident today. He provides a damning account of the cycles of indebtedness, irresponsible management, and hesitant reform after its independence in 1821. Common themes from his work include the reliance on "foreign powers," problematic political leadership, rent-seeking, and opportunism. To balance this important historical background, it may be worth pointing out the aggregate growth of Greece, which moved from abject poverty into one of the worlds' richer countries, and acknowledging that several of the issues pointed out as uniquely Greek features are an unfortunate part and parcel of any organized society. Kalyvas (2015) provides a somewhat more optimistic, if sanguine, account of Greece's triumphs and disasters, and the role of entrenched political economies. The arduous and hesitant progress of the reform agenda in Greece also comes out from the collected essays in Kalyvas et al. (2013), which focus on more recent history and show why reforms, post-crisis, were met with such enmity. Doxiadis (2013) provides an example of more recent structural problems that led to today's financial mess, focusing on business structures. Pappas (2015), taking a political science angle, describes how the military dictatorship of 1967 to 1974 set the ground for the growth of populism, and how populism grew into a stranglehold. It is useful to keep in mind, though, that this shift started having a real impact on the economy when political parties institutionalized their role as providers of employment via positions in the civil service or brokers for deals and protection to a host of special interests, especially from the 1980s to the 1990s, next in the mid-1990s, and then after Greece joined the euro.

26. The use of IT in the Greek state has sadly been as inefficient as the state itself, with many IT expenditures focused on hardware with minimal leverage and interoperability, let alone a focus on business transformation or reform (see chapter 15).

27. It is sobering to see that such efforts as publicspending.gr, aimed at analyzing the use of public funds, have been shunned by the system. Publicpsending.gr was denied access to the servers of the Athens Technical University and had to resort to being hosted outside Greece. As for http://www.transparency.gr/diafaneiatora/ (an initiative that included a hotline to denounce bribes in Greece, aimed at both creating social pressure and potentially raising complaints), it

appears to have been "successfully completed," according to the latest website announcement (accessed on 19/9/2015.) This seems rather ironic given the scope and depth of these problems.

References

Accenture. 2008. *An International Comparison of the United Kingdom's Public Administration*. Dublin. https://www.nao.org.uk/wp-content/uploads/2009/02/0809123_Accenture_report.pdf.

Adam Smith International and Alvarez & Marsal. 2014. Preliminary evaluation of the technical assistance provided to Greece in 2011–2013 in the areas of tax administration and central administration reform. EU Ref. Ares(2014)3045121–17/09/2014. VC/2014/0002. http://ec.europa.eu/about/taskforce-greece/pdf/tfgr/evaluation_report_alvarez_july_2014_en.pdf.

Andrews, R., J. Downe, and V. Guarneros-Meza. 2013. Public sector reform in the UK: Views and experiences from senior executives. Part of COCOPS Research Project.

Aucoin, P. 1990. Administrative reform in public management: Paradigms, principles, paradoxes and pendulums. *Governance: An International Journal of Policy, Administration and Institutions* 3 (2): 115–37.

Bank of Greece. 2010. Monetary Policy Interim Report. Athens: BoG.

Bergvall, D., R. Emery, I. Hawkesworth, and J. Wehner. 2008. Budgeting in Greece. *OECD Journal on Budgeting* 2008 (3): 1–50.

Boston Consulting Group. 2012. A practical guide to change in the public sector. https://www.bcgperspectives.com/content/articles/public_sector_change_management_practical_guide_to_change_in_public_sector/.

Buehn, A., and F. Schneider. 2012. Size and development of tax evasion in 38 OECD coutries: What do we (not) know? *Journal of Economics and Political Economy* 3 (1): 1–11.

CASE (Center for Social and Economic Research) and CPB. (Netherlands Bureau for Economic Policy Analysis). 2013. *Study to Quantify and Analyse the VAT Gap in the EU-27 Member States*. Warsaw.

Cengiz, F., and L. Hoffmann. 2013. Rethinking conditionality: Turkey's European Union accession and the Kurdish question. *Journal of Common Market Studies* 51 (3): 416–32.

Diamandouros, N. 1994. Cultural dualism and political change in post authoritarian Greece. Working paper 1994/50. Instituto Juan March de Estudios e Investigaciones, Madrid.

Doxiadis, A. 2013. *The Invisible Fault: Institutions and Behaviors in the Greek Economy* (in Greek: *Το αόρατο ρήγμα: Θεσμοί και συμπεριφορές στην Ελληνική οικονομία*). Athens: Ikaros (Αθήνα: Ίκαρος).

Drazen, A. 2002. Conditionality and ownership in IMF lending: A political economy approach. *IMF Staff Papers* 49: 36–67.

EKDD (National Center for Public Administration). 2012. *Di@vgiea: The Present and the Future of Transparency in Public Life* (in Greek: Πρόγραμμα Δι@ύγεια : Παρόν και Μέλλον της Διαφάνειας στο Δημόσιο Βίο), *Web report.* http://www.ekdd.gr/ekdda/images/ektheseis_politikis/Policy_Paper _Diavgeia_2.pdf.

Eleftheriadis, P. 2005. Constitutional reform and the rule of law. *West European Politics* 28 (2): 317–334.

EU DG ECFIN. 2011. The Economic Adjustment Programme for Greece. Third Review—winter 2011. Occasional paper 77. http://ec.europa.eu/economy_finance/publications/occasional_paper/ 2011/pdf/ocp77_en.pdf.

European Commission. 2006. Measuring administrative costs and reducing administrative burdens in the European Union. Commission working document, COM (2006) 691 final.

European Commission. 2014. The Second Economic Adjustment Programme for Greece. Fourth review—April 2014. Occasional paper 192. ISSN 1725-3209. Brussels.

Featherstone, K. 2015. External conditionality and the debt crisis: The "Troika" and public administration reform in Greece. *Journal of European Public Policy* 22: 295–314.

Featherstone, K., and D. Papadimitriou. 2008. *The Limits of Europeanization: Reform Capacity and Policy Conflict in Greece.* Basingstoke: Palgrave Macmillan.

Fernandez, S., and H. G. Rainey. 2006. Managing successful organizational change in the public sector. *Public Administration Review* 66 (2): 168–176.

Gritzalis, S., S. Katsikas, A. Mitsos, N. Polyzos, D. Spinellis, M. Stratigaki, and A. Takis. 2012. *From Academia to Public Administration: A Return Trip* (in Greek: *Από το πανεπιστήμιο στη δημόσια διοίκηση: Ένα ταξίδι με επιστροφή*). Athens: Papazisis. (Εκδόσεις Παπαζήση).

Haughton, T. 2007. When does the EU make a difference? Conditionality and the accession process in Central and Eastern Europe. *Political Studies Review* 5 (2): 233–46.

Hlepas, N.-K. 1999. *Local Government in Greece* (in Greek: *Η Τοπική Διοίκηση στην Ελλάδα*). Athens: Sakkoulas (Εκδόσεις Αντ Σάκκουλας).

IMF. 2006. Greece: Report on the observance of standards and codes: Fiscal transparency module. Country report 06/49. Washington, DC.

IMF. 2010. Greece: Staff Report on Request for Stand-By Arrangement. Country report 10/110. Washington DC.

IMF. 2013. Greece: Selected issues. Country report 13/155. https://www.imf.org/external/pubs/ft/ scr/2013/cr13155.pdf.

Jacobides, M. G. 2012. The real problem with Greece. *Business Strategy Review* 23 (2): 64–67.

Jacobides, M. G. 2015. Greece and its misguided champions. *Harvard Business Review Blog.* https:// hbr.org/2015/08/greece-and-its-misguided-champions/.

Jacobides, M. G., R. Portes, and D. Vayanos. 2011. Greece: The way forward. *EU Vox,* November.

Jilke, S., Van de Walle, S., and R. Van Delft. 2013. Public sector reform in the Netherlands: Views and experiences from senior executives. Country report as part of the COCOPS Research Project.

Kalyvas, S. 2015. *Modern Greece.* Oxford: Oxford University Press.

Kalyvas, S., G. Pagoulatos, and H. Tsoukas, eds. 2013. *From Stagnation to Forced Adjustments: Reforms in Greece, 1974–2010.* New York: Columbia University Press.

Kostis, K. 2013. *History's Spoiled Children* (in Greek: *Τα κακομαθημένα παιδιά της ιστορίας*). Athens: Polis Editions (Εκδόσεις Πόλις)

Kotter, J. 1996. *Leading Change.* Boston: Harvard Business School Press.

Ladi, S. 2005. The role of experts in the reform process in Greece. *West European Politics* 28 (2): 279–96.

Ladi, S. 2014. Austerity politics and administrative reform: The Eurozone crisis and its impact upon Greek public administration. *Comparative European Politics* 12: 184–208.

Lane, J.-E. 2000. *New Public Management.* London: Routledge.

LBS. 2013. RedesignGreece. Reforming the public administration: A bottom up, awards-driven initiative. Briefing note. London. *October.*

Machiavelli, N. 1947 [1515]. *Il Principe,* translated by T. G. Bergin. Hoboken, NJ: Crofts Classics.

Maglaras, E. 2010. The complex problem of exploitation of public real estate property. Policy brief 9. ISTAME.

Manos, S. 2015. Answer to GENOP-DEI (in Greek: *Απάντηση στη ΓΕΝΟΠ/ ΔΕΗ*), Capital, June 21. http://www.capital.gr/story/3034964.

March, J. G., and H. A. Simon. 1958. *Organizations.* New York: Wiley.

Matsaganis, M., and M. Flevotomou. 2010. Distributional implications of tax evasion in Greece. GreeSE paper 31. Hellenic Observatory. London School of Economics.

McKinsey & Company. 2012. Greece: 10 years ahead. http://www.mckinsey.com/locations/athens/greeceexecutivesummary_new/.

Ministry of Finance. 2011. The Economic Adjustment Programme for Greece. http://www.minfin.gr/sites/default/files/Quarterly%2BReport%2BMay%2B2011-FINAL.pdf.

Ministry of Finance. 2013. Regular budget expenditure per Ministry (in Greek: *Έξοδα Τακτικού Προϋπολογισμού - Υπουργεία, Νοέμβριος 2013*). http://www.minfin.gr/sites/default/files/financial_files/EX-TAKT-YPOYRGEIA-2013-GR.pdf.

Mouzelis, N. 1978. *Modern Greece: Facets of Under-Development.* London: Macmillan.

OECD. 2011a. Greece: Review of the Central Administration. Paris.

OECD. 2011b. *Government at a Glance*. Paris.

OECD. 2011c. *Public Governance Reviews—Estonia: Towards a Single Government Approach*. Paris.

OECD. 2013. Economic surveys: Greece. http://www.oecd.org/eco/surveys/GRC_Overview_Eng _2013.pdf.

OECD. 2014. *Education at a Glance*. Paris.

OECD. 2015. *Government at a Glance*. Paris.

Olsen, J. P. 2006. Maybe it is time to rediscover bureaucracy. *Journal of Public Administration Research and Theory* 16 (1): 1–24.

Ongaro, E. 2009. *Public Management Reform and Modernization: Trajectories of Administrative Change in Italy, France, Greece, Portugal and Spain*. Cheltenham: Elgar.

Pagoulatos, G. 2005. The politics of privatization: Redrawing the public-private boundary. *West European Politics* 28 (2): 358–80.

Pagoulatos, G., and N. Zahariadis. 2011. Politics, labor, regulation, and Performance: Lessons from the privatization of OTE. GreeSE paper 46. Hellenic Observatory Papers on Greece and Southeast Europe. http://eprints.lse.ac.uk/33827/1/GreeSE_No46.pdf.

Papoulias, D., and H. Tsoukas. 1998. *Directions of State Reform*. Athens: Kastaniotis.

Pappas, T. S. 2015. *Populism and Crisis in Greece* (in Greek: Λαϊκισμός και κρίση στην Ελλάδα). Athens: Ikaros (Ίκαρος).

Parkinson, C. N. 1958. *Parkinson's Law or The Pursuit of Progress*. London: John Murray.

Perry, J. L., D. Mesch, and L. Paarlberg. 2006. Motivating employees in a new governance era: The Performance Paradigm revisited. *Public Administration Review* 66 (4): 505–514.

Peters, B. G. 2008. The Napoleonic tradition. *International Journal of Public Sector Management* 21 (2): 118–32.

Pollitt, C., and G. Bouckaert. 2011. *Public Management Reform: A Comparative Analysis—New Public Management, Governance, and the Neo-Weberian State*. Oxford: Oxford University Press.

Psarakis, A. E., and D. R. Rigopoulos. 2014. Absurdities and mistakes in evaluation: Compulsory quotas (in Greek: Ο Παραλογισμός και τα Λάθη στην Αξιολόγηση: Υποχρεωτικές Ποσοστώσεις). *Economic Review* 926 (September): 552–54.

Schneider, F. 2015. Tax evasion, shadow economy and corruption in Greece and other OECD Countries: Some empirical facts. Speech. http://www.amcham.gr/wp-content/uploads/2015/taxspeeches/friedrich%20schneider.pdf.

Spanou, C. 2008. State reform in Greece: Responding to old and new challenges. *International Journal of Public Sector Management* 21 (2): 150–73.

Spanou, C., and D. A. Sotiropoulos. 2011. The odyssey of administrative reforms in Greece, 1981–2009: A tale of two reform paths. *Public Administration* 89: 723–37.

Stavropoulos, G. 2015. Disciplinary law for public servants (*Το Πειθαρχικό Δίκαιο των Υπαλλήλων του Δημοσίου*). Mimeo (in Greek).

Vafopoulos, M., M. Meimaris, I. Anagnostopoulos, A. Papantoniou, I. Xidias, G. Alexiou, G. Vafeiadis, M. Klonaras, and V. Loumos. 2015. Public spending as LOD: The case of Greece. *Semantic Web Journal* 6 (2): 155–64.

Vasardani, M. 2011. Tax evasion in Greece. *Economic Bulletin* 6: 15–24. http://www.bankofgreece.gr/BogEkdoseis/econbull201106.pdf.

World Bank. 2006. Report on strategic planning and policy management in Lithuania and Latvia. Washington, DC.

World Bank. 2013. Latvia: Maintaining a reform state of mind. *Doing Business Report* 2013: 32–36.

World Economic Forum. 2011. *The Future of Government Lessons Learned from around the World.* Geneva: World Economic Forum.

World Economic Forum. 2012. *The Global Competitiveness Report 2012-2013.* Geneva: World Economic Forum.

15   The Dysfunctional Structure of Greek Public Administration and the Challenges in Reforming It

Panagiotis Karkatsoulis and Efi Stefopoulou

15.1   Introduction

This chapter highlights some of the key problems with the Greek public administration and some of the challenges in reforming it. Section 15.2.1 provides a historical account of the size of the public sector. Section 15.2.2 argues that the public administration suffers from complicated and rigid structures that are not conducive to efficient decision making and policy implementation. Section 15.2.3 provides a case study of administrative complexity. Section 15.3 summarizes some recent attempts at reform. Section 15.4 concludes.

The data used in this chapter were collected and analyzed by the authors as part of a functional review of the Greek central public administration. Some of the collected material has been published by the OECD (2011a).

The preceding chapter in this volume analyzes broader aspects of the public administration, including metrics of performance and the link with the private economy. The present chapter focuses more squarely on issues of administrative structure.

15.2   The Problems

15.2.1   Key Facts and Figures

The public sector grew significantly from the 1980s onward. Most of the growth took place in the "wider public sector," which includes all entities that are supervised by the state but operate under private law, rather than in the "narrow public sector," which includes the ministries, local governments, and all other entities that operate under public law. Governments have used entities in the wider public sector as hiring hubs for their partisan clientele. This is because hiring in public entities that operate under private law is subject to fewer constraints and scrutiny relative to hiring in public entities that operate under public law. Moreover employment contracts under private law allowed governments more flexibility to offer advantageous terms to those they wanted to hire. As a result many people entered the wider public sector under differentiated employment statuses in the early 1980s. Figure 15.1 illustrates the rapid growth of the public sector in the early 1980s. The figure confirms that most of the growth took place in the wider public sector. Figure 15.1 differs from figure 14.9 in the previous chapter in that it is constructed using data from the Ministry of Interior rather than ELSTAT. That data exclude some fixed-term employees as well as most employees in firms that are state-controlled but not state-owned.

The fact that most of the civil servants were hired during the 1980s has led to a disproportionate age distribution. The population of civil servants is aging, and there are today specific ministries where the aging problem is endangering the ministry's sustainability. Figure 15.2 shows that the share of civil servants aged 51 to 65 is around 50 percent in a number of ministries.

Figure 15.3 describes the educational level of civil servants. University graduates make up only 38 percent of the employees in the central administration, while those having completed only secondary education make up 34 percent.

Civil servants are guaranteed permanent employment by the Greek Constitution (article 103). The main legislation governing civil servants is Law 3528/2007 (the Code of Public Civil Administrative Employees and Employees of Public Administration's

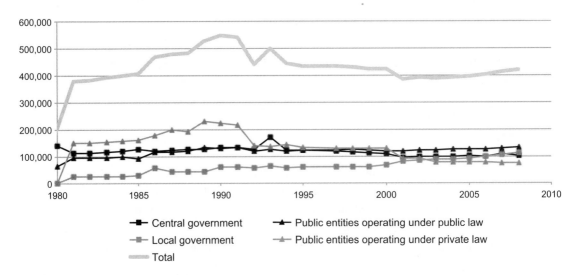

Figure 15.1
Number of civil servants, 1980 to 2008

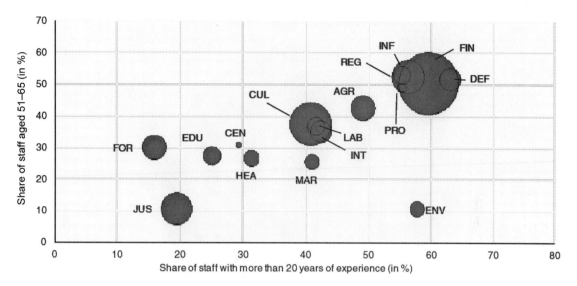

Figure 15.2
Age and experience trends in ministries. A bubble's size is proportional to the number of ministry's staff (central and decentralized services).

Legal Bodies), which includes provisions on their rights, privileges, and obligations. Open-term contract employees are governed by Law 3839/2010 and casual staff may be contracted under the procedures dictated by the Supreme Council for the Selection of Personnel, which is an independent agency that oversees personnel selection.

The recruitment system used in the Greek public service is exceptionally career-based. Entry into the public service is through a competitive examination. No posts are open to direct external recruitment and all applicants have to first enter the public service. Performance assessment is mandatory for almost all employees and takes the form of written feedback from a superior every year. A small range of performance criteria are used, including activities undertaken, values, disciplines and inputs, and interpersonal skills. Performance assessment typically is taken into account for career advancement. However, in practice, implementation of performance assessment is of little importance. Remuneration is not open to negotiation, as base salary and bonuses are based on the recommendations of an independent examining committee.

15.2.2 Administrative Structures
A key problem with the Greek public administration is its rigid structure, which involves thousands of detailed "competences" as sets of regulated tasks. Civil servants

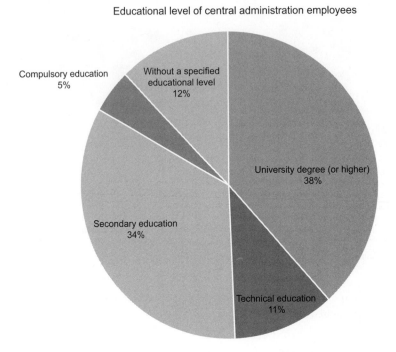

Educational level of central administration employees

Figure 15.3
Educational level of the central administration's employees

can only perform tasks that lie within their competences. Although the initial rationale for a strict regulation of tasks was to safeguard the legality of civil servants' actions, the regulation has led to a bureaucratic inertia that stifles innovation.

To quantify the problem, we measured the competences within each ministry. We clustered competences into two major groups: those that are of a strategic nature (i.e., strategic planning, policy coordination, policy monitoring) and those that are supportive to the first ones (i.e., administrative management, IT support, etc.). We also considered two smaller groups: service delivery and control & audit. The total number of competences that we mapped was 23142.

Since ministries are the strategic hubs of the government in their respective policy areas, one would expect that most of the competences within them would be strategic rather than supportive. Yet the data show that ministries are not so strategic: only 47 percent of the mapped competences were strategic, while 42 percent had a supportive character, 4 percent were relating to service delivery (which is normally carried out at local level), and 7 percent were relating to control and audit (figure 15.4). Even many

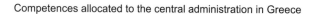

Competences allocated to the central administration in Greece

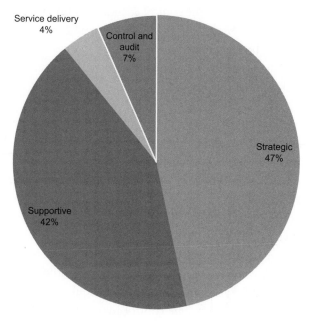

Figure 15.4
Competences allocated to the central administration in Greece

of the competences that were classified as strategic were not so strategic but rather appeared to have been invented to justify the existence of the supportive competences.

The strict regulation of tasks and the large number of competences are a consequence of a tradition of legalism and formalism, burdened with clientelistic pressures. Having an administrative system established on legalism and formalism leads to a negative self-reference, with more competences continuously asked by public agencies to deliver their mandate.

The thousands of competences in existence have not increased efficiency. Rather, they have led to a situation where informed decisions have become hard to make and implement. Indeed being "responsible" for something means that one can handle some issue but cannot decide or act. The implementation of the decision is being pushed forward to the higher level, which instead is supposed to be responsible for taking and not implementing the decision. Therefore there is a constant enforcement deficit.

Special reference should be made to the control & audit competences (7 percent of the total number of competences). Many of them have been accumulated over the past decades by governments as part of a symbolic policy to fight against corruption. In the last twenty years, every minister of public administration has added his own amendments to the patchwork of regulations that define the control & audit function within the ministries. From a normative point of view, Greece with over 1,500 controlling competences and dozens of controlling bodies should have been the champion of the fight against corruption. This is not the case, however: international rankings on corruption (e.g., by Transparency International) place Greece close to the bottom of the EU28 countries.

Additional evidence for the limited success of the public administration in producing efficient decisions comes from a questionnaire, which was circulated in the framework of the functional review to the General Directors of a large number of public agencies (their combined strategic competences exceeding 50 percent of the total). The findings are presented in figure 15.5. The figure shows that only 4 percent of the outcomes produced by the public administration were operational decisions, while 75 percent were studies, notes, and memos.

Public agencies have a never-ending appetite for more competences, and this is evident by the normative means by which competences have been assigned to them. For new competences to be assigned to an agency, a presidential decree should be issued. The issuance of presidential decrees ensures an *ex ante* control by the Court of the State, and this procedure generally involves some intense scrutiny. Nevertheless, only 64 percent of the existing competences were assigned to the ministries by presidential decrees. The remaining competences were assigned by laws and even ministerial decisions. Thus ministers have found ways to assign to themselves some competences with no prior control. Figure 15.6 shows the precise breakdown.

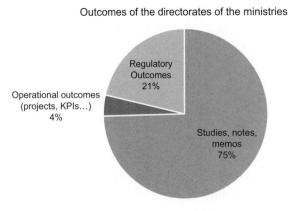

Outcomes of the directorates of the ministries

Figure 15.5
Production of Directorates within the ministries, 2009 to 2010

Normative means by which competences are assigned

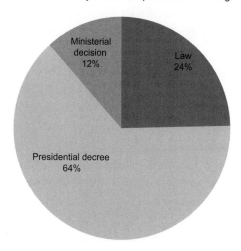

Figure 15.6
Normative means by which competences are assigned

The thousands of competences require just as many intricate structures so they can be performed. The 15 Greek ministries are organized in 149 General Directorates, 886 Directorates, and 3,720 Departments.[1] Personnel staffing all those structures is divided into 1,445 different "branches." Under these circumstances the administration's capacity to organize its tasks and run specific projects is weak. We further illustrate administrative growth and complexity with the case study of the Ministry of Labor in section 15.2.3.

We next turn to the span of control at different levels of the central administration. The span of control varies considerably with administrative level. There are on average five General Secretariats per Ministry, two General Directorates per General Secretariat, six Directorates per General Directorate, and four Departments per Directorate.

One would expect that the span of control gets narrower at higher hierarchical levels because the tasks assigned to higher levels are usually more burdensome compared to those at lower levels. But as the span of control at the lowest level (Departments per Directorate) is just four, there is little room to follow such a rule. The narrow span of control is a result of the over-fragmentation of structures especially at the top levels, which does not depict the real needs of the public organizations but rather reflects the construction of highly esteemed positions for politically friendly affiliates. This argument is made obvious if one looks at the personnel staffing all those structures: 21 percent of the departments of the central administration have no employees, 14 percent of the departments of the central administration have one employee, and 55 percent of the departments of the central administration have up to 3 employees. Figure 15.7 generalizes these observations by plotting the fraction of departments as a function of their number of employees.

The phenomenon of understaffed departments is not a new one in the Greek public administration. A field study carried out in 1994 (Karkatsoulis 1998) in 1,085 Departments in 18 different ministries showed that 113 Departments had one employee, 135 Departments had two employees, 47 Departments had no head and no employees at all, 69 Departments had one head but no employee, and 124 Departments had employees but no heads. The structural inflation in the number of administrative departments causes a number of problems. Coordination across Departments becomes more difficult. Moreover the understaffed departments are either obsolete but still there, so they burden the state budget or they fail to respond to the tasks assigned to them.

A key question is why structural inflation exists and rationalization efforts fail. A driver of the oversupply of administrative structures has been political rent-seeking, namely to provide more highly ranked positions for partisan affiliates. Additionally governments have been reluctant, throughout the decades, to evaluate administrative structures based on the resources they consume and the outputs they produce. This

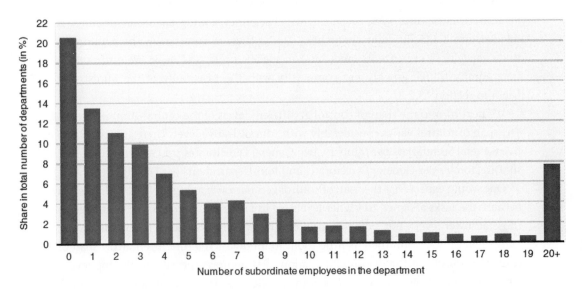

Figure 15.7
Number of employees in a department as measured in 2011
Source: OECD (2011a)

has created no incentive to merge or abolish nonproductive structures. A lack of assessment tools to evaluate the output of each structure has also prevented the emergence of competition between structures. The dispersion of the organizational structures into many buildings has been an additional driver of structural inflation, since it has increased the need for supportive structures.

The administrative structures charged with the coordination of public policies have similar attributes: too many structures have been created, the lines of command and communication are not clear, and overlapping competences result in the problematic situation shown in Figure 15.8. Structural inflation is not confined within ministerial departments. Many agencies and public entities were created and mostly used to accommodate partisan affiliates. These entities operate under private law or public law.

There is no single registry of all public sector entities, and the Greek government (including the General Accounting Office) is not in a position to figure the total amount of public money that all these entities cost. That is the reason why the expenses of some of them are written in the state budget, while for some others money is given to the supervisory ministry, which then allocates the resources to the public entity.

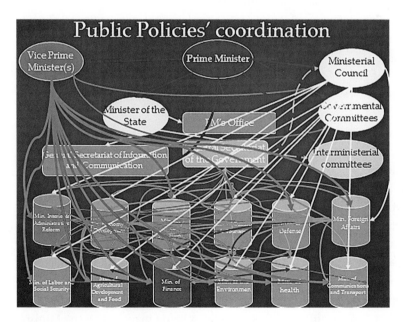

Figure 15.8
Coordination mechanism for public policies in Greece

Dispersion, lack of interconnection, and silos are traits found not only in competences and structures but also extended to infrastructure. The functional review registered the following: 263 leased, 271 owned, and 70 consigned central government's buildings, the majority of which violated the main principles of town planning, safety, and working area quality standards. Obviously information technology and communications cannot offer much help within such a building infrastructure. They can, however, be used as an excuse to increase the demand of ICT equipment to ensure a quick profit to technology resellers: 54,927 terminals, 2,983 servers—but only 332 integrated information systems/databases and only 25 percent of civil servants with an official governmental email account (13,343)—are the evidence of such a claim (Table 15.1). While there are plenty of buildings and digital infrastructures, a deficit in spatial rationality and e-governance is quite evident.

15.2.3 A Case Study: The Ministry of Labor

The Ministry of Labor has been changing its organization once or multiple times a year, and more structural units were added in most of these instances. Between 1990 and 2009, 21 distinct changes took place, establishing new units (e.g., Directorates, General Directorates, or Special Units) and abolishing others.

The two snapshots in figures 15.9 and 15.10 show the structure of the Ministry in 1989 and then again in 2009. The 2009 structure is much larger and more complicated than the 1989 one.

15.3 Reform Efforts

Over the past two decades, there have been efforts to reform the public administration. Some efforts have focused on making regulations (applying to the rest of the economy) simpler and more efficient. Part of those efforts was an attempt to codify legislation. This attempt has not borne enough fruit, as the Central Codification Committee consisted of only few members employed on a part-time basis. As a result fewer than 15 codifications were carried out in five years, and they were mostly static, failing to encompass into the new text any update or amendment that might have been enacted after the codification ended. Although the digital technology is in place and e-rulemaking is no more considered a novelty, the Greek public administration failed to use it to keep the statute book tidied up. The official codification project "Raptarchis" (Ραπτάρχης) remains unfinished. Raptarchis is being managed by the Ministry of Administrative Reform and has taken the form of an electronic database of regulation. However, the database is not up to date, which leads professionals to address their

Table 15.1

ICT infrastructure mapped in the functional review

Ministry	Number of servers	Number of terminals	Number of laptops/ notebooks	Databases that are not a vertical integrated ICT solution	Vertical ICT solutions	Staff with a governmental email account	Percentage of supportive competences over the total of the ministries' competences	Number of staff	Percentage of staff with a governmental email account	Percentage of staff with a terminal	Databases/ total number of vertical ICT solutions
Ministry of Administrative Reform	206	1,811	46	33	11	1,852	56	2,111	88	88	75
Ministry of Finance	1,137	16,890	2,512	2	15	1,225	34	20,931	6	93	12
Ministry of Foreign affairs	357	3,211	51	0	11	55	40	1,285	2	110	0
Ministry of Defense	316	4,314	481	35	26	1,388	37	8,206	58	202	57
Ministry of Development	218	1,303	76	9	8	1,562	32	1,824	85	75	53
Ministry of Environment	65	1,070	23	19	0	1,070	37	990	92	94	100
Ministry of Education	161	1,820	19	30	14	1,314	37	1,568	8	116	68
Ministry of Transport	18	430	55	5	0	380	37	3,122	7	8	100
Ministry of Labor	67	1,565	22	29	1	686	30	1,629	44	103	97

Table 15.1 (continued)

Ministry	Number of servers	Number of terminals	Number of laptops/notebooks	Databases that are not a vertical integrated ICT solution	Vertical ICT solutions	Staff with a governmental email account	Percentage of supportive competences over the total of the ministries' competences	Number of staff	Percentage of staff with a governmental email account	Percentage of staff with a terminal	Databases/total number of vertical ICT solutions
Ministry of Health	32	543	15	3	0	613	47	1,760	38	35	100
Ministry of Agriculture	80	1,857	49	34	6	1,088	37	2,014	49	85	85
Ministry of Justice	113	1,000	10	5	28	279	40	159	92	105	15
Ministry of Public Order	133	12,477	340	2	2	668	44	428	100	100	50
Ministry of Culture and Tourism	163	2,650	30	7	1	1,200	37	8,979	16	35	88
Ministry of Maritime Affairs	12	125	16	5	1	119	31	1,413	15	18	83
General Secretariat of the PM and General Secretariat of the Government	6	40	1	0	0	40	34	94	33	33	0
Total	3,084	51,106	3,746	218	124	13,539	42	56,513	51	81	61

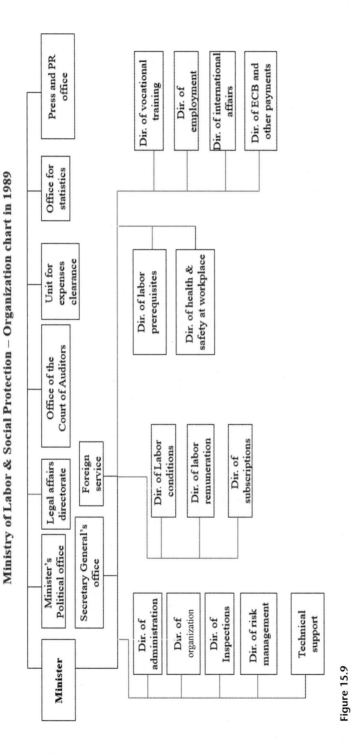

Figure 15.9

Organogram of the Ministry of Labor in 1989

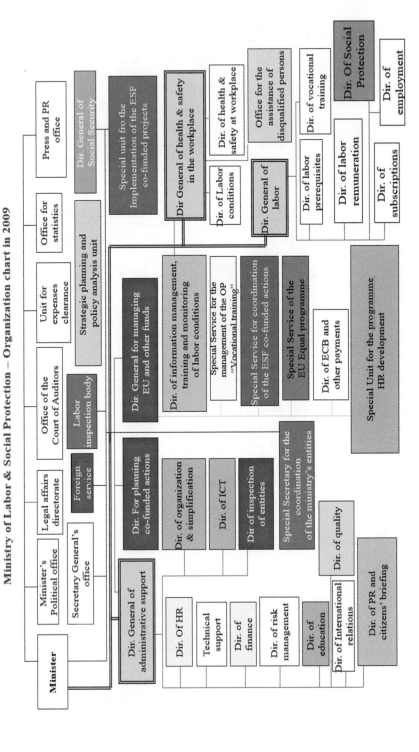

Figure 15.10

Organogram of the Ministry of Labor in 2009

queries on certain regulatory matters to private databases. Moreover several ministerial departments codify the dispersed provisions that affect them using their own legal collections for internal use.

Law 4048/2012 on better regulation was the most important effort to limit the flood of new legislations and regulations. Unfortunately, this law still remains inactive. Although impact assessments are drafted they usually include little evidence and are more of a bureaucratic exercise than a tool to make regulation better. *Ex post* evaluation of enforced laws could also be used as a tool to provide information on the laws' impact.

Law 3853/2010 simplified businesses' licensing procedures but did not establish a single point for licensing. Licensing points include 3,330 notaries, 54 citizens' service centers, and 59 chambers of commerce.

Other reform efforts have focused on improving administrative structures and promoting efficient decision-making. These efforts have often been resisted by politicians, bureaucrats, and public sector trade unions. Law 3032/2004 on goal setting allowed administrative departments and agencies to set goals and evaluate the results of the relevant actors. Nevertheless the implementation of that law was not mandatory. Other reforms complementary to management by objectives (i.e., job profiles, standardization of procedures, performance appraisal) have not been legislated.

An effort to connect budgetary expenditures to policy results has taken place, with the OECD's support, between 2007 and 2010 (Emery et al. 2008). The effort was abandoned just after the outburst of the crisis, as it was opposed by almost all members of the cabinet.

The e-government policy failed to achieve significant results in incorporating ICT (information and communication technology) to the quest for the reduction of bureaucracy. Although sufficient resources were allocated to e-government (through two Community Support frameworks) the Greek public administration is still lagging behind. Technological applications that could decongest the intra-administrative workload are not used to their full potential, and much of civil servants' time is spent copying the paperwork to the ICT systems. Some positive measures such as the online submission and retrieval of certain official documents, and the self-appointed search for documents by the public administration to avoid repeated submission of the same information by citizens, are in place but have not cut bureaucracy significantly. Moreover positive results arising from such initiatives are often neutralized by regulatory inflation.

The EU co-funded projects that were implemented during the past two decades did not follow any strategic plan. This is why the Greek administration is overloaded with ICT infrastructure that does not interoperate. The fact that systems are non-interoperable is often overcome by creating *ad hoc* interfaces.

The functional review's suggestions to the Greek government were to deal with the organizational inflation through re-examination of the existing structures. The Greek government reduced them nominally and without evaluating their efficiency and purpose. Two bills that merged 200 legal entities have also been enacted, but the vast majority of the entities supervised or financed by the state was left intact.

As for the scattered infrastructure, the 40-year-old vision to create a governmental park has not been implemented yet.[2] The lack of a clear-cut policy on public buildings, especially in times of austerity, has resulted to an abandonment of public buildings for financial savings reasons, which consequently has led to the stacking of people and equipment into places that fulfill none of the hygiene and safety in the workplace standards. An example of this ineffective policy is the relocation of the tax offices, which resulted not only in the deterioration of the heavily populated buildings but also in the decrease of the quality of the services provided.

Regarding human resource management the most significant development was the dismissal of 14,000 employees. The majority of the redundant personnel were security guards at schools or cleaners. Layoffs have caused more problems than the ones they were supposed to solve. Moreover the implementation of a modern personnel evaluation system based on job descriptions has been suspended. In the meanwhile early retirement of civil servants has created significant gaps in key services.

To coordinate the administration's activities, in such a fragmented and silo-based environment, the Troika suggested the creation of a central coordination unit. This led to the establishment of the General Secretariat for Coordination (GSC), via Law 4109/2013. Two years after the establishment of the GSC, coordination is still weak. An effort initiated in 2013 to systematically map and electronically follow up the ministries' goals, activities, and results was still in a pilot phase in 2014 and has been abandoned in 2015.

15.4   Conclusion

Our analysis of the problems with the Greek public administration and of the attempts at reforming it leads us to a number of main conclusions. First, an overall strategy of dealing with the problems is still to be formulated. The fragmentation, duplication, formalism, and legalism that are evident in procedures, regulations, and HR management and structures remain to be addressed. Second, the existence of a strategic framework for administrative reform must be accompanied by a series of operational programs and actions that will ensure its implementation. The main problem of public policies in Greece remains the poor implementation of what has been voted in the parliament or adopted in regulation. Third, much work is required to have an evidence-based policy on administrative reform, free from ideological stereotypes.

Notes

1. The numbers refer to the Greek public administration structures as they had been in 2012. Minor changes have taken place since then.

2. See Kyrtsis (2006).

References

Emery, R., D. Bergvall, I. Hawkesworth, and J. Wehner. 2008. *Budgeting in Greece*. Paris: OECD.

Karkatsoulis, P. 1998. Administrative reform (in Greek). *Sakkoulas, Athens*.

Kyrtsis, A. A. 2006. *Constantinos A. Doxiadis: Texts, Design Drawings, Settlements*. Athens: Ikaros.

OECD. 2011a. *Greece: Review of the Central Administration*. Paris: OECD.

OECD. 2011b. Classification of the functions of government (COFOG). In *Government at a Glance 2011*. Paris: OECD.

Timeline of Political and Economic Events Pertaining to the Greek Crisis

The global financial crisis of 2007–2008 turned into a sovereign debt crisis in 2009. Bond yields rose sharply in a number of eurozone countries, including Greece. Greece lost market access in April 2010, and a financial assistance program involving the IMF and European institutions was agreed in May. Unlike typical IMF programs, there was no currency devaluation because Greece was a eurozone member, or a restructuring or default on the debt, although debt restructuring and some forgiveness took place in 2012. The first program was followed by a second in 2012 and a third in 2015. All three programs involved both fiscal tightening (tax increases and cuts in pensions and public sector wages) as well as structural reforms (e.g., in the labor market, the product markets, and the public administration). Although the normal electoral cycle in Greece is four years, four elections took place between 2010 and 2016: a PASOK (Socialist) government was followed in 2012 by a coalition government between New Democracy (Conservative) and PASOK, and in 2015 by coalition governments between SYRIZA (Leftist) and ANEL (Nationalist). A primary deficit of 10.3 percent of GDP in 2009 turned into a primary surplus of 0.4 percent in 2014, and a trade deficit of 10.4 percent of GDP in 2009 was reduced to 1 percent in 2014. These adjustments came at a cost of a large decline in GDP: 25.8 percent in real terms between 2008 and 2014. Greece still remains (as of early 2017) in a financial assistance program.

January 2009	January 7, 2009	Cabinet reshuffle. G. Papathanasiou new Finance Minister
	January 30, 2009	2008–2011 Updated Stability and Convergence program published by Ministry of Finance
February 2009	February 18, 2009	European Commission adopts a report that marks the start of the Excessive Deficit Procedure for Greece
March 2009	March 24, 2009	European Commission recommends that Greece strengthens fiscal adjustment
June 2009	June 25, 2009	Fiscal package of €1.9 bn announced by G. Papathanasiou
September 2009	September 2, 2009	Announcement of early parliamentary elections
October 2009	October 4, 2009	PASOK (Socialist party) wins parliamentary elections. G. Papandreou new Prime Minister, G. Papakonstantinou new Finance Minister
	October 8, 2009	G. Provopoulos (BoG Governor) states that 2009 General Government deficit will exceed 10% of GDP
	October 20, 2009	G. Papakonstantinou informs ECOFIN on 2009 projected General Government deficit of 12.5% of GDP
	October 22, 2009	2008 General Government deficit upward revision by 2.7% of GDP, to 7.7%, in second notification to Eurostat for 2008
November 2009	November 29, 2009	A. Samaras elected as new President of New Democracy (Conservative party)
December 2009	December 24, 2009	Approval of 2010 budget by the Parliament (2010 General Government deficit projection: 9.1%)
January 2010	January 14, 2010	Updated Greek Stability and Growth program published by Ministry of Finance, with planned measures of €10.3 bn
	January 27–31, 2010	World Economic Forum annual meeting 2010 (Davos). Pressures on Prime Minister G. Papandreou for fiscal measures
February 2010	February 3, 2010	K. Papoulias re-elected President of the Hellenic Republic
	February 9, 2010	First package of fiscal measures announced (€4.65 bn)
	February 16, 2010	ECOFIN approves Greece's Updated Stability program. Requests timetable for implementation of budgetary measures by 03/16/2010

March 2010	March 3, 2010	Second package of fiscal measures announced (€4.5 bn)
	March 11, 2010	10-year bond issue from Hellenic Republic (€5 bn, yield 6.25%)
	March 26, 2010	Spring European Council: Eurozone member states ready to participate to a joint financing mechanism with the IMF
April 2010	April 7, 2010	7-year bond issue from Hellenic Republic (€5 bn, 5.90%)
	April 11, 2010	Eurogroup: Financial Support Mechanism for Greece is ready, if needed
	April 22, 2010	2009 General Government deficit of 13.6% of GDP according to Eurostat (first notification for 2009)
	April 23, 2010	G. Papandreou's Kastelorizo Proclamation (Greece requests activation of the Financial Support Mechanism)
	April 27, 2010	Standard & Poor's downgrades the sovereign debt rating of Greece to junk
	April 28, 2010	Spread of Greek 10-year bond exceeds 1,000 basis points
May 2010	May 6, 2010	First Memorandum of Understanding (MoU) approved by the Parliament (Law 3845/2010): loan of €110 bn, €80 bn from bilateral loans with Eurozone members, €30 bn from the IMF; additional fiscal measures of €5.8 bn for 2010
	May 9, 2010	Establishment of the European Financial Stability Facility (EFSF)
June 2010	June 4, 2010	Law 3852/2010 on local government ("Kallikratis Law"): establishment of 325 municipalities in the place of 1,034 municipalities and communities, and of 13 regions instead of 51 prefectures; targeted reduction of local entities to 4,500 from 6,000; targeted savings of €500 million in 2011 and additional savings of €500 million in 2012 & 2013
	June 15, 2010	Law 3853/2010: legal framework for "one-stop-shop"
July 2010	July 15, 2010	Law 3863/2010 on social security: use of full earnings history for the calculation of pensions; increase of the minimum age to claim full benefits to 60 years by 2015; merger of the social security funds to six; minimum guaranteed pension from 01/01/2015
	July 31, 2010	Law 3869/2010 on the settlement of debts of over-indebted individuals ("Katseli Law")
August 2010	August 2010	First review of the Economic Adjustment program completed

October 2010	October 29, 2010	European Council agrees to set up a permanent crisis mechanism to safeguard financial stability of the Eurozone area as a whole. This European Stability Mechanism (ESM) will be based on the EFSF
November 2010	November 7 & 14, 2010	Local government elections. G. Kaminis and G. Boutaris, both of which ran as independent candidates, are elected as mayors of Athens and Thessaloniki, respectively.
	November 15, 2010	Review of 2009 General Government deficit to 15.4% of GDP (€36.1 bn) in second notification to Eurostat for 2009
	November 22, 2010	Ireland requests financial assistance
December 2010	December 2, 2010	Law 3894/2010 on "fast track" procedures for strategic investment
	December 2010	Second review of the Economic Adjustment program completed
	December 16, 2010	Ireland signs MoU on financial assistance with the EC, the ECB and the IMF
	December 17, 2010	Law 3899/2010 on labor relations: predominance of firm-level contracts over sectoral; establishment of a 12-month trial work period
	December 23, 2010	Approval of 2011 Budget by the Parliament. Measures of €14.3 bn for 2011 (instead of €9.15 in the MoU)
February 2011	February 11, 2011	Third review of the Economic Adjustment program completed
	February 2011	DG ECFIN third review report (Occasional paper 77): 2010 General Government deficit of 9.6% of GDP (program definition), instead of a 8.0% target in the beginning of the program
	February 24, 2011	Announcement of Privatizations and Real Estate Development program for 2011–2015 (tentative targeted total proceeds of €50 bn)
March 2011	March 2, 2011	Law 3919/2011: abolition of unjustified restrictions to the provision of professional services
	March 12, 2011	Eurozone summit decision for extension of maturity of May 2010 loans to 7.5 years and adjustment of interest rate by 100 basis points
April 2011	April 7, 2011	Portugal requests financial assistance
May 2011	May 17, 2011	Financial assistance program for Portugal concluded
	May 25, 2011	First protest demonstration outside the Parliament by the so-called indignants

June 2011	June 16, 2011	Negotiations to form a coalition government in Greece fail
	June 16, 2011	Law 3982/2011: simplification of licensing for technical & manufacturing activities
	June 17, 2011	Cabinet reshuffle. E Venizelos new Finance Minister
July 2011	July 1, 2011	Ratification of the Medium Term Fiscal Strategy 2012–2015 (MTFS, Law 3985/2011): additional fiscal measures for 2011 (€6.5 bn); establishment of the Hellenic Republic Asset Development Fund (TAIPED)
	July 1, 2011	Law 3986/2011: establishment of the social solidarity levy
	July 4–8, 2011	Completion of the fourth review of the Economic Adjustment program
	July 21, 2011	Eurozone summit decision for a new loan to Greece (€109 bn): extension of new loan maturity to 15–30 years, with 10-year grace period; private sector involvement program (PSI) with estimated net effect of €37 bn; debt buyback of €12.6 bn
August 2011	August 8, 2011	Athens stock exchange index falls below 1,000 units for the first time since 1997
	August 18, 2011	OPAP wins auction for 35,000 VLTs, at a price of €560 million
September 2011	September 2, 2011	E. Venizelos stops negotiations with the Troika
	September 2, 2011	Ratification of law concerning restructuring of Higher Education (Law 4009/2011)
	September 13, 2011	Law 4013/2011: insolvency process enhancement by abolishing the conciliation procedure and introducing a new rehabilitation procedure
	September 19, 2011	Law 4014/2011: simplification of granting of environmental permits
	September 30, 2011	Law 4021/2011: special duty on real estate (EETIDE)
October 2011	October 26, 2011	Eurozone summit decision on haircut of Greek debt held by the private sector by 50%. Additional financing of €100 bn up to 2014 (incl. bank recapitalization)
	October 2011	Completion of fifth review of the Economic Adjustment program
	October 2011	DG ECFIN 5th review report (Occasional papers no 87): 2010 General Government deficit revised upward, to 10.6% of GDP (program definition)
	October 31, 2011	G. Papandreou announces his intention to have a referendum regarding the offered new loan agreement

November 2011	November 3–4, 2011	G-20 Cannes summit
	November 11, 2011	G. Papandreou resigns. New coalition government supported by PASOK, New Democracy, and LAOS (nationalist party). L. Papademos new Prime Minister
December 2011	December 8, 2011	Ratification of 2012 budget by the Parliament. No additional measures for 2012 compared to MTFS 2012–2015 (€6.7 bn)
February 2012	February 14, 2012	Second MoU (Law 4046/2012): EFSF loan of €144.6 bn; up to €50 bn of the new loan for bank recapitalization; cuts in minimum wages (22% for employed persons of at least 25 years of age, 32% for younger employees)
	February 2012	DG ECFIN Second program report (Occasional paper 94): 2011 General Government deficit of 9.6% of GDP (program definition), instead of a 8.3% projection in the third review of the first program (Feb. 11)
March 2012	March 9, 2012	Completion of PSI, with participation of 95.7% of eligible lenders; general government debt reduction of €107.1 bn
	March 9, 2012	Law 4055: organization of courts and the role of court officials
April 2012	April 6, 2012	Parliamentary elections announced to take place on 05/06/2012
	April 11, 2012	Law 4072/2012 for the improvement of the business environment. Among other measures, establishment of the private capital company legal form
May 2012	May 6, 2012	Parliamentary elections. No party or coalition of parties forms a government
	May 16, 2012	P. Pirkammenos becomes Prime Minister of the caretaker government which will implement the 06/17/2012 parliamentary elections
June 2012	June 17, 2012	New parliamentary elections
	June 20, 2012	Coalition government formed by New Democracy, PASOK, and DIMAR (Moderate left party). A. Samaras new Prime Minister, G. Stournaras new Finance Minister
September 2012	September 27, 2012	Establishment of the ESM (following Germany's ratification)

November 2012	November 9, 2012	Ratification of the MTFS 2013–2016 by the Parliament (Law 4093/2012): fiscal measures of €9.4 bn for 2013; abolition of Easter, Christmas, and summer bonuses for civil servants & pensioners; increase of general retirement age to 67 years; changes in labor relations (collective agreements binding only to signatories; minimum wage becomes floor for wages and salaries throughout the economy; minimum wage becomes determined by the government in the future; severance payment schemes and maximum dismissal notification period reduced; social security contributions reduced by 1.1%)
	November 11, 2012	2013 budget approved by Parliament
	November 26, 2012	Completion of the first review of the Second Economic Adjustment program
	November 26, 2012	DG ECFIN 1st review report (Occasional paper 123): 2011 General Government deficit of 9.4% of GDP (program definition), slightly downward revised (-0.2%) compared to DG ECFIN second program report (Feb. 12)
	November 27, 2012	Eurogroup decision on General Government debt buyback program: interest rate on first program loans lowered by 100 bps; maturity of these loans and of EFSF loans extended by 15 years; EFSF loan interest payments deferred by 10 years; consideration of further debt relief measures if necessary after Greece achieves primary surplus
December 2012	December 3, 2012	Offers for General Government bonds buyback open
	December 11, 2012	Offers for General Government bonds buyback closed
	December 11, 2012	Exchange of General Government bonds of €31.9 bn with 6-month zero coupon bonds of €11.29 bn completed
January 2013	January 18, 2013	Law 4110/2013 on income taxation: elimination of tax allowances and special tax regimes; elimination of the tax allowance for the self-employed; increase of the taxation of profits and reduction of that on dividends
March 2013	March 1, 2013	Hewlett Packard agrees with COSCO to use its terminal as a transit center at the port of Piraeus for Eastern Europe & Middle East
	March 19, 2013	Cypriot House of Representatives rejects 03/16 Eurogroup Adjustment program. Financing envelope (€10 bn) for Cyprus, due to non-guarantee of bank deposits higher than €100,000

	March 19, 2013	Bank holiday imposed in Cyprus
	March 26, 2013	Piraeus Bank acquires Bank of Cyprus, Cyprus Popular Bank, and Hellenic Bank subsidiaries in Greece
	March 31, 2013	Bank holiday in Cyprus terminated
May 2013	May 3, 2013	Second review of the Second Economic Adjustment program completed
	May 8, 2013	Law 4152/2013: temporary special duty on real estate (EETA) replaces EETIDE, as the latter was no longer in force
	May 13, 2013	DG ECFIN 2nd review report (Occasional paper 148): 2012 General Government deficit of 6.3% of GDP (program definition), instead of a 6.6% projection in the first review (Nov. 12)
June 2013	June 11, 2013	Government closes down the Greek Broadcasting Corporation (ERT)
	June 21, 2013	DIMAR pulls out from the government
	June 24, 2013	Reshuffle of Government
	June 27, 2013	ECOFIN agreement on bank recovery and resolution
July 2013	July 23, 2013	Law 4172/2013 on prior actions for the third review of the Second Economic Adjustment program. Emphasis on the restructuring of public sector employment (K. Mitsotakis): abolition of job positions in the public sector made feasible; mobility schemes extended throughout the public sector; 4,200 employees in "mobility status" by end-July 2013, 12,500 by end 2013
	July 24, 2013	Third review of the Second Economic Adjustment program completed
	July 31, 2013	Completion of the first recapitalization of the Greek banking sector: banking assets become concentrated on 4 core banks (Alpha Bank, Eurobank, National Bank of Greece, Piraeus Bank); public funds of €25.5 bn and private funds of €3.1 bn are injected into those banks; an additional €13.4 bn of public funds are used to resolve most of the smaller banks
August 2013	August 6, 2013	Law 4177/2013: Sunday opening for small retailers and large stores
	August 12, 2013	Agreement on the sale of OPAP to EMMA DELTA for €652 million signed
September 2013	September 17, 2013	Law 4186/2013: Establishment of general lyceum, vocational lyceum, vocational training schools, and non-formal educational bodies (lifelong learning centers, colleges)

December 2013	December 12, 2013	Ratification of 2014 Budget. First projection of a 2013 primary surplus, according to MoU definition (0.4% of GDP), one year earlier than expected (balanced primary outcome according to DG ECFIN third review report, July 2013). Forecast of a primary surplus of 1.6% of GDP 2014, without additional measures
	December 31, 2013	Economic Adjustment program for Ireland completed
January 2014	January 1, 2014	Greece assumes 6-month EU presidency
March 2014	March 6, 2014	Results of banks' stress-tests by the Bank of Greece and Blackrock published: capital needs for 4 core banks of €6.4 bn in the baseline scenario. Second recapitalization of the Greek banking sector is completed over the next two months and is covered solely by private funds.
	March 26, 2014	Law 4250/2014: repeals and mergers of public entities; review of the evaluation procedures for civil servants
	March 31, 2014	Completion of Alpha Bank share capital increase by €1,2 bn
April 2014	April 7, 2014	Law 4254/2014 implementing OECD recommendations on repealing barriers to entry and competition in: retail trade (pharmaceuticals, gasoline, books, kiosks); food products (bakery and farinaceous products, dairies, oils and fats, meat processing); building materials (mining and quarrying, cement handling); tourism services (tourist transfers, tourist ports, validation of prices and rates); and road haulage
	April 10, 2014	Completion of Piraeus Bank share capital increase by €1,8 bn
	April 10, 2014	Successful 5-year bond issue from Hellenic Republic (€3 bn, yield 4.95%)
	April 24, 2014	DG ECFIN 4th review report (Occasional paper 192) affirms a 2013 primary surplus of 0.8% of GDP
	April 29, 2014	Completion of Eurobank's share capital increase by €2.9 bn
	April, 2014	Fourth review of the Second Adjustment program completed
May 2014	May 12, 2014	Completion of National Bank of Greece's share capital increase by €2.5 bn
	May 25, 2014	European Parliament elections. SYRIZA (Leftist party) wins

June 2014	June 10, 2014	Cabinet reshuffle. G. Hardouvelis new Finance Minister
	June 30, 2014	Economic Adjustment program for Portugal completed
July 2014	July 11, 2014	Hellenic Republic issues a 3-year bond to raise €3 bn with a yield of 3.5%, but offers amount to only €1.5 bn
	July 14, 2014	Law No 4275/2014: new evaluation system for high-level public servants
September 2014	September 2–4, 2014	Negotiations with Troika in Paris
October 2014	October 13, 2014	Digital share rights auction completed (total offers of €381.1 million)
	October 26, 2014	Results of banks' stress-tests by the ECB published: negligible capital needs of €18 million for Eurobank in the dynamic scenario (taking into account spring 2014 share capital increases)
December 2014	December 29, 2014	Failure of Parliament to elect the new President of the Hellenic Republic
	December 30, 2014	Parliamentary elections announced to take place on January 25, 2015
January 2015	January 25, 2015	Parliamentary elections. Coalition government formed by SYRIZA and ANEL (Nationalist party). A. Tsipras new Prime Minister, G. Varoufakis new Finance Minister
February 2015	February 18, 2015	Election of P. Pavlopoulos as President of the Hellenic Republic
	February 27, 2015	Third Amendment agreement
June 2015	June 26, 2015	Announcement of referendum on 07/05/2015 regarding the new Loan Agreement
	June 29, 2015	Imposition of capital controls and bank holiday
July 2015	July 5, 2015	Prevalence of "No" in the referendum with 62%
	July 5, 2015	A. Samaras resigns. E. Meimarakis new Interim President of New Democracy
	July 6, 2015	G. Varoufakis resigns. E. Tsakalotos new Finance Minister
	July 12, 2015	Eurozone summit: Agreement for new financial assistance to Greece

	July 15, 2015	Law No 4334/2016 (urgent measures for the start of negotiations with the ESM): VAT revision (abolition of the reduced VAT in islands, transfer of products and services to the main VAT rate of 23%); strengthening the independence of the National Statistical Authority; changes in social security (merger of all supplementary funds since 01.01.2015, increase of healthcare contributions for main pensions to 6%, imposition of healthcare contributions of 6% on supplementary pensions, freezing of state funding to the Social Security system during 2015–2021)
	July 17, 2015	Reshuffle of Government. E. Tsakalotos remains as Finance Minister
	July 20, 2015	End of bank holiday
	July 22, 2015	Law 4335/2016: Measures for the implementation of Law No 4334/2015, including the revision of the Code of Civil Procedure, and the transposition of the Bank Recovery and Resolution Directive (BRRD - 2014/59/EU) to Greek Law
August 2015	August 14, 2015	Third MoU (Law 4336/2015): ESM loan up to €85.5 billion for 2015–2018; €25 billion reserve for the banks' potential capital needs; changes in social security (increase of the minimum contribution period for full pension rights to 67 years, or to 62 years for those with 40 years of social security contributions, higher penalty on early retirements by public sector employees (-10% of pensions per year), freezing of the lowest pensions in the private and in the public sector up to 2021); primary balance targets of -0.25% of GDP (2015), 0.5% (2016), 1.75% (2017), 3.5% (2018)
	August 20, 2015	Government resigns, parliamentary elections announced to take place on September 20, 2015
September 2015	September 20, 2015	Coalition government formed by SYRIZA and ANEL
October 2015	October 17, 2015	Further measures for the implementation of the third MoU (Law 4337/2015): budgeting standards in the General Government entities (excluding local governments); strategic plan for the restructuring of the Athens Urban Transportations Organisation (OASA)

November 2015	November 1, 2015 November 24, 2015	Law No 4340/2015 on bank recapitalization and governance: upgraded role of the Hellenic Financial Stability Fund (HFSF) in recapitalizations; qualification standards and evaluation procedures for the members of banks' boards of directors Resignation of E. Meimarakis. G. Plakiotakis new Interim President of New Democracy
	November 30, 2015	Completion of the third recapitalization of the Greek banking sector: following emergency Asset Quality Review conducted by the European Central Bank, 4 core banks are required to raise €13.7 bn; capital raised from private sources, including debt-equity swaps, accounts for €8 bn; banks' capital prior to the recapitalization is valued at only €0.7 bn
December 2015	December 7, 2015	Ratification of 2016 Budget
	December 14, 2015	Concession Agreement between Greek Government and FRAPORT AG-SLENTEL Ltd. (14 regional airports)
	December 16, 2015	Law 4354/2015 on the management of nonperforming loans
	December 22, 2015	National Bank of Greece sells Finance Bank in Qatar National Bank for €2.75 bn
January 2016	January 10, 2016	K. Mitsotakis elected as new president of New Democracy
February 2016	February 8, 2016	Athens' Stock Exchange Index falls below 500 units for second time after June 2012
May 2016	May 9, 2016	Eurogroup decision for Greek debt relief (short, medium, and long-term measures)
	May 11, 2016	Law No 4387/2016 on social security: new calculation method for the new pensions (pensions defined by the sum of the national pension and the proportional pension); merger of all the main social security funds to a single fund (as of 01/01/2017); gradual abolition of the Social Security Benefit (EKAS); social security contributions of employees and self-employed defined solely by their income.

	May 27, 2016	Additional reforms and fiscal measures for the implementation of the third MoU and the completion of the first review (Law 4389/2016): establishment of the Independent Public Revenue Authority; establishment of the Hellenic Corporation of Assets and Participations (HCAP S.A.); ratification of the concession agreement for the management and operation of regional airports; additional fiscal measures of €5.4 bn (fee for the use of cable TV, fee for internet use, increase of the high VAT rate to 24%, "residence tax" for hotels, special solidarity contribution, increase of excise duty on cigarettes, alcohol, gasoline, diesel, heating oil, etc).
June 2016	June 21, 2016	Disbursement of the first sub-installment of €7.5 bn, after Eurogroup's decision
July 2016	July 14, 2016	Hellenic Public Asset Development Fund (TAIPED) accepts offer by Ferrovie Dello Stato Italiane S.p.A. and declares that firm preferred investor for TRAINOSE
August 2016	August 12, 2016	Completion of the transfer of 51% of the share capital of Piraeus Port Authority S.A. to Cosco (Hong Kong) Group Ltd
September 2016	September 30, 2016	Measures for the completion of the second phase of the first review (Law No 4425/2016): transfer of state-owned enterprises to the HCAP S.A. (Thessaloniki Water Supply & Sewerage S.A., Athens Water Supply and Sewerage S.A., Hellenic Vehicle Industry, Attiko Metro S.A., Public Power Corporation S.A.); review of the regulatory framework for the energy sector (establishment of new energy markets, responsibilities of the energy regulatory authority and of the operator of the electricity market (LAGIE)).
October 2016	October 25, 2016	Disbursement of the second sub-installment of €2.8 billion, after Eurogroup's decision
November 2016	November 4, 2016	Reshuffle of Government. E. Tsakalotos continues as Finance Minister
December 2016	December 5, 2016	Eurogroup announces short-term debt relief measures
	December 6, 2016	Law No 4441/2016: simplification of the procedures involved in starting a business; removal of regulatory barriers in road haulage sector and in wholesale trade of pharmaceutical products.
	December 8, 2016	A. Tsipras' proclaims distribution of part of the budget surplus (€617 million)

Index

Access to finance, 29–30
  Eurobarometer survey results in 2005 and
    2009, 270
  and export performance, 122
  index, 143
Accountability
  in education (*see* Evaluation of educational
    units)
  in the justice system (*see* Evaluation of
    judges)
  in privatizations, 193, 197
Adjournments, 563–565
Administrative competencies, 628, 646–647,
    680–683
  and legal formalism, 645–647, 681
Adoption and control of regulations. *See
    also* Codification and drafting of
    legislation
  current system, 146–147
  Law 4048/2012 on better regulation and
    previous reforms, 654, 686–691
  reform proposals, 153–155
Anticorruption policies, 611–613
Antimonopoly policy, 141–143,
    150–152
Appeals, 567–568
Auction design in privatizations
  auctions versus negotiations, 194–195
  discriminatory auction, 194
  reserve price, 195, 201
  uniform price auction, 194

Autonomy
  of educational units, 311, 314, 348–350
    in tertiary education and law 4009/2011,
      344–346
  and management of courts, 554–556

Bank recapitalizations, 43
  first and second recapitalizations, 279–282
  recapitalization versus resolution,
    276–278
  third recapitalization, 282–284
Bankruptcy, 43–44
  corporate, 286–289
  household, 289–291
  procedures, 287–290, 528, 565
  reform proposals, 288–291, 565–566
Banks
  assets and lines of business, 255–257
  bank-sovereign loop, 267–276
  core tier 1 capital, 273, 281–282, 294
  incentives and capacity to resolve
    nonperforming loans (*see* Nonperforming
    loans)
  industry concentration, 280, 297
  liquidity and funding, 269–270, 273–275,
    282–283
  political interference (*see* Political
    interference: in banks)
  recapitalizations (*see* Bank recapitalizations)
  state control (*see* State-controlled firms:
    banks)